The History Social Foundations of American Education

Tenth Edition

John D. Pulliam
Professor Emeritus
University of Montana

James J. Van Patten
Professor Emeritus
University of Arkansas—Fayetteville

PEARSON

Boston   Columbus   Indianapolis   New York   San Francisco   Upper Saddle River
Amsterdam   Cape Town   Dubai   London   Madrid   Milan   Munich   Paris   Montreal   Toronto
Delhi   Mexico City   São Paulo   Sydney   Hong Kong   Seoul   Singapore   Taipei   Tokyo

Vice President and Editorial Director: Jeffery W. Johnston
Executive Editor: Ann Castel Davis
Editorial Assistant: Penny Burleson
Vice President, Director of Marketing: Margaret Waples
Marketing Manager: Joanna Sabella
Senior Managing Editor: Pamela D. Bennett
Production Manager: Susan Hannahs
Senior Art Director: Jayne Conte
Cover Designer: Suzanne Duda
Cover Image: Shutterstock
Full-Service Project Management: Sandeep Rawat, Aptara®, Inc.
Composition: Aptara®, Inc.
Text and Cover Printer/Bindery: RRD/Harrisonburg
Text Font: Garamond

Credits and acknowledgments for material borrowed from other sources and reproduced, with Permission, in this textbook appear on the appropriate page within the text.

Every effort has been made to provide accurate and current Internet information in this book. However, the Internet and information posted on it are constantly changing, so it is inevitable that some of the Internet addresses listed in this textbook will change.

Photo Credits: © H.M. HERGET/National Geographic Stock, p. 1; © North Wind Picture Archives, p. 31; © Bettman/Corbis, p. 89; © North Wind Picture Archives/Alamy, p. 115; © Fine Art Photographic Library/CORBIS, p. 139; © Frances Benjamin Johnston Collection/Library of Congress, p. 171; © Nicola Armstrong/Alamy, p. 203; © Frances M. Roberts/Newscom, p. 235; © Steve Skjold/Alamy, p. 259; © Ian Shaw/Alamy, p. 301; © Juice Images/Alamy, p. 349.

Library of Congress Cataloging-in-Publication Data

Pulliam, John D.
  The history and social foundations of American education / John D. Pulliam,
James J. Van Patten.—10th ed.
    p. cm.
  Rev. ed. of: History of education in America: Upper Saddle River, N.J.: Merrill, c2007.
  ISBN-13: 978-0-13-262613-2
  ISBN-10: 0-13-262613-6
  1. Education—United States—History.   I. Van Patten, James J.   II. Pulliam, John D.
History of education in America.   III. Title.
  LA205.P84 2013
  370.973—dc23

                                                                    2011033277

10 9 8 7 6 5 4 3 2 1

ISBN 10:   0-13-262613-6
ISBN 13: 978-0-13-262613-2

PREFACE

The Importance of Gaining Perspective

As we pass through the second decade of the twenty-first century, times are changing so rapidly that keeping pace in every field is extremely difficult. The knowledge explosion affects all scholars as they seek to find and synthesize the latest research. But beyond the special areas and general knowledge necessary for a strong foundation for understanding the profession of teaching, there is also the profound change in the social, cultural, philosophical, and political environment. There are teachers still active in the profession who recall how fearful Americans were of the communist block and possible nuclear war with the USSR. To many, that may seem like ancient history, but today we have international terrorism, global warming, a recession, and an information explosion with which to contend. To gain perspective as educators, we not only need to understand the teaching profession but also the society that is a foundation for education. For example, modern China with its huge population and outstanding educational system now presents a challenge to American schools never previously seen. Students in India and Japan are being trained in fields like accounting, medicine, and computer science, which allow them to compete with us on a global scale. This is occurring at a time when American schools face budget cuts, teacher layoffs, and the dismal prospect of decline in scholarly competence. It is not enough for teachers to master skills in the profession and keep up with inventions and innovations. They must also deal with the shifting values, beliefs, and cultural standards in the United States and in the world.

In *The World Is Flat,* Pulitzer Prize winner Thomas Friedman points out how globalization, outsourcing, and new information have leveled the competitive world playing field. All knowledge centers on the planet are now connected and more people can collaborate in real time than was ever before imagined. Nations like China and India, which long lagged behind, are now connected to a single global network. If politics and terrorism do not stop it, innovations will lead to greater innovation and prosperity. An American accounting firm may now employ CPAs from India who speak English, understand American tax law, are directly connected through fiber-optic cable, and are happy with lower wages than their counterparts in the United States. We once thought of the masses in Asian nations as starving. Now they are starving for our jobs. A current best-selling book in China is a guide for how to get your Chinese child into Cambridge, Columbia, Harvard, or Oxford. Clearly, to compete, the American educational system must improve. Americans must constantly upgrade and improve their skills if they hope to be successful in a flat world. They must also have better than a mediocre schooling as a base.

The Purpose of This Textbook

This is a book on the foundations upon which rest the American system of education. That is, it deals with the cultural, historical, philosophical, social, and psychological factors that define the educational institutions. The basic concepts and theories that underlie educational practice are presented in compact form. In order to cover as much information as possible in one volume, interpretation is left largely to the reader or to professors who use the book as a text. Issues in American education are legion. There is the raging controversy between traditionalists and revisionists. Superimposed upon this argument is the very different view of educational objectives coming from global sources such as Islam and Chinese communism. Before readers can make sound judgments of interpretation, they must read and retain a great deal of factual information, which the authors have provided. It is paramount that accurate accounts of events be known, but knowing why they took place is more important than the facts themselves.

Authors' Positions

We have checked the accuracy of facts presented in this book and nothing has been distorted or intentionally left out. As educators, we do have opinions concerning policies for American public education, educational theory, and future direction for the schools. Should the reader feel that our views show through the text, we ask that the following be considered.

In 1839 a popular and respected professor at Bowdoin College was accused by some of his students of trying to convert them to his point of view on some current issues. Called before the governing board of the college to answer the charges, the professor freely admitted that they were true. Indeed, he told the board, he often tried to indoctrinate his students. Further, he said that when he was successful it indicated that the student in question was unprepared, had not learned to think for himself or herself, or lacked the mental capacity for successful college work. Students are expected to study the material presented and draw their own conclusions independent of the teacher's views.

New to the Tenth Edition

- ❑ The book includes social and historical information for easy access and reference, including "Focus on the Issues" features to promote critical thinking about educational controversies. Chapter 2 includes Eastern philosophies, including competition for jobs and market share, especially with highly educated and economically motivated people of China, Japan, India, and South Korea. Historical events are linked to the social, cultural, political, and economic forces that created them, making this a social foundations text. Current educational changes are analyzed and explained on the basis of social and cultural influences.

❑ This edition features graphs, photographs, and expanded timelines depicting historical and social foundations, events, people, and significant milestones in American education. Emphasis is placed on demographic change such as the American population becoming majority Hispanic and the educational and economic impact of global population growth.

❑ We have included an expanded treatment of alternative certification, gangs, school violence, and bullying (including cyberbullying). Evaluation of student achievement, charter schools are considered in the light of political and economic forces such as the shortfall of state budgets and potential downsizing of federal funding for education.

❑ Integration of content, updated and modified activities, and study guides at the end of each chapter are used to engage students in social and historical studies, perspective, and research.

❑ This revision includes a section on non-Western philosophies, including Islamic nations and their historical, social, and political influences. "Focus on the Issues" boxes including the Chinese Cultural Revolution have been added.

❑ The text identifies past, current, and prospective laws and litigation, and current educational issues, within all chapters and in the "Then to Now" sections.

❑ This revision focuses on diverse populations, with an emphasis on equity and access for special education, women, and minorities; the effect of political conflict on educational theory and practice; and the pros and cons of the reauthorization of No Child Left Behind legislation prospects in the 112th Congress.

❑ The book features the social and psychological influences on schools caused by dramatic events such as school violence and the continuing global war on terrorism and issues centering on freedom of speech in the light of Wikileaks and social networking on Facebook.

❑ An Instructor's Manual with test questions is available at the Pearson Instructor's Resource Center. Go to www.pearsonhighered.com and click on the "Educators" link. Here you will be able to login or register for a user name and password.

Other Text Features

❑ The end of each chapter provides sections for engaging students in higher-order thinking and "hands-on" learning experiences. "Gaining Perspective through Critical Analysis" presents discussion questions that review significant content areas. "History in Action in Today's Classrooms" suggests activities to get students out of the classroom and engaged in meaningful learning experiences. "What Do You Think?" questions are included at the end of each "Focus on the Issues" box for student reflection and analysis.

❑ This edition includes the most recent legislation, court decisions, and governmental policies and programs initiated by Congress and the Obama administration to improve student access and achievement at all educational levels. Also included is information about universal public school access to the Internet, including safeguards (such as Cyberpatrol and efforts to deal with increases in identity theft).

❏ Chapter 11 on global trends integrates past and future issues and reflects changing demographics and emerging social issues.

❏ Selective chapter bibliographies and a general annotated bibliography have been updated and are provided as guides for more detailed study. The reader is also urged to pursue original documents as well as interpretative histories.

ACKNOWLEDGMENTS

We are indebted to Ann Davis for her support and encouragement to produce a new edition; to Penny Burleson for development support; and to Sheryl Langner for her help with the photos and production guidance. Their readiness to answer our many questions during the writing process was invaluable to us. In addition, Timothy J. Bergen, Jr., Megan Verbeck, and Jennifer Wood, provided secretarial and computer assistance. We would also like to thank and appreciate Sandeep Rawat for his fine organizational skills in overseeing the entire production process, and Evelyn Perricone for professionally copyediting the manuscript.

Lori Foster, with her computer expertise to assist in manuscript completion, was also invaluable. The support, proofreading, and research skills of Alison Verbeck (Washington University Physics Librarian), George Denny and Bart Cohen University of Arkansas, Fayetteville, Wayne Willis, Moorehead State University, Kentucky Brandi Holt and Barbara Fitzpatrick for outstanding editorial & computer assistance. Special thanks also go to Florida Atlantic University doctoral graduate Dr. Susan B. Korb and Janice Oliveira for their assistance with the project. Last, but certainly not least, we want to thank the reviewers for this tenth edition: Jan Carlson, Oklahoma State University; and Anne M. Knupfer, Purdue University.

BRIEF CONTENTS

CONTENTS

Chapter 3   American Education: Our European Heritage and the Colonial Influence   89

CHAPTER 1

INTRODUCTION: APPLYING HISTORY TO EDUCATION TODAY

Lycurgus would never reduce his laws into writing . . . for he thought that the most material points . . . such as . . . the public welfare, being imprinted on the hearts of their youth by a good discipline . . . would find a stronger security, than any compulsion would be, in the principles of action formed in them by their best lawgiver, education.

Plutarch

Being a form of social action, education . . . is rooted in some actual culture and expresses the philosophy and recognized needs of that culture.

Alexis de Tocqueville

1

Greek City States	Roman Republic	BC	AD	Roman Empire	Dark Ages
c 900 Homer	Cato		First Century Hebrew elementary schools		
	Cicero		Quintilian		
Athens Sparta			Tacitus		
		University of Alexandria	360 Julian revived classical learning		
	Fifth and Fourth Centuries Socrates Plato Aristotle Isocrates		529 Justinian closed pagan universities		
		Paradigm Shifts			

Figure 1.1 Selected Historical Figures and Events That Influenced American Education

OVERVIEW

As the world celebrated the close of the second millennium, a group of world-famous scientists met in New York to identify the most profound invention or discovery of the past 1,000 years. Some advocated the voyages of discovery, the internal combustion engine, space exploration, and the splitting of the atom, while others suggested the Big Bang theory of the universe's creation, DNA, or the development of the microchip computer. In the final analysis, however, these experts agreed that no invention was more significant than Gutenberg's use of movable type in a printing press in the year 1440. Thus, the most salient invention in terms of its impact on human life and culture originated as educational technology. Printing and the spread of knowledge did more to alter civilization than anything else. This illustrates just how powerful a force education and the dissemination of information can be.

The Examination of Social Forces.   This book covers the social foundations of education, focusing on the history of education in the United States. It is not confined to tracing events specific to one aspect of the culture, such as the schools, but also deals with the underlying social and philosophical conditions that support those schools. Purposes and goals of educational institutions in a simple agricultural village in colonial or early national America were vastly different from those found in a modern, urban, diverse, multicultural community. Contemporary institutions are best understood by studying the history of how they evolved. Sociology of the community, different concepts of the psychology of learning, conflicting ideas about what values are most important, and issues about how schools should be controlled and supported are fundamental to comprehending education now.

Middle Ages		Renaissance		Reformation
569–632 Mohammed	776–804 Alcuin	1158 University of Paris	1466–1536 Erasmus and humanism	
800 Learning revived by Charlemagne	Chivalry	1225–1274 Thomas Aquinas		1517 Luther's 95 Theses
Monasticism		Scholasticism		1509–1565 Calvin
		Growth of universities		1550 Knox and English Puritans
Social Change		Core Values		

Superimposed upon this is the accelerating rate of change and the vast increase in available information, which alter the learning environment and the curriculum for the future. Most adult Americans matriculated before personal computers and the Internet were universally available, and certainly before there was a global marketplace or an information economy. Therefore, history cannot ignore the social, philosophical, and psychological foundations of education. It must also treat themes such as the rapid rate of social change, new vocational and informational skills, educational issues and reform, and the shifting economy (agricultural-industrial-informational).

In this chapter, we will examine a few of the most important social forces that govern the relationship between educational institutions and the communities they serve. We will also treat educational history as a discipline and survey the intellectual forces that have had a major influence on American schools. Chapter 2 deals with the philosophical and psychological foundations of education.

No educational system is created in a vacuum. Schools exist now to serve the needs of contemporary American society, but like society itself these needs are changing rapidly. A good deal of confusion and conflict now exists about the goals of education and about what alterations should be made. This is easier to comprehend when we examine cultures less complicated than ours is now. Examples are found in colonial villages and nineteenth-century rural communities where agreement about the aims of education and the structure of institutions was easily reached. We will also briefly look at pedagogical models from society's antecedent to ours for comparison.

The authors assume that readers of this volume have some familiarity with modern American education, probably from having passed through the public schools. Firsthand experience is critical, and its great value in teacher preparation is widely recognized. This is why almost all colleges and departments of education require field experience prior to student teaching. But attending or working in a given school may create the false impression that there is universal agreement about the function, philosophy, curriculum, and learning styles. It may not reveal the deep divisions over educational policy found in many communities. This is why a broader historical study of educational institutions and the foundations upon which they rest is necessary for understanding as well as for participating in making changes in the future.

The Link Between Educational Theory and History.   The fundamental link between any educational theory and the historical context in which it developed can never be ignored. No one in contemporary America would deny sexual, class, or racial equality so far as educational opportunity is concerned. Yet, we need look back only to the 1880s for a time when women had no control over their own property and acquired schooling only with permission of their husbands or fathers. Racially segregated schools were commonplace in the United States until the 1950s, while in parts of colonial America only boys from upper classes received formal education.

Today we try to provide schooling for every child, including those so severely handicapped or disabled that special education teachers must be sent to their homes, while those able to attend school are mainstreamed into regular classrooms in order to provide the least restrictive environment. Efforts are made to accommodate children who are not proficient in the use of English through bilingual programs, while the children of aliens not legally living and working in the United States are admitted to schools under the child benefit theory. Equality of educational opportunity is a core value, but there is much concern over the cost of programs that benefit only a small part of the population.

Obviously the ability to succeed in a multicultural, multiracial, society, to work in a global economy, to access the Internet, or to find employment in a foreign business environment were not goals of the founding fathers. Although we must constantly alter the schools to meet current and future needs, we are never free from the influence of the past. Social history shows why French, German, and Spanish are widely taught in American schools while Chinese, Russian, and Swahili are not. Should this be so? That a fifth of the world's people speak Chinese is certainly an argument for teaching that language. Yet, if Chinese were to be taught to all American students, something else in the curriculum would have to be eliminated or time in school would have to be extended. The choice is a philosophical one, closely related to social theory and influenced by history.

As Alvin Toffler demonstrated in *Future Shock*, the pace of change and the creation of new information are the most significant characteristics of modern society. Schools were established for the express purpose of inducting the young into the culture of the society into which they were born and in which they must learn to live as responsible and useful members of the community. This is not so easily accomplished in an age of accelerating change. Schools are major social institutions. As such, they are constantly bombarded with new demands and challenged with alternative ideas about how goals might be achieved. Historical traditions and entrenched values conflict with preparation for an unknown future. American culture has long provided for opposing viewpoints to be passionately expressed, but debate is more intense today because basic values and the public philosophy are at stake.

Presently, the United States is recovering from the worst economic down cycle since the depression of the 1930s. Cold War–era threats of Communist domination and nuclear war have vastly diminished. Nevertheless, the world suffers from poverty, pollution, underemployment, starvation, ethnic strife, Middle East and Afghanistan conflict, threat of Iranian nuclear power, and the violation of basic human rights. That terrorism exists was clearly demonstrated by the attack on September 11, 2001. The appearance of safety and economic well-being does not guarantee that today's students will be free to meet all of their future needs. Education must anticipate the knowledge, skills, and attitudes required for future success. Modern teachers are likely to be overwhelmed by the number and variety of demands made and by conflicting ideas about how these should be met. In this age of information overload—when the number of words electronically stored exceeds the total number in print—it is especially important for educators to have a theoretical base to serve as a guide through the labyrinth of opinions and facts. Misconceptions and misunderstandings can be avoided if teachers have the social, philosophical, and psychological foundations well in hand.

Our present culture has been built over time. The schools have always reflected the dominant ideology of a given period of history. In colonial times, the orientation was toward Europe, building character for salvation, and the preservation of values. There was no distinction between philosophy and theology. It was assumed that the future would be just like the past. Today, we must expect that the current rate of change will continue to accelerate. Our students must "learn" a living, build a foundation for continuing education throughout life, and contribute to solving the world's problems. An understanding of how we evolved to this stage and a study of the sociology, psychology, and theory of education will aid in building a bridge to the future.

Schooling in an Age of Change, as Revealed Through the Past.   The era of electronic communications, cybernation, the Internet, and mushrooming scientific discovery is upon us. Astronomers ponder an expanding universe filled with quasars, visible galaxies no longer in existence, rapidly spinning neutron stars, supernova explosions, and elusive black holes. At the opposite end of reality, quantum physicists study subatomic quarks, which are only virtual because they can never be seen or directly measured. Artificial intelligence and human cloning are on the horizon while superconductors are grown from organic crystal. In history, exact dates are fixed by comparing the decay of radioactive carbon-14 in living tissues with the more stable and common carbon-12.

To understand schooling in this age of exponential change, teachers must know how educational institutions developed, their relationship to society, what dangers and opportunities are linked to them, what future developments can be predicted, and the philosophical implications. In short, the theory and practice of education now are best revealed through the historical, social, philosophical, and psychological foundations. The relationship between these foundations and the schools is more easily seen in societies less complex than ours. The five following historical models illustrate efforts to educate prior to the evolution of many contemporary issues.

In 490 B.C., the first marathon runner arrived in the city-state of Athens to announce victory over the Persians. A school of the time would be located in one of the temples or public buildings, perhaps on the *stoa* (open porch). Students are adolescent boys of the citizenship class. Their status is apparent from their short woolen tunics with classic designs embroidered around the skirt hems. The teacher, a young man from a leading family, is chosen for his dignified bearing and knowledge of the culture. It is beneath his dignity to accept pay for the civic duty and privilege of teaching, although pleased fathers might sometimes give him a present. Responsibility for the education of sons rests with the fathers, who would have taught them basic reading before entering the school. Military training only is a function of the state, and these students spend their afternoons practicing martial arts and athletics. The curriculum this morning is based on the *Iliad,* a copy of which, on rolled parchment, is in the hands of the instructor. Each boy in turn recites a previously learned passage from the familiar poem. The pupils are evaluated for accuracy, attitude, clarity of speech, posture, and enthusiasm. Passing citizens pause to listen to the presentations and to praise good work. The boys understand the importance of learning their culture, which they believe to be the superior one not only in Greece but in the world. Language, literature, manners, customs, skill in debate, and national defense are vital to these boys, who will later proudly take their seats in the assembly of free citizens.

Half a century after the death of Julius Caesar and the dawn of the Christian era, M. F. Quintilian has opened his school of oratory in a room of his spacious Roman home. His fame and success enable him to charge high fees, and graduates of his school find high places in the governmental bureaucracy. Quintilian has written several books on education and invented pedagogical devices such as carved ivory blocks over which children move their fingers to learn Latin letters. The dozen well-dressed and well-groomed students obviously are from wealthy patrician families. They have learned to read Latin and a little Greek at home from their fathers or hired tutors. Now in the Institution of Oratory, they seek skills needed for clerks, legal advisors, and business managers in the service of the wealthy and politically powerful. Quintilian's model is a "good man skilled in speaking." By this he means one able to present logical arguments and to persuade, but also a person of character and integrity. The classroom is light, and one side is open to a fountain in the atrium. On a raised platform, a boy wearing a white toga as befits one running for public office is making a speech in favor of invading Gaul. His speech is judged for logic, clarity, and power to persuade. When finished, the whole class offers a critique, supervised by the master. Students here are motivated because they know upward mobility in the vast empire depends upon skill in speaking and forensics.

In the year 1636, as Harvard College is founded in the American colonies, the Moravian educator J. A. Comenius receives permission from the city fathers of

Amsterdam to open a school. Like most European cities at the time, Amsterdam has no system of public education, but the town council is anxious to promote learning and has raised a modest fund to help support the famous teacher. Comenius agrees to teach 30 boys and girls from Protestant families in the community who cannot afford private schooling and to furnish each with an illustrated textbook of 18 pages. Published in German, the text is used by pupils not prepared in Latin grammar.

Located in a loft above a grain merchant's warehouse, the school is furnished with stools, maps, scientific drawings, and objects designed to arouse students' interest. Comenius is a fatherly figure with a long, flowing beard and gowns appropriate to his office as bishop of the Moravian sect. There is an atmosphere of love and kindness here, with no corporal punishment or harsh discipline. Believing that all children including females should be able to read the Bible for themselves, the parents encourage these youngsters to learn. Everything is made easy by moving from the simple to the complex and from the familiar to the unfamiliar. Comenius believes in a curriculum as broad as life itself, but concentrates here on what each pupil is able to master at a given age. The students are clean and neatly dressed. The teacher makes a real effort to explain why the lessons are important and to create a family-like environment. Students feel fortunate to attend and will be sorry to see the school close in a few months. Civic leaders wish that there were more teachers like Comenius and that similar schools could be provided for all children.

At the dawn of the eighteenth century, a primary school is operating in the town of Deham in Massachusetts Bay Colony. Here, a plain clapboard building has been built by the town and furnished with benches, a fireplace, a board for writing sums with chalk, and an imposing desk on a raised platform for the master. Twenty-five pupils in attendance range in age from 6 to 14. Both sexes are represented, but there are no blacks or Indians or children from non-Puritan families. The teacher is proud of his 3 years of higher education at Harvard College, which gives him status in the community almost equal to that of the local preacher. This is a school of reading with a little writing and simple sums in addition. The *New England Primer*, the *Psalter*, and the Bible are in evidence, while younger children carry hornbooks. Students read and recite aloud. The schoolmaster maintains a stern and severe atmosphere and is ready to use his hickory stick at any sign of inattention or mischief. Learning here is considered a serious matter and a duty for every child. Today the opening exercise is a lecture on the behavior God expects from good children and the consequences of failure to meet those expectations.

Two years after the stock market crash in 1929, 30 pupils are seated in small chairs in a circle around their teacher. This is a fourth-grade class in a public school in Springfield, Missouri. The 16 girls and 14 boys are much alike in that they all come from middle-class homes. Although most are Protestant, there are four Catholic children and one who is Jewish. The teacher is pleased that two of the girls are black because most Negro children attend a school on the other side of town and she believes in integration. A graduate of the Normal school in Warrensburg, she has been steeped in the theory of progressive education and Gestalt psychology. She tries to implement principles such as interest as the guide to all work, scientific study of child development, and freedom to choose styles of learning. The teacher very much admires John Dewey, whom she once heard speak in St. Louis. Before the students arrived this morning, she "seeded" the classroom with potted tulips, wooden shoes, cheeses, and pictures of windmills. The teacher expects that this will lead to spontaneous interest on the part of the children in studying the culture of Holland. The atmosphere here is open and friendly, and the teacher hopes that a better understanding of other societies will improve relations among and between her classroom charges.

SOCIETY AND EDUCATION: SCHOOLS AND THE COMMUNITIES THEY SERVE

World Events That Disrupt Education.   Unexpected, dramatic, and unwanted events may have a shocking impact that destroys the tranquil nature of a culture and upsets the stable balance between society and education. Incidents of school violence create turmoil and fear with which teachers must deal before normal instruction can be resumed. Prime examples of disruption include the Civil War, the Great Depression, the Japanese attack on Pearl Harbor, and the terrorist bombing of the World Trade Center in New York. Such happenings altered the world as we know it, and this is especially significant when the causes and true nature of the occurrence are poorly understood. American adults and pupils in schools could not easily comprehend the reasons why innocent civilians would be attacked or disease-laden letters would be sent. There are few incidents like the September 11, 2001, attack, but those few create profound and lasting consequences. Consider the following examples.

After the election of Abraham Lincoln in 1860, Southern states confidently expected that after a few military setbacks the federal government would allow their secession. No one anticipated a destructive war lasting nearly five years, the impact of the emancipation of slaves, the bitterness of the fighting, or the sacrifices that would be made by every community. Whole academies of young men and their teachers went off to join both armies, and public education in the South suffered for generations following the war. At the end, the Union was preserved, sectionalism and states' rights declined, a new nation emerged, and the Old South was indeed gone with the wind. The Civil War had a major and lasting effect on all aspects of American culture, education included.

America escaped almost unscathed from World War I. There followed a period of prosperity and optimism that was suddenly shattered by the stock market crash of 1929. Most Americans could not comprehend the reasons for the economic collapse and the resulting unemployment, poverty, soup kitchens, and loss of confidence. New Deal efforts to stimulate the economy were not entirely successful and the Depression only ended with the wartime economy of 1941. No aspect of the culture escaped the shattering of the American dream that permeated the society in the 1930s, but education was especially hard hit. Teachers had to work with students from families that had lost faith in the system and who had little hope for gainful employment in the future.

The ravaging surprise attack on Pearl Harbor in December 1941, affected all Americans as much as the destruction of the World Trade Center in 2001. Neither attack was anticipated, and both electrified the people and brought about a unified response. With Pearl Harbor, the enemy was known and the appropriate reaction was clear. Certainly there was fear, but at no other time in American history has the solidarity and resolve of the people been so clearly demonstrated. The educational system geared up with the rest of the nation to defeat the empire of Japan. Yet in both World War II and the recent terrorist attacks, there were aspects that passed the understanding of most Americans. For example, after Japanese military power had been largely destroyed, why would thousands of young men volunteer to train for suicide missions as pilots of kamikaze aircraft? The vast majority of these planes were shot out of the air but those that got through killed many sailors and sank numerous American navy ships. Likewise, following September 11, 2001, many asked why the terrorists hated us enough to commit these hideous acts, and why they would commit suicide to kill Americans. The restoration of order after chaotic events take place requires an effort to understand what happened so that teachers may help students comprehend the nature of the tragedy. History is the best tool we have for making sense out of otherwise incomprehensible events. From feudal times, Japanese society was dominated by the Samurai class of warriors with their strict code called *Bushido*. This required unquestioning loyalty and obedience and placed honor before life. Superimposed upon this were the emperor's divine status and his god-like authority. Military leaders in Japan used this tradition as a basis for training generations of soldiers, including kamikaze pilots. Because they had complete control over the media and the schools, information about military defeats was suppressed while emphasis on fanatic patriotism and loyalty to the emperor continued to the end.

On the opposite side of the world, Islamic people developed a tradition quite different from the Japanese Bushido but with similar results. From 1090, an order of Muslim fanatics known as Assassins emerged in Persia and Syria. They believed it was the will of Allah that they kill Crusaders and other infidels. They interpreted the Qur'an to say that if they were killed while fighting nonbelievers, they would go at once to heaven and be given wonderful rewards forever. The Assassin tradition has been revived many times in history, especially during times of fundamentalist revolution such as occurred recently in Iraq, Afghanistan, and Iran. It has been used in training camps for Islamic warriors and fits easily into the mind-set for terrorists, especially those who believe the United States is the great evil. Historical analysis should help in the discussion of outrageous events that must be part of the healing process before normal schooling can continue. Understanding is just as important as restoring a sense of safety.

Obviously the learning process needs safe and stable conditions and a feeling of well-being. During the Cold War, teachers had to deal with the very real threat of a nuclear attack. Students in schools that have experienced acts of violence by other students need to be calmed and reassured. American society has been vastly altered by the events of September 11, 2001, and the subsequent hunt for the culprits in Afghanistan. The changes brought about by the terrorism directed at the World Trade Center and the Pentagon cannot be ignored by educators. As the famous educational philosopher John Dewey held, schools must simplify, purify, and order the environment so that learning may proceed. All American teachers must now shoulder the difficult task of making students feel safe and comfortable in an age of terrorist fear.

Roots of U.S. Education.   The history of American education has its primary focus on the creation and evolution of schools in the United States. It also requires careful examination of the antecedents, especially those of European and Western civilization. This is not to imply that what happened in Incan, Chinese, or Egyptian culture, among others, is less important, but only that the direct historical roots of our modern system are found in ancient Greece, Rome, and the nations of Europe. As these cultures evolved, many practices and assumptions about schools became traditional. Schools have not existed in all cultures. They were not found in hunting and gathering societies prior to the agricultural revolution. Formal efforts to teach came with civilization, writing, literature, and distinct cultural values. Different answers to fundamental questions emerged quite early.

Upper-class Athenian fathers assumed responsibility for teaching their sons the unique parts of their culture that they believed vital for the good life and the preservation of their city. No provision was made for girls, slaves, lower-class Athenian boys, or foreigners. Sparta, with its warlike traditions, opted for a state-controlled military academy for both boys and girls of the citizenship class. Neither Athens nor Sparta believed in vocational education. Making a living was left to the servile class in Athens and to the Helot slaves in Sparta. Educational theory remained simple until Plato developed his sophisticated system (see Chapter 2). Basic questions such as who would be taught, qualifications of teachers, the curriculum, and how schools would be supported were answered by the ancients in ways that are not currently acceptable. Some things do persist over long periods of time. The *Iliad* was studied in ancient Athens, Rome, eighteenth-century British public schools, colonial America, and frontier colleges in the United States. Even with all the new subjects added and all the programs now required in contemporary schools, it is likely that all students will have some familiarity with Homer's classic poem, although perhaps not for the reasons it was studied in the ancient world.

Cultural Influences on Education.   To understand the importance of the relationship between a culture and its education, we must trace the most salient forces that have shaped and continue to influence communities. Insight may be gained by considering the most uncomplicated culture we can imagine.

A familiar example before the American Revolution is found in Longfellow's classic poem *Evangeline* (1847). Here, the Acadian farmers who make up the tiny village of Grand Pré, Nova Scotia, are all on a first-name basis with one another. Their forefathers are all from Normandy, they speak French, and they belong to the Catholic Church. No extremes of wealth and poverty exist. Everyone lives in a thatched-roof house of wood with similar outbuildings and gardens. All live by farming except Basil the blacksmith, Michael the fiddler, René the notary, and Father Felician. They all share the same customs, beliefs, taboos, and faith. For example, it is universally held that a fever may be cured by enclosing a spider in a nutshell. Decisions are made by mutual agreement with no need for formal government or law enforcement. The Church is the only institution in Grand Pré. Father Felician is both priest and pedagogue, teaching letters to Evangeline, Gabriel, and other village children. Nothing else is necessary because the notary writes the letters, mathematics is confined to measures of grain, and vocational training is by example. Grand Pré has no strife or conflict. It might have remained so had not a distant English king ordered the village burned. It is unlikely that any actual society as ideal as Grand Pré ever existed, but there were many in early America that were almost as simple. Clearly in such places there would be no issues over the curriculum, the qualifications of teachers, who should be taught, or support and control of education.

Since the development of sociology as a discipline by Auguste Comte, Emile Durkheim, and Max Weber early in the twentieth century, systematic efforts have been made to study social change. Space does not permit a full discussion here, but some themes must be treated in order to understand the history of education as it relates to the culture. Among these are the accelerating rate of change, the concept of cultural lag, and the shrinking of core values.

ACCELERATING RATE OF CHANGE

For most of human history, women and men lived out their lives in periods of slow, evolutionary change. As Toffler argues in *The Third Wave*, past sweeping revolutions have been few and there has been time to adjust. The first major revolution came with the domestication of animals and the deliberate cultivation of crops. Before this, everyone had been engaged in hunting and gathering. There were no social classes, no division of labor, no cities, and no stable food supply. Agriculture allowed for civilization to develop, with rulers, priests, soldiers, and artisans living from the surplus that farmers could produce. The population expanded, cities were built, and inventions like irrigation, architecture, philosophy, law, and organized religion flourished. The revolution did not lead, however, to rapid improvement in agricultural methods or technology. It is estimated that in Plato's time seven full-time farmers could produce only enough food to sustain one nonfarmer. Roman farmers tilled the soil by means of a noose around the neck of a horse or ox. The horse collar, which increased the land that one man could break by a factor of four, was not invented until the ninth century. Indeed, many centuries were known for only one major technological change, such as the chimney in the eleventh century, which altered architecture. Long after the Industrial Revolution had started, most Americans lived by farming and saw little need for schools to prepare for anything else.

Change Fueled by Invention.   Breakthroughs in science and technology triggered an acceleration of invention in the eighteenth century known as the Industrial Revolution. This time the change was far more rapid, and almost every aspect of life was affected. From it we got factories, mass production, automobiles, electricity, labor-saving devices, and great wealth. It also brought pollution, slums, environmental destruction, crowded urban areas, and social unrest. It is misleading to conceive of the Industrial Revolution as an event in history—something that had an end. On the contrary, the changes this great transition brought continue to accumulate at an exponential rate. Although we are still adjusting to the huge impact of the Industrial

Revolution, the third wave is upon us. This is a revolution marked by the space age, automation, cyberspace, genetic engineering, computers, and the global information economy. It is a revolution of the magnitude of the agricultural or the industrial age, but this time we must adjust to the change in a single generation.

Most futurists anticipate that we will experience changes as great as this each decade into the future. It is this vastly accelerating rate of change that makes it difficult to plan for and anticipate the future or to get social agreement on what needs to be done with education. As you read these words, think of the new things you have experienced so far in your life. A child born today has a reasonable chance to see the dawn of the twenty-second century. Try to imagine what the world will be like then. More to the point, what must we do to prepare the child for survival and success in that world? World population doubled in the last 50 years to the current seven billion and is expected to reach nine billion by 2050. This rate of growth cannot be sustained. While China has reached zero population growth and Western birth rates are falling, many areas still produce more people than can be fed or educated.

Ogburn Model of Adjustment to Change.   In sociology, the most famous treatment of social change was made by William F. Ogburn. He applied statistical methods to social change caused by advances in technology. Ogburn divided the culture into three parts—the material, the adaptive nonmaterial, and the nonadaptive nonmaterial. Material change is the dynamic and accumulative phase of the culture. Over time, the adaptive nonmaterial adjusts to technological change. For example, automobiles were invented and mass produced before there were licenses, traffic laws, or companies offering insurance, but these adjustments were made. However, the motor car also had an impact on personal freedom, houses built in suburbs, and the value system of adolescents—the nonadaptive nonmaterial culture.

The first four historical models presented were not subject to the stresses of rapid change, but the progressive school of the 1930s certainly was. Since the Great Depression, technological invention steadily gained momentum and became increasingly difficult to fathom. Those currently holding positions on school boards or making decisions about federal aid to education may still think in terms of an economy driven by industrial production rather than one based on computer software and microchips. Ogburn was correct in saying that it is difficult for the nonmaterial culture to adapt. This is reflected also in the work of other sociologists like Gunnar Myrdal, Karl Mannheim, and William Sumner. It is a major theme in Merle Curti's *The Social Ideas of American Educators* (1968) and underpins almost all futures theory.

Social Darwinism.   There are other interpretations of the impact of technological invention as a driving social force. Sumner was a social Darwinist who applied natural selection and survival of the fittest to social change. In his view, schools should be used as sorting and selecting agencies to pick out those of highest ability and to discard the rest. Social Darwinism is no longer widely accepted in the United States, but its influence can still be seen. An example is the familiar comparison of achievement levels in the American comprehensive secondary school, which admits and attempts to retain all students, with European or Japanese schools, which are highly selective in admission. Karl Marx saw materialistic invention as the basis of class struggle, which is the driving force for all human culture. No longer dominant in Eastern Europe, versions of Marxism still influence educational theory in China, North Korea, and Cuba. The explanation of just how accelerating change and the creation of new information alter society may continue to be a subject of debate, but there can be no question about its impact upon all social institutions, including education.

CULTURAL LAG

The crisis facing those who shape education today cannot be explained entirely by the tempo of innovation in the material culture. Ogburn pointed out that scarcity of invention in the adaptive culture along with factors such as conservatism in social habits cause widespread maladjustment in society. He called this "cultural lag" and argued that it is most severe during periods of basic transformation such as the Industrial Revolution. This seems so obviously true that it has become a building block for modern sociology and is fundamental to the work of Pitirim Sorokin, Thorstein Veblen, and most futurists. Lag theory was quickly applied to economics, demography, and social psychology. It clearly shows how failure to adjust to material change causes devastation. An infamous example occurred in World War I when generals and political leaders insisted on following outdated Napoleonic tactics while their armies were killed by machine guns, tanks, poison gas, and airplanes. Culture lag in education happens when communities fall behind a transformation that is taking place. In 1954 the Supreme Court ruled that blacks could no longer be segregated in public schools, but many local districts did everything in their power to block the rule, even closing schools in Prince Edward County, Virginia.

Unequal rates of change create pervasive maladjustments when a series of industrial and technological revolutions occur within a short span of time. Common patterns of thinking and acting upon which collective action is based are disrupted during such periods. Sociologist Robert MacIver argues that serious and numerous lags in the nonmaterial culture can only be resolved by fundamental alteration in normative principles and institutional arrangements. No institutions, not even governments, are more fundamental to the success of society than educational institutions. In our dynamic and fluid world, education must not be allowed to lag behind. What is taught may be vital or useless to the student depending upon the current state of the culture. Skill in using typewriters and adding machines is obsolete, but keyboard skills apply to using computers and accessing the World Wide Web. Library research may teach students to compare numerous sources to verify the validity of a statement. The truth of statements found on the Internet is not so easy to verify. The problem of culture lag is revealed in the history of education, especially the most current history. It is also a problem all teachers face in the future.

Errors and misconceptions in the mass culture are another form of lag that poses a special problem for teachers. For example, in 1911, British physicist Ernest Rutherford developed his model of the atom. He said that the atom resembles a tiny solar system in which electrons orbit the nucleus just as Earth rotates around the Sun. So simple and clear was this model that it became the standard conception of atomic structure for generations of Americans. It persisted even though Niels Bohr had proved two years earlier that it could not be true. Today, science teachers trying to communicate the difficult notion that electrons are both waves and particles that make quantum jumps and appear to be in two places at once must combat the planetary model of the atom. The only part of Rutherford's model still accepted is that atomic structure is largely empty space, but many adults still think of an electron as a miniscule planet.

CORE VALUES

Defining the final objectives of education is not in the hands of professional educators but rests with the wider community. Obviously there are conflicting ideas about the kind of social philosophy schools should encourage, character they should try to develop, subjects they should teach, and methods they should use. These issues are even more fundamental than arguments about support and control of education. Achieving consensus depends upon finding common ground—values upon which the whole community can agree. In a Greek city-state or a colonial village, the community was homogeneous and a core of common values was easily found. In the sophisticated, complex, multicultural, multiracial, and diverse modern society, the task is much more difficult. Some sociologists suggest that the core values in modern America may be breaking up, a condition leading to social chaos. Anthropologist Ralph Linton is credited with the clearest statement about the relationship between core and alternative values (see Figure 1.2). Decisions about the basic standards and norms (called *mores* by Sumner) are based on the cultural core, as are the most fundamental choices concerning education.

Linton held that all cultures have a solid, well-integrated, and fairly stable core of fundamental values and a fluid, constantly changing, and mostly unintegrated set of alternative values not shared by all members. In a simple agricultural village like Grand Pré, the core would be very large in comparison to the alternatives. Choices in such societies are limited to occupation and avocation. The community tolerates no choice in religion, moral values, lifestyles, or expressed opinion. The tyranny of nineteenth-

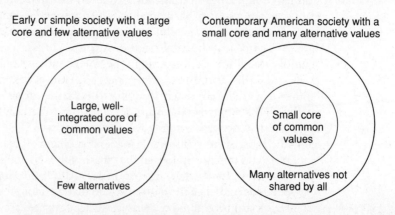

Figure 1.2 Linton's Concept of Core Values

century communities has been well documented in history and literature. There was insistence upon rigid moral standards, customary modes of behavior, and even standard dress. There were certainly positive factors such as kinship, sympathy, and shared joys, but public opinion was almost irresistible. Arguments between members of the community existed, but they did not extend to differences in the core values.

A Myriad of Values. By contrast, modern society contains so many alternatives that the core of shared values is relatively small. Our society has minute division of labor, extreme heterogeneity, profound conflict of interests, and significantly different conceptions of the good life. In the twentieth century, new forces such as industrialization, specialization, urbanization, and improved communications contributed to the decline of the local community. Organized interest groups began to play a more important role because their members shared interests not common to everyone. Our century is a transitional era. It is a peculiarly strategic time in which rapid change has destroyed the old basis of an ordered society. Synthesis of core values, however, may still be found in some parts of the democratic tradition. Values such as equality of educational opportunity still form a core from which decisions may be made.

Although we must not overlook the fact that millions of people, all over the world, have been sincerely and passionately devoted to totalitarian ideology in fascist or communist form, our society is committed to the democratic ideal.

It is very important for education that a core of common values still exists—otherwise, there could be no social consensus concerning essential action. Americans differ sharply about how the school needs of students can best be served, but unite in the view that they must be served. Nevertheless, the search for pedagogical authority is more complicated in our fluid, dynamic, and rapidly changing culture than it was in our earlier history. Schooling in this nation is primarily a state function, but significant roles also are played by the local school boards and the federal government. A core of common values may be larger and more easily agreed upon at the local than at the national level.

Social forces are reflected in the relationship between philosophy and history. Parents in the early national period wanted their children to learn the three *R*'s and values such as patriotism and responsibility, but demanded little more. In the present multicultural nation with its myriad of conflicting religions, ideals, values, and ethnic cultures, much is expected of schools. Even so, some modern adults are primarily interested in seeing that their children learn the skills and information needed for success in the global marketplace. Others place more value on equality of opportunity, a violence- and drug-free environment, or the chance to participate in varsity sports. Whatever happens in the wider culture influences education as well.

Currently, the issue over teaching "intelligent design" as an alternative to evolution causes heated argument. Litigation brought by parents seeking admission for their daughters to all-male football teams led to the creation of new opportunities in sports such as women's basketball and volleyball in high schools and colleges. School violence, especially instances of students shooting students, so profoundly impacted the public mind that demands for security became the number one educational concern in many communities.

FOCUS ON THE ISSUES

Cultural Diversity

A few years ago, John Pulliam, one of the authors of this book, was teaching an extension course for teachers at the American school in Dhahran on the Persian Gulf. While there, the Saudi Ministry of Education asked him to address a group of female candidates for elementary teaching positions at a seminary in be Riyadh. On arriving, he was shocked to find a heavy cloth screen suspended around the podium from which he was to speak. At the time, he was dean of a college of education in a major American university and respected by the Saudis as a scholar. Nevertheless, as a man, a foreigner, and a non-Moslem, he was not permitted to look upon the young women to whom he spoke.

Our history reflects failure to account for cultural diversity. In 1879, the federal government opened the first school for Indians not on a reservation at Carlisle, Pennsylvania. Operated in a military format with uniforms, strict discipline, and rigid schedules, the Carlisle Indian School took no notice of Native American culture. Tribal values such as a casual attitude toward time or belief that young people must be silent in the presence of elders were ignored. To be successful at Carlisle, the Indian student had to abandon his heritage. In effect, he had to adopt the white culture and give up his own.

Likewise, the first schools to admit Negro children following the Civil War assumed that blacks had inferior mental capacity and could benefit only from simple vocational training. Even after school integration in the North, many teachers treated black youngsters differently from whites. Ignorant of black culture, they saw behavioral differences as differences in ability just as they saw girls as unable to benefit from the study of science and higher mathematics.

Not only is America now a multicultural society, but it is also part of a global society in the information age. American teachers now are certain to encounter students with values and traditions unlike their own. Education will fail unless it takes into account racial, cultural, national, and linguistic differences in students.

What Do You Think?

1. Have you visited a country in which you were a foreigner out of touch with the culture? What would it be like if you were a student there?
2. Is it possible that we attribute behavioral characteristics to people based on race, appearance, language, or sex? How can teachers guard against doing this?
3. Trace the evolution of social justice in our society. List two ways in which other nations with diverse cultures achieve social justice.

How You Can Use This Text. A complete history of American education is not possible in a book of this length. Many excellent treatments with more detail are available, and reference is made to most of them. The object of this work is to provide an outline of the most significant educational events, movements, and theories that shaped the American schools. It is designed to provide a sound historical base from which to evaluate modern educational practice and to plan for the future.

The level of information provided is sufficient for candidates preparing to teach and is about what most universities require of graduate students not majoring in educational foundations. This book should therefore prove useful in preparing for teacher certification. It is hoped that you will go beyond this volume for greater breadth and detail, but we believe that a sound foundation is provided within these pages. The broad chronological organization and time lines are designed to help you find topics and organize facts. Information about recent events is as current as possible.

HISTORY AND PURPOSES OF EDUCATIONAL HISTORY

Reconsidering History from New Evidence. On February 23, 1987, the Canadian astronomer Ian Shelton photographed the Large Magellanic Cloud from an observatory in Chile and noted a bright spot that had not been there the night before. He quickly ran outside and became the first person in a century to view a supernova. This one was the brightest seen since Johannes Kepler recorded one in 1604. The discovery by Shelton duly entered the history books as fact in the manner that humans measure time, with the date noted. But the maelstrom exploding with the energy of 200 million suns was not there when Shelton viewed it. Traveling at 196,000 miles per second, light from the supernova required 167,000 years to reach Earth. Our ordinary conception of time in increments of hours, days, and centuries must be recast to accommodate space-time.

To be accurate, we must constantly rethink history. Consider the 5,200-year-old "ice man" recently found in a glacier in the European Alps. Tests on his hair made possible by new forensic technology revealed traces of arsenic. This shows that the ancient fellow was probably involved in smelting the bronze for the head of the axe he carried. Before this discovery, it was not known that the smelting of metals took place in this region at this early date. History does not change, but our techniques for understanding and interpreting it do.

New evidence forces us to reconsider history at all stages. This becomes more difficult as we approach the present. As futurists like Daniel Bell, Joseph Coats, and Robert Heilbroner are fond of pointing out, the rate of change is so rapid that it becomes ever more difficult to understand the forces that shape society. It is easier to demonstrate something in an objective way for times long past where vested interests no longer apply. Educational historians are more comfortable explaining the Freedmen's Bureau role in serving educational needs of blacks after the Civil War than explaining why the gap between white and black school achievement did not decline in the 1990s as it did in the 1980s. The authors will provide as much guidance as possible, but ultimate interpretation of history must be left to the reader. The more independent sources consulted, the better the chances of being right.

Another difficulty with history is the multiplication of records as we move from the past to the future. Significant events were less numerous in former times. Few records and fewer artifacts survive from schools on the American frontier. By contrast, almost every county in the nation has a detailed history that traces local development of public schools. It is easy to enumerate early educational court decisions such as the Dartmouth College Case (1819), but the sheer volume of litigation in the past half century is overwhelming. One could spend a lifetime just reading the briefs pertaining to educational judicial decisions since 1995. By 1947, in the United States, 98.6% of all children through the age of 13 attended public or private schools.

Because modern American education is such an enormous enterprise, its history is also mammoth.

Some long-standing decisions such as that schools should be public, state controlled, tax supported, and open to all are unlikely to be challenged now, but cultural events always demand educational responses. In 1842, the Citadel was founded in South Carolina as a military college for men. With women in military careers and female cadets at West Point, the Citadel found it necessary to admit females. It was soon caught up in the accusations and incidents of sexual harassment that plagued other military training centers. Such events force public schools to look again at sexual equality, bias in programs, and possible discrimination.

The Study of Educational History.   As subjects of study or "disciplines" go, the history of education is relatively new. In a general way, it has been included as part of the field of history, but intellectual, social, and cultural history (of which the history of education is a segment) is much more recent than military and political history. Systematic study of the history of education has developed in America largely within the past century, although there were many earlier accounts of the training of particular individuals or unique groups. Thus, literature contains some history of education, as in the case of the life of Lycurgus in Plutarch's *The Lives of the Noble Grecians and Romans* (1992), which provides considerable information about the training of boys in the ancient Greek city-state of Sparta. Biography is obviously a rich source of information about educational practices in times past, because authors nearly always attempt to account for character development by describing childhood experiences, schooling included. Historians have also been attracted by customs or practices that they considered rare or bizarre, so that atypical educational systems often have been described in some detail.

Modern history of education received its greatest stimulation from the theory that teachers should have, as a part of their professional program, knowledge of the development of at least their own national school system. Obviously, this belief was dependent upon some sort of formal training for teachers that did not occur in the United States until after 1825 and then only to a limited degree.

The common assumption that educational historiography started in the nineteenth century is largely true, even though one may point to numerous efforts to trace school development in earlier times. Quintilian, a Roman educator of the first century, included some history of education in his *Institutio Oratoria*; and Robert Goulet's book, *Compendium on the Magnificence, Dignity, and Excellence of the University of Paris in the Year of Grace 1517*, helps us understand the origins of our modern university as well as linkages with our present secondary educational system. Similarly, Goulet's *On the Origins of the University of Paris,* published in 1517, could be considered educational history. Professor Harry Good identifies Claude Fleury's *Treatise on the Selection and Methods of Studies* (France, circa 1700) as the oldest systematic history of education. There were numerous histories of institutions of higher learning and some efforts to describe higher education generally, such as that of the Puritan minister Cotton Mather, who wrote about New England college programs around the year 1700.

Nevertheless, the history of American education was hardly a field for systematic study until Ellwood P. Cubberley of Stanford University published his *Public Education in the United States* (1934), followed by books of readings in the history of education and critically annotated bibliographies on the subject. Cubberley, who produced his books just after 1900, was a widely respected educator and scholar who had considerable influence upon the inclusion of the history of American education among standard subjects in teacher-training programs. Because normal school education had become common by the beginning of the twentieth century and education departments were by then established in many of the nation's leading universities, courses dealing with history of education in the United States sprang up all over the country. Historians who were not also educators continued to avoid the field. But scholars such as Paul Monroe, with his *Founding of the American Public School System* (1940), and I. L. Kandel, with his *International Yearbook of the International Institute of Teachers College* (1st to 21st editions, 1942–1944, which explored adult education in other countries), contributed vastly to our knowledge.

History of education was identified by its broad area of coverage compared with other kinds of history. The emphasis of historians who were also interested in teacher preparation and school improvement was not simply on the development of the public system of education but also on the social factors that gave rise to the system. In this sense, the history of education may be called the earliest systematic treatment of cultural, social, and intellectual factors affecting the American people. No full understanding of the current educational situation in any nation is possible without knowledge of the evolution of its school system, together with the practices and theories that contributed to its growth. Thus, the educational historians do not limit themselves to a single field of knowledge but draw upon information from such disciplines as economics, sociology, anthropology, and psychology in an effort to get a true conception of educational development. For this reason, their approach should be considered interdisciplinary.

Differing Points of View.   Leading historians of education have been more interested in the application of their studies to professional improvement of teaching than to the study of "pure" history for its own sake. This fact and the educators' point of view have led to disagreements between modern historians of education and professors of history who are interested in studying education. Both groups add to the existing body of knowledge about education. The historian contributes special skill in the detailed study of limited periods, geographical areas, and special topics. Educational historians are usually interested in interpreting broad cultural trends in order to clarify the goals and aims of education, as well as in intensive work on specific topics related to schooling. Historians of education have differed on the interpretation of the facts, especially since scholars entered the field with a strong interest in sociology. Bernard Bailyn (1962) is an example of an author who feels the schools have generally supported educational equality, but Michael Katz (1971), Peter McLaren (1995), and Joel Spring (1990) argue that they have served the special interests of the dominant middle-class whites. Much of the current historical literature in education aligns itself with one of these interpretations of education's role in American culture.

Influence of Recent Changes.   During the past few years, a number of changes have taken place in education that have had a marked influence upon the study of the history of education. Among the more important developments are the following: (a) rapid increase in scientific activity and the accumulation of knowledge, together with an extension of average time spent in school and a major increase in adult education and training by private industries; (b) substantial involvement of the federal government in educational matters, especially after the success of the Soviet space effort in 1957; (c) growth of graduate work in education attributable to a much larger demand for teachers with advanced degrees, bringing many more scholars to the field of history of education; (d) an increased interest in foreign school systems, the role of education in emerging nations, and the problems of social class, racial integration, gender equality, and poverty in America; and (e) the work of critics of the school system in the United States who have taken issue with the organization, methods, and especially the curriculum of our public schools. The history of education is therefore a developing rather than a finished area of study. It is concerned with building a full understanding of the current educational situation through the study of the evolution of educational practices, ideas, and institutions in social context. In a 1964 lecture to the Department of Education of Johns Hopkins University, William W. Brickman described educational history as that branch of history that deals with the development of thought, practice, materials, personnel, administration, organization, and problems of schools. Educational history also includes institutions and organizations that instruct the young and the mature, the mass media, and other learning experiences.

INTELLECTUAL BACKGROUND

American education is Western education, and therefore the intellectual roots for it extend back to ancient Greece and Rome. Socrates, Plato, and Aristotle formed the basis of the school curriculum and also laid the foundation for educational theory. Classical studies especially stressed Latin and the culture of the Greeks and Romans. Humanism in the age of Erasmus (sixteenth century) looked back to Cicero and Quintilian for models of literary style. Leaders of the American Revolution were familiar with writings of classical antiquity and often quoted the ancient writers. (See Chapter 2 for a philosophic discussion of early writers.)

Force of Medieval Tradition.   With the decline and fall of the Roman Empire, an intellectual and social stagnation began in Europe that continued until the several revivals of learning known collectively as the Renaissance. During this era, feudal patterns of social structure and economics developed, and philosophy and learning were handmaidens of the Church. Education was at a low ebb; the monasteries and a few cathedral schools were the chief instruments of instruction. Charlemagne made an effort to revive learning at the end of the eighth century, but theological questions continued to occupy the minds of the learned elite while the great bulk of the people remained ignorant in an "otherworldly" society.

A reintroduction of ancient classical learning, especially the Arabic translations of Aristotle in the thirteenth century, gave rise to the higher level scholarship of Albert the Great and Thomas Aquinas. Medieval universities and the scholasticism of Thomas Aquinas eventually provided a basis for moving beyond the traditions of the Middle Ages. Nevertheless, medieval influences were still very strong at the time of American colonization. They are to be found in the social structure, the dominance of religion, superstitions, and other beliefs widely held by settlers from all parts of Europe.

Impact of the Renaissance.   The Renaissance, or rebirth of learning, began in the 1200s and lasted through the Reformation of the 1500s. Many aspects of this movement had some influence on American development. The Renaissance replaced a religious point of view with a secular one, making man rather than God the focal point with reference to art, literature, and the government. This emphasis on secular concerns, or humanism, was based partly on the transfer of wealth and political power from the Church to laymen and nation-states. The Renaissance also included a revival of interest in the classical culture of ancient Greece and Rome. Humanists studied and imitated the manuscripts of the great writers of the past. They also examined the ancient social order (especially of Rome) and made critical comparisons with their own time. Classicism protested against the narrow religious nature of education in the Middle Ages. Erasmus made editions of the New Testament in Latin and Greek and also criticized the ignorance of the clergy and the injustice of society. Renaissance emphasis on the development of the individual helped to purge ignorance and encourage education. Significant and new inventions made rapid progress in learning possible. As the Renaissance swept through Europe, a great desire for books developed that hand copying or block printing could not satisfy. By about 1440, Johannes Gutenberg had developed his technique for using separate pieces of raised metal type in a press. The resulting revolution in the production and availability of printed information had a profound impact on education in the Western world. The availability of books at a low cost allowed many more members of society to read and think for themselves, instead of accepting everything on the authority of scholars. Growth of cities, revival of trade, exploration, and increased mobility of scholars helped to spread information and expedited the exchange of ideas.

Influence of Scientific Thinking.   From 1500 to 1700, significant changes were taking place in Europe, such as geographic exploration, religious revolution, the growth of nationalism, and the development of science. While the classical humanism of the Renaissance period continued to be the dominant educational force, commercial interests and cultural diversity gave rise to the growth of scientific facts and methods.

Around 1500, Leonardo da Vinci called attention to the importance of observation and experimentation in learning. Francis Bacon (1561–1626) popularized the scientific technique in *Novum Organum* (1863). The astronomical discoveries of Copernicus, Kepler, Galileo, and Bruno challenged traditional conceptions of the universe. William Gilbert made studies of electricity, Robert Boyle examined the chemical properties of gases, and Isaac Newton published basic laws of physics and mechanics. Mathematical support for science was found in the contributions made to calculus and analytical geometry by Leibniz, Descartes, and Newton.

Science was still suspect when the American colonies were founded. Very few learned people accepted the materialism and the concept of a machine universe expounded by Thomas Hobbes or Pierre Gassendi. Nevertheless, the scientific method of thinking did provide a challenge to established beliefs and laid a foundation for the enlightenment of the eighteenth century. William Harvey's theory of the circulation of the blood was discussed at Harvard while that institution remained a theological college strongly opposed to science.

Significance of Religious Revolutions.

Probably no single movement so greatly affected colonial America as the Protestant Reformation and the Catholic Counter-Reformation. The tremendous impact of the Reformation on social, economic, and political life was of paramount importance in the formation of the United States, and some of the influences are still felt today.

In 1517, when Martin Luther posted his Ninety-Five Theses on the church door in Wittenberg, Germany, the Catholic Church was the most important educational agency in the world. At the close of the Thirty Years War, all institutions and every aspect of the culture had been affected. Most of the Europeans who came to America were Protestants, but there were many denominations. Lutherans from Germany and Scandinavia settled in the Middle colonies, especially Pennsylvania. Puritans, Presbyterians, Huguenots, and several smaller sects represented followers of John Calvin. Anabaptists (followers of Huldreich Zwingli [1484–1531]) were persecuted by both Catholic and Protestant authorities, and therefore sought freedom in the New World. Much of the struggle known as the Reformation centered upon efforts to capture the minds of men, and therefore great emphasis was placed upon the written word. Obviously, schools were needed by both sides to foster the growth of each denomination or sect.

Luther's doctrine of the "priesthood of all believers" made it necessary for boys and girls to learn to read the Scriptures. Educational programs intended to give the masses the ability to read the Bible in the vernacular were started by Protestant groups in Germany and wherever Luther's concepts spread. Although the schools were often rudimentary, they offered universal education for all children, regardless of wealth, and were supported by both church and state. Protestants also provided secondary education of higher quality for the elite destined to enter positions in the government or the Church. Although Catholics played a substantially smaller role in colonial America, they were very much part of the Counter-Reformation. Leaders such as Jean Baptiste de la Salle and St. Ignatius of Loyola influenced Catholics in Maryland.

In England, the break with the Catholic Church came when Clement VII refused to annul Henry VIII's marriage to Catherine of Aragon. By the Act of Supremacy in 1534, Henry became head of the Church in England and proceeded to break up the monasteries. The English Church remained very much the same during Henry's time, with the Reformation really starting under Edward VI. Mary I briefly restored Catholicism, but during the long reign of Elizabeth, Anglicanism was firmly established. Anglicanism is a moderate form of Protestantism, which preserves most of the organizational structure of the Catholic Church. English Calvinists who wanted to change or purify the Anglican Church became known as Puritans and were very important in the settlement of New England. Other dissenters from the Anglican faith included some called Separatists, who denied the establishment of religion and held that each man must be free to worship as he thought fit. Followers of John Knox (1505–1572) in Scotland (Presbyterians), Quakers, and Catholics tended to move to America when the political tide was against them in England. For example, the great Puritan migrations in the 1630s took place because of the persecution directed by Anglican Archbishop Laud.

American Colonists: Conservatism and Change.   Students sometimes get the idea that the Renaissance and the Reformation were entirely progressive movements. In fact, they were often reactionary. Humanism looked to the past rather than the future for its model. The Reformation had a tendency to make religion once again the dominant intellectual interest of mankind. Other forces, however, tended to counteract the importance of the Reformation and the Renaissance. The American colonies were an integral part of a great English colonial empire. They were not isolated outposts or temporary communities but a portion of a larger capitalistic scheme brought about by a strong middle class for the purpose of material gain. The rise of capitalism was one of the strongest factors in the development of this nation. Economic motives and interests profoundly affected American civilization from the first. Even the New England Puritan, who came to a "stern and rockbound coast" in order to escape religious oppression, was not without economic concern. The soil in New England was shallow and unproductive. In order to make a living, Pilgrims and Puritans soon turned to timber cutting, ship building, fishing for cod, manufacturing, and trade.

In addition to capitalism, the colonists brought the parliamentary form of government to America. The New Englanders especially supported Parliament against the King. They wished to substitute their own body politic for the authority that had been vested in the crown. Thus, the effort of the Pilgrim Fathers in drawing up the Mayflower Compact, which served as a constitution and defined the responsibilities of the people as well as centering authority in the people, could hardly have occurred without the struggle for parliamentary supremacy that had taken place in the mother country.

Many other potent forces played a part in the intellectual climate out of which American educational institutions developed. The rise of science, British empiricism, the forces of rationalism, and the movement toward greater intellectual discovery all had their effect on the birth of American schools. The point to be made is that American educational and intellectual foundations have roots that run very deep into the European past. Many of the most conservative ideas, such as the evil nature of man, were preserved in America, but there were also factors tending to develop an attitude of change.

FOCUS ON THE ISSUES

Judging the Importance of Historical Events

Do we correctly judge which historical events are important? Take for one example the Acheulian flint hand axe, the longest-lived human invention. This useful cutting tool was found in the oldest communities and probably predates language. The design was passed from generation to generation for thousands of years and may have been independently invented by different cultures. Such stone implements were commonly used by hunting and gathering peoples 500 years ago and are even occasionally seen in use today.

By contrast, the Pony Express had barely become operational when it was superseded by the electric telegraph in 1861. Express riders functioned for a few years only and the entire volume of mail carried was hardly more than a city postal worker now delivers in one day. Why then does every school child know about the Pony Express while the Acheulian axe is hardly remembered? It is because the romantic image of daring young men riding fearlessly through hostile territory to carry a sack of mail from St. Joseph to Sacramento in eight days strikes our imagination and brings to mind our ideas of the romantic Old West. It appeals to images of cowboys and Indians and beliefs about how the nation was settled. The importance of an event or invention is not limited to its actual impact on the culture at the time. It must also be judged by how it altered our concepts of reality and views of the past.

In *The Lord of the Rings* (1954), Tolkien tells us that history becomes myth and myth becomes legend. Did George Washington cut down the cherry tree? Since the first account of this is found in the second biography of Washington by Mason Locke Weems, it appears to be an invention aimed at selling books. Yet it remains in the collective American mind as the model of Washington's honesty.

What Do You Think?

1. Do new programs use the most important events for their headlines or the ones that are judged to be the most sensational?
2. One hundred times more American students are killed in automobile accidents each year than are harmed by incidents of school violence. Why is so much more attention paid to violence?
3. When we consider an educational event, do we always think about how many people will be affected by it and to what degree?
4. Give examples of social change and core values in education and society.

THEN TO NOW

The casual student of history may not immediately see the relationship of the remote past to the age in which we live. Nevertheless, connections do exist between the world of today and those past traditions that were once dominant.

The History of Curriculum. A better understanding of modern attitudes and ideas can be gleaned from an analysis of historical forces. Consider, for example, the curriculum of present schools and colleges. Medieval universities offered studies derived from ancient educational interests reaching back to Aristotle. These were the seven liberal arts that scholars believed to be essential to the life of the mind and the education of men. The basic or tool subjects were grammar, logic, and rhetoric. Advanced studies consisted of arithmetic, geometry, astronomy, and harmony. Although the names have sometimes changed (music for harmony and language arts for grammar), it is obvious that these medieval curriculum offerings are still found in the schools. It is also true that modern groupings into the natural sciences, the social sciences, and the humanities are based on these early subjects and that we still speak of a liberal arts curriculum in reference to such studies. There have been many modifications and additions, but the curriculum of the Middle Ages' universities has not disappeared. The whole idea of a university stems from the medieval organization of a guild of teachers and a guild of students. The modern master's degree is named after the guild practice of awarding master craftsman status for those who had demonstrated excellence in their work. Our most modern research universities still have deans, lecture halls, graduation rites, student organizations, and rectors (presidents), all of which were part of the early universities.

The Spirit of Inquiry and Dissemination of Knowledge.   The rebirth of learning known as the Renaissance has never really ceased. Ideas from the classical past together with the humanism of scholars like Erasmus produced a new desire to understand the forces that shape human society. When modern sociologists attempt to analyze the actions of groups of people, they are involved in the spirit of inquiry that was the heart of the Renaissance. Educators today still debate the role of humanistic studies in an age of scientific research and specialization. Likewise, the invention of the printing press led to improved production and distribution of information that is still accelerating. Modern telecommunications, information superhighways, electronic media, and computer-based research are current aspects of the revolution started by Gutenberg. It also should be obvious that the secular scientific thinking started by Bacon, Galileo, Gilbert, and others has continued to grow and expand at a rapid rate. The study of the history of science in many universities and popular television programs like *Connections* and radio programs like *Science Friday* illustrate the need for understanding the past in order to cope with the present. Current issues over tax support for religious schools may be linked to the struggles of the Protestant Reformation and the Catholic Counter-Reformation.

Identifying Currents of Thought Through History.   Although we are able to get a better picture of the forces that shaped values and attitudes of historical times than we can of the forces that shaped the values and attitudes of today, currents of opinion and climates of thought are difficult to isolate in any age. It is easy enough to mark the founding of the English settlement on the American seaboard with Jamestown in 1607 and to mark the first major school law with the Old Deluder Satan Act of 1647, but it is another matter to trace the cultural forces that shaped the minds and deeds of the colonists. Nevertheless, whatever light can be cast on the intellectual, social, ethical, and philosophic forces that created colonial culture will be useful in helping to gain a better understanding of our own times. Just as the Puritan ethic of early America still casts its shadow over modern educational theory and practice (as in the case of Bible reading and prayer in public schools), so the Puritans themselves were influenced by mainstreams of thought going back at least to medieval times. As difficult as the task may be, cultural and intellectual history must try to identify main currents of thought and influential values that set the parameters of basic cultural beliefs. In this way, history can be a most useful tool in helping us to understand ourselves and the times in which we live.

Because we tend to think in a contemporary time frame, it is important to recall that many of the movements considered in this book occurred over a period of years. The Protestant Reformation and the Catholic Counter-Reformation were not single events like those reported every day on CBS, NBC, ABC, CNN, and Fox News. They were revolutions of many facets of society that took centuries to develop and decades to complete, and their aftermath continues to be felt in contemporary society. Because of the brief treatment given to colonial history in the common school history courses, it is easy to make the error of thinking of the colonial period as brief. Actually, the years between the settlement of Jamestown and the American Revolution cover almost half of the time that has elapsed since 1607. In the passing of nearly two centuries, the changes that occurred in colonial America were dramatic and vast, even though they took place at a slower rate than modern transformations. The revolt against England and the birth of a new nation could hardly have taken place in the conservative climate of opinion that existed in the beginning of the seventeenth century.

Changing World Conditions.   Educational development in colonial America and its influence on the schools of later times can only be appreciated against the backdrop of an earlier Old World culture. What is happening in education today must also be evaluated in terms of changing world conditions. For the first time in history, all of the school-age children in mainland China actually attend school. Mass starvation and continuing ethnic conflicts in East and Central Africa make it impossible for children there to reach their full potential or to achieve educational goals. Currently, nations of the former Soviet Union are in the throes of trying to reconcile Western capitalism with citizens' demands for jobs and the sustenance protection offered by the old communist regime. The Bosnian conflict also reflects a return to the balance of power system so prevalent in history. Russia has emerged as a power broker, influencing competing interests in Bosnia as well as in the Middle East. The continuing pressures of an interdependent global community will influence our economic system. All people are affected by the ways in which natural resources are used, and all are demanding more human services, including education. An airport or a computer is much the same whether it is found in New York, Manila, or Buenos Aires. Our educational history began with influences from many areas and traditions; the future of education also depends on events and developments that are global in nature.

Many causes were at work in the settlement of the American colonies. Adventure, money, love of God, and a desire to convert the Native Americans gave rise to the colonies. Many wished to escape oppressive governments and the hard times in Europe, such as the English depression of 1595. The first settlers were Europeans, dominated by English traditions. Modern society in the United States has been greatly modified by the influx of other people and ideas, but the Protestant religions and the English language remain dominant today although Hispanic culture and language are expanding. This dominance, like that of middle-class values in schools, creates a major educational problem in equal treatment of students whose first language is other than English or who represent religious backgrounds other than Protestant Christian.

Why the Past Illuminates Today.

Most of the time and effort of teachers and administrators in schools is spent dealing with contemporary needs and problems. It is all too easy for us to think of events in the remote past as having no relevance for modern educators, if we think of such events at all. This is a fundamental mistake that may prevent us from making the best decisions for the well-being of our students and their communities. Religious conflicts starting with the protests of Martin Luther are still evident in current arguments over prayer in public schools. Attacks by the "ultra-right wing" on "secular humanism," as well as by various other special interest groups including advocates of home schooling, can be clarified by an understanding of conservative theology, Renaissance humanism, and *laissez-faire* politics. Several states have passed or are considering passage of a law requiring schools to give equal time to the biblical theory of creation and the theory of evolution. It is not enough to link this matter with the work of Darwin or with the Scopes trial in 1925. The educator needs also to consider it in the light of the opposition to scientific knowledge in the time of Copernicus and Bruno. Historical knowledge is vital for placing current issues into perspective and making decisions that will stand critical analysis.

Look to the Evidence.

Sources of educational history include deeds, contracts, oral history, archival records, newspaper morgues, personal correspondence, archaeological discoveries, museums, art, tools, garments, flyers, government documents, artifacts, charters, journals, texts, and diaries of the period, all of which provide avenues to understanding our past. Formal or primary sources for educational theory consist of the original writings of philosophers and treatments of schools of philosophy from idealism to postmodernism. Secondary sources are compilations or interpretations of original works. Educational theory can also be gleaned from values, attitudes, curriculum choices, and criticism of schools, whether or not they are linked to an articulated philosophy.

How Does the History of Education Apply to Educators Today?

As one examines our educational history, one sees that cycles of change occur and reoccur. New terminology often covers age-old educational concepts and innovations. Plutarch's Lycurgus sought critical thinking, discipline, and ethical conduct through education. Today people emphasize these concepts and the importance of character building. Although we have witnessed increased educational and employment opportunities for women, minorities, culturally diverse populations, those who are physically or mentally challenged, and senior citizens, debate over curriculum content, public and private education, and what is ultimately worth knowing continues now as in the past.

GAINING PERSPECTIVE THROUGH CRITICAL ANALYSIS

1. Evaluate the process of making educational decisions in a culture with a large core of common values as compared to doing so in contemporary American society.

2. Describe the significance of each of the following forces on education:

   ❑ Medieval tradition
   ❑ The Renaissance
   ❑ Scientific thinking
   ❑ Religious revolutions

3. Identify three reasons why teachers and other educators can benefit from studying the history of education.

4. Give two examples of modern educators "reinventing the wheel" because they lack historical knowledge and perspective.

5. Compare and contrast the contributions of the Protestant Reformation and the Catholic Counter-Reformation on the development of education in colonial America. Identify some current religious influences on current educational practice. (It will be helpful to have a journal to record historical highlights and watersheds.)

6. Give an example of attempts to develop a classless society.

HISTORY IN ACTION IN TODAY'S CLASSROOMS

1. Interview a retired teacher or administrator. Ask him or her to discuss educational reform cycles and trends during his or her career. Does he or she remember one-room schools? Keep a journal of your findings to share in class.

2. What are some current forces that have shaped educational history as a discipline in recent years? Cite a journal or Internet article to support your opinion.

3. Trace the history of significant religious revolutions. Identify current religious movements and their effect on education.

4. Identify influences that lead to an accelerating rate of change in society, culture, and education. Discuss and answer the questions at the end of the Focus on the Issues features "Cultural Diversity" and "Judging the Importance of Historical Events." These features are found within the chapter.

BIBLIOGRAPHY

Bacon, Francis. *Novum Organum.* Translated by James Spedding, Robert Leslie Ellis, & Douglas Denon Heath in *The Works,* volume VIII. Boston: Taggard and Thompson, 1863.

Bailyn, Bernard. *Education in the Forming of American Society: Needs and Opportunities for Study.* New York: W. W. Norton, 1962.

Barrow, Robin. *Plato and Education.* Boston: Routledge & Kegan Paul, 1976.

Brann, Eva. *Paradoxes of Education in a Republic.* Chicago: The University of Chicago Press, 1979.

Cahn, Steven M. *Classic and Contemporary Readings in the Philosophy of Education.* New York: McGraw-Hill, 1997.

Church, Robert L. *Education in the United States.* New York: The Free Press, 1976.

Clough, A. H. *Plutarch's Lives.* New York: Bigelow, Smith and Co., 1911.

Cremin, Lawrence A. *American Education, The Colonial Experience.* New York: Harper & Row, 1970.

Cruickshank, Donald R., & Associates. *Preparing America's Teachers.* Bloomington, IN: Phi Delta Kappa, 1996.

Cubberley, Ellwood. *Public Education in the United States.* Boston: Houghton Mifflin, 1934.

Curti, Merle. *The Social Ideas of American Educators.* Totowa, NJ: Littlefield, Adams, 1968.

Curtis, Stanley, & M. E. A. Boultwood. *A Short History of Educational Ideas.* 3rd ed. London: University Tutorial Press, 1964.

Fleury, Claude. *Treatise on the Selection and Methods of Study.* France, circa 1700.

Grant, Gerald, Ed. *Review of Research in Education: Section 11 History and Philosophy*. Washington, DC: American Educational Research Association, 1992.

Gross, Richard, Ed. *Heritage of American Education*. Boston: Allyn & Bacon, 1962.

Guvlet, Robert. *The Compendium Universitatis Parisiensis*. Translated by Robert Belle Burke from the Latin original. Philadelphia: University of Pennsylvania Press, 1928. Originally published in 1517.

Gwynn, Aubrey. *Roman Education from Cicero to Quintilian*. Rev. ed. New York: Teachers College Press, 1966.

Harris, Benjamin. *The New England Primer*. New England: Author, 1690.

Holley, Raymond. *Religious Education and Religious Understanding*. Boston: Routledge & Kegan Paul, 1978.

Homer. *The Iliad*. Translated by Robert Fagles. New York: Penguin Books, 1990. Originally published in 800 B.C.E.

Kandel, I. L. *Educational Yearbooks of the International Institute of Teachers College*. New York: Bureau of Publications of Teachers College Columbia University, 1934.

Katz, Michael B. *Class, Bureaucracy and the School*. New York: Praeger, 1971.

Labaree, David F. "Public Goods, Private Goods: The American Struggle Over Educational Goals." *American Educational Research Association Journal* 34, no. 1 (Spring 1997): 39–82.

Longfellow, Henry Wadsworth. *Evangeline*. Boston: William D. Ticknor & Company, 1847.

McLaren, Peter. *Critical Pedagogy and Predatory Culture*. New York: Routledge, 1995.

McMillan, James H., & Sally Schumacher. *Research in Education: A Conceptual Introduction*. New York: Harper Collins, College Publishers, 1993.

Meyer, Adolphe. *Grandmasters of Educational Thought*. New York: McGraw-Hill, 1975.

Monroe, Paul. *Founding of the American Public School System*. 2 vols. New York: Macmillan, 1940.

Mulhern, James. *A History of Education*. 2nd ed. New York: Ronald, 1959.

Perkinson, Harry. *Two Hundred Years of American Educational Thought*. New York: David McKay Company, 1976.

Plutarch. *Lives of Noble Grecians and Romans*. Edited by Arthur Hugh Clough & translated by John Dryden. New York: Random House, 1992. Originally written at the start of the second century A.D.

Pounds, Ralph. *The Development of Education in Western Culture*. New York: Appleton-Century-Crofts, 1968.

Quintilian. *Institutio Oratoria*. Originally published in the first century A.D., 1920–1922.

Ravitch, Diane. *The Revisionists Revisited: A Critique of the Radical Attack on the Schools*. New York: Basic Books, 1978.

Reed, Ronald F. *Philosophical Documents in Education*. New York: Longman, 1996.

Rusk, Robert. *The Doctrines of the Great Educators*. Rev. ed. New York: Macmillan, 1969.

Sherman, Robert, Ed. *Understanding History of Education*. Rev. ed. Cambridge, MA: Schenkaman Publishing Company, 1984.

Spring, Joel. *The American School: 1642–1990*. New York: Longman, 1990.

Spring, Joel. *Images of American Life*. Albany: State University of New York Press, 1992.

Toffler, Alvin. *Future Shock*. New York: Random House, 1970.

Toffler, Alvin. *The Third Wave*. New York: William Morrow, 1980.

Tolkien, J. R. R. *The Lord of the Rings*. Boston: Houghton Mifflin, 1954.

Weems, Mason Locke. *The Life of Washington*. Philadelphia: J. B. Lippincott, 1918. Originally published in Philadelphia in 1800.

Wood, Norman. *The Reformation and English Education*. London: University Tutorial Press, 1931.

CHAPTER 2

SHAPING THE SCHOOLS: PHILOSOPHICAL, SOCIAL, AND PSYCHOLOGICAL FOUNDATIONS

Only in education, never in the life of farmer, sailor, merchant, physician, or laboratory experimenter, does knowledge mean primarily a store of information aloof from doing.

John Dewey

BC	AD	1200–1800	1800–1900
427–347 Plato		Aquinas (1225–1274) Locke (1632–1704) Berkeley (1685–1753)	Kierkegaard (1813–1855) Spencer (1820–1903) Peirce (1839–1914)
384–322 Aristotle		Rousseau (1712–1778) Herbart (1776–1841)	Whitehead (1861–1947) Russell (1872–1970)
	Religious Diversity		Social Reconstruction

Figure 2.1   Time Line for Philosophies of Education

John Dewey, the best-known American educational philosopher and the intellectual founder of the progressive movement, wanted to make schools practical, experience based, and a mirror of life. To do so, he had to combat long-standing educational traditions and the entrenched theories of education grounded in idealism and realism. Shaping any school system requires knowledge of the historical forces in play, a clear understanding of goals determined by philosophy, and consideration of anticipated change. For example, modern China is approaching a population of a billion and a half people. This is largely because of political and economic changes that have almost doubled life expectancy. For the first time in history, all the children in China receive state-supported schooling and, although opportunities are still limited, an increasing number of students go on to higher education. Although communism is in decline in the rest of the world, one cannot hope to understand modern Chinese educational theory without knowledge of the philosophy of Marx and Mao. This knowledge is also critical to American education as the Chinese move into the global marketplace.

Because contemporary American schools look very much the same in organization, structure, and curriculum, it is easy to assume that there is agreement on their philosophic foundations. In fact, as educational issues occur and recur, so do underlying philosophical contentions. A shared public philosophy may support universal schooling with tax support for all American children, but it does not extend to cover what subjects are most important in the curriculum, whether compulsory education is justified, or what ethical training should be included in schools. Shaping schools requires an exploration of alternative views of what is ultimately worth knowing and the various aims, policies, and ideologies expressed in school and society throughout history as well as in the contemporary period. There can be no educational program without clarity of its aims and theory. It is of vital importance for a teacher, a staff member, or an administrator to know what theory underlies his or her school policy and also to understand philosophically the basis for criticism or disagreement from parents or the public.

Modern	
James (1842–1910)	Skinner (1904–1990)
Dewey (1859–1952)	Rawls (1919–2002)
Buber (1878–1965)	Foucault (1926–1984)
Thorndike (1874–1949)	Habermas (1929–)
Wittgenstein (1889–1951)	Derrida (1930–2004)
Humanism	Rorty (1931–)

Focus on the Issues

Philosophical Divisions

Because the standard divisions of philosophy are ancient, extending back to Aristotle, one might get the impression that answers to the most important philosophical questions have been long established. Nothing could be further from the truth. Modern change and new discovery force us to reconsider time-honored conclusions reached by great thinkers of the past.

In metaphysics, the stable and uniform laws of Isaac Newton were thought to govern and explain everything. We are still dependent upon Newtonian physics for most pragmatic decisions but we find his theory inadequate to explain the universe. Albert Einstein proved Newton wrong in his interpretation of time and space. But while Einstein made enormous contributions, he searched in vain for a unifying principle governing universal reality. Now the Hubble Space Telescope reveals myriad galaxies moving away from one another and from us at accelerating speed as if the explosion known as the Big Bang is still in progress. At the opposite end of reality, quantum mechanics allows us to predict the probable behavior of subatomic particles or waves and thus build models that work in fields like medicine and computer science. Nevertheless, we have no exact knowledge of the smallest building blocks of reality and so are dependent on speculation like string theory, for which no scientific proof can be developed with current methods. Metaphysics is therefore a wide-open field today.

Likewise epistemology (theory of knowledge) is affected by scientific discovery that gives new information but also opens new questions. We may have great confidence in our knowledge of fields like cosmology, genetics, and medicine, but there remains much of which we are ignorant. The rules of correct thinking (logic) are entwined with the verification of knowledge, but both are inadequate for dealing with many scientific breakthroughs. In nuclear physics, quarks defy logic by appearing to be in two or more places at the same time and orbit the nucleus of the atom in random or chaotic paths. The uncertainty principle of quantum physics puts in question both the certainty required for epistemology and logical methods of thought. Theory of value (called *axiology;* and especially its branch called *ethics*) is also affected by new invention.

What Do You Think?

1. We now have the scientific ability to clone humans. If we do this, imagine the urgency of the ethical questions. Is a clone fully human? Does a clone have civil and political rights?
2. Can clones be used as slaves or for spare body parts?
3. Does a person have a right to make clones of him- or herself? You can readily see that the great philosophic questions in all divisions have not yet been resolved.
4. Describe cultural and religious diversity. Identify goals of and examples of social reconstructionism in schools and society.

INTRODUCTION TO EDUCATIONAL PHILOSOPHY

Webster's Dictionary defines *philosophy* as the "love of wisdom," which is a literal rendering of the Greek word. Philosophy deals with ultimate questions such as the nature of truth, what is real, and what is of value. Speculative, reflective, and theoretical attempts to answer questions about the basic purposes, goals, and outcomes of formal education are philosophical in nature. Those questions dealing with the nature of knowledge, the characteristics of the educated person, or the structure of the curriculum are the broadest issues for philosophy of education. Those dealing with methods of teaching or the length of the school year have a somewhat less abstract nature. Although the terms are sometimes used interchangeably, educational theory is more focused and narrow in scope than educational philosophy. Before the twentieth century, most American educational philosophy was derived from the great systems or schools of philosophy, especially idealism and realism. Although these positions are still supported with vigor by many policy makers in education, they have been challenged recently by contrasting views expressed by pragmatists, existentialists, futurists, and analytic philosophers, among others.

Traditional philosophy, like other fields of discipline inquiry, is divided into categories. These categories are important because they focus the arguments between schools and illustrate what is most important to individual philosophers. Idealism and realism deal equally with all divisions, pragmatists have little to say on questions of ultimate reality, and analytic philosophers concentrate on rules of valid thinking. The basic divisions are metaphysics, epistemology, axiology, and logic.

Metaphysics is concerned with reality and existence. For education, the conception of reality reflected in the curriculum and the experiences of the student are paramount. Formal education describes and defines reality as it is understood by those in control of the learning environment. Obviously, reality would appear differently to an Athenian citizen in the age of Pericles than to a Puritan minister in colonial New England, or to an astronomer gathering X-ray data on a distant galaxy.

Epistemology is the theory of knowledge and includes the study of how we know. Does knowledge begin with sensations from objects, as realists think? Are pragmatists correct in their belief that we create knowledge by interaction with our environment? Are idealists correct in saying that knowing is the recollection of absolute ideas that have an independent existence of their own? The answers imply stimulating questions about the learner, problem solving, and the use of sensory stimuli. Clearly, knowing and knowledge are critical to any theory of education.

The division known as axiology includes ethics, aesthetics, and the formation of values. Ethics examines moral values; aesthetics deals with the values of beauty and art. All teachers must be concerned with the formation of values by children and the encouragement of behaviors that conform to some conception of that which is true, good, or beautiful. Many educational theories such as idealism and realism hold that values are valid in all times and places (objective theory of value); however, pragmatists and social theorists say that they are culturally or ethically relative. Many of the major conflicts over the impact of the school in the formation of character and in guiding behavior are grounded in axiology.

The final division, logic, is concerned with the rules of valid thinking. The study of logic was once required of all university students but now is limited to the discipline of formal philosophy. It is still basic to the rules of correct argument. Analytical philosophy relies on logic; existentialism subsumes it under personal feeling and individual freedom. Inductive logic is associated with empiricism and pragmatism; realism and perennialism rely on deduction from first principles. A very good way to understand philosophers or schools of philosophy is to study their positions on metaphysics, epistemology, axiology, and logic. Questions about ultimate reality, the nature of knowledge, values, and rules of thinking (even when a given theory is silent on the topic) reveal a great deal about any philosopher or philosophy.

SCHOOLS OF EDUCATIONAL PHILOSOPHY

No Neat and Tidy Boxes.   Neither educational philosophy nor philosophy itself divides automatically into neat categories. The discrete schools, or "isms" as they are often called, have no validity apart from the thinkers whose systems of thought they represent. Just as Aristotle found it helpful to group plants and animals into classes according to their similarities, students of philosophy find that classifying is a good tool for understanding theoretical positions. We must remember, however, that individual members of a school or "ism" do not always agree on every point (see Tables 2.1, 2.2, 2.3, and 2.4).

Most everyone agrees that Plato, Hegel, Kant, Berkeley, and Horne are representatives of idealism, whereas Bacon, Locke, and Hume are British empiricists. However, Albert Camus is called both a logical positivist and an existentialist, and some philosophers defy classification altogether. Names may also be confusing. For example, John Dewey only slightly modified his position during his long career, but is classified by different authors as a pragmatist, an instrumentalist, and a progressive. Most commonly used categories provide a foundation for the study of educational practice grounded in philosophy, but classification schemes may vary. For example, J. Donald Butler in *Four Philosophies and Their Practice in Education and Religion* (1957) includes naturalism as a school, and J. Arthur Cooper in *Exemplars in Educational Philosophy* (1988) created a division called "eternalism." Most of the authors included under naturalism or eternalism are identified in other standard categories.

Drawn from Many Sources.   As we examine the schools, one other disclaimer should be kept in mind. Some famous philosophers such as Rousseau and Whitehead devoted much of their attention to education; others such as Hegel and Bergson did not write on the subject. There are major educational theorists, Comenius and Pestalozzi, for example, who are not recognized as important in general philosophy. Sometimes educational ideas from a variety of nonphilosophical sources are incorporated into a theoretical school. Educational futurism draws from sociology, economics, communications theory, and cybernetics as much as from philosophy. Postmodernism tends to defy analysis in terms of the models used by classical philosophers.

Table 2.1   Alternative Philosophies of Education and Their Exponents

Educational Philosophy	Influences	Rationale	Curriculum
Perennialism (Neo-Thomism)	St. Thomas Aquinas Jacques Maritain Robert M. Hutchins Stringfellow Barr Max Rafferty Mortimer Adler	Stresses intellectual attainment and the search for truth	The Great Books The classics Liberal arts
Idealism (Perennialism)	Plato Josiah Royce Immanuel Kant Ralph Waldo Emerson Herman Horne	All material things are explainable	History Biography Humanities
Realism (Essentialism)	Alfred N. Whitehead Aristotle John Amos Comenius Johann F. Herbart John Locke Harry Broudy	Propositions are true only if they correspond with known facts	Science Mathematics Quantitative subjects Foreign language
Pragmatism	Boyd Bode John Dewey William James Charles Peirce William Kilpatrick	Search for things that work Experimental Democratic	Core curriculum Student centered Revolves around the interest of the student
Reconstructionism	Theodore Brameld George Counts Harold Rugg Ivan Illich John Holt Paul Goodman	Seeks to reconstruct society through education	Current events Social problems Futures research Sociology Political science
Protest Philosophy (Behaviorism, Existentialism, and Postmodernism)	John Paul Sartre Soren Kierkegaard Martin Buber Albert Camus Martin Heidegger A. S. Neill Carl Rogers B. F. Skinner Richard Rorty	Importance of the individual Subjectivity Discover the inner nature of things and people Rejection of logic and reason	Individual preference Psychology Human relations

Developed by Timothy J. Bergen Jr., University of South Carolina, and modified by the authors.

Table 2.2   Educational Implications of Alternative Philosophies of Education

Educational Philosophy	Teacher	Method of Teaching	Examinations
Perennialism (Neo-Thomism)	A taskmaster–philosophically oriented and knowledgeable about the Great Books	Lectures Discussions Seminars	Essay
Idealism (Perennialism)	Serves as the ideal A good role model	Lectures Discussions Imitation	Essay
Realism (Essentialism)	Presents subject in a highly organized and very exact manner	Lectures Demonstrations Sensory experiences Teaching machines	Objective
Pragmatism	A guide One who can present meaningful knowledge with skill	Discussions Projects	Gauge how well people can problem solve
Reconstructionism	Social activist	Real-life projects	Students select, administer, and evaluate Gauge ability as an activist
Protest Philosophy (Behaviorism, Existentialism, and Postmodernism)	Very committed individual Person who is both teacher and learner One who provides a free environment to learn	Learner is encouraged to discover the best method for him/herself	Student should learn to examine him/herself Learner should be aware of sexism, racism, and social control

Developed by Timothy J. Bergen Jr., University of South Carolina, and modified by the authors.

Slow and Homogeneous Development.   American educational philosophy developed slowly. Colonial and early national schools were simple in curriculum, goals, and organization. So long as the general public (consisting largely of farmers and factory workers) was satisfied with the three *R*'s (reading, writing, and arithmetic), conflict was minimal. Common values could be identified in a fairly homogeneous population keenly interested in a better standard of living but less concerned with social and intellectual issues. Before the vast expansion of the high school following the Kalamazoo court decision (1874), secondary education was confined to the college-bound elite. Colleges dictated both the educational theory and the curriculum of the high schools. In turn, colleges and universities reflected the beliefs of their boards, presidents, and faculties. Religious idealism was strong in denominational colleges, Scottish realism dominated state universities, and Thomism governed the Catholic institutions. Science was not in vogue, and no alternative values were tolerated in high schools or colleges.

Table 2.3 Educational Outcomes of Alternative Philosophies of Education

Educational Philosophy	Preferred Architecture	Criticism	Educational Outcome
Perennialism (Neo-Thomism)	Classical	Very elite and aristocratic Must be accepted on faith and absolute truth	An intellectual scholar
Idealism (Perennialism)	Traditional	Elite	An intellectual scholar
Realism (Essentialism)	Efficient Functional	Often fails to deal with social change	Technician scientist
Pragmatism	Flexible Natural	Permissive Very democratic Replace history with social studies	Good problem solver
Reconstructionism	Non-school setting "Schools without walls"	Very utopian Very impatient	Social activist
Protest Philosophy (Behaviorism, Existentialism, and Postmodernism)	Individual preference	Unsystematic Rejects all authority Opposes discipline, order, and logic	Inner-directed Authentic person Committed, involved, cares Independent thinking and nonconformist

Developed by Timothy J. Bergen Jr., University of South Carolina, and modified by the authors.

Philosophical Theory: Origins.   Not only was philosophic conflict rare in American education prior to this century, but the most important educational ideas were imported from Europe. Comenius, Locke, Rousseau, Pestalozzi, Froebel, and Herbart were the respected leaders in educational theory until the twentieth-century American philosophers emerged. Even today, foreign thinkers contribute to many educational theories. With the collapse of the Soviet Union, Russian communism is in decline, but at least a fourth of the world's children are in schools that follow some form of Marxism. Only a handful of Americans accept or contribute to the contemporary school of Marxist education, but it is a vital philosophy in Europe, Africa, and Asia. Existentialism is largely European with some American support, and analytic philosophy of education is about evenly split between British and American authors. However, pragmatism, behaviorism, and social reconstructionism are unique to the United States. Postmodernism as well as social and futures philosophy are still emerging; thus, the major contributors to these educational theories are still emerging. It is useful to examine the various schools in order to understand the basis of contemporary education.

Table 2.4 Non-Western Philosophy

Educational Philosophy	Influences	Rationale	Curricula	Teacher	Method of Teaching	Examinations	Preferred Architecture	Criticism	Educational Outcome
Islamic	Mohammed ******	Spread of Islam Preserve traditions	Conservative Islamic Anti-Western Cultural conformity	Orthodox Moslem Politically correct	Lecture Memorization Rote learning	Objective	Sexually segregated No graphic art Traditional Islamic	Culturally limited Prejudiced against Non-Moslems Not globally ready	Islamic conformity Traditional values Basic skills
Chinese Commu******	******Deng Capitalism	World economic competition Loyalty to State Better living standards	Science Mathematics Technology Foreign languages Loyalty to State	Highly skilled professional Party approved	Modern electronic (where available) Wide range of methods	Highly competitive Failure to pass is a disgrace	Open classroom Ultra modern plant Any available space	Emphasis on jobs Not socially well rounded	Economically competitive Loyal citizen Excellence in training
Oriental (Japan, India, South Korea)	Buddha Hinduism Shintoism Economic growth	Economic growth Job preparation Improved social status	Basic subjects Technical training Computer skills	Mostly professionals Well educated Highly respected	Many methods: traditional to modern	Many different types Usually objective	Various new buildings, but old also used	Emphasis on jobs and technology No social or cultural curriculum	Technician Professional Scientist Globally competitive

Idealism. Plato. Idealism is a very old traditional philosophy, and Plato. (427–347 B.C.) is credited with providing the philosophic principles upon which it rests. The term refers to the reality of ideas, or mind, spirit, and reason. Idealism is in opposition to materialism and realism. Plato held that only mental or spiritual aspects of experience are ultimately real. He used the myth of the cave and the allegory of the divided line to convince his followers that ordinary commonsense objects exist only as copies of absolute ideas or "forms." In the cave, a person held captive from birth experiences only the dim light and shadows on the wall made by his captors and the objects they manipulate. Eventually he breaks loose and emerges from the cave where he experiences the "real" world of sunshine, other people, farms, and the sea. Having once "seen the light," he can never again believe in the reality of the cave.

St. Augustine and Other Idealists.   Because the universal mind is real for idealists and the individual's spiritual essence, or soul, is permanent, the philosophy is compatible with organized religion. St. Augustine (354–430) had been a teacher of rhetoric as a young man. He employed many of the ideas of Plato in the Church and made idealism a Christian theology. The seven liberal arts consisting of the trivium (logic, grammar, and rhetoric) and the quadrivium (music, arithmetic, geometry, and astronomy) were Platonic subjects, modified by the fathers of the Church. They persisted into the medieval universities and are still found in the modern curriculum.

Other famous idealists include René Descartes (1596–1650), George Berkeley (1685–1753), Immanuel Kant (1724–1804), and George W. F. Hegel (1770–1831). Berkeley took the extreme position that physical objects cannot exist on their own, but that they depend on some mind for their reality. Kant's transcendental idealism stated that an object consisted of ideas in our mind but that a thing observed might exist "in itself" independent of the knowing mind. For Hegel's "absolute idealism," both the object itself and the object known to us are ideas of the universal mind. If the universal mind is defined as God, it is easy to see why this philosophy dominated religious institutions and influenced American transcendentalists such as Emerson and Thoreau. American education in the nineteenth century was greatly influenced by Friedrich Froebel (1782–1852) and William Torrey Harris, both idealists. Josiah Royce (1855–1916) and Herman Horne (1874–1946), contemporaries of John Dewey, were idealists in America. In addition, J. Donald Butler was an ardent spokesman for American educational idealism.

Idealists think that only the spiritual is ultimately real and that the universe is the expression of a universal mind or a generalized intelligence. This mind is permanent, regular, orderly, and eternal; the truth it represents is absolute and universal. Through education, the individual mind or soul may come to understand and appreciate these unalterable truths. For idealists, teaching is bringing forth latent knowledge so that a general awareness of universal truths will emerge.

Intellectual disciplines or conceptional systems—such as mathematics, language, ethical studies, history, and the sciences—represent a synthesis of the universal mind. The liberal arts and all other formal intellectual disciplines lead to the highest order of knowledge about reality. Integration of all subjects is important to idealistic pedagogy. Logic and mathematics are powerful tools that cultivate the ability of the student to deal with abstractions and the most sophisticated aspects of the cultural heritage. Vocational subjects, or those that have a practical outcome, are not highly valued. Natural and physical sciences are useful because they deal with cause and effect. History and literature hold a higher place in the curriculum because they provide cultural models. At the top of the hierarchy are the general disciplines of philosophy and theology, which are the most abstract and which transcend time and space. Clearly an idealist school or college would lean heavily toward the arts and sciences and would stress general or what is called "liberal" education of the arts. Idealists will not tolerate an elective system by which students may choose to boycott general education and concentrate on job preparation. Although idealism as a philosophy of education is still found among educators in the United States, it is no longer a dominant theory as was the case in the nineteenth century. The vast expansion of science and technology has also contributed to the decline of idealism. Friedrich Froebel, founder of the kindergarten, followed the tenets of idealism in both theory and practice in his work with childhood education.

Educational aims of seventeenth- and eighteenth-century American colleges included moral and ethical conduct, universal truths and knowledge, and expounding the best ideals of humankind. Although often honored more in the breach than the observance, these idealistic values were taught in colonial colleges as well as in their European models. Religion and idealism were often interrelated in schools and colleges of the period.

Realism.   Realism is a school of philosophy that stresses objective knowledge and information that comes from the senses. These philosophers hold that there is a real world not constructed by human minds that can be known by the mind. Knowledge of reality is the only reliable means of guiding individual and social conduct. Reality is found in the realm of objects and perceptions about objects, and these objects are matter. According to realists, division between object and form does not exist. Human beings can know reality through examination of objects and through reason.

Aristotle.   Plato's student Aristotle (384–322 B.C.) is considered to be the father of philosophic realism. Although he did not reject the existence of ideas or forms, Aristotle found it impossible to separate the study of sense objects from their blueprints or forms. Plato would consider the idea of a rectangular solid in the abstract. Aristotle insisted on examining the object itself. For example, a brick takes the form of a rectangular solid, and that is its basic plan or idea. The brick is made of straw, sand, and clay, and that is its materialistic nature. Aristotle was also interested in the force that made the object (the brick maker) and the purpose for which it was intended, such as a brick wall (final cause). He invented many of the standard ways of looking at things, such as classification into categories and the examination of individuals within a class. We can know objects directly through sensation and indirectly through contemplation or abstraction. When a number of individual objects have the same characteristics, we can generalize about them. This is a spectator epistemology in that the learner is an onlooker who sorts and classifies objects in his or her environment. Spectators may verify conceptions by correspondence with objects in the sense world. This is the empirical principle of John Locke (1632–1704).

St. Thomas Aquinas.   Just as Plato's ideas were adapted to the Church by St. Augustine, those of Aristotle were brought into harmony with Christian doctrine by St. Thomas Aquinas (1225–1274). He held that God is pure reason, and by use of reason, we could come to know the truth of reality. Proofs of the existence of God rely heavily upon observation so that scientific activity, while subordinate to reason, is justified. Aquinas saw philosophy as the handmaiden of theology and, therefore, a tool for reaching God. Knowledge can be gained from sense experience, and reason may be applied to sense data, revealing the divine plan. A proper education recognizes both the material and the spiritual nature of man. Thomism is still the philosophy of education for Roman Catholic institutions and has greatly influenced other branches of Christianity as well.

The term *sense realism* refers to the process of sorting objects in the environment and gaining an understanding of reality through observation and classification. In this sense, Bacon, Locke, Comenius, Rousseau, and Pestalozzi were realists. Sense realism, as in the case of Comenius, may be combined with religious or rational realism. The curriculum should be organized into separate subjects in order to create an efficient and effective means of learning about the real world.

The school then becomes a reflection of the systematic way in which the intellectual disciplines are organized in the university, and those, in turn, reflect the universal order of the world. For the realist, knowledge comes through pursuit of the ordered and disciplined inquiry of bodies of knowledge and subject matters. Realists also value prescriptions to govern intelligent behavior. Such behavior is rational when it conforms to the way objects behave in reality as they follow natural laws or physical laws. The educated person must live according to the rules of civilized social organization and must exhibit rational characteristics.

Modern Realism.

Modern realism has flourished in the scientific era. Herbart combined sense realism with psychology to produce an influential theory of education that dominated professional education in the 1890s. Contemporary realism has benefited from the work of Alfred North Whitehead (1861–1947) and Bertrand Russell (1872–1970). They made their reputations in the field of mathematics, co-authoring the famous *Principia Mathematica*. Whitehead was very much interested in education and produced a book called *The Aims of Education and Other Essays* (1929). He was concerned about process and what he called "living ideas." Such ideas are connected with the experience of learners and are capable of being articulated and communicated to others. He saw this organic process pattern of education as different from the learning of "inert" ideas of the past.

An excellent statement of Whitehead's position is found in Harry Broudy's *Building a Philosophy of Education* (1954). Russell (1932) urged a temperate approach to science and said that education held the key to a better world. He conducted some practical experiments in private education with his Beacon Hill School in Massachusetts and was active in a number of social movements against the atom bomb and all wars. Modern realism has many faces, depending on point of view. All realists agree that sense objects exist, that instruction should be organized according to intellectual disciplines, and that the role of the teacher who presents the curriculum is crucial.

Perennialism.   Realists and idealists are in fundamental opposition on the nature of reality, but their educational theories are much more similar than different. Both want a subject–matter curriculum and see the school as an institution designed for the cultivation of human intelligence. Education ought to concentrate on basic moral, ethical, aesthetic, and religious principles drawn from the collective experience of culture, especially Western culture. These ideals have recently been expressed under a new rubric: *perennialism.* Although the term is of recent origin, perennialism presents a conservative, traditional view of human nature and education. It would not be amiss to say that the founding fathers held perennialist views, because they grounded their beliefs in religious idealism and made the basic assumption that certain ethical principles apply to all people at all times. This was the case for the eternal truth from God that was the foundation for Harvard College and for Franklin's nondenominational academy in Philadelphia. The idea of universal and unchanging truth was not foreign to those who advocated the separation of church and state in the Bill of Rights or to Horace Mann in his struggle to keep schools free of sectarian control. Assuming the rational nature of human beings, realists held that education should stress the recurrent theme of human life as well as knowledge about the objective world.

The most articulate spokespersons for the perennialist position were Robert Hutchins (1899–1986) and Mortimer Adler (1902–2001). Hutchins and Adler established the Great Books Program in 1946 and devised an index by which the answers of classical authors to the great questions could be compared. Hutchins, who was chosen dean of the Yale Law School at a very early age, became the president of the University of Chicago in 1929, at the age of 30. There, he stressed cultivation of the intellect and held that only educational institutions have the power to do so. He opposed specialized or vocational education but favored those subjects designed to develop the mind. Adler had recently reentered the field as a voice for perennialism with his book *The Paideia Proposal* (see Chapter 9). He had the support of former education secretary William Bennett, who shares the basic tenets of perennialism. Another major statement of perennialism, very popular with the intellectual community, is found in Allan Bloom's *The Closing of the American Mind,* which was published in 1987.

Pragmatism.   Pragmatism (from the Greek word meaning "a thing well done") emerged as a uniquely American philosophy just before the end of the nineteenth century. Educational theories such as progressivism, John Dewey's experimentalism, and social reconstructionism are branches of pragmatism. Founded upon modern science and evolution, pragmatism developed a distinctive empirical epistemology opposed to idealism and rationalism. Its themes were practicality, change, growth, and uncertainty as opposed to the order, finality, and fixed truth dominant in older systems. Pragmatists stressed incompleteness, contingency, the consequences of human experience, and a wide open universe. The major figures in pragmatism were Charles S. Peirce (1839–1914), William James (1843–1910), and John Dewey (1859–1952).

Charles S. Peirce.   A classic statement of Peirce's philosophy appeared in a January 1878 article called "How to Make Our Ideas Clear" in *Popular Science Quarterly*.

Peirce said that if we consider the practical effects that an object of our conception might have for our lives, these practical effects define the object. That is, an object only exists "for us" to the degree that it has practical bearings on our life-space—our own existence. Because objects far distant in space called quasars have only recently been discovered, they did not exist for Peirce, but they have important practical bearings (and therefore are real) for modern astronomers and for all of us who have altered our conception of the universe on the basis of their discovery. Peirce argued that the only genuine road to knowledge is the scientific method that is based on human experience and subject to empirical testing.

William James.   William James was a major contributor to educational psychology. Like his brother, Henry, he was a famous author with a national reputation and enormous influence in intellectual circles. In *Pragmatism: A New Name for Some Old Ways of Thinking* (1907), James agreed with Peirce that truth is not absolute but depends on the "workability" or consequences of an idea in actual life. Human experience is of paramount importance for James, and he often spoke of the "stream of experience" or the serial course of events that make up our individual concrete reality. James was not such a "hardheaded" experimental scientist as Peirce and believed that truth is not always objective but that meaning is sometimes found in personal experience that is nonverifiable.

Thus, there is an existential strain in James that is reflected in his keen interest in extrasensory perception. James called upon philosophers to abandon universals, abstractions, and essences in favor of studying human experience (in the laboratory) and reflecting on personal experience (introspection). Peirce was a more systematic thinker than James and soon became upset over what he considered the "bastardization" of pragmatism (even inventing the term *pragmaticism* to distance himself from James), but James remained popular, and his theories were closely related to those of Dewey.

John Dewey.   By any measure, John Dewey was the most important educational philosopher ever produced in the United States, as well as a major founder of pragmatism. Born in Burlington, Vermont, in 1859, the year *On the Origin of Species* was published, Dewey had an average boyhood dominated by New England Puritan values and Protestant Christianity. At the University of Vermont, an edge was put on his intellectual appetite by a course in physiology in which the theory of evolution was taught. Dewey turned to philosophy as a means of bridging the gap between the new science and his belief that the world was shaped by God's moral will. After graduation, Dewey taught school in rural Vermont and Oiltown, Pennsylvania, before entering Johns Hopkins University as a graduate student in philosophy. There, he studied under the idealists George Morris, G. Stanley Hall, and Charles Peirce. Morris introduced Dewey to a system of thought that declared that matter was only illusion. Dewey took his Ph.D. and for 10 years taught philosophy at the universities of Michigan and Minnesota. During this time, he became interested in the vigorous rate of change in technology and society, the growth of democracy, and the economic and social changes caused by industrial expansion and urban development. He became disenchanted with a system of unchanging spiritual reality and began to reject Hegelian idealism for what William James called the "wide open universe." By 1890, Dewey was converted to pragmatism and started his own version of the philosophy, called *instrumentalism* or *experimentalism*. Dewey made pragmatism a comprehensive system of thought dealing with all problems generated by conflicts within the culture. Instrumentalism served to restore integration and cooperation between beliefs about the world in which we live and beliefs about the values and purposes that guide conduct. As much a method as a philosophy, instrumentalism concentrates on the scientific, experimental tools for clarification of ideas about social issues and moral conduct.

Dewey saw the task of philosophy not as knowing the nature of ultimate reality but as understanding and controlling the world. The human mind is an instrument that must be sharpened by experience for use in problem solving and adjustment to the practical situations of human life. Experience, especially collective human experience, provides the best means for coping with a world always in flux. Anticipating Alvin Toffler and the futurists of today, Dewey held that problems cannot be solved with any degree of finality because of constant change and the unknown. Human intelligence and knowledge enable us to adapt our environment to our needs and to adapt philosophic goals to the reality of the situation of life-space in which we exist. Like Locke, Dewey was concerned about the origin of ideas and the problem of how the mind functions. The first of his many books dealt with functional psychology. He accepted the empirical principle that ideas come from experience and are verified by comparison with objective reality. Since action must precede knowledge, there are no *a priori* ideas. Dewey drew upon the naturalistic theories of Rousseau and Froebel but also upon the biological sciences, sociology, and Darwinian evolution. He saw human survival and the progress of the race tied to the means available for solving essential problems. Natural intelligence combined with reconstruction of past experience can be the means only if antecedent action is able to trigger a scientific, rational approach to solutions. Past beliefs, grounded in tradition or drawn from authority, may actually inhibit the survival of humankind. For this reason, Dewey wanted to submit every tradition, attitude, or belief to the experimental test with its corollary of verification by experience.

A central theme in Dewey's educational theory is "the complete act of thought." Although described in many of his writings, his little book *How We Think* (1910) gives the most detailed analysis of the problem-solving process. Dewey held that learning grows out of ongoing activity that must be meaningful to the learner. Activity involves the individual in the relationship between an act and its consequences. This implies that schools must foster purposeful activity by building on the common interests of children, such as communication, inquiry, construction, and artistic expression. Although activity is required for learning, no progress will be made so long as it is a routine activity and the student operates on the basis of habit.

Learning actually begins when a difficulty or problem creates a barrier and prevents an activity from continuing. The problem must be genuine (not imposed from outside by the teacher) and must be defined by the learner, so that he or she knows exactly what blocks the activity. The problem provides motivation, the driving force or interest required for thinking. At this point, information or data concerning a possible solution are gathered. This may be done merely by remembering prior experience or by more sophisticated means such as consulting an expert or using a library. The next step is forming a hypothesis—an educated guess as to how the problem may be resolved. The learner does not jump at once to any hypothesis but first reflects upon the probable outcomes and the possibility of undesirable consequences if the hypothesis is accepted. Finally, the learner chooses the most likely hypothesis to solve the problem and puts it to the empirical test of experience. If it works, the barrier to the activity is removed; if not, the learner has gained further data upon which to operate and may continue the process. Dewey's complete act of thought (activity, problem, data, hypothesis, testing) was taken directly from the scientific research model and is the basis for his pedagogy.

In *Experience and Education* (1938), Dewey defined *education* as the process of continuous reconstruction of experience with the purpose of widening and deepening its social content while helping the individual to gain control of the methods involved. In *Democracy and Education* (1916), he called education a process of living and not merely preparation for future living. Dewey also claimed that education is growth and that as long as growth continues, education must continue as a social process. As the title suggests, *Democracy and Education* argues that the social process of education is best served if the school is a democratic community. Dewey once said that if we are willing to conceive of education as the process of forming fundamental dispositions, philosophy might be defined as the general theory of education.

Dewey's critics often point to the contradictions and inconsistencies in his work. However, few have studied all of his books and articles, and he continued to be a prolific writer and to develop his philosophy until his death in 1952. On becoming chairperson of the Department of Philosophy at the University of Chicago, Dewey gave equal attention to the teacher education unit of which he was also in charge. He became a critic of rugged individualism, free enterprise without controls, outmoded social institutions, and a narrow definition of democracy as a form of government. His educational experiments at the laboratory school in the University of Chicago were used as models by many of his progressive followers, but he became very critical of progressives when he felt their activities were not philosophically sound. In 1916, his *Democracy and Education* was published, making him a national figure in both fields.

Dewey supported child-centered schools without stiff authoritarianism, but he also stressed the importance of integrated subjects in the curriculum and saw the school as a place where experiences could be simplified, purified, and ordered. His open-ended universe and pluralistic reality would not allow him to place limits on what might be studied, but he did think people could be educated so that they could control their own affairs and attain a more satisfactory collective life. Scientific method and experimental thinking can help us improve life and invent better social institutions. Although he rejected supernatural beliefs, as well as militant atheism, Dewey supported a humanistic religious position in books like *A Common Faith* (1934a). He also gave considerable attention to aesthetic development, especially in *Art as Experience* (1934b).

Dewey was not only the most articulate spokesman for pragmatism and the theoretical founder of progressivism, but also the most influential American philosopher of education. He had legions of followers, and many may still be found in schools and institutions of higher education. Many colleges of education such as Teachers College of Columbia University, the University of Illinois at Urbana—Champaign, the University of Texas at Austin, Ohio State University, and Stanford remained centers of Dewey's theory long after his death. Several of his followers like Boyd Bode, Gordon Hullfish, William Kilpatrick, and Bruce Raup became well known in their own right. Criticisms were also numerous, ranging from the serious philosophical issues raised by idealist Herman Horne and the attack on relativism voiced by Allan Bloom to the unfounded political rhetoric expressed by Max Rafferty and Albert Lynd.

Social Reconstructionism.

From ancient times, educational institutions have had the function of transmitting cherished values and preserving the culture. Schools have rarely been the focus of radical social change, but they have been an instrument for social improvement, especially economic improvement. Horace Mann and other early national leaders fostered utopian ideals in education, such as equality of opportunity and ending poverty. Interest in this utopian theme accelerated during the progressive era in American history and the rise of populist parties. The women's suffrage movement, the civil rights movement, the attack on graft, and the work of muckraking authors who exposed corruption and inequality also influenced the utopian theme. Progressive education was also a force in social reconstruction, as illustrated by the appearance in 1932 of George Counts's *Dare the Schools Build a New Social Order?* This book called for complete social revolution and was considered radical even by most members of the Progressive Education Society, but it did raise the question of the role of the school in changing society.

Dewey's belief in education as an instrument for the continuous reconstruction of experience, his championship of democracy as a way of life, and the pragmatic theme of understanding and controlling the world contributed to this position. In 1935, W. H. Kilpatrick, John Childs, Bruce Raup, and Harold Rugg joined Counts in founding the John Dewey Society for the Study of Education and Culture. The society began publishing the journal *Social Frontier*, which attacked the evils of capitalism and called for active participation of educators in social change. This journal was responsible for much conservative criticism of progressive education, but it was also the focal point of those progressives who felt that schools should be active in altering society.

Theodore Brameld.

The most important figure in social reconstruction is Theodore Brameld (1904–1987). Brameld saw a crisis in modern society, with many contradictions and mass confusion regarding goals. He agreed with Isaac Kandel that setting up a utopian model is dangerous because there is no empirical way to define an ideal society. Still, he felt that we must take a holistic approach to alternative possibilities. Brameld's arguments are expressed in books like *Toward a Reconstructed Philosophy of Education* (1962), *Education as Power* (1967), and

Patterns of Educational Philosophy (1971). If the crisis is real (illustrated by wars, the rich–poor gap, pollution, international terrorism, the population explosion, resource depletion, and accelerating technological advance), then merely transmitting dominant social values in traditional schools will not suffice. Brameld wanted to solve the pervasive problems of humankind and direct us toward a global government.

He agreed with Karl Mannheim and Robert Heilbroner that we are about to witness the very end of civilization unless we can quickly and drastically reconstruct our priorities and patterns of behavior. He saw mass confusion about goals and inadequate responses to the world crisis. He thought that nationalism is no longer adequate and that we must create a world government to control nuclear arms and stop environmental destruction. In *Education as Power* (1967), he argues that knowledge is power and that the reconstructionist theory of value might be transmitted through schooling to produce a utopian "civilized civilization." Because values are human-made, it is possible to define ends through social consensus. It is assumed that world peace and economic cooperation are such goals, but no one wants them to be imposed by an outside authority such as a national government. In *Toward a Reconstructed Philosophy of Education* (1962), Brameld says that education is a means for guaranteeing sufficient income to all families; meeting reasonable standards of nutrition, medical care, shelter, dress, and schooling; and utilizing all of the world's natural resources in the interests of the majority of people. Many social theorists and most futurists share this position.

Recontructionism and Politics.   Although many agree that the world crisis is real and cannot be resolved by the United States alone, a global civilization and a world government do not seem realistic. Schools under the direction of local or national governments lack the power to engage in global reconstruction. They can provide, as futurists argue, information on what is happening in our world and prepare students for problem solving and better communication in an age of rapid change.

From a practical standpoint, social reconstructionism has waxed and waned depending upon the political climate. Progressives in the 1930s and 1940s were successful in persuading school authorities that children learn best when they are safe, healthy, properly nourished, and enjoying a pleasant physical environment. This "whole child" philosophy led to hot lunches, health care, counseling services, and the like. The civil rights movement of the Martin Luther King era, the war on poverty, and the liberal social policies of the Kennedy and Johnson administrations fostered social engineering through schools. Racial integration, bilingual programs, special education, Head Start, Educational Talent Search, No Child Left Behind, Race to the Top, and Upward Bound are examples of such efforts at the federal level.

President Barack Obama seeks higher achievement levels and highly qualified teachers at all educational levels but especially in low-performing schools, reflecting own experience as revealed in *Dreams From My Father: A Story of Raced and Inheritance* (1995). The Obama administration stressed the need for state-of-the-art assessment and accountability systems in his Race to the Top program.

Essentialism.   Essentialism is a conservative educational theory that emphasizes the value of certain "basic" subjects and the authority of the teacher. Educators have always attempted to identify what is essential to the knowledge of a learned person. Ancient Athenians thought it essential for boys of the citizenship class to learn the *Iliad*, but they did not think it good for slaves or women to study Homer. Most Americans now think computer literacy is basic, but this was not the case two decades ago. Educational history is filled with debate over what constitutes basic knowledge, which people should receive it, and how it should be transmitted. The essentialist movement in America began as a response to what was considered "soft pedagogy" or "permissive" education supported by progressives. It was recently reflected in the charge of former education secretary William Bennett that schools emphasize process and not content.

William C. Bagley.   In 1938, a group of prominent educators led by William C. Bagley (1874–1946) started a movement that called for intellectual training in schools instead of "child growth and development." They said the essential skills of reading, writing, and arithmetic should be found in every elementary curriculum together with history, literature, and geography. For the secondary school, the curriculum was the Western cultural heritage, including the academic subjects in the arts and sciences. Bagley favored observed data over a strictly rational approach and, like the realists, supported scientific examination of physical phenomena. Michael Demiashkevich, Robert Ulich, and W. E. Hocking soon joined him. By this time, progressive education was on the decline, and essentialism attracted a great deal of public support.

Although the Eight-Year Study showed that students from progressive high schools did well in college, Bagley's argument had merit, and the political climate was right, because of the conservatism of the World War II era.

A Focal Point for Criticism.   Many authors with quite different views who were determined to attack not only progressives but also those they labeled "educationists" soon supported essentialism. Arthur Bestor, Jr., in *Educational Wastelands* (1953), Albert Lynd in *Quackery in the Public Schools* (1953), and Max Rafferty in *Suffer, Little Children* (1962) were especially shrill in their condemnation of all educators. Although their motivation was largely political, they attracted a great deal of public support and caused essentialism to become the focal point for all criticism of public schools and teacher education programs. In discussing the "diminished mind," Mortimer Smith accused John Dewey of destroying the ability of Americans to think. Some of the arguments were no more grounded in fact than the anticommunist "witch hunts" of Joseph McCarthy. However, they got a similar response from the mass media, and by 1960 "education bashing" became popular.

More serious, if less colorful, were the arguments for more rigor in curriculum; these arguments came after the formation of the Council for Basic Education in 1946. Indeed, modern educational history describes a pattern of back to basics movements followed by liberal responses like team teaching and nongraded schools, followed again by back to basics. Sometimes the cycle is fostered by comparison with foreign schools, as was the case with Admiral Hyman Rickover and

James B. Conant, following the Soviet success with *Sputnik* in 1957. More recently, the cycle was initiated by education secretary T. H. Bell and his National Commission on Excellence in Education, which produced *A Nation at Risk* in 1983.

Humanism.   Humanism is not so much a philosophy of education as it is a point of view based on literary studies and the assumption that the proper study of mankind is man. All systems of philosophy give some attention to human values and the human condition. The roots of humanism go back to ancient Greece, where the sophists claimed that "man is the measure of all things." In Europe, during the fourteenth and fifteenth centuries, humanism flourished as the intellectual core of the Renaissance. Desiderius Erasmus (1466–1536) contributed to humanism by trying to move the Church away from ceremonies and toward ideal Christian living. Early American literary humanists rejected the Puritan belief that man is sinful by nature and agreed with Comenius that the human condition could be improved through education. Franklin, Jefferson, Emerson, and Thoreau are counted among American humanists, as are all Deists. Literary and classical humanism flourished after World War I and was represented by such advocates as Nicholas Murray Butler, Abraham Flexner, and Mark Van Doren. Drawing from the newer disciplines of psychology, political science, anthropology, and sociology, they spoke less to the supernatural nature of man than they did to his distinctively human faculties as a guide for moral conduct. Humanists support the utilitarian concept of the greatest good for the greatest number but oppose the dominance of science, materialism, and values drawn from mass behavior. Humanistic educators find too great an emphasis on vocationalism and technology in schools and urge more attention to literature and the classics.

There is a strong tie between humanists and perennialists. Indeed, Robert Hutchins and Mortimer Adler may be classified as both perennialists and humanists. Humanists say that people have distinctive qualities—such as reason, moral conscience, aesthetic taste, and religious instinct—that are quite different from those of animals. While giving priority to the literary and linguistic arts, humanists stress the heritage of Western culture, especially the classics of Greece and Rome. Such subjects lead to a well-rounded development of the intellectual, moral, aesthetic, and religious capabilities of humankind.

Neo-Thomists and mainline Protestants support humanism; fundamentalist Christians do not. Using the powerful tool of the television ministry, many "born-again" Christians have launched a particularly vicious attack on what they call "secular humanism." Although the term seems to have been invented for atheistic humanists, as used by Jimmy Swaggart and Jerry Falwell, it includes liberal Christian ministers and all professors in secular universities. This blanket definition, which includes such strange bedfellows as scientists and biblical scholars under the rubric "secular humanism," has confused the issues. Falwell has claimed that secular humanism is a religion, something that all humanists would deny. Literary humanists have suffered from the conservative attacks, and their influence in education has been weakened. A curriculum example is the support for giving creationism (or intelligent design) equal space with the theory of evolution in school textbooks.

Analytic Philosophy of Education.   The analysis of concepts in philosophy is as old as the formal study of ideas; logic can be traced back to Aristotle. Certainly the meaning of various concepts and arguments is central to building any philosophy or educational theory. Pragmatists such as Peirce wanted to make ideas clear, but Dewey used terms like *democracy, interests,* and *growth* without giving them precise meaning. With the decline in emphasis on formal logic in universities and the rise of political and media slogans, the use of logic and the analysis of language gained in importance. Analytic professors now dominate many departments of educational philosophy in universities. They point out the absurdity of taking a phrase such as *self-actualization* from Maslow and making it an educational goal without understanding what Maslow really meant or how hard it would be for all students to attain such a goal. They challenge political statements of the "Lake Wobegon" sort that say all students should be better than average.

Although the roots of analytic philosophy are found in logic, British empiricism, and nineteenth-century efforts to clarify meaning in literature, its major foundation is contemporary realism and logical positivism. An Englishman, George E. Moore (1873–1958), developed the analytic branch of realism with emphasis on ordinary language. His colleague, Bertrand Russell, leaned toward formal language and the precise terms used in the sciences and mathematics. Moore's "A Defense of *Common Sense*" (1925) dealt with the meaning of propositions found in common language and pointed out that many issues in philosophy are attributable to misunderstanding because of abstract and technical language. Russell's formalistic approach became popular with scientific Americans, especially after he began lecturing at Harvard in 1914.

The logical positivist roots of analytic philosophy originated with a group of European scientists and mathematicians known as the "Vienna Circle." Ludwig Wittgenstein (1889–1951) was an Austrian philosopher who contributed to positivism and greatly influenced the Vienna Circle. He studied with Russell at Cambridge and became a British subject after World War I. Wittgenstein held that the job of philosophy is not to discover truth but to resolve problems and clarify ideas obtained from other fields. He wanted to deal with the language about data as opposed to the study of metaphysical statements from the great philosophical systems. Vienna Circle members Rudolph Carnap and A. J. Ayer interpreted Wittgenstein to mean that all propositions must be publicly verifiable and capable of replication.

With the growth of modern science and new disciplines, experts have used special language. An example would be computer language terms such as those used in BASIC or COBOL. Analysts foster communication by dealing with the real meaning of terms, their truthfulness, and their reliability. They translate specialized language into ordinary meaning that can be used for educational policies.

Because of increased specialization and advanced technology, communication between experts in different fields has become more difficult. Information that comes through the mass media shows a vast range of truthfulness, reliability, and validity. Clearly, an analysis of knowing, such as that developed by Gilbert Ryle in *The Concept of Mind* (1949), has value now. Modern analytic professors of education like Israel Scheffler, R. S. Peters, Jonas Soltis, Henry Perkinson, and Richard

Pring offer no metaphysical statements or models of schools. Instead, they clarify meaning so that those who make policy or develop curriculum may understand exactly the theories upon which they build and the consequences of their own position statements. Analytic philosophy is not a speculative system, but it provides a means for making educational ideas clear, precise, and meaningful.

Protest Philosophies.   The philosophical foundations upon which schools rest that we have so far examined assume an ordered universe, the validity of reason, logic in the curriculum, and an individual governed by ethical rules in an intelligible world. Plato believed that a person with a rational soul could not choose to do wrong if he or she clearly understood what action was right. Yet, it is obvious that a child may misbehave knowing the behavior is wrong and that an adult may act for psychological rather than logical reasons. Many theories hold that the social order is not fair or reasonable, and some say the universe is not subject to rational analysis. Such thinking leads to protest against the schools, the society, customs, moral rules, and the assumption that truth corresponds to reality. Behaviorism, existentialism, and postmodern philosophy are treated as protest positions. They are seldom the foundations for schools, but they raise troubling questions with which all educators must deal.

Behaviorism.   Psychology and education are closely related. Dewey and James were psychologists, as well as philosophers and progressives, and adopted Gestalt psychology as their own. A few modern psychologists have developed a position sufficiently broad and with enough followers so that it is meaningful to speak of their educational philosophies. Among these are Jerome Bruner, Abraham Maslow, Carl Rogers, and especially Burrhus Frederick Skinner (1904–1990). Although best known for his programmed instruction derived from the principles of operant conditioning based on laboratory experiments with animals, Skinner has moved behavioral engineering into the realm of utopian planning, the nature of humankind, social values, and a definition of the good life.

Born in Susquehanna, Pennsylvania, Skinner taught psychology at the University of Minnesota and Indiana University before returning to Harvard, where he had taken his Ph.D. Earning a reputation as one of the most important contemporary psychologists, his work on animal behavior is a major contribution to knowledge. Building on the foundation of Ivan Pavlov (1849–1946), who began experimentation on conditioned reflexes in Russia, and the American behaviorists Edward Lee Thorndike (1874–1949) and John B. Watson (1878–1958), he developed laws of behavior and created teaching machines. Had he confined his work to "rat in a box" psychology, as it is sometimes called, there would be no behavioristic theory of education; but he went beyond the experimental laboratory in his books *Walden II* (1976) and *Beyond Freedom and Dignity* (1971). Behaviorism is grounded in realism, especially the materialistic branch, which maintains that behavior is caused by environmental conditions. Instead of concentration on mind or consciousness, behaviorists look at observable facts that can be empirically verified. Skinner thought philosophers who attempted to deduce a concept of human nature from *a priori* generalizations or introspection had made errors. Although he did not deny genetic influence, he opposed the traditional views of humankind that assume there are internal drives and hidden forces that define humans. Humanists argued that human beings possess distinctive qualities that are absolutely different from animals and that are not the product of evolution. Skinner treats humans as animals subject to the same environmental controls and evolutionary forces as any other living organism, different only in degree, not kind.

Increasingly in contemporary society, environmental forces control our behavior. Some of these, such as inflation and population growth, may be accidental; others, such as advertising to make us want particular products, are intentional and manipulative. Skinner argues that because we understand the power of such forces to modify behavior, we ought to use them deliberately to construct a society of the most benefit to all. This was the theme of the utopian new Walden, where everything was done with cooperation but according to plan. Few are neutral about Skinner's theories. A common charge is that he abolished "mankind" through scientific analysis. He is interested in the complexity and uniqueness of people, but he sees people as mechanical and animal in nature. Critics suggest that the same behavioral engineering techniques he advocates might produce a nightmare society such as Orwell's *1984*. Skinner replies that we are likely to get such a society by not planning or attempting to control and modify human behavior.

Skinner believes in a sophisticated science of human behavior and maintains that value judgments are just as much a part of science as any other field, including philosophy. Behavior (including aggressive behavior) is explained by positive reinforcement. It is not helpful to condemn the culprit in crime or the extermination of Jews in World War II. Rather, we should look for ways to remove the positive reinforcement of such behavior. Knowing is not just a cognitive process; it is environmental, behavioral, and psychological as well. The "good" for Skinner is merely that which is rewarded; if we want to shape cultural evolution, we must find ways to reinforce that behavior that the culture defines as desirable. He points out that, historically, cultural change has been blind, accidental, or random. He holds that although we may not have a blueprint for the perfect society, we can develop better social arrangements, and education is one of the best ways to design a better culture. Again, positive reinforcement (not punishment) is the most effective way to alter institutions, because human action is shaped by rewards.

Obviously, behavior depends upon actual possibilities. In ancient Athens, the automobile was not a possibility, and it had no part in shaping the culture. For modern American adolescents, driving an automobile is rewarding. It gives a feeling of power and freedom, and the teenage subculture regards "wheels" as one of the most important status symbols. For contemporary culture, the automobile is very important, and our behavior of driving and prizing cars is reinforced.

Behaviorists view the child as a highly conditioned organism even before entering school. Whatever has gone on before, including contradiction in the values exhibited by parents or the environmental control of institutions such as churches, will have an impact on the school environment. Because teachers must engage in the modification of behavior, it is important that they know what goals they wish to achieve and how to reach them with efficiency. Skinner does not see this process as evil but as a means for expanding possibilities and developing a preference for a better kind of civilization. Behaviorists can demonstrate that operant conditioning actually works. Successful techniques for classroom management and control are grounded in the theory, as well as instructional methods such as those of Madeline Hunter. Skinner's influence is enormous in spite of strong opposition to his ideas. Nevertheless, behaviorism is a growing educational philosophy, especially in the United States.

Existentialism.   Existentialism (and its psychological counterpart, phenomenology) is a protest against institutional controls, formalism, and social norms rather than a systematic philosophy. Existentialism provides a means for examining life in a personal way, reflecting on commitments and choices, and considering the temporary nature of human life. Existentialists do not believe that we inhabit a meaningful or explainable world. The philosophy includes a theme of hope, but there is also a theme of desperation and anguish. One cannot find a model of a school based upon existentialism. The closest thing might be the schools of the American Summerhill Association (based on the work of A. S. Neill in England), which stress freedom of choice, authenticity, and personal development. Martin Buber (1878–1965) offered some existential-based suggestions about education in *I and Thou* (1958); and critics like Holt, Leonard, and Illich reflect an existentialistic point of view. The philosophy forms a foundation for taking issue with almost all of the activities that take place in public and private schools.

Roots of existentialism go back to the admonition of Socrates to "know thyself" and the sophists, who said that "man is the measure of all things." Descartes, Pascal, and Dostoevsky stressed the idea of personal freedom and responsibility. Albert Camus, Gabriel Marcel, Friedrich Nietzsche, and Edmund Husserl, who founded phenomenology, developed the modern theme. The influence on American education has come since World War II and is largely based on Soren Kierkegaard (1813–1855), Martin Heidegger (1889–1976), Jean Paul Sartre (1905–1980), and Martin Buber.

Existentialism's primary focus has been on the nature of human existence. According to Sartre, existence precedes essence and we are "condemned" to be free. Unlike realists or idealists, existentialists think people create their own essence by choosing what they will be. This is quite different from Kant's charge that we have a duty to be moral or Mill's belief that we must act in the best interests of the greatest number. We must choose to conform, rebel, commit suicide, live independent from social norms, love, hate, or be directed by peer values. Although others seek to impinge upon our freedom to make choices, we are totally responsible. The authentic person is one who is aware of his or her freedom and is willing to take the responsibility for self-direction and self-definition.

Choices and the manner in which they are made determine what human beings we will become. Each person's situation is unique; the world is only temporary, and each of us must carry the burden of our own upcoming death. Existentialists will not tell us that our choices are right or wrong, only that our freedom is total, that our existence is determined by the choices we make, and that the universe is indifferent to human wishes and desires. We may choose to keep up with the Joneses, take our values from the mass media, or work only for money in a meaningless job; but such choices lead to an unfulfilled life of desperation and anguish and cut off possibilities of loving, creating, and being.

The very nature of existence poses a metaphysical question of central interest to existentialists, and their theory of value is important; but the philosophy is not concerned with logic or epistemology. Some aspects of phenomenology relate to the formation of values and ethical questions in education. Examples would be Abraham Maslow's stages of development and the theory of moral development in the work of Lawrence Kohlberg. Because schools operate on rules, conformity, acceptance of the curriculum, homework, following directions, teacher authority, and the like, students who insist on individual choice and challenge regulations are hard to manage.

Should Schools Exist?

Some existentialists think that schools should not exist. Others, like George Leonard, object to the "hidden curriculum" of social expectations and peer values transmitted by the school environment. They think that once the veneer of civilization is stripped away, the savage nature of man and the misery of the human condition will be revealed. No set of values or established body of knowledge can replace individual experience with its personal motives, choices, and responsibilities.

Existentialism is very troublesome for educators because it attacks the fundamental assumptions of systematic philosophies upon which schools rest. The themes of desperation, alienation, death, and despair are not compatible with schooling. Absolute freedom to choose is a challenge to all social organizations and the institutions of civilization. Yet, the awful price we pay for giving over our choices to others and allowing them to determine our fate is the basis for a critical examination of all philosophies. Examples include the mass suicide in Jonestown, Guyana, and the Heaven's Gate group suicide in Rancho Mirage, California; in both cases, many lost their lives because they put their trust totally in others. The influence of existentialistic writers is increasing and can hardly be dismissed by policy builders or those who create educational theory, even though it is a difficult matter to deal with in schools.

Postmodernism.

The postmodern writers form less of a school of philosophy than a complex set of reactions to modern philosophy and its presuppositions, models, logic, and analytic methods. Some themes such as the nonrational character of existence and the inclusion of all types of experience as reality are related to the existentialism of Sartre, the nihilism of Nietzsche, and the phenomenology of Husserl. Postmodernists oppose essentialism, idealism, and all forms of realism including Marxism. Jean Francois Lyotard claims that his position precedes modern philosophy because it does not assume that knowledge provides an accurate picture of reality and rejects all philosophical assumptions since Plato. Reason is not sovereign for Lyotard, and no grand scheme such as democracy or economic determinism is valid. Postmodern thought also includes feminist challenges to social norms as found in the work of Judith Butler, Helene Cixous, and Martha Nussbaum. Feminist authors say that the schools reflect a society that is sexist and patriarchal, even extending to the language and the curriculum.

Leading postmodern writers include Michael Apple, Michel Foucault, Henry Giroux, Jurgen Habermas, Barry Kanpol, and Richard Rorty. Rorty's ideology of postmodernism is an extension of some of the basic philosophical premises of John Dewey. The other authors offer alternatives to the philosophical ideas of the enlightenment era. Concepts of structure, dogmatism, rationalism, modernism, positivism, and any other preconceived notion of knowledge are replaced in postmodernism by ideas of ambiguity, questioning, unsystematic narration of perceptions, and freedom from any superimposed knowledge systems. Even language and its structure are under intense scrutiny because of the limitations on truly knowing. Postmodernism is a blend of the liberating message of existentialism with the humanism of pragmatism and the critical theory of Marxism. Jacques Derrida's deconstructionism examined hidden meanings in language built up through culture and historical processes.

Postmodernists criticize any universalistic explanations of the cosmos, replacing them with a transformation of liberation that includes concerns of "marginalized" people (those who have not always been heeded by mainstream thinkers). This celebration of diversity focuses on liberating individuals from age-, class-, gender-, and race-based prejudices. Reaching the feelings, attitudes, and aspirations of individuals through exploration of their own account of educational politics and struggles within their school settings is achieved through micronarratives (or present-oriented dialogue). These insights into the attitudes of educators about their individual struggles and triumphs within schools provide meaningful structures that can be interwoven in metanarratives of school research findings.

As with pragmatism, postmodernism finds democracy and its institutions always in flux, change, and modification. As Dewey noted, change is a function of democracy. Change gives democracy its uniqueness and ability to meet conditions requiring innovation in theory and practice. As in existentialism, postmodernism seeks meaning in situational context, texture, and consciousness raising. The Marxist call for liberation from forms of modernism or industrialism that encroach on human freedom is found in postmodernists' attunement to an age of postindustrialism or global communication/information networks.

Postmodernists seek to build a more humane society through reaching all levels, gender, ages, and races. They seek to re-create and reinvent democracy to achieve more economic and social justice. Susan Hekman, Kate Campbell, and other feminist authors find postmodernism helpful in delineating alternatives to masculine-oriented theories from the Enlightenment forward. Kai Erikson's account (1982) suggests that this is a necessary liberating approach, as can be seen from the 1637 trial of Ann Hutchinson, whose banishment from Massachusetts Colony was attributable to in no small part to Governor Winthrop's view:

> For if she had attended her household affairs, and such things as belong to women, and had not gone out of her way and calling to meddle in such things as are proper for men, she had kept her wits, and might have improved them usefully and honorably in the place that God set her. (p. 82)

The feminist struggle for liberation continues through postmodern literature in our twenty-first century.

Non-Western Philosophy.

When Rudyard Kipling wrote "Oh East is East and West is West and Never the Twain Shall Meet," there was no mass media, no Internet, rapid transportation, United Nations, or global economy. On a political and economic level, the "flat world" has forced the meeting, but East and West are still poles apart on matters of governmental policy, human rights, ecology, ethics, social priorities, and philosophy. One thing is certain, those who pass through the American educational system must be affected by what goes on in the rest of the modern world. The great variation in Oriental societies means that their impact is far from uniform. An example is the densely populated Korean peninsula. North Korea is atheistic, communistic, militaristic, and a threat to world peace. Its autocratic one-party dictatorship preaches hatred of America and all things Western. Poverty, economic instability, border fights, and a constant show of military power are characteristic of North Korea. The nation causes unrest if not fear in the region and worldwide. By contrast, South Korea is a modern nation with a high standard of living, considerable individual freedom, an outstanding educational system, and growing democratic ideals. Because American support allowed them to stay free of domination by the communists, South Korea has become a major economic force in the world and a strong trading partner for the United States. In the Orient, Japan and Taiwan are closer to the American value system than South Korea.

Beyond the Americas and Europe, some population centers have enormous impact on America while others have much less. China, Japan, and India are nations with huge economic and social impact on America while Bangladesh, Egypt, Indonesia, and Nigeria have much less. It is no longer true that nations with the strongest economies, highest levels of technology, most developed educational system, and best access to global information influence America most. More than half of the world's people dwell in non-Western cultures and some understanding of their culture, belief, attitudes, and characteristics is vital to Americans.

Islam.

Religion has always influenced philosophy in Western culture, but there has been a division between theology and secular thought. Augustine, Comenius, and Buber were both philosophers and religious leaders, while Camus, Marx, and Nietzsche were nonbelievers. Some communist governments oppose religion; some use religion to support its government. People in India generally embrace it, and Islamic nations see no separation between religion and government, or even between religion and law. Approximately one billion people claim to be Christian, and an equal number are Islamic, although the Islamic faith is growing faster.

Buddhists and Hindus account for another billion, while at least two billion in China, the former Soviet Union, and North Korea say they are atheists. Many profess local or tribal beliefs and not all religions are mutually exclusive. Most Japanese people have some Buddhist and some Shinto beliefs. Gandhi himself said he was a Hindu, a Moslem, a Buddhist, a Christian, and a Jew. A nation like China, which still holds the Marxist position that religion is "the opium of the people," stands in stark contrast to Iran, which is an Islamic theocracy. Of course, Islamic law cannot take precedence over civil law in nations with mixed Moslem and non-Moslem populations such as Indonesia and Nigeria. Today, in contrast to Mao's era when religion was banned or strictly prohibited, churches and Buddhist temples are seen throughout the country with increasing membership.

Of the three great Abrahamic monotheistic world religions, Christianity and Judaism are usually considered to be Western, while Islam is not. This does not take into account the large number of Moslems living in Europe and America, or Christians in the Orient. Indonesia is 78% Islamic, while nearby Papua, New Guinea, and the Philippines are Catholic. In London today the most popular name for a baby boy is Muhammad. Demographers say France will have more Islamic people than Christian within a quarter of a century.

Some regions defy classification. Africa is mostly Islamic in the North and Christian in South Africa, while the middle regions are a mixture of both and include tribal and traditional beliefs.

The word *Islam* means "submission to God." The religion was founded by Muhammad in Arabia in the year 622. The Qur'an, the main religious text of Islam, is considered the divine revelation of Allah to Muhammad. Although Islam recognizes earlier prophets such as Abraham and Jesus, Muhammad is the Prophet.

Islamic belief teaches that all Moslems must follow the five pillars of the faith: The first is to say with conviction that there is no God but Allah and that Muhammad is his prophet; the second, to say five ritual prayers every day while kneeling and facing Mecca, as well as a Friday noon prayer, which must be said in a mosque; the third, to give alms to the poor beyond the amount required by law; the fourth, to keep the fast during the holy month of Ramadan; and the fifth, to make the Hajj, or pilgrimage to Mecca, once in a lifetime. The first four pillars are regularly observed by all Moslems, but followers in many poor and remote areas, such as Bangladesh, cannot make the Hajj.

Islamic guides also include the Sunna, the traditional portion of Islamic law that consists of the sayings and deeds of Muhammad, and the Sharia, which is religious law. These documents include references to other obligations, such as spreading the faith by all means, including the sword. Such references have been used by Islamic extremists as justification for violent acts and the killing of "infidels."

Although there are major divisions within Islam, such as the Shiites, the Sunnites, and several smaller groups, an Islamic tenet that any belief held by a majority of the faithful must be true has helped to unify the scattered believers.

The greatest impact on the Islamic world comes not from the nations with the largest populations, but is exerted by those with the most prestige and who have learned to use mass media effectively. Sparsely populated Saudi Arabia was the birthplace of Muhammad, and controls access to Mecca and the Hajj. As an oil-rich nation and a member of Organization of the Petroleum Exporting Countries (OPEC), Saudi Arabia provides support for the pilgrimage and other religious activities and economic leadership in the Middle East. Saudi Arabia has also brought a measure of stability to the region through its close ties with the United States.

Other Islamic countries have also received much attention. U.S. military involvement in Afghanistan and Iraq, conflict in the areas around Israel, pirating in Somalia, and terrorist recruitment in Yemen have all contributed to this. Pakistan's history of external as well as internal conflict, including war with India, a hostile border with Afghanistan, and Al-Qaeda hideouts in its northern mountains, makes it a standard news headline. By contrast, the huge Moslem populations in Indonesia and Bangladesh, and the smaller ones in Egypt, Turkey, and Morocco, tend to be ignored by the mass media. Because they play a lesser part in world affairs, they have less of an impact on the impressions of Islam held by people in the West than do countries like Iran.

The center of the Persian Empire in ancient times, Iran has a long history of violence and turmoil. Islamic art and architecture flourished there in the seventh and eighth centuries, but Afghans, Ottomans, and Turks fought for control of the area before European expansion, and the decline of Persian power led to control by Russia and Britain. Iran became an independent nation in 1943, but nationalization of its oil industry led to the Iranian monarchy. Headed by Mohammad Reza Shah Pahlavi, the Shah of Iran, the government was backed by oil companies and many Western governments, including the United States. A period of westernization followed, marked by the arrival of things like makeup and shorter skirts for women, American movies, and expensive automobiles in Tehran.

The period was relatively short-lived. After a conservative Islamic revolution led by clerics including the Ayatollah Khomeini overthrew the Shah in 1979, it reinstated old dress codes, religious values, and an anti-Western position. In addition, Iran began spending more and more of its oil riches on military hardware and a large army.

Khomeini died in 1989, but the theocracy he established continues. Iran leads the Moslem world in anti-Western sentiment, and the curriculum of its religiously controlled and gender-segregated schools still contains material filled with animosity toward the United States. The ongoing fight over nuclear arms in Iran continues to be a major source of conflict for the United States and its allies.

Although peace is also a primary goal of Islamic philosophy, the bombing of the World Trade Center on September 11, 2001, by Moslem extremists, the ensuing "war on terrorism," and militant rhetoric from Iran have caused many Americans to fear and distrust Moslems. Despite the wariness and misunderstanding on both sides, most of the billion Moslems on the planet wish only to be left alone to live their lives and worship Allah as the Qur'an dictates. The recent revolutions in the North African Arab states may impact Islamic beliefs.

Japan.   Geologically, the island nation of Japan is smaller than the state of Montana, but it contains almost half as many people as the United States. It has the third largest economy in the world, has seven of the ten largest banks, and is of great influence internationally. Few who recall Pearl Harbor in 1941 could have imagined that Japan would emerge as the Asian nation with beliefs, values, and aspirations most closely reflecting those of Americans. Not only has Japan created a huge industrial economy highly competitive in the global marketplace, but it has embraced many democratic institutions. Education is valued highly in Japan and fully half of the students there go on to college.

Only 15 percent of the land in Japan can be farmed. Fuel and raw materials must be imported. Japan cannot sustain itself without foreign trade, but its motivated and highly trained work force has made it a leader in the production of everything from automobiles to television sets and electronics. Its stock market is second only to Wall Street while its standard of living is the highest in the Orient. Its life span is highest in the world. This success is something of a mixed blessing, because Japanese workers demand the highest pay in the region, making them less competitive than labor in China, India, and Indonesia.

At the end of World War II, Japan was in chaos. It was devastated physically, economically, politically, and socially. Emperor Hirohito declaimed his divinity and a democratic constitution was adopted. The United States rebuilt the infrastructure and provided funding for new factories. In return for military bases, America also furnished protection and prohibited the growth of the Japanese army and navy. There were protests, but Japan benefited by spending little on the military and having more funds for economic expansion. Japan's social, cultural, political, and economic revolution had a profound effect on attitudes, ethical standards, philosophy, and beliefs. While old traditions such as Buddhism, Shintoism, and worship of the emperor still remain, Japan has become more like the West than other nations of the Orient. It has not had a long experience with democracy, but so long as the people live well, it is unlikely that the Japanese will return to the imperialism, autocracy, or military dominance of the past. Individual freedom, human rights, and the status of women have vastly improved in Japan while the educational system is outstanding for its excellence.

The people of Japan came mostly from China, as did their earliest traditions. The empire can be traced back to 660 B.C. Chinese art and literature had a profound impact on the culture. For more than 700 years, warrior-kings known as *shoguns* ruled Japan in the name of the emperor. Through the code of Bushido, these autocratic leaders controlled military forces and exercised absolute power over the people. Japan pursued an isolationist path until Commodore Matthew Perry forced its ports to open for trade. Power struggles followed between the Shogunate and the emperors, with foreign nations backing the emperors. Social and economic reforms led to modernization in the reign of the Emperor Meiji and Japan became an industrial power in the Orient. Nationalism and a desire for empire building led to a modern military structure. Japan invaded Manchuria, defeated Russia at sea, and began the conquest of China. By 1941, Japan was a powerful military and industrial empire bent on control of all Asia. There was devotion both to the state and to the emperor and loyalty that was fanatic. This continued until the defeat (August 15, 1945) and American occupation (August 28, 1945) of the Japanese islands.

Most modern Japanese identify themselves as both Buddhists and Shinto but they are open to other systems of belief, including Christianity. Because neither of these belief systems has a united theology, many of the ideas overlap and are not mutually exclusive. Buddhism entered Japan about 600 B.C. and has remained a major force. The branch known as Zen has had much influence in recent times. Yoga and meditation are associated with Zen and are very popular with modern Japanese, as are martial arts like karate. Karma is also widely accepted as a belief, although not associated with Hinduism as in India. Throughout Japan images of the Buddha are found intermingled with Shinto shrines. Buddhist priests are used for many ceremonies, although Shinto priests are more numerous.

Shinto (the way of the gods) originated as a primitive animistic cult of nature not unlike Druidism in Europe. The writings of Confucius were an early influence as later was Buddhism. Shintoism has many gods or spirits thought to govern health, good fortune, and fertility. The Sun Goddess was once the most important deity and was claimed by many to be a direct ancestor of the emperor, hence the rising sun on the flag. It is not clear how much influence Shintoism has on behavior or philosophy today, but ceremonies like funerals, marriages, and childbirth almost always employ Shinto priests and often take place in temples. The Japanese are sophisticated about modern culture. They are materialistic, pragmatic, and realistic in their views and conduct, but also very much influenced by the old religion and value system.

India.   The huge subcontinent of India is the most densely populated region of the Orient. Even with the Moslem nations of Bangladesh and Pakistan removed, more than a billion people live there. The people are also characterized by cultural diversity. Great Eastern cities like Hong Kong in China and Singapore in Malaysia were trade centers under European influence for such a long time that they are almost nations in themselves. Bombay, Calcutta, and Delhi under British control developed a similar cosmopolitan society. Modern India is developing into a major industrial and service economy, but two-thirds of its people are still engaged in agriculture. The values and belief in rural villages are changing more slowly than in urban centers. The nation is also a melting pot of religious and ethical diversity. The division between India and Pakistan caused much turmoil and strife, but Moslems still make up about 10 percent of the population. Hinduism is dominant but Buddhism is still influential. There are also numerous Christians, Sikhs, and other minorities.

Buddhism originated in Nepal and quickly spread throughout India and Southeast Asia. Gautama Siddhartha (563–482 B.C.) was the founder and is the Buddha, although there were Buddhas before him and will be more. There are no gods in the system. Gautama taught that existence is suffering and the cause of suffering is desire. To end suffering one must give up all desire, including the desire for salvation. Good actions are rewarded and evil ones punished either in this life or in a long series of lives resulting from *samara*, or the cycle of death and rebirth. Individual *karma* depends on previous life or lives. Buddhists and Hindus share the belief that all living things have souls and that lower life forms such as insects reflect evil behavior in former life. The aim of life must be to break the circle of reincarnation and to be absorbed into the cosmos (*nirvana*). There would be no persistence of the personality for a person who achieves nirvana, but that person would become part of the universal soul. This is difficult to achieve and is approached through the noble eightfold path. This path includes right views, right resolve, right speech, right action, right livelihood, right effort, right mindfulness, and right concentration. Obviously, these have little meaning without interpretation. It is provided by priests in Buddhist temples and by literature. Each major division has its own version of theology.

Hinduism.   The roots of Hinduism go back some 3,000 years. It is characterized more by a philosophy and a way of life than a religion. Although there are many gods in the system, Hinduism has no individual founder and no fixed theology or dogmatic structure. Brahma, creator of the universe, Shiva the destroyer, and Vishnu the preserver are most important. Brahma is equated with the universal soul with which all individual souls will unite when the illusion of time and space (*Maya*) is overcome. Hinduism's sacred literature includes the Veda, the Upanishads, and the Bhagavad Gita. Many theological tracts and commentaries contain prescriptions for divine favor. There are almost as many divisions and sects as gods, and temples devoted to various deities are found throughout India. Many old customs such as child marriage, the rite of *suttee*, and the caste system have largely died out, but karma, the transmigration of souls, the sacred nature of animals, and the desire to be free of the cycle of death and rebirth remain strong. Hindus participate in the worship of gods or spirits at different shrines and tend to be tolerant of other beliefs. The religion supports peaceful coexistence and nonviolent political action.

By far the most influential philosopher in India was Mahatma Gandhi (1869–1948). Gandhi was the most important political leader in the fight against the British for independence. His use of nonviolent noncooperation such as refusal to pay taxes or obey unjust colonial law proved very effective. He became a figure of immense international moral and ethical stature who shaped thought not only in India but worldwide. With the exception of communism, the philosophy of Gandhi has had the greatest impact on the Orient. He was, of course, deeply disappointed with the separation of India from Pakistan on the basis of religious beliefs. His theory supports peace, tolerance, ending poverty, and international cooperation.

Perhaps no nation of the East has had a greater variety of influences than India. Its long history as a British colony caused much unrest and may have retarded economic development, but the railroad system and the English language helped to move the nation forward. Modern India has internal violence and a history of war with Pakistan. It still contains many poverty-stricken areas but the standard of living is improving. Education is valued highly and its highly trained professionals compete successfully on the global market for jobs. Its growing industrial power makes India an international player not far behind China and Japan. Cultural and social values are taught by the families and the wider society, leaving Indian schools with more time to concentrate on mathematics, computer science, language skills, and technology. These schools are able to produce a well-trained, competent workforce in minimum time.

China.   For planning the future of education in America, some understanding of the social, historical, and philosophic evolution of modern China is essential. Not only does China account for one-fifth of the world's population and the second largest economy, but it is rapidly becoming the dominant power in the Orient. One need only visit any American store to see how many Chinese goods are offered on the American market. Competition in education is also keen and growing. Ninety-seven percent of the children in China attend kindergarten. For every child in American public schools, eight pass through the compulsory nine-year educational system in China. Many Chinese students go on to attend their own country's universities or to study abroad. More Chinese are able to speak English than there are people in the United States. Huge numbers of Chinese compete with the best and the brightest for high-paying jobs in fields like accounting, engineering, computer science, and medicine. Not only do the Chinese have an improving standard of living and great future expectations, the communists have brought about a kind of loyalty, pride, patriotism, and enthusiasm not previously seen in the nation.

Western thought has always had difficulty understanding the Oriental mind and so the "inscrutable Chinese" have remained an enigma. Modern communistic Chinese philosophy is even more perplexing because it is still emerging and seems full of contradictions. How can China be both a communistic and a capitalistic society? How can it build a global economy while trying (with limited success) to censor information coming from sources like Google? The answer seems to lie in the course of history.

Three factors are paramount in analyzing the modern mind-set in China. First, for 1500 years religion, literature, rules of ethical conduct, and values based on Confucianism and Taoism were dominant while the imperial government remained static. Although bitterly attacked by the Red Guards during the Cultural Revolution, traditional beliefs die hard and were never completely eliminated. Second, the catastrophic events in the twentieth century—from the foundation of the republic through two world wars, the Japanese occupation, famine, chaos, and civil war—changed everything in China. From this turmoil, the new nation arose from the ashes like the phoenix. Third is the emergence of the unique system of Chinese communism, which differs not only from Western democracy but also from the theories of Marx, Engels, Stalin, and even Mao.

Confucius, born about 550 B.C., was an ethical teacher who urged social reform, scholarship, morality, peace, and justice. His sayings were collected in *The Analects* and the writings of his follower Mencius. Filial piety is a dominate theme in Confucian thought as is *jen*, or sympathy for others. The golden rule of the system is that subordinates must be treated the same as superiors. Extremes are to be avoided in favor of the "middle way" toward peace and harmony. For more than a thousand years, scholarship in China centered upon the classical literature of Confucianism and was required for admission to public office. Its emphasis on family law, respect for elders, and traditional values were universal. Acquiring knowledge was stressed, but foreign literature, science, and external criticism were discouraged.

While Confucius acquired almost divine status, his system had little emotional appeal and was overshadowed by Taoism and Buddhism. Taoist thought stems from Lao Tzu, who developed the theory of the way or path to self-realization in the sixth century B.C. Taoist ethics emphasize patience, simplicity, and the harmony of all natural things. A major theme is the balance between the *yin*, or female principle, and the *yang*, or the male principle. As a religion, Taoism dates from the first century A.D. and Buddhism entered China about the same time. Zen Buddhism, called *Ch'an* in China, stressed mind to mind or master to disciple communication and meditation, leading to tranquility and *saturi* ("awakening"). For the agrarian population, ancestor worship and fertility cults were also important. Christian missionaries reached China in the nineteenth century, although the number of converts was small. Although the Soviet Union under Stalin came down hard on the Russian Orthodox Church as an enemy of the people, Maoist China had no well-organized religion to combat and tended to ignore local and family beliefs. Opposition to religion was more politically than theoretically motivated, as with the suppression of Lamaism in Tibet.

It is likely that events in the century just past have done more to shape the Chinese worldview than all the earlier traditions and beliefs. The end of imperial rule saw foreign intervention, British seizure of Hong Kong, the Opium War, the Boxer Rebellion, regional starvation, and conflicts between local warlords. At the turn of the century, Sun Yat-sen started the nationalist revolution but was opposed by a rival government in Beijing. Later, the Kuomintang government allied with the Communist Party of China, but Chiang Kai-Shek turned against the communists in 1930, leading to civil war and the Long March by Mao and his followers. Japan took advantage of the chaos to establish the puppet state of Manchukuo, which was followed by the invasion and occupation of large areas of the north and east. There followed atrocities such as the rape of Nanking and the Japanese appropriated everything they could from China. When the allied forces defeated Japan, the civil war between communists and nationalists resumed. The USSR supported Mao while the United States supported Chiang, but the communists had by far the greater popular support and in 1949 the People's Republic of China was established. The nationalists fled to Taiwan, but America continued to recognize nationalist China to the dismay of the mainland.

At midcentury, the new China was facing economic collapse and even starvation. Mao was the undisputed leader but except for the Party and the army he had few resources. Germany and Japan were rebuilt with American aid, but China had to build from scratch with limited help from the Soviets and only hostility from the West. Fear of communism, continued support for Taiwan, the Korean War, and the Chinese conquest of Tibet kept relations cool even after China became a nuclear power and gained a seat on the UN Security Council. Mao began to collectivize agriculture; large landowners were deposed but there was no industry beyond Hong Kong (returned by the British in 1997) and a few coastal cities. The government launched large-scale social and economic reforms such as the Great Leap Forward. New factories were built with new cities to support them and workers moved from rural areas. Commerce and international trade were encouraged. A steam railroad system was built to use abundant coal and plans were made for the huge hydroelectric dams on the Yangtze that displaced a million people when completed. There were failures such as backyard smelters for steel production and Soviet-style collective farms. The second Five Year Plan did not meet goals and the power of Mao began to decline. The dictatorship of the proletariat was harsh and dissent was crushed, but many social changes were effective. Facing an increase in population growth it could not sustain, the government limited family size by arbitrary means such as abortion and severe punishment of those who did not comply. The old preference for sons over daughters (perhaps from Confucianism) led to female genocide if the firstborn was a girl. Small families are still the rule in China, which provides a great deal of parental support for the education of each child. In 1966, the Cultural Revolution was launched. It was intended to purge the Communist Party of opponents to Mao and instill correct revolutionary attitudes. Intellectuals and others suspected of revisionism were attacked and humiliated. Red Guards destroyed books, cultural centers, historical sites, and caused terror. By the time of Mao's death in 1976, chaos nearly caused civil war and the army had to restore order.

In the United States, George Washington is honored as the father of the country and so in China Mao Zedong is venerated as the larger-than-life founder of the People's Republic of China. Maoism is the basic theory of government, although it has been much modified by modern Party leaders. Mao was born in a peasant family in Hunan province in 1893; he always respected the common working people. This was reflected in his plain blue coat and soft cap, which was his uniform even as head of state. He received a classical education of high quality, which is shown by his publications that number more than 2,000.

Like many young men of the period, Mao was attracted by democratic principles of Sun Yat-sen. These included nationalism, democracy, freedom from oppression and a guaranteed livelihood. As a Christian, Sun did not think communism was right for China, but both he and Chiang Kai-shek accepted Russian help. Mao read Marx and Engels, rejected religion, and helped to found the Chinese Communist Party. In 1927, the Kuomintang government purged the communists and Mao led the Long March to Yenan, which became his base. For the next 20 years, his attention was occupied by organizing the Red Army, civil war with the nationalists, and fighting Japan. His philosophy was formed during this time, although many of his positions remained fluid. Mao admired Stalin's organizational skill and power, but the Soviet model of collective industry and agriculture seemed ill-suited to China and a unique version of Marxism began to emerge. Over time, Mao became an international figure best known for guerrilla warfare and revolutionary movements and later as a communist theoretical leader.

Communism is based on the communal ownership of property. It asserts that social and political relations depend on economic production. Value is produced by labor but the owners of the means of production (capitalists) appropriate profits for themselves and deny the workers fair value for their labor. The resulting class struggle leads to the overthrow of the capitalists and the creation of state socialism. In this system, production and the distribution of wealth would be democratically controlled (from each according to their ability and to each according to their need). Mao accepted this, but he knew the theory was expected to apply to industrial workers in nations like England and Germany and would require modification for the enormous poverty-stricken agricultural nation of China. He was pragmatic enough to base economic policies on experience and consequences. The concept of a classless society remained basic, but Mao and his prime minister Zhou Enlai tried economic experiments like those of the Soviets. The Great Leap Forward was somewhat successful, but the second Five Year Plan less so. It is not clear whether this, declining health, or fear of loss of power, led to the disaster of the Cultural Revolution, but Mao became quick to blame others. His power had eroded by the time of his death in 1976 but he remains the most important of modern Chinese leaders. His "Little Red Book" once rivaled the Bible as the volume with the most copies in print and in China it had as much status.

Following the death of Mao, a power struggle emerged between the Gang of Four (which included Mao's widow) and moderates led by Deng Xiaoping. Although he had been dismissed during the Cultural Revolution, Deng emerged as the dominant new leader and introduced economic modernization on a grand scale. China had to make do with whatever measures would work. Lacking medical schools and the resources to bring in foreign doctors, every tenth person was trained for minor medical work such as setting bones or curing infections. When collective farms did not produce, more freedom was given to farmers along with new methods and machinery. These acts seem closer to the utilitarianism of Jeremy Bentham (the greatest good for the greatest number) than to Marx. From the time of Deng to the present, China has relaxed socialistic bans on capitalistic practices in order to build a global economy. This has been applied to industry, commerce, trade, and environmental controls, but not to social reform. The crushing of the student revolt in Tiananmen Square, limitation on human rights and free speech, and the imprisonment of Nobel Peace Prize winner Liu Xiao reflect a restrictive government. Facing a population explosion it could not support, the Chinese government limited family size by the most arbitrary means, including abortion and genocide of female infants. These harsh measures worked and the one-child policy has now been in effect for 30 years. There are obvious benefits but also a shortage of women to be future wives and mothers. China has also made progress internationally. Its huge size and commercial power make it a force for stability and world peace. The magnificent handling of the Beijing Olympic games and efforts to curb military threats from North Korea have won worldwide acclaim.

Many political and economic revolutions occur in which one government is replaced by another without greatly altering the basic philosophy of beliefs of the people, but this is not the case with the communist revolution in China. A whole new culture has been created with far-reaching consequences that have destroyed many traditions, challenged the most basic beliefs, and stood old institutions on their heads. Most of the people are happy with their new wealth, and economic prosperity is a strong antirevolutionary force, so it is unlikely that future change will be sudden or violent. It is almost certain that demands for greater freedom and human rights will accompany increased wealth and the emergence of a middle class. The Chinese have yet to define all the factors that united their materialistic capitalism with Mao's brand of communism. There are half a billion members of the Chinese Communist Party. This gives the party a huge populist base that is missing from other communist nations and should keep a small elite from holding autocratic power.

Growing pains will continue for the People's Republic of China. It is not easy to move tens of millions of rural workers to new cities supporting highly specialized factories feeding a global market. China has one city making zippers, another umbrellas, while a textile center processes one-third of the world's socks. Money for these enterprises came from lifting restrictions on foreign capital, but now the Chinese save and invest over 20 percent of their wages, making outside investment less necessary. Whether it is cultural, ethnic, social, or genetic, contemporary Chinese have a superior work ethic and seldom miss an opportunity even if it requires moving or the breakup of a family. China has many millionaires from commerce, building factories or real estate speculation. The infrastructure has been widely expanded. Old steam railroads of Mao's time now have electric trains running at speeds of 260 miles per hour. The Three Gorges Dam is the largest in the world. Power plants and airports abound. China has the fastest supercomputer on earth. Six million cars are added to the roads in China every year and all transportation is expanding. Unlike North Korea or Iran, the Chinese are not hostile toward the United States, but are curious about the American system and future.

When Mao came to power, China was largely illiterate. One of his earliest accomplishments was the building of a universal, compulsory, free educational system for both sexes. Revolutionary communist attitudes were taught, but also basic skills, English, music, and art. Today this system has progressed and is one of the best in the world. Most Chinese children learn social skills, English, and music in day care centers or private schools starting at age three. Almost all attend kindergarten. There are few distractions, well-trained teachers, and pressure to succeed. The school year averages 41 more days, longer than in America, and there are weekend classes. Sporting events are carried on outside of the schools and coached by volunteer Party members, not teachers. Of the qualified secondary-school graduates who apply, only one in ten is admitted to the excellent Chinese universities. Even so, these universities produce four times as many college graduates as do the ones in America. Overproduction of college graduates creates underemployment issues.

It seems certain that China will continue to change and that greater freedom and democratic values will emerge. If the economy continues at its present growth rate of 10 percent or better a year, the Chinese will pass American within two decades. Education will continue to be a high priority. Not only does China control much of the world's manufacturing and commerce, but it also produces large numbers of highly qualified workers, mostly fluent in English to compete on the global job market. The particular combination of Confucian, Taoist, Buddhist, communist, capitalist, and family values that make up the modern Chinese worldview may be hard to define, but it is clear that American schools will have to improve if they expect to successfully compete with China in the future.

Chaos Theory.   Although chaos is a mathematical phenomenon, an increasing amount of research is done in other areas such as ecology and the social sciences. Some scientists believe the twentieth century will be known for three theories: relativity, quantum mechanics, and chaos. Physics now includes the study of chaotic systems and how they work in the social sciences. Chaos theory has opened the possibilities of a hidden wealth of rich, dynamic structure for predicting and making policy decisions for large-scale social systems. This will be helpful in dealing with issues faced by educational policy makers. A recent social systems development has been the move away from large-scale models to use simpler, better-defined assumptions about small-scale behavior. This will be helpful in many areas. For example, there are areas where social and physical dynamic systems interact in complex ways, as in the spread of infectious diseases such as AIDS. Understanding such linkages will be helpful in understanding and perhaps controlling their spread (Brown & Blake, 2004).

Social and Futures Philosophy.   Strongly related to social reconstructionism and the theories of John Dewey, social and futures philosophies are emerging as important bodies of thought aimed at understanding a world of accelerating change. Joel Feinberg tells us that social philosophy is less well defined than most of the other conventional branches and that social philosophy of education is even more elliptical, because it embraces philosophical matters from political science, sociology, and anthropology while including skills of analysis and critical thinking. Although the theory has roots in the Enlightenment and in the works of Comenius, Locke, and Rousseau, it is mainly a twentieth-century development.

Social and futures philosophy is especially concerned with the study of the school as a social institution and concepts like freedom, human rights, leadership, ideology, power, equity, and justice. Social and futures thinkers rely equally on work from philosophy and work from other disciplines. For example, they rely on William F. Ogburn's *Social Change* (1950), Marshall McLuhan's *Understanding Media* (1994), Arnold Toynbee's *A Study of History* (1946), and Kenneth Boulding's *The Meaning of the Twentieth Century* (1965). This interdisciplinary basis means that these theorists are interested in all social issues. General statements of the futures philosophy are found in the works of Alvin Toffler and Edward Cornish. Jim Bowman, Christopher Dede, Draper Kauffmann, and Harold Shane have developed the educational theory.

Insofar as social philosophers deal with ultimate reality, they accept the metaphysics of realism. Logic is of little interest to them, although many accept the urge to clarify language as voiced by analytical thinkers. The real thrust of the movement is epistemology and axiology. These philosophers have historically criticized "received" notions such as the accepted social role of the school, the end of preparing to enter the job market, and the notion that existing bodies of knowledge define the path to the good life. They look to the kind of information a learner must have for survival in the future, and they consider how the society might be reconstructed through education to meet new technical, social, and environmental needs. This aspect of the social philosophy has, in the current century, taken on a strong normative component, as it attempts to set forth new designs and scenarios of teaching and learning, research and study, knowledge and values, and the theoretical dimensions of special institutions. Spencer Maxcy of Louisiana State University has developed a statement of social philosophy of education, as has Harold Hodgkinson.

As the name implies, social philosophers of education are concerned with the deeper, more theoretical dimensions of social issues as they are related to education. They have criticized the accepted social role of the school. Futurists are interested in those social arrangements that will allow us to survive with a maximum realization of the human potential. They see education as a means of inventing the future and restructuring society so as to resolve the most pressing human problems and to take advantage of new opportunities provided by technological invention. This aspect of social philosophy of education has a strong value orientation as it attempts to set forth new designs and scenarios of teaching, learning, research, and study. Values and ethics, freedom, human rights, equity, justice, ideology, leadership, and the proper use of power are major areas of interest for futurists and social philosophers.

Qualitative methods of educational inquiry are increasingly used in research. Elliot Eisner, James Swartz, and others address the utility of qualitative research. William Pinar talks of the need to reconceptualize education, to move from traditional means of telling the truth about schooling to a better understanding through psychological/biographical/literary techniques and the adoption of more naturalistic methods. Philosophy, social science, and futurism join hands to provide a more workable set of solutions to the social problems facing human society. A branch of social philosophy called *hermeneutics* argues that the primary function of thought is seeking an understanding of the conditions we face as humans. The business of social and futures philosophy is edifying rather than providing data or statistical analysis of present conditions and interpreting social change.

Philosophy and Technology.

Upon first examination it would seem that technology and philosophy are mutually exclusive fields of human inquiry, but this is not strictly true. From ancient times, it was noted that the sun and moon followed precise paths across the sky and their movement could be predicted without exception. At the beginning of the nineteenth century, the Marquis de Laplace developed the theory of scientific determinism. Most philosophers and scientists, including Samuel Johnson and Benjamin Franklin, accepted the idea that a set of precise laws governed the universe and that once these were known, everything would be within the power of human minds to know.

In 1900, the German scientist Max Planck found that X-rays and other forms of light could only be emitted in certain groups that he called *quanta*. This was followed in 1926 by Werner Heisenberg's famous uncertainty principle. Heisenberg found that in order to predict the future position and velocity of a particle, one must be able to measure the present position and velocity accurately. This cannot be done because the more accurately one measures the position, the shorter the wavelength of the light and therefore the higher the energy, which alters the velocity. This uncertainty principle had profound implications for the way we view the universe and was the death blow for scientific determinism. It led to the development of quantum mechanics.

Quantum mechanics cannot predict a single definite result for an observation. It does tell us how many possible outcomes there are and gives the probability of each one of these. Quantum mechanics has turned out to be very useful for dealing with subatomic particles like electrons, photons, and quarks. It underlies all modern science and is fundamental to the technology of transistors, integrated circuits, and computers. It is a method of dealing with the behavior of the smallest parts of matter we can identify when these sometimes appear to be waves and other times to be particles. The large-scale structure of the universe and the force of gravity seem to be governed by Einstein's general theory of relativity, which does not take into account the uncertainty principle, even though the basic building blocks of matter must.

Philosophers have had difficulty in keeping up with new scientific theories, especially because one must specialize in physics and mathematics to understand them. Ludwig Wittgenstein, one of the most famous philosophers of the twentieth century, gave up on ultimate reality and held that the only remaining field for philosophy was the analysis of language. But the fact remains that with all the scientific and technological advances, we still do not know the ultimate nature of reality. Even if we had certain proof of the Big Bang theory of the universe's creation or absolute knowledge of the structure and behavior of subatomic particles, the philosophic questions still remain. The "what" of the universe does not tell us the "why." One function of education for the future might be to give students enough background in fields like astronomy and physics so that they can understand the discoveries that are being made and contribute to the ongoing philosophic inquiry.

FOCUS ON THE ISSUES

The Cultural Revolution

One of our students once shared with the class her experiences in China's cultural revolution in the 1960s. Mao called for a thousand flowers to bloom, encouraging people to speak out in 1958. Yet when he felt his regime was threatened, he called for a purge of bougeoisie intellectuals. A young girl and her brothers watched as their father, president of a large university in north China, was dragged through the streets with a huge metal sign roped around his neck calling him "bougeoisie intellectual." He was paraded by Red Guards shouting out insults and slogans such as "Down (opening paren) with the bougeoisie intellectual." No classes were taught for several years as many professors and administrators were labeled as "bougeoisie intellectuals" or "capitalist road takers." They were humiliated, physically abused, and made to clean toilets or work on the farms. Many died in the purge.

Part of Mao's denouncement of education was also reflected in his policies in the late 1960s and early 1970s, during which millions of youth from junior high to high school were sent to farms and remote rural areas for "reeducation" from "workers, farmers, and soldiers" who were considered the leaders of the country. These youth lived in rural homes with no facilities and worked in the fields with the farmers all year round. Our student and her family were eventually left alone to rebuild their lives while Mao's wife was condemned as part of the Gang of Four who mislead the country.

Although there has been never an apology from the Chinese government for the tragic loss of lives and unmeasurable economic reversal under Mao, the new leaders in China in the 1980s supported the intellectuals and education moved forward. The cultural upheaval was "designed" to understand and appreciate the lower classes, the working classes, and the rural classes.

What Do You Think?

1. Compare and contrast the Cultural Revolution in China with that of Iran after the demise of the Shah.
2. What did Mao plan for the Cultural Revolution and what happened to upset his plan?
3. Give three examples of threats to intellectual freedom in our era.
4. Define humanism and an inclusive society and educational system. Describe Chinese child rearing in Amy Chua's popular book, *Battle Hymn of the Tiger Mother*. Your reaction?

PSYCHOLOGY AND EDUCATIONAL THEORY

Teacher education programs include at least one course in general psychology and one in psychology of education. The part of modern educational psychology that will be discussed in this section is the history of child study and psychology. Obviously this topic is important to understanding how schooling developed in America, while the relationship between philosophy and psychology is fundamental to knowledge of educational theory.

Psychology and Learning: Historical Development. *Education of the Elite.* Assumptions about the nature of mind and learning underpin all educational efforts. As we have seen, Plato wrote about the three divisions of the soul and the need to make reason paramount. Because he believed that only a small part of the population is ruled by the faculty of reason, his schools were set up to identify and educate only those able to become philosopher-kings. The curriculum focused on pure ideas and abstract sciences like geometry. Both sexes were admitted to the schools described in the *Republic*, but any child lacking either interest or ability was encouraged to drop out. Those who did so (the vast majority) were relegated to lower positions in society. Plato's highly elitist system has had vast influence, causing many to believe schools should sort out the best and the brightest and concentrate on subjects designed to strengthen the faculties of the mind.

Dualism. Aristotle studied with Plato in the Academy. He did not reject Plato's notion of pure ideas or forms, but he did hold that the mind is undivided and independent of the body. This dualism of mind and body was dominant throughout the Middle Ages and was reinforced by René Descartes in the sixteenth century.

Experience. A major revolution in psychological thinking came with the empirical principle and the origin of ideas from experience in John Locke's "Essay Concerning the Human Understanding" (1690). Locke's epistemology holds that there are no innate ideas—that everything in the mind comes from experience through the sense organs. Because the mind has no content at birth, it is like a blank tablet upon which experience writes. The measure of the validity of an idea comes from the experimental process of comparing it with sensory data from the real world, not from logical analysis. Locke and other empiricists such as David Hume (1711–1776) restricted human knowledge to the experience of ideas and impressions, making the flow of ideas through perception paramount. Because of the rise of empiricism and sense realism, there has been a debate over what part of the understanding is genetic and how much depends upon the environment. The education profession leaned toward the environment in the nature–nurture controversy, in part because it had no control over anything else. Today, work on DNA and genetic engineering casts new light on this debate.

Pedagogy. Although philosophy still ruled psychology, as it did until scientific laboratories were developed, several efforts to improve the understanding of mental activity and learning were made by leading educational theorists. John A. Comenius (Komensky), the seventeenth-century Moravian educational reformer, created lessons in graded order to accommodate stages of learning. By working from the simple to the complex and the familiar to the unfamiliar, he made teaching easier and was one of the first to propose a science of pedagogy.

Naturalism and Phrenology.   In 1762, the French philosopher Jean-Jacques Rousseau published his educational book *Emile*. Advocating freedom for the child, this work called for relying on the natural interests of youngsters through a series of developmental stages. Rousseau saw no need for external rewards or punishment to be used in education. Instead, he suggested altering the environment and using activities such as field trips to stimulate the natural curiosity and inquisitiveness of the learner. These ideas were quickly applied to schools by Johann H. Pestalozzi in Swiss villages and to early childhood education by Friedrich Froebel in Germany. Both Pestalozzi and Froebel saw education as the natural harmonious development of all the child's natural faculties and powers. Both had tremendous influence in Europe and later in America (see Chapter 5). Stephen Tomlinson in his *Head Masters: Phrenology, Secular Education and Nineteenth Century* (2005) analyses the role of phrenology in education.

Words like *intelligence, consciousness*, and *mind* were still vague and mystical at the end of the nineteenth century. The German physician Franz Joseph Gall ascribed cerebral functions to various areas of the brain and claimed that the shape of the skull could determine mental abilities. This "phrenology" was popular for a time and drew the support of the American educator Horace Mann. The major theory for educational leaders continued to be faculty psychology, or the belief that the mind is divided into separate powers. This fosters mental discipline and the idea of transfer of training.

The Doors of Perception.   In 1892, the Committee of Ten of the National Education Association (NEA) based its recommendations on faculty psychology. A protest against this psychology was led by the German philosopher Johann F. Herbart. Toward the middle of the nineteenth century, he became interested in Pestalozzi's methods and developed a metaphysical theory of pluralistic realism that rejected faculty psychology. Herbart refused to believe in innate ideas but developed a theory of learning from sensory experience that formed the basis of pedagogical method for his many followers (see Figure 2.2). The mind is divided into two parts: the conscious and the subconscious. Ideas enter the conscious mind as perceptions delivered by a sense organ (the eye). The conscious mind associates the perception with others that are similar (a child's block, a box, an ice cube) and then pushes the perception through the division between the parts of the mind (the limen). Associations create an "apperceptive mass." An idea thrust into the subconscious for storage may be remembered by fishing for the associations with which it is identified. Thus, to remember someone's name you fish for associations such as with whom you last saw the person. When dreaming, the limen is open and ideas flow from the subconscious to the conscious without order. Education must concentrate on

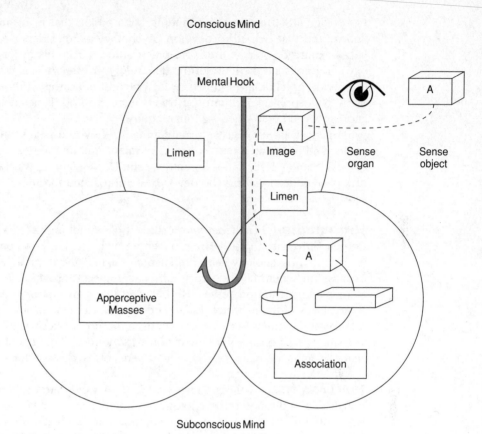

Figure 2.2   Herbart's Conception of the Human Mind

association and apperceptions. We expand our knowledge by making connections between old ideas and each new one.

Biology and Psychoanalysis: A Time to Experiment.   Psychology as a science developed in Europe and to some degree in America before the beginning of the twentieth century. Herbart sought clues to mental development in the facts of physiology. Darwin's work on evolution stimulated others to study the child's nature from a biological standpoint. Pavlov's conditioned reflex experiments on animals in Russia created a new wave of interest in psychology. Of even more significance was the founding of the first experimental psychology laboratory by Wilhelm Max Wundt at Leipzig in 1878. Wundt trained a great many American psychologists, and he is often regarded as the father of structural psychology. Other European leaders included Ebbinghaus, who worked with nonsense syllables to measure memory, and Freud, who developed psychoanalysis from the dynamics of motivation in personality formation.

Although not strictly an experimental psychologist, William James (1842–1910) did much to create a link between education and psychology. His *Principles of*

Psychology (1890) was an outstanding contribution that made him internationally known and that helped to develop psychology as an independent area of study. James extracted some of the more practical ideas from his major work in psychology and published them under the title *Talks to Teachers*. This was the first attempt to provide psychological guidance for practical educators. Although his work was partly philosophical and introspection was his method, James helped to make psychology a valid field of educational inquiry.

American psychologists, heavily influenced by Europeans, attacked formal discipline and formulated new concepts of mind. Among the first were Edward Titchener, G. Stanley Hall, James M. Cattell, John Dewey, and Edward L. Thorndike. The history of educational psychology is best approached through the various types or schools of psychology.

Structuralism.   Titchener was a student of Wundt and a leading psychologist at Cornell University for 30 years. Concerned with the study of consciousness, Titchener treated psychology as an impersonal science and approached it atomistically. That is, Titchener and the structuralists attempted to isolate and analyze the basic elements of mental processes. He believed that a microscopic examination of the basic blocks of the nervous system and psychic elements would lead to a complete science of the mind. Because structuralism did not concern itself with the living organism, its relationship with education was indirect. Members of this psychological school dominated many college departments of psychology for years.

Functionalism.   William James and John Dewey were the first to identify functionalism as a division of psychology. For them, a study of consciousness could not be isolated from feelings, sensations, thoughts, and activities of the living organism. In 1900, as president of the newly formed American Psychological Association, Dewey called for the application of psychology to social and educational practice. For Dewey, the complete act of thought is the same for a child in school as it is for a scientist working on a problem in a laboratory. Both go through the same five-step process:

1. Engaging in an activity
2. Discovering a problem
3. Gathering data
4. Forming a hypothesis
5. Testing

Learning can only occur when students are engaged in genuine activities rather than in artificial ones imposed by the teacher. Problems occur when activity is blocked. Children learn how to gather data from simple sources such as their own memories or from more complicated sources such as libraries. Hypothesis formation is merely the posing of a possible solution to a problem, and the learner must examine what consequences might occur if the hypothesis is accepted. Only by testing the proposed solution against empirical evidence can learning be completed. Dewey's *Psychology* (1887) and *How We Think* (1910) described his functional theories.

His *Human Nature and Conduct* (1922) is a statement of the interaction between the individual and his environment.

Connectionist Psychology or Associationism.
Edward Lee Thorndike (1874–1949) was a student of William James and James McKeen Cattell. Building on Herman Ebbinghaus's curve of learning and forgetting and on studies of animal learning made by Lloyd Morgan in England, Thorndike began a series of learning experiments with animals. After a series of trial and error activities, the animal would chance upon the "solution" that released food. Further trials in the same puzzle box resulted in the animal's making the proper response more rapidly than at first. This led Thorndike to his "law of effect," which he also extended to human activity. He found a very strong effect from rewards but also discovered that punishment was a less effective means for the control of behavior. Following Pavlov's lead, Thorndike assumed a connection between stimuli and responses. He developed this into *S–R* bond psychology using the equation Learning = Stimulus = Response. If stimulus *A* is known to be associated with response *B*, repeat *A* until *B* is produced without hesitation whenever *A* occurs. Teachers rapidly accepted Thorndike's laws of learning, which they found to be highly useful devices for classroom instruction.

Because Thorndike had an impeccable reputation as a scientist, his pioneering experiments opened new fields of psychological research at the time when modern conceptions of pedagogy were being born. He was one of the first to understand that education and psychology were closely linked. Psychology forms the foundation for the science of education, and schools furnish subjects and data sources for psychological research.

Behaviorism.
Associationism or connectionism gave rise to the psychological school known as behaviorism (the logical extreme). John B. Watson (1878–1958) is generally regarded as the founder, but his student, Karl Lashley, also contributed to this strictly objective division of psychology. One of the best-known scholars in the field of behaviorism was B. F. Skinner (1904–1990) of Harvard.

Although he had studied with Dewey, Watson believed that psychology should be confined to those activities that could be verified by an outside observer. Behaviorism discarded consciousness as a subject of investigation and refused to use the method of introspection. It limited its findings to laboratory experiments that could be controlled and dealt only with those factors capable of analysis. Behaviorists believe that we have no right to project our feelings or ideas onto the subjects that we investigate. For example, if a person gives a piece of meat to a dog, it is legitimate to describe the dog's behavior (i.e., the animal jumps up, drools, opens its mouth, and eats the meat). However, it is not legitimate to say that the dog "likes" the meat because that projects the attitudes or feelings of the human onto the dog, and there is no evidence to support the statement.

Watson held that environment is far more important than heredity in the determination of human behavior. He rejected innate ideas and most instincts. His experiments with infants caused him to conclude that almost all emotional responses are learned. Watson held that if the environment could be strictly controlled, any normal

FOCUS ON THE ISSUES

Behavior Modification

Behaviorism relies on operant conditioning to control the actions of animals and people. This "rat in a box" psychology developed by Watson and Skinner is so universally effective that we are constantly bombarded by its simple system of rewards and punishments. Advertisers promise that buying their products will make us beautiful, healthy, and sexy. Video games and casino slot machines allow us to win until the habit of playing is established and we are hooked. Parents offer increased allowances or trips to Disney World for kids who bring home good report cards and withhold privileges when they do not. Teachers shower praise or award gold stars for high achievement and depend on techniques of behavior modification for classroom management. Simply put, operant conditioning works.

It works, however, at a price. If the reward (or withholding the reward) is outside of the task itself, then the motivation is linked not to the behavior but to the desired reward. Behaviorism may be used to teach one to be a competent piano player but not to love music or to play for the sake of playing. Many of the world's greatest artists (Vermeer, for example) received neither money nor praise for their work but continued to produce wonderful products. Knowledge and wisdom are not produced by methods that bring success on tests of achievement. It is much like the mirror of Erised in *Harry Potter and the Sorcerer's Stone* (Rowling, 1998). Interest is keen and behavior is changed, but the mirror gives us neither knowledge nor truth. Likewise, external rewards in education produce results but do not create a love of learning or a desire to master fields of knowledge. The same results do not come from reading a book because it is good and reading it because it is required and the reader will be tested on the content. Behavior modification will continue to be used but it leads to training rather than to education in the best sense of the word.

What Do You Think?

1. What things do you most enjoy doing for their own sake and not for external reward?
2. Young people universally enjoy learning to drive. Immediate feedback when the wheel is turned or the brake is applied is rewarding. Can teaching be made as exciting as driving for students?
3. A bird in a cage pecks on a piece of bright metal and is immediately rewarded with food. Is this the best model we can develop for teaching humans?

child could be raised to be a mechanic, an athlete, a professional person, or a thief. Lashley was able to demonstrate that even human glands could be conditioned.

The early work of the behaviorists helped to discredit many theories about learning that were held by other psychologists. They did a great deal to foster objective evaluations of experiments. Sometimes their claims were extravagant, and certainly many educators objected to what they described as "rat in a box" psychology and the restriction of investigation to a fractional part of human behavior. Nevertheless, behaviorism won the respect of scientists in other fields, and its rigorous techniques helped to support objective educational research.

B. F. Skinner's work spans the period from early behaviorism to the present. In the late 1930s, he began a series of animal learning experiments in which he taught animals to perform complex tasks. He accomplished this by giving the subject a reward after each step of the task was successfully accomplished. Out of this grew the idea of programmed instruction and teaching machines. During World War II, new programs for using electronic devices in teaching were developed by Skinner and his students. Computer-assisted instruction, now used in numerous aspects of education, was adapted from the work of behaviorists. Skinner's books—*Science and Human Behavior* (1953), *Walden II* (1948), and *Beyond Freedom and Dignity* (1971)—have had a profound effect upon educators in modern America. Few of the findings of Skinner and other behaviorists have been scientifically rejected. The criticism of behaviorism normally comes from those who say it is too narrow, mechanical, and nonhumanistic.

Gestalt.   At about the same time that behaviorism began to influence education in America, German Gestalt psychology also became important. *Gestalt* is a German word meaning "form or pattern," and it refers to the whole configuration or sum of integrated experiences present at any one time. The apparent motion created by flashing a series of photographs in the cinema is not explained by examining individual still pictures, nor can music be understood merely through the study of notes. Max Wertheimer, Kurt Koffka, and Wolfgang Kohler started Gestalt psychology in Germany. Beginning in 1914, Kohler began a series of experiments on the island of Tenerife using apes as subjects. He concluded that learning takes place as sudden insight rather than by simple trial and error. This led to the examination of the pattern perceived by the learner in his or her total environment, rather than to an atomistic consideration of essential elements in the learning process.

Kurt Lewin (1890–1947) was a German Gestalt psychologist who migrated to the United States when Hitler came to power. He believed that behavior is the result of energy derived from the needs or wants of the individual and the organism's efforts to meet those needs. Lewin's psychology is called *field theory* because of the emphasis of the life-space or field of the individual as he or she perceives it. Lewin used the term *vector* to describe the attractive or repulsive forces that motivate the organism to act.

Modern humanistic psychologists such as Abraham Maslow and Carl Rogers have been highly influenced by Gestalt, field, and holistic psychological theories. Members of these schools have had at least as much impact on American education as behaviorists.

Modern Developmental Psychology and Stage Theory.   A major thrust of educational psychology in recent years has been directed toward the relationship of curriculum and methods to stages of development in children. Conflict exists between various theories of development, but there is agreement that poor pedagogy results from attempting to teach information or concepts before the learner has reached the stage at which such information and concepts can be understood.

How to Increase Motivation.   David Ausubel (1963) distinguishes between learning by reception and learning by discovery. Reception learning requires the student to internalize material in order to recall it at a later date (as on a test). Discovery learning does not present material in finished form but sets up an environment in

which something has to be discovered or invented by the student before it can be assimilated. Discovery learning emphasizes the process; reception learning concentrates on the product. Ausubel contends that discovery learning motivates the student to understand how new knowledge is generated and stimulates the learner; however, it is an inefficient method for delivering large amounts of information. Ausubel therefore believes that a balance must exist between process and product and that schools that offer discovery learning foster the progress of children and make education interesting.

Jerome Bruner is recognized for his efforts to apply scientific methods to teaching and for his research on the formation of concepts in children. Bruner is interested in the structure of subject matter. He believes that the teaching of particular subjects can be integrated into the way the students see the world so as to permit learners to discover the basic principles of the discipline under study. Motivation therefore should be stimulated by the subject matter itself and not from external appeals to interest or the arrangement of consequent events. Obviously, this idea differs from Skinner's operant conditioning. Bruner believes that it is possible to teach any subject in some intellectually honest way to any child at any developmental stage.

Stages of Learning: Gagné and Piaget.

Child psychologist Robert Gagné is well known for his contributions to programmed instruction. He believes that children pass through developmental stages of learning that are determined by what is to be learned. Gagné identifies eight conditions for learning:

1. Signal learning occurs when infants learn responses to a general cue.
2. Stimulus–response learning is more precise and voluntary.
3. Chaining is the result of putting together previous responses.
4. Verbal discrimination is the association of names with objects.
5. Multiple discrimination is identifying and classifying groups of stimuli.
6. Concept learning is the ability to identify important differences and similarities between sets of stimuli.
7. Principle learning is relating one complete concept to others.
8. Problem solving is using several principles for dealing with a new situation.

Gagné urges educators to give more attention to the way in which instruction is sequenced because he holds that no learning stage can be skipped. Because Gagné believes that it is the nature of the skills to be learned that determines the sequence of stages, the curriculum must be ordered accordingly. Ausubel, Bruner, and Gagné all see the subject matter or the learning tasks as central to learning stages. However, Piaget holds that stages are related to the maturation and development of children.

Jean Piaget was born in Neuchatel, Switzerland, in 1896. He began his career as a zoology assistant at the age of 11 and published papers on mollusks at the age of 15. Piaget worked with Alfred Binet in Paris on standardizing tests of intelligence and became interested in the levels of logic used by children taking such tests. Building on Rousseau and Pestalozzi, Piaget attempted to establish a body of psychology to give support for educational techniques truly adapted to the laws of mental development. For many years, he carried out experiments on learning tasks with children in the J. J. Rousseau Institute. He was active in the field until he died in 1980.

Piaget believed that the two fundamental characteristics of a child's learning and cognitive development are organization and adaptation. Organization is described as the systematizing of information into meaningful patterns. These patterns are used to structure new information so that it does not seem random or chaotic to the learner. Adaptation is the process of coping, or integrating new information into existing perceptions and patterns. Intelligence for Piaget must follow from our ability to organize and adapt. Like Dewey, Piaget saw human beings as born active, curious, interested in communication, and with a need to assimilate information. His principles of organization and adaptation are in basic agreement with the theories of Bruner and Gagné.

Piaget and his followers urge educators to be realistic about what children can accomplish at each stage. Tests have shown that many freshmen entering universities still think on a concrete level. Even after a person has reached the formal level of operations, it is common to revert back to earlier stages under stress. Teachers, in the view of Piaget, must avoid abstract and theoretical tasks if any of the learners in their classrooms are still operating in a nonformal way.

What's Recent Counts.   Jerome Kagan challenges the belief that early experiences are crucial to later development. For Kagan and his associates, the most recent experiences are more important than the earliest ones. His research shows dramatic improvement when children from deprived backgrounds are exposed to an enriched environment. Rather than dealing with stages of development, Kagan urges teachers to create a stable and positive learning situation. Past experiences of the teacher and of the student are less significant to Kagan than a sense of involvement and experiences that are supportive of intellectual growth. Kagan believes that the environment is all important, and he is optimistic about programs like Head Start. His cognitive interpretation of child development states that learners do best in an environment characterized by moderate discrepancy from their existing worldview. Uncertainty and challenge are emotionally satisfying, but the shock of something totally new may create resistance in the learner.

Understanding Words.   In *Thought and Language*, Vygotsky (1985) noted that thought and speech are the key to the nature of human consciousness. Thus, understanding child development entails a totality of understanding words, thoughts, and motivations. He finds four developmental states:

1. Primitive or preverbal thought
2. Experience with physical properties (self and objects around the child)
3. Use of external and internal signs as aids in solving internal problems
4. In growth of constant interaction between inner and outer operations

Vygotsky, like Dewey, placed emphasis on the cultural ingredients in human development.

Other Contributions to Educational Psychology.   Benjamin Bloom's mastery learning concept has had considerable influence on the theory and practice of teaching in modern America. Mastery learning calls for individualized instruction, with each student going at his or her own pace. Students must demonstrate that each level and condition of learning has been mastered before going on to the next level. Bloom is also known for his two taxonomies, the cognitive and the affective. Values and attitudes in the affective domain must be understood as different from the intellectual tasks of cognition. Split-brain research and its implications for educators have supported this distinction. Neurologists like J. E. Bogen and Michael Gazzaniga claim that education has stressed verbal skills to a fault and that both language and nonlanguage techniques are needed.

Cognitive psychology contrasts sharply with the behaviorism of B. F. Skinner. It emphasizes complex intellectual processes that cannot be explained by the analysis of simple stimulus–response situations. Since 1970, cognitive psychology has become the dominant theoretical force, but most schools still reflect the behaviorist approach. Cognitive psychologists like Robert Glaser thought this would change before the end of the twentieth century. Other psychologists such as Albert Bandura and Richard Walters concern themselves with the way people acquire behavior appropriate to social circumstances. Loud expressions and slang language may be appreciated in an informal meeting of peers but are not appropriate in a classroom setting. These psychologists build on the principles of Skinner to form a theory of social learning.

Noam Chomsky of Massachusetts Institute of Technology (MIT) has criticized Skinner on quite different grounds. He sees Skinner's learner as a robot responding to external stimuli only. Chomsky believes that all human beings have an inborn inclination to master language, regardless of the environment. His theory of transformational grammar states that learners respond not only to the environment but also to internal events.

Another area of psychology that has created considerable educational interest in recent years is described as humanistic and phenomenological. Carl Rogers is known for client-centered or nondirective therapy. He feels that psychology has focused on the experimental laboratory and Freudian theory instead of human growth and the potential of humankind. In books like *On Becoming a Person* (1962), Rogers concerns himself with the infinite possibilities of human development, creativity, and how people can help each other to become more fully human.

Abraham Maslow.   Abraham Maslow is one of the best-known humanistic psychologists. He has focused on counseling and identified the needs that are basic to the educational environment. Maslow's hierarchy of needs is included in the basic preparation of many American teachers. Basic needs such as food and shelter always take priority over other needs. This is not different from the position of the progressives, who believed that before a student can be taught, the school must see that he or she is properly fed and physically well. Safety and security needs come next in Maslow's scheme. Beyond security, we all have needs for affection and love. A desire for self-esteem and the respect of others takes the next place on the hierarchy.

The final need is for self-actualization. Teachers will do well to consider these needs in the light of recent events such as school violence and terrorist attacks.

THEN TO NOW

The philosophies of education discussed in this chapter are certainly the major ones in contemporary America, but many educational decisions are made without any obvious link to a theoretical foundation. As Dewey once put it, philosophers may argue with one another, but "burly sinners" run the world. It is certainly true that many people who make decisions about education do so without a philosophic foundation or one that is pragmatic in the narrow sense of the word.

Educational Goals. Chairperson of the National Commission on Teaching and America's future, North Carolina Governor James Hunt, in *What Matters Most: Teaching for America's Future* (1996), again stressed high academic standards both for teachers and for students as well as reinventing teacher preparation and professional development to achieve success at all educational levels. Hunt received the American Educational Research Association's (AERA) first Distinguished Public Service Award for his work in enacting educational policies based on educational research as governor of North Carolina. His address to the 2003 meeting was titled "How I Know That We Can Make Every School Work and Help Every Child Learn" (*AERA News*, 2003).

The Goal of Citizenship. Nel Noddings, in the *Kappan* (1996), calls for a broader goal of education. Students should learn to become good neighbors, concerned guardians of the natural world, and honest colleagues in whatever activities they pursue.

A few philosophical positions such as existentialism would be in total opposition to Hunt's "Education for Economic Growth," but most would think his views myopic to the extreme. Idealists and perennialists would argue that job preparation is secondary to character building, value formation, citizenship training, and a broad understanding of Western civilization. Social and futures theorists would say that Hunt's position is counterproductive to meeting even his narrow objective, because future economic growth depends on solving social problems, protecting the environment, and creating a stable world order.

It is reasonable to expect that a child born today will be a functioning member of society in the end of the twenty-first century. If conditions change at the rate of present experience (and there is good reason to think they will alter even more rapidly), the world the future will be a different one indeed.

Agreement on Educational Policy. There is a seeming contradiction between the support for individual freedom found in Rousseau's *Emile* (1762) and his effort to develop for the inhabitants of Poland a social contract that had mechanisms of social control and public schools. Futurist Fred Kierstead has expanded this conflict in order to define the meaning of the "general will" as the authority for making educational decisions. For Rousseau, the will of the people, expressed through popularity polls or single votes, was not as trustworthy as the general will. The general will was the true belief of the people as a body over time. If there is validity in the theory, we still have the problem of how to find the general will now and in the future. Politics, media campaigns, personalities of leaders, and current events may cloud our perception of what the people really want.

Philosophy may be the best tool we have for clearing away the barriers and reaching agreement on educational policy. It is unlikely that we will ever get total agreement from everyone. The comet that appeared in the sky during the spring of 1997 was an object of beauty and scientific significance for most of us. We accepted the astronomers' explanation of its existence. Yet, a handful of members of the cult called Heaven's Gate believed the comet was a ship from outer space sent to take them away. Their belief was so strong that they took their own lives in order to speed the process of leaving Earth. Clearly, there are those who passionately believe what most of us consider nonsense.

In his *Education and Work for the Year 2000: Choices We Face* (1992), Arthur Wirth argued that we must give ourselves freedom and flexibility to explore alternatives and opinions. As educational philosopher Maxine Greene noted, Wirth's book dealt with the continuing tension between our democratic tradition and demands for technological revolution. John Dewey's concept of continuous reconstruction of experience as the basis for solving problems and planning action is compatible with Wirth. So are the ideas of futurists Kenneth Boulding, Alvin Toffler, Wendell Bell, Daniel Bell, and John R. Platt. As John Dewey put it, democracy is the form of social organization most conducive to problem solving because only in a democracy are people free to inquire. Through freedom of inquiry, the mechanisms of democracy may be used to shape the schools and resolve conflicts over such issues as teaching methods and curriculum. Democratic education may also be the means by which people can secure the civil and political freedoms necessary for the good life. This goal is obviously much broader than Governor Hunt's job preparation. Can we achieve both?

As the twenty-first century develops, movement toward a more democratic and free market society in Russia and China encourages optimism among futurists that a global democratic educational system might be possible. Already there is worldwide competition for the best jobs; American children must learn how to speak foreign languages, how to access the Internet, and how to use multicultural interpersonal skills if they are to be successful. Concerns over human rights violations in China, ethnic conflict in Bosnia or the Middle East, or the peace efforts between Arabs and Israelis clearly indicate an unstable world culture. The great fear of nuclear war no longer threatens the globe, but philosophical differences over educational goals are even greater in the international scene than in the United States.

Unlike the West Germans or the Japanese, ordinary Americans are directly involved with the governance of their schools. Americans are also inconsistent in the way they choose or represent values and philosophies. Thus, school board members often share a vague belief in an idealistic world order or universal mind while

FOCUS ON THE ISSUES

International Terrorism

Iroquois, Huron, and Mohawk braves descended savagely on the isolated town of Deerfield that frigid morning in 1704. The predawn raid occurred without warning so that farmers hardly had a chance to reach their guns before they were felled by arrows and tomahawks. Indians were also armed with French muskets provided as part of the French and Indian War against English settlers. Fifty men, women, and children were slain within an hour. Eighty-eight prisoners were marched off through heavy snow; those who could not keep up were hacked to pieces. One old man survived with his scalp completely cut away and an eye missing. Curiously, a silver cup belonging to the local schoolmistress was later found in the burning ruins of the village. . . .

A cold wind was blowing off the Big White River near the mouth of Wounded Knee Creek that December day in 1890. Troops of the U.S. Army stood guard over a large band of Sioux who had been taken in previous days of fighting. The Sioux had been disarmed and were held in an area from which escape was unlikely. Suddenly, a shot rang out. The startled Native Americans began to mill about. Poorly trained white soldiers began to panic. Rifle fire increased and Gatlin guns opened up. Two hundred Sioux warriors died in the bloody massacre. . . .

In an impoverished town in Alabama, a 15-year-old girl told her brother that she had been raped by a young Negro man named Jim Pryor. The brother rounded up his relatives and friends. They burst into the Pryor household and dragged the sleeping Jim out into the street. Someone produced a rope and the struggling black youth was hung on a telephone pole. There was no arrest, no trial, no supporting evidence, and no defense. The sheriff did not like what the lynch mob had done but he had little evidence against them. In addition, he was coming up for reelection. Blacks in the community had no power to do anything and the incident was passed over with no investigation. The year was 1923. . . .

These are clearly incidents of terrorism in which the victims were attacked and died without recourse. They differ from 9/11, car bombings in Israel, or explosions in American embassies overseas because they were incidents caused by American to Americans in our own history. All of us are now involved with the war on terrorism if only through paying for the huge costs of increased airport security and the invasion of Iraq. International violence permeates the mass media. We are keenly aware of fighting from Palestine to Sudan and concerned about possible future attacks at home. Because Abraham Maslow has demonstrated that learning requires students to have a safe environment, teachers must help students to overcome fear and to deal with the reality of international terrorism while avoiding hysteria. It may help to understand that terrorism was not invented by Nazis, ethnic hatred in Bosnia, or Islamic extremists.

What Do You Think?

1. During the Cold War, Americans feared nuclear attack by the Soviet Union. Was this different from the current fear of attack on the United States?
2. In the global culture, are Americans viewed as people who support world peace?
3. How can teachers help students to understand international attitudes?

spending their time on such mundane matters as buying buses, reviewing complaints about "lax" discipline, or trying to head off the demands of teachers for better pay. Parents and community citizens may exhibit keen interest in the success of the local high school's varsity football team and very little interest in the school curriculum, although they would not list varsity sports as the purpose of secondary education.

Consistency is not a characteristic trait of Americans. Obviously, better understanding of the theoretical basis of education is required to clarify issues and meet future needs. Historical trends reflected in alternative philosophies of education enable students to assess current issues and policies more effectively.

GAINING PERSPECTIVE THROUGH CRITICAL ANALYSIS

1. How do proponents of idealism, realism, and pragmatism differ in terms of educational practice? Which philosophy is most appealing to you? Why?
2. Describe the effects the protest philosophies have had on educational policy in terms of the curriculum and the roles of the teacher, administrator, staff, and student.
3. Name two social reconstructionists, and discuss their contributions to educational policy and practice.
4. Analyze the contribution of existential thought to today's education practices and policies.
5. How does the quote that opens the chapter reflect Dewey's belief that theory and practice should always inform each other and not exist in isolation?
6. Give examples of psychological theories in educational practice.
7. Identify the dual role of psychology.
8. What were the major contributions of American psychologists to education?
9. How did John Dewey develop a theory of economic and social justice for society and democracy?
10. Compare and contrast the educational, social, and political systems of China and the Middle East Islamic countries.

HISTORY IN ACTION IN TODAY'S CLASSROOMS

1. Describe your philosophy of education and how it applies (or will apply) to your educational practice.
2. After observing a teacher or administrator, attempt to determine that person's philosophy of education. Factors to consider include classroom organization, diverse student populations, teaching methods, and lesson planning. Make an appointment to discuss your observations and validate your findings.
3. Obtain permission to audiotape or videotape an interview with an experienced teacher or administrator. Find out how his or her philosophy of education has evolved through the years. Share your findings with your class. Discuss and answer the questions at the end of the features "Philosophical Divisions," "Behavior Modification," and "International Terrorism." These features are found within the chapter.
4. Using the Internet, find one site that would be useful in obtaining information on, or ideas about, educational philosophy.

BIBLIOGRAPHY

Adler, Mortimer. *The Paideia Proposal*. New York: Macmillan, 1982.

American Educational Research Association. "Aera Honors Hunt for Public Service in Education." *Aera News* (April 23, 2003). Available at: www.scienceblog.com

Apple, Michael. *Ideology and Curriculum*. London: Routledge & Kegan Paul, 1979.

Ausubel, D. C. *The Psychology of Meaningful Verbal Learning*. New York: Grune & Stratton, 1963.

Bagley, William C. "An Essentialist's Platform for the Advancement of American Education." *Educational Administration and Supervision* 26 (1938): 241–256.

Bell, Daniel. *The Coming of the Post-Industrial Society: A Venture into Social Forecasting*. New York: Basic Books, 1976.

Bell, T. H. *A Nation at Risk*. Washington, DC: National Commission on Excellence in Education, April 1983.

Bestor, Arthur. *Educational Wastelands*. Urbana, IL: University of Illinois Press, 1953.

Bestor, Arthur. *The Restoration of Learning*. New York: Knopf, 1955.

Bloom, Allan. *The Closing of the American Mind*. New York: Simon & Schuster, 1987.

Boulding, Kenneth. *The Meaning of the Twentieth Century*. New York: Harper & Row, 1965.

Brameld, Theodore. *Education as Power*. New York: Holt, Rinehart and Winston, 1967.

Brameld, Theodore. *Patterns of Educational Philosophy*. New York: Holt, Rinehart and Winston, 1971.

Brameld, Theodore. *Toward a Reconstructed Philosophy of Education*. New York: Holt, Rinehart and Winston, 1962.

Broudy, Harry S. *Building a Philosophy of Education*. Upper Saddle River, NJ: Prentice Hall, 1954.

Brown, Allison, & Blake LeBaron. "Has Chaos Theory Found Any Useful Application in the Social Sciences?" *Scientific American's* "Ask the Expert" website (2004). people.brandeis.edu/~blebaron/ge/chaos.html

Buber, Martin. *I and Thou*. 2nd ed. Translated by R. Gregory Smith. Edinburgh: T. & T. Clark, 1958.

Butler, J. Donald. *Four Philosophies and Their Practice in Education and Religion*. New York: Harper & Row, 1957.

Campbell, Kate, Ed. *A Critical Feminism: Argument in the Disciplines*. Philadelphia: Open University Press, 1992.

Chua, Amy. *Battle Hymn of the Tiger Mother*. New York: Penguin, 2011.

Cooper, J. Arthur. *Exemplars in Educational Philosophy*. Minneapolis, MN: Alphia Editions, 1988.

Cornish, Edward. *The Study of the Future*. Washington, DC: World Future Society, 1977.

Counts, George. *Dare the Schools Build a New Social Order?* Carbondale, IL: Southern Illinois University Press, 1932.

Cuban, Larry. *How Teachers Taught: Constancy and Change in American Classrooms, 1890–1980*. New York: Longman, 1984a.

Darwin, Charles. *On the Origin of Species*. London: John Murray, 1859.

Dewey, John. *A Common Faith*. New Haven: Yale University Press, 1934a.

Dewey, John. *Art as Experience*. New York: Penguin Putnam, 1934b.

Dewey, John. *Democracy and Education*. New York: Macmillan, 1916.

Dewey, John. *Experience and Education*. Toronto: Macmillan, 1938.

Dewey, John. *Psychology*. In *The Early Works 1882–1898*, Volume 2. Edited by Jo Ann Bonsdston. Carbondale, IL: Southern Illinois University, 1887.

Dewey, John. *How We Think*. Boston: DC Heath, 1910.

Dewey, John. *Human Nature and Conduct*. New York: Modern Library, 1922.

Eggen, Paul D., & Donald Kauchak. *Educational Psychology: Windows on Classrooms*. Upper Saddle River, NJ: Merrill/Pearson Education, 2000.

Eisner, Elliot W. *The Enlightened Eye: Qualitative Inquiry and the Enhancement of Educational Practice*. New York: Macmillan, 1991.

Erickson, Kai. *Wayward Puritans: A Study in the Sociology of Deviance*. New York: John Wiley & Sons, 1982.

Fineberg, Joel. *Social Philosophy*. Upper Saddle River, NJ: Prentice Hall, 1973.

Giroux, H. A. *Postmodernism, Feminism, and Cultural Politics*. New York: State University of New York, 1991.

Giroux, Henry. *Theory and Resistance in Education: A Pedagogy for the Opposition*. Boston: Bergin & Garvey, 1983.

Griffin, David Ray, & Huston Smith. *Primordial Truth and Postmodern Theology*. SUNY Series in Constructive Postmodern Thought. Albany: State University of New York Press, 1990.

Gutek, Gerald. *Philosophical and Ideological Perspectives on Education*. Upper Saddle River, NJ: Prentice Hall, 1988.

Hekman, Susan J. *Gender and Knowledge: Elements of a Postmodern Feminism*. Boston: Northeastern University Press, 1990.

Homer. *The Iliad*. Translated by Robert Fagles. New York: Penguin Books, 1990. Originally published 800 B.C.E.

Horne, Herman. *The Democratic Philosophy of Education*. New York: Macmillan, 1935.

Hunt, James B., Jr. "Education for Economic Growth." *Kappan* (April 1984). Reprinted in *Justice, Ideology, and Education*. Edited by Edward Stevens, Jr., & George H. Wood, Eds. New York: McGraw-Hill, 2002.

Hunt, James B., Jr.. *What Matters Most: Teaching for America's Future*. New York: National Commission on Teaching & America's Future, 1996.

Hutchins, Robert. *Great Books: The Foundation of a Liberal Education*. New York: Simon & Schuster, 1954.

James, William. *Pragmatism: A New Name for Some Old Ways of Thinking*. New York: Longman, Green, 1981. Originally published in 1907.

James, William. *Principles of Psychology*. Boston: Henry Holt, 1890.

Johanningmeier, Erwin. *Americans and Their Schools*. Chicago: Rand McNally, 1980.

Kanpol, Barry. *Towards a Theory and Practice of Teacher Cultural Politics: Continuing the Post Modern Debate*. Norwood, NJ: Norwood Publishing, 1992.

Kierstead, Fred D., & Paul A. Wagner, Jr. *The Ethical, Legal and Multicultural Foundations of Teaching*. Madison, WI: WCB Brown and Benchmark, 1993.

Kliebard, Herbert. *Forging the American Curriculum: Essays in Curriculum History and Theory*. New York: Routledge, 1992.

Kliebard, Herbert. *The Struggle for the American Curriculum*. Boston: Routledge and Kegan Paul, 1986.

Kneller, George. *Existentialism and Education*. New York: John Wiley & Sons, 1958.

Kohlberg, Lawrence. *The Philosophy of Moral Development: Moral Stages and the Idea of Justice*. San Francisco: Harper & Row, 1981.

Lather, Patti. *Getting Smart*. New York: Routledge, 1991.

Lefrancois, Guy R. *Psychology for Teaching: A Bear Is Not a Cowboy*. New York: Thomson Learning, 1999.

Lefrancois, Guy R. *Theories of Learning: What the Old Man Said*. New York: Thomson Learning, 2000.

Leys, Simon, Tr. *The Analects of Confucius*. New York: Norton, 1997.

Locke, John. *An Essay Concerning Human Understanding*. London: William Tegg, 1689.

Lynd, Albert. *Quackery in the Public Schools*. Boston: Little Brown, 1953.

Lyotard, J. *The Postmodern Condition: A Report on Knowledge*. Minneapolis: University of Minnesota Press, 1984.

Lyotard, J. *Post Modern Explained*. Minneapolis: University of Minnesota Press, 1993.

Lyotard, J. *Toward the Post Modern*. Atlantic Highlands, NJ: Humanities Press, 1991.

Mao Tse-Tung's Quotations, The Red Guard Handbook. Introduction by Stewart Fraser. Nashville, TN: International Center George Peabody College for Teachers, 1967.

McLuhan, Marshall. *Understanding Media*. 2nd ed. Cambridge, MA: MIT Press, 1994. Originally published in 1964.

Meadows, Donela, & Dennis Meadows. *The Limits to Growth*. New York: Universe Books, 1972.

Moore, George E. "A Defense of *Common Sense*." In *Contemporary British Philosophy* (2nd Series). Edited by G. H. Muirhead. London: Allen & Unwin, 1925.

Morris, Van Cleve. *Existentialism in Education*. New York: Harper & Row, 1966.

Neill, A. S. *Summerhill*. New York: Hart, 1960.

Noddings, Nel. "Rethinking the Benefits of the College Bound Curriculum." *Kappan* (December 1996): 285–289.

Obama, Barack. *Dreams from My Father: A Story of Race and Inheritance*. New York: Times Books, 1995.

Ogburn, Wiliam F. *Social Change*. New York: Viking, 1950. Originally published in 1922.

Ormrod, Jeanne Ellis. *Human Learning*. Upper Saddle River, NJ: Merrill/Pearson Education, 1998.

Orwell, George. *1984*. New York: Harcourt Brace Jovanovich, 1949.

Ozmon, Howard, & Samuel Craver. *Philosophic Foundations of Education*. 6th ed. Upper Saddle River, NJ: Merrill/Pearson Education, 1999.

Park, Joe, Ed. *Selected Readings in the Philosophy of Education*. New York: Macmillan, 1958.

Peirce, Charles S. "How to Make Our Ideas Clear." *Popular Science Quarterly* (January 1878).

Perkinson, Henry. *Since Socrates: Studies in the History of Western Educational Thought*. New York: Longman, 1980.

Pinar, William, & William M. Reynolds, Eds. *Understanding Curriculum as Phenomenological and Deconstructed Text*. New York: Columbia University, Teachers College Press, 1992.

Plato. *The Republic*. Translated by Benjamin Jowett. New York: PF Collier and Son, 1901. Originally published in 360 B.C.E.

Rae, Greg. (2004/2005). "Chaos Theory: A Brief Introduction." Available at: www.umho.com/grae/chaos/

Rafferty, Max. *Suffer, Little Children*. New York: Devin-Adair, 1962.

Rogers, Carl. *On Becoming a Person*. New York: Houghton Mifflin, 1961.

Rogers, Carl. *Philosophy and the Mirror of Nature*. Princeton, NJ: Princeton University Press, 1987.

Rorty, Richard. *Objectivity, Relativism and Truth*. New York: Cambridge Press, 1991.

Rousseau, Jean-Jacques. *Emile*. Translated by Allan Bloom. New York: Basic, 1979. Originally published in 1762.

Rowling, J. K. *Harry Potter and the Sorcerer's Stone*. New York: Arthur A. Levine Books, 1998.

Russell, Bertrand. *Education and the Modern World*. New York: W. W. Norton, 1932.

Ryle, Gilbert. *The Concept of Mind*. Chicago: University of Chicago Press, 1949.

Sartre, Jean Paul. *Being and Nothingness: An Essay on Phenomenological Ontology*. New York: Philosophical Library, 1956.

Sarup, Madan. *Marxism and Education*. London: Routledge & Kegan Paul, 1978.

"Shanghai Tops International Test Scores" (December 7, 2010). Available at: www.washingtonpost.com

Simpson, Douglas, & Michael Jackson. *The Teacher as Philosopher*. New York: Methuen, 1984.

Skinner, B. F. *Beyond Freedom and Dignity*. New York: Alfred A. Knopf, 1971.

Skinner, B. F. *Science and Human Behavior*. New York: Macmillan, 1953.

Skinner, B. F. *Walden II*. New York: Macmillan, 1976. Originally published in 1948.

Slavin, Robert E. *Educational Psychology: Theory and Practice*. New York: Pearson Publications, 2000.

Strike, Kenneth, & Jonas Soltis. *The Ethics of Teaching*. New York: Teachers College Press, 1985.

Thomlinson, Stephen. *Phrenology, Secular Education, and Nineteenth Century*. Tuscaloosa, AL: University of Alabama Press, 2005.

Toffler, Alvin. *Future Shock*. New York: Random House, 1970.

Toynbee, Arnold. *A Study of History*. Oxford: Oxford University Press, 1946.

Vygotsky L. S. *Thought and Language*. Cambridge, MA: The M.I.T. Press, 1985.

Whitehead, Alfred. *The Aims of Education and Other Essays*. New York: Macmillan, 1929.

Wirth, Arthur. *Education and Work for the Year 2000: Choices We Face*. New York: Jossey-Bass, 1992.

Woolfolk, Anita E. *Educational Psychology*. Upper Saddle River, NJ: Pearson Education, 2000.

CHAPTER 3

AMERICAN EDUCATION: OUR EUROPEAN HERITAGE AND THE COLONIAL INFLUENCE

It being one chief object of that old deluder, Satan, to keep men from the knowledge of the scriptures, . . . it is therefore ordered, that every township . . . after the Lord hath increased them to the number of fifty householders, . . . shall . . . appoint one within their town to teach all children as shall resort to him to read and write. It is further ordered, that where any town shall increase to the number of one hundred families . . . they shall set up a grammar school, the master thereof being able to instruct youth so far as they may be fitted for the university.

Old Deluder Satan Act, Massachusetts Laws of 1647

Protestant Reformation			Glorious Revolution
1601 English Poor Law	1620 Plymouth Colony	Social change	1664 New Amsterdam became New York
		Class society	
1607 Jamestown	1636 Harvard College		
1619 Black slaves in Virginia	1642 Massachusetts compulsory school law	1647 Old Deluder Satan Act	1689 English Act of Toleration

Figure 3.1   Time Line for European Heritage and Colonial Influence

Modern conceptions of reality are highly influenced by images gleaned from the mass media and systems of electronic communication. A recent Pew Research study found over 74 percent of American adults over 18 use the Internet while most children aged 12 to 17 have Internet access. Added to film and television, this constitutes a media saturation that determines perception. It is therefore not surprising that most Americans think of the colonial era in history in terms of Benjamin Franklin toying with a kite in an electrical storm, the witch trials in Salem, or Mel Gibson playing the title role in *The Patriot*. Such images provide useful glimpses of history, but they hardly reveal the century and a half during which England ruled its American colonies. Before the American Revolution, the colonies were more isolated from one another than from Europe and only the larger cities on the Atlantic seaboard had good means of communication with each other. School accounts of events in the last decades of the eighteenth century emphasize the unfairness of British policies and paint a grim picture of George III. Furthermore, where kings exist today, they are regarded as mere heads of state and not as superhuman. Yet even those who emigrated from England seeking religious freedom regarded the king and the royal family as belonging to a special class and did not question his divine right to rule.

The idea that all men are created equal was revolutionary indeed and did not emerge in the earlier colonial period where British social classes and social stratification dominated. America differed from England only in that it was easier here to break away to start a new life on the frontier and there was a chance of economic improvement through ability or hard work. Otherwise, the social system and its prejudices remained in vogue in the American colonies. Women were universally considered inferior beings who could not hold property or engage in politics and who had no rights beyond those given by their fathers or husbands. Native Americans, although often respected, were thought inferior to whites, while the mentality of children was ascribed to African American slaves. Others were simply ignored by the culture. Persons with disabilities or physical handicaps were sometimes the

French and Indian War		Boston Massacre	
1690 *New England Primer*	1751 Franklin's Academy in Philadelphia		
			1763 Treaty of Paris ended the French and Indian War
1693 College of William and Mary, Virginia	1762 Rousseau's *Emile* published in France		1765 Stamp Act

object of pity and sometimes believed to be God's punishment for the sins of parents and other times special children of the gods. Colonial literature does not acknowledge the existence of homosexuals except through some vague reference to Sodom and Gomorrah.

Accustomed as we are to rapid change, it is difficult to imagine the colonial culture in which everything remained very much the same for generations. Except for an increase in population, farms in New England and plantations in the South looked very much the same from the mid-1600s to the mid-1700s. The Industrial Revolution had hardly started in England by 1776 and did not reach America until the following century. Every village had its smithy and there was trade in timber, but manufacturing was not encouraged by British rulers and only the central colonies developed brisk commerce. Colonial life was theocratic, with the presence of God assumed in everything. In December 2000, Irwin Victoria reported in the *Christian Science Monitor* that a number of states have implemented "a moment of silence" for prayer, meditation, or other silent activity. There are supporters and dissenters over the moment of silence in public schools, but our colonial forefathers could have never understood what the fuss is about.

The first American educational theory and practice tended to reflect European patterns, but the instances of transplantation without modification were few. The settlements of the Spanish in Florida and the French in the Mississippi Valley copied European institutions, including schools, as closely as the new environment would allow. This was true in St. Augustine, which was founded by Pedro Menendez in 1565, and in the French settlements at Montreal, Quebec, Kaskaskia, and New Orleans. Spanish monasteries were educational as well as religious institutions, and the duty of teaching Native Americans the Spanish language was required by royal order in 1643. Convents and schools founded by French and Spanish Catholics reached much of North America, including California, where Father Junipero Serra was active.

British colonials, however, began to incorporate distinctive new features in the models they took from their homeland. The apprenticeship system, elementary reading schools, the Latin grammar school, and even Harvard College were not exact duplicates of their English counterparts. The Reformation had suggested the principle of universal education, but in England it had also allowed church property to be used for secular purposes, nearly destroying elementary schools. Philanthropists, therefore, began endowing British charity schools, whereas the upper-middle-class children attended schools taught by private masters for fees. In America, charity education provided by such agencies as the Society for the Propagation of the Gospel in Foreign Parts (SPG) became popular. The SPG, an agency of the Anglican Church, provided money, books, teachers, and physical facilities for American children who otherwise would have had no opportunity to attend school. Of course, philanthropic education usually had special interests attached, such as furthering the cause of a particular religion or fostering a set of values esteemed by those who contributed funds.

The English pattern of high-quality private schools catering to the children of the well-to-do and supported by tuition was not followed to a great extent in the colonies. Secondary educational institutions modeled on Westminster, Eton, or other English "public" schools were uncommon in America. Private venture schools tended to offer practical courses such as surveying, navigation, or bookkeeping. In those areas where religion was the driving force of a community, education became an instrument for social control through transmitting and preserving the beliefs of the sect. The authorities in England had often discouraged such efforts. All schools underwent changes as a result of cultural forces in the colonies and the experience of coping with the American wilderness. Apprenticeship and the tutorial system remained dominant educational practices in the colonies, as was the case in England.

Generally the educational aims of colonial schools and teachers represented stability, tradition, authority, discipline, and preordained value systems that were marks of idealism and classical realism. Many of the European educators (discussed in Chapter 4) reflected the ideology of idealism and classical realism; Friedrich Froebel's educational writings reflected idealism, and the others reflected various forms of realism.

COLONIAL MELTING POT

Theories of educational idealism and realism were modified in theory and practice in colonial America. Modifications may be attributed to environmental difficulties, such as the struggle to produce food, the communication problem, disease, isolation, and hostile natives. Economic stresses and strains have always played a part in education. Other changes were caused by the new intellectual climate illustrated by the many nonconformist or religiously dissenting settlers and the shift of the center of civil authority represented by the signing of the Mayflower Compact. Of course, the colonists remained Englishmen and the crown retained sovereignty until the American Revolution, but local control and some degree of political independence began to emerge quite early.

Dissatisfaction with conditions in the homeland caused the migration of thousands of individuals who were not anxious to restore the agencies of their grief and oppression. The availability of free land and the desire of the English to encourage settlement made it possible for almost every group of people to find a place where they could practice their own religion and follow their own lifestyle. For example, Quakers sought freedom from restrictions on their religious activities, and indentured servants wanted freedom from bondage and the opportunity for social advancement. Many colonial communities were similar to Longfellow's Grand Pré (described in Chapter 1).

However, the European school itself was not the object of attack by dissatisfied groups. The fact that educational facilities in the homelands were often decadent and offered very limited opportunity for the children of many who stayed behind did little to harm their reputation in America or undermine the attempt to imitate them. In an effort to preserve the European civilization of which they were a part, the colonists tried to copy the educational institutions they knew best. English textbooks and school methods were widely accepted in all the American colonies. Nevertheless, schools in the colonies were not merely transplanted but also revolutionized in spirit and sometimes in form. Although the colonies were never a melting pot in the sense of mixing all the people together into one homogeneous mass, cultural diversity and the presence of many different religious denominations had a considerable influence on colonial schools.

Colonial legislatures, royal governors, proprietors, and stock companies were delegated educational authority along with political powers by the British crown. However, the degree to which civil governments took an interest in education differed greatly from one colony to another. Established churches and European governments exchanged mutual support in seventeenth-century culture. This alliance was also found throughout the colonies, although the nature of established churches differed considerably from Puritan New England to Anglican Virginia. Some degree of religious toleration developed in Rhode Island, Pennsylvania, New York, and Maryland.

RELIGIOUS SECTARIANISM

Religion played a very important part in colonial schools and colleges, both in the conduct of the institutions and in the curriculum. Although Bible reading and prayer continued to be a major part of common school practice well into the national period, control of education gradually shifted away from sectarian authorities. Just as the states in modern America delegate authority to local school boards, so the colonial governments allowed private individuals and religious groups to establish schools of their own. This practice was partly attributable to the failure of governments to support schools with tax revenues and partly to the rise of numerous religious sects that demanded the freedom to educate children in their own way. As a general rule, the central civil government did not engage in close supervision of schools that were built and financed by local or church agencies. This was true throughout the colonies in the eighteenth century and was especially obvious in frontier settlements.

In a very real sense, the desire for greater religious freedom contributed to the doctrine of separation of church and state. Roger Williams was driven from Massachusetts partly for supporting such separation, and he made it a policy in his Rhode Island settlement. The various sects eventually obtained freedom of worship, and because there was no consensus concerning religious principles to be taught in schools founded by civil authorities, the various denominations conducted and controlled their own schools. In New England, the selectmen of a town, the general court of the colony, or the ministers constituted ultimate educational authority. Royal governors and towns gave charters for schools in the Middle colonies. In the Anglican South, the Bishop of London was responsible for licensing teachers.

SOCIAL CLASS IN THE COLONIAL ENVIRONMENT

English feudal structure was not equally superimposed on all parts of the American colonial culture, but social class stratification was marked. Southern plantations usually contained every social class from slaves to owners of estates. Virginia reflected British class divisions almost exactly, and even feudal practices such as primogeniture (passing an estate to the eldest son) and entail (making sale or exchange of real property unlawful) were found in that colony. Indentured servants and at least a few slaves lived in all of the colonies. New England had no gentlemen–planter class; however, ministers and magistrates had great prestige, and Puritan emphasis on work and frugality soon produced wealthy merchants. Middle colonies like Maryland had a well-developed middle class consisting of artisans and skilled workers, but the middle classes grew everywhere as trade developed and the population increased. Scarcity of labor, and especially of skilled labor, made it easy for the ambitious man to improve his social status through hard work. It was difficult to prevent a servant from becoming an independent frontier farmer.

Although social-class mobility was a feature of colonial society, the schools remained class centered. Latin preparatory schools and theological colleges favored the upper classes. For many years, Harvard College class roles were arranged by social rank. Public demand for new skills resulted in a special school—the academy—that catered to the practical requirements of the commercial class. Nevertheless, many students obtained only rudimentary education, and many of the earlier settlers of the lower classes could not read or write. Even in New England, where schools were in operation by 1636, the level of instruction was low and not all children could attend. Individuals who did not adhere to acceptable religious beliefs were excluded from economic and educational opportunities. Before American independence, there were trends toward a more flexible and democratic school pattern, but the rigid class system and the strong religious atmosphere continued to influence education until comparatively recent times. Opportunities for success were limited for those who were not in the religious mainstream of the day.

Few experiences in England fitted colonists for the difficulties of sustaining life in a wilderness, and the colonies were not similar in climate, landforms, or population. Thus, quite different lifestyles emerged. The South concentrated on agriculture and created great plantations with a social system resembling that of England, and economic complexity in New England led to towns and villages sufficiently dense in population for the maintenance of schools.

Each colony also had different community patterns. Land was too cheap to sustain the feudal privileges of Southern planters, and soon a new breed of small farmers and hunters emerged. These rough-and-ready pioneers were not at all like the gentlemen who owned large estates planted in indigo, rice, or tobacco. They were not cultured or highly educated, and they had little leisure time to pursue the intellectual graces commonly acquired by wealthy slaveholders. But they soon became a political and economic force. This new class of independent people had little use for the classics or the Latin grammar schools, but they wanted their children to have the basic skills of reading and writing. In England, the sons of working men and farmers seldom had an opportunity for formal schooling. In America, the possibility for a better life in the future for children of all classes created a demand for some sort of schooling in every community. The most common practice among working- and middle-class parents was to apprentice their sons to skilled tradesmen or shopkeepers.

THE SOUTHERN COLONIES

Of the English colonies on the eastern seaboard, Maryland, Virginia, the Carolinas, and Georgia most closely resembled the British homeland in cultural and social patterns. Economic factors were responsible for most of the migration of English gentlemen to the South. They were not dissatisfied with conditions in the homeland and therefore expected to replicate English institutions in America without substantial change. Southern planters devoted their energy to business and the development of their estates. They remained loyal to the Anglican Church and the values of the British landed gentry. Plantation owners emphasized the enjoyment of the cultured life, which included gambling, dancing, literature, music, art, books, and the breeding of fine horses.

Religion was reverently practiced through prayer and church attendance, but it did not become the dominating force of life as in New England. There was no Puritan zeal for having every person taught to read the Bible. The clergy was responsible for interpreting scripture, and clerical authority was vested in the Anglican hierarchy. Educational matters also rested with the decisions of the Archbishop of Canterbury or the Bishop of London. Because both church and state favored the landed gentry and large estates were the rule, social equality did not develop in the South. Those not favored by conditions of birth and wealth were expected to be satisfied with their station in life and the decisions made for them by their "betters." In 1671, Governor Sir William Berkeley of Virginia held that every man should instruct his own children according to his means:

> I thank God, there are no free schools nor printing, and I hope we shall not have
> them these hundred years, for learning has brought disobedience, and heresy, and
> sects into the world, and printing has divulged them, and libels against the best
> government. God keeps us from them both. (Mill, 1859, pp. 190–191)

FOCUS ON THE ISSUES

The Curriculum

The famous author Mark Twain was a notoriously poor speller. Asked about that, he replied that he had always admired a man who could think of more ways than one to spell a word! From colonial times, spelling was a major subject of the elementary curriculum and occupied fully a quarter of the school day. It seems odd now that so much time was devoted to so few subjects; but it was justified then because letter writing was the only means of distance communication, so orthography and writing were significant. Colonial and early national schools offered few subjects, so more time was available. The recitation method in common use allowed teachers to line up students and have them spell words orally, moving to the head of the class when they spelled correctly. Masters with little or no training could control a school using this technique, although most students remained idle most of the time. Spelling bees were popular as community entertainment and the ability to spell became a mark of distinction. Orthography held its place as the queen of subjects for many years.

Until Joseph Rice demonstrated conclusively that students spending 15 minutes a day learned to spell just as well as those devoting two hours on it, orthography continued to dominate the elementary curriculum. In the 1930s progressive educators decided that sounding out words was bad pedagogy and insisted on the sight method. The failure of the sight method is shown by a generation of poor spellers and the popularity of the modern program Hooked on Phonics. With modern spell checks on computers, the importance of teaching spelling has declined. Most students today learn keyboard skills early but only a few years ago high schools required most students to take two semesters of typing. The demands on the curriculum continue to grow while the time devoted to learning tends to shrink. With competition from abroad, the globalization of the economy, and the information age, we can ill afford to spend time on subjects only because of tradition.

What Do You Think?
1. Of the subjects you studied in elementary school, which are of most value?
2. Are there some topics that could be eliminated or cut down?
3. What was not included in the curriculum of your youth that would have been helpful to you?
4. Identify the pros and cons of a national curriculum/national standards in view of historical local control of schools.
5. Trace the evolution of a class society to an open democratic society through social change.
6. Identify the pros and cons of rugged individualism and self-reliance.

Berkeley no doubt spoke for many Virginians, but some free schools did develop in spite of the opposition. Occasionally a parish built and maintained a school that was open to children who could not pay tuition. There were numerous endowments for schools such as those provided in the wills of Benjamin Syms (1634) and Thomas Eaton (1659), both of whom gave land and goods for the maintenance of an "able schoolmaster" to teach poor children. Nevertheless, free schools remained rare in Virginia, and large areas of the South had no formal education of any kind.

The planters did devote a good deal of time to intellectual pursuits beyond the instruction of their children. The art of writing letters was highly developed, and many newspapers were circulated. Even the remote plantations usually had a good collection of books from England and other European nations. Some private libraries were excellent: that of William Byrd contained some 4,000 volumes. An excellent account of the intellectual and social life of the colonial South is found in the diary of Philip Fithian. Fithian was a graduate of Princeton and served as tutor to the Carter family of northern Virginia. Tutorial education was common practice in the South.

Leading elements of the social order attempted to copy the customs and mores of wealthy Englishmen in everything, including schools. Southern educational institutions reflected more English ideals than schools in other parts of the colonies, and every planter who could afford it wished to send his son to Oxford or Cambridge Universities or the Inns of Court (London law schools) for training.

Rigid Southern social-class distinctions allowed few opportunities for the indentured servants, the slaves, and the poverty-stricken freedmen to engage in cultural pursuits or to improve their minds. The persons lowest in social rank were entirely dependent upon the wealthy and powerful for what little education they received. Skills needed to operate farms and plantations were not taught in schools, nor was education received very clearly related to success.

Gentlemen thought of themselves as natural political leaders, as well as guardians of refined manners, learning, justice, hospitality, and religion. No effort was spared to initiate sons of the planter class into the intellectual pursuits of their fathers. They were given generalized readings in the Greek and Roman classics, French was widely taught along with English literature and the Bible, and studies such as painting and architecture were commonly included.

No single educational pattern developed in the Southern colonies, making it difficult to generalize. Although diversity of educational practice was at a maximum in the South, public interest in education was at a minimum. Virginia had money earmarked for education as early as 1618, but the revocation of the charter for the Virginia Company seven years later stopped these funds. From that time until 1660, Virginia passed laws that required children to be taught religion, although public financial support was lacking. Because Southern leaders came from the upper classes of England, the Anglican Church dominated—and exercised considerable influence over the existing educational programs. Law or the church, however, only indirectly controlled schools, because education was considered a private matter left in the hands of individual citizens. Exceptions were apprenticeship education, which was carefully regulated by law, and efforts of philanthropic or religious societies in behalf of the poor, Native Americans, and slaves. Attempts to convert Native Americans met with slight success; however, continuous appeals were made for giving slaves the rudiments of a religious education, especially the entreaty that Christianity would make them more content and harder working.

Schools for those not favored by birth were limited in the Southern colonies. Early efforts to provide endowed schools for all children, including Native Americans, failed. Some laws required education for pauper children, but little was actually done. Like England, the Southern governments made an effort to keep the poor from starving and to see that children of paupers learned a trade, but the Virginia law requiring training of "bound" boys was not passed until 1705. Virginians saw nothing odd in imposing requirements upon parents and ministers for religious instruction without giving financial aid to education. Teachers in private schools were seldom examined on their qualifications beyond the ability to read and write but were expected to prove their orthodoxy in religion.

Meager efforts were made to establish chartered or publicly aided schools in the Carolinas. Maryland fared a little better with a provision in 1671 for a "School or College" and a system of secondary county schools founded in 1728. Duties on tobacco and fines for crimes were used to support such schools, but only a small proportion of the population had access to them. Maryland had a quasi-public corporation made up of church and government officials to make policy and secure funds for schools in each county. Georgia was the last Southern colony to be settled, and little progress toward an educational program was made there before the Revolution.

Tutorial Schools.

Tutorial schools existed throughout the South, although they varied widely in form. Very wealthy planters hired learned tutors to train their sons and frequently their daughters as well. When there was time and interest, a similar tutorial system was also used by others attached to the plantation, such as the sons of foremen or managers. Teachers were often Anglican ministers who served churches in the proximity of the estate, but private schoolmasters were also employed to teach. Sometimes, it proved cheaper or more expedient to buy the teaching services of an indentured servant. Many well-trained Scots who knew Latin and Greek were included in the shiploads of indentured persons entering Southern ports, and their time could be purchased at a lower rate than that of skilled labor. Private tutorial schools were sometimes sufficient to prepare boys for college in England. The curriculum was usually classical, but practical subjects such as surveying and mathematics were by no means excluded. Girls were instructed in French, music, dancing, and polite manners by their tutors, and for them the instruction was terminal. Boys who had mastered Lily's *Latin Grammar* (1540) were often sent to one of the private preparatory schools (great public schools) in England.

Travel was considered to be a major part of education, even for boys who did not attend Latin grammar schools or colleges in England. Such educational leaders as James Blair and the Reverend Thomas Bray of Virginia maintained high standards of scholarship. The universal employment of tutors indicated a greater interest in education by American planters than by their English counterparts.

Old Field Schools.

One Southern innovation was the old field school. This was a local elementary school built by members of a community on one of the fallow "old" fields that had lost its productivity through overuse. Sometimes Anglican ministers taught in these schools as they did on the plantations, but the masters were often persons with very little education. Old field schools were usually maintained by private subscriptions with some sort of scholarship or other provision for impoverished scholars. Control of the schools, including the securing of teacher and materials, was in the hands of the local community. These schools were similar to later ones established in frontier towns during the national period. They commonly were in operation for only a few months each year.

Dame Schools.   In most colonies, including those in the South, dame schools could be found. These were not really schools at all but consisted of rudimentary instruction given by a woman in her own home, usually while she carried on household duties. The lessons were limited to the alphabet, counting, prayers, the catechism, and perhaps reading a few sentences from the Bible. A standard instrument in the dame school was the hornbook, which consisted of a single printed page that was attached to a wooden paddle and covered with a transparent film made by boiling down the horns of cows. Hornbooks often were inscribed with the alphabet, numerals from one to nine, and the Lord's Prayer. They were a means of keeping "letters faire from fingers damp" and were used throughout the colonies. Dames who offered instruction were often barely literate themselves. According to Harry Good and James Teller (1973), one is recorded as saying, "'T' is little they pays me and little I learns 'em" (p. 235).

Secondary and Higher Education.   Plans for a Latin grammar school were made in Virginia before 1630. Property bequeathed by Syms and Eaton apparently was used for such classical schools. Thomas Jefferson graduated from a Latin school before entering William and Mary College. Nevertheless, because of the preference for sending sons to preparatory schools in England and the sparse early population, few secondary schools developed. Some towns were able to maintain academies. Those in Charleston were supported by a combination of fees and grants. Some academies were classical schools for college preparation, and others taught only practical or commercial subjects. William and Mary was the only institution of higher learning in the Southern region during the colonial period. It began granting degrees in 1700.

Charity Education.   Other educational measures were taken by philanthropic societies, most of which were organized by religious institutions. The Anglican Church encouraged slaveholders to teach their charges Christianity. Charity schools were operated in England, and this idea soon spread to America, for the training of orphans and paupers. The SPG of the Anglican Church was, by far, the most active group; it raised funds in England and used the money to send out teachers and to buy textbooks for the colonies. Many able instructors (often young ministers) brought their knowledge and missionary zeal to the colonial schools for the poor. The best charity schools and also the most numerous ones in the Southern and Middle colonies were provided by this Anglican society. It printed and distributed books on history, agriculture, and mathematics, as well as religious tracts.

Perhaps the most conspicuous thing about education in the South before the American Revolution was the lack of public interest in schools. Several factors contributed to this attitude, some of which continued to affect public schools in the national period. It was strongly believed by the dominant planter class that each man was responsible for the education of his own children. Further, it was against the prevailing custom to tax one person for the education of the sons of others. Southern colonies had widely scattered populations not concentrated in cities and towns. Even if the people had wanted an educational system, physical remoteness made one almost impossible. Secondary schools of either the Latin grammar or practical academy type did not develop. The classes most interested in education could afford to hire tutors or to send their sons to England; many of the smaller landowners and pioneer hunters were more concerned with the practical skills necessary for survival than with formal schooling. Also, the Southern attitude toward religion failed to bring about the New England emphasis on education as a means of salvation. Southern colonial education remained very much like education in England. Nevertheless, many of the most learned and able leaders in the revolutionary period were from the South.

THE MIDDLE COLONIES

Diversity and *parochialism* are perhaps the words that best describe the colonial settlements of Delaware, New Jersey, New York, and Pennsylvania. Settlers from Holland, Germany, Sweden, England, Wales, and Scotland came to the Middle colonies in large numbers. Disparity in religion was even more pronounced than differences in nationality; thus, the colonies became a potpourri of faiths, languages, and ethnic cultures. It is said that 13 languages were spoken in Dutch New Amsterdam before it became New York in 1664. So many different religious denominations were represented in the region that toleration soon became a necessity. The Quakers of Pennsylvania were theoretically opposed to persecution.

Commerce and trade worked better in an open society, and no single religious sect had the numerical power to force its will on the others. Although the Catholics in Maryland had been protected in Lord Baltimore's time, religious freedom was limited there after 1654. Rhode Island as well as other Middle colonies then became the haven for all persons escaping from any form of religious persecution. It was this freedom that attracted the Pietist scholar Francis Daniel Pastorius (1651–1720), who was the best-educated man in America at the time. Pastorius wrote a primer called *Methodical Directions to Attain the True Reading, Spelling, and Writing of English*, published in New York in 1698. New York, like Philadelphia (the largest British city in America during the eighteenth century), was a center for intellectual activity.

Mennonites, Quakers, Lutherans, Calvinists, Moravians, Huguenots, Separate Baptists, and Episcopalians established educational practices of their own. Small numbers of Dunkards, Jews, disciples of John Hus, and other minor sects emigrated to America and set up schools. In short, the Middle colonies were the ones with the largest number of national and religious groups; therefore, they tended to develop many kinds of schools. There was also a considerable urban growth in this area and constant communication with the most sophisticated centers of Europe. Intellectual freedom (and tolerance) was possible in the central coastal cities to a degree unheard of in New England or the South. Blacks, Native Americans, and other minority pupils were sometimes admitted to Middle colony schools.

From its very beginning, the Dutch West India Company accepted its obligation to provide schools, and it demanded careful records showing every expenditure down to and including paper and ink. All nine villages chartered in New Netherlands probably had schools. The schoolmaster was not only a teacher but also a minor church official. He was picked for his orthodoxy and had other duties such as reading Scriptures on Sunday, digging graves, and acting as church sexton. When the English became dominant, Dutch schools continued to exist very much as they had before, but they became parochial institutions supported by local church congregations or private schools supported by towns.

Except for insisting on the right to license teachers, practically no laws were made concerning schools. The SPG of the Anglican Church was responsible for the majority of the common schools in New York, which were intended for the poor and thus were charitable institutions. These enjoyed the favor and support of the governor and his offices but were seldom entirely free, with each student paying what his family could afford. This system of charging different amounts was known as the "rate bill" and was widely adopted. Private instruction was sometimes similar to the plantation schools of the South, but individual tutors were rare.

Private venture schools in towns sometimes taught such practical subjects as bookkeeping, geography, and navigation. Each denomination was permitted to set up its own school system, and therefore schools were nonpublic in nature and intolerant of individuals representing other views. Nevertheless, religious differences kept the schools out of the hands of the central civil government and made them the responsibility of the churches. It was common in the Middle colonies, therefore, to have many sectarian schools together with a considerable number of charitable institutions for education.

In areas where the Quaker faith was strong, there was much support for primary education. Pennsylvania, with its Quaker commonwealth, had many laws regulating morality, including punishment for such offenses as drunkenness, dancing, gambling, and profanity. Nevertheless, jailing for debts was abolished, and a great deal of freedom of speech and religion was allowed. Because the colony was open to all creeds, Pennsylvania attracted Mennonites, Moravians, Lutherans, and Anglicans, in addition to the large numbers of Quakers.

Denominational Influence.

Dissenting factions in Pennsylvania caused many Quakers to fear for the unity of their church and to be suspicious of college education, but they remained active in their support for elementary schools. Quaker schools were excellent in quality. They taught reading, writing, arithmetic, and probably bookkeeping as well as religion; and they were not closed either to the poor or to girls. Quaker teachers received apprenticeship training, the first teacher education in America. The record shows that some control was used: The Council of Philadelphia rebuked Thomas Meking for teaching in a Friends public school without a license. Quaker schools provided the first American education for freed blacks. Smaller religious sects known as "dissenters" also established schools and colleges. The "log college" opened by Presbyterians in 1726 trained boys for the ministry. In Philadelphia, the William Penn Charter School taught both the classics and an English curriculum. The German scholar Francis Pastorius taught there. Baptists and Moravians set up denominational schools that were also open to the public. Governor Nicholson set aside land for a free Catholic school in Maryland.

Academies. Vocational education was more significant in the Middle colonies than elsewhere in colonial America. English poor laws of 1562 and 1601 proposed the establishment of working schools; they also forced apprenticeship for the poor. William Penn was influential in bringing the idea of trade training for pauper children to Pennsylvania, and John Locke's concern for practical subjects was well known in the colonies. The academy, a terminal secondary school that prepared students for a vocation, did not become highly significant until the national period. Nevertheless, both elementary and secondary schools in the Middle colonies offered such practical subjects as merchandising, navigation, trade, and mechanics. Benjamin Franklin's academy in Philadelphia opened in 1751 and became a model for others. Although it was organized in part as a Latin school, the academy was intended for the heterogeneous population of Pennsylvania. Franklin was particularly interested in training teachers for rural schools and in training officials for the government. The seeds of the American comprehensive high school, which offered vocational subjects, were planted in the private and parochial schools of the Middle colonies.

Latin Grammar Schools. Secondary schools of the Latin grammar type were necessary for college preparation. New York, Pennsylvania, New Jersey, and Maryland had such schools. Higher English schools and Latin schools existed together in Quaker Pennsylvania, and denominational support for both was common. The teachers were usually ministers who had no church to serve; the purpose was college preparation, leading eventually to political or church positions. Latin secondary schools and colleges were strictly for men. The curriculum often included Juvenal, Ovid, Virgil, Caesar, Cicero, and Horace, with perhaps some Greek grammar.

Religious sectarianism was a major force in Middle colony education, even though freedom of choice was respected. Schools were used for propaganda, and there was often bitter condemnation of other groups, especially Catholics.

Common Schools. Private education in Pennsylvania was largely the prerogative of the upper classes. However, there were some accommodations for sons of workmen and artisans of the middle class. A night school teaching writing and some mathematics was opened in Philadelphia in 1731. Navigation, surveying, and mathematics were taught in another night school in the same city. Later in the eighteenth century, private evening schools for accounting, mathematics, and modern languages were advertised in many cities. Public lectures on natural science, astronomy, and mechanics attracted large crowds. Private circulating libraries were available for a fee. Journals, books, and newspapers were numerous in larger cities. Philadelphia continued to be a major center for learning throughout the colonial era. Although New England led in universal education during the colonial period, there was a great deal of school activity at the elementary level in the Middle colonies.

Higher Education. The Middle colonies also had their share of denominational colleges as well as the College of Philadelphia (established in 1755), which was the only nonsectarian institution of higher learning. The College of New Jersey (Princeton) was established by Presbyterians in 1746. King's College (Columbia) was an

Anglican effort of 1754, and the Dutch Reformed Church founded Queen's College (Rutgers) in 1766. The College of Rhode Island (Brown) was created by the Baptists in 1764. Of the nine colonial colleges in America, five were in the Middle colonies. Early graduates of American colleges often found work as tutors to well-off children in the Middle colonies and the South.

The cultural variety that characterized the Middle colonies made education quite different from that of both the North and the South. Particularly significant were the early influences of settlers from Holland and the later emigration of large numbers of Germans. There was no one single powerful ruling church, and therefore no establishment of religion. Tolerance was greater than in New England or in the South, and many more sectarian schools developed. Class differences in the Middle colonies were less distinct than in the South, and the central colonies became a melting pot for many nationalities and many social positions. But by and large, less interest was shown in educational development in the Middle colonies than in New England.

THE NEW ENGLAND COLONIES

In many ways, education in New England was most significant for the growth of later American schools. The influence of parliamentary rule and the Christian duty of educating each child caused the theocratic governments in New England to take great interest in schools. The Puritans wanted a state church ruled by congregations rather than by bishops and a government that substituted the authority of the people for the divine right of a king. New England colonies made laws requiring education of the children but left details to local communities—thereby creating the traditions of local autonomy and the district system. These colonies provided both for universal elementary education and for the training of ministers, a practice that tended to perpetuate the English dual system of education. But it is wrong to assume that Puritan efforts fostered religious freedom or democracy.

Puritan Philosophy. Part of their educational interest stemmed from a concept of the nature of man that is found in the Calvinistic creed. The Puritans assumed that man is by nature evil, having fallen in the sin of Adam. Man is not only bad, but he also has an active nature that must be controlled to prevent the devil from becoming his master. This notion of man's being bad and active gave rise to the establishment of schools in order to prevent idleness and show mankind the way to overcome the evil in his nature. Assuming that man is depraved, there must be an effort to bring him to salvation. This, together with the Protestant notion of the priesthood of all believers, made it mandatory that the New England Puritans establish elementary schools.

In Massachusetts, New Hampshire, and Connecticut, Puritans were determined to build their own religious orthodoxy in the way Calvin had suggested. They established theocracies in which the church and state ruled by means of public disapproval, whipping, banishment, and fines. It was common for them to use the General Court and the authority of the minister to enforce conformity both in behavior and in belief. Such positive support of religion required not only the creation of schools but also that every child be able to read and understand both the Scriptures and the capital laws.

Numerous Puritan ministers wrote works in theology and philosophy that reinforced this educational theory. In his book *A Family Well-Ordered* (1699), Cotton Mather dwelled upon the duties of parents and the obligations of children. John Cotton reflected the same view. And even the learned Jonathan Edwards (1703–1758) made his idealism the servant of a narrow Calvinistic theology. The views of these Puritan theorists are clearly seen in the religious nature of textbooks like the *New England Primer* of 1690. This textbook includes the following verses:

> *In Adam's Fall*
> *We Sinned All*
> *. . . Thy Life to Mend*
> *This Book Attend*
> *. . . The Idle Fool*
> *Is Whipt at School*
> *(p. 22)*

As previously stated, in New England the farm land was not especially fertile, and people turned early to such occupations as shipbuilding, manufacturing, and trade. A merchant class developed that had need of people who could take care of business accounts and work with all sorts of business documents. It was therefore an economic necessity to have large numbers of people able not only to read and write but also to cast accounts. Even so, the New England schools were primarily established for the propagation of the Gospel and the control of new generations. It was usual for children to spend only a few years in the common school. However, Latin grammar schools were established for the elite.

The Pilgrims insisted that the parents take care of education. As early as 1642, however, the General Court of Massachusetts came to the conclusion that many parents were neglecting the training of their children. Therefore, the court ordered that the selectmen of every town should require that all parents and masters undertake the education of their children. After a short time, it was found that this provision was not working well. In 1647, therefore, the General Court passed its famous Old Deluder Satan Act. This law required every town to set up a school or to pay a sum of money to the next larger town for the support of education. A precedent was thus made for requiring the towns (or townships) to take the responsibility for establishing and maintaining schools. The theocracy not only required education but also set both the curriculum and the standard procedures for operation. These early efforts of Massachusetts were soon picked up by other parts of New England.

The first tax on property for local schools was in Dedham, Massachusetts, in 1648. New Hampshire required towns to support elementary schools as early as 1693. Taxes were used to pay the wages of teachers and to build school buildings, but tuition fees were universally charged in the New England colonies. The curriculum of the early New England schools was almost entirely religious, for these institutions were viewed officially as being indispensable to the stability of Puritan society. Such books as the Bible, the *New England Primer,* and the catechism were widely used in schools. Education was for salvation as well as for getting along in life. It was a primary duty of parents to bring their children up according to the orthodox religious beliefs of Puritan society.

The Puritans feared leaving an illiterate ministry to the people. For this reason they established Harvard College (1636) almost as early as the town schools. The college was primarily for the education of ministers of the Gospel, although after a few years students preparing for professions such as law attended as well.

Once the college had been established, it was necessary that Latin grammar schools be provided so that the boys wishing to enter Harvard could get the necessary preparatory studies. The first of these schools was established in Boston. A famous teacher, Ezekiel Cheever, taught for over 50 years in the Ipswich Grammar School and in the Boston Latin Grammar School; his teaching had considerable influence on the prestige of the teaching profession in the New England area. Almost no curriculum choice was offered in any of the colonial schools, and the methods were both fixed and harsh. It was ordained that schoolmasters be examined and certified by the minister of the town or the adjoining towns where the school was to be held. Education was generally narrow, limited, elementary, and moral in character. In Massachusetts, it was common for masters who failed to carry out their responsibilities adequately to be fined and sometimes even thrown out of their jobs.

Educational Conditions.
In the lower schools, there was normally one master for a room full of children of various ages. The local minister and the selectmen of the town provided supervision of the school. Buildings were of the log cabin or clapboard variety, furnished with benches, a fireplace, shelves around the walls for writing, and a few small windows. The master usually had a chair and lectern, but the meager equipment seldom included blackboards or maps. A whipping post was commonly erected by the school door. Severe floggings were administered for misbehavior or breaking the rules, because Puritan philosophy called for literally beating the devil out of the child. According to the law in Massachusetts, children could be confined in stocks for some offenses, and fathers had the right to execute their children if they could not be controlled, although this extreme was never practiced. There are records of pupils who were tortured by having a stick of flat wood (whispering stick) placed like a bit between their teeth, pupils made to kneel on hard pebbles, and pupils made to wear heavy wooden yokes. The school in colonial New England was not a pleasant place, either physically or psychologically. Great emphasis was placed on the shortness of life, the torments of hell, and the fear that one's behavior might not be acceptable for salvation. Children in dull and grim schools memorized passages such as:

> *I in the Burying Place may see*
> *Graves shorter there than I;*
> *From Death's Arrest no Age is free,*
> *Young Children too must die.*

Oh God may such an Awful Sight
Awakening to Me be,
That by Early Grace I shall,
For Death Prepared be.
(Ford, 1987, p. 123)

The elementary curriculum consisted of the four *R*'s: religion, reading, writing, and arithmetic. Boys and girls entered the school at the age of six or seven. They began with the hornbook or a similar instrument printed on stiff paper called a *battledore*. Next they were given the *New England Primer;* a crudely illustrated reading text that included the "Westminster Shorter Catechism"; a picture of the martyr John Rogers being burned at the stake in England; a dialogue between Christ, a youth, and the devil; and John Cotton's "Spiritual Milk for American Babes Drawn from Both Breasts of the Testaments for Their Souls' Nourishment." Many children remained in school only 3 or 4 years and did not progress beyond the primer. For those who remained longer, there was the Psalter (Book of Psalms) and the Bible. Paper was scarce and of very poor quality. It came in large, unlined sheets and had to be folded, sewn together, and marked with pieces of lead in order to make a tablet for the children. Students provided hornbooks, crude slates, and quill pens. Often the masters would canvass the community to determine the availability of books, and whatever they found would be used as reading material for older pupils.

The school normally operated 6 days each week, except in the summer. There were long periods of prayer and Bible reading both morning and evening. Most of the subject matter was memorized by the student and tested in a cue and recitation session before the master. There were no group activities or mass assignments. Students were not encouraged to express opinions or to ask questions. The word of the master and the text were regarded as absolute authorities. Teachers had no pedagogical training as such, but in New England the schoolmasters were often among the best-educated members of the community. The pay was extremely low, and many communities required masters to "board around" in order to save money.

Latin Schools and College Programs.

Boston had a free Latin grammar school, and many other New England towns developed secondary schools supported by tuition. These "higher track" schools for the social and intellectual elite were intended to prepare boys for college and were always taught by college graduates—often ministers. Boys usually entered the Latin school at the age of eight after having learned to read English at home or in a lower school. The curriculum consisted of 3 years of Latin grammar "accidence" and practice in parsing Latin sentences. Thereafter, the scholars began to "make Latin" and to translate Latin literature into English. The program continued from 6 to 8 years and included some Greek and Hebrew in the last 2 years. All the students in the Latin grammar school hoped to be admitted to a college, as that was the entire purpose of such schools. Entrance requirements for Harvard College (1642) indicated the curriculum of that institution:

When any Schollar is able to understand Tully, or such like classical Latine
Author extempore, and make and speake true Latine Verse and Prose, . . . and

> *decline perfectly the Paradigm's of Nounes and Verbes in the Greek toungue:*
> *Let him then and not before be capable of admission into the College.*

Because the first Puritan ministers were graduates of Oxford and Cambridge, colleges in New England closely copied those English institutions. Until 1653, Harvard was a 3-year college with a fixed course offering one subject at a time, so that the president could teach all classes. Classical and theological studies were the mainstay of the program. Aristotelian logic and physics, arithmetic, geometry, astronomy, grammar, rhetoric, dialectic, etymology, syntax, and prosody were taught for the purpose of disciplining the mind. Upperclassmen studied Greek and Hebrew grammar, and there were occasional lectures in history and natural science. Students were expected to declaim once a month, and great stress was placed on study of the Bible. For a degree, the student had to present evidence of his ability to read the Scriptures in Latin and to resolve them logically, "with all being of godly life and conversation."

Yale College was founded in 1701 and Dartmouth in 1769. All three New England colleges were Congregationalist and similar in curriculum. They were theological seminaries, not schools for professional men in other fields such as law, medicine, or science.

Religious Cycles.   Education in New England during the colonial period was highly influenced by religion, but the degree of religious activity varied greatly. Harvard and the early town schools of Massachusetts were established during the time of religious enthusiasm of the great Puritan migration. Economic interests and secular views soon created apathy, which caused a decline of educational zeal. Between 1661 and 1681, enrollment at Harvard dropped steadily, and the district schools had difficulty obtaining support. But in the first half of the eighteenth century, there occurred a fervent religious revival known as the "Great Awakening." Although the movement was largely evangelistic, it sparked renewed interest in schools at all levels. Yale College opened at the beginning of that period of new religious enthusiasm and produced the most famous preacher of the time, Jonathan Edwards. Edwards was an eloquent speaker, well known for his fiery "Hell and Damnation" sermons. He was also a learned scholar and the author of many pamphlets widely used in schools and colleges. The Great Awakening and the efforts of Edwards caused numerous conflicts, such as the issue over predestination that split the "Old Lights" from the "New Lights," but it also caused a major revival of educational activity. The new demand for ministers led Eleazar Wheelock to found a school in Connecticut in 1754; it was later moved to New Hampshire and renamed Dartmouth College. The College of Rhode Island, founded by the Baptists, was also a product of the Great Awakening.

New England schools were crude in form, narrow in curriculum, and poorly supported, but the significant fact remains that they existed in quantity. Long before the United States became a nation, traditions of education, including the ideas of universal schooling and public support, had been formed. Americans had already started to demand what was to become standard—better education for children than their parents had enjoyed.

THEN TO NOW

Life in pre-Revolutionary colonial American culture seems to bear very little direct relationship to present conditions, at least at first glance. Educational institutions such as dame schools, academies, old field schools, and Latin grammar schools have long since disappeared. Of course, the New England pattern of district schools, compulsory education, taxation, and distinct educational levels continues to exist in highly modified form. More important than the schools, however, is the vast heritage of beliefs, values, and attitudes inherited from the Puritans. Modern citizens are more highly influenced by the colonial past than they might imagine, because systems of value tend to persist over generations. As the theory of culture lag suggests, materialistic and technological inventions occur rapidly, and concepts of proper conduct and ideas about the good life change so slowly that they appear to remain constant. Alteration of values is likely to be slow and evolutionary, while changes in material aspects of the culture are quick and revolutionary. This is obviously important, because schools have a major role in transmitting the core values from one generation to the next.

Teaching values or value clarification is always difficult, but it is even more complicated in a multicultural society in which some children come from families more influenced by the Puritan ethic than others. Choosing and reinforcing values for survival and maximum realization of the human potential in the present and the future are central to the socialization function of education. Socialization can hardly be accomplished without a basic understanding of the Puritan ethic of the old Massachusetts Bay colony. Puritan beliefs about the evil nature of the children and their support for corporal punishment are no longer popular, but the basic values are found in the "pioneer spirit," the work ethic, and middle-class values.

Puritan Values.   Because the Puritans held that God allowed his elect to prosper and that idle hands did the work of the devil, they stressed productive work and striving for economic improvement. Today, schools support justification of one's existence through hard work and social service. Puritans were not supposed to display their wealth; therefore, they invested in land and various commercial enterprises. Living a frugal lifestyle, saving money, preparing for the future, and investing were New England values that proved useful to business and commercial interests. These values are not limited to the Puritan tradition (they are practiced also in Japan), but they are central to the American cultural core. One should not overlook the fact that Puritans were intolerant to dissenters in their time. Social ostracism was often used to gain conformity to their values. The credit card economy has tended to undermine values of thrift and frugality.

Socialization requires that the most important aspects of the dominant culture be taught. Using models of accepted behavior and sanctions, schools attempt to get students to accept and internalize values cherished by the institutions and the leaders of the dominant culture. The following are some of these values that can be traced to the Puritan heritage:

- ❑ Respect for authority
- ❑ Postponing immediate gratification

- ❑ Neatness
- ❑ Punctuality
- ❑ Responsibility for one's own work
- ❑ Honesty
- ❑ Patriotism and loyalty
- ❑ Striving for personal achievement
- ❑ Competition
- ❑ Repression of aggression and overt sexual expression
- ❑ Respect for the rights and property of others
- ❑ Obeying rules and regulations

Without making a judgment about these values, it may be pointed out that teaching them creates certain problems. Ours is a multicultural society in which minority and ethnic groups differ in the emphasis they place on traditional values of the majority culture. Contemporary American society is also stratified, and the various social classes do not exhibit the same esteem for all behaviors prized by schools. For example, American Indian and Hispanic cultures have had a more casual attitude toward time than the middle-class Caucasian society. As a result, they cherish punctuality less, and their children may not understand the school's demand that homework be turned in on time.

Economically and socially challenged at-risk youngsters seldom have the future orientation that is the ordinary time frame of the middle class. Living for the immediate moment and letting tomorrow take care of itself is an attitude sure to be in conflict with schools that require planning and a postponement of rewards. Some ethnic groups may discourage competition, even when schools encourage it. Urban African American youngsters are not apt to appear neat to white teachers, even when their appearance is quite acceptable to their parents and peers. The "macho" image that many socially and economically challenged boys need to create for peer acceptance makes them seem rude and loud in school. Expression of sexual interest may be tolerated and encouraged within some communities in ways likely to be unacceptable and punished in middle-class schools. Extreme concern about respect for property and the need to be still while others speak may be more difficult for students with no experience in valuing such behavior.

Puritans were not tolerant of any violation of their social norms. They were quick to condemn and punish any who dared to challenge the authority of the institutions or to break the rules. Middle-class teachers may insist upon modern versions of the Puritan ethic, but many students find that ethic incompatible with their own cultural backgrounds. The critical literature on contemporary education indicates that children of ethnic groups and minorities are more likely to fail in school if the school attempts to teach values foreign to them. This is the message of Ebonics supporters.

Of course, Puritans did not believe in democracy; however, modern education must attempt to promote democratic values in order to deal constructively and creatively with the confusions and conflicts of the modern world. Puritans also had the church, the family, and the local community in absolute support of their educational efforts, while contemporary schools exist in an environment of special interests and conflicting beliefs.

Multidimensional Values.   Not all middle-class people from the dominant culture support the traditional values of the schools. Sociologists say that there are emerging values in American culture that are in conflict with the traditional ones. The family as a socialization agent often needs additional support, and as that duty is passed to schools, the schools need support. Single-parent households often struggle to make ends meet, relying on schools to pick up some of the child-care duties. These are examples of emergent values in conflict with traditional ones. The peer subculture of American adolescents is unconcerned with older traditional belief systems. Rock and roll, rap, punk, freaking, grinding, booty dancing, the nasty, hip hop, and funk music; experimentation with drugs; and permissive attitudes toward sex often reflect the interests of teenagers. Educators strive to encourage healthy lifestyles through sex and drug education. Some parents find these efforts in conflict with their values systems.

Another potent force in value formation is the mass media. Television and the Internet may foster values in conflict with those of traditional schools and the Puritan ethic. A few television programs may urge people to immediately gratify their every desire, to "buy now and pay later," and to enjoy life without concern for future consequences. Many members of the modern society have little faith that honesty really is the best policy or that patriotism is a higher value than individual gratification. Computer software such as "cyberpatrol" is designed to block student access to offensive material, and educators are working to assist students in developing critical and selective viewing skills.

Dissolution of the traditional family unit with its support network, single-parent families, multiple-partner parents, the challenges of AIDS (HIV), teenage suicide, teenage pregnancy, an increase in crime (on and off school campuses), random violence, children killing or maiming other children, children whose health has been affected by parental use of drugs, and inner-city riots are part of the American culture of the twenty-first century. Reports of child abuse grew exponentially in the early 2000s, and there are few solutions in sight. The harsh youth discipline of Puritan days, acceptable then, would be classified and reported as child abuse today. Whatever the causes of these challenges to the social fabric—whether increased unemployment, lack of skills to cope with an increasingly complex society, emotional instability, or uncontrollable drug use—there are ever growing numbers of families and children at risk. These challenges lead to social fragmentation that conflicts with the goals of consensus and social unity in democracy. To deal with these issues, there are increasingly strident calls for character, values, and moral education in our schools.

Minority, single-parent, and nontraditional families are less likely to agree with the Puritan ethic than middle-class, majority culture parents. If they do agree with the ethic, they are less able to reinforce the values of schools at home. Some Americans reflect the fierce independence shown by the early colonists. An example is the litigation known as *Wisconsin v. Yoder* (1972), in which Amish families won exemption for children from the compulsory education laws of the state. Like early colonists, the Amish were willing to challenge secular authority on religious grounds and define their own values. Another example is the home-school movement. Some parents wish to teach their children at home in order to "protect" them from values taught at school. Vouchers and charter schools are available in many states to increase parental school choice and to cut down on local, state, and federal regulations.

Some educators also believe the school should work for diversity, tolerance, open-mindedness, and the development of self-concept. They do not agree with the function of transmitting an authoritative body of knowledge, and they do not want the school to impose values on children. Nevertheless, modern American schools still reflect many Puritan values, as seen in current reform reports calling for more effort and discipline.

It remains to be seen just how effective the schools will be in supporting traditional values or in teaching emerging ones. It may be that some of the Puritan values are not at all appropriate for a future learning society in which leisure and cooperation are envisioned. Schools tend to be quite conservative, but there are many other institutions that carry cultural values. In Puritan America, the family and the church supported values taught in schools. Contemporary society finds the schools often in conflict with such agents as the mass media and advertising.

At present, the Evangelicals, the Christian Coalition, and other fundamentalist conservative religious groups support some of the values of the Puritan ethic; other groups push for diversity, free choice, and multiculturalism. President George W. Bush stressed family values during his two election campaigns. Laurel Walters, in his 1993 article "Religious Right Win Seats on School Boards Across the US," noted that religious right candidates won school board elections in 12 states in 1992–1993. People for the American Way is also working to elect school board candidates to represent its point of view. These groups represent increased public interest in education decision making. Both groups are active as we enter a new millennium. Tolerance and an appreciation of the energy and contributions of a diverse population are essential in our democratic society. Kansas school authorities recently reinstated the teaching of evolution after it had been replaced by creation science by conservative interest groups, but dialogue continues on this topic. This demonstrates the continual pendulum swinging between conservative and liberal interest groups and its effect on public schools. Rifkin, in *The Empathic Civilization*, finds the pathway to a sustainable future is through engagement, replenishment, integration, and holism rejecting divisiveness of the past and the development of social responsibility.

Historical Perspective.   Educators need to understand the historical link with the colonial past. Although the Puritan heritage can be overemphasized, its contributions are important in understanding the present culture and preparing for a viable future. Beliefs of the early settlers of colonial New England still cast a shadow over values in modern American society. Those who do not appreciate this historical fact are ill-prepared to understand the value conflicts that are central to so many modern educational issues.

GAINING PERSPECTIVE THROUGH CRITICAL ANALYSIS

1. What does the Old Deluder Satan Act of 1647 demonstrate about the relationship between religion and education? (A review of the chapter opening quotation will help you with your answer.)

2. Compare and contrast the roles of religion and social class on colonial education and on education today.

3. How did the culture and history of the Southern colonies make educational practice different from education in the New England and Middle colonies?

4. Identify the goals of the tutorial, old field, dame, and charity schools. Compare the goals of these colonial schools with the goals of public schools today.

5. What reasons can you give for the differences between school discipline in colonial times and discipline in public schools today?

6. Compare educational facilities, instruction method, and curriculum content in colonial days with the current state of education.

HISTORY IN ACTION IN TODAY'S CLASSROOMS

1. Find an example of multicultural literature that "fits" the melting pot theory. Share the book or article with your class and describe why you chose it. (See Glossary.)

2. Interview a teacher or an administrator. Ask him or her about school discipline in the past and present. What are his or her opinions about civility, responsibility, and character education in the past and present? Add these findings to your journal.

3. Define core values, alternative values, and culture lag (covered in Chapter 1). Show how these terms apply to colonial education and to a modern multicultural school setting.

4. Write a brief dialogue or drama that exemplifies cultural lag in practice. Trace the origin of settlers in the United States. Identify diverse cultures of our nation's early founders.

5. Discuss and answer the questions at the end of the feature "Spelling and the Curriculum." This feature is found within the chapter.

BIBLIOGRAPHY

Butts, R. Freeman, & Lawrence A. Cremin. *A History of Education in American Culture*. New York: Rinehart and Winston, 1953.

Church, Robert. *Education in the United States: An Interpretive History*. New York: The Free Press, 1977.

Cohen, Sheldon. *A History of Colonial Education, 1607–1776*. New York: John Wiley & Sons, 1974.

Curti, Merle. *The Social Ideas of American Educators*. Patterson, NJ: Littlefield, Adams, 1959.

Edwards, Newton, & Herman G. Richey. *The School in the American Social Order*. Boston: Houghton Mifflin, 1963.

Eggen, Paul D., & Donald Kauchak. *Educational Psychology*. Upper Saddle River, NJ: Merrill/Pearson Education, 2000.

Ford, Paul Leicester, Ed. *The New England Primer*. New York: Dodd, Mead and Co., 1987. Originally published in 1690.

Founding of Harvard College, America. Vol. 2. 1642, pp. 155–157. Available at: education.byu.edu/edlf/archives/prophets/founding_fathers.html

Gay, Geneva. *At the Essence of Learning: Multicultural Education*. West Lafayette, IN: Kappa Delta Pi, 1994.

Good, Harry, & James Teller. *A History of American Education*. 2nd ed. New York: Macmillan, 1973.

Havinghurst, Robert, & Daniel Levine. *Society and Education*. 5th ed. Boston: Allyn & Bacon, 1975.

"Internet User Profiles Reloaded." Pew Research Publications (January 10, 2010). Available at: pewresearch.org/pubs/1454/demographic-profiles-internet

Jernegan, Marcus. *Laboring and Dependent Classes in Colonial America, 1607–1783*. New York: Frederick Ungar, 1960.

Knight, Edgar W. *Education in the United States*. Boston: Ginn and Co., 1951.

Lefrancois, Guy R. *Theories of Learning: What the Old Man Said*. New York: Thomson Learning, 2000.

Lily, William. *Latin Grammar*. London: Thomas Berthelet, 1540.

Mather, Cotton. *A Family Well-Ordered*. Morgan, PA: Soli Deo Gloria Ministries, 2001. Originally published 1699.

Mill, J. S. *On Liberty*. London: J. S. Parker and Son, 1859.

Miller, Perry, Ed. *The American Puritans: Their Prose and Poetry*. Garden City, NY: Doubleday, 1956.

Morrison, Samuel Eliot. *The Intellectual Life of Colonial New England*. New York: New York University Press, 1956.

Pastorius, Frareis Daniel. *Methodical Directions to Attain the True Spelling, Reading, and Writing of English*. New York: William Bradford, 1698.

Potter, Robert. *The Stream of American Education*. New York: American Book Company, 1967.

Rifkin, Jeremy. *The Empathic Civilization*. New York: Penguin, 2009.

Rippa, S. Alexander. *Education in a Free Society: An American History*. 7th ed. New York: Longman, 1992.

Rippa, S. Alexander, Ed. *Educational Ideas in America: A Documentary History*. New York: David McKay, 1969.

Van Til, William. *Education: A Beginning*. Boston: Houghton Mifflin, 1974.

Victoria, Irwin. "Prayer and Giggles During 'Silent Moment.'" *Christian Science Monitor* 1 (December 11, 2000): 9.

Walters, Laurel. "Religious Right Win Seats on School Boards Across the US." *Christian Science Monitor* 1 (August 9, 1993): 20.

Warren, Donald, Ed. *History, Education, and Public Policy*. Berkeley, CA: McCutchan, 1978.

Woolfolk, Anita E. *Educational Psychology*. Upper Saddle River, NJ: Allyn & Bacon/Pearson Education, 2000.

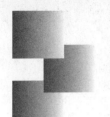

CHAPTER 4

AMERICAN EDUCATION: THE AMERICAN REVOLUTION

Although I do not, with some enthusiasts, believe that the human condition will ever advance to such a state of perfection as that there shall no longer be pain or vice in the world, yet I believe it susceptible of much improvement, and most of all, in matters of government and religion, and that the diffusion of knowledge among the people is to be the instrument by which it is to be effected.

Thomas Jefferson

American Revolution		
1776 Declaration of Independence	1780 English Sunday school founded by Robert Raikes	1785 Northwest Ordinance Land Grant
Thomas Paine's *Common Sense*	1781 Battle of Yorktown	1787 Constitutional Convention
Adam Smith's *Wealth of Nations*	1783 Treaty of Paris ended war with England	1789 Constitution accepted without mentioning education

Figure 4.1   Time Line from the American Revolution to the War of 1812

Before the time of the Revolutionary War, the population of the American colonies had grown to more than 2.5 million people. An expanding frontier fostered perseverance, ingenuity, self-confidence, and a defiant individualism among the Western settlers. This frontier character was unique to America, as was the mixture of nationalities and religions found in the Middle colonies. The district system with its decentralization and local control continued to dominate New England schools before and after the Revolution, and the idea of free, compulsory, universal education was central to the ideal of self-government there. Although schools varied widely in number and quality in the New England colonies and later in the New England states, America looked to Massachusetts, Rhode Island, and Connecticut for educational leadership. Religious denominational or parochial schools remained common in the Middle colonies until the country became independent, but such sectarian schools were weakened by the withdrawal of English financial support and by the separation of church and state. (Please refer to Figure 4.1 for a time line from the American Revolution to the War of 1812.)

DEMOCRATIC IDEALS

The rising tide of democracy threatened a dual system of education in which the elite enjoyed good schools and the masses were largely ignored. This factor accounts for the shrinking influence of Latin grammar schools and the vast growth of the academy. The revolutionary period saw academies—with their emphasis on practical subjects such as bookkeeping, navigation, and surveying—increase in popularity. Town schools in the most populated areas and even crude schools of the remote frontier settlements became more numerous as the eighteenth century closed, and

French Revolution		War of 1812
1791 Bill of Rights ratified	1798 Joseph Lancaster and Andrew Bell start monitorial schools	1805 New York Free School Society
Philadelphia Sunday School Society	1802 West Point founded	1806 New York monitorial Schools
	1803 Louisiana Purchase	1812 State Superintendent appointed in New York
Individualism Self-reliance		

such educational institutions did not cater to an aristocracy. Southern educational patterns altered little during the revolutionary era, except that students did not study in England and many of the charity schools were closed.

CHANGES IN COLONIAL CULTURE

American capitalism provided general growth and prosperity in the economic order and in intercolonial trade before the Revolution. New York, Boston, Philadelphia, and Charleston became large cities with sophisticated populations interested in all sorts of European ideas. There was a diffusion of culture between the various parts of the colonies, as well as much travel and correspondence. Newspapers like the *Boston News Letter* and other periodicals such as *Poor Richard's Almanac,* published by Benjamin Franklin, stimulated colonial intellectual life. At the outbreak of hostilities in 1775, there were 37 newspapers in regular publication.

College, private, and city libraries were found throughout the colonies, although many did not permit the free circulation of books. Subscription libraries were available at a small fee. Only a few Americans published books before the Revolution, but British volumes were for sale in most large towns. Bookstalls had the works of Bacon, Locke, Boyle, Newton, Swift, Milton, Hume, Voltaire, and Addison, among others. Learned professions like law and medicine made progress in the late eighteenth century and gained in respect. Experiments in science and medicine were as popular as speculation in philosophy. The American Philosophical Society, which developed from a proposal by Franklin, brought Americans into contact with the learned world of Europe. Not many colonial minds were on a par with the cosmopolitan Benjamin Franklin or the theologian–philosopher Jonathan Edwards, but there were well-educated, widely read, cultured Americans before the Revolution. Leaders in public life like Patrick Henry, John Adams, and Thomas Jefferson were much influenced by intellectual changes in Europe.

THE SHIFT IN THE COLONIAL MIND

Dissatisfaction with conditions in Europe was one reason for the first American settlements, but this feeling shifted to dissatisfaction with English colonial policies such as mercantile capitalism. The American Revolution was a combination of native efforts and contributions from foreign thinkers and movements. Political philosophers like John Locke and Jean-Jacques Rousseau, whose effect on education was both direct and indirect, provided the rationale for the American experiment in self-government.

Locke's Influence.   The English philosopher John Locke (1632–1704) not only provided a theoretical basis for the Declaration of Independence but also contributed to American educational thought. Locke's political ideas concerning the inalienable rights of humanity and the contract relationship between a people and its government were accepted almost without qualification by Thomas Jefferson and other leaders in the movement for independence. The high reputation Locke enjoyed among Americans caused his philosophical writings to be widely circulated in the colonies and later in the United States. Locke had severely altered the direction of educational thought through his denial of the existence of innate ideas and his insistence that the mind at birth is passive and like a blank tablet (*tabula rasa*) upon which experience writes. He believed that all our ideas come from experience and that the measure of the truth of an idea is its correspondence with concrete, objective, commonsense reality (empirical principle). Emphasis on experience, good study habits, a utilitarian curriculum, and sense-realism aided the scientific and practical elements in American education.

Franklin's belief in self-education for practical utility, his broad interest in empirical science, and his desire to provide educational opportunity for anyone who wanted to learn were all in keeping with Locke's theories. The emergence of a strong middle class with large numbers of lawyers and merchants was an event of the late colonial period that helped to support Locke's ideas. Franklin and Locke emphasized the secular aspects of education as opposed to the ecclesiasticism of the schools supported by religious organizations. Although sectionalism, a lack of money, disunity, and religious sectarianism prevented any common educational program in colonial America, the theoretical foundation for free, universal, and public schools was laid.

Comenius.   An outstanding spokesperson for the power of education in improving the human condition was John Amos Comenius (Komenski) (1592–1671). Born in the village of Nivnitz in Moravia, Comenius became bishop of the Moravian Brethren, a Hussite religious sect persecuted by both Lutherans and Catholics. In spite of exile, the murder of his family, and the destruction of his library, Comenius managed to develop a philosophy of education and to write some of the most influential schoolbooks produced in Europe. His *Great Didactic and Door of the Languages Unlocked* (1632) (an introduction to Latin grammar) was produced while he was rector of the Gymnasium at Lissa, Poland. Influential Englishmen invited Comenius to present his plan for universal knowledge and a world university to Parliament, but the English Civil War of 1642 prevented his appearance. For six years he wrote textbooks for Latin schools in Sweden and later established a school at Sárospatak, Hungary. There, Comenius developed his idea of schools in graded order from "the school at the mother's knee" to the university. In 1658, while living in Amsterdam, he published his *Orbis Sensualism Pictus* (1657), the first popular illustrated textbook for children. Cotton Mather claimed that Comenius was invited to become president of Harvard in 1654. He was a highly respected educator whose ideas fell on fertile soil in America.

Although the religious background of Comenius caused him to accept the doctrine of original sin, he agreed with Locke that ideas come from experience and that our sense organs are our teachers. This sense-realism lent support to empirical investigation, practical education, and the potential of science. Comenius believed that war could be prevented if scholars were brought together to work out solutions to international problems. To this end, he proposed a pansophic university with functions faintly similar to those of the United Nations. He felt that universal education could improve civilization through the discovery and dissemination of practical information on subjects such as economics, medicine, agriculture, and sanitation.

Although a linguist himself, Comenius believed that primary instruction should be given in the vernacular. He encouraged the publication of dictionaries, textbooks, and encyclopedias in order to simplify instruction. He thought that a science of education was possible and that teachers could be trained to practice it. Comenius influenced American education through his textbooks, his support for science, and his belief that education must be practical. The growth of the academy and the concept of self-education made popular by Franklin were also part of the educational theory of Comenius.

Impact of European Movements.

Impact of European Movements. The sense-realism of Comenius, the empiricism of Locke, and the scientific movement in Europe paved the way for new conceptions of people and society. The verbal or humanistic realism of John Milton advocated encyclopedic studies and general education. In place of the narrow religious view and conservatism of the New England Puritans, Englishmen were substituting a secular, realistic, liberal worldview.

The life of the mind in the American colonies varied from theological arguments in the early Puritan settlements to broad scientific and secular issues addressed by men like Franklin in the urban centers of the Middle colonies. The scientific revolution of seventeenth-century Europe reached America by degrees and had a major impact after 1750. Findings of the Royal Society of London for Improving Natural Knowledge excited American interests and stimulated discussion, especially of the physical sciences. Empiricism, sense-realism, and scientific discovery foreshadowed the movement of the late seventeenth and early eighteenth centuries known as "the Enlightenment."

The Enlightenment was a rational, liberal, humanistic, and scientific trend in thought that vastly altered the climate of opinion in Europe. It was grounded in the natural and social theories of Comenius and Locke but found new expression in the works of Diderot, Voltaire, Rousseau, Hume, Paine, and Kant. Kant described the Enlightenment as the liberation of man from his self-caused state of minority. The Enlightenment was a protest against authority that insisted upon man's ability to understand the universe without divine revelation. It held that men as individuals have worth and dignity and that they are able to judge truth for themselves. It fostered belief in a universe governed by natural law that reason could penetrate. The Enlightenment was a protest against both the authority of Christian dogma and absolute monarchs. Its leaders sought a balanced social order free from the control of a single powerful class.

Enlightenment thought favored autonomous economic enterprise and parliamentary forms of government. It created an attitude of distrust for despotic monarchs and all other forms of strong centralized government. British mercantile capitalism, which exploited colonies as sources of raw materials and dumping grounds for surplus manufactured goods, was attacked by the theorists of the Enlightenment. Scottish economist Adam Smith, with his ideas of value placed on labor, *laissez-faire*, and a free market, appealed to leaders of the Enlightenment.

Humanism looked to the past, through a study of classics, for solutions to problems of the world. Great interest was shown in the social and governmental arrangements of ancient Greece and Rome. Men like Jefferson used classical models for the new republic and for institutions such as the University of Virginia. Sense-realism placed humankind (not God) at the focal point and sought knowledge through ordinary experience or scientific observation. American revolutionary leaders were much influenced by books written by liberals like the humanitarian Montesquieu. Cultural changes of the Enlightenment helped to plant the ideas that grew in the fertile soil of a comparatively free society and that became the timber of revolution. It should also be remembered that more than 150 years of colonial growth and development before the Revolution provided ample time for a major alteration of values and beliefs. The intellectual climate of 1776 was far different from that of 1620.

COLONIAL LIBERALISM

By no means were all of the colonial settlers conservative and narrow in their beliefs, in spite of restrictions imposed by Puritan and Anglican authorities. James Oglethorpe proposed colonization of Georgia as an experiment in humanitarianism after he had visited English prisons. The Quakers of Pennsylvania were not only tolerant of other religious beliefs but also concerned about the dignity and worth of all persons without regard to color, creed, or social position. Catholics in Maryland brought a different tradition to America, and they were hardly in a position to resist religious freedom.

The Puritans were outspoken in their opposition to secular authority that over-ran the "just bounds" that they defined as God's word and the common interest, although they were not willing to grant religious freedom. Even so, Roger Williams, Thomas Hooker, Jonathan Mayhew, and John Wise were Puritans who dissented from church authority with considerable success. Puritan schools were dominated by orthodox teachers like Ezekiel Cheever, who was praised by Cotton Mather as much for his preaching as for his pedagogy; but tolerance and liberalism became widespread ideals before the Revolution.

Other systems of thought had considerable influence on the cultural climate before the United States emerged as a nation. The Puritan theologian Jonathan Edwards was hard pressed to defend his religion against science. Samuel Johnson was attracted to the idealism of Bishop Berkeley, while Deism (the belief that God created the world and then withdrew to let it operate according to natural law) was popular with many intellectuals. The naturalism of Rousseau and his concept of government were known in America, although his influence on education was severely curtailed by the conservative reaction that followed the war for independence. Adam Smith's *Wealth of Nations* appeared in 1776 and became the basic economic theory of the new nation. Thomas Paine was one of the great champions of the American Revolution because of such writings as *Common Sense* (1791), which had an enormous circulation and which proclaimed independence. However, Paine's *Age of Reason* (1793) was considered radical in the conservative period that followed the Revolution, and its author lost his influence in the United States.

EDUCATIONAL CHANGES IN THE LATER COLONIAL PERIOD

Several of the colonial colleges were founded in what could be called the revolutionary era. Harvard College, William and Mary College, Yale College, and the College of New Jersey were founded between 1636 and 1746. King's College, the College of Philadelphia, the College of Rhode Island, Queen's College, and Dartmouth College were all founded between 1750 and 1776. Some of the political leaders in the movement for freedom from England were products of the colonial colleges, which were basically conservative institutions. The total enrollment of the nine colonial colleges operating on the eve of the Revolution was about 750 students.

On the secondary level, Latin grammar schools declined in importance with respect to the academy. Academies were more democratic in organization and far more geared to the needs of an expanding economy. Franklin's first effort at Philadelphia in 1751 was secular, practical, and widely copied. Courses in Latin and Greek were included in some academies, but modern languages, including French and German, were more popular. Gauging, drawing in perspective, merchant's accounts, logic, chronology, astronomy, and rhetoric were added to the older subjects of history, geography, bookkeeping, writing, surveying, and navigation.

Academies and some private-venture secondary schools flourished in the larger towns in the decades before the war. As colonial interest shifted from religion to shipping, commerce, and agriculture, civil town governments became more important in education. Many efforts were made to obtain town schools in which children without means could receive rudimentary training, and town schools often had secondary departments for those who could pay.

Elementary schools continued to operate with crude instruction and equipment. Several factors led to the decline of certain kinds of schools, but the educational tradition continued. The early New England writing school, which had never been in great demand, expired before the Revolution. In Pennsylvania, the SPG gave up in disgust after 1763, and the decline of New England theocracies made schools more difficult to support. Massachusetts, Connecticut, and Rhode Island did not abandon efforts to educate all the children, but some towns were without schools, and many provided them for only a few winter months. Denominational efforts such as the Reverend William Tennant's Log College (a classical secondary school for training Presbyterian preachers) declined after 1742. Nevertheless, elementary education was provided for most colonial children who could pay a small fee. A larger and more prosperous population gave rise to more schools in the Middle colonies than had been the case earlier.

THE WAR AND AFTER

The Revolutionary War directed men's energies away from education and science, as De Witt Clinton observed years later. Illiteracy increased because rural schools had to close their doors and because even the larger-town Latin grammar schools were crippled. British occupation of New York caused schools to be abandoned there. New England schools continued to operate, but they suffered from a lack of funds and teachers.

Higher education was restricted in part because many talented teachers were Loyalists. Books were scarce because many of them came from England and because colonial printers could not maintain their presses without outside English supplies. Yale College was broken up into groups centered in different towns, and Harvard's buildings and those of the College of Rhode Island housed provincial troops. Dartmouth had neither money nor books, and classes had to be discontinued at the College of Philadelphia. The Colleges of New Jersey and William and Mary also suffered but were not closed.

British support, as in the case of the Anglican SPG, was cut off and never revived. Lack of money and the interruption of the normal economic process made the operation of educational institutions almost impossible. Teachers and scholars joined the fighting forces, and school buildings were converted into barracks. Tory or Loyalist teachers were turned out of their schools. Sometimes, the schools were burned and libraries were scattered or destroyed. Nevertheless, the conflict was restricted to certain parts of the colonial territory, and areas that escaped destruction continued with education. Peace allowed for a restoration of many schools, even though the money was scarce and authority uncertain.

Sway of Independence.   The Revolution not only dealt harsh blows to intellectual life in America, but it also provided the seeds for intellectual activity independent of Europe. As long as the colonists were tied to the value system of the mother country, it was almost impossible for the native culture to rival the established and sophisticated English life of the mind. But the Revolution broke those ties and stimulated considerable literary activity, expressed in antimonarchical and pro-democratic pamphlets and books. Further, the heroes of the Revolution were elevated to a dignified and popular social and political status in the new nation. Their ideas gained immediate support. Many revolutionary leaders attempted to put ideas central to the struggle for liberty—such as natural rights, freedom, equality, patriotism, and resistance to tyranny—into the laws. A free press and freedom of speech called attention to the need for schools if the new government of the people was to be successful.

EFFORTS OF EDUCATIONAL FOUNDERS

Many of the men who contributed to the birth of the new nation had plans for schools or other educational institutions. For a variety of reasons, including the national debt of $75 million (which seemed a staggering sum at the time) and Federalist conservatism, few of these plans were actually realized.

Freedom of Religion.   Patrick Henry first became involved in the struggle for religious freedom in 1763, when he defended a group of Virginia farmers against Anglican ministers who were suing for their back pay. He lost the suit, but the jury fixed the pay of the ministers at one penny, which was a victory for the opponents of established religion. James Madison and Thomas Jefferson carried the banner of freedom of religion during the war. They offered a bill in 1776 to exempt dissenters from paying the church tax. In 1779, Jefferson sponsored a bill establishing religious freedom, but it was unsuccessful. Patrick Henry proposed a law in the Virginia legislature that would have provided tax support for teachers of the Christian religion, without regard to denomination. Madison feared the creation of a "multiple establishment of religion," and in 1785 he managed to push through Jefferson's earlier proposal. Virginia became the first state to have a law guaranteeing freedom of religion. Jefferson returned from his mission in France in 1787. Finding no constitutional guarantees for individual rights, he refused to support ratification of the Constitution without the series of amendments known as the Bill of Rights.

The First Amendment specifically prevented Congress from making any law respecting the establishment of religion or prohibiting religious practice. Connecticut, Maryland, Massachusetts, and New Hampshire did have constitutional provisions for tax-supported religion, but they abolished these provisions by 1833. Although the long-range effects of disestablishment and religious freedom were beneficial to public schools, the immediate result was to take away public funds that had been used to support church-related schools. Separation of church and state also gave rise to educational problems that persist today, such as the issue over prayer and Bible reading in public schools. Nevertheless, sectarian control over public education was broken by the provision for religious freedom.

National University.   James Madison and Charles Pinckney attempted to include in the Constitution a provision for a national university. Although it failed, several national leaders including Washington expressed interest in the idea. His farewell speech to the army emphasized the need for the promotion and diffusion of knowledge. Several times Washington attempted to get Congress to establish a national university, and he left part of his estate to the proposed institution. John Jay, James Monroe, and John Quincy Adams shared the desire for a national university with Washington, Jefferson, and Madison. The university was never built, partly because Congress failed to act and partly because of legal and financial arguments.

Plans for a National System.   Despite the omission of education from the Constitution, revolutionary statesmen made a number of proposals for a national school system. In 1795, the American Philosophical Society offered a prize for the best essay on the subject of a national system of education. Many plans were submitted, including those of Benjamin Rush, Noah Webster, Samuel Smith, Samuel Knox, and Pierre DuPont de Nemours. Knox and Rush shared the prize. All these plans were founded on the theory that a public system of education is necessary for a free and self-governing republic. Consideration was given in the plans for public control, public support, a practical curriculum, compulsory attendance, and all levels of schools including a national university. The plans differed; however, one in particular, designed by Rush, offered a very extensive system with supervision of schools and academies for teacher training. Support for an American school system also came from essayists such as Robert Coram of Delaware and Revolutionary War officer Nathaniel Chipman. In spite of the interest, Congress rejected all plans for a national system.

REVOLUTIONARY PERIOD EDUCATIONAL LEADERSHIP

Many men aided the cause of schools during the period of the American Revolution. Benjamin Franklin lent his great prestige to all intellectual and cultural causes, although he supported practical self-education more than public schools. Benjamin Rush, a signer of the Declaration of Independence, wrote numerous essays on education, in addition to his plan for a national system. Perhaps the most important influence of the era came from Noah Webster and Thomas Jefferson.

Noah Webster.   Known as the "Schoolmaster to America" because of the popularity of his textbooks, Noah Webster (1758–1843) was a major educational force for many years. His *Compendious Dictionary* (1806) was the first of a series of dictionaries and lexicons that made his name a household word in the United States. While keeping a classical school in New York, Webster began his *Grammatical Institute of* *the English Language,* of which the first section, often revised, became the famous "blue-backed speller." It is estimated that this book had sold 19 million copies by the time of Webster's death, and by all measures it was the most successful textbook ever produced in America. He also wrote books on grammar, reading, and history, all with a strong patriotic and nationalistic flavor. As a young man, Webster was caught up in the liberal ideas of the Enlightenment and the Revolution. He supported free schools, a national language as a band of union, and separation of church and state.

The French Revolution shocked Webster, and he repudiated his earlier republican principles in favor of conservative federalism. His later works stressed religious morality, respect for government, and a patriotism that sometimes bordered upon the fanatic. He believed that all books, schools, masters, and programs for the schools of the republic should be strictly American and even suggested that the first word taught to an infant should be *Washington*. Webster called for strict teaching and supported traditional methods of instruction, but he was against corporal punishment. He wanted education for girls because they would be the mothers of future citizens and the teachers of youth. Webster felt that no legislature should ignore the need for free schools in which all American children could learn the virtues of liberty, just laws, morality, hard work, and patriotism.

Thomas Jefferson. Jefferson's contribution to education would constitute ample material for an entire book. He provided the ideology for extending educational opportunity to all citizens and argued that no democratic society is safe without an educated population. For more than 50 years, Jefferson was personally active in efforts to put his educational theory into actual practice. As a young man he worked to reform the schools of Virginia, while much of his old age was devoted to building the University of Virginia. The basic theme of Jefferson's educational policy was academic excellence with equality of opportunity for all. He was not, like Hamilton, a supporter of strong federal government, and therefore his efforts to improve schools were on a local and state level.

Jefferson's Bill for More General Diffusion of Knowledge in Virginia was widely circulated and used as a model. The plan called for a state system of free elementary schools with local control. Secondary schools were to be tuition institutions, with a provision for scholarships to meet the needs of poor but gifted boys. A state university was to crown the educational system. Jefferson submitted three bills to the Virginia Assembly, but he was not successful in passing any of his proposals except that for the University of Virginia. His effort to overcome the danger of an ignorant populace was very modest; the bill called for only 3 years of public schooling. His organizational pattern with decentralized control and localization of financial responsibility became popular even though Virginia failed to adopt the plan. For example, Edward Coles became governor of Illinois in 1818 and promptly submitted a plan for a school system in that state that borrowed many of Jefferson's ideas.

After attempting to reform the College of William and Mary, Jefferson became convinced that an entirely new university was required. Few institutions have reflected one person's views as closely as the University of Virginia reflected those of Thomas Jefferson. Not only was he the driving force for the creation of the university, but he organized the curriculum, hired the faculty, planned many of the buildings, purchased and catalogued the books for the library, and generally supervised the entire operation. In 1825, Jefferson saw his creation open with 40 students. The University of Virginia became the first state university and the first one with a "modern" curriculum.

EARLY GOVERNMENT PROPOSALS

It was the prevailing view of the founding fathers that while knowledge was the best guardian of liberty, education did not belong in federal hands. James Madison wanted a general tax for schools, and Samuel Knox argued that private schools were subversive in a republic. But such reasoning did not convince the Constitutional Convention. The Constitution, therefore, contains no reference to education, although the First Amendment and the Tenth Amendment ensure state control and nonsectarian public schools. Other measures significant in the development of education came out of the early national period.

Early National Legislation.
In 1785, Congress outlined regulations for the national territory west of the Alleghenies, north of the Ohio River, and east of the Mississippi River. This Northwest Territory was to be laid out in townships consisting of 36 sections. By the Ordinance of 1785 (also called the Northwest Ordinance), the sixteenth section (one square mile) in each township in the territory was reserved for the support of schools within the township. A second Ordinance two years later authorized not more than two full townships in each new state to be reserved for a university. The act contained a statement that schools and education should forever be encouraged for the benefit of human happiness and good government. These acts became a precedent for land grants to the states for public schools and colleges. By later acts, most new states entering the Union received federal land for educational purposes.

In 1802, Congress established the national military academy at West Point. This was the first of many federal acts that created special educational institutions with specialized functions. West Point had the first American training center for engineers.

State Efforts.
Seven of the state constitutions adopted before 1800 mentioned education. Those of Pennsylvania, North Carolina, and Vermont called for the establishment of schools in each county, with some public financial support. The Pennsylvania Constitution, accepted in 1776, became a model for several others. It required that the state pay salaries of teachers in public schools. New Hampshire and Massachusetts stressed the need for wisdom and knowledge as a means of preserving liberty, but their constitutions did not require schools. Massachusetts legalized its traditional local district school system and, in 1789, admitted girls to district schools. New York made public lands and certain other funds available to free schools.

Before 1812, the Union had grown considerably with the purchase of the Louisiana Territory in 1803 and the admission of the new states of Vermont, Kentucky,

Tennessee, Ohio, and Louisiana. The constitutions for these states all indicated some concern about education, and several set up a system of schools that was enacted into law. As the nation grew, each new state adopted a constitution modeled after those that were admitted earlier. Having educational provisions in the state constitutions became a tradition.

OTHER EDUCATIONAL MOVEMENTS

Lacking public school systems and the ability to obtain laws for education, a number of leaders tried to support schools by other means. Many church-related institutions continued to offer charity education as they had in the colonial period.

Monitorial Schools.   Monitorial schools originated in England through the work of Joseph Lancaster and Andrew Bell. This type of school provided for inexpensive education that could be given to the masses by a minimum teaching staff. Students of ability were selected as monitors or student teachers, and the master instructed these monitors. The monitors, in turn, taught the lessons they had learned to small groups of pupils. Simple lessons were memorized, and slates or chalkboards were used. The Lancasterian monitorial system allowed one teacher to instruct hundreds of children. One of these schools appeared in New York City in 1806, and the idea spread. Lancaster himself came to America in 1818; while in America, he promoted his mass education program until 1830. After 1830, complaints of "factory" type schools, excessive uniformity, and inability of monitors to maintain discipline led to the eventual demise of the monitorial school.

Sunday Schools.   Another English educational plan introduced in America was the Sunday school. Not a church school in the modern sense, the purpose of the Sunday school was to provide basic education to the poor. Its champion, Robert Raikes of Gloucester, wanted to rescue children of factory workers from their filth, ignorance, and sin. Because the children worked in the mills all week, schools could be provided only on Sundays. Several religious groups, especially Methodists, supported the Sunday school with money and teachers. Children were supervised and given instruction in rudimentary principles during their free time on the Sabbath.

In 1791, a Sunday School Society was organized in Philadelphia. American Sunday schools developed in most of the major cities. They were primarily for the poor but were not confined to factory or mill workers. Generally, the schools operated from 6 to 10 o'clock on Sunday morning and again from 2 to 6 o'clock in the afternoon, leaving time for worship. Although they could hardly have provided more than the bare fundamentals of education, these institutions taught many children to read.

Free School Societies.   School societies were organized to develop monitorial schools, Sunday schools, and free public schools in certain areas. The Connecticut school societies were authorized to be district school authorities, while the New York Free School Society promoted several types of education. The New York group founded schools for girls and for the poor; the group later became the Public School Society of New York. It was assumed in this period that students who could afford private schools would attend them, and indeed they did. Public schools and free schools carried the stigma of poverty because they were charity institutions.

SCHOOL IDEAS AND THE CURRICULUM

Independence brought about the development of a unique American culture and a set of national institutions. Education was a reflection of this new spirit, as were self-reliance, optimism, individualism, and democracy. Farmers wanted more education for their children because education was a mark of achievement and a step up the social ladder. The population of the new nation grew rapidly, increasing more than tenfold in a single century after the Revolution. Much of this growth came through immigration from European nations other than England. For these new citizens, education was the means of becoming "real Americans."

Improvements in transportation brought about social consciousness that was lacking in isolated colonies. This social consciousness fostered an exchange of ideas and a national feeling that aided schooling. The start of the American Industrial Revolution shifted many people from rural to city areas, especially in the Northeast. Factory workers created special needs for free elementary education on a much larger scale. Doctrines of freedom and equality gave rise to free speech and a free press, which in turn fostered democracy.

But there was also a conservative reaction to the War for Independence. Those who feared the education of the masses and federal control opposed liberals who fought for a free public system on the national level. Lack of money and opposition to direct taxation prevented the building even of a national university. However, there was keen interest in the building of state universities, and these universities became a unique American cornerstone of higher education. Educational interest was also expressed in state constitutions, land grants, school societies, and philanthropy. The start of free public schools for all the people can be found in the period before the War of 1812.

Separation of church and state did not take religion out of the schools. Both sectarian and public schools of the revolutionary era continued to use textbooks that were religiously centered. The Bible and the *New England Primer* were by no means expelled. Use of *Cheever's Accidence*, the "Westminster Catechism," and the Psalter continued in New England schools after independence.

New Materials.   Changes did occur, however, in fields like mathematics, commerce, history, geography, and English grammar. Lindley Murray's *English Grammar* (1795) and the *Universal Geography* (1796) of Jedidiah Morse appeared before 1800. Samuel Goodrich wrote texts in reading under the pen name of Peter Parley, and Nicholas Pike's *A New and Complete System of Arithmetic* appeared in 1788. Noah Webster entered the field with his *Grammatical Institute of the English Language* in 1783.

In 1812, New York provided for a superintendent of common schools but later abolished the office. Supervision was almost nonexistent in the revolutionary period, except in monitorial schools and in those operated by school societies. There was little effort to train teachers. Methods remained as crude as they had been earlier, with memorization the central concern. Liberal ideas from Europe and the frontier brought about changes in textbooks but not in the conduct of the schools, for it was still believed necessary to keep strict discipline by means of corporal punishment. Difficult subjects were learned for their value as a "discipline" to exercise the faculties of the mind. A more enlightened theory of learning was not to develop for more than 50 years.

THEN TO NOW

Anyone interested in describing an educational system must look for answers to several fundamental questions. The following are among the most important: Who will be educated? What institution will control education? Who will provide the financial support? Why do certain groups get a different quality of education?

A National System Fails to Win Approval.   The colonial era was a period of transition from European educational patterns to ones more appropriate for life in the American environment. As we have seen, Southern planters retained the English family-supported tutorial system, and New England towns adopted a district system with some tax support. By the time of the rebellion against the British, no uniform educational policies had been established. Sectional differences in attitudes toward public schooling continued in the states as in the colonies.

The great liberal leader Thomas Jefferson understood the need for citizens of a republic to be educated, but he did not believe in a federal system of schools. His Bill for the More General Diffusion of Knowledge proposed to the Virginia legislature in 1779 was a very modest plan that combined elements of an aristocratic attitude with a desire to broaden the educational opportunities of poor but able students. Even so, Jefferson's ideas were too liberal to gain the support of his colleagues from the South. Far-reaching plans for a national system of education such as those designed by Robert Coram, Benjamin Rush, and Noah Webster met with even more opposition. Yet whether education should be public or private, supported centrally or locally, and managed by parents or governmental agencies are issues that are still debated.

Financing State Systems and Testing Controversies.   Although the 50 state systems of public schools have been operational for many years, Americans are still divided on numerous educational issues. An example is the argument over tuition tax credits for parents who send their children to private schools. These credits and the debate over the various voucher plans constitute significant support and control disputes about which many modern Americans obviously disagree. Another public concern is a disparity in school finance between rich and poor school districts. Many states are under federal court orders to equalize school funding. Other points of disagreement include the use of standardized test scores for ranking and placing students as opposed to authentic assessment or the use of a balance of evaluation measures and evaluating progress on a continuing basis using portfolios in which students narrate their backgrounds and goals. Although some educators advocate alternative forms of assessment that do not rely on a competitive evaluation system with a percentage of students bound to fail, others including major urban political leaders use standardized test results to have students with low scores repeat grade levels.

Another example is the rejection by a growing number of parents of educational outcomes in which children are assessed on standards of performance that include values of tolerance and cooperation. Pennsylvania and other states are modifying outcomes assessment programs because of parental complaints that their children had to learn about and accept diversity in American culture. The philosophy of outcomes continues to be practiced but under different terminology. Under President Obama's Education Secretary Arne Duncan, the No Child Left Behind Act (NCLB), during a difficult political and economic environment, may be modified to meet the objections of state educational leaders. Obama stresses the importance and role of charter schools in his Race to the Top.

In a November 1993 election, Californians voted on a school-voucher system to expand parental choice of schools. Under the proposal, parents would receive half the amount spent on each public school student, or about $2,500. Parents could choose private, parochial, or public schools. Although the voucher proposal was rejected by a large margin of Californians, several states have implemented a voucher system, and others are considering the concept. California has a number of charter schools, but the populace again rejected vouchers in 1997. A small New Jersey school district has proposed vouchers that will enable parents, regardless of their income, to send their children to any public or private secondary school, including religious schools. In November 2000, voters in Michigan and California rejected ballot voucher plans. The Obama administration supports charter schools and accountability for results, especially for at-risk students (Condon, 2010). Some 4,000 children attended church-related schools in Cleveland through a voucher program in 2000. A federal appeals court ruled against Ohio's voucher plans on the basis of government support of religion. The Supreme Court, in *Zelman v. Harris* (2002), reversed the appeals court decision and upheld the Cleveland voucher program. In *Hibbs v. Winn* (2004), the Supreme Court ruled that constitutional challenges to state tax benefits like tuition tax credits are legal. There is strong opposition to the voucher proposal by several civil rights groups, and the Bush administration's voucher plans face intense opposition. The Florida voucher system, a centerpiece for parental choice, has been rejected by several courts in the state. Vouchers were rejected in 2006 by the State Supreme Court, but Governor Charlie Crist has expanded the program for disabled and high-poverty students (Matus, Solochek, & Bousquet, 2010). Governor Rick Scott seeks to expand options for public school students, giving them more opportunities to transfer to other campuses, enroll in charters schools, and take classes online ("Governor Rick Scott," 2011).

Establishing National Standards.   Many of the founding fathers of the United States feared that leaving education in the hands of private families, churches, local communities, or philanthropic societies would not guarantee the survival of a democracy. Nevertheless, they were unable to promote a national system of education at any level. Considerable effort was made to obtain a national university, but even that modest proposal was finally defeated. Education was not mentioned in the Constitution. Under the Tenth Amendment, the power to create, maintain, and govern schools fell to the states by default. Today there is continued conflict over what powers rightfully belong to the federal government, to the states, and to local school boards.

One of the major current issues in American education centers on the influence of political and governmental forces on community educational practices. The states were very slow in passing educational laws, even though the right was stated in the enabling acts incorporated in several state constitutions. Responsibility for public education was assumed by the states in the 1830s, modified by federal aid to education in the Kennedy–Johnson era, and restored to the states under the administrations of Reagan and George H. Bush. The Clinton administration moved toward national models for educational standards, curricula, and assessment to meet the need for achievement equity among schools. An education bill establishing national standards and testing passed Congress and became law in January 2002. With a larger popular vote margin in his reelection, George W. Bush continued his efforts to expand NCLB to include high school student assessment. The Obama administration continues the drive for excellence in education in a difficult political environment. Some 4.5 billion in his Race to the Top program was offered to states for their most innovative educational policies (Martin, 2010).

Local Power Versus State Control.   Early national practices allowed religious organizations, free school societies, and monitorial schools to fill the void before state systems were developed. Laws provided for a great deal of autonomy to be delegated to local school boards, while funding came largely from local property taxes. Under these conditions, it was natural for the district school authorities to consider themselves all-powerful and beyond much control by the state. In the early national period, leaders like Horace Mann and Henry Barnard built their respective state school systems without taking away the policy-making power of boards of education. Since World War II, the tradition of local autonomy has resulted in considerable conflict with state legislatures. State governments and state departments of education now take a more active role in teacher certification, establishing lists of approved course materials and even mandating the curriculum. Many states now have a provision for academic bankruptcy, whereby the state department of education takes over school districts when school achievement standards are not met.

Local Power Versus Federal Control.   Federal pressure on local schools comes through court-ordered plans of desegregation, laws for equal educational opportunity—including opportunities for disabled, disadvantaged, and limited English proficient children—and regulation of programs supported by federal taxes. There exists a great deal of resentment over the involvement of the central government in matters many consider to be the business of local boards. School boards and parents often feel that the bureaucrats in Washington have no understanding of local conditions and needs. Public sentiment for getting the federal government out of the schools and restoring local control was clearly demonstrated in the Reagan victory in the election of 1980. Although there is increasing federal school funding together with a movement toward national standards for education, some parental rights groups are seeking passage of a Parental Rights and Responsibilities Act. Parental rights and school choice remain a goal of some citizens in the early 2000s.

Much of the criticism of modern education from sources like *A Nation at Risk* is federal or national in origin; however, the reforms mandated are to be carried out at state or local levels. There is more widespread public approval of a move toward testing and accountability for student performance. There is also criticism of penalties and excessive regulations in NCLB.

The Clinton administration sought higher national achievement standards and the Bush and Obama administrations continued that effort. With few exceptions, both political parties and the public place education improvement high on their agendas, although funding may limit implementation of some programs. In December 2000, Congress passed a record $42 billion education budget. Funds for reducing class size, upgrading teacher skills and quality, improving reading and math, renovating school facilities, and special education grants to states were included. Also Pell grants, and Gear Up and Trio programs, together with comprehensive school reform, accountability, and twentieth-century after-school programs, were included. A bipartisan coalition found education as a national priority. Although education spending increased, by 2005 budget deficits and the costly Iraqi War made it difficult to obtain further funding. Educational reform for the Obama administration was a top priority. With an economy in a free fall, the Obama administration, like the Bush administration, poured money into the financial system through a stimulus program. Under the American Recovery and Revitalization Act, 48.6 billion was sent to states to help for fiscal relief. Funds were also available to prevent teacher layoffs (Reyna, 2009).

Two points need to be made here. First, the history of the early national period clearly indicates that education is a state function even though the states have traditionally permitted a high degree of local control. Second, although the federal Constitution did not deal with education, there has been a long tradition of federal aid to the states and to local schools as well. People who are trying to understand the current issue over local, state, and federal control of education should remember that all three levels have had input into educational policy since the founding of the nation.

Federal Education Acts.   Granting federal land to the states for educational purposes began with the Northwest Ordinance of 1785. During the Civil War era, this practice continued with the Morrill Act, which used federal land grants to create universities.

Congress also established a number of schools for specific purposes and encouraged vocational education through legislation such as the Smith-Hughes Act. Recent federal acts such as the National Defense Education Act, the Elementary and Secondary

Education Acts of 1965, the Equal Opportunity Act, the National Service Legislation of 1993 (the National and Community Trust Act), and the Education of All Handicapped Children Act of 1975 (better known as Public Law 94-142) are merely current extensions of federal involvement in education that reaches back to American historical beginnings. The 1990 Individuals with Disabilities Education Act (IDEA) and the Education Amendments of 1997 extended provisions of Public Law 94-142 to all citizens from ages 2 to 21. Provisions of both acts are under continuing review by congressional committees to clarify various provisions. The acts require inclusion, or placing students with physical and emotional challenges in regular classrooms. The 2005 funding reauthorization act, "Improving Education Results for Children with Disabilities," expanded, defined, and clarified services for the nation's exceptional children.

FOCUS ON THE ISSUES

Divided We Stand

Abraham Lincoln expended most of his energy as president in an effort to preserve the Union, but it was not until after Appomattox that the idea of "one nation, indivisible" gained universal support in America. Regional differences remained strong and sectional issues continued. Clearly, after the Civil War most people thought of the United States as a single unified nation. At times, such as following the Japanese attack on Pearl Harbor in 1941 or the bombing of the World Trade Center towers in New York, there has been universal national support. "United We Stand" billboards appeared everywhere after 9/11 and the war on terrorism had little opposition. Even now, those who believe our invasion of Iraq was a mistake and that American security would be better served by not alienating the world's vast Moslem population support our armed services overseas. We must remember, however, that loyal American citizens have been and still are sharply divided on many disputes that permeate our society, such as the justification for the Vietnam War, the invasion of Iraq, or troops in Afghanistan.

At the beginning of the Obama administration the nation faced a severe recession with failing banks, high unemployment, and a crisis in the housing industry. The nation was severely divided on how to deal with these problems and with health care reform. International affairs such as war in Iraq and Afghanistan and nuclear bomb production in Iran also contribute to a difference of opinion among the American people. Clearly, political controversy and national issues affect education. Of particular concern is the disagreement about how public money should be distributed among educational institutions and how schools should be controlled. Opposing view about national testing, charter schools, alternative teacher certification, and the teaching of creationism (or intelligent design) are examples. United we stand on some issues, but certainly we are divided on others. This is a real problem as the United States attempts to improve the quality of its schools with no clear mandate about how this can be done.

What Do You Think?

1. Should education be immune from public controversy?
2. Can it ever be?
3. Identify pros and cons of Race to the Top with distribution of federal funds for innovative, experimental educational programs based on competitive proposals from state school districts.
4. Describe rugged individualism and self-reliance in education and society. Should our teacher methods be based on cooperation or competition?

Formation of the U.S. Department of Education.   The mood of the nation has often been reflected in political activity that has a direct bearing on education. The history of the United States Department of Education is an example. As we have seen, many of the founding fathers wanted to establish a federal system of education. In 1829, Congressman Joseph Richardson proposed a federal committee on education to coordinate the state programs. Congress squelched this proposal, but the idea kept emerging. Charles Brooks of Massachusetts (a Unitarian minister and school reformer) devoted 30 years to efforts at getting a national system. Although he failed, he stimulated educators to form communications networks to gather data and influenced Congress to consider federal aid to the South after the Civil War. Following the war, the National Association of School Superintendents proposed a bureau of education.

In somewhat reduced form, the bill creating a department of education was passed and signed into law by President Andrew Johnson in 1867. Henry Barnard, who had also lobbied for such a department, became the first commissioner. Barnard was not popular in Washington, and the department was soon reduced to a bureau in the political turmoil following Johnson's near impeachment. General John Eaton, Barnard's successor, toned down the office and made its function mainly one of collecting information. For almost a century after its creation, the United States Office of Education kept a low profile and concentrated on statistics. Then, in the 1950s, with the black revolution and the civil rights movement, latter-day reformers found the Office of Education to be a useful instrument for implementing the reforms of the Great Society.

In the Kennedy–Johnson years, the Office of Education gained great power and status. It was authorized to distribute vast sums of money to compensate for the inequality of educational opportunity and to stimulate plans for school integration. The Office of Education was placed in the Department of Health, Education, and Welfare; and its staff grew to enormous size. Under President Carter, it became a separate cabinet-level Department of Education.

The administration of President Reagan, however, took a very dim view of social engineering through federal spending and reduced both the budget and the influence of the department. All through history, the progress of education has been linked to the whims of politics and public attitudes. It should be remembered that the reason we do not have a federal system of public schools in the United States is because of the political climate at the time of the writing of the Constitution.

Political Attacks on Educational Institutions.   Another example of politics and education is shown by the attempts of politicians to control higher education. During the American Revolution, criticism and attacks were directed at conservative colleges because they were considered to be insufficiently patriotic. William Smith, the president of the College of Philadelphia, was an Anglican minister accused of Tory sentiments. In 1776, the legislature investigated the college, dissolved the board of trustees, and dismissed the faculty. The legislature created a new board and a new institution called the University of the State of Pennsylvania. The old college continued

to function without legal status, and finally, in 1789, the two institutions joined to form the University of Pennsylvania. The case of the College of Philadelphia is similar to that of Dartmouth College (discussed in Chapter 5). The point is that political influence over education is nothing new in American history.

Periods of political unrest foster attacks on institutions of education. Notable modern examples include the investigations by Senator Joseph McCarthy following World War II and the controversy over loyalty oaths for teachers (*Wieman v. Updegraff*) in the 1950s. Although education is legally a state function, all levels of government are involved in educational matters. The arguments over control and support of education that began in the period of the Revolution are very much alive today and may be expected to continue into the future.

Educational Artifacts and Technology: No Steady History.

Inventions and discoveries that have dramatically altered the human condition have no steady or evolutionary history but consist of dramatic breakthroughs commonly followed by periods of inactivity. Thus, ancient Romans invested in aqueducts and sophisticated plumbing for baths and fountains while later Europeans living in the Middle Ages not only lost the technology but attributed the ruins to a race of magical super beings.

A parallel situation is found in contributions to education and learning. In today's world of mass media and electronic communications, it seems strange that so much of human history passed with few developments in education and that some of the important inventions were not passed on to other cultures. Nevertheless, progress before modern times was slow and sporadic.

Consider writing, the ultimate foundation for educational progress and schools in all cultures. Pictographs or symbols representing specific things such as heavenly bodies, men, or animals are found in cultures as diverse as the Chinese, Egyptian, and Incan, so we may assume independent invention. It was, however, the Sumerians who developed true writing in the third millennium B.C. The Sumerians of Mesopotamia developed a strong sense of personal property, creating a need to mark objects for ownership, especially when artifacts were presented to the gods. Names or identification marks scratched in the wet clay soon gave way to individual cylinder seals that could be rolled into the damp tablets. This evolved into cylinders for special purposes such as contracts for business or marriage, with names and dates added on the clay tablet with a wedge-shaped stylus made of wood or bone. Some seals may have been made of wood, but many were cut into bronze. Numerous examples have been recovered by archaeologists.

Unlike Egyptian papyrus pith paper or Roman velum, clay tablets do not disintegrate in dry climates, so many thousands have been recovered from ancient sites in the Fertile Crescent. Legal documents are sometimes found encased in their own envelopes or sheaths with identification marking on the outside clay layer. These Sumerian written records are the oldest form of writing anywhere, and some words such as *crocus*, *myrrh*, and *saffron* are still in use. These early people created symbols for syllables as well as words and developed lexicons and grammars. A thousand years passed before the next major change came in writing with our present alphabet, invented by the Phoenicians.

In addition to the keyboards on our computers, everyone today has access to a vast array of pens, pencils, crayons, and markers. Oddly, the Egyptians, Greeks, and Romans failed to develop a pen or pencil and relied on reeds with frayed ends for writing. Marking fluids were made from various combinations of oils, soot, berry juices, and vegetable dyes until the Greeks learned to extract ink from marine animals. The quill pen was an invention of the Middle Ages and was the mainstay of handwriting for a thousand years. Not until 1828 did a metal point fitted into a wooden pen come into common use. Fountain pens were early twentieth-century inventions while the ballpoint instrument appeared in 1948.

Limestone, charcoal, lead, and chalk have always been used for temporary marking when available. In early America chalk was scarce, and so soft stone was used for doing sums on slates and blackboards. Sometimes, blackboards were "whiteboards" painted or whitewashed and written upon with charcoal. The story of young Abraham Lincoln doing mathematical exercises with charcoal on the back of a shovel reflects common conditions on the American frontier. Graphite was discovered near Keswick, England, about A.D. 1500. First used as a mold for cannonballs, graphite was cut into small slabs for marking in the days of Elizabeth I. The earliest pencils were wrapped in sheepskin, but the wooden holder developed in Italy became standard. Pencil making was a cottage industry until the French learned to mix ground graphite with clay and fire it in a furnace to make a thin pencil filler. Thereafter cheap manufactured pencils became standard tools for writing practice in schools everywhere.

Educational technologies often follow those of manufacturing and industry. Everyone is familiar with the standard school desk and seat made of wood with cast-iron side supports. Rows of such desks were bolted to the floors of American schools for generations, and some are still in use today. Iron and steel production in America were not well developed until the coming of the railroads. In 1829, with George Stephenson's locomotive Rocket and a year later with Peter Cooper's locomotive Tom Thumb, the steam rail industry was born. The need for strong, cheap metal rails stimulated the iron and steel industry, which revolutionized American manufacturing. At the time, Horace Mann was calling for improved, standardized public schools. He drew plans for cast-iron school-desk supports that could be made at little expense as a by-product of the railroad rail manufacturing, and thus began the common school basic furniture industry.

The Role of History of Education.

Educational issues and the visions of Webster, Jefferson, Locke, and Comenius are often reflected in current educational debates. Bilingualism versus English immersion, the relation of the government and its citizens, experience and learning, the role of the church and state in education, international and global education, controversies over economic globalization, collective bargaining, academic freedom, decisions on what is ultimately worth knowing, and professional versus general education remain issues for schools and society. Governmental gridlock occurs when narrow margins between the political parties lead to conflicts as single special interest groups seek to promote their ends through the law and political power. This leads to social fragmentation as these single interest groups often push legislation for interests detrimental or not beneficial for the larger population.

GAINING PERSPECTIVE THROUGH CRITICAL ANALYSIS

1. Name three European philosophers who helped to shape colonial thought before the Revolutionary War. How did each of them influence American educational practice?
2. What was the significance of the thinking and writing of Noah Webster and Thomas Jefferson on education? (A review of the chapter opening quotation will help you with your answer.)
3. How did societal changes lead to curriculum modifications during the American Revolution?
4. Do you think you would have had more effect on American education as a member of Congress in colonial times or today? Give three reasons for your answer. Identify the influence of government gridlock and social fragmentation.
5. What were the primary differences between monitorial schools, Sunday schools, and free school societies established during the period of the American Revolution? Give examples of similar efforts to expand educational access and opportunity today.
6. Examine the literature on the Northwest Ordinance, and relate the content of the ordinance to school finance issues then and now.

HISTORY IN ACTION IN TODAY'S CLASSROOMS

1. Interview a retired teacher or administrator. Discuss his or her perceptions of the changing role of women and curriculum changes throughout his or her career. Add the findings of your interview to your journal, and share them with your class.
2. Using the library, the media, or the Internet, review current legislation that supports either national control or state/local control of education in your area. Use your journal to record the results of your search.
3. Give examples of expansion of social consciousness and social justice in the educational and occupational treatment of women and minorities from a historical perspective.
4. Discuss and answer the questions at the end of the Focus on the Issues feature "Divided We Stand." This feature is found within the chapter.

BIBLIOGRAPHY

Arrowood, Charles Flinn. *Thomas Jefferson and Education in a Republic*. New York: McGraw-Hill, 1930.

Bergen, Tim. *Foundations of American Public Education*. New York: McGraw-Hill, 1994.

Best, John Hardin, Ed. *Benjamin Franklin on Education*. Teachers College, Columbia University Bureau of Publications, no. 14. New York: Columbia University Press, 1962.

Butts, R. Freeman, & Lawrence A. Cremin. *A History of Education in American Culture*. New York: Holt, Rinehart and Winston, 1953.

Church, Robert, & Michael Sedlak. *Education in the United States: An Interpretive History*. New York: Free Press, 1976.

Clinton, Bill, & Al Gore. *Putting People First*. New York: Random House-Time Books, 1992.

Comenius, John Amos. *The Great Didactic and Door of the Languages Unlocked*. Translated/edited by M. W. Keating. London: A and C Block, 1896. Originally published in 1632.

Comenius, John Amos. *Orbis Sensualism Pictus*. Translated to English by Charles Hoole. London: Printed for J. Kinton, 1659.

Condon, Stephanie. "Obama Calls for Big Education Reforms—More Charter Schools, Longer School Year." *Political Hotsheet* (September 27, 2010).

Davis, David. *The Problem of Slavery in the Age of Revolution, 1770–1823*. Ithaca, NY: Cornell University Press, 1975.

French, William M. *American's Educational Tradition, an Interpretive History*. Boston: DC Heath, 1964.

Gay, Peter. *John Locke on Education*. New York: Teachers College Press, Columbia University, 1964.

"Governor Rick Scott Won't Push School Voucher Expansion—For Now." *Orlando Sentinel* (February 10, 2011).

Gutek, Gerald. *An Historical Introduction to American Education*. New York: Thomas Crowell, 1970.

Hansen, Allen O. *Liberalism and American Education in the Eighteenth Century*. New York: Macmillan, 1926.

Hoff, David J. "Clinton Gives Top Billing to Education Plan." *Education Week* 1 (February 12, 1997): 34.

Hofstadter, Richard, & Wilson Smith. *American Higher Education: A Documentary History*. Chicago: The University of Chicago Press, 1961.

Homstad, Wayne. *Anatomy of a Book Controversy*. Bloomington, IN: Phi Delta Kappa, 1995.

Jefferson, Thomas. "Letter to Pierre DuPont de Nemours, April 24, 1816." In *Jefferson on Religion in Public Education*, edited by Robert M. Healey. New Haven, CT: Yale University Press, 1962, p. 181.

Ketcham, Ralph. *From Colony to Country: The Revolution in American Thought, 1750–1820*. New York: Macmillan, 1974.

Martin, Patrick. "Obama Education Plan Boosts Privatization, Victimizes Teachers." *World Socialistic* website www.wsws.org (accessed March 31, 2010).

Matus, Ron, Solochek, Jeffrey, & Bousquet, Steve. "Crist Approves Historic Expansion of School Vouchers." *St. Petersburg Times* (April 23, 2010).

Meyer, Adolphe. *Grandmasters of Educational Thought*. New York: McGraw-Hill, 1975.

Morse, Jedidiah. *Universal Geography*. Boston: J. T. Bukingham, for Thomas Andrews, 1796.

Murray, Lindley. *English Grammar*. York, UK: 1795, 1805 (also Boston: Thomas and Andrew, 1796).

Paine, Thomas. *Age of Reason*. Paris: Barrois, 1793.

Paine, Thomas. *Common Sense*. Philadelphia: W and T Bradford, 1791.

Perkinson, Henry J. *Since Socrates: Studies in the History of Educational Thought*. New York: Longman, 1980.

Pike, Nicholas. *A New and Complete System of Arithmetic*. Newburry-Port: John Myeall, 1788.

Ravitch, Diane. *National Standards in American Education: Citizens Guide*. Washington, DC: Brookings, 1995.

Reyna, Ryan. "State Opportunities Under the American Recovery and Reinvestment Act: State Fiscal Stabilization Fund." *National Governors Association Center for Best Practices* (March 24, 2009).

Smith, Adam. *Wealth of Nations*. 2 vols. London: Dent & Sons, 1904. Originally published in 1776.

Thayer, V. T. *Formative Ideas in American Education*. New York: Dodd, Mead, 1965.

Travers, Paul, & Ronald Rebore. *Foundations of Education: Becoming a Teacher*. Upper Saddle River, NJ: Prentice Hall, 1987.

Ulich, Robert, Ed. *Three Thousand Years of Educational Wisdom*. 2nd ed. Cambridge: Harvard University Press, 1963.

Walsh, Mark. "New Jersey District Proposes Vouchers for High Schoolers." *Education Week* (February 12, 1997): 6.

Webster, Noah. *Compendious Dictionary*. Hartford, CT: Hudson & Goodwin, 1806.

Webster, Noah. *Grammatical Institute of the English Language*. West Hartford, CT: Hartford, 1783.

Woody, Thomas. *Educational Views of Benjamin Franklin*. New York: McGraw-Hill, 1931.

CHAPTER 5

AMERICAN EDUCATION: 1812–1865

I believe in the existence of a great, immutable principle of natural law, or natural ethics—which provides the absolute right of every human being that comes into the world to an education; and which, of course, proves the correlative duty of every government to see that the means of that education are provided for all.

Horace Mann

Jacksonian Democracy		
1817 Thomas Gallaudet established school for the deaf in Boston	1821 First American high school, Boston	1827 Massachusetts required high schools
1818 Robert Owen's infant school	Emma Willard's school for girls	1832 New York school for the blind
1819 Dartmouth College case	1825 Friedrich Froebel published *Education of Man*	1837 Calvin Stowe's report on Prussian schools
University of Virginia	Henry Barnard visits Prussian schools	Horace Mann made secretary of Massachusetts school board
Marginalized Women		

Figure 5.1 Time Line of American Education 1812–1865

Before the War of 1812, education was virtually a religious enterprise, with the exception of some academies and free school societies. The period from 1812 to the Civil War was a transitional one during which educational leaders such as Horace Mann, James C. Carter, and Henry Barnard forged the first links in what has evolved as a free, public school system, supported and controlled by the state. The rise of nationalism and Jacksonian Democracy, the Industrial Revolution, and the forces of westward expansion, immigration, and population growth provided impetus to the concept of universal education. There was a rebirth in the growth of the elementary or common schools. Academies supplanted the elite-oriented Latin grammar schools, which flourished until their peak in 1850.

More important in this era was the birth of the American high school, an institution that would, in time, become the vital force of secondary education. This period saw the passing of the Morrill Act and the subsequent establishment of land grant colleges. European ideas were transplanted by innovations such as those of Victor Cousin, Joseph Lancaster, and Margarethe Meyer Schurz. The curriculum was expanded. The sectarian stronghold gave way to a more secular orientation, and the concept of teacher training was realized in the establishment of the first normal school in 1839.

Missouri Compromise		Civil War
1839 First American normal school, Lexington, Massachusetts	1848 Attempt to teach the profoundly retarded, Boston	1855 German-speaking kindergarten
		1860 English kindergarten in Boston
1840 Rhode Island compulsory education	1849 New York general tax for schools	1861 M.I.T. founded
1846 Laboratory sciences in colleges	1852 Massachusetts attendance law	1861 Civil War begins
		1862 Morrill Land Grant College Act
Adult Education	Americanization	

SOCIAL, POLITICAL, AND ECONOMIC TRENDS

The period of time from the War of 1812 through the Civil War is often referred to as the age of the common man. This is true in part because of the impact of Jacksonian Democracy and the social, political, and economic developments of the nation. Throughout the land, the advancement of the common man carried the banner of education as a basic right and opportunity that should not be denied any citizen.

Common School Ideal.   The doctrine of equality of all citizens demanded mass education and made a system of separate schools for the elite social classes unacceptable. Equality led to the belief that all should read in order to participate in government and to have the opportunity to improve. The idea that schools could provide a ladder by which one might climb socially and economically was widespread. There was a demand for general education and for vocational skills as well. The attitude supported local control with no federal regulations. It was felt that common schools should be public in curriculum and tax-supported. In limited-resource communities, the poor— including minorities, whites, and women—were often excluded from political, social, and economic equality. Separation of church and state was upheld, but no restrictions were placed on nondenominational religious instruction in public schools.

FOCUS ON THE ISSUES

Teacher Qualifications in Frontier Schools

Still sits the school-house by the road,
a ragged beggar sunning;
Around it still the sumacs grow,
and blackberry-vines are running.
Within the master's desk is seen
deep scarred by raps official;
The warping floor, the battered seats,
the jack-knife's carved initial*

These lines from Whittier's *In School Days* well describe the physical school common on the American frontier. By the latter part of the nineteenth century, especially in the trans-Mississippi West, such schools were often taught by young women with some education. Before that, instruction was commonly delivered by men with scanty learning and no pedagogy. Schools were crude affairs of short duration and unreliable support. Few schoolmasters made a career of teaching; most only taught until some better opportunity came along. Girls and boys ranging in age from kindergarten years to young adults were lumped together in one room. The master often had to prove he could control the school by sheer strength and bravery. A custom grew up of locking out the schoolmaster at Christmas time unless he provided a treat of eggnog. This vile concoction, consisting of eggs, milk, sugar, and whiskey, was served out to all children. As small sums of money from state sources became available to augment local taxes or subscription, some method of certification began to emerge. Often some official such as the lieutenant governor or secretary of state assumed the duties of school supervision for states newly admitted to the Union. They were in charge of state school funds and licensing of teachers. When Illinois became a state in 1818, a man who had been teaching in a country school saw Ninian Edwards on the capital steps in Vandalia. Recognizing Edwards as the state school officer, the man approached and asked if he could obtain certification. Edwards asked the man if he could make eggnog. The candidate told Edwards that while he had not made eggnog himself he "had seen it did." Edwards replied that his case was a bit doubtful, but since Illinois needed teachers, he issued the man a certificate from a sheaf carried in his pocket.

What Do You Think?
1. Consider all you must do today to become a certified teacher. Are the rules sufficient to make sure incompetent people are excluded?
2. Should the United States have a national system of teacher certification? Compare and contrast traditional versus alternative certification programs.
3. Trace to evolution of social and economic justice for marginalized women, adult education and Americanization.

*Source: Poets Corner John Greenleaf Whittier, selected words, "In School Days." Available: www.theotherpages.org/poems

---

Impact of the Industrial Revolution.   The Industrial Revolution began in Europe before the American Revolution and slowly spread to other nations including the United States. British inventions including Watt's steam engine, Arkwright's spinning frame, and Cartwright's power loom were instrumental in moving toward an industrial economy for which Adam Smith supplied the economic theory. Machines made of wood and driven by water or wind evolved into factories with iron mechanical devices powered by steam.

At the opening of the nineteenth century, agriculture dominated the American economy. This was still the case in the South and West at the opening of the Civil War, but not in the Northeast and Midwest where textile mills, coal mining, iron and steel plants, commercial enterprises, food-packing companies, and railroads became dominant. The steam engine was the catalyst of change, and railroads transformed agrarian communities into mill towns with job opportunities for expanding populations. Major cities on the Atlantic coast became nerve centers for short rail lines, but soon distant inland points like Cleveland, Chicago, and Atlanta were connected. Railroads were not so numerous in the South, but lines were built to carry cotton to market after Eli Whitney invented the cotton gin in 1793. The open hearth and Bessemer process made malleable iron and steel available for rails and engines, creating yet another industry. As always is the case, material invention precedes social adjustment so that no provision was made for the vast changes created by the new economic order. Slums, crowded conditions, pollution, abuse of labor, poverty, and social unrest were also caused by the Industrial Revolution. The greatest impact of this technological change occurred after the Civil War, but it altered American society long before that.

Not only was the Industrial Revolution uneven in its spread across the nation, but it also contributed to extreme sectional differences. It is often pointed out that the United States lacked a sense of nationalism before 1865 and that loyalty was centered in various regions instead of in the nation as a whole. The Whiskey Rebellion of 1794 established the federal government's power to tax, but it created vast resentment among local farmers who lived by converting corn into liquor. High tariffs could not be equally good for farmers and factory owners. Black slaves were considered an economic necessity in the South, but their use violated a growing sense of human rights elsewhere. An illustration of the power of sectionalism is found in the life of Robert E. Lee. Except for the aged Winfield Scott, Lee was the best-known American soldier at the time of the Fort Sumter attack. As such, he was offered the command of the Union Army. But while Lee was a dedicated career officer and opposed secession, he could not lift his sword against his neighbors and fellow Southerners. He therefore resigned his commission and offered his services to Virginia.

Education and the Industrial Revolution. One effect of the change from an agricultural to an industrial economy was a demand for a terminal secondary school to prepare boys for the work for which they were destined. After 1830, considerable pressure was generated for the expansion and improvement of public schools. The industrial working class became a political factor. Workers in urban areas could not afford to send their children to private schools. They wanted a better opportunity for their sons and daughters than they had enjoyed. Factory labor was often recruited from the vast numbers of foreign-born people who crowded into cities. These immigrants joined forces with others supporting public education. Today, Arizona and

California are moving away from bilingual programs in favor of one year of English immersion before students are integrated in all-English classrooms. This follows years of primary instruction practice in the student's native language, especially Spanish. Foreigners entering the United States in the nineteenth century made no demand for instruction in anything but English. They desired universal free schools, but they expected their children to learn the national language. Indeed, they saw English usage as a requirement for entering the job market.

In the industrial East, the growth of cities and factories tended to increase the desire for schools and decrease the opportunity many children had to attend them. Factories often employed entire families. Some youngsters began working 12-hour shifts at the age of 8. The severity of the problem is illustrated by the fact that in the 1830s, two-fifths of New England's workforce was made up of children under 16 years of age. Child labor, the lack of safety devices or worker's rights, extreme poverty, and crowded slums added to social problems of the day. Many reformers hoped to use education as a means of overcoming the difficulties produced by the Industrial Revolution. Women and girls in urban factories worked under sweatshop conditions with little opportunity for a better life. Under a *laissez-faire* philosophy, employers saw no requirement to improve the conditions of work. This led to greater demands for reform by workers and social leaders, and public education for all children.

Public School Support.
Throughout this period, there was an increase in the political power of the ordinary man, and aristocratic birth came to be a political handicap. Private philanthropy, even by such a popular organization as the Public School Society of New York, could not really provide the answer, and increased agitation for tax-supported schools became commonplace. Bands of factory workers in cities formed working men's societies; these organizations tended to give their support to public education. Because they were important politically, the working men's societies had considerable effect.

The theory behind taxing every person for the education of all children was eventually accepted in most parts of the country, and the belief that schools must be both free and tax-supported developed into general public policy before the Civil War. This did not mean that all states had established their school systems before 1865 or that all resentment of tax support for education had disappeared. However, the American people had generally accepted the notion of public support for common school education.

There was some feeling, particularly expressed by the *New York Working Men's Advocate,* that the public schools ought to board children so that those from poor families would not feel inferior to the sons and daughters of the rich; they felt that by doing so, equal educational opportunity would be a reality. This argument of 1830 serves as a reminder of some of the present controversy over civil rights legislation. It was also held that the curriculum ought to be the same for all students and that, rather than the classics, a practical education including the rudiments of the English language should be the basis.

Today the population explosion has manifest implications for education, but even in the early national period demographic changes had their educational impact. From 1820 to 1850, the centers of commerce, especially cities like Boston and New York, jumped vastly in population. Rapid growth of the cities and the subsequent surge of poverty and slums made reform and public concern with educational matters much more important. By 1845, the flow of people from foreign countries was so pronounced that as many as one-third of the residents in cities like Boston were foreign born. The nation's population exceeded 30 million in 1860.

Nationalization.   Many immigrants had customs and languages different from those of the native-born population; therefore, the schools became a major instrument in the transfer of the American culture to the foreigners. One aspect of this "Americanization" was not limited to the newcomers. The two wars with England and the rapid growth of America had nurtured a growing nationalism. This nationalism resulted in the educational principle that schools should pursue the inculcation of patriotism—love and respect for America, its ideals, its history, and its potential. Frontier equality aided public education through the belief that people ought to have equal educational opportunity without the stigma of charity. Hence, the new states with large frontier communities tended to provide for education as they provided for universal suffrage. Many ethnic groups including Germans, Italians, Irish, and Dutch maintained their cultural identity while their children mainstreamed into the American culture through the public schools.

Frontier Impact.   Frederick Jackson Turner (1861–1932), an American historian, became famous for his theory of the significance of the frontier in American development. He thought that an abundance of free land strengthened the democratic ideals and that western expansion provided a safety valve that prevented social revolution caused by economic stress. His view of the impact of western expansion and the moving frontier dominated American historical thinking for decades.

Other historians challenged Turner's ideas, but it is certainly true that free land, westward expansion, and the constant development of new outposts of civilization were significant factors in the creation of the United States. Although it is true that there was a certain amount of anti-intellectualism on the frontier, it is also the case that most pioneer farmers wanted their children to have the rudiments of an education. The frontier towns were raw and unsophisticated but never dominated by only one class of people. Doctors, lawyers, and well-educated ministers were present along with farmers, ranchers, prospectors, and scouts. Pioneer virtues of thrift, hard work, self-reliance, and independence were often reflected in attitudes toward social institutions such as schools. The theory of minimum public education for every child found wide acceptance on the frontier, but getting tax money for schools often met with a good deal of opposition. The egalitarian view that one man was just as good as any other without regard to wealth, family, or social status became commonplace on the frontier and in American schools. The frontier fostered individual freedom and lack of governmental restraint—values that often made it difficult to support and regulate schools. There was also a general distrust of classical or "foreign" education on the American frontier, with reliance being placed on practical wisdom and basic skills like reading.

The first quarter of the nineteenth century was remarkable in many ways; it brought about the beginning of the state school systems that still exist in one form or another today. During this time of common school revival, the older colonial educational programs that had developed in Massachusetts and the other New England states were reestablished. Of course, there was widespread opposition. Many newspapers were against taxes for the support of schools, and it was not possible to raise revenues with the speed necessary to develop a genuinely good school system. But well before the Civil War, all the states had given at least some attention to the question of developing a system of public schools for the children of all the people.

First State Programs.   The founders of the American common schools did not think it necessary to guarantee a democratic system of education for all the people. The earliest state provisions usually created an *ex officio* superintendent of schools, whose other duties might include, for example, serving as secretary of state. It was also common to empower local groups interested in education to establish an educational corporation for the purpose of building school buildings, hiring teachers, and whatever else seemed necessary to the making of a school. But the states moved slowly in the passage of laws that set up their various educational systems. The state superintendent of free schools or common schools, or the state superintendent of public instruction, as the officer was sometimes called, often had very feeble powers. Even when the states passed laws necessary for a real school system, they tended to be very slow in the enforcement of those laws. For a long time it was difficult to collect school taxes and nearly impossible to ensure compulsory attendance, even when such attendance was a legal requirement. Hence, the development of the state school systems varied as the people's interest tended to wax and wane. Educational progress was hindered by the old tradition that children should be educated first by their parents and second by the church. However, in the long run, frontier democracy overcame the prejudices against public schools.

THE AGE OF THE COMMON SCHOOL REVIVAL

Educational historians often refer to this period, 1812 to 1865, as the Age of Common School Revival. It was during this time that the old New England demand for universal common education became an ideal for the American people. The common elementary school was established in the North and West; it had the task of building social, political, and moral character needed in a democracy. In addition, it was concerned with the teaching of basic skills. The battle for free public education, supported and controlled by the state, was centered on the common school.

As the curtain rose on the nineteenth century, the condition of elementary school education was most depressing. The SPG (The Society for the Propagation of the Gospel) withdrew its efforts after the split with England, and there were few schools that were for the benefit of the masses. Most existing schools required tuition, although some scholarships were available. Education was traditional, and discipline was harsh. In the few public schools, most of which were in New England, the teachers' workloads were heavy, and only the fundamentals were taught. For the most part, school buildings and equipment were very poor, even in the private schools and academies. Textbooks, blackboards, and all working materials were in extremely short supply. Buildings were not kept up, lighting was not adequate, and quite often one poorly trained teacher was in charge not only of one school but also of an entire district.

Teachers who possessed only an elementary school education were frequently hired. Of course, teachers in the Latin grammar schools and academies were educated, but there was certainly no formal teacher-training system. There were some teachers of ability, but frequently men who were dreamers or who could not succeed in other professions became schoolmasters. Perhaps people of better quality and training would have been attracted to teaching if the pay and conditions could have been improved, but this was beyond the settlers' capability in most of the newer areas of the country. Even on the frontier, some well-educated and excellent teachers could be found, but in most cases the quality of teaching was extremely low and the children could expect to gain little learning in return for the brief time and small fees that were required of them.

State Funds and State Laws.   Permanent school funds had been set up by a number of states during the early national period. Connecticut used the money from the sale of its Western Reserve for this purpose in 1795. New York and Virginia also had provisions for standing school funds before the passage of laws that set up their state systems. Although much educational support came from these funds, the tendency to rely on them probably retarded efforts to get real tax support.

One of the first education acts commonly passed by states was a provision that local districts might tax themselves to support schools if the people in the district agreed. Such a law was passed in Pennsylvania in 1834. Although no district was required to provide schools, more than half of the Pennsylvania districts did so. There was a great deal of opposition to school taxes in Pennsylvania, especially among Catholics and German-speaking farmers. Accordingly, the state senate voted repeal of the 1834 law, and it was expected that the house would agree. At this point, one of the most unusual developments in the history of American education took place. An appeal was made to Thaddeus Stevens to support the repeal. Instead, Stevens made one of the most eloquent appeals known for free public schools. He offered a substitute law that would strengthen the public schools rather than repeal their support. Stevens used the common man ideal, the need for equality, and the argument that public schools cost less than jails or welfare programs. Stevens was able to carry the day, and Pennsylvania accepted his substitute bill. Three years later, Massachusetts passed a school law that established the right to use tax money for public schools. Other states soon passed similar legislation.

Curriculum Improvement.   Changes in the curriculum came gradually. Development was slow partly because most states could not afford teacher education or schools that offered much beyond the basic *R*'s. English grammar and spelling gained a place in school programs in the early national period. In western frontier towns, spelling sometimes was stressed more than reading and writing. American history was offered in some form to boys and girls who remained in school beyond 3 years. Geography was introduced into many of the elementary schools before 1825. Arithmetic was much improved by the addition of new texts and materials, but many pupils were taught only addition and simple multiplication "to the rule of three." As in colonial schools, reading, grammar, spelling, and (later) history and geography were taught by the recitation method. In 1836, William Holmes McGuffey began to publish his readers; they sold over 120 million copies by 1920. These readers stressed individual virtue, literacy, hard work, and moral development. The readers—with the theme of "rugged individualism" and "*laissez-faire*" important to industrialists during the period—were used to indoctrinate pupils into a middle- and upper-class value system.

Graded Primary Schools.   Parents customarily taught their children to read and write before sending them to school; therefore, primary education was not considered the responsibility of the state. In Boston in 1818, primary schools were set up to take over this function. The schools were taught by women and eventually were consolidated with grammar and writing schools; this union led to the formation of the 8-year elementary school, a structure that is still prevalent in many areas today.

The start of a graded elementary school, though not uniform throughout, can be traced to 1818, when the Boston Primary School was organized into six classes, with the grammar or secondary school forming the seventh. In 1823, the grammar school was also divided into reading and writing sections. Many of the town schools had two rooms. Children were placed in the primary or the advanced room according to age. The person in charge of the older students was called the "principal teacher," a title that eventually led to an administrative distinction. The introduction of McGuffey's *Eclectic Readers* contributed to the grading movement as did the work of John D. Philbrick as principal of the Quincy Grammar School in Boston after 1848. Of course, many schools remained with no grades or divisions, especially in rural areas.

In 1850, 45 percent of the nation's youngsters attended school, and half of the states had established their school systems before the Civil War. Quality remained poor in most schools. The typical common elementary school of 1860 was a crowded one-room institution with poor lighting, bad ventilation, inadequate furniture, and no special equipment. The poorly educated and untrained teachers did not have a program to follow, and much of the time was spent in individual recitations. Severe discipline and corporal punishment stifled creativity and imagination. Nevertheless, schools were growing in number, and the principle of direct tax support for elementary education had been generally accepted.

BIRTH OF THE AMERICAN HIGH SCHOOL

Secondary education in the early national period consisted of the Latin grammar school, the academy, and the high school. Latin grammar schools were strictly for the preparation of the college-bound elite, and they charged high fees. Academies also charged tuition, although some had scholarships for poor students. A booming economy and the religious revival known as the Second Great Awakening contributed to the development of academies. Many were boarding schools that provided a protected moral environment for students. By 1860, there were 250,000 students enrolled in 6,000 academies. However, the middle and working classes made a growing demand for terminal secondary education with free tax support. Increasing urban growth and industrial expansion also contributed to the birth of the public high school.

In 1821, Boston opened the English Classical School and renamed it the English High School in 1824. This first American high school was established to meet the needs of boys who did not plan to attend college. Boys as young as age 12 were admitted by examination; however, very few poor or working-class youngsters were involved. English, mathematics, history, science, geography, philosophy, bookkeeping, and surveying were taught. Massachusetts passed a law in 1827 that required towns of 4,000 or more to create a high school, but not all towns complied.

At first, high schools grew slowly. There was competition from well-established academies and opposition to taxation for secondary schools. Still, the idea of a free secondary school or a "college for all the people" appealed to the middle class and grew in popularity. In 1826, Boston opened a female high school under the direction of Ebenezer Bailey. So many girls applied for admission that the school was closed for lack of funds. In 1855, Boston established another school for girls that included teacher training in a "normal" department.

There were no electives in these high schools. Students were expected to take all of the courses offered; however, there was a choice between an English, a classical, or a commercial curriculum. Entrance requirements and standardization of courses varied. There were arguments over whether high schools should be terminal institutions only. When the Civil War began, there were over 300 high schools, of which one-third were in Massachusetts.

HIGHER EDUCATION BEFORE THE CIVIL WAR

Except for the College of Philadelphia, all the colonial institutions of higher learning had been church related. In spite of efforts to make them democratic, most colleges remained sectarian and aristocratic. Classics, theology, and mathematics dominated their curricula. Control was vested with religious leaders and with the wealthy. Although it was possible to prepare for college in a low-cost academy and some students worked their way through college by teaching school during vacation periods, only a small fraction of the population attended college. A majority of the students were preparing for the ministry or for a life of leisure that their families could provide.

Dartmouth College Case.   The struggle over the question of public or private control of colleges came to a head with the Dartmouth College issue. Dartmouth had been founded through the efforts of Eleazar Wheelock, who was succeeded by his son John. A dominant figure, John Wheelock came into conflict with the college's trustees. In 1815, the board removed Wheelock from the presidency of Dartmouth; however, in 1816, the successful Jeffersonian Democrats converted Dartmouth into a state university and restored Wheelock. As a result, the students and faculty rebelled, and the trustees filed suit to recover the college. In 1818, the case reached the U.S. Supreme Court. John Marshall wrote the decision; it held that a private educational institution could not be taken over by a state against its will. This decision clearly established the right of private as well as state colleges to exist and to solicit gifts or grants for support.

State Universities.

State universities were chartered first where no institution of higher learning existed. They reflected the theory of the Enlightenment that education should promote social improvement and individual happiness. Georgia chartered its university in 1785 and opened it in 1800. North Carolina chartered its university in 1789, Vermont in 1791, and South Carolina in 1801. There was also Blount College in 1794, which later became the University of Tennessee. None of these colleges grew rapidly. They were state universities in name; however, all were under the control of a private board, and the curriculum included a large measure of classical studies.

New Programs and Reforms at State Universities.

The best known of the early state universities was that of Virginia, and Thomas Jefferson dominated it. There was a degree of academic freedom there: Professors could select their own textbooks, and they held tenure. The curriculum was also much more liberal than at other colleges. Jefferson called for professors of ancient languages, modern languages, mathematics, natural philosophy, natural history, medicine, moral philosophy, and law. This was the first attempt to include such professional studies as law and medicine in a university program, and the students could select (or elect) the program they wished to follow. In September 1825, there were over 100 students attending the University of Virginia.

While the new program at Virginia was getting underway, an effort was made to reform Harvard. George Ticknor, a professor of modern languages, proposed a series of changes based upon European universities that he had visited. Among his reforms were the departmentalization of the university, strict examinations, teaching by the lecture method, and student election of some subjects. These reforms would have created a university similar to those of Germany, which had very high standards of scholarship. The reforms were unpopular with faculty members, and Ticknor was forced to resign in 1835. Resistance to change was also demonstrated by the Yale Report of 1828. This report placed stress on the status quo, emphasizing classical languages and theology as a means of gaining discipline over the mind. It put little faith in science and held that the foundation of a superior education is grounded in traditional subjects. The Yale Report called for recitations rather than lectures and placed stress on the "superintendence" of the faculty over all student activities. It supported the idea that traditional studies are a good foundation for all vocations, including the learned professions. The Yale Report was a clear statement of the conservatism that continued to dominate most colleges until after the Civil War.

In addition to Harvard and Virginia, Union College in New York and Brown University began using the elective system. The major growth in higher education before 1860 was in the private and denominational colleges. Private and church-related colleges accepted the principles of the Yale Report and rejected the elective system. In 1810, there were about 30 private colleges and more than 50 in 1830. Eastern missionaries were especially active, founding colleges in western states like Ohio, Indiana, and Illinois. After the sponsorship of the Society for Promotion of Collegiate and Theological Education in the West, which united Presbyterian and Congregationalist efforts, even more western denominational colleges were established. Methodists were also active. Many graduates of Princeton and Yale believed that creating new colleges was a way of reforming society and expressing religious beliefs. There were 182 American colleges in operation before the Civil War, although some of these offered only secondary instruction. Many of them ceased to exist before 1900.

State universities were also set up in the areas of westward expansion before 1861. In 1837, the University of Michigan was authorized to begin offering literary, scientific, and practical courses; there was also a branch for the education of primary school teachers. Indiana, Kentucky, Missouri, Mississippi, Iowa, Wisconsin, Minnesota, Louisiana, and California chartered their state universities prior to 1860. Many of these institutions did not reach university status until later.

Technical Schools.   Technical and scientific education began to increase with the foundation of the Rensselaer Polytechnic Institute in 1824. The Lawrence Scientific School at Harvard opened in 1847, and Yale created the Sheffield Scientific School in 1852. There was a great demand for people trained in scientific and engineering skills long before most universities developed professional schools. West Point–educated engineers were too few to meet the need, and there were no universities where one could study agriculture. By 1850, there was considerable pressure for the establishment of scientific, agricultural, and engineering colleges.

Adult Education and Cultural Improvement.   An adult education movement developing during the early part of the nineteenth century gave considerable attention to public schools as well as the educational improvement of older citizens. In 1826, Josiah Holbrook of Massachusetts organized the first lyceum, or association of men and women for cultural advancement. By 1832, a national lyceum movement had been organized for the improvement of useful knowledge and the advancement of public schools. Lyceums especially encouraged female teachers and invited them to participate in local educational movements for better support of and higher quality in common schools. Lyceum meetings were similar to county institutes. The nonsectarian character of the lyceum provided common ground for persons of divergent religious persuasion to discuss educational matters.

Other literary and cultural activities helped to give indirect leadership to the school cause. Ralph Waldo Emerson and Walt Whitman idealized the common man. Transcendentalism supported raising the educational level of the whole people as a means of social improvement. Newspaper editorials and publications of workingmen's

societies, such as the *Mechanics' Free Press*, continued to urge free schools throughout the nation.

Morrill Act.   In 1857, Justin Morrill, a congressman from Vermont, offered a bill
for the grant of public lands to the states for colleges that would teach agriculture and
the mechanical arts. The precedent of federal land grants of large size for schools and
colleges had been established by the Ordinance of 1785. Morrill had the support of
the farm interests in the South and West, but there was fear concerning the federal
control of education. The Senate passed the bill, but President Buchanan vetoed it.
Congress passed it again when Lincoln became president, and it became law in 1862.

The Morrill Act granted each state 30,000 acres of public land for each senator
and representative it had in Congress. The land was to be used for the endowment
and maintenance of at least one college in each state for the teaching of agriculture and the mechanical arts. Military science and tactics were also required, but the
states retained control of the administration of the colleges and the remainder of the
curriculum. Some states used the money to develop existing colleges; others created
new agricultural and mechanical universities. The actual building of these state institutions did not occur until after the war years. Congress made a number of supple-
mentary cash grants to these colleges in later years (Figure 5.2).

AMERICAN EDUCATIONAL LEADERSHIP

Political Leaders.   Political support for educational reform came from many
parts of society. De Witt Clinton of New York was a political leader who showed
great interest in educational matters. He often urged that the legislature establish tax-
supported common schools and institutions for teacher training. In 1827, Clinton was
largely responsible for creating a fund for aiding academies and promoting teacher
education. He promoted the creation of the first office of superintendent of schools
in New York, to which Gideon Hawley was appointed in 1812.

Governor Wolf of Pennsylvania charged in 1833 that his state had failed to meet
the constitutional demand that required the legislature to provide poor children
with free education. Thaddeus Stevens helped put Pennsylvania at the forefront of
the fight for common schools. Archibald Murphy in North Carolina, Calvin Stowe in
Ohio, and Edward Coles in Illinois called for complete educational programs in
their states. Governors and influential political leaders in all parts of the nation
attempted to persuade the various legislatures to pass school laws and provide tax
support. Of course, there was opposition and not many political figures had the
success of Horace Mann and Henry Barnard, but many were trying.

Literary Support.   Barnard's Connecticut *Common School Journal,* William Russell's *American Journal of Education,* and the *Academician,* all of which appeared in
1818, are examples of early educational journals that aided the common school cause.
The mission of the Western Literary Institute was to create favorable public opinion
for free schools, according to John Prickett, who founded the organization in 1831.

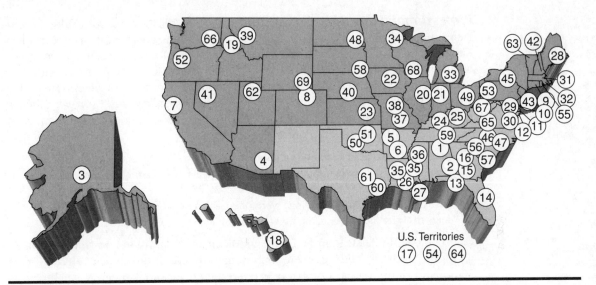

FIGURE 5.2 Land Grant Universities as Designated by State Legislatures

1. Alabama A&M University
2. Auburn University
3. University of Alaska
4. Arizona State University
5. University of Arkansas, Fayetteville
6. University of Arkansas, Pine Bluff
7. University of California
8. Colorado State University
9. University of Connecticut
10. University of Delaware
11. Delaware State College
12. University of the District of Columbia
13. Florida A&M University
14. University of Florida
15. Fort Valley State College
16. University of Georgia
17. University of Guam
18. University of Hawaii
19. University of Idaho
20. University of Illinois
21. Purdue University
22. Iowa State University
23. Kansas State University
24. Kentucky State University

25. University of Kentucky
26. Louisiana State University
27. Southern University
28. University of Maine
29. University of Maryland
30. University of Maryland, Eastern Shore
31. Massachusetts Institute of Technology
32. University of Massachusetts
33. Michigan State University
34. University of Minnesota
35. Alcorn State University
36. Mississippi State University
37. Lincoln University
38. University of Missouri
39. Montana State University
40. University of Nebraska
41. University of Nevada, Reno
42. University of New Hampshire
43. Rutgers, The State University of New Jersey
44. New Mexico State University
45. Cornell University
46. North Carolina A&T State University

47. North Carolina State University
48. North Dakota State University
49. Ohio State University
50. Langston University
51. Oklahoma State University
52. Oregon State University
53. Pennsylvania State University
54. University of Puerto Rico
55. University of Rhode Island
56. Clemson University
57. South Carolina State College
58. South Dakota State University
59. Tennessee State University
60. Prairie View A&M University
61. Texas A&M University
62. Utah State University
63. University of Vermont
64. University of the Virgin Islands
65. Virginia Polytechnic Institute & State University
66. Washington State University
67. West Virginia University
68. University of Wisconsin-Madison
69. University of Wyoming

Source: Information from Robert O'Neil, Chairman. *Factbook.* Washington. DC: National Association of Land Grant Colleges, 1989, pp. 39–41.

Professional Educators.   Cyrus Peirce, Samuel Hall, Edward Sheldon, and Henry Barnard pioneered the normal school movement. Sheldon, the school superintendent in Oswego, New York, implemented Pestalozzi's educational concepts in the United States. Catherine Beecher, Emma Hart Willard (founder of the Troy Female Seminary), and Mary Lyon were among the promoters of education for women. In 1962, Frederick Rudolph, in *The American College and University*, identified historical challenges to women's education. He wrote of the fears of men, such as Reverend John Todd, who dreaded coeducation:

> Must we crowd education on our daughters, and for the sake of having them "intellectuals" make them puny, nervous, and their whole earthly existence a struggle between life and death?
>
> Early female college buildings were often only two stories, since there were fears that any more stair climbing would completely unsex women! (p. 360)

Caleb Mills in Indiana, John D. Pierce in Michigan, Calvin Wiley in North Carolina, and John Swett in California were important early educators. James Carter, Horace Mann, and Henry Barnard probably exerted the greatest influence.

Carter.   James G. Carter (1795–1845) was a pioneer educational reformer who worked his way through Harvard University by teaching in the Massachusetts district schools. He is often called the "father" of the Massachusetts school system and of normal schools. Carter was largely responsible for the passage of the Massachusetts school law of 1827; the law provided for public secondary schools in that state. He made an effort to influence Massachusetts to establish public normal schools for the training of common school teachers, and he helped to set up the state board of education in 1837. Carter wrote essays on popular education in which he attacked the antidemocratic character of the private schools that existed in the early national period. He feared that private education, and especially private academies, would give rise to a differentiation between the classes of citizens, a differentiation that would be detrimental to America. Hence, in addition to his direct work with the schools—work that included not only his efforts to pass school laws but also some personal experiments with private schools—Carter contributed vastly to the belief in democratic education for all people without regard for social class or wealth.

Mann.   Horace Mann (1796–1859) was perhaps the best known of the important leaders in developing the American public school system. Mann worked with Carter to persuade the Commonwealth of Massachusetts to establish a board of education; then he resigned from the legislature in order to become secretary of that board. During his 12 years as secretary, he was the country's most active leader of the movement for common school education. The *Common School Journal*, of which Mann was editor, was circulated throughout the nation and in foreign lands as well. Mann often received letters from educational reformers and others interested in schools beyond their own states, and he gave many lectures and made public appearances in the cause of education. Mann became the acknowledged leader in American school organization, and he created a revival in Massachusetts that spread throughout the land.

The 12 annual reports published during his period as secretary of the board contained much information about how the schools could be improved. Mann was an enemy of the old district schools of Massachusetts, and he believed that education should be little influenced by private or religious societies. He succeeded in obtaining the support of the state legislature for liberal taxation, which increased educational opportunities through new buildings and better salaries for teachers. From 1839 to 1840, Mann organized three of the first normal schools in the country. He also created 50 new high schools and had a marked effect on increased attendance in public schools at all levels. He worked, too, for improvement of teaching methods and for a better curriculum for the common schools. He attempted to use the schools to improve social conditions as well as to provide an opportunity for those who were on the bottom of the economic order.

Mann's work was so respected that his influence was very great throughout the United States. His system for Massachusetts was widely copied as the development of common schools and high schools progressed in the rest of the nation.

Barnard.   Henry Barnard (1811–1900) played a role in Connecticut and Rhode Island that was similar to the role played by Mann in Massachusetts. He was secretary of the board of education in Connecticut, principal of a normal school there, and beginning in 1845, the state superintendent of Rhode Island. Barnard's major contribution came through his editorship of educational publications, particularly the *American Journal of Education,* published between 1855 and 1881. Barnard initiated the teacher's institute movement in 1839 and became a popular disseminator of information about better schools. As a member of the Connecticut legislature, in 1838, he sponsored a successful law similar to the Massachusetts bill of 1837, which created a state school board. He became the first secretary of the board of education and stirred much interest in education, although the legislature soon abolished his office.

Next, Barnard moved to Rhode Island. There, after a two-year campaign to awaken the citizens to the problems of the schools, he managed to get a law passed creating public schools and served as commissioner until 1849. Connecticut made some efforts to reverse its previous error in firing Barnard by setting up a normal school and inviting him to be its principal. He held both positions for a number of years, and during this time he also produced many letters, articles, and educational studies. Barnard was also chancellor at the University of Wisconsin, president of St. John's College at Annapolis, and the first U.S. commissioner of education from 1867 to 1870. His greatest success lay in democratic philosophy and his ability to rouse public interest through the dissemination of information about education. Barnard is sometimes called the "father of American school administration," as well as the founder of American educational journalism.

EUROPEAN INFLUENCES

Although it is true that American education was formed and molded by many factors that were uniquely American, the importance of transplanted European movements should not be underestimated. In the period from 1810 to 1865, the influence of European ideas was quite evident in the evolution of American preschool institutions.

Infant Schools.   The infant school of England, originated by Robert Owen and modified by Samuel Wilderspin, ministered to toddlers from the age of three. Owen's version encompassed a sort of informal education centered around health, physical training, and spontaneous activity. Wilderspin defined the school's function in more traditional terms, and his schools have been described as "intellectual packing-houses." In 1818, Boston made provisions for the first American infant school, with an allocation of $5,000. Dubbed the "primary school," this institution catered to children who had attained their fourth birthday. Within a decade, similar schools had sprouted in New York, Philadelphia, and Providence. Both originators influenced the American infant school, or primary school, but the Wilderspin format enjoyed the greatest development.

By midcentury, the primary school had been absorbed into the common elementary schools. Infant schools were started to help the children of poor factory workers, but they did not satisfy the demand for free public schools.

Kindergartens.   European educators instituted the kindergarten as the proper foundation for education. The "garden of children" nurtured growth with the concept of activity, accenting the importance of play, songs, and stories. Froebel's educational ideas formed a complex and sophisticated philosophical position, but the kindergarten movement in America only encompassed the outward manifestations of his theory. Strangely enough, the kindergarten met with stern resistance in Froebel's homeland of Germany; its greatest development was in the United States. In the midst of a wave of German immigration following the Prussian Revolution in 1848, Margarethe Meyer Schurz, a former pupil of Froebel, established the first American kindergarten. Formed in Watertown, Wisconsin, in 1856, Mrs. Schurz's school was really a German kindergarten on American soil, with German language as the means of communication. Elizabeth Peabody, who in 1860 established in Boston the first English-speaking kindergarten, considerably fostered the growth of American kindergartens. In 1873, the kindergarten was brought into the realm of the public schools, because of the efforts of Superintendent William T. Harris in St. Louis, with the assistance of Susan E. Blow, who published *Educational Issues in the Kindergarten* in 1908. The movement was expanded in the private arena with contributions of philanthropic societies. In the early years, kindergartens served children from ages three to seven. By the 1970s, they served ages three to five and were found throughout America.

The kindergarten has become a stable part of the modern educational system, with more than 90 percent of America's five-year-olds enrolled. Many of the ideas made operational by the progressives in the twentieth century trace their roots to Froebel and the kindergarten.

European School Model.   If the American schools were not altogether adequate, there was at least an awareness that better programs for education were available in other parts of the world. The influence of reports on European education can hardly be overemphasized, and the most influential of the lot was by Victor Cousin. His detailed monograph on Prussian schools was first published in 1831 and translated into English in 1834. It was widely circulated in America, and its impact can be judged from the fact that shortly after it gained prominence, a number of important educators journeyed to Europe with the intent of studying the European systems and Prussia's in particular. Calvin Stowe's visit resulted in his treatise, *Elementary Education in Europe* (1837). Mann made the trip in 1843 and gathered material for his famous *Seventh Annual Report to the Massachusetts Board of Education*. Although he disapproved of Prussian purposes, Mann found great merit in their efficient methods, universality, high-quality buildings, broad curriculum, and significantly effective teacher training. Almost all the American educators who had an opportunity to visit schools on the European mainland returned with favorable impressions. They used German or Prussian schools as a model for making the American educational program more uniform and efficient.

European Educational Theory.   Although some of the advances made in European schools were the result of national or political forces, there was also a new philosophic basis for change. In addition to Comenius and Locke (discussed in Chapter 4), major educational concepts were developed by Jean-Jacques Rousseau (1712–1778), Johann Basedow (1734–1790), Johann H. Pestalozzi (1746–1827), Johann Herbart (1776–1841), and Friedrich Froebel (1782–1852).

Rousseau.   Rousseau was a critic of conventional civilization, which he viewed as depraved and artificial. Rejecting the doctrine of original sin, he held that the basic nature of man is good and only social institutions—such as governments, churches, and schools—cause evil. Rousseau demanded a return to nature and an opportunity for the child to pass through natural stages of development without being molded by degenerate social forces.

Although better known for his *Social Contract,* Rousseau's *Émile* became a major educational classic. In it, he advocated emotional, intellectual, and educational freedom for children. Distrusting books and standard pedagogical techniques of his day, Rousseau believed that children should learn directly from experience. Thus, physical activity, field trips, learning by doing (including manual or vocational experiences), freedom to pursue natural interests, and play were advocated as means for developing the latent potentialities of the child. Rousseau suggested that people be aware of "negative education," by which he meant protecting the student from the influences of superficial social institutions. Rousseau's attack on formalism and support for natural interests had little direct influence on American education until the period of John Dewey and the progressive educators. However, his effect on European educators and schools had an indirect bearing on American schools at an earlier date.

Basedow.   The German educator Johann Basedow attempted to put many of Rousseau's ideas into operation in his Philanthropinum. This school was open to all students, regardless of wealth or class. It stressed natural development, teaching through conversation and sense experience, play, physical activity, and object lessons. Basedow included health, sex education, vocational training, and "world citizenship" in his curriculum. He wrote *Elementary Work*, a book on his theories, and he advocated teacher training. One of the teachers at the Philanthropinum, Christian Salzmann, later created his own school. Salzmann required his students to learn gardening, pursue gymnastics, and develop vocational skills; but there was also time for play, nature study, and formal classes. Other disciples of Basedow, such as J. H. Campe and Johann Guts-Muths, developed German children's literature and the physical education program for the German states.

Pestalozzi.   The Swiss educator Johann H. Pestalozzi experimented with some of the more practical ideas of Rousseau's *Émile* and applied many of his own theories as well. Pestalozzi's major books included *Leonard and Gertrude, How Gertrude Teaches Her Children, Book for Mothers*, and the *Evening Hours of the Hermit*. Pestalozzi conducted schools at Neuhof, Stanz, Burgdorf, Hofwyl, and Yverdon. Starting with his own son's education, about which he kept a careful diary of observations, Pestalozzi developed educational programs for impoverished children and methods that were useful for teaching the children of the common people.

Pestalozzi looked upon the child's mind as a union of separate moral, physical, and intellectual faculties. He believed that education was the natural, progressive, and harmonious development of the natural faculties and powers. He trusted children's natural instincts and thought they should provide the motives for learning. Instead of threats and corporal punishment, Pestalozzi believed that cooperation and sympathy could produce discipline in a homelike atmosphere. He saw education as a mutual effort by the student and the teacher, an effort that produced mutual respect. Like Rousseau, Pestalozzi believed that the child unfolds or develops through various natural stages, according to the principle of growth. He thought that sense impressions were the foundation of all knowledge. Pestalozzi wanted to develop each child's potential to the maximum, and therefore spoke of educating the "hand and the heart" as well as the "head." Moral education and vocational training were just as important to Pestalozzi as intellectual subjects.

For Pestalozzi, education was based on actual observations rather than on books and theories. He relied on object lessons to develop the child's senses of sight, touch, and sound. Plants, animals, music, tools, and the natural environment were important in his education. Unlike the earliest sense realists, he did not view the mind as a passive receptor of sense impressions. He insisted that the mind is active in perceiving, analyzing, and selecting. Pestalozzi believed that society could be improved through adequate educational opportunity for all. Teachers from all over Europe came to observe his methods, and Pestalozzi offered them training. He believed that the basis for teaching should be close observation of children's attitudes and activities.

In England, Charles Mayo made the ideas of Pestalozzi popular. American followers included Joseph Neef, who wrote *Methods of Instruction*, and Edward Sheldon, who created the Oswego movement (see Chapter 6).

Froebel.   Since the advent of the kindergarten, educational leaders have been much influenced by Friedrich Froebel's theories concerning education of the very young. Froebel became a follower of Pestalozzi while teaching at a small private school at Frankfurt, Germany. In 1816, he opened a school of his own, and 6 years later published *The Education of Man*. At Blankenburg, Froebel finally was able to establish his educational institution offering programs for children between the ages of three and eight. (The German term for his school was *Kleinkinderbeschaftingung-sanstalt;* that term was later reduced to *kindergarten*.)

Froebel was basically an idealist who looked upon the child as the agency for the realization of God's will in human nature. A mystic, Froebel believed that the spirit of the child could be linked with the absolute through the unity of experience and divine nature. From a practical standpoint, the significance of Froebel was in his conception of the educative process as something that must begin with a child of three or four years of age. Early childhood educational activities centering on play, music, and physical activity made him famous. Froebel created new respect for children, especially for their individuality and for the dynamic and active qualities of their nature. Froebel's program supported constructive use of objects, storytelling, and cooperative social activities. Children were free to express themselves and to build good relationships with others in the kindergarten. Although later educators often disagreed with Froebel's mystical concepts, his efforts to create early childhood education had a profound effect. Froebel greatly influenced both Maria Montessori and John Dewey.

Growth of Academies.   The Age of the Common School Revival was also a time of expansion for academies. Those that developed in colonial times were terminal private-venture schools with practical programs. Many of those in operation before the Civil War offered college preparatory courses. Some were denominational; a local board or city government governed others. Most academies charged tuition, but several enjoyed some sort of private endowment as well. Various schemes for public support of academies were tried, and a large number did benefit from some degree of public finance. The curriculum of the academy was never fixed; many offered a wide range of courses. Reading, writing, grammar, arithmetic, and higher mathematics were usually offered. Chemistry, botany, mineralogy, logic, moral philosophy, and natural science were sometimes in the program. Many academies offered modern languages and music. Some claimed to prepare students for teaching and other professions. A large number of academies admitted girls, and some were designated as "female seminaries" or schools for girls only. After 1860, academies declined in number, largely because of the vast increase in public high schools. The census of 1850 numbered 6,085 private schools and academies in the United States. New York had over 800 incorporated academies. Both Ohio and Virginia chartered more than 200 before 1860. The majority were located in eastern states, but there were frontier academies in newly settled regions as well. Many academies closed after a few months because of lack of support. Some were only elementary schools, and others were largely vocational. However, most American communities had access to some sort of academy for those who could afford tuition.

Normal Schools and Institutes.

Private academies for the training of teachers did not satisfy educational leaders like Mann, Barnard, and the Reverend Charles Brooks. Brooks began a campaign for state normal schools in Massachusetts in 1835, using the Prussian model of teacher education as a guide. Brooks had some influence on the school board; in 1838, when Edmund Dwight offered $10,000 for educational improvement, three normal schools were founded. The state matched Dwight's grant and used the funds for salaries and operating expenses of the teacher-training institutions. In 1846, the normal school at Bridgewater got its own build-ing. The term *normal school* came from the model or practice school in which the standard or normal curriculum and methods were observed. Cyrus Peirce, the first principal of the normal school at Lexington, stressed the review of common subjects and practice teaching under his own observation.

New York created a state normal school at Albany in 1844, but state money was also used to subsidize private academies for teachers. David Page, a principal at Albany, wrote *Theory and Practice of Teaching*; the book became a standard text for teacher education. Only 12 normal schools were created in the United States before the Civil War. Many districts were satisfied with the untrained young ladies they hired as elementary teachers.

Henry Barnard started the teacher's institute. This was a meeting of a group of teachers for instruction; it usually lasted only a few weeks. County superintendents of schools often conducted institutes for teachers in summer months. A similar effort was made by the National Education Association (NEA) Teacher Center, which was popular in the 1870s.

Educational Opportunity for Women.

The growth of academies provided a much greater opportunity for secondary and higher education for women. A few girls' schools in colonial times offered courses in ornamental needlework, polite manners, music, French, and other subjects deemed proper for females. Many of the academies in operation before 1860 expanded the curriculum. There was some op-position to teaching girls Latin, logic, and the sciences, but all other courses were of-fered in at least some of the schools for girls. Coeducation was rare; most academies admitted one sex or the other, but not both. Employment of male teachers only, except in the dame schools, ended during the early national period. Horace Mann and other educational leaders encouraged women to teach in elementary schools. It became common for many academies to offer courses in "schoolkeeping" for girls. Preparation of common school teachers was largely confined to a review of the com-mon branches and a series of highly moralistic lectures on the "duties" of teachers; however, it was often the only teacher training available. Samuel Hall's *Lectures on Schoolkeeping* was the basic text for teacher training until normal schools such as Edward Sheldon's opened in 1853 in Oswego, New York.

FOCUS ON THE ISSUES

Opportunities for Women

Women in modern tribal cultures and the more traditional Islamic states do not enjoy the degree of equality and freedom they have in the United States. Emerging female equality in China, Indonesia, and Russia has not yet reached American levels. In this nation we are not surprised to see female army officers, airline pilots, business executives, or medical doctors, although men are still more numerous in these fields. Historically, however, women were regulated and forced to accept subservient roles. In colonial and early national America, females could not own property, vote, engage in litigation, or make public statements without the permission of their fathers or husbands. Work outside the home was long forbidden to women. The first professional positions open to them were elementary teaching and nursing. Female teachers in the nineteenth century were not allowed to date, marry, travel alone, drink alcohol, or smoke. They could be fired for any "inappropriate" behavior or for failure to attend church regularly. When girls were admitted to secondary schools, male authorities decided that physical education would be bad for future childbearing and that subjects like science and mathematics were too stressful for the delicate female brain. The long struggle of Susan Anthony and Elizabeth Stanton to give women rights over their own children and suffrage shows how stubborn male resistance to female emancipation can be. Law, management, engineering, and medicine remained male-only occupations until after World War I. This author recalls a local citizen wanting to speak to the high school principal about 30 years ago. The principal, an attractive female in her late twenties, was taken by the man to be a secretary and he demanded to see the principal when "HE" arrived. In spite of the voting rights, women in the highest professional roles, and equality of educational opportunity, there remains a perception of male domination. This may account for the militant feminist movement and many incidents of sexual harassment. But times are changing. Asked to write a poem, a third-grade girl from Bend, Oregon, came up with this:

> *Girls go to college to get more knowledge.*
> *Boys go to Jupiter and just get stupider.*

Obviously, she was not buying into the idea of male superiority.

What Do You Think?
1. The proliferation of sports for both sexes has gone a long way toward equality. Have other parts of the curriculum kept pace with sports?
2. Female elementary principals outnumber those who are male, but there are still more male secondary principals and superintendents. Is this just a lag or a reflection of public attitude?
3. How does the worldwide lack of equal rights for women affect American schools?

Catherine Beecher, Mary Lyon, Almira Phelps, and Emma Willard were leaders in the movement for girls' secondary education. In 1821, Mrs. Willard opened the Troy Female Seminary, and Mary Lyon founded Mt. Holyoke Female Seminary in 1837. Catherine Beecher founded the American Women's Education Association, and Almira Phelps wrote a series of *Lectures to Young Ladies*. The efforts of these female educators helped to establish the first coeducational college program at Oberlin in 1838.

Polly Welts Kaufman, in *Women Teachers on the Frontier,* wrote about women sent by the National Board of Popular Education in the decades before the Civil War to teach in the South and West. Some 600 women were sent to teach in Missouri, Ohio, Indiana, and other western and southern states. Many remained and settled in the West. The board accepted only those women who could prove membership in an evangelical church as well as tell about their conversion experiences. Reasons for women choosing to leave their homes in the East included better job opportunities, adventure, and missionary zeal. Their curriculum included Bible readings, singing programs as advocated by Horace Mann, and instilling high ideals in their pupils. Although teachers' salaries have improved in recent years, one may still find a gap in teacher salaries between men and women. The perception of women teachers' worth was expressed in an 1855 *Annual Report of the School Committee of Concord, Massachusetts*. According to the report, town officials found that students improved more when female teachers rather than male teachers taught them.

> Sure, this being the fact, it is not good economy to employ a man to teach those
> Schools, when the services of a woman of the best qualifications, can be obtained
> for two-thirds or three-fourths the expense. (Kaufman, 1984)

Minority Education.   Very little progress was made in providing educational opportunity for minority children before 1861. Early schools that had been established for Native American children by missionaries were largely unsuccessful because the teachers misunderstood Native American culture and attitudes. An occasional student learned to read English, but formal schooling was almost nonexistent for the Native American population.

In the colonial period, many slave owners permitted blacks to read. Some felt it was their duty to teach slaves something about the Bible and the tenets of religion. A few free blacks made their way into Quaker schools in the North, which were open to all. In 1833, a Quaker teacher named Prudence Crandall was criticized for admitting black girls to her school in Connecticut. In 1846, Benjamin Roberts of Boston filed suit because his son was forced to attend a segregated school for black boys. The Massachusetts Supreme Court held that the school committees had a right to keep schools segregated. However, by 1857, Massachusetts passed a law preventing discrimination. The school laws in most states before the Civil War did not provide for black scholars. Those of Indiana and Illinois specifically required schools for white children.

Even in the South, blacks were occasionally educated. John Chavis was a teacher and a licensed Presbyterian minister before North Carolina passed a law against black preachers in 1832. Most southern states prohibited the teaching of blacks after Nat Turner's rebellion of 1831.

THEN TO NOW

Assimilation.   The Age of the Common School Revival was a period in which equality of educational opportunity was stressed. Horace Mann was a great champion of education for all. He and Henry Barnard believed that the schools had the power to unite the United States into an integrated national community. Economic, social, racial, ethnic, and religious diversity were to be subsumed under one democratic system of education that would unite all the people into a single indivisible nation. Education was to be used as the chief instrument for assimilating the foreign born into the mainstream of American life and culture.

Schools did have a considerable measure of success in creating a single culture. Some 35 million immigrants came to America in the nineteenth century, and they were Americanized largely by the public schools.

Equality Not Gained. Still, the aim of Mann and Barnard to achieve equality and social integration was not fully realized. Contemporary concerns about equality for ethnic groups and blacks are clear indications that the melting pot ideal has not been fulfilled. Rather, an appreciation for the richness of a cultural mosaic is emerging. Mann also wanted to move away from the extreme differences between rich and poor. He believed that a strong nation must provide opportunity for all and that differences between the haves and the have-nots must be reduced. Although many Americans have achieved affluence in the modern era, there are still many who are poor or the victims of discrimination.

Black education in the South was almost nonexistent before the Civil War and very limited in northern states. President Lincoln liberated about four million slaves, almost all of them illiterate. The Fourteenth Amendment (ratified in 1868) specified that states should not deprive any person of life, liberty, or property without due process of law. Nevertheless, blacks remained second-class citizens. Jim Crow laws of the 1880s were passed to "keep the Colored in their place" (Sandifer, 1969), and discrimination was universally practiced.

The separate but equal doctrine of *Plessy v. Ferguson* in 1896 legalized racial segregation until 1954. Private black colleges and those created by the Second Morrill Act helped to improve the quality of teachers; however, black schools lacked funds, and the extreme poverty of the people made progress very slow. States claimed to provide equal support for black and white schools, but many actually put more dollars into education for the majority race (Figure 5.3).

Desegregation. This difficulty has not been resolved in the modern era. An end to legal segregation and plans for achieving racial balance in school systems have had considerable impact, but problems remain. Many American cities are still segregated *de facto*. This situation is not improving in many areas that are becoming almost totally populated by one race or ethnic group. Affluent blacks (and other minorities) who represent the professions or the middle class have little difficulty in assimilating with white society. Integration in schools works well when all the students come from a similar socioeconomic background. However, there are major problems when black children from urban slums are placed in classrooms with students from more affluent families. The issue is especially clear when busing is used as a means of bringing together students from different races, ethnic groups, and socioeconomic backgrounds. Demographic patterns in many large cities are shifting so rapidly that efforts to integrate schools are frustrated. Atlanta, Houston, Washington, DC, and

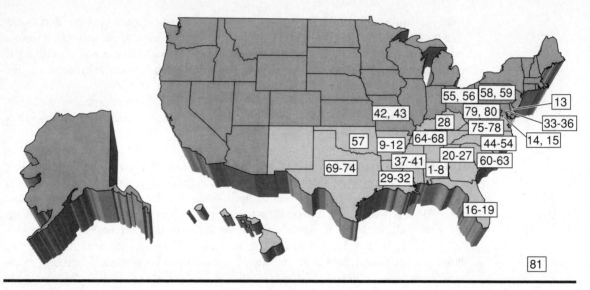

1. Alabama A&M University
2. Alabama State University
3. Concordia College
4. Miles College
5. Oakwood College
6. Stillman College
7. Talladega College
8. Tuskegee University
9. Arkansas Baptist College
10. Philander Smith College
11. Shorter College
12. University of Arkansas, Pine Bluff
13. Delaware State University
14. Howard University
15. University of the District of Columbia
16. Bethune-Cookman College
17. Edward Waters College
18. Florida A&M University
19. Florida Memorial College
20. Albany State College
21. Clark Atlanta University
22. Fort Valley State College
23. Morehouse College
24. Morris Brown College
25. Paine College
26. Savannah State College
27. Spelman College
28. Kentucky State University

29. Dillard University
30. Grambling State University
31. Southern University
32. Xavier University of Louisiana
33. Bowie State University
34. Coppin State College
35. Morgan State University
36. University of Maryland: Eastern Shore
37. Alcorn State University
38. Jackson State University
39. Mississippi Valley State University
40. Rust College
41. Tougaloo College
42. Harris Stowe State College
43. Lincoln University
44. Barber-Scotia College
45. Bennett College
46. Elizabeth City State University
47. Fayetteville State University
48. Johnson C. Smith University
49. Livingstone College
50. North Carolina A&T State University
51. North Carolina Central University
52. St. Augustine's College
53. Shaw University
54. Winston-Salem State University

55. Central State University
56. Wilberforce University
57. Langston University
58. Cheyney University of Pennsylvania
59. Lincoln University
60. Benedict College
61. Chaflin College
62. South Carolina State University
63. Voorhees College
64. Fisk University
65. Knoxville College
66. Lane College
67. LeMoyne-Owen College
68. Tennessee State University
69. Huston-Tillotson College
70. Paul Quinn College
71. Prairieview A&M University
72. Texas College
73. Texas Southern University
74. Wiley College
75. Hampton University
76. Norfolk State University
77. St. Paul's College
78. Virginia State University
79. Bluefield State College
80. West Virginia State College
81. University of the Virgin Islands

Figure 5.3   Colleges and Universities with Large Black Enrollment (60 percent to 98 percent)

Source: Information from the Editors of the *Chronicle of Higher Education, the Almanac of Higher Education II.* University of Chicago Press, 1995, pp. 321–390. (Figures complied by the U.S. Department of Education.) Additional information (and update to 2005) is available from the National Education Data Resource Center (NEDRC).

Newark are cities that experienced dramatic increases in the number of minority students just when they began to implement plans for desegregation. Federal judges have recently approved unitary status for school districts under desegregation orders on the basis of good-faith efforts to assure equity and access for minorities as well as changing population patterns. Multiracial and multicultural population growth has resulted in an increase in majority–minority communities.

Desegregation efforts are illustrated by the Little Rock, Arkansas, school districts, which are under federal court–approved desegregation plans. Ann S. Marshall, former federal monitor for the Federal District Court in the Pulaski County, Arkansas, school district, reported that in 1993 the three districts of the system—Little Rock, North Little Rock, and Pulaski County—had a racial black–white enrollment of approximately 60–40, 50–50, and 30–70, respectively. The districts created magnet schools that sought to draw more students from throughout the district, but the end result was the proportions noted. In 1999–2000, there were five racially identifiable schools, some of which continue. These were schools with such a high black enrollment that they were designated double-funded incentive schools. The double funding was designed to compensate for the racially isolated environment and to provide an incentive for white students to transfer to these schools. The incentive funding has ceased. By 2009–2010 the racial black–white balance of the districts was 59–33, 67–22, and 44–56 with five incentive schools in operation.

In 1995, the District Court withdrew its monitoring and supervision of North Little Rock School District in the area of student assignments, but enrollment trends continue to be published because enrollment and racial balance in the district remain a factor in majority-to-minority transfers and in the proportion of students eligible for magnet school enrollment. A 2000 Pulaski County Special School District plan included requiring yearly reporting on one-race classes, as well as studying disciplinary practices with African American students, particularly male students at the secondary level. The court granted the Little Rock district partial unitary status. The case filed in 1982 continued, as a federal court judge in 2004 ordered continuation of court monitoring for at least two years. On February 23, 2007, the Little Rock School District was granted unitary status and is no longer under court supervision.

The Immigration Effect.   Demographic studies indicate the United States will be a majority–minority population by 2050. The dominant groups will be Hispanics and Asian Americans, with Caucasians a minority. Penny Loeb and colleagues, in an article entitled "To Make a Nation" (1993), notes that in the 1980s, over 8.6 million newcomers, mainly from Asia, Latin America, and the Caribbean—the greatest influx since the 1920s—came to the United States. Although all parts of the country were influenced by an increase of 63 percent between 1980 and the 1990s over the previous decade, most foreign-born arrivals settled in five states—California, New York, Texas, Florida, and New Jersey. Currently the influx of Hispanics in the South has created a challenge for school administrators. Hispanic populations in Arkansas, Georgia, and North Carolina have soared. There is an urgent need for school funding for the population influx as well as for teachers who speak Spanish. Some groups are calling for immigrant restriction and reduction, while businesses require entry-level workers to take jobs others do not want. In some school districts where blacks were formerly in the majority, African American board members are concerned with the growing Latino population (Jordan, 2004). With a major recession in 2010, there has been a decline in immigration and a tightened national policy for illegal immigration. Arizona passed a law requiring immigrations to carry registration documents at all times. The federal government justice department has brought lawsuit to challenge Arizona law and affirm federal government authority in immigration policy (Meissner, Doris and Ziglar, James W, 2010). In the first three months of 2010, more than 1,180 bills and resolutions related to immigrants and refugees were introduced in state legislatures and border enforcement has been tightened ("Factbox—Illegal Immigration in the United States," 2010).

By late 1997 and through 2010 federal legislation restricting immigrant inflows and benefits such as food stamps, aid to families with dependent children, supplemental security income, and Medicaid was being explored for both illegal and legal immigrants. However, rather than restrict immigration, the Hudson Institute issued a report entitled "Workforce 2020" that suggested increasing immigration of skilled workers would compensate for an aging workforce.

By 2005, a number of states sought measures to deny government benefits for illegal immigrants. However, undocumented alien reform immigration legislation has gained wide congressional support. The Safe, Orderly, Legal Visas and Enforcement Act of 2004 (SOLVE) is designed to unite immigrant families, encourage them to become legal, and develop temporary worker programs with protections as well as providing paths to citizenship. There are an estimated 9 to 12 million undocumented aliens in the United States. SOLVE has widespread support from a number of immigration advocacy groups including the National Council of La Raza, the National Asian Pacific Legal Consortium, and the AFL-CIO. Efforts are being made in states and nationally to provide in-state college tuition to undocumented immigrant students. D.R.E.A.M., for example, is a Nebraska proposal to grant legal permanent residency to undocumented students who live in the state after completing 2 years of college or 2 years of U.S. military service ("Immigrant Workers Freedom Ride Coalition," 2004). Striving for tolerance and appreciation of diversity in our population is a continuing goal of educators now as it has been in the past. The controversy over immigration continues unabated at the turn of the first decade of the 21st century.

Implementing Equality for Minorities and Students with Special Needs.
Much effort has been devoted to creating and expanding public schools, including high schools. Educational leaders like James Carter did their best to make schools available to all and to improve their quality. The goal of providing equal educational opportunity to everyone and of having excellent programs is still a difficult one to reach. Private school and home schooling enrollment growth is a factor in providing for an expanding school population.

Even before Thurgood Marshall (as lawyer for the National Association for the Advancement of Colored People, or NAACP, in 1954) argued that segregated schools are inherently unequal, there was general agreement that minority schools had lower standards. It could have hardly been otherwise, because those schools enrolled many poor, disadvantaged, at-risk diverse student populations. Black schools had less equipment, worse buildings, and teachers with very limited training. Some researchers find school resegregation occurs because of changing demographics. Beyond question, minority students have gained a great deal since desegregation. It stands to reason that placing children in better schools will benefit them. Still, many schools have not been integrated, and critics say that progress in those that have been is not satisfactory. Lower overall achievement sometimes occurs when children with a poor educational background are placed in the same classrooms with those who have done better. Historically, labeling students on the basis of preconceived biases has prevented some minority students and women from acquiring access and equity in education. Local, state, regional, and national efforts are being made to assure continued quality education for all students. The No Child Left Behind Act (NCLB) may be modified with a name change to reflect input from educators about the strengths and weaknesses of the act. Arne Duncan, Education Secretary, has initiated waivers for states wanting to opt out of NCLB requirements.

Mainstreaming of students with special needs has often enhanced self-esteem, increased life skills, and improved achievement levels. The current attacks on remediation, social promotion, and soft pedagogy reflect public dissatisfaction with student academic achievement levels and with educational standards. Although there has been criticism of inadequate funding for implementing NCLB, there is widespread support for accountability, benchmarking, and closing the achievement gap.

Ethnic and minority groups often argue that attempts to teach the same values in all schools and Americanize all youth take away the unique characteristics of children who are not of the white, middle-class, dominant culture. Teachers in some school districts with large black populations have been encouraged to communicate and instruct in Ebonics (the subculture language of inner cities and other centers of minority populations). Supporters believe educators should understand the dialogue of minorities in order to effectively bridge racial divides and improve communication between teachers and pupils. Others believe, as did Noah Webster, that pupils need to be taught English language skills for common values and citizenship in the nation.

History reveals the continued efforts to achieve Horace Mann's call for an absolute right of all citizens to an education. Exploring alternative methods of teaching students from different language backgrounds contributes to universal education.

GAINING PERSPECTIVE THROUGH CRITICAL ANALYSIS

1. Name the similarities and differences between the impact of the Industrial Revolution on historical educational policies and practices and the impact of technology on today's policies and practices.
2. Give your interpretation of the purpose and contribution of the common school revival to educational theory and practice.
3. Name three educational leaders who contributed to the development of public school systems. What policies and practices initiated by these leaders are still used today?
4. Compare and contrast the educational opportunities available for minorities and women in early America with opportunities for those groups today.

5. What examples of English, classical, and commercial curriculum are still found in today's high school curricula?

6. Trace efforts to achieve equity and access for minorities in America's schools. Find commonalities and differences in treatment of multicultural populations then and now.

HISTORY IN ACTION IN TODAY'S CLASSROOMS

1. Contact people, organizations, and institutions in your community to determine the educational and employment opportunities available for women and minorities.

2. Interview a staff member or community leader of one of the organizations or institutions that try to create educational opportunities for women and minorities. Explore his or her perceptions of equality and excellence available to the population he or she serves. Add the findings to your journal.

3. How has federal legislation increased access for minorities in educational opportunities and employment since World War II? Discuss and answer the questions at the end of the features "Teacher Qualifications in Frontier Schools" and "Opportunities for Women." These features are found within the chapter.

BIBLIOGRAPHY

Bailyn, Bernard. *Education in the Forming of American Society.* New York: Random House, 1960.

Binder, Frederick. *The Age of the Common School, 1830–1865.* New York: John Wiley & Sons, 1974.

Bouvier, Leon. *Florida in the 21st Century.* Washington, DC: The Center for Immigration Studies, 1992.

Bouvier, Leon. *Shaping Florida: The Effects of Immigration.* Washington, DC: The Center for Immigration Studies, 1995.

Brown, Ann. *Federal Monitor to the Office of Desegregation Monitoring.* Little Rock: U.S. Government Printing Office, 1993. ("1999–2000 Enrollment and Racial Balance in the Little Rock School District and Pulaski County Special School District," report filed with U.S. Eastern District Court, Arkansas, March 29, 2000.)

Brubacher, John. *Henry Barnard on Education.* New York: McGraw-Hill, 1931.

Burton, Warren. *The District School as It Was.* Boston: Lee & Shepard, 1897.

Butts, Freeman. *The American Tradition in Religion and Education.* Boston: Beacon Press, 1950.

Bystydzienski, Jill M. *Women in Cross-Cultural Transitions.* Bloomington, IN: Phi Delta Kappa, 1994.

Cremin, Lawrence, Ed. *The Republic and the School: Horace Mann on the Education of Free Man.* New York: Teachers College Press, 1957.

Curti, Merle. *The Social Ideas of American Educators.* New York: Littlefield Adams, 1966.

"The First Kindergarten in the United States," regarding the Watertown Wisc. School of Mrs. Carl Schurz. Available at: jwa.org/encyclopedia/article/Schurz-margarethe-meyer

"Factbox—Illegal Immigration in the United States," *Reuters* (July 22, 2010). Available at: in.reuters.com/assets/print?aid=INIndia-50313620100722

Good, Harry G., & James D. Teller. *A History of American Education.* New York: Macmillan, 1973.

Gutek, Gerald L. *American Education in a Global Society.* New York: Longman, 1993; Westview, 1997.

"Immigrant Workers Freedom Ride Coalition" (2011). Available at: www.foodfirst.org/en/node/1277

Jordan, Miriam. "Report Warns Influx of Hispanics in South Creates School Crisis." *The Wall Street Journal* (December 9, 2004): B1, B2.

Kaufman, Polly Welts. *Women Teachers on the Frontier.* New Haven, CT: Yale University Press, 1984, xvii–xxiii, 6, 22. (*Annual Report of the School Committee of the*

Town of Concord, Year Ending April 1, 1855, Concord, Massachusetts, 1855, p. 15.)

Loeb, Penny, Dorian Friedman, Mary C. Lord, Dan McGraw, & Kukula Glastris. "To Make a Nation." *U.S. News and World Report* (October 4, 1993): 47–54.

MacMullen, Edith Nye. *In the Cause of True Education: Henry Barnard and Nineteenth Century Educational Reform.* New Haven, CT: Yale University Press, 1991.

Mann, Horace. *Lectures and Annual Reports on Education* Cambridge, MA: Cornhill Press of Boston, 1867.

Mann, Horace. "Tenth Annual Report (1846)." In *The Republic and the School: Horace Mann,* edited by Lawrence A. Cremin. New York: Teachers College Press, Columbia University, 1957, p. 63.

Pratte, Richard. *Ideology and Education.* New York: John Wiley & Sons, 1977.

Rudolph, Frederick. *The American College and University.* Athens: University of Georgia Press, 1990, 360. Originally published 1962.

Rusk, Robert, & James Scotland. *Doctrines of the Great Educators.* New York: St. Martin's Press, 1979.

Sandifer, Jawn A., Ed. *The Afro-American in United States History.* New York: Globe Book Company, 1969.

Silver, Harold, Ed. *Robert Owen on Education.* Cambridge, MA: Harvard University Press, 1969.

Veblen, Thorstein. *The Higher Learning in America.* New York: B. W. Huebsch, 1918.

Woody, Thomas. *A History of Women's Education in the United States.* New York: Farrar Strauss, Octagon Books, 1966.

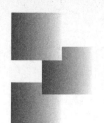

CHAPTER 6

AMERICAN EDUCATION: 1865–1918

We want education for ourselves . . . adequate, expertly taught, and continuing through the elementary grades, through high school and as far beyond that as proven gift and desert show is clearly for human welfare, no matter what the race, sex or religion of the recipient. This education is a public duty and should be at public expense. It should continue beyond school years, and in the form of adult education for all.

W. E. B. Du Bois

Reconstruction	Herbartian Movement	Progressive Era
1865 Slavery abolished by Thirteenth Amendment	1870 School superintendents in 28 American cities	1890 Second Morrill Act provided black A. M. and N. colleges
1868 Fourteenth Amendment protects life and property	1874 Kalamazoo case made tax support legal for high schools	1893 Rhode Island begins special education programs
1869 Fifteenth Amendment guarantees civil rights	1890 National Herbart Society	Social conflict

Figure 6.1 Time Line of American Education 1865

MODERN–DAY DIFFERENCES

Compulsory Attendance.   Because historical interpretation is influenced by personal experiences, it is sometimes difficult to understand the conditions of times past. Twenty-first-century teachers, administrators, and law enforcement officers find it difficult to enforce compulsory attendance laws. Almost every school has at least a few students who do not want to attend and who will not cooperate. Oftentimes, these children are from dysfunctional homes or are involved in drug or alcohol abuse. Sometimes, they are so socially maladjusted that they threaten others with violence. Apart from counseling and disciplinary action, there is very little that educational authorities can do to keep such students in school, but every state requires attendance at public or private school, normally through the age of 16. These laws were enacted in the late nineteenth and early twentieth century throughout the United States. Their historical purpose, however, was not to force children to attend but to prevent others from keeping them out of school. As America became one of the great industrial economies of the world, labor organizations brought great pressure to end child labor. Political leaders and social reformers attacked the parental practice of putting children to work and taking their wages. When public schools became the norm, it was widely accepted that every child should have the opportunity to attend, and this was the reason for compulsory attendance laws. Today, some believe that compulsory attendance is obsolete, but it is a firmly grounded tradition and the laws are likely to persist.

Technology in the Classroom.   All of us tend to think of schooling in terms of our own educational experience. Just how much computer-assisted instruction

Urban and Industrial Growth		Social and Political Reform
1909 Junior high school in Berkeley, California	1913 Thorndike published his *Educational Psychology*	1916 Dewey published *Democracy and* *Education*
1910 Junior college in Fresno, California	1914 Smith-Lever Act encouraged agriculture	1917 Smith-Hughes Act encouraged vocational schools
Vast growth of high schools		
Child labour	Minority/Prejudice	Racism

one received and how sophisticated the electronic information was depends on how long ago the education took place and where one went to school. Virtual high schools, e-mail photos, blackboard, online courses, videoconferencing, PowerPoint presentations, and new delivery systems are part of our education culture. If this new image-morphing computer technology is not familiar, neither is the lack of technological support suffered by teachers in history.

The recitation method used before the Civil War was inefficient and crude. It devoted the attention of the teacher to one student at a time and ignored the rest. One reason for the slow development of group methods was that there was no way to duplicate or copy materials. Tests were given orally or questions were written on the blackboard, but copying a test by hand for each student was just too much labor for teachers. By 1875, the hectograph appeared. This crude instrument allowed for ink transfer on a shallow pan or box filled with gelatin. Several copies could be made from a prepared master. Eventually, a flexible master was placed on a drum so that copies could be cranked out on a machine. Such duplicating or other copying devices were in common use until electronic copiers such as photocopying machines were developed. The first typewriters were for the use of the blind, but L. C. Scholes made a commercial model in 1867. Most schools had manual typewriters available to teachers by 1900, and an electric model was invented in 1935. Making carbon copies on typewriters was tedious at best, but eventually typed duplication masters were made available.

Making copies of materials for students is only one of many examples of the very slow growth of educational technology before the modern period. Maps, laboratory equipment, vocational training devices, and mathematical calculators underwent a similar evolution. So did school libraries and reference materials for research.

Computers, electronic copies, desktop printing, and the Internet make conditions of teaching altogether different from those of past historical periods. It is easier to understand history and to anticipate future change when the slow rate of past invention is compared with the accelerating rate today.

Stimulus for Change in Education.   Wars are by no means the only significant checkpoints in educational chronology, but the period between the Civil War and World War I saw the development of the modern American school system. Westward expansion and the growth of industry, agriculture, and population put vastly increased demands upon existing schools and required the building not only of new schools but also of whole new educational systems. By 1890, the frontier had almost ceased to be, and with the addition of New Mexico and Arizona to the Union in 1912, the continental United States was formed. Industrial growth carried with it the new problem of educating children in the urban slums and the need for Americanizing immigrants on a grand scale. Natural increase and immigration swelled the population from just over 30 million in 1860 to more than 100 million by 1920.

Before 1860, the northern states had largely developed the outlines of their educational systems, and some had made substantial progress in bringing state education to all the people. States were not uniform in their growth; those first to be settled usually developed their systems earlier. By 1873, laws for the organization of a state school system, including the school tax and some form of state control, were to be found all over the nation. Before World War I, public school education in America typically included an 8-year elementary school and the 4-year high school. State universities capped the systems, although only a small percentage of the people could take advantage of them. Public kindergartens, junior high schools, and junior colleges were found in only a few areas before 1920 and were not yet a significant part of the public school organization.

Educational theory passed through a series of stages that included sectarian dominance, *laissez-faire*, slavish copying of European models, and the scientific progressive movement. Professional training for teachers and administrators became firmly established as an ideal with the growth of normal schools and colleges or departments of education in the universities. Compulsory attendance, expanded curriculum, fully graded common schools, public high schools, and large increases in spending for buildings and equipment marked the period. However, the late nineteenth century witnessed extreme sectional differences in educational structure and quality.

INHIBITED DEVELOPMENT OF EDUCATION IN THE SOUTH

The Civil War interfered with education all over the nation, causing schools to be closed and governmental revenues to be directed to the immediate expenses of the conflict. But northern states were able to continue their school programs in spite of the reduction in available money and the loss of many teachers. Sometimes, an entire student body and faculty went off to join the army, as in the case of Illinois

College at Jacksonville, Illinois; however, elementary schools in the Union states continued to operate through the wartime years. It was not so in the South; there the battle devastation and increased sacrifice to support the war severely crippled the embryonic school systems. Southern states spent many years recovering even the low educational level they had enjoyed before the national strife, and some of the scars are still visible in the slower school development of the rural South.

Southern Collapse.

The war left southern states in physical and economic ruin—with crops destroyed, buildings burned, livestock slaughtered, and the labor force demoralized. Civil authority broke down, courts were nonexistent, and four million black citizens were without economic resources or leadership. Presidents Lincoln and Johnson hoped to enlist the cooperation of former Confederate leaders in rebuilding the South, but the radical Republicans in Congress wanted to punish the southern states. In the struggle, Andrew Johnson was nearly impeached, and a military reconstruction government dominated by northern interests was imposed. These governments—consisting of "carpetbaggers," former slaves, and fortune seekers—failed to obtain the support of the southern white majority.

Very little real progress had been made by 1876, when the radical reconstruction government finally ended and the Union army of the occupation was removed. Southerners, bitter about their treatment after the conflict and fearful of black power, set about to undo the acts of the reconstruction era. Measures providing for public education, especially where racially mixed schools were concerned, were either ignored or removed from the books. Sectional hatred and opposition to black schools might have paralyzed education even if money had been available, but the war and the waste of the first postwar governments left the South bankrupt.

Newfound freedom did nothing to improve the living standards of the southern blacks. Most of them were as economically dependent and as subject to exploitation as they had been in slavery. Economic expansion was slow to develop, and both races remained poor, especially small farmers and sharecroppers. Industry received a boost in the 1880s with the founding of textile mills. Tobacco products, lumber, and even steel mills in Alabama contributed to a stronger economy. But agriculture continued to be the mainstay of the southern economy, and very little tax money was available for school purposes until the twentieth century. Many southern statesmen deplored the low level and retarded growth of public schools but were powerless to provide adequate support.

African American Education.

Some money for educating the newly freed citizens came from private and church associations that sent teachers to the South in considerable numbers. The Peabody and other philanthropic funds provided some assistance, but control remained in the hands of whites. In 1869, there were about 9,000 such teachers, working mostly in schools for freedmen. Several societies for the aid of freed slaves were formed, the most important of which were the American Freedman's Union (secular) and the American Missionary Association (religious). Congress established the Freedmen's Bureau in 1865. Its head, General O. O. Howard, considered education to be the most pressing need of blacks in the South.

There was considerable enthusiasm for schooling among former slaves in the period immediately following the war, but adults soon learned that education was something for which they had neither the time nor the preparation. The economic support was often sporadic, and it appears that many of the schools were very ill-equipped and of poor quality. Social liberals and political propagandists among the teachers from the North were unpopular. Like all things "Yankee," the freedmen's schools became objects of attack once the power of the reconstruction government was broken. Although the South was still organized as a series of military provinces, new constitutions were adopted that included provisions for education. But for all practical purposes, the states of the South were bankrupt. As a result, little more than a paper system of education existed in 1870.

Hoar Bill.   In 1870, a bill was introduced in Congress by George F. Hoar of Massachusetts; the bill would have established a federal school system in southern states. The measure was designed to compel the establishment of a system of instruction and the appointment of a federal superintendent in all states where a minimum standard was not met. Textbooks were to be prescribed by the United States Commissioner of Education, and the schools were to be supported by a centrally collected direct tax. The bill was defeated partly because of the opposition of the National Education Association (NEA) and Superintendent Wickersham of Pennsylvania. They felt that national control over part of the nation's schools could not be tolerated, although gifts of federal money with local autonomy could be. Roots of the modern-day issue over federal aid to education can be seen in the arguments over the Hoar Bill.

Blair Bill.   A second effort to get national aid for states unable to maintain schools came in the form of a proposed national school fund from the sale of public land in the tradition of the Ordinance of 1785. When it appeared that this plan would not be adopted, Senator Henry Blair of New Hampshire introduced a bill in 1882 to help states with the greatest educational need. The Blair Bill (in final form) provided for $77 million to be divided among the states in proportion to the number of illiterates in each. The money was to be used as each state saw fit, provided that it was used only for education. This measure passed the Senate three times but was never successful in the House of Representatives. No further bills of this nature were proposed until recent times, although the federal government continued to aid colleges through the Morrill Act of 1890.

Philanthropy.   Private agencies made an effort to fill the educational void in the South and to stimulate greater local effort. George Peabody gave $2 million for this purpose. A board of trustees headed in turn by Barnas Sears, Horace Mann, and J. L. M. Curry administered the Peabody Fund. Under the direction of Curry, a Southerner, the money was used to develop a limited number of high-quality schools as models. The Peabody Fund went to normal schools for female teachers of both races and to what became the George Peabody College for Teachers in Nashville. Agents who supervised private funds also visited schools and opened lines of communication between groups interested in school improvement.

Southern Associations.   Thirty years after the Civil War, the Conference for Education in the South was organized, and numerous meetings were held for the purpose of improving education. Out of this grew the Southern Education Board and the General Education Board (1903). The Southern Association of Colleges and Schools was established, as well as many private boards that were connected with philanthropic societies, such as the Carnegie Foundation and the Rosenwald Fund. Although stimulation and information were given, the public systems tended to make only limited progress before 1920. Only meager tax support was available in agricultural areas, and even southern cities were poor by northern standards.

The educational conservatism of the prewar period and hostility toward schools introduced in the reconstruction era dampened interest in public schools. The most negative factor of all was insistence on separation of white and black schools. This segregation required the building and maintenance of a dual system with duplication of buildings and teachers in states that could least afford them. Because schools for white children were given significantly more support because of a stronger community tax base together with segregation, funds were distributed unevenly, leading to lower levels of education for African Americans. This was a major factor in keeping the educational level of southern states lower than that of the rest of the nation for several decades.

In the early 1900s, the South was still marked by short school terms (70 days in North Carolina), high illiteracy, ineffective administration, poorly trained teachers, and meager tax support. Salaries of southern teachers in 1900 averaged about half that of northern teachers, and black teachers were paid lowest of all.

NATIONAL AFFAIRS AND PROGRESS

If progress was slow in the southern states between the Civil War and World War I, those years also marked the transition from an old agrarian to a modern, industrial America. In less than half a century, wounds of the Civil War were largely healed, and America entered the era of industrial world powers. Territorial expansion had given way to a greater and faster development of northern industrial capacities. The growth and development of industry was at least as important a factor in the population growth figure as immigration. Because of a favorable attitude by the government, untapped industrial resources, and cheap labor, the Goulds, the Carnegies, and the Rockefellers were able to build vast industrial empires and accumulate great fortunes. Many of the industrial barons were interested in education and helped to found colleges, universities, and better public schools.

Industrial Exploitation.   The other side of the Industrial Revolution had a negative effect on education. Exploitation of children and working men was widespread, and immigrants in the cities commonly labored 16 hours a day. The growth of great industry swallowed up the small businessman, and there was much corruption in government at all levels. City slums also presented a different kind of educational problem. The need for reform was seen, but many of the people in power sought to make more severe laws and develop additional penitentiaries, rather than to cure the problem through education.

The Republican Party dominated politics and held control of the presidency between the end of the Civil War and the election of Woodrow Wilson in 1913, with the single exception of the two terms of Grover Cleveland. Distinctly the party of business, industrial, and commercial interests, it did not promote mass educational reform supported by federal and state governments. What was done for the education of the masses in the cities was done largely through private enterprise and with the interests of individuals who saw most clearly the need for reform. The dissatisfaction of the laboring masses began to show itself in the latter part of the nineteenth century. Numerous labor reform parties came into being in the 1870s, and the agrarian and labor groups organized the Independent or Greenback Party in 1874. Later, several independent groups organized the Populist Party, which became part of the Democratic Party in 1896 and came very close to electing William Jennings Bryan over William McKinley. The tremendous increase in industrial growth in the urban areas of the United States—especially obvious in the northern and eastern sections—together with the growth of large corporations controlling vast amounts of wealth, changed the nature of American society considerably. There was a strong belief in a hands-off, or *laissez-faire*, governmental policy. During this period, the basic nature of American society changed from rural to urban. The great cities were beginning to take present-day shape, and the idea of the independent farmer class as the dominant one in America was beginning to fade.

Agricultural, Population, and Vocational Changes.

There was also a revolution in farming, attributable to inventions like McCormick's reaper as well as the new scientific knowledge about agriculture that had been greatly advanced by the agricultural colleges set up under the Morrill acts. However, the farmer did not immediately benefit from the better technology, because the increase in production caused prices to fall. Hence, the period from 1865 to 1900 saw the rise of many farm organizations designed to aid the plight of the farmer with his decreasing income. This, too, was the beginning of the organized labor period in America. The Knights of Labor gave way to the American Federation of Labor, and the union movement was well under way by 1900.

The character of the population changed at this time. Immigrants coming to the United States had previously been largely from northwestern Europe, especially England, Ireland, Germany, and Scandinavia. But the people who arrived after the Civil War came from other parts of Europe such as Spain, Russia, Austria, Hungary, and Italy. There were also a few from non-European nations such as China, Japan, and Mexico. Chinese workers helped build the transcontinental railroad. Because of economic and labor problems in the 1870s, some Americans in western states sought to restrict Chinese immigration; this restriction led to the 1882 Chinese Exclusion Act.

Immigration laws were relaxed in the following decades. However, discrimination has occurred against minorities and newcomers throughout our history. Societies and individuals are prisoners of the intolerance of the ages in which they live.

Butts and Cremin (1953) noted that after the Civil War, groups that had been excluded from public elementary schools—Negroes, Indians, Chinese, and Mexicans, as well as those with mental or physical handicaps—were increasingly provided access as a matter of right rather than as charity. The immigrant population became radically different during this period of time; Eastern Europeans and non-Europeans arrived, making language and cultural assimilation considerably more difficult. Tremendous growth in communication and the transportation system, together with an increased centralization in American life, also had an effect on the educational needs of the people.

THE PUBLIC SCHOOL IDEAL

A major principle of education put into practice after the Civil War was that public education should be free to all. In contrast with the European dual system in which elementary education was for the lower classes and secondary reserved for the elite, the United States established a ladder system by which one might advance from the first grade through college in a series of yearly steps. In theory, at least, each child was free to begin at the lowest level and progress as fast as his or her abilities would allow. It was an American belief that the schools could be used for advancement up the social ladder, and the person of ability could qualify for a high-paying job by acquiring education.

This was an age of social revolution in which the industrial and financial leaders accumulated great wealth as industrial and technological expansion increased. With the commercial production of petroleum starting in 1859, the opening of the West to farmers and ranchers, and the joining of the Union Pacific with the Central Pacific to make the first transcontinental railroad line in 1869, growth of wealth and commerce accelerated. Although wealthy families seldom sent their children to public schools before 1900, class distinctions were foreign to the educational ideal. Laboring and middle-class families demanded high-quality public schools for their sons and daughters. Training for making a good living was important, but so too was education for citizenship, morality, and self-improvement. The common elementary school for all citizens was established in theory before the Civil War. It became a reality between 1865 and 1900 for the majority of Americans. Before World War I, the theory was extended upward to include secondary education. The standard American high school became a major part of the educational program and cultural experience of the nation. Dewey's *Democracy and Education*, published in 1916, addressed the role of education in a pluralistic society.

THE AMERICAN PUBLIC HIGH SCHOOL

The academy reached its zenith of popularity by the middle of the nineteenth century and declined rapidly after that time. Growth of high schools in the United States was slow at first. In 1875, there were fewer than 25,000 students enrolled in public high schools. In the 1880s, more students attended high schools than academies, and by 1890, some 2,500 high schools enrolled more than 200,000 students. By 1900, there were more than 6,000 high schools and over 500,000 students.

Kalamazoo Case.   Although the age of the common school revival clearly established the principle of free, tax-supported elementary schools, considerable controversy continued over taxation for high schools. Public secondary schools in some states were financed from common school funds while others charged tuition. Because one major function of high schools was to prepare students for college and because high schools were not patronized by all children, some citizens felt the states had no right to tax the public for support of these schools. Others, led by such spokesmen as California superintendent Ezra Carr, argued that high schools were an important part of the basic public educational system.

The best-known case dealing with tax support for high schools came after the town of Kalamazoo, Michigan, created a public secondary school in 1858. Three taxpayers brought suit to restrain the school board from collecting and using taxes to support the high school. The case reached the state supreme court, which decided in favor of the school authorities in 1874. The opinion, written by Justice Cooley, held that high schools are common schools and that they constitute a vital link between elementary schools and the state university. He pointed out that the absence of public secondary schools would discriminate in favor of the rich and thus prevent others from entering college. Although other cases were tried, the Kalamazoo decision became a precedent that established the right of the several states to levy taxes for public high schools. This precedent contributed to the vast growth of high schools in the period before World War I.

Curriculum.   High schools offered both traditional and practical programs, but the emphasis was usually placed on the college preparatory curriculum. In spite of the fact that only about a tenth of the students in high schools in 1900 expected to enter college, the "classical" course was taken by a majority of youngsters. Latin and algebra were the subjects that had the highest enrollment. Sometimes the college course was divided so that a student could elect an English or a scientific major, but there was no free choice of subjects. Many schools had whole programs or courses such as the manual or commercial training courses for the terminal student (not college bound). Many students studied the English classical course, even if they had no plans for higher education.

The English Classical School, established in Boston in 1821, was modified over time, changing its focus from foreign languages (as in the Latin grammar school) to English literature and practical and vocational studies. The change in focus was designed to meet the needs of an emerging middle commercial class (Butts & Cremin, 1953; Meyer, 1957). The English Classical School still exists and was recognized for going green on energy saving and environmental protection. A few high schools offered specialized vocational courses, and some offered preparation for teaching. The comprehensive high school curriculum contained a wider variety of subjects, including vocational and business education. Vocational education included training in the trades, agriculture, carpentry, mechanics, and technical job skills. Business or commercial curricula included keyboard typing skills, accountancy, and bookkeeping. There were private trade and venture schools meeting increased demands for job skills in both vocational and business education. Physical education, art, music, and religion were included in the subjects offered by many high schools at the end of the nineteenth century. There was very little standardization. Some high schools offered as a 4-year course what others gave in one semester or 1 year.

Standardizing Associations and the National Education Association.

The United States had developed a large number of secondary schools. Many difficulties arose concerning the subjects of the curriculum, the length of time spent on each subject, and the quality of the instruction. Associations of standardization were created to deal with these issues. They also considered the preparation of teachers, the length of the school year, libraries, physical facilities, and graduation requirements. The New England Association of Colleges and Secondary Schools was founded in 1789. Next came the Middle Atlantic States Association (1892), the North Central Association (1894), the Association of College and Preparatory Schools of the Southern States (1895), and the Northwest Association of Secondary and Higher Schools (1918). All of these organizations had the purpose of improving and making standard the offerings of various secondary schools and some colleges.

In 1857, 43 leaders from 10 state teachers' associations organized the National Teachers' Association in Philadelphia. In 1870, this organization merged with the National Association of School Superintendents and the American Normal School Association to form the NEA. The NEA held an annual convention and published reports dealing with all aspects of education. Later, it became involved in defining the functions and standards for schools at all levels. Congress granted a charter to the NEA in 1905.

Committee of Ten.

Confusion over standards in secondary schools, curriculum issues, and the argument between "modernists" and "traditionalists" caused the NEA to take action in 1892. In that year, the NEA appointed the Committee of Ten to examine the high school curriculum and to make recommendations about methods, standards, and programs. Commissioner W. T. Harris and Harvard's President Charles W. Eliot were well-known members of the committee. There were four other college presidents, two headmasters, one professor, and one high school administrator, but no high school teachers. College interests dominated in the Committee of Ten, and the report was a bastion of educational conservatism.

One of the major weaknesses of the committee's report was that it based its findings on the psychology of mental discipline. The assumption was made that all subjects for general education had equal value for training the mind's powers, such as expression, memory, reasoning, and observation. At a time when faculty psychology (which listed active powers—each of which could be strengthened through use of the mind, such as hunger—and intellectual powers, such as memory) and mental discipline were already under attack, the Committee of Ten held that all of its recommended subjects were of equal value for building sound mental habits in children. There were subcommittees on Latin, Greek, English, the modern languages, mathematics, the physical sciences, the biological sciences, history, and geography. These subjects represented vested interests and were given support by the committee, but vocational and commercial courses were largely ignored. In every case, the purpose of studying a subject was held to be mental discipline and exercise of the powers of the mind. It was also held that any recommended subject that was studied for one period each day for 5 days each week for a year was equal to any other recommended subject studied for the same length of time, which became standard units for academic measurement.

The Committee of Ten influenced the Committee on College Entrance Requirements (established in 1895) and the subsequent work of the Carnegie Foundation for the Advancement of Teaching. The result was the establishment of the standard unit of credit for high school subjects (Carnegie unit), the support of traditional subjects and faculty psychology, and the limitation of any new or innovative high school programs. The Committee of Ten recommended intensive study in high schools of a few subjects for long periods of time. It supported an 8-year elementary school followed by a 4-year high school. No special subjects or methods were recommended for students who expected to terminate their formal education with high school graduation.

Accreditation. The NEA Committee on College Entrance Requirements not only defined units of study in secondary schools but also recommended a set of constant or core subjects to be taken by all students. In 1902, the North Central Association set up a Committee on Unit Courses. The committee required 15 units for high school graduation and recommended at least three units of English and two of mathematics for college entrance. Those recommendations became standard requirements in accreditation for all high schools. The College Entrance Examination Board was also established.

Cardinal Principles. In 1918, the NEA appointed a Commission on the Reorganization of Secondary Education. This commission recognized the high schools as instruments for social integration and building values. It warned against specialized schools that would divide the population of students and supported the idea of a comprehensive secondary school offering a variety of subjects and courses.

The commission provided some theoretical basis for the later development of a truly comprehensive secondary school. However, it is best known for issuing its seven Cardinal Principles of Secondary Education, which became standard objectives for teachers, school boards, and administrators. The following are the seven principles:

1. Health
2. Command of fundamental processes
3. Worthy home membership
4. Vocation
5. Citizenship
6. Worthy use of leisure time
7. Ethical character

Obviously, these principles could serve as a guide for curriculum and methodology, but they did not fill the need for a carefully articulated educational philosophy. The meaning of each principle may be interpreted in a variety of ways.

Rapid growth of high schools continued even though most of them, before 1920, were noncomprehensive and strictly college preparatory in curriculum. By 1900, the public high schools were almost all coeducational, and more than half of the students were girls. In the early decades of the twentieth century, high schools doubled in enrollment every 10 years, until they became common schools in fact as well as name.

Reorganization. Public high schools retained the same general characteristics and organizational structure well into the twentieth century. In addition to a principal and his or her staff, the schools usually had departmental divisions with a chairperson or "head" for each major program area or department.

Charles W. Eliot was an enthusiastic supporter of both college and high school electives. He was one of the first to suggest a new school organization that would provide more choice for high school students. Basically, Eliot wanted to extend the high school courses downward into elementary education. G. Stanley Hall, author of the first book on adolescents and no friend of Eliot's proposal, felt that reorganization was necessary to meet the needs of older elementary pupils who were no longer children. Others believed that the elementary and high schools did not provide a smooth transition from childhood to young adult life. It was felt that the opportunity for advanced elementary education of a general sort as well as some industrial and commercial training should be provided outside the senior high school. The Committee on College Entrance Requirements had recommended the division of elementary and secondary schools into year-year blocks, and the Committee of Ten had considered reorganization of some type.

As a result of these and other suggestions, junior high schools were created in Columbus, Ohio, and Berkeley, California, in 1909. Other cities soon followed, and the junior high school became a common institution in the United States after 1930. Typically, the elementary school was reduced to six years, with junior and senior high schools requiring 6 years together. This 6–3–3 plan was not always used; some schools retained a 4-year high school and used a 6–2–4 system. Reorganization is still in process today, with many schools experimenting with a 4–4–4 or other "middle school" plan. The junior high school stressed socialization, guidance, individual differences, and survey or exploratory courses of a general nature.

VOCATIONAL AND INDUSTRIAL EDUCATION

The history of vocational education spans a long period of time in America. Apprenticeship was first used for vocational training when literary and religious education was the only prerogative of the school. However, by 1820, eastern cities saw the establishment of a few mechanics' institutes for technical instruction. Worcester Polytechnic Institute was opened in 1868, and there were some manual labor

schools built along lines suggested by the European educators Pestalozzi and Fel-
lenberg. Manual training demonstrations were given in Philadelphia in 1876. Some
cities had manual and vocational courses in high schools by 1890.

Shop work of various kinds replaced manual training in many high schools, but
some secondary schools were designated as manual training high schools with no
college preparatory courses. The vocational value of shop work was considered
part of general education, and special trade training was avoided in favor of
mechanical principles. Students learned general skills on the transfer-of-training theory rather than how to make specific articles. The need for skilled workers and the
desire for high school education for those not bound for college caused the manual
training movement to gain speed after 1880. Columbia University began training
teachers for manual training classes, and an industrial education association was
organized in 1884.

Gradually the movement for training teachers of manual arts spread through the
universities. Some labor leaders feared that industrial education would develop a
surplus of cheap trained labor, but labor generally approved of industrial and vocational education. In general, manufacturers were also in support of this movement,
but the opposition from traditional educators with classical backgrounds was more
difficult to overcome.

Smith-Hughes Act.   The vocational school movement continued to grow from
1907 to 1917, receiving its greatest boost in 1917 when the federal Smith-Hughes
Act was passed. This law provided federal aid for the states by paying vocational
teachers' salaries in the high schools and aiding teacher-training institutions in the
education of such teachers. The states were required to match the federal grant on a
dollar-for-dollar basis. In an effort to provide aid for the child trying to make a choice
between vocational subjects, the Vocation Bureau and Breadwinner's Institute was
established in 1909.

Vocational and manual training also received support from new experiments
and theories in education. John Dewey attracted attention by insisting that children
learn through activities. His book *School and Society* (1900) made this point. New
interest in psychology led to the beginning of professional guidance for students in
industrial and vocational schools. Guidance developed slowly, and vocational high
schools were the first to offer counseling services.

Demand for practical vocational skills and scientific information was especially
great among the farmers of the nation. Farmers' Institutes started in 1854 and led to
an interest in agricultural education on both the high school and the college levels.
Colleges that resulted from the Morrill acts of 1862 and 1890 gave college status to
agriculture and the mechanical arts. Demonstration farms, agricultural experiment
stations, and training for improvement of agricultural techniques were provided by
these colleges and by the Department of Agriculture, which was established in
1862. The Hatch Act of 1887 provided federal funds for agricultural experiments. In
1914, Congress passed the Smith-Lever Act, which created agricultural extension
programs for farmers and led to vocational agriculture courses and 4-H clubs. Many
high school students took advantage of federally funded vocational work, but often

vocational agriculture was the only practical course offered in rural secondary schools. There was no attempt to offer general federal aid to public schools until after World War II.

PAROCHIAL AND PRIVATE EDUCATION

Obtaining exact figures on school enrollments before 1900 is difficult because neither schools nor reporting techniques were standardized. Statistics on public and private sectarian schools were often reported together as late as 1870. Although the states of the West and South were behind those of the North and East in percentages of children enrolled in public schools, it is clear that very rapid growth in all states took place between 1860 and 1900. In 1900, about 90 percent of the American secondary school students attended public high schools.

Catholic doctrine has always insisted the state should have only a secondary role in education while the parents and the church have primary responsibility. Catholic schools existed in such areas as New Mexico, California, and Louisiana early in American history, but intolerance and discrimination by the states prevented rapid growth on the eastern seaboard. In colonial America, only Pennsylvania allowed Catholics to conduct schools. However, the appointment of Father John Carroll as Superior of Missions in the United States and the guarantee of religious freedom in the Bill of Rights provided a foundation for Catholic education in America. With the large influx of Irish Catholics during the first half of the nineteenth century, interest in parochial schools increased. By 1840, Catholics had created 75 elementary parochial schools, 25 high schools, and 6 colleges. Many Catholic children attended public schools, but there was great controversy over Protestant creeds and the use of the King James Version of the Bible in public schools. Catholic children were often punished if they objected to non-Catholic religious practices. In 1854, the Maine Supreme Court rejected a Catholic plea to exclude the Bible from the public school curriculum, although the Ohio Supreme Court upheld a similar Catholic plea in 1872.

The Third Plenary Council of Baltimore in 1884 required all parishes to provide schools for Catholic youngsters. As a result, Catholic parochial schools increased in number to about 3,000 in 1884. Secondary Catholic schools were developed through Jesuit leadership partly in an effort to train boys for the priesthood. Parish high schools were largely an extension of the parochial school. They emphasized Latin, literature, grammar, and religion. Few, if any, vocational courses were offered. By 1910, there were more than 300 Catholic high schools in operation in the United States.

The Lutheran Church founded the largest number of non-Catholic parochial schools. There were also schools created by Quakers, Jews, and other religious groups. Much smaller in numbers than the Catholic schools, these sectarian efforts nevertheless provided alternative educational opportunities for students in many parts of the nation. An interesting discussion of these issues appears in *Great School Wars* (1988) by Diane Ravitch.

Oregon Case.   Bitter public reaction against parochial schools has existed in the United States for many years. Discrimination has been expressed in many ways, and direct efforts have been made to outlaw parochial schools. The most famous case occurred in the state of Oregon in 1925 and has remained unchallenged. The Oregon legislature passed a law that required all children to attend public schools through the eighth grade. The Society of Sisters of the Holy Names of Jesus and Mary and the Hill Academy brought suit against Governor Pierce in an effort to keep their schools. Although the state supreme court upheld the state law, the Supreme Court of the United States declared the action unconstitutional. It held that the state has a right to inspect and regulate private and parochial schools but that the state does not have a monopoly on education.

In addition to religious schools, a number of private schools and academies continued to operate. These were sometimes military schools or elite college preparatory institutions for wealthy children. Military academies declined after World War II, but other kinds of private schools grew rapidly in number and the voucher system now allows for new educational experiments.

HIGHER EDUCATION

Colleges and Universities.   Higher education had a steady growth during this period, and as a result of the Morrill Act of 1862 almost every state created a land grant college. Industry and scientific agriculture were emphasized by these institutions, but they were by no means confined to such subjects. The land grant schools grew slowly at first because they lacked the prestige of liberal arts colleges. However, they had the support of science and were powerful as a democratizing influence. Nine of these colleges developed into state universities, and many added colleges of engineering, home economics, and education. The Morrill Act of 1890 made $15,000 annually available to each of the original institutions, resulting in vast expansion. By 1918, many state universities became major institutions of higher education. Efforts to develop private colleges met with limited success. A high percentage of the sectarian colleges founded before the Civil War closed by World War I, but others were created. Some degree-granting colleges were really only secondary schools, although there were high-quality denominational colleges as well as good secular universities.

New University Model.   The most significant development in higher education during this period was the establishment of graduate programs based on the German example. Early supporters of this idea included Henry P. Tappan (later president of the University of Michigan) and Louis Agassiz, who developed science programs at Harvard. It was not, however, until Johns Hopkins University opened in 1876 that a real scientific research university existed in America.

Johns Hopkins was a wealthy Baltimore businessman who provided a large endowment for a university that would include a medical school and hospital. Much of the credit for the success of Johns Hopkins University goes to its first president, Daniel Coit Gilman (1831–1908). Gilman was a Yale graduate who became president of the University of California before being selected for Johns Hopkins. He was a keen administrator and a careful judge of talent. Gilman selected professors who had not yet reached national status but who had demonstrated their potential ability. The new institution had a graduate school aimed at creating new knowledge and supporting scientific investigation rather than merely transferring information and skills. It required graduate students to do research as a regular part of the program and provided the necessary laboratory equipment and other support. Inquiry, observation, freedom to seek truth without institutional restrictions, and high-quality scholarship became standard at Johns Hopkins. The idea that faculty members should do research and publish the results of their work also found favor there.

Professional Schools.

Johns Hopkins was the first American university to have a medical college with full-time professors. In the post–Civil War period, professional schools rapidly replaced the private practices of "reading law," apprentice doctors, and self-education for ministers. In 1899, there were 532 reported professional schools operating in the nation, about half of which were departments in colleges and universities. The practice at Johns Hopkins of requiring college graduation for admission to the medical school was rare, and numerous professional programs were offered for short periods of time. Low standards from a lack of state supervision were common until after 1900, when regulations began to increase. The growth of graduate schools had a major effect on professional schools because of the training they offered to college and professional schoolteachers. Graduate departments and professional schools began to differentiate between universities and liberal arts colleges, even when such colleges referred to themselves as universities.

Curriculum Changes.

Because traditions in education are very strong, change normally meets with great resistance. College faculties have always been very conservative with regard to altering the curriculum. Nevertheless, colleges did begin to expand their offerings in the period under consideration, in spite of great faculty reluctance. Science and research made the addition of many courses necessary, although most colleges merely added the new programs without altering or eliminating the old. Agriculture, mechanical arts, and military science gained a foothold in higher education because of the Morrill acts. The 65 colleges and universities established under these acts by 1900 obviously had a profound effect on the curriculum. Massachusetts Institute of Technology began instruction in 1865, with theoretical support for scientific and practical subjects provided by Herbert Spencer and T. H. Huxley. Darwin's *On the Origin of Species* (1859) caused a great deal of interest in the intellectual world, and such scholars as John Fiske at Harvard soon discussed evolution. The tycoons of the "gilded age" gave substantial gifts to higher education, and in return they influenced the curriculum. Practical, utilitarian, and business courses often had the support of philanthropists, as did conservative views of social change and classical economics.

Before the Civil War, it was unusual to allow students free selection of courses or programs in colleges. Although George Ticknor had experimented with electives, the real development of the college elective system came when Charles W. Eliot was president of Harvard. By 1894, Harvard required only French or German, English composition, and some work in physics and chemistry; all other courses could be selected by the students. Educational conservatives bitterly opposed the elective system, but leading universities soon adopted it to some degree, although a core of "disciplinary" courses was often required. The major effect of the elective system was to break the hold classics had on higher education and to allow the introduction of popular modern subjects such as history, sociology, psychology, economics, and the sciences. Breadth of the curriculum and the freedom to examine various theories or ideas became part of the university ideal.

Although coeducational colleges existed before the Civil War (Oberlin, 1833; Antioch, 1852; and Iowa, 1856), their major development came between 1860 and 1920. By 1880, about half of the colleges and universities admitted women. Vassar, Smith, Wellesley, and Bryn Mawr were women's colleges that offered programs equivalent to colleges for men. Affiliated or "coordinate" colleges for women also were established, such as Radcliffe at Harvard. At the turn of the century, there were still some doubts about higher education for women. Frederick Rudolph wrote, in *The American College and University* (1962, pp. 326–327), that as late as 1895 the faculty at the University of Virginia believed that women students were often physically unsexed by the strain of study. He also wrote that a Vanderbilt student stated that no man wants to come home at night and find his wife testing some new manufacturing process for oleomargarine or in the observatory sweeping the heavens for a comet. Rudolph also noted that a foreign visitor to Wellesley opined that this is all very well but how would it affect their chances for marriage. In addition, Rudolph noted that the suspicion would long linger that coeducation deprived women of some of their infinite charm and gentleness and robbed men of some of the sternness and ruggedness on which society depended for its protection. A wide curriculum was offered for women, but teaching was still the only career generally open to females in 1918.

MINORITIES AND PREJUDICE

Before the terrorist attack on New York City, a bearded man with Arabic features and a turban would have created no interest. Following 9/11, such a person might have been viewed with suspicion. Attitudes toward people exhibiting different characteristics from the majority have often been negative. This is a major problem for education.

Half a century ago the landmark *Brown v. Board of Education, Topeka* paved the way for blacks to be integrated into American public schools. In the next half century, according to demographers, Hispanics will be the majority, with blacks and whites constituting the two largest minorities. The way in which minorities have been treated by the majority in this country is hardly something of which we can be proud.

SCHOOLS AND COLLEGES FOR MINORITY GROUPS

The adoption of the Fourteenth Amendment in 1868 gave black Americans citizenship, but few opportunities for higher education existed then. In 1826, the first college degree granted to a black student went to John Russwurm; only 28 black college graduates were recorded before the Civil War. Northern colleges that opened to African Americans after 1860 found many ill-prepared for college work because of the inadequate segregated public schools from which they came. Progress in literacy rates is clear, however, in the increase in the literacy of black Americans from 10 percent in 1866 to over 90 percent in 1936. According to Edgar Knight, 132 blacks received Ph.D. degrees in this same time period.

Black schools and colleges in the South developed through the efforts of educators like Booker T. Washington. Hampton Institute for Negro Higher Education had been established in Virginia in 1870 under the sponsorship of the American Missionary Association. Washington became a student there, arriving on foot and with only 50 cents to his name. When Washington graduated in 1875, he was recommended by Principal Samuel C. Armstrong as a teacher for a proposed black normal school at Tuskegee, Alabama. Under Washington, Tuskegee Normal and Industrial Institute became a model of black education and its director a national figure. Washington received an honorary degree from Harvard University and became the recognized leader of black education. Realizing the attitudes of white Americans in the South, Washington agreed to a subservient role for blacks in return for practical and

---

Focus on the Issues

Sanchez Encounters Prejudice

The education building at the University of Texas is named for the late professor George I. Sanchez. Sanchez was a distinguished professor of history and philosophy of education and one of the first Hispanic faculty members at the Austin campus. He had many graduate students and insisted that they be bilingual. To this end, he required his advanced students to address him in Spanish while he spoke to them in English. On a trip to Star County in south Texas, he and a doctoral candidate were following this format. Stopping for lunch at a local café where Mexicans were not welcome, they were watched closely by the proprietor. Finally, the owner said to Dr. Sanchez, "I'll serve you but if that Mexican with you wants to eat he will have to go out to the kitchen." The student had no Latino features while Sanchez looked very much Mexican American. Professor Sanchez told this story because it amused him, but it shows how ignorant prejudicial assumptions can be.

What Do You Think?
1. Are you a member of a minority group?
2. If the status of your group changes, will that affect the way you are treated?
3. Great efforts have been made to eliminate prejudicial practices in schools, but the general culture still carries bad attitudes toward some groups. What can teachers do to help resolve this problem?
4. Trace the issues of child labor, racism, prejudice, and social conflict in our schools and society.

vocational education. His Atlanta compromise speech is a classic political conces-
sion. At Tuskegee, Washington stressed hard work, vocational skills, and economic
advancement. He won wide support among whites in the South, and although his
institute became a model for black colleges, his willingness to accept social discrimination has drawn much criticism. Washington always avoided the demand for
social and political equality made by W. E. B. Du Bois and his followers. Washington sought to improve the status of African Americans within the social and economic system; Du Bois sought social, economic, and political reforms to expand
equity and access for minorities.

Minority education outside the South grew slowly but steadily during the period
between the Civil War and World War I. A few liberal colleges like Antioch admitted
black students early, but discrimination was practiced in most areas of the nation.
Numerous black agricultural, military, and normal colleges were established with
funds from the second Morrill Act, and these colleges always included programs for
teachers. Federal money was badly needed, and the black agricultural, military, and
normal schools soon became as important as Tuskegee and various church-related
black colleges. These colleges admitted Native Americans, Asian Americans, and
other minority students. Numerous northern state universities were open to minorities, but the number actually admitted was small, attributable in part to entrance
requirements that screened out graduates from the poor public schools. Public
school segregation was maintained either legally or *de facto* almost everywhere (see
Figure 5.3).

Native American Schools.   Most of the formal education provided for Native
Americans was through philanthropy or missionary efforts until the Office of Indian
Affairs was opened in 1819. Thereafter, schools of various kinds were supported by
government grants, although religious organizations continued to operate the majority of mission schools for Native Americans. A number of Native American scholars
attended Hampton Institute, and in 1879, a Native American training school was
authorized for Carlisle, Pennsylvania. Except for boarding schools on reservations
and a few specific programs aimed at training for vocations, very little was done by
federal or local government to meet the needs of education for Native Americans.

TEACHER EDUCATION

Although colonial teachers were sometimes college graduates, there was nothing
available to them that might be considered professional training. Academies and
female seminaries in the early national period often advertised pedagogical programs that consisted of a review of basic elementary subjects and some lectures on
keeping school. It was long considered adequate for secondary teachers to have
only a sound knowledge of their subject field, without any training in psychology or
methods of teaching.

The first normal schools were academically low-level institutions, a problem
that continued to exist until they were made into 4-year colleges in the twentieth

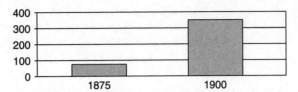

Figure 6.2 Phenomenal Growth of Normal Schools

century. Early normal schools usually had some sort of practice teaching and a course in mental philosophy, but there was no sound theoretical foundation. Some private normal schools and academies for teachers offered programs with higher academic standards, but they also lacked a professional basis. Nevertheless, the growth of teacher education was rapid in the latter part of the nineteenth century (see Figure 6.2). In 1871, 114 schools for teachers replied to an inquiry about programs and enrollments made by the United States Bureau of Education. At least 70 normal schools were receiving some state support in 1875. By 1900, there were 345 normal schools reported in the United States (see Figure 6.2).

Women outnumbered men in the state normal schools; the sexes were about evenly divided in private schools for teachers. A great many students in normal schools already held teaching certificates, and most had some teaching experience before entering the program. Large numbers of teachers attended normal schools for short periods, but only about a third of the public school teachers were normal school graduates. Many normal school programs were offered for 2 years or less and usually were below university level. Most had meager equipment, insufficient support, poor facilities, and an underpaid staff.

Before World War I, however, these institutions began enlarging their curricula and requiring high school graduation for admission. Some, such as Illinois State Normal, were able to erect expensive modern buildings and develop college-level courses. Both the number and quality of normal schools improved very rapidly in the last decades of the nineteenth century and the first decades of the twentieth. Nevertheless, normal schools, high school normal departments, academies, or college departments provided fewer than half of the trained teachers needed to staff public schools. Underpaid young women with little or no education beyond elementary school and perhaps a summer institute continued to teach in district schools.

Sheldon and the Oswego Movement.

A much better conceptual framework for the professional training of teachers was provided by Edward Sheldon. Sheldon became secretary of the Board of Education of Oswego, New York, in 1853. He visited a number of cities in order to find ways of improving the schools, and in 1859 in Toronto, Sheldon came across a Pestalozzian program produced by the Home and Colonial Training Institution of London. Instruction there was based on charts, pictures, manuals, and objects developed by Charles and Elizabeth Mayo, who had been teachers in schools conducted by Pestalozzi.

Having purchased materials worth $300 and secured the services of Margaret E. M. Jones to demonstrate them, Sheldon proceeded to reform the Oswego schools along lines developed by Pestalozzi. The success was impressive, and in 1866, the New York legislature made Oswego a state normal school. Teachers flocked to the new program, and Oswego soon became the most famous teacher-training institution in the United States. Graduates of the school found jobs in various parts of the nation, and thus the Oswego movement influenced regions far beyond New York.

Some of the improvement attributed to the Oswego movement came from the enthusiasm of Sheldon himself, but new techniques of learning and respect for the unique personality of the child were also important. Object teaching began with something familiar to the environment of the child and moved to an abstract description of the object. Geography was taught from the local community outward, until the whole nation and the world could be understood. Study and discipline through mutual understanding and respect were also stressed. Unfortunately, the term *object lesson* was also used by textbook companies who merely wanted to sell books, and some other normal schools made highly formalized lesson plans out of what the Oswego movement had intended to be flexible. Nevertheless, Oswego provided a new model of teacher education that included new principles, better psychology, creative methods, and an effort to understand how children learn.

University Departments of Education.

For many years, pedagogy and teacher training were excluded from universities. Faculty members in the academic disciplines held all professional education in low esteem, and many had contempt for teacher-training programs. In 1879, W. H. Payne, spurred on by the Kalamazoo case, was able to fill the nation's first successful permanent chair of pedagogy at the University of Michigan. The trustees turned down President Barnard of Columbia when he proposed a department of education in 1882. Instead, he assigned Nicholas Murray Butler to offer Saturday lectures for teachers. The interest was so great that over 2,000 teachers applied for Butler's lectures, but the trustees again refused to authorize a department of education or even a senior elective in pedagogy. Finally, Butler organized the New York College for the Training of Teachers. In 1892, under strong opposition, that college was accepted as an affiliate of Columbia University. Faculty and administration traditionalists feared that a move toward a professional college would be detrimental to the university's historical general education and liberal arts tradition. Vocationalism and specialization were not viewed as part of the university mission.

Teacher education at the college level began at Washington College in Pennsylvania in 1831 and at New York University in 1832. The University of Iowa had a chair for didactics (education) in 1873. By 1900, professors of pedagogy were to be found in many universities, although sometimes only one professor constituted the whole department. New York University offered graduate work in education in 1887. Starting about 1890, teacher-training institutions tended to become degree-granting colleges that required secondary school graduation for admission. The scientific study of education and psychology came to be linked with certification. A body of educational theory slowly developed out of work done in education at universities and graduate schools. Nevertheless, the normal school stigma continued to plague departments of education. In a 1992 article in *Change,* Harvard President Derek Bok argued that good teachers would not be produced so long as pedagogy is restricted to the fringes of the universities. Bok worked to stress and improve teaching, and in 1991, the Harvard Center for Teaching Learning, founded in 1976, was named after him.

DEVELOPMENT OF EDUCATIONAL PHILOSOPHY

Theology and philosophical idealism dominated American educational theory before 1900. Before World War I, William James, Charles Peirce, and John Dewey made contributions to pragmatism, but their influence was much greater during the Progressive era of the 1930s. It was so difficult even to provide the rudiments of education to the whole population that little effort was made to define educational goals, to equate theory with psychological principles, or to work out the logical educational positions. Once schools were established, a host of new educational demands were made, and many began to debate the proper role of education. The early influence of Rousseau, Pestalozzi, Froebel, and other European philosophers continued to be felt, but American educational theory also began to develop (see Figure 6.3).

Harris.   William T. Harris, who developed a public kindergarten in 1873 as part of the school system in St. Louis, Missouri, was superintendent of schools there from 1867 to 1880 and United States Commissioner of Education from 1889 to 1906. He was one of the best-known school administrators in America, and his ideas had wide influence throughout the nation. Harris was philosophically an idealist, a follower of the German philosopher Hegel, and a traditionalist in education. As an idealist, Harris believed education should emphasize the cultural subjects and prepare children for harmony with the absolute order of the universe as well as for life in an Industrial nation. As a traditionalist, Harris stressed universal values of right and wrong. Teachers

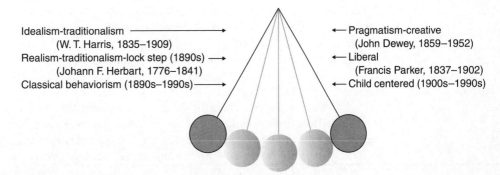

Idealism-traditionalism
   (W. T. Harris, 1835–1909)
Realism-traditionalism-lock step (1890s)
   (Johann F. Herbart, 1776–1841)
Classical behaviorism (1890s–1990s)

←— Pragmatism-creative
   (John Dewey, 1859–1952)
←— Liberal
   (Francis Parker, 1837–1902)
←— Child centered (1900s–1990s)

Figure 6.3 Cycles of Educational Trends

should teach and represent the best ideals of humankind while instilling moral and ethical values in their students. He accepted some of the methods of Pestalozzi but was basically opposed to the manual training movement, science, and materialism. As U.S. Commissioner of Education, a member of the major committees of the NEA, and a leader in the National Herbart Society, his influence was very great. Harris was the great spokesman for the idealistic-traditional theory of education.

Parker.   Quite a different educational position was taken by Francis W. Parker, who was principal of schools in Carrollton, Illinois, before the Civil War. His school career was interrupted by the conflict, in which he served as a colonel in the Union forces. Parker studied in Germany, becoming familiar with the practices of Pestalozzi and Froebel. He returned to America to become superintendent of schools in Quincy, Massachusetts, and later was head of the Cook County Normal School in Chicago. Parker was a democratic individualist with a practical outlook. He followed Pestalozzi closely with regard to and respect for the creative activity of the child. Parker experimented with many kinds of school programs, including the core curriculum that attempted to relate subjects of the curriculum through such interrelated studies as history and geography. Parker provided the background for the work of John Dewey and the Progressives.

The total impact of Pestalozzi and Froebel was relatively light, although kindergartens did develop and university scholars began to study the child as an individual. Public education changed very little before the American Herbartian movement started around 1890.

Herbart.   Johann F. Herbart (discussed in Chapter 2) was responsible for a much greater revolution in American education than any previous European thinker had been. Herbart held that the aim of education was attainment of good moral character and that such character could be acquired only through the process of analyzing the social interests of man to discover ideals appropriate for education. The first step in character realization was the "many sidedness of interest." Although he used the word *interest,* Herbart was really referring to a stimulus to learning. He once said that the person who lays hold of information, and because of that information reaches out for more, takes "interest" in it. In the study of history and literature, Herbart saw a core for the curriculum that could encompass or could be co-related with all other subjects. His principles of co-relation and concentration, by which he meant relation with emphasis at the core, became central to his doctrine. Despite Herbart's insistence on the social and moral aims of education, he took an intellectual approach to the learning process. He also developed a psychology that is still of some value today.

Herbart was an associationist—that is, he believed that we have to account for every new idea on the basis of ideas already in the mind, and hence we must consciously relate or associate new ideas with previous experiences. For Herbart, there could never be a totally new idea. He believed that we receive impressions to the conscious mind (presentation). These presentations are then associated with other ideas that lie together in masses in the subconscious part of the mind. When a new idea in the mind is related, it is transferred from the conscious to the subconscious mind and becomes part of an "apperceptive mass." The idea will not appear in the conscious mind again until it is needed to clarify some new presentation. Herbart's own psychology was not rigid, and his insistence upon the mind as a unity tended to break down the older faculty psychology, which understood the mind to be divided into separate faculties, abilities, or powers.

American Herbartianism.   Herbart's followers in America used his insistence upon association and interests to develop a very rigid educational program. This program came to be known as the "Five Formal Steps of Teaching and Learning." The following are the five formal steps:

1. *Preparation*, in which old ideas useful in learning new materials are called to the learner's mind
2. *Presentation*, or the actual giving of the new material
3. *Association*, in which new material is compared with and related to the old
4. *Generalization*, in which rules, definitions, or general principles are drawn from specific cases
5. *Application*, in which general principles are given meaning by reference to specific examples and practical situations

These Herbartian steps were made popular by Charles De Garmo, Charles McMurry, and Frank McMurry, who were among the early leaders of the American Herbartian Association. It must be remembered that during the late 1800s most teachers were largely without training, and there was no rational philosophy of education. The formal steps of the American Herbartianists filled a void in educational theory, and hence the influence of Herbart through his American followers became dominant in this country in the 1890s. Unfortunately, the set methods of Herbart's led to a "lock-step" in American education; the same subjects were taught in the same way using the same methods and the same textbooks in every public school from Boston to Berkeley. The beneficial part of this uniformity was that it became possible for children to transfer from one school to another without a change in curriculum or loss of time; however, the respect for individuality, new ideas, and creativity, which had been so much in the theories of Froebel and Pestalozzi, was largely lost. Although difficult to identify philosophically, Herbart tended to be a realist and a traditionalist—a realist in his emphasis on fact-centered knowledge and a traditionalist in his focus on uniformity and conformity within educational systems.

Protest Against Rigid Systems.   One of the first to raise a cry against the rigid lock-step school was John Dewey (discussed in Chapter 2). His influence was first felt in the closing years of the nineteenth century, and his importance increased considerably during the first three decades of the twentieth century. Dewey continued to write until the 1950s. However, his greatest amount of influence on education came in the 1930s, when the Progressive Education Association was at the height of its popularity. Dewey felt that Herbart and his followers had emphasized formal methods to the extreme and that they failed to account for natural growth and individual differences. He attacked schools for being antidemocratic and the curriculum for being subject centered. For Dewey, education had to be part of life itself.

Other developments also contributed to the changing climate of opinion out of which new educational theories evolved. In 1859, Charles Darwin published his *On the Origin of Species*, a book that set off the explosive theory of evolution. The theories of scientific evolution and social Darwinism challenged the conceptions of man and the universe held by conservative educators. Evolutionary principles contributed to the formation of the philosophy of pragmatism by Charles Peirce and William James. Pragmatism emphasized the practical questions of how we can understand and control the world instead of the metaphysical question of how we can know reality. Herbert Spencer and others applied the theory of evolution to society in order to explain the existence of social classes and social institutions. Resulting studies in sociology altered traditional conceptions of humanity and opened new windows through which to view education. Evolutionary science became part of the curriculum in universities, but it created an issue in public schools, where it was often banned. The conflict of religion and science culminated in the Scopes trial, a trial that involved the teaching of evolution in Dayton, Tennessee, in 1925.

Schools continued to grow in number before World War I. Children tended to remain in school longer, teachers received more training, and education became a subject for university study. New scientific subjects were added to the high schools, and public high schools became the standard American secondary schools. Child study and psychology led to new concepts of method and new interest in the individual child.

THEN TO NOW

Social and Educational Problems from War.   Events leading up to the American Civil War (and the conflict itself) bear a strong relationship to numerous conditions in the modern era. Extremely bitter sectional and ideological arguments not only caused the Civil War but also altered the attitudes of people for generations. Although the Union survived, negative feelings about Civil War issues continued to dominate political life into the twenty-first century. Social and educational problems created by the freeing of slaves plagued the nation, and the burden carried by the impoverished South caused a very low level of public schooling for both races. Black struggles for equality, reflected by the militant self-help and return-to-Africa movement of Marcus Garvey in 1917 and the civil rights activism of Dr. Martin Luther King, Jr., in the 1960s, may be traced to this era. No struggle divided and alienated the American people like the Civil War until the outbreak of the conflict in Vietnam. The bitterly contested 2004 presidential election brought foreign issues to the surface. The return of American military from Iraq leaves it to historians to determine its aftermath. The Afghanistan conflict, going on 11 years, is a divisive issue for citizens.

American involvement in Southeast Asia during the 1960s and 1970s caused caustic criticism of national policy, especially on university campuses. Like the Civil War, Vietnam raised ugly moral issues, created an erosion of patriotism, and shook the very foundations of the national culture. Just as the Civil War closed schools, promoted illiteracy in most of the South, and led to a system of schools segregated by race, Vietnam also created a major educational crisis. The war caused violence in colleges, alienation of students from their parents' values, and the withdrawal of financial support to educational institutions.

Tracing modern issues over desegregation of schools to the Civil War period is easy, but the total impact of the Vietnam era on education and the American culture may not be known for generations to come. The effect of the Iraq and Afghanistan wars on society and education remains to be written, but Congress has passed a bill to provide education for returning veterans similar to the GI Bill for World War II (Pelosi, 2008).

The quick victory in the Persian Gulf War of 1990–1991 provided some counter-balance to the Vietnam episode, although determining America's role in foreign conflicts—such as those involving the Congo, Somalia, Bosnia, Kosovo, Israel, Palestine, Iraq, Afghanistan, and Haiti—continues to be a challenge. The United States continues to face challenges such as the war on terrorism sparked by the attacks on the World Trade Center and Pentagon in 2001. The Afghanistan elections, in 2004 and 2010, although faced with claims of fraud, was an effort to build a more stable society whose future remains uncertain.

Libya's rejection of terrorism and efforts to join the world community won worldwide support. The Egyptian popular revolution of 2011 swept through the Middle East with an unpredictable end for democratic aspirations. The U.S. elector-ate remains deeply fragmented and divided over a variety of issues including the Iraq and Afghanistan Wars, stem cell research, immigration, budget deficits, conser-vative versus liberal values, and the membership of the Supreme Court.

Concepts and Values, by Generation, 1920 to Today.   Intellectual and cul-tural historians argue that life conditions have major effects on the attitudes, values, and beliefs of all people. Thus, it is necessary to identify the most significant forces that shape values and concepts about the good life for each generation.

Those who grew up in the 1920s held establishment values. World War I, pro-hibition, and the Model T Ford influenced them. Young people were interested in gin and jazz, but close family ties and patriotism dominated the nation. Although the Scopes trial created a major issue, education remained conservative. By the 1930s, the economic crash had taken place, and the nation was in the Great Depres-sion. There was mass unemployment, soup lines, and social unrest. Radical eco-nomic solutions including socialism were suggested, and Franklin Roosevelt became popular with his New Deal. Great emphasis was placed on the value of the dollar, and those who grew up in the 1930s are still very security minded. This was the age of progressive education and radical school reform.

At the beginning of the 1940s, the dominant interest was keeping America safe from the Germans and the Japanese. World War II touched every family, and patriotism permeated the culture. This was an age of working women, geographic mobility, rationing, and support for the armed forces. People became used to the idea of scarcity and waited for better times when peace would be restored. Education turned back to the basics, and the GI Bill increased enrollment in colleges. When the war ended, Americans bought all the things they could not obtain in a wartime economy. Some 50 million TV sets were sold in America, and children began growing up with Howdy Doody and Captain Kangaroo. Crew cuts gave way to longer hair, children were materialistically indulged, and Elvis Presley personified the rock-and-roll age. School desegregation began in the 1950s, and Martin Luther King, Jr., gained a great following. The Korean conflict was considered a great tragedy, but it did not draw the patriotic support common in World War II. Hedonism, materialism, affluence, and the mass media influenced people growing up at this time.

The 1960s saw rapid economic growth, the space program, computers, and Vietnam. Alternative lifestyles were manifest in the hippie subculture, and campus rebellion shocked conservative Americans. Those who grew up in this period recall the bitterness over the Vietnam War and the conflict between generations. It was an age of assassination but also of continued financial growth and affluence. Education focused on school integration, equal opportunity, and the needs of the culturally different child. By the end of the decade, deep-rooted value conflicts had divided Americans to a degree quite similar to the era of the Civil War.

By 1970, inflation and a weaker economy were evident. Many people began to fear a return of the conditions of the Great Depression of the 1930s. Some 20 million mothers entered the workforce in order to improve family income. The energy crisis was taken seriously, and there were concerns about environmental deterioration. Richard Nixon and Watergate caused the erosion of respect for government, while the people began to distrust motives of oil companies and other industrial corporations. Music, the mass media, fast foods, and automobiles were major interests of the young. Drug abuse and alcoholism became widespread among students. Educators concentrated on computer-assisted instruction, a relevant curriculum, and compensatory education for the culturally deprived.

The 1990s and 2000s saw increasing social, political, and economic fragmentation as individuals, communities, business, and industry sought either to maintain or expand their share of an ever-smaller state and federal budget. Shortly after taking office, George W. Bush was confronted with 9/11, a war on terrorism, and stabilizing the economy. Airlines were especially hard hit, and by 2005 many major corporations were facing bankruptcy and financial exigencies. Although the economy stabilized, the continuing Iraq and Afghanistan conflicts became a heavy human and financial burden. Litigation increased in all economic, social, political, religious, and educational institutions during the period. Because performance accountability required ranking and rating of faculty in terms of publication, research, teaching, and fund acquisition, collegiality gave way to adversarial relationships in higher education. In the early 1900s, muckrakers exposed corrupt business and ethical issues in individual and institutional life; in the 1990s, corruption and lapses in morality and ethics were exposed. Upton Sinclair's 1906 *The Jungle* and The Teapot Dome Scandal provided an impetus for the reforms of the

Progressive era. In our twenty-first century, television and newspaper reporters uncover similar ethical and moral lapses among political, military, and business-industrial institutions and their personnel. Exposes of corrupt corporate officials and policies swept America in the early 2000s. Whistleblowers and modern-day muckrakers exposed corruption. The nation faces the challenge of increasing numbers of children living in poverty. Edelman (1996), Feldmann (1996), Kozol (1995, 2000), and Francis (1996) reported on the need for educational and governmental assistance for the working poor.

During the early 2000s, the economy took a nosedive with a dot.com down cycle. President George W. Bush stressed tax reduction. Federal Reserve Chairman Alan Greenspan and the board lowered Federal Reserve fund rates as efforts were made to deal with a cyclical downturn. President Barack Obama was confronted with a major economic recession and expanded a stimulus plan started by his predecessor. Obama stressed assessment, accountability, and testing, as well as vouchers and charter schools. "Raise to the Top" became vision of Education Secretary Arne Duncan.

By 2010, support for national educational standards grew as the National Governor's Association and the National Council of Chief State School Officers sought adoption of common standards for academic content (Education Week, 2010).

Changes in Basic Values.   There is a strong tendency in America for each new generation to reject the ideas and the values of the generation just past. John Dewey and the Progressives rebelled against the lock-step schools and the rigid systems of Herbart's followers. The counterculture did not accept the materialism and the need of security so characteristic of the Depression era and the period of affluence following World War II. Such beliefs were scorned in turn by the youth of the 1970s and early 1980s. It is also probably true that change in basic value orientation takes place more rapidly in an age of accelerating economic and technological invention than in a more stable environment.

The Civil War was a time of social and ethical conflict. When it ended, the old South had disappeared, and the whole of American society was altered. The black revolution and the demand for civil rights evolved slowly from the Civil War to the 1950s, but certainly these movements began in the aftermath of that conflict. Likewise, the whole of American society was changed by the turmoil of the Vietnam era. Changes of this magnitude necessarily have an impact on education and the socialization of the next generation. Periods of revolutionary conflict and social change may be followed by conservative reactions, but history has shown the culture is never restored to what it was before the conflict. Rapid, though uneven, transformation of American society has been evident since the 1860s. American values and the culture of the people can never again be what they were in the antebellum South or the period before the Vietnam conflict.

This is also the case in the rest of the world. The student rebellion in China and the struggle to achieve human rights altered the values of that nation for the future. Events in Eastern Europe and the former Soviet Union vastly changed perceptions of the Communist bloc and the concept of the Cold War. By 1990, the social and political revolutions in nations like Poland, Hungary, and Romania had altered the nature of Europe and changed global social relationships. NATO was expanded to include Eastern Europe, and Russia became involved in the organization. As the European Common Market expands, it will pose a threat to American economic dominance and power. Regional trade organizations in Asia, Europe, and the Americas as well as proponents and opponents of globalization will affect our future. Lack of international support for the preemptive strike in Iraq with an emerging costly internal insurgency will require new strategic military and diplomatic initiatives. These events will continue to have great impact on the world. Education must always prepare students for change if it is to be successful.

Educators and politicians of the 1990s and early 2000s addressed growing value conflicts through conflict resolution, sensitivity training programs, and a commitment to moral, ethical, and character education at all levels of the educational system. Programs in multiculturalism, cultural diversity, and English limited proficiency reflect a continuing expansion of the nation's social consciousness. At the same time, home and private schooling are expanding, partly because of the many religious and secular value conflicts in society. History of education continues to show that W. E. B. Du Bois's call for universal education as a public duty and at public expense is as timely in the twenty-first century as in the twentieth.

GAINING PERSPECTIVE THROUGH CRITICAL ANALYSIS

1. Name two actions by the federal government that impacted the education in the southern states after the Civil War. How are these actions affecting educational practices today?

2. Discuss the discrepancy between W. E. B. Du Bois's call for universal and free education and the actual funds allocated for it. (A review of the chapter-opening quotation will help you with your answer.)

3. Analyze the contribution of the Kalamazoo case ruling to public schools.

4. What impact did the Smith-Hughes Act have on early educational practices, and what effects do we still see on today's vocational education?

5. What current philosophy of education is the closest equivalent to the philosophy of the Oswego movement? Give reasons for your choice.

6. Why was there so much opposition to the founding of Teacher's College at Columbia University?

HISTORY IN ACTION IN TODAY'S CLASSROOMS

1. How do the Cardinal Principles apply to today's educational system? List at least three applications in your journal.

2. Make a time line in your journal that shows the significance of the National Education Association (NEA) between 1857 and 1998 in regard to educational equity and access for women and minorities.

3. Did the NEA leadership exercise its organizational power to change traditional views of women and minorities or did the association's actions reflect public attitudes during various historical periods? Give examples of positive action, inaction, or evasive action of the NEA concerning improving the lot of women and minorities. Add the findings to your journal.

4. Use your journal to record a sample budget for a classroom using a $300 limit. List the philosophical or historical ideas that influenced your decisions. Compare your purchases with those of Edward Sheldon. Discuss and answer the questions at the end of the Focus on the Issues feature "Sanchez Encounters Prejudice." This feature is found within the chapter.

▜ BIBLIOGRAPHY

Beale, Howard. *A History of Freedom of Teaching in American Schools*. New York: Octagon Books, 1974.

Bok, Derek. "Reclaiming the Public Trust." *Change* 24, no. 4 (July/August 1992): 19.

Bok, Derek. *The State of the Nation*. Cambridge: Harvard Press, 1996.

Boring, Edwin G. *A History of Experimental Psychology*. New York: Appleton-Century-Crofts, 1957.

Butts, Freeman. *The Education of the West: A Formative Chapter in the History of Civilization*. New York: McGraw-Hill, 1973.

Butts, R. Freeman, & Lawrence A. Cremin. *A History of Education in American Culture*. New York: Holt, Rinehart and Winston, 1953.

"Common Standards Judged Better Than Most States," *Education Week* (July 21, 2010). Available at: www.edweek.org/ew/articles/2010/07/21/37fordham.h29.html?tkn=YLNFLyhtPuP19

Counts, George. *Secondary Education and Industrialism*. Cambridge, MA: Harvard University Press, 1929.

Cubberley, Ellwood. *Readings in Public Education in the United States*. Boston: Houghton Mifflin, 1934.

Dewey, John. *School and Society*. Chicago, IL: University of Chicago Press, 1900.

Edelman, Marion Wright. "We've Got More Wallet Than Will, Says Children's March Leader." *Arkansas Democrat Gazette* (May 27, 1996): 6A.

Feldmann, Linda. "More Children of Working Parents Now Live in Poverty." *The Christian Science Monitor* (June 4, 1996): 3.

Francis, David R. "Despite Growth, Families Suffer to Prosper in the U.S." *The Christian Science Monitor* (August 7, 1996): 1, 8.

Herbart, John Frederick. *Outlines of Educational Doctrine*. New York: Macmillan, 1909.

Kandel, Isaac. *History of Secondary Education*. Boston: Houghton Mifflin, 1930.

Karier, Clarence J. *Shaping the American Educational Experience: 1990 to the Present*. New York: Free Press, Macmillan, 1975.

Knight, Edgar, & Clifton Hall. *Readings in American Educational History*. New York: Appleton-Century-Crofts, 1951.

Kozol, Jonathan. *Amazing Grace: The Lives of Children and the Conscience of a Nation*. New York: Crown Publishers, 1995.

Kozol, Jonathan. *Ordinary Resurrections: Children in the Years of Hope*. New York: Crown Publishers, 2000.

Mayer, Frederick. *A History of Educational Thought*. 3rd ed. New York: Merrill/Macmillan, 1974.

Meyer, Adolphe E. *An Educational History of the American People*. New York: McGraw-Hill, 1957.

Nassaw, David. *Schooled to Order*. New York: Oxford University Press, 1979.

Pelosi, Nancy. "GI Bill for the 21st Century" (2008). Available at: www.democraticleader.gov/issues

Ravitch, Diane. *Great School Wars*. New York: Basic Books, 1988.

Reavis, George H., & Carter V. Good. *An Educational Platform for the Public Schools*. Bloomington, IN: Phi Delta Kappa, 1996.

Rudolph, Frederick. *The American College and University: A History*. New York: Vintage Books, 1962.

Sheldon, Edward. *Autobiography*. New York: Ives-Butler, 1911.

Vaughn, Preston. *Schools for All: The Blacks and Public Education in the South, 1865–1877*. Lexington, KY: University of Kentucky Press, 1974.

Warren, Donald. *To Enforce Education: A History of the Founding Years of the United States Office of Education*. Detroit, MI: Wayne State University Press, 1974.

Washington, Booker T. *Up from Slavery: An Autobiography*. New York: Doubleday, 1938.

Weinberg, Meyer. *W. E. B. Du Bois: A Reader*. New York: Harper & Row, 1970, p. 147.

Westerhoff, John. *McGuffey and His Readers: Piety, Morality, and Education in Nineteenth Century America*. Nashville, TN: Abingdon Press, 1978.

CHAPTER 7

DEVELOPMENT OF MODERN AMERICAN EDUCATION AFTER 1918

Quantification, mechanization and standardization: these are then the marks of the Americanization that is conquering the world. They have their good side; external conditions and the standard of living are undoubtedly improved. But their effects are not limited to these matters; they have invaded the mind and character, and subdued the soul to their own dye.

John Dewey

World War I		Great Depression
1919 Progressive Education Association	1929 George Reed Act	1932 George Counts Dare the School Build a New Social Order
1923 Daytona-Cookman Collegiate Institute (Bethune-Cookman College)	1930 School year became 172 days and all states had compulsory attendance	1937 George Reed Act
1925 Oregon case guaranteed right of private schools	1932 New Deal educational programs	1930–38 *Eight-Year Study* confirmed value of progressive schools

Figure 7.1 Time Line for American Education After 1918

Several volumes could be written on the subject of educational expansion, change, and controversy since World War I. The most obvious feature has been the tremendous growth at all levels in the numbers of students, teachers, and facilities. Secondary education grew during this period until it became standard for almost all children, just as the elementary school had done in the previous century. Higher education expanded, especially in the years following World War II, so that some kind of college or university experience was enjoyed by more than two-thirds of all American high school graduates. Many cities in the United States now contain more individuals engaged in formal schooling than could have been found in the entire colonial area at any one time. Sophisticated training offered by industry, early childhood education (public and private), the federal government, expanded school choice (vouchers and charter schools), assessment, cultural diversity, and mass media illustrate agencies and techniques now active in education that were not significant in earlier times. Education is now big business in terms of money spent on training teachers, physical plants, developing materials, and serving students.

This magnification of educational enterprise raised new issues concerning the relationship of school and the society. Advances in technology, fluid social order, economic cycles, wars (both hot and cold), and conflict over the meaning of democracy led to a reevaluation of educational aims.

World War II	Cold War	
1941 Military training for national defense	1950s Loyalty Oaths	1963 Education Facilities Act
1944 G.I. Bill for college tuition	1954 *Brown v. Board of Education* in Topeka	1964 First Surgeon General's Report on Smoking and Health
1945 UNESCO	1957 *Sputnik*	1965 Head Start Program
1947 Truman Commission Report	1958 NDEA	1981 Identification of AIDS
		1984 Carl D. Perkins Act

MAJOR EDUCATIONAL CHANGES

National Unity Through Education.   Integration of all Americans into a national community was a goal of early leaders such as Mann and Barnard. Schools were viewed as social ladders for individual and group improvement and as the means for "Americanizing" immigrants. Since World War II, the civil rights movement, the black revolution, the growing Hispanic population, and the educational problems of children from various social, economic, religious, ethnic, and racial backgrounds have received much more attention. Desegregating schools, helping the culturally disadvantaged, and meeting social needs in urban centers have become major goals of American education, and schools have made great strides in these areas. However, large numbers of children are still excluded from equal educational opportunity, and national unity though social integration has not been realized. Much current educational theory centers on the role of school in solving major cultural problems and on the kind of education that will be required to prepare the young for meeting the challenges of an uncertain future.

Changes in Education, Mid-1900s to Today.   Among the more significant changes in education during the last half century are the following seven.

    1. *A broader educational philosophy* with social as well as individual objectives, illustrated by progressive education, deconstruction,

postmodernism, social equity, aggression control, constructivism, inclusion, and social reconstruction movements.

2. *New areas of educational concern* such as vocational guidance, standardized testing, tech-prep programs for employability, special education for the physically and mentally challenged and the gifted, English for speakers of other languages (ESOL), and English as a second language (ESL).

3. *Reorganization of schools* to include junior or middle high schools, junior or community colleges, night schools, and correspondence courses, as well as an explosion of graduate education, changes in graduate and undergraduate delivery systems to include Saturday and weekend classes, on-site classes in industry and business, external degree programs for individuals not able to take time off from work for further education, home study television classes with proposals for 3-year bachelor's degree programs, compressed video and blended learning degree programs, advanced placement or honors programs, and college credit for work experience. Online learning programs for kindergarten through 12th-grade students will give students control over time, pace, and place.

4. *New emphasis* on health, welfare, violence prevention, improved buildings and equipment, partnerships between schools, businesses, and community and service learning (credit given students for civic participation such as helping the elderly, and a wide variety of community projects).

5. *Enormous increase in attendance* at all levels and an extension of the years of formal schooling for the average student including adult education and lifelong learning. Elderhostels are an example of continuing education efforts.

6. *Extension and improvement of teacher training,* Master of arts in teaching programs (often 5-year programs), congressional legislation to survey teacher education content and practices, and the scientific study of education through research.

7. *Impact of cultural changes* such as mass media of communications; research conducted by private organizations; development of the Internet with search engines such as Bing, Alta Vista, AskJeeves, Looksmart, Microsoft MSN, AOL, Yahoo, Internet Protocol, and Google; IPhones, IPods, digital images, and growth in distance learning programs at all educational levels; cell phones, wireless systems, location tracking (global positioning system, or GPS), and multimedia systems combining telephone, computer, entertainment services, and research queries into information superhighways; and the increased role of the federal government in educational affairs such as the No Child Left Behind Act (NCLB) as well as The American Recovery and Reinvestment Act.

Availability of Educational Materials; Lifelong Learning.   Historically, many famous Americans including Benjamin Franklin and Abraham Lincoln were self-educated. This required a high degree of motivation and self-sacrifice. Franklin subsisted on potatoes and used his wages to buy books while Lincoln borrowed all the reading material he could find in his frontier settlement. The availability of educational materials expanded vastly in the modern period with resources such as school, university, Internet, and public libraries.

With the onset of World War II, men and women prepared for work in business and industry. Men were quickly trained to fly aircraft, drive tanks, or manage military logistics. Standardized tests with multiple methodologies of personality assessment classification were developed and refined to predict, sort, and categorize men and women for military assignments. After the war, testing spread from the barracks to the classrooms, as group tests for use in the nation's schools were developed (Meyer, 1957). Hundreds of thousands of women left homemaking and trained to produce wartime material in the nation's industrial plants. With peace, almost everyone had to be reeducated for different jobs with the help of the GI Bill and other governmental programs. Adult education, retraining for new jobs, and lifelong learning became a reality. No one today expects to stop learning after leaving school, because skills and information quickly become obsolete.

The computer and the Internet have so vastly altered the learning environment that all levels of schooling have changed. It is now common for a preadolescent child to write a sophisticated story or produce a well-researched paper that would have passed for college work a decade ago. Most homes now have Internet access, and devices such as the Connected Touch Pad provide access in places too small for PCs. Schools will certainly continue to function as the electronic age advances, but their role will no longer be to provide or transfer information that can be found elsewhere. Change continues to accelerate with Spintronics (a whole new class of electronics based on the spin of the electron), quantum information science and technology, virtual online external degree programs, and electronic publishing (Jeffry, 2000).

These changes are not without problems. Plagiarism is easy via the Internet, and there are few controls. Cyber crime including identify theft led Congress to pass the Fair and Accurate Credit Transaction Act (FACTA) that provides consumer protections. Cyber law is frequently out-of-date as soon as it is written. Accessing information does not mean that it is always well evaluated or properly applied, as vast quantities of online materials are of questionable value or just plain wrong. Nevertheless, the electronic information age will continue to govern future educational theory and practice. Inventions in this field come rapidly, and education must adjust. It is hard to realize that the dollar value of software is now greater than that of manufactured goods in America.

Perhaps the most difficult problem for educators in the United States today is how to provide varied, realistic, general, and individual education for all children and produce the experts necessary for a technology-media-oriented democracy at the same time. Can we really be equal and excellent, too?

Social, Political, and Economic Influence.
Many of these changes, and others less dramatic, began in the nineteenth century and were developed in recent decades; however, there were also innovations that came about as a result of

economic and social changes during the two world wars. Older concerns with physical expansion gave way to new problems of technological discovery and scientific development. Reforms in government pursued legal measures to prevent waste and exploitation of dwindling natural resources. Contact with the sophisticated culture of Europe during World War I and the economic crisis that followed the conflict altered many of America's basic conceptions. Woodrow Wilson's failure to persuade America to join the League of Nations and the isolationism, fatalism, and inflation of the postwar era did not destroy European influences.

The decade-long depression that started in 1929 shook American optimism and altered the government's role in economic affairs. When Franklin Roosevelt became president in 1932, the immense task of economic rebuilding began. The New Deal program attempted to place 11 million unemployed persons in various types of meaningful jobs and to establish emergency measures to solve the economic crisis. It was not, however, until the beginning of World War II that the United States found its way out of the Depression and into a new era of war-boom and postwar prosperity.

FOCUS ON THE ISSUES

Divergent Views

Returning from a meeting in Texarkana, a vocational agriculture teacher was driving through a remote rural area when he happened to see a farmer holding a small hog. He stopped and stared in disbelief while the farmer lifted his pig to the lower branch of a tree, where the animal proceeded to eat an apple. The teacher said, "What a ridiculous way to feed a pig. I have never seen such a colossal waste of time." The farmer shrugged and replied, "What is time to a pig?"

This illustrates that perceptions vary significantly from person to person. During the recession at the start of the second decade of the twenty-first century, massive economic bailouts for corporations and financial institutions were passed by Congress. To many, this huge cost to the taxpayer and increase in the national debt seemed not to be justified. Others believed that it was the only way to keep the nation out of a full-blown depression. There was little agreement about what caused the economic collapse and less on how the problem should be addressed. Some issues center on social or cultural beliefs. Among traditional Navajo people, it is customary to toss a pinch of pollen toward the east at daybreak to greet Dawn Boy and bless the day. Many Christian fundamentalists view this practice as pure paganism or even as devil worship. Although public education must be governed by majority rule in a democracy, we must understand that very different views of school issues exist in our society. Divergent views are even greater in the global society where Islamic or communist ideas may prevail.

What Do You Think?

1. Evolution is considered fact rather than theory by the scientific community, but religious fundamentalists consider it an attack on their beliefs and push for teaching intelligent design as an alternative theory. How can teachers deal with both views?

2. Seeing exactly the same evidence, two well-intentioned persons may reach opposing conclusions. How does this impact on such educational governance as school board policy?

3. Identify key components of progressive education as well as the search for consensus or unity within diversity for a democratic society.

World War II caused a rapid increase in the rate of technological advancement and stimulated American interest in the international situation, leading to an ideological struggle against communism culminating in the Cold War of the 1950s. The impact of space achievements resulted not only in federal support for advancement of science, mathematics, and foreign languages in the schools, but also in efforts to locate and train the exceptional pupil who could be a leader in scientific and military development. Under Truman and Eisenhower, programs developed that provided a greater amount of social security and a higher rate of employment, but the nation was faced again with a need for protection against external aggression. America became involved in the United Nations (chartered in 1945), and the need to develop peaceful coexistence with communistic countries dominated American foreign policy. American efforts to limit communist expansion led to commitments in Korea, Berlin, and Vietnam.

The leadership of John F. Kennedy brought new reforms and policies to the internal social development of the country, including economic stimulation and programs of health and medical care for the aged. Vast increases in federal aid to education, the war on poverty, and greater federal expenditure for education marked the presidency of Lyndon Johnson. It is important to remember that the United States contained a population of about 100 million in 1918 compared with over 300 million today, with an increasing number of Hispanic, Asian, and other immigrants entering the country each year. Social mobility and new industry gave rise to teeming cities with very different educational problems from those of agrarian communities. Americans became the most affluent people in history (with persistent pockets of inner-city and rural poverty), and an increase of wealth produced demands for amenities, more education, and solutions to new kinds of problems.

Today, more than 50 percent of our high school students express interest in attending a college or university. Although education is still the road to economic advancement, the role of the schools in social change, education for leisure, and the evaluation of major institutions now takes on new significance. The trend of beginning school earlier and staying in school longer has by no means reached its zenith. A major educational problem of the twenty-first century centers on the need for both general education (common school experiences for all children) and increased specialization. Adult education and lifelong learning are requisites for students and workers in order to keep up with rapid changes in technology and a mobile social structure. Special efforts to improve at-risk student achievement levels are underway at all educational levels. Corporations such as Wal-Mart and Tyson initiated programs to help their employees and their children enroll in language and degree programs.

EVOLUTION OF THE MODERN INSTITUTIONAL STRUCTURE

A serious argument rages among educators over the adequacy of the current educational system in meeting the needs of our young people. Many studies show that children are capable of learning such skills as reading at a younger age than we had previously supposed. However, children mature at different rates so that starting all six-year-olds in the first grade is psychologically unsatisfactory.

Many students seem to benefit from early childhood education, such as a structured nursery school or a Montessori school. Most American communities now offer some preschool educational experience of a formal type. Although some people became interested in the educational ideas of Maria Montessori as early as 1911, the rapid growth of Montessori programs for young children has taken place only in the last few decades. A major problem for Montessori and other preschool programs is that most are supported by private tuition. A notable exception is the federally funded Head Start program operating in all 50 states. The program provides comprehensive developmental services for America's low-income at-risk children from age three to five.

Many children who could benefit from formal educational experience prior to entering kindergarten are from families unable to pay the fees, and Head Start is not available to all. Since 1970, kindergartens have been publicly supported as part of the public school system in almost all American communities. Before that date, some kindergartens were private and some cities had none at all. Some schools now offer developmental programs for kindergarten-age children who are found through testing to be immature. Today a large number of American pre-kindergarten children are in day-care centers that often have educational programs, and most of them teach social skills.

Currently day-care centers, most privately owned, are widely available for children at risk, but vary in effectiveness. Some nonprofit centers supported by a combination of private, community, and federal funding and volunteers—such as the Community Child Care Center of Delray Beach, Florida, nationally accredited by the National Academy of Early Childhood programs—offer expanded services from the age at which children can walk through age five. Among the clientele are abused, neglected, at-risk children from low-income working poor, refugees, teen parents in school, and those in job training. Parents are also assisted in dealing with drug use, AIDS, aggressive or dysfunctional behavior, and inadequate job skills. Immigrant and minority communities with a large number of single parents with transient partners are given special assistance for employability in conjunction with some day-care centers like the Community Child Care Center. Many day-care centers offer services to families.

Elementary Programs.   Before the beginning of the twentieth century, the modern school system had emerged as a single track from the elementary grades through college. American schools are still divided into 50 different state systems, with a great deal of control vested in local boards and state departments of education. However, the past 50 years have clearly demonstrated a trend to build larger units, standardize programs, and put more schools under the jurisdiction of centralized administrative units. Research into the advantages and disadvantages of large versus small schools currently continues.

In 1893, the NEA appointed a Committee of Fifteen on the organization and programs of primary and grammar schools. The committee stressed good English usage including literature, United States history, geography, writing, arithmetic, physical science, and music. It suggested manual training for boys and cooking or sewing for girls, along with Latin for children in the eighth grade. The effect of the recommendations was to standardize the curriculum of elementary schools throughout the nation.

Most modern elementary schools do not extend beyond the sixth grade. Although curriculum changes have taken place, elementary students still devote the majority of their time to skill subjects such as reading, writing, grammar, and mathematics. Having combined history and geography into "social studies," they added biological sciences, and replaced arithmetic with the "new math" of the 1960s (which focuses on formal math structure).

Art, music, and physical education are often the first courses to be cut during budget shortfalls, even though research has shown that achievement in mathematics and music is interrelated. However, social studies now receive more attention than spelling. Physical education might consist of organized sports, calisthenics, or merely free play at recess or noon, although efforts are made to employ full- or part-time instructors in the field. Many subjects such as sex education, aggression control, multicultural studies, and health education have been added to the curriculum. Sometimes state legislatures have taken it upon themselves to pass laws requiring the teaching of additional subjects such as drug education and, more recently, character and aggression control education. Senator Robert Byrd inserted a provision in the 2005 budget to require all schools receiving federal funding to give lessons on the Constitution every September 17 ("Schools Must Teach About Constitution," 2005). Educators have experimented with curriculum, and much new information has been added. However, there have been more changes in attitudes and methods than in basic subjects.

The School Survey.   Educational leaders as early as the period of James Carter and Horace Mann looked hard at the adequacy of schools in various states, but it was not until 1910 that a formal survey of schools took place. In that year, Superintendent William Kendall of Indianapolis was invited to visit and make a report on the schools of Boise, Idaho. His survey covered teachers, curriculum, organization of schools and buildings, and attitudes of citizens toward their educational system. By 1914, the school survey was an established practice, but not many were as detailed as the three-year, $100,000 New York City survey.

Early surveys used the services of well-known educators and ranked the subject system against others regarded as comparable. Nothing more sophisticated than observation was used as a tool for measurement. Criticism of the large numbers of changes recommended and failure to consider the limitations of resources caused surveys by teams of experts to be unpopular. *The Thirteenth Yearbook of the National Society for the Study of Education* offered suggestions about how surveys might be conducted by local educators with only slight assistance from experts. Data from a 1926 survey of secondary school units with "regular" and "reorganized" (referring to various types of junior-senior combinations) high school enrollments (see Figure 7.2) showed that over 60 percent of the 18,157 high schools in the United States had an enrollment of 100 pupils or less.

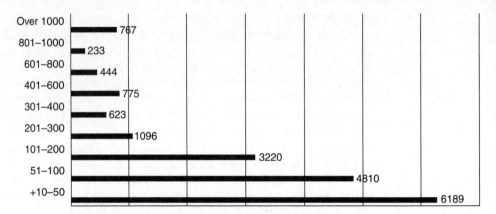

Figure 7.2 Distribution of U.S. Public High Schools by Enrollment for 1926

Note: The average number enrolled in the 18,157 schools was 211.4. De Witt Clinton High School of New York City was the largest school with an enrollment of 8,611.

Source: From the U.S. Bureau of Education *Bulletin,* 1927, No. 3, Statistics of Public High Schools. Cited in Department of Superintendence *Seventh Yearbook* (p. 208), 1929. Washington, DC: Department of Superintendence of the National Education Association.

Detailed surveys are still conducted in the United States. They serve a variety of purposes such as planning for consolidation, desegregation, new building, curriculum change, and administrative reorganization. Surveys are also used by organizations for accrediting schools and evaluating programs.

Savoie (2010) noted that the 111th Congress passed the 21st Century Green High Performing Public School Facilities Act authorizing 6.4 billion dollars for school modernization and renovation for fiscal year 2010. Additional funds would be provided for school districts affected by hurricanes and other natural disasters.

Consolidation. One of the earlier shifts in design resulted from the consolidation of one-room district schools in rural areas. Local elementary schools were first built just far enough apart to permit scholars to walk from their homes. Concentrations of population, the wide use of automobiles, and a reduction of the number of farm families made it possible to build united schools that were larger and more efficient. Just after World War I, about 70 percent of the public school buildings in the United States were of the one-room variety, which were expensive to maintain, lacking in equipment, poorly supervised, and without specialization. Consolidation has reduced the number of one-room schools to less than 5 percent of the total. Today, even sparsely populated communities often have modern multiroom physical plants, complete with gymnasium, cafeteria, and modern equipment. Bus service is normally provided by consolidated school districts. School consolidation continues to be a work in progress in rural areas, including Arkansas Act 60, passed by the Arkansas State Legislature, requires consolidation when school districts fall below 350 students. Fifty-seven of the small school districts were consolidated in 2004 with continuing controversy, protest, and lawsuits. Further consolidation will occur when districts fall below 350 (Robinson, 2004). Kellar Noggle, former Executive Director of the Arkansas Association of Educational Administrators, reported that 124 out of 1,000 Arkansas public schools did not meet some form of state curricular or licensure standards. Although most were minor credentialing issues, schools on probation two years in a row are subject to strict oversight. School consolidation is designed to pool resources and facilities. The *Digest of Educational Statistics 1999* and *2004* gives a picture of the dramatic decline of one-teacher, one-room schools (see Figure 7.3). The report found some 463 one-room, one-teacher schools, with the majority in Montana (82) and Nebraska (97). There were 366 in 2002. The others are in rural areas throughout the country. We may expect they will disappear in the future.

The modern elementary school has changed in both consolidated and urban school districts. Elementary schools are not as directly linked to colleges (although there are more cooperative programs between universities and elementary schools) as are high schools. This link allows more flexibility in the curriculum and scheduling. Team teaching, block scheduling, programmed instruction, and minicourses for student electives—such as introduction to foreign languages, vocational education, keyboarding, computer literacy, teaching machines, and computer-assisted instruction—are used in connection with other innovative programs in instructional technology. The organization, administration, structures, and curriculums of schools in America are not fixed or final. Further evolution of schools and programs may be expected in the future. Many schools have specially trained teachers for art, speech correction, guidance counseling, and so forth. Extracurricular activities, such as team sports, and federally subsidized lunch programs are commonly found in elementary schools.

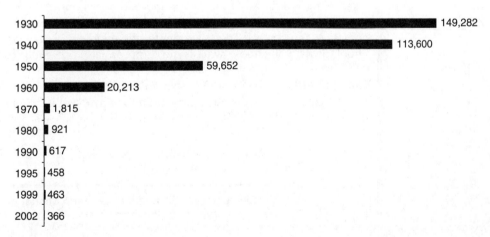

Figure 7.3 Decline of One-Room Schools
Source: From *Digest of Educational Statistics 1996, 2004* (p. 96), by Thomas Snyder, Washington, DC: U.S. Office of Education. National Center for Educational Statistics.

Junior High and Middle Schools.   Eight-year elementary schools and 4-year high schools are still found in the United States, but other organizational plans are more common. Junior high schools increased slowly in number during the first half of the twentieth century, but their number increased markedly in the past 30 years. Middle schools or mid–high schools are now found in many communities. Since the middle of this century, the 6–3–3 or 6–6 plan of organization has become more common than the traditional 8-year elementary school followed by a 4-year high school. Some cities have experimented with a 6–2–4 or a 4–4–4 organizational plan (see Table 7.1). The 2-year community college has sometimes been added as an extension of the common school system.

The typical junior high school consists of seventh, eighth, and ninth grades. Part of the theory behind junior high schools relates to a need for vocational or terminal secondary education. Their success and popularity can be attributed in part to an exploratory curriculum with general courses in science and introductory work in various fields. Students receive guidance concerning their abilities and limitations. They study fewer subjects (with a different teacher for each course), but greater detail is given than for elementary subjects. It is assumed that junior or middle high school students no longer need the security of belonging to one classroom with one teacher, and they are expected to have a longer attention span than younger children.

Perhaps the most important reason for the popularity of the 3-year junior middle high school is that it separates youngsters just starting the adolescent period of life from both older and younger students. This separation contributes to the development of social skills. Children of all ages are not crammed together into a matrix of social and intellectual competition. Some middle schools have innovative multi-age-teaming child-centered programs. Junior high schools may be attached to an elementary or high school or may be completely separated. New York City and a few other school districts are moving toward the historical format of first through eighth grades and away from junior and middle school concepts. Cromwell (1999) finds the kindergarten through eighth grade (K–8) model revolves around intimacy, the basics, and control. There is room for the middle school and K–8 concept. Each school district will choose what is most appropriate to its individual culture.

High Schools.   The most important thing about the American high school in the past 50 years is its phenomenal growth. In the sense that it caters to a range of abilities, interests, and goals, the secondary school has become a school of all the people,

Table 7.1 Combinations of Organizational Plans for Public Schools

Elementary	Middle	High School
6	3	3
6		6
6	2	4
4	4	4

just as the elementary school was in an earlier period. In 1920, there were about 2.5 million U.S. secondary school students (approximately a third of the population between the ages of 14 and 17). In 1965, there were more than 15 million secondary school students—approximately 85% of the high school age group. There are a number of vocational or technical high schools, especially in large cities, but the typical American secondary school has become the "comprehensive" public high school.

Comprehensive is a term used by scholars such as James B. Conant who have studied the program of the high schools in detail. Basically, it refers to a secondary school that has a program designed to meet the various needs and interests of students, regardless of whether or not they expect to attend college. Vocational courses have long been offered by high schools, but the major emphasis is still on college preparation. With the increasing affluence of the American people and the growing scarcity of jobs for which little training is required, college preparation is not likely to lose ground as high school's major purpose. According to the *Digest of Education Statistics: 2009* and the *Statistical Abstract of the United States 2009*, college enrollment increased 41 percent between 1970 and 1980 and 20 percent from 1980 to 1992, or from 12.1 million to 14.6 million, a record level. Over 15 million students were enrolled in higher education institutions in 1994. A record public and private higher education projected 2011 enrollment of 19,713 was reported by the U.S. Census Bureau/*Digest of Education Statistics*. Nevertheless, the purpose of secondary education and the program of the high schools continue to be the most hotly debated issues in American education. There is a trend toward dual enrollment in high school and college courses.

Shortly after the Kalamazoo decision ensured tax support, the public high school took on qualities of both the academy and the classical school. It offered courses that were practical and cultural on the one hand and college preparatory on the other. Training of the mind became equated with preparation for life, and the college preparatory course was considered to be the best mental training. Electives were offered in high schools, but curriculum was shaped by what colleges would accept for entrance.

The Committee of Ten of the NEA's report in 1892 emphasized that high schools were for the elite. The twentieth century gave rise to an increase in national wealth, an improved living standard, and a need for a better trained labor force. High schools were forced to cater to the needs of the entire population in a growing industrial democracy. The NEA Commission on the Reorganization of Secondary Education, meeting in 1918, developed the Cardinal Principles of Secondary Education. In contrast with the college-centered and mental-discipline-oriented Committee of Ten, these principles stressed guidance, a wide range of subjects, adaptation of content and methods to the abilities and interest of students, and flexibility of organization and administration. In addition to fundamental processes and academic subjects, high schools began to stress health, citizenship, vocational preparation, ethical development, and the worthy use of leisure time. In short, they became comprehensive.

A demand for experts to improve industry and to help win the Cold War resulted in more science courses; and new subjects such as driver training, mental hygiene, nutrition, and personal relations reflected the needs of individuals in a complex society. The American comprehensive high school has received harsh criticism, especially from those emphasizing traditional subject matter and academic excellence. There is still a question of whether or not the high school should be specialized and, if so, how specialized and how early in the student's career. In 1945, a Harvard committee published *General Education in a Free Society;* the book suggests that specialization on the secondary level is unsound. Others have joined the battle to extend general education through the high school on the grounds that modern society demands generalized knowledge of many areas for true human fulfillment and good citizenship. Other nations such as China do not stress general education in their schools.

The American high school has provided universal education for the nation's youth. Regardless of the variation in school facilities and achievement levels, few other nations have an institution serving such a broad-based student body. Record levels of enrollment are occurring in our twenty-first century. Public elementary school enrollment (K–8) is projected to be 38.8 million, while it is 371 billion in the 1998–1999 school year. Total public education expenditures were $589 billion in 2009–2010 and average pupil expenditure was $10,190 (National Education Association, 2010). Some 7.4 percent of the gross domestic product is spent on public education at all levels (*Digest of Educational Statistics 2002, National Center for Education Statistics 2002*). Savoie (2009) noted Congress passed a 21st Century Green High-Performing Facilities Act authorizing $6.4 billion for school renovation and modernization projects for 2010. Additional funding would be provided to school districts affected by hurricanes.

Higher Education.   Because of the phenomenal growth of colleges and universities, high schools in the United States have never entirely lost their college preparatory function. With the exception of the period of the Great Depression, college enrollments have had a steady increase, but the great explosion in size and number of colleges has taken place since World War II. Colleges have become more utilitarian and scientific in nature, although the liberal arts college is still a major American institution. With the addition of colleges and universities of a professional nature (education, agriculture, engineering, commerce, architecture, computer information systems, criminal justice institutes, food science, dentistry, and veterinary medicine) and the creation of separate departments within colleges, higher education has become very specialized. Practical and scientific courses were in demand before World War I, but the expansion of industry and the explosion of knowledge have made college training indispensable to many occupations that previously needed little formal schooling. Clark Kerr (1911–2003) developed the concept of a multiuniversity, multicampus, state university system in California that has served as a model in other states. The system provides additional resources to students living at a distance from the flagship university.

Minority Women.   Mary McLeod Bethune (1875–1955) recognized the need for advanced education for minority women. She had a lifelong commitment to the improvement of education and the socioeconomic status of African American women.

Bethune was born in Mayesville, South Carolina, and was educated in a mission school (Scotia Seminary) and in the Moody Bible Institute. Bethune taught in Florida and Georgia from 1897 to 1903. She founded the Daytona Educational and Industrial Training School for Negro Girls in 1904. The curriculum included reading, writing, spelling, arithmetic, cooking, cleaning, sewing, and religion. With financial support from white liberal tourists from the North and blacks and whites in the community, the school was maintained. Bethune often had her students sing in tourist hotels to raise funds for the school. In 1923, the school was merged with Cookman Institute of Jacksonville, Florida. Daytona–Cookman Collegiate Institute became Bethune–Cookman College. Bethune was president of the college from 1904 to 1942 and from 1946 to 1947.

Bethune used a variety of prestigious national positions to advance the cause of African American education. Bethune held leadership positions in the National Association for Colored Women and its Florida Sunshine State Affiliate. Bethune was a consultant to the United States contingent at the founding conference of the United Nations in San Francisco. Appointed director of the Negro Affairs Division of the National Youth Administration (1936–1944) by President Franklin Roosevelt, she served as a powerful advocate for civil rights of African Americans. During this period, Bethune was a consultant to the United States Secretary of War in the selection of the first female officer candidates for the armed forces. Her energy, persuasive skills, and ability to build bridges between the races served as a model in her time.

Bethune used the differences in the philosophies of Booker T. Washington, who stressed working within the system, and W. E. B. Du Bois, who sought political change, to advance the cause of African American women. Bethune used the ideas of Washington and Du Bois as engines for social change while working within the arena of political reality. Through work and an iron will, she raised national awareness of the lack of social, educational, and economic opportunities for black women. She raised social consciousness and was a model for future minority change agents. Her contributions to higher education remain not only in the hearts, minds, and lives of those she influenced but also in the college that carries her name (McKissack & McKissack, 1987; Smith, 1995).

Hundreds of new special occupations resulted from the changes brought about by scientific research in the universities. Veterans returning from World War II demanded and got practical courses from colleges and universities that had previously offered only liberal education. Governmental support of veterans' education through the GI Bill stimulated a trend toward considerable federal interest in higher education. Large numbers of students attended colleges and graduate schools through grants made by the National Defense Education Act of 1958 or other scholarships. The 500,000 students enrolled in college in 1918 seems a very small number compared with today's figure, which exceeds 16 million students. It seems fair to predict that college enrollments in America will follow the same general growth trend as that of high school enrollments 50 years ago. Already, graduate schools are growing more rapidly than colleges did in the nineteenth century. Between 1984 and 1994, full-time male graduate student enrollment increased by 25 percent compared with 62 percent for women. Part-time graduate student enrollment shows the same trend. Enrollment of men during the period increased by 8 percent compared with a 30 percent increase for women.

The *Digest of Educational Statistics* and *Projections of Educational Statistics to 2008* further reveal an increase in Hispanic and Asian graduate student enrollment from 1976 to 1994. There are projections that 9.2 million women may be enrolled in higher education by 2008. They will constitute 57 percent of college enrollment while an estimated 6.2 to 6.9 million men will be enrolled in higher education by 2008. In the 2001–2002 school year, some $291 billion was spent on higher education. The *Chronicle of Higher Education* (2004) in "Status of Women in Academe" found for the first time that American women are earning more Ph.D.s than men. Minority enrollment continues to increase in 2010 in part because of the national recession. Yet overall, the majority of professors in the country's top research universities are men. In addition, more women are earning Ph.D.s in the social sciences and humanities than in the physical sciences.

In the 2000s, we face many new challenges in higher education. Among them are demands for more information, including graduate and retention rates especially for minorities and athletes, faculty workload, staff and administration evaluation, class size, and other measures of accountability. Higher education institution audits are being explored in many states, such as Oklahoma, to ensure maximum effectiveness in cost control. In addition, Congress passed the Students Right to Know and Crime Awareness and Campus Security Act in 1990, with an expanded list of crimes to be disclosed in The Higher Education Amendments of 1998. The legislation requires higher education institutions to publish graduation and crime rates on each campus including "hate crimes" to be reported by "category of prejudice."

Higher education institutions are facing a new form of competitiveness in alternative degree programs. Distance learning through accredited degree programs—such as that offered via email by Phoenix University—is leading traditional colleges and universities to explore Saturday, weekend, compressed video, and other forms of flexible delivery systems. The Cooperative Research and Technology Act of 2004 (CREATE) allows the government to approve patent applications on inventions that have been made collaboratively among multiple organizations. It is an attempt to spur the development of new technologies involving universities and corporations. There is a trend to put upper divisions in community colleges and many community colleges are offering 4-year degrees. Universities are offering a variety of delivery systems including programs and degrees by distance learning. There is also a trend to offering licensure programs such as advanced paralegal programs.

Junior or Community Colleges.   A direct result of the expansion in higher education not accommodated by existing colleges was the junior college movement. Two-year terminal colleges, often staffed by senior high school teachers, began to appear before World War I. There have been both private and public junior colleges, but those with public control and tax support have increased most rapidly in recent years. The government established some junior colleges during the Depression

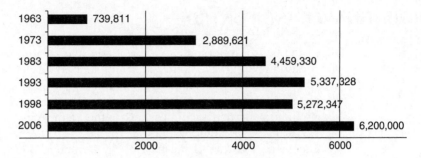

Figure 7.4 Growth of Public 2-Year Community Colleges

Source: From *Digest of Educational Statistics, 2000* (p. 228, Table 199), by Thomas Snyder, Washington, DC: U.S. Office of Education. National Center for Educational Statistics.

years, but city or state junior college boards have developed the greatest number. Municipal junior colleges have often provided the first 2 years of standard college education, thus taking some of the pressure off colleges and universities. Public junior or community colleges are either free or charge a very low tuition, and students usually live at home while attending them.

The junior or community college therefore offers an extension of educational opportunity to students who could not otherwise afford higher education. There is a vastly increased demand for more junior or community colleges of both the terminal (associate degree) and the nonterminal type (entry-level job skills/transfer courses for senior colleges). Financing is a serious problem in communities that direct a major portion of school taxes to the lower public schools. By 1997, more than 1,473 junior and community colleges were operating with a combined enrollment of over 5 million students (see Figure 7.4). By 2008, there were over 11.5 million students (Pew Research Center, 2009) and the number continued to grow from a severe national recession. Community college enrollment grew by 14 percent in the 1990s, five percentage points more than all higher education (Longley, 2005). National efforts are underway to expand opportunities for education through the fourteenth grade or the community college level. These efforts revive the Truman Commission's 1947 report recommending expanding universal education through the community college. Adelman (2005) examines diverse groups of traditional age populations served by community colleges.

The average length of time spent in school has expanded at both ends of the continuum. Many students now have the opportunity to attend kindergarten (K) before starting public school at the age of six. Quite a large number of school systems have public kindergartens, with the K–6–3–3 or K–4–4–4 plans being most common. Public kindergartens are found in all but the smaller rural schools. Day-care centers and Montessori schools for pre-kindergarten youngsters are available in most cities, but they usually require tuition. Head Start programs make an effort to give underprivileged children some of the preschool experiences enjoyed by middle-class youngsters.

SCHOOL FINANCE AND CONTROL

An issue that is developing into a major educational argument in America concerns the location of authority and the source of support for public schools. Although this has always been an issue in education, the voucher and charter school movement is bringing it to the forefront. As the federal government becomes more active in providing money through such measures as the Elementary and Secondary Education Act of 1965, 1999 Reauthorization Act, the 2009–2010 American Recovery and Reinvestment Act, the role of the national government in education becomes larger. Many leaders feel that the schools ought to remain in local hands, and they fear that federal aid to education will eventually lead to complete federal control of schools. However, national authorities have allowed a good deal of local administration of federal funds when local and state governments have been unable to raise sufficient money for high-quality schools. We can predict that the argument over federal control of schools will continue, although it also seems likely that a larger share of future school finance will be handled by the states and national government.

Local and State Control.   Educational support and control in the United States has been a curious composite of local, state, and national functions. Because education was not considered a federal responsibility by the founding fathers, each state set up its own unique educational system. Many of the states have similar laws, but each is autonomous with regard to public schools and educational requirements within its own borders. Although the states have guarded their authority over schools and generally opposed federal financial aid, local school boards have been granted a considerable degree of freedom in managing the schools. State boards of education have served largely for making policy, and state superintendents or commissioners have been responsible for administration and general supervision. States differ widely in their method of selecting boards and executive school officers: They are sometimes elected, sometimes appointed by the governor, and sometimes appointed by the state legislature.

Most states have well-organized educational offices with specialists for inspecting schools, certifying teachers, and allocating funds that are distributed by the state. There are normally smaller administrative units presided over by township, county, or district superintendents. Cities often have independent school districts with superintendents who work directly for the locally elected board of education and who perform the functions otherwise delegated to county superintendents. There is no uniformity with regard to the size and type of school districts in the United States. One superintendent and board of education in a metropolitan area may be responsible for hundreds of schools at all levels. At the other end of the extreme is the school board and executive officer governing only one small school building, although this is becoming rare with the increased focus on cost-effectiveness through consolidation.

Although teachers' salaries are uniform in some states, it is still common to find adjacent school districts that differ in money paid to teachers and otherwise expended for the education of children. The inequality of educational opportunity in various districts has encouraged state and federal participation in education.

School Finance. In the twentieth century, states began to play a much more important role in school finance. State funds originated as early as 1795, when Connecticut sold its vast Western Reserve lands and put the money in permanent school funds. Most states have such funds, drawing money from public land sales, taxes, special appropriations, and so forth. Historically, the states have used their meager allotments for giving state aid to local districts that agreed to tax themselves for schools and for making payments to districts unable to obtain sufficient local revenues for a minimum standard. By and large, the concentrated wealth and population of cities, as compared with that of rural communities, has made it relatively easy for urban areas to levy taxes and support schools. Local taxes have paid the lion's share of public school costs, and the states have confined their administration to a minimum. However, state funds have encouraged the keeping of accurate records of attendance, school inspection, and the establishment of accepted minimum standards. Between 1930 and 1970, the percentage of locally raised public school funds dropped from about 83 percent to 51 percent.

As the proportion of local support has fallen, state and federal support has increased. Quite naturally, the larger governmental units have begun to place more restrictions on the money that they have collected and distributed. Such restrictions have usually been confined to general rules for the use of money, but there is no question that centralized control is increasing. Throughout the nation there is increased litigation over school funding as low-income school districts seek additional funds. Over 20 states have had their school funding systems declared unconstitutional by state and federal courts. George W. Bush supported having dollars follow the child by giving parents more choice through vouchers, charter schools, and opportunities to select public schools. With his reelection to a second term, school choice and faith-based initiatives expanded, although federal court rulings may limit this expansion as noted in *Hibbs v. Winn* (2004). The Obama administration has used stimulus money to support education excellence initiatives and supports expansion of charter schools.

States use a variety of means for funding public schools including sales tax, state income tax, lotteries, state property tax, fees, and licenses on items such as automobiles. Miller (2004) reported that there were lotteries in 39 states (including the District of Columbia). Other states earmark a portion of the proceeds for public education. However, funds are often inadequate, and the relationship between local and state sources creates a political problem. School districts have the power to raise only *ad valorem* property taxes within district boundaries. If the wealth of the district is low, it may not be possible to meet school funding needs even if the voters in the district support the levy. When this occurs, schools can turn to the courts to force the states to fund a larger part of the school budget. For example, more than 100 school districts in Montana sued the state in 1988 on the grounds that they did not have the power to raise enough taxes to meet state-mandated requirements for a basic education. The state supreme court agreed with the schools and required the legislature to provide a means for additional state funding for all public schools in Montana.

There is increasing litigation in the states over equity in school district financing. Federal and state court rulings continue to address the need for adjusting the balance between rich and poor districts as well as expanding educational opportunities for all children. There is an increase in class-action lawsuits to roll back tax increases, which has affected public school financing. The Fayetteville, Arkansas, school district faced such a rollback in 2000. The National Council of State Legislatures has created an information clearinghouse on school finance. The center will track information on funding formulas in the 50 states and keep a website on all aspects of school finance. Hoff (2004) discussed efforts to redistribute funds from wealthy to poor school districts (Robin Hood). Texas and Vermont found Robin Hood politically controversial and moved toward other funding methods for poor districts.

Historically, the federal government has been interested in the improvement of higher education and in specialized training in such subjects as agriculture. Local property taxes are still widely used for school finance, but they are neither sufficiently flexible nor adequate to care for the changing population distribution. Knowledge of the federal government's emergence as a major educational agency is vital to an understanding of the current issue over support and control of the schools.

FEDERAL PARTICIPATION IN EDUCATION

(The U.S. government's involvement has increased so much in the past few years that only major areas of activity are discussed here.) The United States Office of Education has grown rapidly in size and influence, largely from the need for administering federal funds and advising participants in federal projects. The office has had a varied history, having been moved from the Department of the Interior and given separate status in 1930, moved again to the Federal Security Agency in 1939, and made part of the Department of Health, Education, and Welfare (HEW) in 1953. Large grants made through HEW to schools and universities contributed to the importance of the Office of Education, and it was made a separate cabinet-level position under the Carter administration. Cutbacks in federal spending in the Reagan administration created some loss of prestige, and some members of Congress suggested that it should be abolished. The future of the office of Secretary of Education will depend upon politics and federal policy concerning finance.

The 111th Congress passed a record high education American Recovery and Reinvestment funding bill for education and the workforce. With members of Congress on both sides of the aisle concerned about record high and growing budget deficits, there will be efforts in the 112th Congress to decrease expenditures.

Support for Industrial and Vocational Education.   Among the earlier efforts of Congress to aid education were acts designed to fill a need for industrial and

vocational education. Through the Smith-Hughes Act (1917), the George-Reed Act (1929), and the George-Dean Act (1937), Congress attempted to promote vocational education in public schools. The Federal Board of Vocational Education was created in 1917 and, after 1919, was given the additional task of supervising training of people with disabilities.

Ten years later, the Capper-Ketcham Act extended the previous Smith-Lever Act to cover education in home economics and agriculture. During World War I, the government found it necessary to train many technicians, but industrial inactivity during the Depression resulted in a great shortage of trained technicians and engineers. The National Defense Training Program of 1940 provided courses for more than seven million workers during World War II. The Rural War Production Training Program trained farm youth for industry and for jobs in food production. Vocational training also benefited from the National Defense Education Act (1958), but the Vocational Education Act extended previous legislation to cover any skilled, technical, or semiskilled occupation and included provisions for keeping potential dropouts in school.

The original purpose of federal efforts to promote vocational and industrial education was to provide the nation with skilled workers and technicians when other agencies had failed to do so. Clearly, this was the same rationale that fostered the agricultural and mechanical colleges developed from the Morrill acts. However, Congress has increasingly turned its attention to vocational education that may improve the economy, keeping children in school longer, fighting poverty, and creating new jobs for the unemployed. The Workforce Investment Act, 2010, supported by the National Council on Literacy, remains to be funded.

Other federal funding focuses were the Carl D. Perkins Vocational and Applied Technology Education Amendments and the Assistive Technology Act of 1998, designed to address the needs of at-risk individuals and those with disabilities. Funding authorization was provided in 2006 for proposals for state institutions serving individuals with disabilities or incarcerated individuals ("Request for Proposals," 2011). The Association for Career and Technical Education is developing recommendations for reauthorization of Perkins (Alisha, 2011). Further legislation to strengthen vocational education in order to fight against unemployment and provide employable skills seems almost certain.

New Deal Acts.   Attempts to improve the national welfare and increase equality of opportunity were made through the so-called New Deal legislation passed during the administration of Franklin D. Roosevelt. The Civilian Conservation Corps employed young men and gave them vocational training, especially in conservation and building trades; and small grants were given to needy students through the National Youth Administration. The Works Progress Administration subsidized teachers' salaries for programs in job training for adults and aliens and for nursery schools. The Public Works Administration provided loans for communities to use in building schools and libraries. In 1935, the Secretary of Agriculture was authorized to distribute surplus foods to schools, and this led directly to the National School Lunch Act of 1946 (an act that continues to make both food and money available to school lunch programs). Loss of tax funds for schools during the Depression led to loans to school boards through the Reconstruction Finance Corporation. This trend led to legislation such as the Economic Opportunity Act (EOA) of 1964. The 106th Congress passed a 2001 appropriations bill with provisions for a variety of youth support services including community-wide safe schools and healthy students programs to prevent youth violence and drug abuse.

Title I of the EOA set up the Job Corps to train youth between the ages of 16 and 21 for useful employment and citizenship. Job Corps training centers were built around the nation. Students were given training in basic skills as well as in vocational subjects. There continues to be a work–study program for high school students who need to earn money and one for college students with financial need. Title II of the EOA authorized aid for adult education and cultural enrichment programs for children from disadvantaged families. The Head Start program was aimed at children from three to five years of age who would not normally have had the advantage of nursery schools or kindergartens.

Wartime Measures.

Wartime activity also contributed to the involvement of the federal government in education. During World War I, the government trained technicians, and troops drilled on college campuses. In World War II, loans were made to students majoring in critically needed fields such as medicine. Congress began giving assistance to those school districts that absorbed large numbers of children of military or defense personnel. Laws aiding such affected areas were extended in 1950 and 1966. In addition, equipment purchased by the government for special war training was later turned over to schools, and surplus property was made available to all nonprofit educational institutions.

During World War II, women were called upon to enter the workforce. Thousands of "Rosie the Riveters" helped build aircraft, ships, and tanks for the military. Their wartime contributions proved that women workers were dependable, efficient, productive, and capable. Since that time, women have increasingly entered the workforce. They constitute 60 million people, or over 48 percent, of our nation's workforce in the twenty-first century.

In an effort to meet the needs of veterans whose schooling had been interrupted by military duty, the Servicemen's Readjustment Act of 1944 (the GI Bill) was passed. This measure has provided subsistence and school cost allowances for veterans who have continued their education, and it has resulted in the expansion of colleges to accommodate them. The effort to assist returning veterans through government support had its critics. One university president said the GI Bill would open higher education to a flood of unqualified students and depress academic standards, while another saw the bill as a threat to higher learning and said that education was not a device to prevent mass unemployment. Veterans—many from poor families, many at-risk minority students—flooded the nation's colleges. In 1947, a peak year, some 1,150,000 veterans attended school. A report by the Syracuse University Research Institute found a far greater percentage of the population could benefit from higher education than previously thought possible. The Syracuse report found veterans were more serious, contributed more to society on graduation, and received higher grades than nonveteran classmates. The GI Bill was revived for veterans of the Korean War, and the benefits were increased for Vietnam veterans in 1972 and Desert Storm veterans in 1991. Those who served in Afghanistan and Iraq also have a GI Bill for education.

National Defense Education Act. A new period of federal activity in education started with the Cold War and with the Soviet success in launching *Sputnik*, the first space satellite. The National Defense Education Act (NDEA) of 1958 was designed for the purpose of giving aid to education as a means of strengthening the nation. NDEA loans have been made to prospective teachers in amounts up to $5,000, and half of the loan has been cancelable through service as a public school teacher after graduation. Funds have been made available for laboratory equipment and other materials to improve instruction in science, and fellowships have been offered to persons training to be college professors. State testing and guidance to find and encourage able students, an extension of vocational education, and research on new educational media have also been financed by NDEA funds. Out of the John F. Kennedy and Lyndon B. Johnson administrations came a host of federal measures designed to promote equality of educational opportunity, fight poverty, and strengthen defense. The Higher Education Facilities Act of 1963 made funds available for the construction of college buildings, with matching sums provided by the college or state.

EXPERIMENTS AND INNOVATIONS IN THE TWENTIETH CENTURY

Francis W. Parker tried out many new ideas in school organization and curricula in the late nineteenth century and built the foundations for an experimental program in the Cook County Normal School. John Dewey expanded Parker's ideas into his experimental school—which was truly a laboratory for testing educational innovations—at the University of Chicago. The laboratory school lasted only 7 years, but it was a child-centered school that experimented with democratic organization, nontraditional methods and equipment, and a curriculum based on the natural needs and interests of children (activity curriculum). Many of the ideas that appeared in Dewey's 1916 educational classic, *Democracy and Education*, were tried in the laboratory school, and the Dewey school gave rise to new educational experiments by the progressive educators.

Progressive Education. Even before the organization of the Progressive Education Association in 1919, schools were being organized according to the liberal ideas of Rousseau, Pestalozzi, Froebel, Parker, and Dewey. In 1907, Marietta Johnson pioneered a School of Organic Education at Fairhope, Alabama. Teachers did not assign tasks in her school, so students were free to follow their own interests. Natural growth and development according to nature replaced early emphasis on reading and accumulating knowledge. Johnson's program followed Rousseau's *Émile*. The curriculum included nature study, physical education, music, handicrafts, field geography, drama, storytelling, games, and number concepts.

Professor Junius L. Meriam established a similar school under the supervision of the University of Missouri. Meriam's school had a flexible time schedule with no rigid periods for drills, exercises, or formal lessons. Others soon followed the lead of Meriam and Johnson. The Cottage School of Riverside, Illinois, and the Little School in the Woods at Greenwich, Connecticut, were activity-centered institutions. John and Evelyn Dewey reported on a number of these efforts in *Schools of Tomorrow* in 1915.

Within a few years of the beginning of progressive education as a movement, the number of private experimental schools increased rapidly. The founders undertook few sound statistical studies of their programs, but they and others who were critical of traditional schools did highly publicize them.

Progressive Education Association (PEA).

Although the PEA existed as an organization only from 1919 until 1955, its influence on American education was profound. Marietta Johnson joined with Eugene R. Smith of the Park School in Baltimore and Stanwood Cobb (a Naval Academy instructor) to organize the society. Aimed at the coordination of educational reform among private school leaders, the group was highly influenced by the theories of John Dewey. At an organizational meeting of the association held in Washington, DC, on March 15, 1919, the 85 charter members adopted the following seven principles:

1. Freedom to develop naturally
2. Interest as the motive for all work
3. The teacher as guide, not as taskmaster
4. Scientific study of pupil development
5. Greater attention to all that affects the child's physical development
6. Cooperation between school and home to meet the needs of a child's life
7. The progressive school as leader in educational movements

Charles W. Eliot agreed to become the first honorary president of the PEA, lending his prestige to the organization. The journal *Progressive Education* appeared in 1924 and continued to be a major publication until 1957.

In the early 1920s, the membership of PEA consisted largely of teachers and parents in private schools, but by the late 1930s there were more than 10,000 members. Most of the professional educators in colleges and universities joined, as did the superintendents and administrators of many public school systems. In addition to the experimental schools supported by the organization, there were annual public conferences devoted to educational reform. Scientific study of pupil development and strong cooperation between schools and the society were major beliefs of PEA. William H. Kilpatrick, developer of the project method, was a major spokesman for progressive education and made the views of John Dewey popular among many educators at all levels. With Ellsworth Collings, Kilpatrick recommended that the school organize its work through a series of activities that would develop the student's purposeful effort. His projects included drills, problems, appreciation activities, and creative or construction projects.

The PEA soon broke into camps with quite different interests. The Social Frontier group, led by George S. Counts, wanted to use education as a means for social revolution and reform. Dewey and his followers were interested in a sophisticated educational theory and careful research. Other progressive educators merely developed new methods or supported freedom for children.

Extended School Use.   Not all the early innovations were aimed at the individual development of the child. In Gary, Indiana, William Wirt tried intensive use of the school facilities to relieve social problems caused by unexpected urban growth. In an effort to meet the failure of the culture to provide for the needs of city children, the school offered a longer day with constantly open and supervised workshops, gymnasiums, laboratories, auditoriums, and playgrounds. To give all children the opportunity for extended school participation, schools were kept open on Saturday and during vacation periods. Adult night classes were offered, and pupils did their own repair and maintenance work. Costs were kept low by the platoon system, by which work in classrooms, laboratories, and workshops alternated with activities scheduled in auditoriums, playgrounds, and gymnasiums, so as to keep all facilities continuously occupied. This plan for maximum school use spread widely in the United States; by 1929, more than a thousand schools were using a platoon organization. Today, scheduling one school day early in the morning and another beginning in the afternoon relieves crowding in some schools.

Other important efforts to relate the schools to the needs of the society were made by Carleton Washburne in Winnetka, Illinois, and by Helen Parkhurst in Dalton, Massachusetts. The Winnetka plan divided school offerings into creative and group activities and common essentials such as science and basic skills. Work in the essentials was by units and given at the student's own rate of learning, a practice now common in schools using programmed instruction. The Dalton laboratory plan incorporated Dewey's educational principles and many of the methods suggested by the Italian educator Maria Montessori. Both the Dalton and the Winnetka plans sought to develop the whole child and were concerned with physical and social as well as intellectual education.

Influence of Experimental Programs.   Although the early experimental schools did not become standard in America, they served as models for a different approach to basic educational questions. Ideas put into practice in laboratory or innovative schools were often adopted, with modifications, into the programs of the more traditional institutions. Sometimes new schools were created in response to criticisms of existing conditions and were intended to serve as contrasts with older plans.

Charles W. Eliot prepared a report for the General Education Board in 1916, in which he called for changes in American high schools. Partly at the urging of Eliot, the Lincoln School was established as an experimental arm of Teachers College, Columbia University, and it continued to operate until 1948. Today, many of the leading teachers' colleges and universities that have departments of education maintain laboratory schools. Research and development centers for testing all sorts of educational innovations are appearing in teaching-training institutions. Sophisticated statistical processes and refined methods of testing have given a new dimension to educational testing, and the growth of graduate programs has created an explosion in research. Doctoral dissertations in the area of educational psychology alone now provide us with a vast body of knowledge concerning the effectiveness of various pedagogical techniques.

PROGRESSIVE EDUCATORS AND THEIR CRITICS

By 1928, Dewey had become critical of the PEA for its lack of sound social philosophy. His arguments against experiments lacking in theory were expressed well in *Experience and Education*, which appeared in 1938. By the 1930s, the interest of the progressives shifted from a reaction against formal subject matter and harsh discipline to the social and economic problems of the whole culture. Many of the members continued with their experiments in natural development, the activity curriculum, and the child-centered school; however, the possibility of the schools as leaders in improving or reconstructing society became the theme of progressives like George Counts.

Although the progressives continued to meet until 1955, their organization was divided into factions with different points of view, and their efforts provoked a growing amount of controversy. Meanwhile, significant projects were being carried on that were to alter major educational concepts. The *Eight-Year Study* of the PEA involved 30 high schools interested in experimentation and exploration. They altered the secondary curriculum and made it conform to known laws of learning and the various social environments. The report, published in 1942, showed that students in the progressive high schools did at least as well in college as their counterparts in traditional secondary schools and that they were better oriented to adult life.

Life Adjustment Education.   In 1945, a group of educators launched the "life adjustment movement." This group was theoretically related to the progressive education movement, and its concern was mostly with those students who were not preparing for college. The life adjustment movement was aimed at a greater equalization of educational opportunity and was critical of any program that was not suitable for the majority of young Americans. The movement was short-lived because of the bitter attacks from many segments of the American people. The life adjustment movement had the support of several educational organizations and the United States Office of Education, but was severely condemned by many college professors and by those interested in the subject-matter curriculum.

Dr. Charles Prosser pointed out that high schools failed to meet the needs of the 60 percent of the students who were not being trained for a vocational skill. In 1947, Commissioner of Education John Studebaker called attention to the 20 percent of children who did not enter secondary schools and to the 40 percent who dropped out before graduation. Attention was also given to the wide range of individual differences among secondary school students and the effect of family or cultural background on achievement. Twenty-nine states developed some kind of curriculum revision associated with life adjustment by 1954. Many school systems became interested in how to meet the needs of those who seemed not to benefit from standard courses. Studies were made of the holding power of secondary schools (dropout rate) and of the relevance of programs in the view of students.

Because of the heavy criticism by those interested only in intellectual development and a great public fear that academic standards were being lowered by life adjustment, the program was terminated in the late 1950s. Nevertheless, life adjustment gave attention to the concern for equal educational opportunities and the problems of cultural deprivation; this development later brought about programs such as Head Start and the Job Corps. A basic issue remains in American education over whether we should concentrate on educating the whole child or whether intellectual excellence has priority. Many believe that neither meeting the psychological needs of the child nor developing the mind is enough. Few would argue that mastery of the essential subjects—particularly those that can be called tool subjects—is not important, but the great challenge is one of relating the experiences of the child to the cultural environment. American schools continue to have large numbers of students who leave school because they are bored, poorly adjusted, unable to compete, or merely uninterested in the programs offered. Today, numerous school systems are attempting to offer alternative high schools, work-study programs, storefront schools, or "schools without walls" in an effort to meet the needs of students for whom the regular educational program is unsatisfactory. This is exactly what the life adjustment plan intended to accomplish.

Another progressive innovation that seemed to offer a possible solution to some of the social problems in modern America was the community school. Based on such books as John Dewey's *Schools of Tomorrow*, the concept centered upon organizing the curriculum around the lives of students and involving members of the community as resources. The school was to be used for all sorts of community projects such as recreational activities and as a local center for communications. It was also expected that students and adults would work together on problems that involved the whole community. With grants from the Sloan Foundation in the 1940s, several universities established experimental community schools, but only a few remain in operation. George Leonard's *Education and Ecstasy* (1969) describes a future school of this kind.

Critics of Progressive Influence.
Idealists, realists, essentialists, and others with a philosophy opposed to pragmatism were critical of progressive education from the beginning. Dewey himself believed that many of the members of the progressive movement had been too quick to adopt new programs or methods without a proper theoretical base. Boyd Bode, one of the outstanding leaders of progressive education, criticized the determination of educational needs by looking at the individual child, rather than the society and the child together. Bode insisted that the meanings of liberty and democracy are linked and that people must make a moral commitment to the kind of society they want before content and authority in education can be established.

In addition to philosophic criticisms, a number of studies of academic achievement revealed certain weaknesses in the students who attended progressive schools. These studies were not conclusive and most were less impressive than

The Eight-Year Study, which was favorable to progressive schools, but they provided support for those who disagreed with progressive theory. It should be remembered that although the progressive movement had great influence on public elementary schools and colleges of education, the effect on secondary schools was slight and practically nonexistent on the academic disciplines in the universities. Some of those who blame Dewey and the progressives for the ills of education and society attribute more influence to the progressive movement than the historical evidence supports.

In the 1950s, equality of educational opportunity took on a new aspect. Life adjustment had been concerned with the terminal student, but during the Cold War years, the great cry was for the academically talented student to receive adequate training. Arthur Bestor, James Conant, John Gardner, and Hyman Rickover were among prominent critics making new demands on education. They claimed that equality of opportunity did not mean the same education for everyone and that the national welfare demanded special provisions for the gifted.

THEN TO NOW

One of the great tragedies of American education is that we keep reinventing the wheel. Often, ideas that hold great promise for improving teaching and learning are discarded with the movement that brought them about. For example, the psychological concepts of Herbart were rejected by the progressives and by John Dewey himself. This happened because of Dewey's reaction against lock-step programs and rigid systems that developed from the followers of Herbart in America such as Charles DeGarmo. Actually, the ideas of Herbart were well ahead of their time and might have been retained by those who sought to reform teacher-centered methods and formal steps of instruction. Herbart taught that the mind is a unitary organism, and therefore he could not support mental discipline or faculty psychology. He understood the need for relating one subject to another and so developed a core curriculum. Long before psychoanalysis, Herbart studied the relationship of the conscious to the subconscious mind and suggested a logical means by which new ideas from experience may be assimilated and stored by the learner. These ideas were not in conflict with the basic theories of the progressives. Indeed, they might have proved very helpful to the same progressive educators who scorned them because they were identified with the American Herbartian movement. Progressives turned to Gestalt psychology, but many current notions about educational psychology were anticipated by Herbart and might have been used to improve the educational environment for generations.

Exactly the same thing happened with progressive education in its period of decline. As we have seen, progressives ruled education in the 1930s, but by 1940 there was much criticism of their child-centered programs and permissive practices. William Bagley, an essentialist, sought more discipline, effort, and intellectual focus than the progressives. The progressive movement ceased to exert much influence after the conservative reaction in education triggered by World War II. Beyond question, many progressives were extreme in their views, and their schools were by no means perfect. Nevertheless, progressive education brought about numerous experiments that are of great pedagogical value today. That most American teachers are not well versed in their own professional history means that they must begin from scratch in order to create new methods and programs. Progressives anticipated and worked with numerous plans and ideas that today are called educational innovations. This point is well made by Judith Ford in an unpublished doctoral dissertation called "Innovative Methods in Elementary Education: A Description and Analysis of Individualized Instruction in the Progressive Movement in Comparison with the Innovative Modern Elementary School" (1977).

The progressive educators tried, in some form, most of the current practices designed to improve instruction. An exception is computer-assisted instruction, as computers and teaching machines were not available in the 1930s. The following are some of the most obvious parallels.

Inquiry-Based Instruction.   This method is often associated with Piaget and science teaching. John Dewey was a strong advocate of laboratory instruction and discovery learning. Almost all of the progressive schools used inquiry as a major method, and records exist of their success.

Mastery Learning.   Modern mastery learning is usually associated with Benjamin Bloom. Recall and application of learning to a problem-solving situation were mainstays of progressive schools. Ellsworth Collings best demonstrated it in the McDonald County Rural School in 1905.

Individual Contracting.   Using individual contracts with students to stimulate specific learning is now a practice in many schools. The formal writing of contracts with specific behavioral goals is current, but the idea of students participating in choosing what and when they would learn goes back to Helen Parkhurst and the Dalton Contract Plan of 1919.

Differentiated Staffing.   Many professional educators now support differentiated staffing. Having all teachers trained in the same way seems inefficient and wasteful. Master teachers, general teachers, learning specialists, teaching assistants, instructional materials specialists, clerks, and nonprofessional staff members might make up a better team for instruction. The progressives used community resource people in their schools. They did not hesitate to bring in people with different training for various school-related tasks. J. Lloyd Trump, who first urged differentiated staffing in schools, was influenced by the progressive experiments. Paraprofessionals currently assist teachers and administrators.

Flexible Scheduling.   The Gary Platoon Plan organized by William Wirt in 1915 used flexible scheduling. Most of the progressive schools were not tied to the clock or the calendar. They pioneered programs that used whatever time was necessary to accomplish learning without regard to filling days with even blocks of time or earning units of credit. Numerous modern schools use computers to program flexible individualized schedules. Block scheduling has been implemented to assist in achieving teaching effectiveness.

Individualized Instruction.
Today, a body of literature supports the idea that individualized instruction may be superior for many students. Carleton Washburne experimented with such a plan at Winnetka in 1919. Most progressives allowed students to progress at their own speed, a practice that required special individual assignments and evaluation. The history of progressive education shows that individual instruction worked better than group instruction for some learning but that it required more time of teachers. Progressives supported the social interaction of groups for certain subjects (such as social studies) but used individualized projects as well. They understood that each child is unique and that there are many styles of learning. In some ways, the progressive schools were similar to modern alternative schools, almost all of which use individualized instruction.

Open Classrooms.
In spite of all the modern literature on the subject, the progressives pioneered open classrooms. Marietta Johnson's School of Organic Education at Fairhope, Alabama, was an early example. Freedom for students to move about, small-group activities, an informal atmosphere, inquiry, and freedom of expression were characteristics of progressive education. The best of open classroom instruction is described in progressive literature.

Team Teaching and Nongraded Schools.
John Dewey himself created teams of teachers to work with students in the laboratory school at the University of Chicago. Like the progressives who followed him, Dewey was aware that several teachers working together can provide a richer educational environment and better evaluation. Although the progressives did not establish nongraded schools in name, they did allow students to learn at their own rate of speed and were not bound by any external standards. Progressives wrote about the perils of self-contained classrooms and rigid programs that require all children to achieve the same goals within a given span of time.

The period from 1918 to 1960 represented a cycle of regression and progress in education and society. The Depression era of the 1930s gave way to educational expansion and increased federal initiatives for economic and social justice with a renewed interest in improving intergroup, intercultural, and interpersonal relations. *Brown v. The Board of Education* (1954) led to efforts for desegregated and integrated schools. During the same period of the 1940s and 1950s, Congress passed the Alien Registration Act in June of 1940. In February of 1950, Senator Joseph McCarthy started his anticommunist "witch hunt" and hysteria. By 1952, 30 states had enacted loyalty oaths, eventually leading to Supreme Court decisions declaring such academic freedom restrictions an unconstitutional infringement on the First and Fourteenth Amendments. *Wieman v. Updegraff* (1953) was one of several court rulings finding loyalty oaths offensive to due process rights.

As we move toward a multiethnic, multiracial society, globalization will affect all aspects of our educational system. Financial, transportation, governmental, and institutional systems are all affected by globalization as our world gets smaller through superinformation Internet communication systems.

GAINING PERSPECTIVE THROUGH CRITICAL ANALYSIS

1. What impact did World Wars I and II have on education? Interview educators who served in or lived during World War II. Identify changes that occurred in public school curriculum during the period.
2. Identify the contributions of the 1893 National Education Association Committee of Fifteen to the educational curriculum. What current organizations and institutions affect the educational curriculum? Name four major current changes in school curriculum that can be attributable to external organization influences.
3. Examine the effects of the school survey on educational policy making. Interview a school administrator to identify the use of current school surveys.
4. Trace the history of school consolidation. Give examples of continuing efforts for school consolidation. What are the pros and cons of school consolidation?
5. How did American educational policy makers respond to Russian space exploration success with *Sputnik?*

HISTORY IN ACTION IN TODAY'S CLASSROOMS

1. Trace the history of school finance and control. How have schools been financed? How are states currently financing education? What are the pros and cons of litigation for funding equity?
2. Examine the trends for local and state control of education with increased federal initiatives for educational excellence and closing the achievement gap between majority and minority students.
3. Identify major initiatives of the progressive education movement. What current examples of progressive themes in education and society can you identify?
4. Give examples of innovative and experimental educational programs. What are some such programs that continue in the present time? Discuss and answer the questions at the end of the feature "Divergent Views." This feature is found within the chapter.
5. Identify the current work of muckrakers. Give examples of continuity from the past to the present of uncovering ethical and moral lapses in our society.

BIBLIOGRAPHY

Adelman, Clifford. *Moving into Town—and Moving On.* Washington, DC: U.S. Department of Education, 2005.

Sonny, Alisah. "ACTE Launches Perkins and School Reform Task Force" (April 26, 2010). Available at watchblog: www.actonline.org/ctepolicy

Binet, Alfred, & T. H. Simon. *The Development of Intelligence in Children.* Baltimore: Williams and Wilkins Co., 1916, p. 318. (Cited in Karier, Clarence J. *Shaping the American Educational State 1900 to Present.* New York: The Free Press, 1975, p. 162.)

Brown v. Board of Education, Topeka, 347 U.S. 483 (1954).

Conant, James Bryant. Introduction. *General Education in a Free Society.* Cambridge, MA: Harvard University Press, 1945.

Conant, James Bryant. *The American High School Today: A First Report to Interested Citizens.* New York: McGraw-Hill, 1959.

Butts, R. Freeman, & Lawrence Cremin. *A History of Education in American Culture.* New York: Holt, Rinehart and Winston, 1953.

Cromwell, Sharon. "K–8 Schools: An Idea for the New Millennium?" *Education World* (1999): 1–5. Available at: www.educationworld.com.

Dewey, John. "America—By Formula." In *Individualism—Old and New.* New York: Capricorn Press, 1962.

"Dollars to Students, Not Districts." *Wall Street Journal* (January 12, 2000): A 18.

Eliot, Charles. *Changes Needed in Secondary Education.* New York: General Education Board, 1916.

Fry, Richard. "College Enrollment Hits All-Time High Fueled by Community College Surge." *Pew Research Center* (October 29, 2009). Available at: pewsocialtrends. org/pubs/747/college-enrollment-hits-all-time-high-fueled-by-community-college-surge/

Hibbs v. Winn, 542 US88 (2004).

Hoff, David J. "Robin Hood on the Ropes in Texas School Aid Tilt," *Education Week* (May 12, 2004): 1, 24.

Holmes, Natalic Cartes. "Clinton Signs Record Education Increase." *American Association of School Administrators (AASA) Leadership News* (December 22, 2000). Available at: www.aasa.org/

Jeffry, R. "Kentucky's Virtual University Creates Fund to Spur Other On-Line-Education Programs." *The Chronicle of Higher Education* (November 24, 2000): A54.

Karier, Clarence. *Shaping the American Educational State: 1900 to the Present.* New York: The Free Press, 1975.

Leonard, George. *Education and Ecstasy.* New York, New York: Delacorte Press, 1969.

Lewis, Laurie, Cyle Snow, Elizabeth Farris, Becky Smerdon, Stephanie Cronen, Jessica Kaplan, & Bernie Green. *The Condition of America's Public School Facilities.* Washington, DC: U.S. Department of Education, National Center for Educational Statistics, 1999.

Longley, Robert. "Enrollment Grew by 14 Percent During the 1990s." (2005). Available at: usgovinfo.about. com/od/consumerawareness/a/commcollege.htm

McKissack, Patricia, & Frederick McKissack. *The Civil Rights Movement in America.* Chicago: Children's Press, 1987.

Meyer, Adolphe E. *An Educational History of the American People.* New York: McGraw-Hill, 1957.

Miller, Donald E. "Schools Lose Out in Lotteries." *USA Today* (April 14 2004). Available at: www.usatoday.com/ news/opinion/editorials/2004-04-14-miller_x.htm

National Center for Educational Statistics. *Digest of Education Statistics: 2009.* Washington, DC: U.S. Department of Education, 2010.

Noggle, Kellar, Executive Director of Arkansas Association of Educational Administrators, personal phone conversation, July 23, 2004.

President's Commission on Higher Education. *Higher Education for American Democracy, Vol. 1, Establishing the Goals.* New York: Harper, 1948, pp. 38–39. (Cited in Butts, R. Freeman, & Lawrence Cremin. *A History of Education in American Culture.* New York: Holt, Rinehart and Winston, 1953, p. 522.)

Prosser, Charles. *Secondary Education and Life.* Cambridge, MA: Harvard University Press, 1939.

"Rankings and Estimates." *Rankings of the States NEA Research* (2011). Available at: www.nea.org/home,

"Request for Proposals for State Institutions Serving Individuals with Disabilities or Incarcerated Individuals, 2011." The Carl D. Perkins Career and Technical E ducation Act of 2006 (2010–2011). Available at: www.highered.nysed.gov/kiap/colldev/VTEA   Robinson, David. "57 Smallest Districts History." *The Morning News, Arkansas* (July 1, 2004): 7 A.

Savoie, Sonny. "Funding for Green Schools Gaines Momentum in Congress." *United States Green Building Council National School Boards Association.* Washington, DC, June 2009.

"Schools Must Teach About Constitution Every September 17 Under Little Noticed Provision." *Your School and the Law* (January 12, 2005): 2.

Smith, Elaine M. *Mary McLeod Bethune Papers.* New York: University Publications of America, 1995. Snyder, Thomas, Ed. *Digest of Educational Statistics.* Washington, DC: U.S. Office of Education, 2002.

Snyder, Thomas, Ed. National Center for Educational Statistics. Washington, DC: U.S. Office of Education, 2002.

U.S. Census Bureau. *Statistical Abstract.* Washington, DC (2010). Available at: www.census.gov/compendia/statab/2010

U.S. Congress. *Appropriations and Budget.* Senate Document 106-30. 106th Cong., 2d sess., 2000. National Governors' Association. Available at: www.gpoaccess.gov/serialset/cdocuments/sd106-30/index.html

U.S. Department of Education. "The Status of Women." *The Chronicle of Higher Education* (December 3, 2004): A 11.

Wieman v. Updegraff, 344 U.S. 183, 73 S.Ct. 215 (1952).

Workforce Reinvestment Act (1998). www.doleta.gov/ USWORKFORCE/WIA/wialaw.pdf

Chapter 8

American Education: 1960–Present

Cold War	Vietnam Conflict	
1964 Economic Opportunity Act	1965 Head Start	Mainstreaming
	Higher Education Act	
		Service farming
	Rebellion on college campuses	
1965 Elementary and Secondary Education Act	1967 Bilingual Education Act	Volunteerism
	1975 Public Law 94–142 provided education for those with disabilities	Mentoring

Figure 8.1   Time Line for American Education 1960–2000

The success of the former Soviet Union's 1957 *Sputnik* launch shifted emphasis from life adjustment to excellence and led to the National Defense Education Act, which greatly increased technical and scientific offerings in American high schools and colleges. Currently over 100 companies are funding projects in science, technology, engineering, and math to 100 communities where students are most in need (Khadaroo, 2010).

The 1960s were also dominated by concerns for equality of opportunity. A new concern for civil rights, and efforts to meet the needs of children, followed the *Brown* case. Ethnic and multicultural studies became popular, and in schools with many non-English-speaking students, bilingual programs were started. School reorganization and busing to create integrated schools dominated the 1960s and 1970s. Programs like project Head Start were created to help the lower-class youngster compete in middle-class schools. Some critics felt that integration and equality efforts diverted efforts from the drive toward excellence. The lack of literary and humanistic emphasis in school programs concerned others. Public support for education was declining by 1980. Renewed focus in raising school standards nationwide is a major goal of the Barack Obama administration as in former administrations. A National Council for Accreditation of Teacher Education (NCATE) Blue Ribbon Panel has developed principles that frame clinical experience as central in education preparation (Zimpher & Jones, 2010). (These issues are discussed in detail in Chapter 10.)

Inclusion

1979 Secretary of Education as a cabinet position	1990s Massive educational reforms in most states
1981 Education Consolidation and Improvement Act	1990–2005 Inclusion—disabled, minorities, women,
1983 *A Nation at Risk*	2000 Assessment, accountability
	2004 Clark Kerr (1911–2004)

ACADEMIC FREEDOM AND THE EDUCATIONAL PROFESSION

Early twentieth-century American schoolteachers could not smoke, drink alcoholic beverages, or express political preferences without fear of losing their jobs. Although this situation has improved, educators are still attacked for personal actions and what they teach. Thus, a teacher who asks children to read Huxley's *Brave New World,* or advocates adding fluoride to water, or supports racial integration, might be branded a communist by those who fear such ideas. The schools themselves are targets. Frequently, a school board, a superintendent, or even an entire school system will find itself under violent attack from organized groups or powerful individuals. During the Joseph McCarthy era, mere accusation of "red influence" was sufficient to frighten many school officials into firing teachers or removing books from the school libraries. In some cases, however, school boards have been willing to stand up to criticism and make their assailants prove their case, if they have one.

In the 1980s, public school teachers came increasingly under attack from the religious "new right," which accused them of teaching values clarification or secular humanism. Teachers have often been unable to fight because of lack of support from a strong professional organization, a scarcity of financial backing, or the reluctance of some school administrators to take a stand. Thus, a teacher who has a controversial point of view or who refuses to sign a loyalty oath could be asked to resign quietly in return for "keeping his or her record clean." Significant increases in the quantity and quality of teacher training have been made recently, but teachers still lack autonomy to control the admission requirements to their own profession. Teachers find it difficult to identify an agreed-upon and enforceable professional code of ethics or to develop an organization that represents them all. American public school teachers still lack the academic freedom enjoyed by most university professors. Tenure has been dropped for faculty and administrators in most public schools and some colleges. The Florida Education Standards Commission, like other states, has developed a Code of Ethics and the Principles of Professional Conduct of the Education Profession in English and Spanish. The commission has also developed Florida Educator Accomplished Practices for the preprofessional, professional, and accomplished levels.

Although tenure was under attack in the 2000s, major research universities continued to support it in order to recruit topflight faculty. Divergent educational practices in the United States are reflected in teacher education. Many normal schools early in the twentieth century were more like secondary schools than colleges. For years, a shortage of teachers created a reluctance to enforce general standards of certification. Large numbers of rural teachers were given certificates on the basis of passing examinations or on the strength of a year or two of college work. Although temporary or emergency certificates are no longer issued except under unusual circumstances, state requirements differ with regard to the number and type of professional courses demanded.

Without exception, normal schools did become 4-year colleges, and most state universities developed departments, schools, and colleges of education. The 45 teachers colleges in 1920 had grown to four times that number by 1940. The Depression years caused the first oversupply of teachers, giving rise to higher minimum standards. After World War II, most teachers were prepared with a general or liberal college education, specialized knowledge of the field to be taught, professional courses including methods and psychology, and practice teaching. Beyond question, American teachers are better qualified to practice their profession than ever before in history. Nevertheless, there is considerable criticism of teacher education.

The education of American teachers is a persistent national problem. Parents complain about the performance of teachers, university professors question their subject matter competence, administrators feel the universities certify people who cannot cope with school problems, and teachers themselves often feel ill-prepared to work with children, especially those from diverse cultures. The University of Missouri like other universities has a Teacher Development Program dealing with problems of schools, community, and society to address those issues. Radical critics such as Ivan Illich question having teachers trained and certified at all.

Formal and informal surveys and studies reveal that seasoned teachers rate field experience as the most relevant and beneficial part of their training. In 1972, the Commission of Public School Personnel Policies in Ohio reported that 78 percent of the teachers who had graduated from the 53 teacher education institutions in the state thought student teaching was their most valuable preparation. This study also indicated that educational practice or student teaching is insufficient,

FOCUS ON THE ISSUES

Teacher Education: Pedantic Pedagogy

Before the development of laboratory psychology and stage theory, the notion that the mind is divided into separate faculties or powers dominated educational theory. Faculty psychology stressed the exercise of each area of the mind, such as memory, but failed to relate the areas or link one subject to another. Further, it took no notice of attitudes, emotions, feelings, or motivation of students. The child was viewed as an empty vessel to be filled with facts by means of rote memorization.

The infamous Mr. Gradgrind so vividly described by Charles Dickens in *Hardtimes* has become a model of the worst sort of teacher, who follows faculty psychology as method. Indeed, *gradgrind*, or just *grind*, has entered the language to describe a bad or difficult school experience. This cold, aloof, sterile, and demanding schoolmaster was obsessed with pounding facts into the heads of reluctant students without regard for their needs, interests, or prior learning. It may be recalled that he severely criticized a student for failing to know the dictionary definition of a horse although she knew all about horses from her home experience. Many students have found their teachers to be without interest in their personal lives and out of touch with their vital interests. This is evident from the following anonymous poem from a nineteenth-century college for women.

> *Miss Buss and Miss Beale*
> *Cupid's darts do not feel.*
> *How different from us,*
> *Miss Beale and Miss Buss.*

What Do You Think?

1. When you teach, how can you avoid the "gradgrind" image?
2. Do teachers spend enough time relating one subject to another and showing the relevance of a subject to the lives of pupils?
3. What do you need to know about students in order to be a really effective teacher?
4. What is the role of mentoring and service learning in education and society?

poorly supervised, and comes too late in the course sequence. In-service training for teachers already certified and working is also criticized for being of little use to the teacher in actually improving methods, classroom management, communication skills, and techniques for student motivation.

Field Experience.   A major problem of teacher education is providing sufficient field experiences and practice teaching. Institutions of teacher education now usually require many hours of observation and work in schools or with children in other settings prior to practice teaching. There is general agreement that at least 1 year of internship would be a vast improvement over a semester of practice teaching with one cooperating teacher. By 1980, Florida and Oklahoma had passed laws requiring teacher candidates to spend a fifth year in schools as teacher interns before granting full certification. One problem is that teachers are not paid well enough to justify the extra year of entry-level training. Nevertheless, many colleges of education continue to move toward a 5-year plan, with some instituting a Master of Teaching in education degree. Because on-site experience has proved beneficial for entry-level teachers, university–public school partnerships are increasing.

Competency-based teacher education (CBTE), or performance-based teacher education, is now used in many university-based education colleges. CBTE stresses development of specific skills or categories of behavior directly connected to meaningful and observable student learning. Instead of merely having students accumulate credits in various courses, CBTE attempts to offer methods and content selected for their ability to accomplish the goals of professional training effectively and expediently. Researchers are exploring value-added analysis to their work. Measuring student progress over time rather than a fixed-in-time test result may yield more reliable data on which to base education decisions. A school can identify at-risk pupils and evaluate school effectiveness through different grade levels.

Some colleges are now cooperating with urban school districts to provide experiences for teacher interns designed to prepare them for work with the special educational problems of children in the ghettos of large cities. Others have developed teaching centers where professional teachers, practice teachers, college professors, and students can have interaction.

Charles Silberman pointed out that new teachers are often thrust into a situation fraught with anxiety and fear, which is not always alleviated by experience. The techniques most frequently used to help teachers overcome their problems are in-service training and graduate courses. In-service programs often include workshops, guest speakers, and seminars, but vary from one district or system to another. Some schools have no in-service education for teachers, and the programs in others are inadequate for real professional growth.

The American Association of Colleges for Teacher Education devoted much of its energy in 1989 to the difficult task of identifying a common knowledge base all teachers should share. This proved challenging, especially for elementary teachers. There is still much disagreement concerning the makeup of a common knowledge base. Graduate courses in education for teachers are popular because many schools require teachers to obtain a master's degree within a few years from the time of employment, and salary increases are often tied to the acquisition of graduate credit hours or advanced degrees. Graduate work in psychology, administration, adult education, statistics, and educational philosophy is certainly valuable, but there is a minimum of clinical experience or training designed to aid teachers in procedures of instruction and curriculum development. Of course, many teachers use graduate schools of education as a means of preparing themselves for positions as administrators, college teachers, or research workers. Currently a growing number of states are adopting national standards for their schools based on the recommendations of the National Association of Governors and Chief State School Officials (Lewin, 2010). Eight states have agreed to implement a Blue Ribbon NCATE panel's proposal to make clinical practice the centerpiece of teacher education curriculum (NCATE News and Press Releases, 2010).

Continuing Professional Education. The fact that large numbers of teachers believe that they are poorly prepared, combined with learning problems of so many underachieving students, supports the development of new programs. When more certified teachers than jobs are available, administrators can be more selective if they know what skills and what type of teacher training is most effective. Currently with an economic recession and layoffs, there is a national teacher surplus, most evident in California. Many persons now entering the field of education are serious about becoming as skilled and professional as possible. They are demanding clinical training of the sort provided in professional fields such as medicine. Pressures are building for college faculty members to become more directly involved with students and teachers in actual learning situations. Typical of such efforts is the University of Missouri master's program (Teaching Fellowship Program) enabling students to get their degree by teaching for a year at a partner school (Teaching Fellowship Program, 2010).

A National Commission on Teaching and America's Future report (2010) *Team Up for 21st Century Teaching and Learning* found common principles in effective learning communities. Shared values and goals, collective responsibility, authentic assessment, self-directed reflection, stable settings, and strong leadership support were principles common in case studies and research reports. Teacher and administrative reduction because of a lack of funding were common in many school districts. Almost a third of all teachers leave the field in their first 3 years, and half leave before their fifth year. Difficult students and low salaries are often reasons given for leaving the profession. Mentoring was helpful in recruiting and retaining teachers. Wise (2004a) suggested a team approach to high teacher turnover, especially in hard-to-staff schools, with poor teaching talent distribution and the persistent achievement gaps. He envisioned a National Board for Professional Teaching Standards with a certified team leader directing. In addition, another senior teacher, two novice teachers, two underprepared teachers, and six half-time student teachers will be completing their teacher preparation. In addition, Wise suggested four interns working half-time and for half-pay, together with a half-time university faculty member. The team model would be economically feasible, offer mentoring and support as needed, and be effective in closing the achievement gap of minority students. Current NCATE President James G. Cibulka seeks to incorporate new types of data-driven assessment preparation programs. The Performance Assessment for California Teachers (PACT) developed in Stanford will be the basis for the development of an instrument that states may use to evaluate teachers across their careers. PACT is comprised of embedded assessments such as case studies and analyses of student work; a subject-specific teaching event designed to capture teaching acts, from planning to reflection and assessments of teaching in content areas that are distinct from the teaching event (Cibulka, 2010).

Illich has suggested that teachers should have easy access to learning webs—centers where teaching, learning, and communication skills can be developed. Centers where teachers can voluntarily meet to exchange experiences, thoughts, feelings, and suggestions for improving practice are now being suggested nationwide. Such a center was created in Bay Shore, New York, in 1972, and pilot programs have been established for teacher centers in Vermont and Florida.

Cibulka (2009) is working toward a redesign of NCATE to make it more productive and more cost-effective while transforming America's school system to support higher levels of student achievement and success with an increasingly diverse school population.

The goal of the American Federation of Teachers, the National Education Association, NCATE, and other professional organizations is to use all avenues possible to improve the teaching–learning environment, maintain safe schools, raise standards, and improve achievement levels.

Accountability.   The philosophy behind accountability is that with adequate facilities and support systems all children can learn. Arthur J. Wise, president of NCATE, noted that 45 states and the District of Columbia have integrated NCATE's professional review of teachers colleges with their own review. NCATE was founded in 1954 by the American Association of Colleges for Teacher Education, the Council of Chief State School Officers, the National Association of State Directors of Teacher Education and Certification, the National Education Association, and the National School Boards Association. By late 2004, NCATE had accredited 575 teacher-preparation institutions with an additional 100 colleges seeking accreditation (Wise, 2004b). NCATE is aligning teacher-preparation standards with national standards for advanced certification and quality assurance.

October 22, 2010, the governing boards of NCATE and Teacher Education Accrediting Council (TEAC) approved a merger. A new organization, the Council of Accreditation of Educator Preparation, will replace the current organizations within two years. As of January 31, 2011, NCATE had 673 member institutions with 100 more seeking accreditation, TEAC is in the process of accrediting 200 schools. The goal of the merger is to improve instruction quality and student achievement levels. Alternative teacher certification programs such as Teach for America have yet to be accredited by these organizations (Sawchuk, 2010). (Nell Noddings and other authors focus on creating a homelike, nurturing environment in schools to meet the needs of at-risk and disadvantaged students.)

Title II of the Higher Education Act of 1998 was designed to make teacher-preparation programs more accountable. Blair, in an *Education Week* (2001) article, "Education Schools Strain to File Report Cards," notes that the nation's 1,300 education colleges and alternative teacher-preparation programs must submit data on state test passing rates and numbers of students in each program, together with faculty-to-student ratios. The report cards also documented whether a program has been approved by the state or has been labeled "low performing." Although the information was due by April 9, 2001, there has been difficulty gathering the data, finding some degree of uniformity in the information obtained, and organizing the data for state and federal reporting agencies. Reporting deadlines may continue to be extended. *Education Week* publishes a yearly Report of the States to rate the quality of state K–12 education systems.

Although there has been criticism of the complexity of the process, many find it assists in developing collaboration among teacher-education schools. The end result may be a better understanding of the unique challenges in educating teachers in the various states and, in time, more uniformity in the process and outcome of teacher-preparation programs. Ranking teacher-education programs in the states and submitting the data to the Federal Education Department and then to Congress may result in an unintended bureaucratic nightmare. Efforts are being made to deal with these issues with a focus on recruiting and retaining highly qualified teachers.

Elementary and Secondary Education Act. Federal aid to education took another big step with the Elementary and Secondary Education Act of 1965. This measure provided funds for textbooks and other instructional materials and services in public and private elementary and secondary schools. The primary purpose was to ensure that children from low-income families had access to adequate materials. State and local governments, rather than federal agencies, had control of the funds. The act also included $100 million for research in the field of education to be administered by the United States Office of Education. This act was extended for four more years in 1966, at a cost of about $12 billion. In 1981, the Education Consolidation and Improvement Act provided funds for better-quality programs and the encouragement of consolidation efforts. Federal block grants also targeted low-income and minority areas for special funding. With the economy in the worst recession since the Great Depression and a massive budget deficit, renewal of the Elementary and Secondary Education Act (No Child Left Behind) will be a challenge for the 112th Congress and White House.

Higher Education. Secretary of Education Arne Duncan, reflecting the Obama administration focus on international education, called for strengthening higher education foreign language programs to meet increased competition from abroad (Johnson, 2010). The Race to the Top program seeks to encourage states to apply for funding for innovative experimental programs to raise educational standards. Obama also has strongly supported charter schools.

In 1965, the Higher Education Act (which includes the Education Professions Development Act of 1967) was enacted. Since then, it has provided large sums of money for the acquisition of books and other library materials in colleges, improving and extending teacher-education programs, strengthening programs related to community problems like housing and poverty, supporting developing institutions of higher education, giving financial assistance to students through grants and loans, and developing the National Teachers Corps.

Teacher Corps trained teachers and college students to supplement instruction in schools with numerous low-income students. The education given Teacher Corps trainees included living in the neighborhoods near the schools and studying ethnic and minority culture. In 1980, Teacher Corps shifted from teacher training to in-service education. The Higher Education Act provided about 25,000 graduate fellowships for teacher trainees yearly, supported research and development in colleges of education, and established a National Advisory Council on Quality Teacher Education. Cochran-Smith (2005) reported on various alternative teacher-education programs including Teach for America. She noted that teacher education is embedded in the multiple and changing contexts of local institutions and regions and continues to be subject to the interpretation and social interactions of individuals and groups. Runningen and Rower (2010) reported on Obama's goals of making college more affordable, lifting graduation rates and focusing on preparing students to compete in a global economy. The national goal is having the United States with the highest rate of college graduates in the world by 2020. Arne Duncan, Education Secretary, stressed the goal of improving college completion rates through increasing Pell Grants for low-income students with tax credits that help parents cover tuition expenses.

Federal Involvement.   Although the federal government entered the educational arena in a big way in the 1960s, new legislation dropped off after the Johnson administration. One reason is that the shortage of teachers at the time of the National Defense Education Act changed into an oversupply of teachers by 1970. Another reason is the fear of federal control over local schools. In the early 1980s, the mood of the nation favored reduced federal spending and a cut in bureaucracy. Equality of educational opportunity can hardly be guaranteed with local taxes alone. Central tax collection and distribution by the national government appears to be the only way of ensuring equal education for the mobile American population. A number of educators have suggested some sort of federal equalization fund to make up for differences in economic support between states. Of course, fear of federal control has also caused many of the states to take steps for the reformation of their own tax laws. Inequality exists within school districts or cities, such as that demonstrated in the Rodriguez case of San Antonio, Texas. Although Rodriguez did not win, pressure was put on state legislatures to make taxation more equitable.

Congressional funding for education has not been uniform. Bills passed during the Kennedy and Johnson administrations were not always funded under Richard Nixon and few new federal education measures were proposed during that administration. President Ford signed a new elementary and secondary education act into law as one of his first official acts. In spite of the economic recession of the 1970s, efforts to provide federal help for schools and local educational programs did not end. Less money was provided in the 1970s than in the 1960s, but the impact of federal aid continued. The Department of Health, Education, and Welfare used the withholding of funds (or the threat of such withholding) as an instrument for enforcing plans for racial integration. This was continued under President Carter, but President Reagan voiced strong opposition to using the power of the federal government to control local action. The courts of the 1980s also took a less vigorous stand, as in the 1981 Los Angeles case when busing to achieve racial balance in schools was not supported. However, federal courts reinstalled court control over several school districts (including Kansas City in 2000) to ensure that state standards were being met for at-risk inner-city students.

One of the burning issues in American education is the control and support of schools. Public opposition to national educational policy is illustrated by the controversy that included student clashes surrounding the integration of South High School in Boston in 1974. In June 1974, U.S. District Judge W. Arthur Garrity, Jr.'s, Boston school desegregation order led to violent clashes between whites and blacks. Stabbings and brutal beatings occurred as court-ordered busing led to a community backlash. From 1972 to 1999, the white and middle-class student population changed from 60 percent of the 90,000 school district enrollment to 15 percent white, 49 percent black, 26 percent Hispanic, and the rest Asian American and Native Americans (Hendrie, 1999). On the one hand, many laypeople want less federal government in educational affairs and fear that local school boards are vanishing. On the other hand, many believe that federal funds and programs are necessary, and a growing number of states are supporting national standards. Arne Duncan, Secretary of Education, representing the Obama administration, has poured billions of dollars in education to improve outcomes and teacher quality that includes accountability and assessment. Stimulus funds were used to reduce teacher layoffs during the recession.

New Methods. Efforts are being made to introduce students to methods such as the use of programmed learning, distance learning, team teaching, individualized instruction, laboratory techniques, and new methods of computer research. Most states now require student teachers to be competent in instructional technology before they can be certified. A better understanding of remedial reading and learning disabilities is sometimes demanded. The knowledge explosion, the way learning is affected by mass media, social problems of students, and the development of new techniques require that teachers continue their training as long as they work. An example is Media Literacy classes where students learn Smartboard, Movie Maker, and creation of Ning accounts (online social networks) like Facebook.

A variety of programs have been developed to deal with cross-cultural language and academic development (CLAD), as is the case in California. With an increasingly diverse limited-English-proficient population, teacher-education programs are being developed with specialized credentials in working with bilingual student populations (BCLAD). Bilingual education has been controversial, and English immersion in California and Arizona is being implemented. Bilingual advocates continue to defend their programs often on the basis of respecting the language and culture of diversity. Arkansas has an ESL emphasis in a master's degree secondary education program and is expanding the program to include kindergarten through Grade 12 (K–12) to meet demands of an expanding Hispanic population. Florida Atlantic University, Boca Raton, as well as other universities have developed special programs for speakers of languages other than English.

Critics Outside the Profession. Several critics who had never worked in professional teacher education nor made a study of teacher-training institutions argued that good teachers are made through mastering subject matter. Admiral Hyman Rickover, history professor Arthur Bestor, Jr., business tycoon Albert Lynd, and columnist Dorothy Thompson were among the critics of professional education. They argued that knowledge of subject matter and a good liberal education can replace a knowledge of child psychology in the training of teachers. This same point of view was expressed earlier by perennialists, the Great Books advocates, and the Council for Basic Education.

The Carnegie Corporation provided funds for a study of teacher education conducted by James B. Conant, former president of Harvard University. Conant published his conclusions in 1963, making the colleges primarily responsible for selecting courses for teachers. This study negates the role of the states in teacher certification. In the late 1980s, California began selecting master teachers and giving them extra pay to coach newly certified teachers. This mentor project worked well, but as educational reformer John Goodlad pointed out, it was limited to the techniques of the model master teachers at a time when more revolutionary changes were needed. Wise (2000/2001) noted that a changing economy has adults looking into teaching as a second career. Over 130 accredited teacher-preparation programs have alternate route programs that reduce financial barriers to entry. In half of the second-career programs, the teacher candidate becomes the teacher of record, under supervision, while still enrolled in courses; in other programs candidates become interns, substitutes, or teaching assistants. The university and school district collaboratively plan coursework. Courses are designed to accommodate a working adult schedule and include online, weekend, evening, and summer offerings. Most states now have alternative certification degree programs for those holding advanced degrees and want to enter the teaching profession.

Innovations.   Innovations now found in many elementary schools include team teaching, nongraded schools and classes, block scheduling, virtual on line schools, aggression-control programs, and tokenism (food, games, money, tickets, and a variety of other reinforcers for learning). Other initiatives include school uniforms, obesity monitoring, cultural diversity and sensitivity programs, assistive technology, individualized instruction, open classrooms, and looping (the same teacher stays with students through first and second grades and the cycle repeats with a new group of students). Portfolios, rubrics, frameworks (teachers may draw up their own tests, using state guidelines), and programmed learning are also used for student assessment Virtual grade books give students and parents responsibility for checking their own grades. Turnitin, a program to check for student cheating/plagiarism and YouTube, are used more frequently in classes.

In contrast with the self-contained classroom, team teaching provides for the cooperation of a group of teachers working together with children. A team of teachers with a leader might be responsible for all the instruction of children who normally would be assigned to the primary grades (first, second, and third). Teams normally use some large-group, some small-group, and some individual instruction. Advantages include more time for planning, better evaluation of the progress of pupils, the opportunity for teachers to help one another improve practice, and flexibility in meeting the needs of students.

Nongraded schools allow children to progress at their own rate without locking them into the content of a given grade. A student in a graded school who is unable to satisfy the requirements of a given area (say third-grade reading) must be either retained or promoted at the end of the year. In nongraded schools, students who need a year and a half to master third-grade reading are neither punished by failing the grade nor promoted beyond their ability to cope. Florida allows student to complete K–12 through off-campus Internet programs.

Children mature at different rates, have different interests, and are not all motivated in the same way. Experiments in individualized instruction are designed to meet needs through a flexible program that allows each student to participate in planning his or her own program of instruction. Some individual instruction plans operate by providing a large number of groups at different levels for various subjects. A low teacher–pupil ratio and adequate support (including a high-quality instructional materials center) are needed for successful individualized instruction.

Herbert Kohl and others who advocate the open classroom say that the standard curriculum prevents creativity and good communication. By Kohl's standards, not many American elementary schools are "open." However, many schools now offer pupils a wide choice of activities and provide numerous opportunities for self-expression, the development of interests, and creative activities. Open classrooms provide for greater student interaction and scheduling and instructional flexibility; self-contained traditional classrooms provide for a more structured teaching and learning environment. Both the open and traditional classroom models are frequently modified to incorporate the best practices in each method.

Programmed learning, including computer-assisted instruction, is used in connection with other innovative programs. These programs are often found in classrooms and the media centers of schools with open or individualized plans for instruction. Various forms of technology—including voice-over-Internet protocol, personal digital assistants, wireless Internet access, convertible tablet PCs, and global and mobile positioning systems—are in use and all require constant updating. Universal adapters, badge computing, closed-circuit television, videophones, microfilm, VCRs, tape recorders, PowerPoint presentations, CDs, interactive video systems, computer video networks, virtual reality systems, computer-slide-overhead projector combinations, and projectors for slides and films are also used in traditional schools. In our twenty-first century, powerful computers—including new high-speed, high-RAM chip systems; prototypes having ever-increasing speed; more powerful gigahertz chips that can provide for voice recognition, fingerprint authentication, and wireless video in computers and cell phones; and increased hard drive space with multimedia capacities—are becoming more common and less expensive. New classrooms have multimedia equipment built in; so there is ready access to a variety of instructional methods including ability to access classrooms and students in other nations.

The Internet.   The Pew Internet and American Life Project, which tracks Internet usage, found that over 79 percent of the U.S. adult population uses the Internet. In addition, 28 percent of Americans and 59 percent of all Internet users have used a wireless laptop; over 82 percent of Americans have a cell phone—and of those, a growing number have a cell phone that lets them send and receive email. Sales of Apple IPhones and Google Android have soared, increasing social and business networking. The National Center for Education Statistics reported 99 percent of all schools have Internet access and 94 percent use broadband connections for high-speed access. More specifically, 92 percent of all classrooms have Internet access. High-poverty schools have improved the ratio of student per computer from 6.8 students in 2001 to 5.5 in 2002. The digital divide or gap for those without or with limited computer access has closed because of lower-cost computer systems enabling schools to increase the number and quality of computer systems. This progress continues. Davis (2010) discusses the expanding use of Ning and Skype systems to expand global student and classroom social networking. Vega (2010) notes the new web code, the fifth version of Hypertext Markup Language (HTML5), will make it easier to view media content and get information without downloading extra software.

Furthermore, Internet browsers such as Google and Yahoo are changing the way students gain access to knowledge bases. Students can network to contact experts in fields of interest. Twitter and Facebook increase social networking and Pew found civic engagement is taking place in cyber space. Online self-help networks, support groups, chat rooms, and listservs have become the public square where people connect up and come to each other's mutual aid (Boase et al., 2006).

Efforts have been made to connect all public and private educational systems in the country with the Internet. Public schools and universities now have email, Internet, and Telnet highways allowing students and faculty ready access to worldwide library and research facilities, as well as political, social, religious, and economic information. The Integrated Services Digital Network technology provides rapid access to national and international multiple information channels. New search engines provide the widest access to information in the world.

Philanthropic groups have provided new computers and software for public schools, libraries, and universities. The Bill and Melinda Gates Foundation is one of the major philanthropic organizations committed to improving access to technology. IBM has developed software that gives individuals a broad menu of personalized web pages for use virtually anywhere, from desk to handheld devices. Although controversial, cell phones are incorporated in some classes. With a website, Poll Everywhere (2010) surveys can be conducted by texting answers to a website. Finding can immediately be displayed. A Poll Everywhere on Smartboard allows students to use cell phones to text a site and see their answers online. Students can get involved to access knowledge. Recently parents request reports about student behavior be text messaged rather than through phone calls.

Twenty-first-century elementary schoolchildren find it hard to imagine a world without computers. Few inventions in history have been able to cross boundaries, borders, cultures, and languages as easily and effectively as the Internet. One can frequently find Chinese, Iranian, European, African, South American, and other international students spending hours at the 24-hour university computer centers. Sitting side by side, they use chat lines with intensity and spend hours exchanging messages with other students throughout the world. Portable high-power laptop computers make access to information universal. USB flash drives and CDs provide a way of carrying massive amounts of information from one location to another with ease. Internet providers such as Earthlink, MSN, and AOL assist individuals in accessing and disseminating information rapidly.

It seems safe to predict that multimedia systems will have increased utilization as America becomes a lifelong learning society in the information age. The rapidity of technological change requires constant adjustment to new challenges, from copyrighting material found in cyber space and intellectual property rights to monitoring students who can easily complete class assignments by downloading information or simply buying or copying complete research papers from the Internet.

Acohido and Swartz (2004) noted that personal computers have never been more powerful, nor more dangerous. Cyber-crook schemes generate spam, phishing emails (scam email directing consumers to bogus web pages and tricking them into surrendering personal information), and viruses. Compromised PCs are being transformed into obedient zombies slotted into underground networks to broadcast spam, carry out identity theft, and even conduct cyber blackmail. Major software companies are striving to provide computer security, but it remains a challenge to eliminate software flaws. Ash (2010a) reports problems with hackers inside and outside the school system. Efforts are being made to update what students are allowed to do on school computers; to require log-in procedures; to create separate networks for students, teachers, and administrators; to update antivirus software frequently; as well as to inform students of consequences of hacking. Schools also have content filters to comply with The Children's Internet Protection Act.

Recent Growth.
In recent years, there has been an unprecedented growth in school enrollments at all levels, from elementary school through college. About 55 million students enrolled in public school (K–12) in the fall of 2009, and vast technological developments affecting education in disseminating knowledge and enhancing learning have occurred.

Boys and girls who enter the first grade after years of exposure to television, the Internet, and other mass media bring new vocabularies and new experiences into the classroom. Teaching machines (computer-assisted instruction), team teaching, individualized assignments, and nongraded organizations are now being tested in schools and college research centers. Language laboratories, developed by the Army Specialized Training Program, have made a considerable impact on the teaching of foreign languages.

The knowledge explosion has encouraged thinking about a year-round school and the lengthening of the school week through longer hours or Saturday classes. If this is not done, a growing number of high school students will enroll in advanced placement courses in colleges. We may still expect the average school year to lengthen from 185 days to more than 200 days within a decade. The proliferation of subjects seems only to have begun as the scientific explosion continues to gain momentum. There is still the task of providing adequate challenge for the gifted child, appropriate work for the child with mental retardation, and adequate guidance for all.

A New Century–the Twenty-First.
Globalization and immigration, legal and illegal, have challenged policy makers in their efforts to improve educational achievement levels. This is partly attributable to language and cultural differences.

Although historically there have been 50 varying educational policies as each state determines curriculum content and local governance, a competitive economic environment requires some way of uniformly evaluating student performance. Although local control has been an article of faith in American education from colonial times, a modern trend toward state centralization of school, curriculum content, and student achievement exists. Blouin (2000) reported on a U.S. Department of Education–funded model program to provide high-quality data to improve decision making at the school district and state levels. The information gathered includes performance on standardized achievement tests, data on school lunches, and special student services received, as well as race and gender. Administrators and teachers can access the database to improve their educational efforts. Teachers can also track individual students' test scores over time to determine achievement levels. The Data Delivery system provides information that is easily accessible through websites. Researchers Ronna Turner and Sean Mulvenon of the University of Arkansas, Fayetteville, have developed statistical guidelines for instruction improvement and assessment. Mulvenon (2004) has analyzed educational reform measures in higher education calling for more "Intrapreneurs." A growing number of states are using data-based evidence for teacher assessment and evaluation. A partnership between K–12 teachers and the University of Arkansas, Fayetteville, is improving science and math learning through inquiry-based instruction as a potential model for improving science and math education in middle schools. The program, K–12, I Do Science, has a second round of National Science Foundation funding (Jaquish, 2011).

Assessment.   Although there continue to be unforeseen negative effects of performance assessment, the trend toward standardized measurement of student and school achievement levels is increasing nationwide. Savoye (2000) reported on Cincinnati's legislation to pay teachers on the basis of their performance. A commission, with two-thirds of its members being teachers, developed an evaluation system built around 16 categories. Teachers will be identified as distinguished, proficient, basic, or unsatisfactory. The score will determine teacher placement in pay levels of accomplished, advanced, career, novice, and apprentice. New teachers must pass apprentice level by the second year and novice by the fifth year to renew contracts. Savoye also noted that concerns about objectivity are dealt with by use of peer reviews. Provisions are included in the plan to eliminate it if the costs are too high or by 70 percent vote by teachers. By 2005, Ohio school administrators worked with the Milken Family Foundation to reward teachers for knowledge and skills and growth in student achievement. Milken found pay for performance would be ineffective without other components such as continuing professional development Turner (2010) notes that states are pushing to pay teachers based on performance. A judge in Arizona ruled a performance pay program in the state is unconstitutional because it is open to only 28 of the 230 school districts. Teacher unions are opposed to the concept. Sawchuk (2011) reports that the Florida Education Association plans a lawsuit against a bill ready for the governor's signature. It will put all teachers on one-year contracts, end tenure, permit districts to extend contracts only to teachers with good evaluations, and requires all school districts to establish performance-based salaries by July 1, 2014. Research on Pay for Performance reforms is limited. Pay for performance for teachers has increased nationwide in the second decade of the twenty-first century. In the annual *Education Week* report card, Ohio received A for standards and accountability, B for efforts to improve teacher quality, and C and C+ for school climate and resources, a high ranking among the states (Skinner, 1996). Many states are examining pay for performance to improve education outcomes especially in communities with high rates of poverty and at risk children. The Teacher Incentive Fund supports pay for performance, financial incentives to help high-poverty schools recruit more quality teachers. Traditional salary increments based on teacher longevity are being reexamined with the Obama administration's Race to the Top program (Chait & Miller, 2009).

Marshall (2000) reported on teacher, parental, student, and administrator division, discord, confusion, low morale, and chaos created by Florida's distribution of some $152 million, most of which was earmarked for schools with improved student test scores on the Florida Comprehensive Assessment Tests (FCAT). Schools are graded mainly on FCAT test scores. Often schools with at-risk students, English deficient and physically and mentally challenged students, and low-income families are rated low, either D or F. Since outstanding teachers in these schools often received limited or no funds because of the difficulty of identifying and measuring outstanding performance for merit increases, the state provided $1.3 million to the Palm Beach County School district to attract and retain teachers at low-performing schools (Travis, 2001). Tanner (2000) noted that while the regular curriculum is put on hold, teachers often spend weeks teaching to standardized tests that frequently emphasize mechanics. He wrote, however, that performance assessments can be helpful when used as an instructional approach to teach reasoning and problem solving as Dewey did in the late 1890s. There are no easy answers or shortcuts to improving student achievement, and a multitude of initiatives will continue to be deployed to seek increased accountability for results. The National Conference of State Legislatures reported on continuing struggles for adequate school funding to meet new state assessment standards. The major concern is what to do about students who will not pass tougher tests. Michigan has a lawsuit challenging its tests, especially in regard to students with special needs. Poor-performance schools are being taken over by states, closed, or turned over to corporations to manage. Federal courts have ruled against states seeking to opt out of No Child Left Behind Act (NCLB) because of penalties for noncompliance and funding issues. Arne Duncan is responding to funding as well as addressing educational administrators concerns in reauthorization of NCLB (see Johnson, 2010). He is also encouraging the use of detailed databases on achievement levels and teaching effectiveness to close the educational achievement gap for low-income at-risk students.

IDEA. President Ford in 1975 signed the Education for All Handicapped Children (PL 94-142) to provide all children with a free and appropriate education. The Individuals with Disabilities Education Act (IDEA 1997) provided for Individualized

Education Programs (IEPs) for special education students. An IEP team determines whether or not it is appropriate for a student to take state-mandated standardized tests under a philosophy of inclusion in classroom activities. If it is appropriate, the IEP team determines any modifications that may be needed for measuring student achievement. If it is not appropriate, each state is developing special examinations appropriate for the exceptional student. The 106th Congress and the president provided the highest funding in the history of IDEA. The federal contribution to IDEA was raised from 12 percent in 2000 to 15 percent in 2001. Senators Chuck Hagel and Tom Harkin in the 108th Congress introduced a bill to mandate full federal funding (40 percent) for IDEA for the first time in 29 years. A House bill introduced by Representative Charles Bass included the request for full funding, at 40 percent of the national current average per-pupil expenditure, for all children with disabilities. In spite of a burgeoning deficit, a large trade deficit, and a rapidly rising national debt, IDEA funding continues to be a national priority (IDEA Reauthorization Update, 2004–5). President Barack Obama on February 17, 2010, signed legislation doubling current funding for IDEA. Although this is one of the largest funding infusion in special education, it still falls short of the 40 percent goal ("President Signs Legislation," 2010).

Special Assistance.

Miller (2004) finds special education is one of the fastest growing areas of school budgets nationwide. The number of children who qualify for special education has grown nearly 40 percent in the past decade, with some 6.6 million children ages 3 to 21 diagnosed with special needs. Federal funding increases are needed for special education. With over $50 billion spent on special education annually, the federal government contributes from 10 to 18 percent. Meanwhile, educators are wrestling with which children belong in special education or need extra help from counseling, in addition to greater playground supervision. Educators are exploring whether special assistance should be for reading, writing, and arithmetic, or should include interaction with others and social skills. A Department of Education task force suggested reducing the number of youngsters labeled learning disabled, resulting in protests from special education advocates. Parental lawsuits for special education cases are proliferating, and NCLB is being modified to meet the assessment needs of special education youngsters. The Council for Exceptional Children is working on advocacy for program funding as Congress and the Obama administration battle with an unprecedented economic crisis resulting in cuts to educational programs (2010). Ash (2010b) reports on cyber schooling or going virtual in special education. The program requires parental support and is helpful for students with behavioral and social problems.

Other initiatives include substance abuse prevention, mental health, maternal and child health, and preventing obesity through better nutrition and twenty-first-century community learning programs. Many federal, state, corporate, and volunteer groups are working to provide special assistance programs for the nation's poor and marginalized population. The nation's historic commitment to equity, access, and equality continues.

THEN TO NOW

If American education is to meet the great challenges of the future, it must be efficient, flexible, professional, and stimulating. Schools cannot afford to reinvent and test programs or methods that were tried and tested in the past. Educators need to learn about both the success and the failure of earlier educational experiments and to use those experiments as guides in making a better-quality learning environment. The educational reforms of the late 1980s, responding to *A Nation at Risk* and other critical reports, seemed to ignore history. Former Secretary of Education William Bennett wanted to restore a classical curriculum with intellectual rigor for the college-bound elite. Wide support for this initiative by conservative groups and authors like Diane Ravitch and Allen Bloom obscures the goal of progressive education for all.

Providing mentoring and volunteer resources to assist elementary children in reading and mathematics is another major initiative. Teachers, students, faculty, administrators, and parents are increasingly communicating through email systems and accessing knowledge bases through the Internet. Danielson and McGreal (2000) identified historical perspectives in research on teaching designed to improve student achievement levels. Research studies on teacher effectiveness and clinical supervision in the 1960s were followed by analysis of learning styles in the 1970s. Discipline models, effective schools, cooperative learning, and brain research predominated in the 1980s. During the 1990s, research on teaching expanded to include critical thinking, content knowledge and pedagogy, alternative assessment, multiple intelligences, collaborative learning, cognitive learning theory, constructivism, and authentic pedagogy. By the 2000s, teaching research was directed toward authentic pedagogy, engaged teaching, empowering teachers and administrators, assessment models, accountability, and teaching for understanding. These research efforts were designed to use quantitative and qualitative studies to meet the needs of an ever more diverse student population. Teacher education continues to face economic, political, and cultural challenges as it adjusts to new demands as the Obama administration and Congress fund the Race to the Top.

Meanwhile, over 1.3 million students will fail to graduate in the class of 2010. The dropout crisis is concentrated in a very small number of school systems. One in every five dropouts nationwide can be traced to just 25 individual school systems out of roughly 11,000 school districts in the United States (Diegmueller, 2010). Communities with high poverty, crime, and violence are part of the reason that students at risk drop out.

The history of education reveals a continuing effort to include more of the population in accessing equitable education and workforce opportunities. From the Olde Deluder Satan Acts of 1642 and 1647 to the nation's latest appropriations and budget, Congress, the executive branch, and state legislatures work to provide more opportunities for upward mobility through education as well as caring for youth welfare. An example is the Children's Internet Protection Act, requiring all schools that receive technology funds under the Elementary and Secondary Education Act (ESEA) to use filtering software and have an acceptable use policy that has been developed with public input.

The history of American education can never be finished. Innovations in education and cultural changes in the society continue to make new demands. We can only expect that past traditions and trends of development will provide some indication of the future paths of our schools.

GAINING PERSPECTIVE THROUGH CRITICAL ANALYSIS

1. Trace the development of teacher-education preparation programs. What alternative teacher-preparation programs exist in your state? Discuss the pros and cons of such programs.
2. Cite historical issues in academic freedom for educators. What role do professional organizations play in protecting teachers' academic freedom? Identify basic components of your state's code of ethics.
3. Trace the conflict between state and local control of schools and funding sources. Who is winning the battle? Use current research from recent periodicals or the Internet to support your opinions.
4. List the major contributions of the federal government to education policy making between 1960 and 2011. In your opinion, which contributions had the greatest impact? What actions have been taken in the past year by the federal government that impact education policies and practices? Suggested sites include the U.S. Department of Education (www.ed.gov) and the Library of Congress (www.loc.gov/).
5. Identify trends of the National Council for Accreditation of Teacher Education. Examine your state's education standards and professional competencies on the Internet and give four examples of how the standards improve education. (Florida's Professional Competencies for Teachers of the Twenty-first Century as well as professional standards of other states are available online.)
6. Identify the role and function of mainstreaming in our classrooms.

HISTORY IN ACTION IN TODAY'S CLASSROOMS

1. Use your journal to record the major events in the history of academic freedom. Have there been changes in the way teachers are viewed by the public over time?
2. Check periodicals and the Internet to discover at least one case where a teacher has been dismissed for lack of academic freedom protections. Discuss the issues involved. Are teachers professional educators or servants of the state?
3. Contact and ask your state legislative representative to discuss his or her perceptions of recent efforts to improve student achievement levels. Try to determine if he or she views teachers as professionals or as servants of the state. Add the findings to your journal.
4. Visit a child welfare services agency in your community. What social and psychological interventions are being used to deal with children and their families?
5. The Internet would influence which phase of Dewey's act of thought process? Discuss and answer the questions at the end of the feature "Teacher Education: Pedantic Pedagogy." This feature is found within the chapter.
6. Find a copy of national standards for your particular content area of interest by using the library, contacting a professional association, or using the Internet. Analyze the standards in terms of current literature dealing with the pros and cons of such standards. Identify the pros and cons of high-stakes testing and the No Child Left Behind Act. Suggested sites include the National Council for Accreditation of Teacher Education (www.ncate.org) and American Youth Policy Forum (www.aypf.org).
7. In your journal, list at least three reasons supporting separate programs for gifted and talented students and at least three reasons for not supporting such programs. Suggestions include the Council for Exceptional Children at www.cec.sped.org and www.ericec.org/.

BIBLIOGRAPHY

Acohido, Byron, & Jon Swartz. "Are Hackers Using Your PC to Spew Spam and Steel?" *USA Today* (September 8, 2004): 1B, 4B.

Acohido, Byron, & Jon Swartz. "Tech Industry Presents Less-Than-Unified Defense." *USA Today* (September 9, 2004): 1 B, 2B.

Allen, Michael. "Teachers Preparation Programs in the United States, Response to Congress's Mandated Request." Available at: www.tqsource.org/publications/NCCTQBiennialReport.pdf

Ash, Katie. "Hacker Patrol: Schools Work to Prevent Security Breaches." *Education Week, Digital Directions* (Spring–Summer 2010): 30–31.

Ash, Katie. "Going Virtual in Special Education." *Education Week, Digital Directions* (Spring–Summer 2010): 46–47.

Blair, Julie. "Education Schools Strain to File Report Cards." *Education Week* (March 28, 2001): 1, 30.

Blouin, Melissa. "Measuring Performance in the Schools." *University of Arkansas Research Frontiers* (Fall 2000): 28–29.

Boase, Jeffrey, John Horrigan, Barry Wellman, & Lee Rainie. *The Strength of the Internet Ties.* Washington, DC: Pew Internet and American Life Project, 2006.

Brown, Ellsworth. *The Making of Our Middle Schools.* New York: Littlefield, 1970.

Burton, Warren. *The District School as It Was.* New York: Arno Press, 1969.Orginally published in 1928.

Butts, Freeman. *Public Education in the United States: From Revolution to Reform.* New York: Holt, Rinehart and Winston, 1978.

Carroll, Tom. "Introduction to Learning Teams." In *Team Up for 21 Century Teaching and Learning* (June 2010). www.nctaf.org/documents/Teamup-CE-Web.pdf

Chiat, Robin, & Raegen Miller. "Paying Teacher's for Results." *Center for American Progress* (May 18, 2009): 1, 2. Available at: www.americanprogress.org/issues/2009/05/performance_pay_poverty.html

Cibulka, James G. "Taking Assessment to the Next Level: Incorporating New Types of Data Driven Assessment in Preparation Programs. Measuring What Matters." *The Newsletter of the National Council for Accreditation of Teacher Education* 19, no. 2 (2010). Available at: www.ncate.org/public/Newsroom/NCATENews-PressReleases

Cibulka, James G. "An Introductory Message from Jim Cibulka, NCATE President." *NCATE Newsletter* (May 15, 2009): 1.

Cochran-Smith, Marilyn. "Taking Stock in 2005." *The Journal of Teacher Education* (January–February 2005): 3–7.

"Congress Orders Landmark Study of Teacher Education Programs." *Association of Teacher Education Newsletter* (Spring 2004): 4.

Cremin, Lawrence. *The Transformation of the School.* New York: Alfred A. Knopf, 1961.

Cubberley, Elwood. *Public Education in the United States.* New York: Houghton Mifflin, 1934.

Danielson, Charlotte, & Thomas L. McGreal. *Teacher Evaluation to Enhance Professional Practice.* Alexandria, VA: Association for Supervision and Curriculum Development, 2000.

Davis, Michelle R. "Social Networking Goes to School." *Education Week, Digital Directions* (Spring–Summer 2010): 16, 17.

Diegmueller, Karen. "Graduation in the United States." *Education Week, Diplomas That Count* (June 10, 2010): 25.

Feistritzer, Emily. *Profiles of Teachers in the U.S.* Washington, DC: National Center for Educational Information, 1986.

Galley, Michelle. "Texas Model: Go Directly to Class Without Teacher Training." *Education Week* (March 10, 2004): 20.

General Accounting Office/Health, Education, and Human Services Division. *School Facilities: America's Schools Report Differing Conditions.* Washington, DC: Author, June 1996.

Gutek, Gerald. *An Historical Introduction to American Education.* New York: Thomas Crowell, 1970.

Hendrie, Caroline, "Judgment Days." *Education Week* (June 2, 1999). Hirsch, E. D. *The Schools We Need: Why We Don't Have Them.* New York: Doubleday, 238.

Hohn, Robert L. *Classroom Learning and Teaching.* New York: Longman, 1995.

Hurd, Nancy K. Personal conversation and site tour. Delray Beach, CA: Community Child Care Center, December 2000.

Individual with Disabilities Education Improvement Act of 2004, final version passed by Congress and signed by President George Bush as H. R. 1350. The American Counseling Association. Available at: www.Thomas.loc.gov/cgi-bin/query/z?c108:h.1350.enr

Jaquish, Barbara. "Capturing Joy: K-12, I Do Science." *University of Arkansas Research Frontiers* (2011).

Johnson, Marlene. "Secretary of Education Arne Duncan Stresses the Importance of a Global Education." *NAFSA* (May 7, 2010). Katz, Michael. *Class, Bureaucracy, and Schools.* New York: Praeger, 1971.

Khadaroo, Stacy Teicher. "Obama: CEOs Joining To Push Math, Science Education." *The Christian Science Monitor* (September 16, 2010).

"Legislators' Group Opens Clearinghouse to Track School Finance." *Education Week* (February 28, 2001): 19.

Lewin, Tamar. "Many States Adopt National Standards for Their Schools." *New York Times* (July 21, 2010). Available at: www.nytimes.com/2010/00/21/education/21standards.html

Marshall, Toni. "School Bonuses Fuel Strife and Confusion." *South Florida Sun Sentinel* (December 3, 2000): 1, 4A.

McCabe, Melissa. "Salary Adjustments." *Education Week* (Special Issue: Quality Counts, No Small Change) (2005): 24–26.

McKissack, Patricia, & Frederick McKissack. *The Civil Rights Movement in America.* Chicago: Children's Free Press, 1967.

McLaughlin, Milbery. *Evaluation and Reform: The Elementary and Secondary Education Act of 1965.* Cambridge, MA: Harvard University Press, 1975.

Miller, Sara B. "Demand on Special Education Is Growing." *The Christian Science Monitor* (August 24, 2004): 1, 3.

Moe, Terry. *Special Interest: Teachers Unions and Public Schools.* Washington, DC: The Brookings Institution, 2011.

Moorefield, Story. "The G.I. Bill." *American Education* (August–September 1974): 25.

Mulvenon S. "The Impact of Educational Reform on Higher Education: A Greater Need for Academic Intrapreneurs." *All Things Academic* 5, no. 2 (2004): 1–4.

National Council for Accreditation of Teacher Education. NCATE News and Press Releases (December 27, 2010).

Noddings, Nel. *Caring: A Feminine Approach to Ethics and Moral Education.* Berkeley: University of California Press, 2003.

NSF/Project Scope Display 2006. "Alternative Routes to Teacher Certification." Washington, DC: The National Center for Alternative Certification, September 15,

2004. The National Conference of State Legislatures (2002). Available at: www.ncsl.org/

Olson, Lynn. "Pay Performance Link in Salaries Gain Momentum." *Education Week* (October 13, 1999).

Pitsch, Mark. "E.D. Officials Begin Task of Marketing Their Proposal to 'Reinvent' the Elementary and Secondary Education Act." *Education Week* (September 29, 1993): 22.

Poll Everywhere. (2010). www.polleverywhere.com/

"President Signs Legislation to Double IDEA Funding." *Council for Exceptional Children* (July 18, 2010): 1–4.

Pully, Brett. "Rites of Passage." *New York Times* (June 16, 1998).

Rainie, Lee, & Dan Packel. *Sixteen Million Newcomers Gain Internet Access in the Last Half of 2000 as Women, Minorities, and Families with Modest Incomes Continue to Surge Online.* Washington, DC: The Pew Internet and American Life Project, February 18, 2001. Available at: www.pewinternet.org/Reports

Rainie, Lee, et al. *The Future of the Internet 2010 Survey Results.* Washington, DC: The Pew Internet and American Life Project, Pew Research, 2010. Available at: www.slideshare.net/PewInternet/2010-6510FutureoftheInternet

Robinson, David. "57 Smallest Districts History." *The Morning News, Arkansas* (July 1, 2004): 7A.

Rippa, Alexander. *Education in a Free Society.* 2nd ed. New York: David McKay, 1971.

Runningen, Roger, & Kate Anderson Rower. "Obama U.S. Needs More College Grads." *Arkansas Democrat Gazette* (August 10, 2010): 2A.

Savoye, Craig. "City Tries Paying Teachers for Results." *The Christian Science Monitor* (December 5, 2000): 1, 4.

Sawchuk, Stephen. "Merger Lies Ahead for Accrediting Bodies of Teacher Preparation." *Education Week* (November 3, 2010): 6.

Sawchuk, Stephen. "Bill to End Tenure, Create Merit Pay Awaits Florida Governor's Signature." *Teacher Beat* (March 16, 2011). Available at: www.blogs.edweek.org

Sawchuk, Stephen. "Reaction Pours in to Performance-Pay Study." *Teacher Beat* (2010). Available at: www.blogs.edweek.org

Skinner, Ronald A. "State Report Cards." *Education Week* (Special Issue: No Small Change) (1996): 129.

Snyder, Thomas D. *Digest of Educational Statistics.* Washington, DC: U.S. Office of Education, Office of Educational Research and Improvement, 1999, pp. 1–5 (One Room Schools, Table 97).

Snyder, Thomas D. *National Center for Educational Statistics, Encyclopedia of Educational Statistics, Projections of Educational Statistics.* Washington DC: U.S. Office of Education, 1999, 2000. Available at: nces.ed.gov

State by State List of Accredited Institutions. NCATE (January 31, 2011). Available at: www.ncate.org/StatebyStateListofAccreditedInstitutions/tabid/539/Default.aspx

"Surf Report: Bullying and Conflict Resolution." Wisconsin government, Wisconsin.gov.home. Available at: www.ecb.org/surf/

Tanner, Laurel N. "Critical Issues in Curriculum Revisited." *The Educational Forum* (Fall 2000): 16–21.

Teaching Fellowship Program MU Partnership for Education Renewal. (2010). Available at: www.education.missouri.edu/

Turner, Dorie. "States Push to Pay Teachers Based on Performance." *USA Today* (2010). Available at: www.usatoday.com/news/education/2010-04-8-teachers-pay

Turner, Ronna, & S. W. Mulvenon. "Using SAS To Conduct Public Studies: As an Instructional Guide." *SIG Newsletter for Measurement Services* 1 (December 2004).

Travis, Scott. "Bonus Checks for Some Teachers Create Tension." *Sun-Sentinel South Florida* (February 9, 2001): 3B.

Tyack, David. *The One Best System: A History of American Urban Education.* Cambridge, MA: Harvard University Press, 1974.

Vega, Tanzia. "Privacy Backers Rap New HTML." *Arkansas Democrat-Gazette* (October 18, 2010): 1B, 5B.

Vygotsky, Lev S. *Thought and Language.* Cambridge, England: Cambridge University Press, 1962.

Watson, John B. *Behaviorism.* New York: W. W. Norton and Company, 1924.

Wise, Arthur J. "Creating a High Quality Teaching Force." *Educational Leadership* (December 2000/January 2001): 18–21.

Wise, Arthur J. "High Quality Alternative Routes to Teaching: More Programs Now Geared to Adults in Transition." *National Council for Accreditation of Teacher Education Quality Teaching* (Fall 2004a): 1, 2, 7.

Wise, Arthur J. "Teaching Teams: A 21st Century Paradigm for Organizing America's Schools." *Education Week* (September 29, 2004b): 32, 44.

Zimpher, Nancy, & Dwight Jones. "Work of NCATE Blue Ribbon Panel on a Fast Track." NCATE (Spring 2010): 7.

CHAPTER 9

EDUCATIONAL REFORM AFTER 1980: THE SEARCH FOR EXCELLENCE

Hope for the future rests with our ability to use and relate effectively all those educative and potentially educative institutions and agencies in our society—home, school, church, media, museums, workplace and more.

John I. Goodlad

Nixon	Ford	Carter	Reagan
1974 Watergate scandal, loss of respect for government	1976 Bicentennial NEA politically active	Continuation of social engineering in education	Stress on basics
High inflation, revolt of taxpayers	1979 Separate Department of Education	Bilingual programs for growing Hispanic minority	New power of political and religious right
Drop outs Digital Divide at-risk children		Achievement Gap	Conservative social and fiscal policies and rise of the fundamentalist "New Right"

Figure 9.1   Time Line of Educational Reform

THE GREAT AMERICAN EDUCATIONAL REFORM MOVEMENT

As demonstrated in previous chapters, the period of American history from the Kennedy to the Obama administrations was dominated by the social reform movement. Rejecting the old Darwinian concept of survival of the fittest, social engineers and educators joined forces in an effort to attain equality of opportunity, "create the great society," "build a bridge to the twenty-first century," and "race to the top."

Aside from school lunch and health measures, the first such programs concentrated on racial desegregation of the schools. Egalitarian programs focusing on culturally deprived, urban poor, at-risk, English language learners and disadvantaged students soon followed. Thus, project head start, talent search, magnet schools, child-care centers, upward bound, and mainstreaming were superimposed on integration plans such as busing to achieve racial balance. The influx of vast numbers of Spanish-speaking children (the largest minority population in the United States) fostered bilingual programs, and federally sponsored enrichment agendas were followed in the cities. In the early twenty-first century, bilingual education has been

Bush		Clinton		G. W. Bush
1980s *A Nation at Risk*	1986 Gramm-Rudman	1993 National Service Trust Fund	2002 High-stakes testing Teacher shortage	2002 Leave no child behind
Other national reform reports	1986 Holmes Group	1988 Shortage of teachers	1994 Whitewatergate	2006 Polarizations Social Fragmentation Intelligent Design Electronics Eavesdropping Controversy Hurricane Katrina New Orleans Middle East conflict
	1984 Responses by Ernest Boyer, John Goodlad, and Theodore Sizer	2001 IDEA Inclusion full funding for learning disabled		
		2000 Effort to impeach President Clinton		

subject to review. There is a trend toward total English immersion in several states, while bilingual education is an option in others.

Progress was made toward an equal and democratic society in the 1960s and 1970s, although not at a rate that satisfied critics like Illich and Kozol. Almost all federal money earmarked for education was allocated for these projects, and virtually every school district was affected to some degree. When new ideas for the improvement of education appeared in the early 1980s, such as those espoused in B. Othanel Smith's *A Design for a School of Pedagogy* (1980), there was insufficient public support for implementation.

It should come as no surprise that concentration on access to schooling and equity would have a leveling effect on overall achievement. After all, when the population of students expanded to include minorities, the disadvantaged, and those with exceptional needs, some regression might have been expected. College boards, for example, once taken only by elite college-bound high school students, declined as the numbers of pupils taking them expanded. John Gardner, among others, had previously raised the question of whether the public schools could be both equal and excellent. Although the two goals are not mutually exclusive, sterling success in scholarship requires effort and money, as does efforts for equality.

Reform Agendas.   More than 30 examinations of public education in the United States closely followed the publication of *A Nation at Risk*. Some were sponsored by special interest groups, several emerged from the work of commissions and professional organizations, and a few represented individual efforts (see Figure 9.2). By 2005, calls for educational reform had become part of the social, economic, and educational culture. The public, educators at all levels, corporations, and politicians vied with each other to present a variety of strategies for improving educational delivery systems and student achievement across income levels.

As legal and illegal immigration expands a multiracial, multicultural society, both corporations and educators will continue to emphasize understanding and respect for diverse cultures. For the first time, the 2000 and 2010 census provided an opportunity for respondents to identify more than one racial background. Over time this will require cooperation among racial groups to provide federal funding to disadvantaged, at-risk, and poverty pockets. African Americans will join Hispanics (Latinos) and other cultural and racial groups in seeking assistance at federal, state, and local levels. There were over 308 million citizens in 2010 and by midcentury 62 percent of the nation's children will be minorities up from 44 percent currently (U.S. Census Bureau, 2010). The challenge for the future will be a search for unity within diversity to prevent social fragmentation.

A Nation at Risk.   *A Nation at Risk*, issued by the National Commission on Excellence in Education, had an impact similar to *Sputnik's* launch in 1957. Educators criticized the report for focusing too much on high schools, using too narrow a sample and dated information, being biased in favor of a business model, and comparing comprehensive American schools with limited-population elite schools in Germany and Japan. Nevertheless, *A Nation at Risk* caught the attention of both the public and educators. The report made a strong case for the urgency of reform if the nation was to retain its place in the modern world. Although it was followed by a myriad of other studies and reports, there is no question that *A Nation at Risk* had the most influence.

In international comparisons, the report showed that American students never were first or second, and often were dead last, as ranked against other industrial nations on 19 academic tests. About 13 percent of the nation's 17-year-olds and 40 percent of minority youth were functionally illiterate. Some 23 million adults could not pass simple tests of reading, writing, and comprehension. Half of the population of gifted students failed to match their tested ability in school performance. The average achievement of secondary students was lower than in 1957. Nearly 40 percent of high school seniors could not draw inferences from written material, and only a third could solve a mathematical problem requiring several steps.

The report pointed out that college boards (SAT test scores) declined steadily from 1963 to 1980. On average, verbal scores dropped 50 points and math scores 40 points. The proportion of students demonstrating superior achievement also declined dramatically. Between 1975 and 1980, remedial courses in mathematics offered by 4-year colleges increased by 72 percent, so that they came to make up a

The Paideia Proposal: An Educational Manifesto, Mortimer J. Adler, on behalf of the members of the Paideia Group, 1982.

The Troubled Crusade: American Education 1945–1980, Diane Ravitch, 1983.

A Place Called School: Prospects for the Future, John Goodlad, 1983.

Academic Preparation for College: What Students Need to Know and Be Able to Do, Educational Equality Project, The College Board, 1983.

Action for Excellence: A Comprehensive Plan to Improve Our Nation's Schools, Task Force on Education for Economic Growth, Education Commission of the States, 1983.

High School: A Report on Secondary Education in America, Ernest L. Boyer, The Carnegie Foundation for the Advancement of Teaching, 1983.

Making the Grade, Report of the Twentieth Century Fund Task Force on Federal Elementary and Secondary Education Policy, 1983.

Horace's Compromise: The Dilemma of the American High School, Theodore R. Sizer, 1984.

A Study of High Schools, Theodore Sizer, cosponsored by the National Association of Secondary School Principals and the National Association of Independent Schools, 1984.

In Search of Excellence: Lessons from America's Best Run Companies, Thomas Peters and Robert Waterman, 1984.

Investing in Our Children, Report of the Committee for Economic Development, 1985.

A Nation Prepared: Teachers for the 21st Century, Report of the Carnegie Task Force on Teaching as a Profession, 1986.

Time for Results, National Governors' Association, 1986.

Cultural Literacy: What Every American Needs to Know, E. D. Hirsch Jr., 1987.

The Forgotten Half: Non-College Youth in America: An Interim Report on the School-to-Work Transition, Report of William T. Grant Foundation's Commission on Work, Family and Citizenship, 1988.

Teachers for Our Nation's Schools, John Goodlad, 1990.

Horace's School: Redesigning the American High School, Theodore R. Sizer, 1991.

Results in Education: 1990, Report of the National Governor's Association, 1991.

Savage Inequalities: Children in America's Schools, Jonathan Kozol, 1991.

Shared Vision: Policy Recommendations for Linking Teacher Education to School Reform, Calvin Frazier, 1993.

The Basic School, Ernest Boyer, 1995.

The Schools We Need and Why We Don't Have Them, E. D. Hirsch Jr., 1996.

What Matters Most: Teaching for America's Future. National Commission on Teaching and America's Future, 1996.

Horace's Hope: The Future of the American High School, Theodore Sizer, 1996.

The Public Purpose of Education and Schooling, Edited by John I. Goodlad and Timothy J. McMannon, 1997.

Knowing What Students Know: The Science and Design of Educational Assessment, The National Research Council, 2001.

National Governors Association and State Education Chiefs Launch Common State Standards, 2010

The Death and Life of the Great American School System: How Testing and Choice Are Undermining Education, Diane Ravitch, 2010

Shame of the Nation, Jonathan Kozol, 2005.

Figure 9.2   Major Educational Reform Reports

fourth of the mathematics curriculum. Average achievement scores of college graduates also fell between 1975 and 1980. Business and military leaders were cited as saying that high school graduates were so deficient in such basic skills as reading, writing, spelling, and computation that they were forced to spend millions of dollars for remedial training courses just to bring workers and trainees up to the ninth-grade level.

A Nation at Risk was credited with creating the momentum for educational reform, but it did not offer a model for high-quality education. Almost nothing in the report dealt with pedagogy; concentration was on mechanical solutions, which were regarded by the profession as bureaucratic and simplistic. No means of implementing excellence while maintaining equality was suggested. The report sought more basic courses, more homework, longer school years, more required courses, and better pay for teachers. Most educators saw this as a Band-Aid solution at a time when a major new direction was needed. They saw little help for improving schools, such as Eastside High School in Paterson, New Jersey, where principal Joe Clark won both admiration and blame for maintaining discipline with a bullhorn and a baseball bat. As discussed in Chapter 10, Gerald W. Bracey, David C. Berliner, and Bruce J. Biddle found research flaws in the various reform reports that seriously understated student performance and achievement.

Educational Policy.   After nearly 20 years of neglect except for social measures, education again became a top national priority, appearing as a major agenda item in presidential elections from 1984 through 2008. In 1984, 30 governors organized task forces on schooling, as did hundreds of school boards. Universities made efforts to strengthen relationships with schools, and the private sector offered its own reform package. The National Governors' Association report, *Time for Results*, advocated a national board to certify teachers, performance and pay links, school choice, school buildings open all year, and academic bankruptcy for schools and school districts not meeting standards. In 1991, the same group issued *Time for Results in Education: 1991*, which concluded that there was uneven and slow implementation of the earlier proposals for sweeping reform. In "Verbal, Math Scores on S.A.T. Up for Second Straight Year" (1993), Millicent Lawton found 32 states reporting efforts toward developing higher education standards and/or new or improved assessment measures. Although some view the educational efforts of the governors to be political public relations endeavors, a technological base is in development for sharing results of educational reform throughout the nation.

In *A Shared Vision: Policy Recommendations for Linking Teacher Education to School Reform* (1993), Calvin Frazier noted few results from the reform reports of the 1980s and suggested part of the fault was in teacher-training institutions. Frazier called for more input from lawmakers, clear assignments for everyone involved in school reform, clear standards for teacher-education programs, licensure of new teachers, and additional funds for effective school reform.

In *Horace's School: Redesigning the American High School* (1992), Theodore Sizer discussed his eight years of managing the Coalition of Essential Schools and found the reform movement of the 1980s to have little effect on the lives of his fictional English teacher or his students. The follow-up book, *Horace's Hope: The Future of the American High School* (1996) shows some potentially positive effects of the current debate raging in education. Out of the debate over charter schools, vouchers, standards, and visions, Sizer finds a foundation being built, from the bottom up, for a more effective educational system that will serve well in the next century and an emerging community of individuals committed to education change and effectiveness.

Diane Ravitch, in *The Death and Life of the Great American School System* (2010), criticizes an educational reform movement based on choice and testing. Her account, as a strong advocate of public schools, continues the call for liberal arts education presented in the Yale Report of 1819 and the Harvard Report of 1945, as well as *A Nation at Risk*. Ravitch calls for transformative education based on a commitment to educational values and effective neighborhood schools.

Caroline Hoxby (2000), in *Would School Choice Change the Teaching Profession?*, finds school choice policies would improve teacher and student effectiveness and achievement. The National Research Council's report *Knowing What Students Know: The Science and Design of Educational Assessment* (2001) stressed that school assessments should be available in usable forms for multiple constituencies to make more fair and valid inferences about student achievement. The report emphasized the importance of developing measurement instruments based on increased knowledge of how students learn and how such learning can be more effectively measured. In addition to calling for increased funding for assessment research, the assessment committee recommended training teachers in more effective use of tests that measure individual student progress and competence. Demma (2010) notes that the National Governors Association and State Education chiefs are seeking to have common state academic standards to establish clear, consistent goals for Grades K–12. "The Common State Standards" report sets universal high standards and high expectations for students across the country in language arts and mathematics. This is an effort to deal with 50 differing state standards and seek a common thread of uniformity in expectations contrary to historical emphasis on local control of education.

The Business Model.　　*A Nation at Risk* took economic competition as its cause for being. *Action for Excellence* (Education Commission of the States, 1983), by the Task Force on Education for Economic Growth, stressed that public education must prepare students with greater scientific and economic knowledge and provide them with computer literacy to compete in a changing world market. It suggested a partnership of state and corporate support while delegating needs of specialized groups and minorities to state and corporate leaders. *America's Competitive Challenge* (1983), a report by the Business-Higher Education Forum, argued that federal funding should upgrade university facilities and that industry should invest more in educating its workers. It suggested that industry and the universities work together to better use all educational resources.

As Naisbitt pointed out in *Re-inventing the Corporation* (1985), American corporations spent $60 billion annually on education and training. Their programs are so vast that they offer an alternative to traditional university training; of course, these companies apply business measures of efficiency and cost effectiveness to their programs. Much corporate support is similar to that described in Raymond E. Callahan's *Education and the Cult of Efficiency: A Study of the Social Forces That Have Shaped the Administration of the Public Schools* (1962). Callahan describes how schools came under the influence of efficiency experts at the turn of the century.

Henry A. Giroux (1999) found the corporatizing of American education reflects a crisis of vision regarding the meaning and purpose of "democracy" when market cultures, market moralities, and market mentalities may be shattering community, eroding civic society, and undermining the nurturing system for children. Deron Boyles in *American Education and Corporations* (2000) analyzed the growing use of schools as sites for consumer materialism. Waddell (2001) notes the problem of using school websites for advertising, and that some ads contain information inappropriate for children. Some school districts and states are using online advertising to help pay for laptop computers. Waddell notes that even when school districts seek to prohibit online advertising, the Internet is so expansive that school officials find it difficult to enforce restrictions.

Successful commercial enterprises have been able to compete in a changing world market and have their own measures of efficiency. This period's most popular book dealing with the ways in which business and industry have tried to recapture excellence is *In Search of Excellence: Lessons from America's Best Run Companies*, written by Thomas J. Peters and Robert H. Waterman in 1982. Their belief is that what works for the private sector can also be used by public institutions, such as schools.

The business community demanded, and successful corporations provided, a pattern for educational improvement with much public support. In 1966, 44 business leaders and 40 governors attended a National Education Summit calling for tougher standards with accountability, workforce skills, and the improvement of education for global competition. A nonprofit resource center, Achieve, to provide assistance in improving academic and student assessments as well as the use of technology in schools, was created in 1996 by the nation's governors and corporate leaders. The network now includes over 35 states reaching over 85 percent of all public school students. Achieve launched the American Diploma Project network to make career and college readiness a priority ("Achieve," 2010).

Former President Clinton, who addressed the summit meeting, noted that school populations are diverse in race, income, ethnicity, and background. Schools, he noted, have fractured authority and financing and are burdened by social problems. The Clinton, Bush, and Obama administrations stressed: (a) having standards accompanied by accountability; (b) rewarding and demanding higher standards of teachers; (c) holding schools accountable for results; (d) seeking business/community help in school district reinvention of their budgets; (e) having more options, including charter schools; (f) making school safety a priority; (g) keeping schools open longer; and (h) getting the business community involved in expanding technology in classrooms. Clearly, partnerships between school districts and business, school districts and universities, are occurring more frequently throughout the nation.

In the corporate and educational sector, the concept of diversity views multiculturalism in education and the workforce as a strong tree with many different yet equally important branches (Kleiman, 2001). Schmitt (2001) reported an increase in majority–minority populations revealed by the 2000 census. Bruce Katz, director of the Brookings Center on Urban and Metropolitan Policy, and Alan Berube (2001), reported that for the first time nearly half of the nation's 100 largest cities are home to more Hispanics, blacks, Asians, and other minorities than whites. Seventy-one of the American cities lost white residents. Immigration and higher birthrates among foreignborn are changing the complexion of U.S. cities. Although a small part of the population shifts may have occurred as people who previously identified themselves as white in the 2010 census identified themselves as multiracial, the population shift shows the volatility and complexity of change in the United States.

The Paideia Proposal.   Mortimer Adler, longtime advocate of the Great Books curriculum and philosophical companion to Robert Hutchins, wrote the *Paideia Proposal: An Educational Manifesto* in 1982. His plan, which advocates giving the same quality of schooling to all, requires a program of study that is both liberal and general. All side tracks, specialized courses, and vocational training are eliminated and in 12 years of schooling only one choice is allowed, that of a second language.

Adler identifies three distinct modes of teaching and learning, rising in successive gradations of complexity and difficulty from the first to the 12th year. All three modes are essential to the overall course of study. *Mode One* represents the acquisition of organized knowledge from didactic instruction, lectures, and responses, using textbooks and other aids in these subject areas: language, literature and the fine arts, math, natural science, history, geography, and social studies. *Mode Two* represents the development of intellectual skills (skill of learning)—by means of coaching, exercises, and supervised practice—in operations of reading, writing, speaking, listening, calculating, problem solving, observing, measuring, estimating, and exercising critical judgment. *Mode Three* represents enlarging the understanding of ideas and values by means of Socratic questioning and interaction with major contributions to literature. The requirements also include physical education, care of the body, computer skills, manual arts, and an introduction to various careers.

Tanner (1991), in his book *Progressive Education at the Crossroads: Crusade for Democracy*, discussed Dewey's experimentalism in historical perspective. Experimentalism had been viewed in an adverse light in the 1960s through the 1980s by radical revisionists, critical theorists, and neo-Marxists. Tanner noted that Dewey and his followers fought to uphold the democratic-liberal traditions in popular education in the face of great opposition. While Adler stressed the liberating influence of the liberal arts tradition, Dewey viewed the problems of public education as interconnected with social, political, economic, and cultural problems. Dewey saw the school and society as intertwined, with the school as a miniature society.

Boyer, Goodlad, and Sizer.   Three names that constantly appeared in the reform literature of the mid-1980s were Ernest Boyer, John Goodlad, and Theodore Sizer. The three had been associated with studies of education long before the critical reports emerged, and each developed a plan for improving schools. In a 1984 *Phi Delta Kappa article* called "The Rising Tide of School Reform Reports," Patricia Cross of Harvard credited Boyer, Goodlad, and Sizer with the most influential reform books from within the educational profession.

Boyer's most important contribution was a report for the Carnegie Foundation for the Advancement of Teaching in 1984 entitled *High School: A Report on Secondary Education in America*. In a 1996 tribute to Ernest Boyer (1928–1995) in *Educational Leadership*, Vito Perrone noted that Boyer always encouraged educators to maintain a human face in schools, to create an integrated curriculum, and to integrate classrooms and neighborhoods.

Boyer's detailed studies of secondary education tend to support some of the disturbing accounts of teaching conditions described earlier by sociologists like Dan Lortie in *Schoolteacher*. Boyer thinks that the teaching profession is in deep crisis in this nation, and he says teachers are fully aware of their situation. Teachers are deeply troubled not only about low salaries but also about loss of status, bureaucratic pressures, lack of recognition, and a poor public image.

Flexibility and freedom are keys to Boyer's ideas of reform. According to Boyer, reforms will fail unless teachers at the local level are supported by the public and given real professional status.

Goodlad, a recognized expert in curriculum, made a major contribution to the reform literature in *A Place Called School: Prospects for the Future* (1984), which says schooling problems have reached such crippling proportions that the entire public education system could collapse. Goodlad and McMannon's edited book entitled *The Public Purpose of Education and Schooling* (1997) continues the conversations about improving education, by recognizing the complexity of the educational process. Goodlad, like Dewey, noted that democracy and the nation's educational infrastructure are inextricably entwined and sensitively interdependent. According to Goodlad, monetary solutions are not sufficient to regain excellence. In his plan for educational renewal, Goodlad does not abandon the quest for social equality that dominated schooling in the 1960s and 1970s. He is keenly aware of the denial of access to knowledge and access to effective teaching for racial minorities and those relegated to lower tracks through testing. The disadvantaged students are those who might gain most from varied pedagogical techniques and individualized instruction. They are the least likely to benefit from those reforms that pursue excellence by increasing the proportion of failures.

Goodlad announced his sponsorship of 12 such school–university partnerships at the 1986 American Association of Colleges of Teacher Education (AACTE) meeting in Chicago. His *Teachers for Our Nation's Schools* (1990) called for autonomous centers of pedagogy in colleges and universities in order to have the same authority exhibited by medical and law schools.

Sizer, who published *Horace's Compromise: The Dilemma of the American High School* in 1984, also supports more experimentation on the local school level as a means for altering the high degree of standardization and sameness common to educational institutions. He favors designating certain schools as experimental units with license to try innovative approaches. School-based management should be used to move more authority to individual units and provide more instructional options. The involvement of teachers, parents, students, community leaders, and representatives of business and industry should be encouraged. The school principal must have authority for allocation of resources and must act as instructional leader. In *Horace's Compromise* (1984), Sizer recommends that individual schools be relieved of mandated curriculum, allowing experimentation based on the unique conditions of each community. Schools within schools should be set up as laboratories.

Boyer, Goodlad, and Sizer set the scene for continued examination of the process and product of education. The balance between child-centered and subject-centered education that Dewey wrote about in *The Child and the Curriculum* (1902) confronts twenty-first-century educators.

While the pendulum is currently swinging toward intellectual discipline through high-stakes testing policies, parental voices are increasingly calling for alternative methods of evaluation for students at risk. Michael Apple (2001) views the current push for standards and tests as running the risk of affixing labels on children at risk and their teachers. Apple notes that although there are increasing calls for more flexible forms of assessment, declining state resources tend to result in more traditional standards and testing to the detriment of minority and culturally diverse populations of students.

Comment and Criticism.   *Action for Excellence, Making the Grade,* and *A Nation at Risk* were political documents that gave vivid accounts of American education in decline with little regard for accuracy. Their aim was to get action from state and federal policy makers and from the public. The practical school administrator got very little guidance from these reports in terms of actual school improvement.

The drive for educational excellence should also include at-risk children, as noted in the Committee for Economic Development's *Investing in Our Children, Savage Inequalities: Children in America's Schools* (1985) and the William T. Grant Foundation's *The Forgotten Half: Non-College Youth in America: An Interim Report on the School-to-Work Transition* (1988). These works call for greater recognition of the education, social and economic needs, and aspirations of these children. Non-college-bound students deserve the same opportunities as college-bound students to excel in society and in the workplace.

In *Cultural Literacy* (1987), E. D. Hirsch suggested that all educated persons should have knowledge of the best ideals of humankind. Lack of such knowledge, Hirsch noted, is at the base of our literacy challenge. Hirsch reiterated this theme in *The Schools We Need and Why We Don't Have Them* (1996). He emphasizes the importance of content, commonality, and coherence in the curriculum, as well as the importance of rediscovery of a sense of community to preserve the fragile fabric of our society. Hirsch seeks an educational system designed to provide our children universal competence to lessen the us-versus-them mentality in society and education.

"Academic Preparation for College, 1983–1987" (1997) synthesized the judgment of hundreds of high school teachers and college professors concerning the knowledge and skills students should bring from high school to college. It set high standards and a rigorous course of study for English, mathematics, science, social studies, foreign languages, and the arts. There were also the required competencies in reading, writing, speaking, reasoning, mathematics, and study skills. It appealed mostly to elite schools, where most students are collegebound and where resources are adequate. On the negative side, many who are concerned about dropouts and teaching minimum competencies to average children saw the report as unrealistic. Nevertheless, "Academic Preparation for College" provided a comprehensive curriculum model and a specific plan for reform.

What Matters Most: Teaching for America's Future (Hunt, 1996) reflects the continued search for higher standards in education. The report calls for a crusade to improve student achievement levels through a comprehensive approach to redesigning, restructuring, monitoring, and licensing schools and educators to reach higher standards throughout the system. Special emphasis is placed on a National Board for Professional Teaching Standards.

Zollers, Albert, and Cochran-Smith (2000) reported on a multiyear collaborative self-study designed to teach social justice. Zollers and her colleagues found that social justice involves faculty recruitment/retention/mentoring, student admissions/advising, and review of frameworks and knowledge that guide coursework and curriculum. The authors' study was a response to changing demographics as diversity permeates all levels of the educational system.

Hunt and Carroll (2003), in "No Dream Denied: A Pledge to America's Children," found teacher attrition to be a major challenge, with teachers leaving the profession in low-income urban schools at a troubling rate. In 1999–2000, leaving teachers exceeded entrants by 23 percent. Large turnover affects teaching quality and student achievement levels. Hunt and Carroll called for development of small learning communities with shared leadership and technological support to retain experienced, effective teachers.

Education must be accountable. No sector of society is without responsibility for teaching and learning. It is in the national interest for the federal government to regulate, legislate, and fund national school programs. Local districts are responsible for implementing programs, the delivery of educational priorities, legislation, regulations, and funding. The fundamental building block of educational renewal consists of the recruitment and training of high-quality teachers.

The reform reports and studies of the 1980s through the early 2000s had many points in common. They called for revised curriculums, stronger requirements, greater student efforts, and higher admission standards. Some suggested beginning education earlier and extending the school day and year. At least eight studies demanded a revision of vocational courses. Much of the state-level activity that followed the reports was directed toward regulations such as teacher and pupil testing, stronger academic standards, and mandated curriculum requirements.

A student of history might wonder if the twenty-first century will be spent correcting the overregulation of the 1980s, 1990s, and early 2000s. These decades were spent addressing the permissiveness and neglect of earlier decades, but will possibly be part of the problem rather than the solution for the rest of the twenty-first century.

School Effectiveness.   The dismal statistics that pointed to failure and mediocrity in American education in the 1980s were by no means descriptive of all institutions, as averages ignore data that fall at the upper or lower ends of the scale.

Older studies of school effectiveness have been used as the basis for new research. Weber's 1970 study of reading achievement in inner-city schools found that strong leadership, high student expectations, a good atmosphere for learning, use of phonics, individualization of instruction, careful evaluation, and enough trained reading teachers made an outstanding program. In 1981, Zerchykov cited administrative leadership, frequent monitoring of student progress, stress on basic skills, and realistic instructional expectations as factors creating school effectiveness.

Time-on-Task.   Two other terms were widely used in the school effectiveness literature of the mid-1980s. *Time-on-task* dealt with the actual part of each day spent on instruction, as opposed to time used for announcements, passing through halls, taking attendance, and the like. *Efficiency* focused on the most cost-effective means of accomplishing educational goals in order to maximize scarce resources.

Defined as academic learning time or engaged learning time, time-on-task did allow students to spend more time on learning. Students are ontask when they are actively engaged in activities that match their abilities and interests.

However, the California Beginning Teacher Evaluation Study of 1977, which studied this topic in detail, showed that only rather small gains could be made by cutting down wasted time. Current research shows that sizable increases in achievement require sizable increases in time, if time is the only variable modified. Better use of time is essential, but it might not be sufficient to achieve excellence. Likewise, the effective school research shows that as efficiency increases, there is little room for additional improvement through more efficient methods. For example, in January 1983, 85 percent of high schools, 68 percent of middle schools, and 42 percent of elementary schools had microcomputers in use for instruction. The amount of idle time was so small that more efficient utilization of computers would accomplish very little. Real improvement in computer-linked instruction must come from buying more and newer machines or making existing computers available during hours when school is not in session because they are already nearing maximum use during the regular school day. Studies also show that regardless of the numbers of computers in classrooms, adequate instructional software and the instructor's ability to teach students effective computer skills are essential.

Other research indicates there is not a strong or consistent relationship between student performance and school resources, at least after variations in family input are taken into account (Hanushek, 1997). However, in reviewing school finance reform in Kentucky, Adams and White (1997) found increased equal opportunity resulted as funds were distributed more uniformly throughout the state's school districts. Court decisions requiring more equitable distribution of resources between school districts are essential for equal access and opportunity. The task is not easy, as revealed by the number of states under court orders to improve school funding formulas.

Educational Goals.   The Bush and Clinton administrations, reacting to the 1990 work of the National Governors' meetings on education, adopted national education goals for the year 2000 designed to encourage more effective schools through focusing on learner outcomes.

Although the goals were widely heralded as a base for educational excellence, few professional educators believed they would be achieved by 2000, because of restricted financial resources as well as potential social and political roadblocks to reform. *What Matters Most: Teaching for America's Future*, a 1996 report by the National Commission on Teaching and America's Future (Hunt, 1996), reiterated *Goals 2000*. Chaired by North Carolina Governor James B. Hunt and comprised of a large spectrum of education and corporate leaders, the commission called for, among other things, the following:

❑ Establishing a professional standards board, requiring accreditation for all schools of education, and licensing teachers based on demonstrated performance including tests of subject matter and teaching knowledge

❑ Organizing teacher-education and professional development programs around standards for students and teachers and developing extended graduate-level teacher-preparation programs that provide a yearlong internship in a professional development school

❑ Putting qualified teachers in every classroom, providing incentives for teaching in teacher-shortage areas, eliminating barriers to teacher mobility, and increasing the ability of low-wealth districts to pay for qualified teachers

❑ Encouraging and rewarding teacher knowledge and skill, developing a career continuum for teaching linked to assessments and compensation systems that reward knowledge and skill, setting goals and enacting incentives for National Board Certification in every state and district, and seeking to certify 105,000 teachers in this decade, one for every school in the United States

❑ Creating schools that are organized for student and teacher success, investing more in teachers and technology and less in nonteaching personnel, providing venture capital for challenge grants, and selecting, preparing, and retaining principals who understand teaching and learning and who can lead high-performing schools

In "A Framework for Appraising Educational Reforms" (1996), Ernest R. House states that the best educational reforms would focus on greatly reducing the administrative hierarchy, transforming the purpose and structure of the central staff to a small strategic staff, reducing the size of schools to 300 to 400 students, making schools relatively autonomous and unregulated, and providing opportunity for schools of choice. House identified factors that reflect a corporate/industrial model such as national goals and standards, decentralization, open markets, performance, and self-assessment.

In *The Principalship: A Reflective Practice Perspective* (1991), Thomas J. Sergiovanni stresses the importance of the moral aspect of leadership for the future. He notes that moral leadership re-centers people as centers of action, not merely as recipients of action. Carr and Harris (2001), in *Succeeding with Standards: Linking Curriculum, Assessment, and Action Planning*, wrote of the need for making achievement an adventure in success. Graduation challenges, inquiry fairs, and other activities to show-case student performance together with community-wide celebration of student suc-cess are powerful, positive tools for effective learning and improved student achievement.

President Barack Obama, confronted by a major prolonged recession, seeks to have a twenty-first-century education that includes state-of-the-art assessment and accountability systems, recruit and retain talented teachers, challenge state and school districts to dismiss ineffective teachers, encourage charter school develop-ment, and target low-income schools with at-risk students to ensure a complete and competitive education from childhood to adulthood. Arne Duncan, Secretary of Education, is committed to responding to concerns of states and school districts about reauthorization of the No Child Left Behind Act. The American Recovery and Reinvestment Act has provided an over $150 billion two-year stimulus package for education to help school districts during the national recession (Sawchuk & Robelen, 2009; Obama, 2010). Race to the Top was a program providing $4.3 billion to encourage competitive, innovative, experimental programs proposals to improve education, especially for low-performing, low-income schools and communities. Duncan is pushing for accountability, merit pay, raising standards, and closing the achievement gap (Paulson & Kadaroo, 2010).

The National Conference of State Legislatures (NCSL), representing lawmak-ers in all 50 states, concluded after a 10-month study that the No Child Left Behind (NCLB) Act is unworkable and called for changes to fix it. The state law-makers called for more flexibility in implementing the act as well as waivers to use state testing programs already in place (National Conference of State Legis-latures, 2005).

Reform Initiatives in States and Cities.

The pursuit of excellence did not begin with *A Nation at Risk*, but the national reports certainly stimulated renewed activity. According to *Action in the States* (1984) by the Education Commission of the States, school reform was a high-priority item everywhere. All but five states had legislatively enacted initiatives or were awaiting action by the legislature or the state board. The states have generally followed the public demand to cut down on curriculum offerings not considered basic—such as art, music, and physical educa-tion—and to require more "solid" courses.

State educational reform plans are diverse because of demographic factors, the existing level of educational achievement, and the economic conditions. Some states call for continuous staff development, school-based accountability, and curriculum updating through reaccreditation.

In "The Socratic Approach to Character Education" (1996), Elkind and Sweet address character education increasingly being incorporated into the curriculum in response to vandalism and crime in the nation's schools. Some curriculum changes reflected public interest in the environment, nuclear war, and energy issues as well as international and multicultural concerns.

Several state and city schools implemented reforms and fiscal restructuring. All the changes dealt with what Linda Darling-Hammond (1993), director of the National Center for Restructuring Education at Columbia University, referred to as a new school reform model designed to develop communities of learning, grounded in grassroots of democratic discourse. She saw these reforms as a way to reach empowerment and educational freedom for educators of students in a learning community.

The Chicago School Reform Act of 1988 required basic changes in Chicago public school governance. The act sought more involvement from local stakeholders in school governance and policy making. By 2001, Chicago had implemented annual testing from kindergarten through eighth grade, mandated improvement plans, placed penalties on low-performing schools that failed to improve, and allowed parents to transfer children to any school in the system that would accept them. Anne Lewis (2001) noted that Chicago schools have improved but only minimally. She added that the Consortium on Chicago School Research in reports for the Annenberg Challenge found that children do better on skills tests when teachers challenge them to think.

In *City Schools Leading the Way* (1993), Forsyth and Tallerico noted that the Illinois state law provided for increases in parental input in Chicago's school policy. Forsyth and Tallerico also added that Boston was another city school system that moved toward decentralization, accountability, and increased input from parents, teachers, and administrators.

The widely watched 1990 Kentucky Educational Reform Act has been positive to date. Under a Kentucky Supreme Court order (*Rose v. Council for Better Education*, 1988), the state moved toward equal opportunity and an efficient system of education for all school districts. The districts were reevaluated and reconstructed to meet the court order. An independent research group, the Kentucky Institute for Educational Research, indicated over 90 percent of entry-level teachers reported being moderately to extremely well prepared to establish a positive learning environment, communicate high expectations, design instruction that is developmentally appropriate, use different teaching strategies for different instructional purposes, and communicate the core concepts of their discipline (National Council for Accreditation of Teacher Education (NCATE), 1997). Kentucky continues to receive high marks for the progress.

Gehring (2001) reported that teachers in a Washington State school district have started giving student grades on employability to prepare them for workplace success. Work habits, commitment to quality, attendance, punctuality, communication, and interpersonal skills are graded in addition to the regular academic achievement.

In Oakland, California, the California Teachers Association opposed the plan, but the superintendent and the school board voted to give administrators bonuses for higher student test scores on annual state tests (Stricherz, 2001). Low-performing school districts in Pennsylvania are subject to improvement plans, which encompass proposals for private contractors to run the schools, management and fiscal reviews, and teacher-training programs that include parents. Schools that did not improve by 2003 were to be taken over by a three-person control board named by the state (Johnston, 2000).

The concept emerging in the state and city school reforms responded to Arthur Wirth's (1992) call for more democratic participation in public school policy making. Yet, as McKersie (1993) noted, pitfalls exist in implementing reform when there is failure to recognize that the educational enterprise is complex, that there are many voices representing many interests, and that politics involves compromise and consensus to achieve necessary funding for implementing innovative educational reforms. Impediments to educational reform beyond funding limitations include increased costly litigation as various interest groups seek to implement their own agendas, often to the detriment of the overall school programs.

Local Reform Initiatives.

Historically, some of the most impressive efforts to achieve excellence in education have been initiated at the local or district levels. Examples include the Dalton Plan of the Progressive era and the Philadelphia Parkway Program of the 1960s and 1970s. Urban school reform in Atlanta in the 1970s also showed how a failing district could be made into an outstanding one with local effort. Most of the alternative schools in the United States were developed without state or national leadership.

Laboratory schools, schools-without-walls, and magnet schools intending to draw students to a superior and specialized program were created by school districts. Larger school districts with considerable resources, a highly professional staff, and active community leaders have been able to establish models of excellence in education. Sometimes the leadership has come from the superintendent and sometimes from the school board, the parent–teacher organization, or reform-minded citizens. John Dewey insisted that the school and the community work as a unit for high-quality education. John Goodlad often stated that the community should be the major educator of the child. Educational historian Lawrence Cremin argued that the community should serve to interlock all educative agencies within and outside of the school.

Following *A Nation at Risk*, most local school districts in the United States began to evaluate performance standards and accountability. Student outcomes were evaluated in terms of behavior and competence. While state boards focused on learner achievement, many individual schools looked at the relationship between the curriculum and student performance.

Wolf, Borko, Elliott, and McIver (2000) reported on four schools that sought to meet the standards of the Kentucky Reform Act of 1990. Each of the four exemplary schools, their administrators, and faculty took local control of the statewide initiative. They worked diligently on connections and relationships, built a foundation of trust in one another, and engaged in constant dialogue that supported and provided the foundation for professional and personal growth that enriched their lives and led to improved achievement levels for pupils. Internalizing the spirit of the reform— being the best one can be and maintaining high expectations of students—led to involvement, commitment, nurturing, and caring, all of which contributed to positive results. In the end, all school success is local, requiring total commitment of administration, faculty, and staff.

Financial Crunch.   The Reagan administration created the National Commission on Excellence but made it plain that the federal government would not fund its recommendations. According to the National Education Association (2006), it would cost almost $24 billion to implement the recommendations, and if the school year were lengthened, it would cost about $40 billion. Even decreasing class size by one or two students would require millions of dollars, and increasing teachers' salaries across the nation would carry a staggering bill. President Reagan maintained that schools need more discipline, not more money; his educational leaders (T. H. Bell and W. Bennett) said that states and local districts would have to finance the reforms.

This, of course, was more realistic for some states than for others. California was in better shape to finance reform than states that had suffered recession, such as Michigan, Oregon, and the industrial northeast. Sun Belt states that were doing well before the period's decline in oil prices were hit with major cutbacks in 1984. The decline was most dramatic in Louisiana, Oklahoma, and Texas. None of the states that depend on agriculture for revenue were able to adequately fund reforms or salary increases for teachers.

In every state, education must compete with demands for prisons, bridges, roads, and sewer systems, and education must compete with its own needs to repair physical plants or meet safety requirements. By 1994, many states including California and Florida had difficulty funding education because of a sluggish economy. The National Center for Educational Statistics in 2000 estimated that $127 billion was needed to repair America's school buildings, replace defective equipment, and eliminate hazardous asbestos. Currently the Afghanistan conflict and burgeoning national deficits make education and domestic funding difficult.

Much of the money for excellence in education needs to be raised at the local district level, but this had become increasingly difficult in the mid-1980s. Arkansas, a poor state ranked low in educational achievement, passed tough new standards for schools, to be implemented in 1987. The cost of these standards was estimated at $298 million. State revenues were to provide part of the funds, but local districts were to pay for new teachers in subjects not formerly offered.

A state tax shortfall in 1985 reduced the school fund by $25 million. Local millage elections were held in 120 districts in 1984 and 242 districts in 1985. In 70 percent of these elections, higher millages were passed, indicating strong local support for high-quality education. The local efforts were not enough, and Arkansas trailed the national average per pupil expenditure in 1986 by $1,136, demonstrating that it was unrealistic to expect local districts and state governments to fund reforms without federal help. By 2004–2005, expenditures per student reached $6,202 (National Education Association, 2005). Arkansas received an A or 7th in ranking for standards, assessments, and accountability and showed overall improvement in 2010, demonstrating a commitment to raising educational achievement levels ("Quality Counts," 2010).

States are being asked to assume most of the costs for educational excellence at a difficult time. The taxpayers' revolt characterized by California's Proposition 13, which limited spending in that state, was followed by balanced budget legislation in 17 states between 1977 and 1981.

In *Nordlinger v. Hahn* (1992), the Court upheld the constitutionality of California's Proposition 13, which protected the rights of existing homeowners. By mid-1993, six state supreme courts had ordered legislatures to fund schools more equitably. Most states in 1993 faced severe financial restrictions with increased demands for educational staff and facilities in the face of growing enrollments and decreased finances.

By late summer 1997, Baldauf noted that many states had large budget surpluses, squirreling away some $20 billion in reserve funds. By 2010 all state governments except Arkansas, North Dakota, Montana, and Alaska faced deficits. There is, however, caution in expenditures because in a cyclical economy this year's surplus can be next year's deficit. Regardless of the caution, school districts in many states received increased funding.

The 2001 and 2005 national budget greatly increased the amount of funds destined for education, with provisions for special education and for children at risk, and persistent calls for additional funding. The Committee for Education Funding, a nonpartisan school advocacy coalition of 100 organizations, hailed congressional efforts to increase education funding for the future. Although political machinations could change the outcome, a budget resolution to increase education funding by over $350 billion over 10 years was passed by the Senate. The resolution included full funding of IDEA, increased Pell Grants, Head Start, TRIO and college work-study funding, and funding toward hiring 100,000 new teachers.

Gramm-Rudman Hollings Act.
Congress passed the Gramm-Rudman Hollings Act in 1985. The bill, a response to President Ronald Reagan's supply-side economics, slashed the federal deficit by reducing federal expenditures for social and welfare programs. National defense, social security, and interest on the national debt were exempt, so that all cuts aimed at reducing the deficit came from programs like education, highways, and welfare. The Reagan administration opposed new taxes and threatened to veto any that were passed. The immediate impact of Gramm-Rudman was to cut programs such as Title 1, a program that undeniably helped raise the reading and mathematics scores of disadvantaged youngsters.

There was considerable national feeling that Gramm-Rudman would not achieve a balanced budget and that the cost to society was too high. Several constitutional challenges to the bill were made in late 1986. By 1997, both political parties supported increased funding for education, although there were often different priorities.

According to Berliner and Biddle (1995), although expenditures for education have increased, much of the increase has gone to programs for special education. By 2004, efforts had been made to raise teachers' salaries in most states. Burgeoning enrollment approaching 55 million public school students because of immigration and increased birth rates among low-income families led to overcrowded classrooms in Florida and other states. Many school districts were engaged in school building and upgrading programs to meet the needs of a growing student population. *Education Week's* 2005 report, "No Small Change: Targeting Money Toward Student Performance, Quality Counts," found that 43 states and the District of Columbia include adjustments in the finance formulas to provide extra money for students with certain characteristics like poverty, disabilities, or lack of fluency in English.

With the NCLB requiring all students to have a highly qualified teacher by 2005–2006, there was action to improve teacher quality. *Education Week's* earlier 2003 report "Quality Counts" (with support by the Pew Foundation) found that 33 states and the District of Columbia required subject-knowledge tests as part of teacher certification, and 29 states and the District of Columbia require all high school teachers to have majored in their primary subject ("If I Can't Learn from You," 2003).

The National Education Association (2010) reported the average classroom teacher salary in 2009–2010 was $55,350. Nevertheless, Florida and a number of other states reported teacher layoffs because of an economic recession.

FOCUS ON THE ISSUES

Educational Reform: Past and Present

Attempts by the greatest U.S. educational leaders to improve schools have often met with strong opposition. For example, Horace Mann's effort for reform in the first half of the nineteenth century failed. Mann, Secretary of the Massachusetts Board of Education (1837–1848), fought for educational improvement during his term of office. Mann's annual reports included recommendations for uniform textbooks, qualified teachers, timely school education reports, curriculum improvement, use of corporal punishment only as a last resort, universal and free public education, extended school years, examination of teachers, and the use of schools to improve humanity. Yet all his proposals for educational reform were criticized. Calvinists fought Mann's proposals to have schools teach what was common to Protestant creeds, the Bible read without comment, and teachers exemplifying Christianity by their lives. The Calvinists called Mann's proposals godless skepticism that would lead youth to infidelity.

American culture is undergoing vast change and must accommodate different views. The number of Moslem students is increasing rapidly while students from Oriental nations can be seen in most cities. In China, membership in the Communist Party requires a declaration of atheism. We may think of America as a Christian nation, but we must understand and be open to those from different cultures, religions, and ethnic backgrounds.

What Do You Think?

1. Mann questioned why algebra, which not one person in a thousand ever uses in the business of life, was studied by twice as many pupils as bookkeeping, which even the day laborer needs. How would you respond to Horace Mann's question?
2. Identify current controversies about the role of religion in public education.
3. List five criticisms of the No Child Left Behind Act from education literature together with recommended changes for reauthorization of the act.
4. What steps can teachers and students take to encourage respect for and understanding of diverse cultures, ethnicities, mores, and folkways?
5. Identify steps educators have been taking to address issues of dropouts, digital divide, at-risk children, and achievement gaps.

Rebuilding Versus Restructuring.   The American school system, designed in the early national period under the leadership of school reformers like Horace Mann, reflected the influence of the old New England colonial district and catered to the needs of a new democracy. The nation then was dominated by agriculture, making a common school with summer vacations and local control quite acceptable. With the rise of industry, standardization of the curriculum and a delivery system based on a Newtonian mechanistic model were adopted. The school system became a closed machine with top-down administration, predetermined standards, lock-step definitions of content by grade, and fixed rules of behavior. Obviously, the system worked well to prepare students for the factory or the office. With its emphasis on assimilation, conformity, and traditional values, it was able to handle the masses of European immigrants and the growing American population. Mass production philosophy and assembly-line concepts lent themselves to efficiency in the production of trained workers at low cost.

New needs began to emerge with the world wars, the Great Depression of the 1930s, social unrest, the rising affluence of the middle class, the human rights movement, and the demands of minorities for status. Superimposed upon these changes were the new requirements of the information age, a service economy, and a global culture. New programs were tried in an effort to cope with changing life conditions, social mobility, and new expectations. These included open classrooms, individualized instruction, alternative schools, nongraded schools, team teaching, and charter and magnet schools. In general, these innovations were added to the existing system, but they did not become the dominant pattern. Many were simply tried for a time and then withdrawn, allowing the old system to emerge again.

The home school movement of the mid-1980s is an example. With individual computers, communications networks, and many parents working at home, it became possible to give children a basic education without recourse to the schools. Although parents keep many students at home for religious or cultural reasons, the home school movement is also growing among well-educated citizens who prefer to provide their own educational programs for their children. States have initiated testing programs to evaluate the learning of home-educated children when they wish to transfer to public schools.

Private education in the United States represents another alternative that has not lost its popularity. Many private and parochial schools are very traditional. They often have high achievement because of a select student body and/or rigorous discipline and conduct standards, strong parental support, high-quality teachers, and a demanding curriculum. Nevertheless, private schools are not subject to state regulations and controls (unless they request state accreditation) and are free to pursue innovative programs and alternative learning techniques. Very few private schools adopted radical or innovative programs by 1986. The growth in private education has been among religious fundamentalists and others dissatisfied with the quality of public education. Evangelical fundamentalists such as Jerry Falwell and various conservative groups gave support to private religious schools in the 1980s. In cities like Seattle, other parents chose to send their children to private schools deemed to be of high quality.

Viadero (2004) reported on a study commissioned by the American Federation of Teaching (AFT) that found charter school students lag behind regular public school students. Recent studies show considerable variability in charter school results, although there is considerable federal support for expanding charter schools (Croft, 2010).

At best, federal responses to the reform demands must be described as piecemeal. One thrust is the policy of deregulation, first applied to the airlines. Deregulation attempts to remove federal controls from business and industry in keeping with the free market theory and competition. Of course, most of the federal regulations concerning schools were applied to the use of federal money. As fewer dollars flow from the national treasury into school programs, the question of federal control becomes less significant. However, Milton and Rose Friedman argued in *Free to Choose a Personal Statement* (1980) that governmental rules and regulations restrict the freedom of citizens in educational matters. Of course, most laws regulating education are made by the states, and it is unlikely that those laws will be repealed. The free market concept also supports funding plans that would allow parents to spend their vouchers at a school of their choice, public or private. Many educators believe that vouchers would dismantle the public school system, especially in the large cities where there are many disadvantaged and minority children. Deregulation advocates want choice and options for parents, while others believe that federal funds for the nation's poor, at-risk, special-needs, and limited-English-proficiency students are necessary and threatened by deregulation proposals. Florida's voucher plan has been declared unconstitutional by lower courts (in 2005) and recently by the Florida State Supreme Court. Currently legislative proposals would expand Florida's voucher plan and increase the amount allocated to each student (Hansen, 2010).

Volunteerism.   Barn raising, or helping neighbors replace farm buildings destroyed by fire or weather, was a community effort in colonial days and continued through the twentieth century. Efforts to rekindle a spirit of service and helping others have likewise been spreading through America's school districts. The Reagan, George H. W. Bush, Clinton, George W. Bush, and Obama administrations stressed the importance of volunteerism in America. The first African American secretary of state, Colin L. Powell, helped start American Promise—The Alliance for Youth—and is an ardent advocate of volunteerism to improve the quality of life for youth in America. By 1997, several states were implementing mandatory community service as part of high school graduation requirements. Maryland was one of the first states to make student service mandatory for graduation. Students were given opportunities to choose things they were interested in and later to use their experiences for class papers. Naturally, community volunteer agencies were receptive to student assistance. Federal court decisions, although subject to reappraisal, have upheld mandatory community service for graduation. There will be increased volunteerism as school districts expand options in the curriculum for service learning.

Goodlad's call for focus on entire schools, not just teachers, curriculums, or organization, is a more holistic approach. The Rand Corporation's study of school effectiveness (1987) argued that increased expenditures on traditional practices would do little good. Patricia Cross (1984) of Harvard called attention to the mechanical solutions to the crisis of the 1980s and suggested that the old educational structures may be inadequate to cope with diversity. Others describe current reforms as ordinary and conventional.

Year-round schools and strengthened academic requirements, together with a greater emphasis on achievement and performance outcomes than on increased spending, reflect future trends. In "Verbal, Math Scores on S.A.T. Up for the Second Straight Year" (1993), Lawton found that although SAT scores were up, verbal scores were still a point below the 1983 average. Improvements in SAT scores were attributed to increased nationwide demands for more rigorous academic studies. In the late 1990s and early 2000s, reform efforts continued to yield results as international comparisons showed that American students have improved in math and science, although international studies varied in their conclusions. Some studies show that U.S. schools have islands of excellence together with underfunded, poorly performing ones. Gehring, in an *Education Week* (2001) summary of an Organization for Economic Cooperation and Development report, found the United States lagging 17 other countries in secondary school graduate literacy. The 2004 Condition of Education survey (Snyder, 1997) notes that 13 percent of all persons ages 16–24 were neither enrolled in school nor working, a decrease of 16 percent from 1986. By 2009, of 34 countries in the International Student Assessment, the United States ranked 14th in reading, 17th in science, and 25th in math. The highest ranking countries were South Korea, Finland, Singapore, Hong Kong, and Shanghai in China and Canada (*USA Today*, 2010).

Meanwhile, some parents choose alternatives to public schools. Home schooling is one parental option. A new trend is having groups of children taught by mothers who have expertise in individual academic fields.

ACHIEVING EXCELLENCE IN TEACHER EDUCATION

As the public system of education experienced change in America, major consequences accrued for teachers and teacher-educators. In periods of teacher shortages, colleges and universities with teacher-education programs were under great pressure to admit more students in order to feed the market. This caused officials to pay slight attention to standards, especially when the funding for the institutions of higher education was enrollment driven. The shortage ended with the matriculation of the baby boom generation, but it is likely to return with heavy competition for skilled workers, improving salaries, better working conditions, and the retirement of a major segment of the teachers in service. At this writing, a severe recession has led to teacher, staff, and administer lay-offs. The Obama administration implemented a stimulus program February 13, 2009, the American Recovery and Reinvestment Act, to provide funds to retain teachers and to invigorate the economy.

Status of Teachers.   The 1980s may be characterized as a period of professional decline at the very time when better professional performance was demanded. Teaching was one of the first professions open to women in the United States. As more men entered the teaching field, the low salaries of teachers became unacceptable, and teachers began to organize in order to improve their situation. Organizations like the NEA and the AFT eventually became powerful enough to influence federal policy. The creation of the Office of Secretary of Education in 1978 was at least partly a response to the growing power of teachers' organizations. The reduction of the scope of that office in the Reagan administration cannot be separated from what President Reagan viewed as political opposition by teachers. Strike and work stoppages have not improved the image of teachers in the public mind, nor have the professional organizations. Although able women now have the choice of many professions outside teaching, traditional lower salaries for teachers have contributed to inequality for women, because the teaching force remains heavily female.

Efforts to increase faculty, staff, and administrative salaries continue as states and communities vie for teachers. In many states, restricted finances limit progress toward salary increases. Oregon faced a limited tax base created by a voter-mandated restriction on property tax increases. By cutting other programs, the legislature found the money for adequate funding of schools, but it also revoked the teacher tenure law at the same time. Starting in 1998, Oregon teachers were all on two-year contracts. This tenure change reflected a demand for greater accountability, but it lowered the prestige of teaching. The current trend is to eliminate all tenure for public school teachers and administrators. Tenure is under attack in higher education, although it is a highly valued and desired recruiting tool and will probably/remain along with provisions for frequent post-tenure review.

The *Occupational Outlook Handbook, 2010–2011*, notes that the national medium average salary of public school teachers in 2008 ranged from $47,100 to $58,830. The American Federation of Teachers (2000–2006) reported beginning teachers with a bachelor's degree earning an average of $41,106 in 2000–2006 with an estimated average salary of elementary and secondary public school teachers at $47,100–51,180. Charter teachers' beginning salaries in 2000–2006 were $34,817. Median salaries were $52,530 for accredited librarians in 2008; from $23,442 to $51,508 for economists in 2008; from $44,050 to $149,110 for computer systems analysts in 2009; $63,100 for human resource managers in 2009; and an average of $35,160 to $57,110 and up in 2008 for inspectors and occupational health and safety officers, depending on educational degree level.

California, New Jersey, and Connecticut had the highest teachers' salaries in 2008–2009 (American Federation of Teachers, 2010). Although the states and the federal government were facing cyclical ups and downs in educational finances from 2008 to 2011, many efforts were underway to increase teachers' salaries through various state and local tax increases as well as through lotteries. However, federal stimulus money to keep teachers employed was a temporary measure during a major recession. Nagourney (2010) noted that the Los Angeles laid off 2,200 teachers in 2009 and cut a week from its school year because of the recession.

Georgia implemented an innovative model program to provide free tuition (through lottery funding) to any higher education institution in the state for motivated and prepared students. Arkansas provides higher education scholarships through a lottery. This has provided unique opportunities for students at risk but with good academic records to continue in higher education.

A Trend of Negative to Positive Factors.   Low salaries were by no means the only problem facing teachers. In *High School* (1984), Ernest Boyer reported that teachers are deeply concerned about the loss of status, a negative public image, little recognition for their work, and bureaucratic pressures imposed by the board or the administration. Recruiting better students to become teachers is difficult when many teachers in service feel frustrated or are seeking to leave the profession, because, traditionally, teachers have been the best recruiters. By 1986, numerous teachers, along with parents, advised students not to become teachers. In May 1985, the Corporate Forum on Education and the Economy created the Task Force on Teaching as a Profession to study the declining ability of the profession to attract promising future teachers.

Boyer, reflecting an earlier study by Emily Feistritzer (1985) on the teaching profession, stated that students preparing to teach have lower SAT scores than other college students and that the standards in colleges of education are low. As departments, colleges, and schools of education began to strengthen entrance requirements in response to the national criticism, state departments were slow to deny teaching positions to unqualified people. Feistritzer reported in 1984 that all but two states made provision for issuing an emergency or other substandard teaching credential; but the same boards directed their departments to license only teachers who passed tests such as the National Teachers Examination (NTE). National studies find highly qualified teachers are the most important ingredient in improving educational achievement levels. Coming out of a major recession will make it challenging to recruit and retain good teachers, especially as state and national budgets have required massive educator lay-offs.

Albert (1997) reports that although there are continuing problems—such as critics questioning public school teacher competence, violent kids, crime in schools, and one in six first-year public school teachers leaving the profession—teaching is gaining in prestige. Salaries are better, teachers feel more respected, individuals are leaving other jobs to become teachers, and more college freshmen are interested in teaching than at any other time since the mid-1970s. Individuals in the late 1990s and early 2000s have shown interest in the teaching profession because they want to make a difference in society. This trend is timely, because the Department of Education reports that, regardless of the current economic down cycle, some two million teachers will be needed in the next decade to replace retiring teachers.

School Crime/Violence.   Challenges to the education profession include increasing crime on certain school campuses. Miller (2004) found that 7 percent of public schools accounted for 50 percent of the total violent incidents reported. In addition, 2 percent of schools accounted for 50 percent of the most serious violent incidents.

Principals reported that students living in neighborhoods with high or mixed levels of crime were more likely to report a violent or serious crime than students living in neighborhoods with a low crime level. The 2006 National Crime Victimization Survey (Dinkes et al., 2009) showed that 909,500 secondary school students experienced theft in 2006; 43 percent of middle school students reported weekly incidents of school bullying. There were 767,000 violent crimes spread across 26.4 million 12–18-year-old students in 2006 (Mayer & Furlong, 2010).

Teachers and administrators are not immune to the rapid increase in school crime. According to the Florida Educational Coalition Crime and Violence Survey, pupils physically attack over 6,000 teachers nationwide each school day. Monitoring of everyone who enters the facility is a nationwide practice. In Palm Beach County, one of the largest districts in the nation, many schools have a variety of surveillance systems including X-ray and television cameras in classrooms and halls. Students learning to become teachers must be fingerprinted before entering public schools for observing, participating, and practice teaching with supervision. Some students report that public schools feel like prisons with so much control of an "inmate" population.

Miller (2004), in *Education Statistics Quarterly,* reported that according to school principals, 71 percent of public elementary and secondary schools experienced at least one violent incident during the 1999–2000 school year (such as rape, sexual battery, physical attacks or fights, or robbery with or without a weapon). In all, approximately 1,466,000 such incidents were reported in public schools. Reporting is now required under the 1996 Gun Free Schools Zones Act. Obviously, a major goal of governmental, parental, and educator organizations is to provide safe schools. Interesting enough, with notable exceptions, foreign nations experience violence outside of but seldom in schools. Character education and conflict resolution are being incorporated into the curriculum to address the issues of school violence and vandalism. Despite the criticism of a zero tolerance, school administrators tend to support such policies to maintain a proper learning environment. Although there is a record of declining crime and violence in schools, severity has increased.

Educators believe that the causes of increased school crime include social fragmentation, single-parent families, latchkey children, easy access to drugs and weapons, and identification with gangs, poverty, and intolerance. Hate crimes are growing on the campuses of our public schools and colleges. Workshops and seminars on conflict resolution and sensitivity training are being developed to address the issue. Paton (2005) notes a trend toward states prodding schools to teach how to resolve conflicts peacefully. School violence is an international challenge. Israel and other countries have local monitoring systems that connect academic outcomes with school safety conditions (Astor et al., 2010).

Although typical responses to student violence are increased restrictions and law enforcement personnel on school grounds, Raywid and Oshiyama (2000) called for smaller classes and mutual respect among all the school's constituents, reciprocity among students (and between them and adults), responsibility to self and the greater community, and a reverence for civility and comity.

Bullying.   Deerfield Beach in South Florida witnessed middle school students age 13–15 engaged in acts of violence. In one case a boy brutally attacked a girl, kicking her in the head repeatedly with steel-tipped shoes. She was in a coma and is now learning to talk and move with severe head injuries. In another case, several boys doused another boy with alcohol, setting him afire. He was so severely burned that he required intensive wound care for an extended period of time ("Learn About Bullying," 2010). Teen-on-teen violence has increased in severity. Physical bullying includes punching and kicking; emotional bullying encompasses keeping certain people out of groups and sending cruel text messages, emails, or voice mails. There have been several instances of young students committing suicide because of cruel text messaging. Research on bullying shows a link with poor academic performance (Swearer et al., 2010). Although over 44 states now have antibullying statutes, fewer than half have policies about whether schools should intervene in electronic communication, which almost always occurs outside of school and on weekends when children have more time to socialize online (Hoffman, 2010). Massachusetts law requires schools to have an antibullying curriculum, investigate acts of bullying, and report serious cases to law enforcement. Student texting, cell phone calls, and the Internet often give culprits cover through lack of supervision and anonymity. Sexting has become a major problem in middle schools. The National Campaign to Prevent Teen and Unplanned Pregnancy (2008) found 20 percent of teenagers 13 to 19 years of age had sent nude pictures of themselves to male and female friends. Parents, teachers, and law enforcement officials are developing intervention programs to address the issue. School personnel including teachers need to model civility, comity, respect, and courteousness for students and peers (Engel & Sandstrom, 2010).

The report *Safe at School: Addressing the School Environment and LGBT Safety Through Policy ad Legislation* by Stuart Biegel and Sheila James Kuehlcall for state legislatures to adopt prohibitions against bullying, which include cyber bulling, harassment and intimidation, and a hostile environment. Lesbian, gay, bisexual, and transgender students have higher rates of depression and suicide (McCord, 2010), and are often targets of bullying. A recent National School Bullying Summit found in 2000 that one out of three elementary school students and one out of nine secondary schools students reported some form of bullying, with over 900,000 such reports (*NBC Nightly News*, 2010). There are no easy answers to the complex factors behind school violence and bullying. However, Raywid and Oshiyama believe schools that view students as multidimensional (that is, seeing more than student's academic side) can build a more humane school environment.

Changes in Teacher Education.   The National Commission on Excellence and other groups created awareness for the need to improve education. At first the focus was on secondary schools, but soon the focus spread to colleges that prepare teachers, because not much progress toward excellence can be made unless the quality of teacher-education programs is addressed.

There was a clear mandate for schools, colleges, and departments of education (SCDEs) to revise their programs in order to achieve excellence. Organizations like the NCATE had started this process long before the national reports appeared. More stringent NCATE standards were adopted in 1984. Not all SCDEs are NCATE accredited, but many states also adopted the standards of the organization as a model for quality teacher-education programs.

A survey undertaken by the American Council on Education in 1984 (Troyer & Pace, 1984) showed that 9 of 10 colleges with teacher-education programs had minimum requirements, but 8 of 10 had initiated higher admission standards. Most were requiring some exit test for certification, such as a satisfactory score on the NTE. Graduation and certification requirements are not always the same, but colleges were attempting to conform to the state testing requirements.

In the 1990s and 2000s, SCDEs raised standards, required higher GPAs, and implemented 5-year programs. Exit testing was required in more states. In 1994, the AACTE issued a report on the status of multiculturalism; it identified a continuing need to meet the demand for teachers of color. More women and ethnic minority faculty and student recruitment continue to be a mission of SCDEs to teach student populations that reflect dramatic growth in people of African American, Hispanic, Asian American, and Native American ethnicities.

The teacher-education programs satisfied state and NCATE standards and conformed to the major suggestions found in the national reports of 1983. However, many professional educators argued that a 4-year college program was not adequate to prepare candidates for the new demands of teaching. At the very least, it was suggested that an entry-level teacher with a bachelor's degree needed further education along with experience in order to become a master teacher. In-service programs for teachers were therefore stressed to continue the education of new professionals and to upgrade the skills of experienced teachers. By 1986, it was agreed that a 4-year college commitment and an equal or longer commitment by a school district to continue teacher education were needed. In our twenty-first century, there is much discussion of exactly what knowledge base is essential to prepare every American teacher. The Yale Report of 1828 and the Harvard Report of 1945 raised the same question about "what is ultimately worth knowing." Traditionalists call for the liberating liberal arts, the best ideas of humankind; the progressives call for problem solving, critical thinking, and a process of inquiry that is not memorization or restricted by limits of the past. Revisionists of various persuasions call for teaching Third World philosophies, narratives of oppressed persons, and writings through the lenses of those from diverse cultural and ethnic backgrounds.

In the late 1990s and 2000s, NCATE has stressed expanding its accreditation program to cover more of the 1,314 state-approved teacher-preparation schools. Jeanne Ponessa, in *Education Week* (1997), notes that the National Commission on Teaching and America's Future, a privately organized panel, calls for NCATE accreditation together with licensing under the Interstate New Teacher Assessment and Support Consortium and master certification by the National Board for Professional Teaching Standards. An alternative accreditation group, the Teacher Accreditation Council, was formed in 1997. However, NCATE remains the nation's major education accreditation agency. NCATE's standards are followed in 28 states, whether or not those states seek national accreditation. A 2001 article by Leibbrand, "Accrediting Body Changing the Status Quo in Teacher Preparation," shows teacher accreditation and preparation standards have been raised for colleges of education in all areas. The article also referred to a National Council of State Legislatures report that shows NCATE to be a cost-effective means to upgrade teacher preparation in the states, and the National Alliance of Business with the Business Roundtable called for all colleges of education to be accredited. In 2001, NCATE enforced new, rigorous standards of professional preparation, licensing, and advanced certification on the 600 institutions that it accredits. The organization currently is using state–NCATE partnerships in over 46 states to reduce costs and to eliminate duplication of effort. NCATE, seeking continuous review of its accreditation procedure, has implemented a policy for third-party testimony to include the various populaces—faculty, administrators, students, alumni, and cooperating K–12 teachers, as well as other interested community organizations.

In "Groundbreaking Teacher Preparation Standards to Be Used Beginning Next Year" (2000), Arthur Wise, former NCATE president, said it is not enough for a faculty member to say "I taught the material." The 2001 standards include performance-based accreditation based on results that the teacher-education candidate knows the subject matter and can teach it effectively in a real classroom. Olson (2005) noted that for the past five years teacher-preparation schools have revamped how they collect data about their students. There were 656 NCATE-accredited schools in 2011 with 70 school in the process of accreditation. The effort is a work in progress.

Preparing for NCATE visits is time-consuming and expensive, and a difficult challenge for a school's faculty, administration, and staff. NCATE, however, helps the profession stay on target and, through a cooperative effort with state departments of education and other professional education associations, provides channels and models for improving teacher effectiveness and student achievement levels. In the fall of 2011, NCATE is implementing virtual focused visits, and current NCATE president James G. Cibulka is calling for a clinical model for teacher preparation (Fagan, 2011).

Five-Year Programs and the Holmes Group.   Long before *A Nation at Risk* was published, some major universities like Stanford had given up undergraduate teacher education to concentrate on graduate studies. Certainly it is true that growing numbers of teachers take advanced courses and most expect to earn a master's or specialist degree during their careers. By the mid-1980s, numerous universities were offering graduate-level courses for certification to accommodate degree holders and transfer students from other fields, even if they continued to offer the basic 4-year teacher-education program. Some states like New Jersey allowed local districts to provide the training for certification to prospective teachers with degrees in subject fields.

A similar approach was taken by a subset of the National Association of State Universities and Land Grant Colleges, called the Holmes Partnership (after former Dean Henry Holmes, of Harvard's Graduate School of Education). Under the leadership of Deans Judith Lanier of Michigan State and John Palmer of the University of Wisconsin, the organization is committed to a broad strategy of reform for teacher education and could influence the course of teacher education, as has occurred with NCATE, AACTE, Association of Supervision and Curriculum Development (ASCD), and AERA. The Holmes Group intends to make the education of teachers intellectually sound, to create relevant and defensible standards of entry into the profession, to connect schools of education with public schools, and to base teacher education on state-of-the-art research.

Gabriel (2005) suggests involving teachers in the decision-making process, and elevating them to leadership roles as a means to accomplish significant positive change in education. *A Nation Prepared: Teachers for the 21st Century* (Carnegie Forum on Education and the Economy, 1986) tied giving teachers more control over schools to increased accountability; it also recommended phasing out undergraduate education programs. School to university/business/community partnerships are part of many 5-year programs. Many university administrators are working to provide alternative avenues for promotion and tenure for those engaged in university to public school cooperative ventures.

Nancy Faust Sizer and Theodore R. Sizer, in "A School Built for Horace" (2001), discussed the challenges and opportunities of developing a charter experimental school designed to implement the best of educational reform ideas. In the school, with 340 students, the children who ages 12 and up have a personal learning plan that includes a contract among student, school, and the family. Students are promoted through three divisions, regardless of age, by public presentation of portfolios and exhibitions for older students. The school had a waiting list for the academic 2001 year. School admission is open on a lottery basis to any child, wherever he or she lives. Sizer (2005) noted that charter schools continue to deserve vigorous encouragement and support for their quality, variety, and imagination.

A detailed Rand Institute study, "Improving Student Achievement," showed variations among the states in school reform effectiveness, with more rural northern states having the highest average achievement scores and southern states usually among the lowest. The more urban northern states generally fell in the middle of the score distribution. The level of expenditures per pupil and its allocation affected student achievement, particularly for states with disproportionately higher numbers of minority and disadvantaged students. Authors Grissmer, Flanagan, Kawata, and Williamson (2000) found higher achievement scores, higher public prekindergarten participation, lower teacher turnover, and higher levels of teacher resources with lower pupil–teacher ratios. Hanushek (2001) analyzed the Rand study and suggested a larger database would yield more in-depth analysis.

Alternative Teacher Training. Alternative programs are being developed each year by colleges in an effort to build more relevance and skill into teacher education. Teach for America and Teacher Corps require interns, who have received advanced degrees in fields other than education, to live and work in school communities (often lower economic areas with large numbers of minority disadvantaged students) while receiving instruction in theory. Teach for America will place the largest and most diverse teacher corps in its 20-year history in 2010. There were 4,500 new teachers, one-third people of color—11 percent African Americans all committed to teach in underserved schools for two years. Although criticized by education unions, and others for teaching without having completed their preparation programs, Teach for America continues to grow ("Teach for America," 2010).

Many states are developing some sort of alternative certification for would-be teachers with college degrees but no preparation in pedagogy. Teacher for America participants serve in underserved communities for 2 years. Distance-learning teacher-education degrees will require new monitoring systems to ensure adequate preparation for working in ever more complex teaching–learning environments.

Colleges of education now offer programs to help middle-class teacher candidates understand the problems of lower-class students. Many colleges of education offer special courses and degree programs for English as a second language (ESL) students. The National Center for Alternative Certification, in "Alternative Routes to Teacher Certification," reported that 48 states, plus the District of Columbia, have some form of alternative teacher certification. Alaska and Oregon as yet do not have alternative certification programs. Since 1980, an estimated 500,000 persons have entered the profession through these programs, with an increasing number of higher education institutions initiating their own alternative teacher certification programs. Individuals in alternative programs are often older, nontraditional second-career seekers like retired military or former teachers whose families have been raised and who want to return to teaching. Nationally over one-third of new teachers being hired come through alternative routes to teacher education. With the exception of a slight drop in alternative certification during the recession in 2008–2010, the trend is increased use of alternative certification programs, with inner cities increasingly relying on such programs. As these programs expand, there has been less use of emergency and other temporary substitutes. Nontraditional students with advanced degrees are increasingly entering teaching careers. There is continuing research to determine the effectiveness of alternative teacher training. Oklahoma, as other states, has specific requirements for assuring quality teachers from alternative programs. Applicants with no teaching experience are required to participate in a residency program with same duties and responsibilities as other participants; 3 years to complete a block of up to 18 semester hours or 270 clock hours of professional education. The hours may be reduced by advanced degrees, work experience, or a combination of both. In no case will the required number of hours be reduced to less than 6 semester hours or 90 clock hours. The license is valid for one year, but can be renewed and pre-student teaching field experience and student teaching is waved (Charboneau, 2010). There are over 4,900 public charter schools enrolling over 1.5 million students including 400 new ones opening in 2009–2010 ("National Alliance," 2010). Recently, the Ninth Circuit Court of Appeals struck down a rule making it easier for some alternative-route teachers to be considered "highly qualified" before completing their alternative certification program (*Renee v. Duncan*, 2010). Carrie James, spokeswoman for Teach for America, believes the court ruling will be appealed or counteracted by congressional legislation (Walsh, 2010).

Reform in Educational Administration.
Arthur Levine (2005) of Columbia University Teachers College and a research team surveyed 28 educational administration preparation programs. Recommendations included eliminating the education

doctorate (16 percent of all doctoral degrees) for administrators and developing a master's of educational administration degree. According to Levine, only major research universities should offer the research Ph.D. degree in educational administration. He stressed the importance of high standards, commitment to quality instruction, and ending university dependency on "education students as cash cows" for income. Levine's report criticized the quality of off-campus degree programs.

Doctoral programs in school administration have become much more research oriented, and management skills taken from business administration have been added. Many educational administrators seek more practitioner-oriented doctoral programs and question the applicability of research-oriented programs to their ongoing careers. However, there is a national trend toward requiring more faculty and student research in institutions with doctoral programs. Superintendents learn more about school law, school finance, personnel management, conflict resolution, inclusion, information technology, university to school collaboration, managing change, human rights, accountability, assessment, litigation, and site-based management. Principals devote more time to evaluation of teachers, in-service training, and serving as instructional leaders. Accountability, safe schools, gender equity, diversity, and effective schools have become key goals in the administration field.

Educational administrators traditionally were successful teachers who were promoted and then learned management skills on the job or with continued graduate training. This pattern still exists to some extent in America, but the level of required training has increased to the point where administrators must expect to spend additional years in the graduate classroom before assuming a principalship or a superintendency. State requirements for administrative certification have also been strengthened, demanding a specific course of study as well as experience. Alternative certification programs designed to encourage managers from industry and business to become school administrators have been implemented in some states. Some school board chairpersons believe there should be a school administrator for operations and management and one for the academic affairs. Competition for the better jobs is keen, and the salaries are high by educational standards. Administrators who can articulate goals, inspire workers to work harmoniously toward those goals, maintain good relations with the public and school board, and demonstrate leadership are much in demand. Michelle E. Rhee, Chancellor of Washington, DC, schools did a good job in raising standards and closing the achievement gap, but her polarizing style, lack of compromise skills, and a changing political climate led to her resignation (Aarons, 2010). She recently has been selected to work with newly elected Florida Governor Rick Scott's educational team.

Nevertheless, high turnover and early burnout continue to plague the field of school administration. The average longevity of superintendents in large districts is less than three years. Divided school boards, single-interest groups, and managing budgets are continuing challenges for administrators. Pros and cons of data-based decision making also create administrative pressures as statistics and research often do not take into account the necessary people-centered rationale for the schools' existence.

Information Access. Professional improvement and information sharing have been greatly enhanced by the major organizations in administration. These provide a forum in which administrators can discuss problems and evaluate possible solutions with peers from similar school districts. Administrator organizations publish journals, maintain links to professors in the leading universities, and apprise administrators of changing regulations. The National Association of Secondary School Principals is one of the oldest and best-respected professional organizations. The American Association of School Administrators holds major conventions and attracts superintendents as well as political and academic leaders from across the nation. The National Council of Professors of School Administration and the University Council for Educational Administration serve the needs of those who train administrators and foster the dissemination of research. Elementary principals have their own organization, and all major associations have local and state affiliates. Much of the debate over the best responses to the reports demanding school reform has taken place in these organizations and on their useful and valuable websites.

By 1985, educators began to stress the importance of the human element in schools. It became gradually clear that because education is a complex process, caution had to be used in implementing massive changes envisioned by reform reports. Literature in administration began to reflect the impact of "unintended multipliers" of reform reports such as elitism, teacher flight, lower morale, loss of creativity, and high dropout rates when oversimplified solutions are applied. Currently, there is a student and teacher backlash against high-stakes testing in many states.

Research shows that administrative leadership at the school-building level is critical. The Connecticut School Effectiveness Project of 1982 recommends leadership by a principal who understands and applies the characteristics of instructional effectiveness as one of seven measures of good schools. (The others were a safe, orderly environment; a clear school mission; a climate of high student expectation; high time-on-task; frequent monitoring of student progress; and positive home–school relations.)

A school principal who can achieve balance between strong leadership and maximum autonomy for teachers will help to achieve excellence. Some critics say that studies of principals as instructional leaders conducted in inner-city schools may not apply to others. Goodlad (1990) doubts that principals can maintain a higher level of teaching expertise than teachers. Not all principals have the ability to become the exceptional, charismatic leaders that researchers describe. It is clear, however, that principals must devote much of their time and energy to instructional improvement if excellence is to be achieved. Maintaining effective relations with funding agencies, state and national governmental funding processes, and community organizations is vital to ensure adequate resources. School administrators' organizations maintain links with legislative bodies to influence budget decisions as they affect education.

Business Model. Educational administrators in the 1980s accepted many ideas from business, such as the Peters and Waterman (1982) conclusion that excellent organizations have profound respect for individual workers and stimulate unusual effort by ordinary people. They sought university programs to help them deal effectively with multiple changes in a democratic system of education. Collective negotiation with teachers and fact finding for bargaining were added to the themes of accountability, organizational climate, and managing change for excellence. Other trends for educational administrators were increased emphasis on ethical values, maintaining order and discipline in schools, and dealing with federal disengagement from the schools. Performance pay gained adherents from teacher unions, major foundations, Secretary of Education Arne Duncan, and the Obama administration in an effort to improve student learning (Richardson, 2010).

Special Needs.   The American Association of School Administrators is seeking to make IDEA funding mandatory. Rather than be subjected to the political budget process, advocates for full funding of inclusion and special education for physically, mentally, and emotionally challenged citizens seek to have mandatory ongoing resource allocation. Pressure is being placed on Congress for mandatory funding for IDEA by a number of professional education organizations including the NEA, the AFT, the National School Boards Association (NSBA), the National Association of Secondary School Principals, the National PTA, and the American Speech and Hearing Association. According to the Council for Exceptional Children ("IDEA Funding," 2003), Congress has promised for 25 years to fully fund IDEA, yet funding is at 14.8 to 19 percent. Full funding or 40 percent of the average per special-education student is the goal of special-education advocates. In 2001, the average per pupil expenditure was estimated to be $7,066. With 6,138,000 students served under IDEA, schools are qualified to receive $17.35 billion in federal funds, yet they only receive $6.34 billion.

From the early days of the republic, our country has been committed to expanding the nation's social network to cover an ever-larger portion of at-risk special needs citizens through local, state, and national efforts.

Zirkel (2001), in "Sorting Out Which Students Have Learning Disabilities," points to the challenge of parents shopping around for psychologists and physicians who will diagnose their children as learning disabled in order to get special help to excel in school. In his *Phi Delta Kappan* article, Zirkel notes that parents may bring attorneys or disability advocates to a school and threaten legal action. School administrators who believe that an accommodation is unwarranted may have difficulty making tough decisions in the face of such pressure. Zirkel noted that 41 percent of college freshmen who reported in 1998 that they had a disability came from the "learning disability" category, compared with 15 percent in 1988. In addition, the percentage of students with more traditional and visible disabilities had declined significantly. For instance, the proportion of visually impaired students went from 32 to 13 percent, and that of orthopedically impaired students went from 14 to 9 percent.

Special-education students are a diverse group. Although 67 percent have specific learning disabilities or speech or language impairments, fewer than 12 percent have disabilities associated with significant cognitive impairments, such as mental retardation or traumatic brain injury. There is continuing concern that minority students are overrepresented in some special-education categories—and many children are misidentified for special education simply because they did not receive effective education in the first place ("Special Needs, Common Goals," 2004).

In *Educating for a New Millennium,* Shane and Tabler (1981) stipulated the importance of basing the organization and administration of education on local control so that those most familiar with community needs would make priorities and deploy resources. They also called for an alternative to the bureaucratic model of administrative structure common to schooling and business, an idea also supported by both Goodlad (1990) and Boyer (1984, 1995). Fenwick W. English (2001) fears that total reliance on using hard data as the only reliable source of information may drive out and replace the value of other forms of information that are crucial to understanding human interaction and affective learning and teaching.

In *New Schools for a New Century* (1995), Kenneth J. Tewel views the administrator's role as building new teacher relationships through listening and problem solving to expedite the change process. By building staff and teacher support for change through improving communication, administrators can eliminate barriers to school restructuring. Involving teachers in the change process is seen in the current experimentation with flexible scheduling designed to reform the traditional seven- or eight-period day. Block scheduling is designed to increase time available for students to learn in a changed classroom environment.

Administration and the Law.
Because the responsibility of enforcing laws rests on school administrators, they must be especially sensitive to the legal aspects of reform. Following the lead of the Supreme Court in the *Brown* decision of 1954, education has become recognized as a legal right for all citizens. By the 1970s, this right was extended to those with special needs. The 1975 Education for All Handicapped Children Act made it incumbent on all districts to provide to children with special needs education in the "least restrictive environment." Superimposed on this law were the various state regulations concerning excellence. Every state in the nation has made some effort to improve education through legislation. Laws mandated curriculum reform, graduation requirements, student evaluation, longer school days and years, and plans to reward teachers through career ladders or master teacher programs. Another responsibility was responding to the increased number of lawsuits brought against schools. Lawsuits have increased dramatically since 1980 and range from cases involving accidents to those accusing schools of failing to provide equal access to education. Litigation in the field of special-education inclusion has increased exponentially in the past few years, and recently special education has been in litigation in some areas initiated by home schooling parents. Funding for home schooling special education is currently under review.

Challenges will continue to be opportunities to improve more effective educational delivery systems in our schools and communities. The NCLB Act, up for reauthorization, with a divided Congress and nationwide school district administrators calls for modification, will be formulated as a new model. Meanwhile, Arne Duncan is granting school district wavers from compliance with requirements of the act and at-risk students.

THE SEARCH FOR EXCELLENCE CONTINUES

Throughout our educational history, educators served as conduits for an expanded social consciousness. From the early days of the republic, education was seen as vital for future generations. Although many efforts such as the Old Deluder Satan Act of 1647 were honored more in the breach than in the observance, a foundation for an educational system was laid.

Debate and controversy over innovations and progress will continue in the future as in the past. Demands for higher standards are met with concerns for students at risk, students with special learning needs, and limited-English-proficiency pupils. Aristotle's golden mean, or a sense of balance, is needed to deal with excellence and support for the "best one can be" for at-risk students with reasoned inquiry and analysis. There are voices for redesigning teacher and administrative preparation programs through systemic change; there are also voices that recognize much reform hype is for public relations and political purposes. However, educators are working to improve student outcomes with some success, a fact often underreported by the media. A 1999 Teacher Quality National Center for Educational Statistics report (Snyder, 1999) identifies both progress and challenges in the education profession.

Meanwhile administrators, teachers, and staff will have to avoid hardening of the categories and prepare for emerging instructional delivery systems such as distance learning. History of education teaches us that there will be "new wine in old bottles," as old models are wrapped in new language. However, continued change in society and education is the story of our text.

▊ GAINING PERSPECTIVE THROUGH CRITICAL ANALYSIS

1. Compare and contrast areas of agreement and disagreement among major educational reform reports. What impact have the reform reports had on educational effectiveness?

2. Do you agree with John I. Goodlad that schooling and education should not be synonymous? (See chapter-opening quotation.)

3. What role has the business community had on educational reform? How can educators monitor corporate advertising in schools? Identify pros and cons of pay for performance contracts.

4. Name three ways in which *A Nation at Risk* has impacted educational policies and practices. Share your list with your classmates, and add all of the findings to your journal.

5. Use the Internet and the library to find articles dealing with the effectiveness of two educational reform movements of the past on education practice today. Identify the pros and cons of high-stakes testing.

6. Analyze the constraints teachers face when entering the profession. Discuss the social, political, and financial challenges.

7. Compare and contrast the strategies for improving both the teaching and the learning environments in Horace Mann's time with those of the current National Council for Teacher Education, NCATE, the National Education Association, and Phi Delta Kappa.

8. Identify current criticisms of educational outcomes and interview a teacher or administrator to gain that person's responses to such criticisms.

9. Describe the pros and cons of the No Child Left Behind Act. With a divided Congress, what outcome do you foresee for reauthorization?

⊞ HISTORY IN ACTION IN TODAY'S CLASSROOMS

1. Attend a parent–teacher conference. Identify suggestions for achieving excellence in student performance and teacher delivery systems. What (if any) major themes were discussed? If no suggestions were apparent, discuss your impressions of the purpose and outcome of the meeting. Add the findings to your journal.

2. Visit a temporary-help firm in your area to discuss the training programs offered to temporary workers today. What are the reasons for offering this training? Compare these programs with classes offered in the business education department of your local high school. Does the agency provide substitute teachers for public schools?

3. What are the main themes of the No Child Left Behind Act? Why do you think there is so much controversy over implementation of the act? Envision alternative scenarios for efforts to close the educational achievement gap. With a new 113th Congress, what changes might be made to the act and why?

4. What other strategies can be used to measure instructional and student learning improvement besides standardized tests?

5. Identify strategies to address diversity, multicultural issues, and cultural uniqueness in our schools and society. Discuss and answer the questions at the end of the feature "Educational Reform: Past and Present." This feature is found within the chapter.

⊞ BIBLIOGRAPHY

Aarons, Dakarai. "Rhee Reflective in Aftershock of D.C. Primary." *Education Week* (September 22, 2010): 1, 17.

"Academic Preparation for College 1983–1987." *Postsecondary Educational Opportunity*. The Mortenson Research Seminar on Public Policy Analysis Opportunity for Post Secondary Education no. 66 (December, 1997).

"Achieve." *American Diploma Project Network* (2010). www.achieve.org/

Adams, Jacob E., & William E. White. "The Equity Consequence of School Finance Reform in Kentucky." *Educational Evaluation and Policy Analysis* (Summer 1997): 165–184.

Adler, Mortimer. *The Paideia Proposal: An Educational Manifesto*. New York: Macmillan, 1982.

Albert, Tanya. "Common Theme Is Behind New Popularity: Service." *USA Today* (February 25, 1997): 1A–2A.

Alexander, Lamar. *Time for Results*. New York: Report on Education by the National Governor's Association, 1986, 1991.

"Alternative Teacher Certification." National Center for Alternative Certification (2010). Available at: www.teach-now.org/intro.cfm.

American Association of Colleges for Teacher Education. *Teacher Education Pipeline: Schools, Colleges, and Departments of Education Enrollments by Race, Ethnicity, and Gender*. Washington, DC: Author, 1994.

American Council on Education, Business-Higher Education Forum. *America's Competitive Challenge: The Need for a National Response*. Washington, DC: Author, 1983.

"An Older and More Diverse Nation by Midcentury." Washington, DC: U.S. Census Bureau (August 14, 2008). Available at: www.census.gov/newsroom/releases/archives/population/cb08-123.html

Apple, Michael. "Markets, Standards, Teaching and Teacher Education." *Journal of Teacher Education* (May/June 2001): 194–195.

Ashton, Patricia, & Rodman Webb. *Making a Difference: Teacher's Sense of Efficacy and Student Achievement*. New York: Longman, 1986.

Astor, Ron Avi, Nancy Guerra, & Richard Van Acker. "How Can we Improve School Safety Research?" *Educational Researcher* (January/February 2010): 75.

"Average Salary of Arkansas Teachers 9th Lowest in the Nation, Union Surveys Say." *The Arkansas Democrat Gazette* (May 19, 2001): 1B, 3B.

American Federation of Teachers. *Average Teacher Salaries*. Washington, DC (2006–2007). www.aft.org

Otis, Andrew. "Average Teacher Salaries in U.S". *AFT Reports* (July 23, 2011). www.moneyandbusiness.com/careers/career-development/career-paths/average teacher

Baldauf, Scott. "States Weigh Whether to Save or Spend Surpluses." *Christian Science Monitor* (June 19, 1997): 4.

Berliner, David C., & Bruce J. Biddle. *The Manufactured Crisis: Myths, Fraud and the Attack on America's Public Schools*. New York: Addison Wesley, 1995.

Biegel, Stuart and Shiela Kuehl. "Safe at School: Addressing the School Environment and LGBT Safety Through Policy and Legislation." National Education Policy Center (2010). www. nepc.colorado.edu/publication/safe-at-school

Boyer, Ernest. *High School: A Report on Secondary Education in America*. Boston: Houghton Mifflin, 1984.

Boyer, Ernest. *The Basic School: A Community for Learning*. San Francisco: Jossey-Bass, 1995.

Boyles, Deron. *American Education and Corporations: A History of affirmative Action*.New York: Garland Publishing, 2000.

Bracey, Gerald W. "The Sixth Bracey Report on the Condition of Public Education." *Phi Delta Kappan* (1996). Available at the journal's archives: www.pdkintl.org

Brown v. Board of Education, Topeka. 347.U.S. 483 (1954).

"Bullying." *NBC Nightly News Report, NBC University*. (September 5, 2010, 5:30 P.M.). Washington, DC.

Callahan, Raymond E. *Education and the Cult of Efficiency: A Study of the Social Forces That Have Shaped the Administration of the Public Schools*. Chicago: University of Chicago Press, 1962.

Cardman, Michael. "Establishment Puts Weight Behind Full Funding Bill." *Education Daily* (2001): 3–4.

Carnegie Forum on Education and the Economy. *A Nation Prepared: Teachers for the 21st Century*. New York: Carnegie Corp., 1986.

Carr, Judy F., & Douglas E. Harris. *Succeeding with Standards: Linking Curriculum, Assessment, and Action Planning*. Alexandria, VA: The Association for Supervision and Curriculum Development, 2001.

Chao, Elaine L., & Kathleen P. Utgoff. *The Occupational Handbook 2010–2011*. Indianapolis, IN: JIST Publishing. Available at: www.bls.gov/oco/ "Connecticut School Effectiveness Project" (1982). www.eric.ed.gov/ERICWebPortal

Committee for Economic Development. *Investing in Our Children. Savage Inequalities, Children in America's Schools*. New York: Author, 1985.

Croft, Michelle. "Charter Schools: A Report on Rethinking the Federal Role in Education." Brookings Institution (December 16, 2010). www.brookings.edu/

Cross, Patricia. "The Rising Tide of School Reform Reports." *Phi Delta Kappan* 66, no. 3 (November 1984): 167–172.

Darling-Hammond, Linda. "Reframing the School Reform Agenda." *Phi Delta Kappan* (June 1993): 753–761.

Demma, Rachel, Jodi Omear, & Kate Dando. "2010 Governors' Education Policy Advisors Institute" and "National Governors' Association and State Education Chiefs Launch Common State Standards." Washington, DC: The Center for Best Practices National Governors' Association, April 25–27, 2010, and June 6, 2010; www.corestandards.org/articles/8-national-governors-association-and-state-education-chiefs-launch-state-academic-standards

Dewey, John. *The Child and the Curriculum*. Chicago: University of Chicago Press, 1902.

Dinkes, R., J. Kemp, & K. Baum. *Indicators of School Crime and Safety*. NCES 2009-022/NCJ 226343.Washington, DC: National Center for Education Statistics, 2009.

Douglas, Mitchell, et al. *California Beginning Teacher Support and Assessment Evaluation Study*. Riverside, CA: California Educational Research Cooperative, 1977. (Also, San Francisco, CA: Far West Laboratory for Educational Research and Development, 1977.)

Editorial Projects in Education. *From Risk to Renewal: Charting a Course for Reform*. Washington, DC: Author, 1993.

Education Commission of the States. *Action for Excellence*. Task Force on Education for Economic Growth. Denver, CO: 1983.

Education Commission of the States. *Action in the States: Progress Toward Educational Renewal*. A Report of the Task Force on Education for Economic Growth, July 1984.

Elkind, David H., & Freddy Sweet. "The Socratic Approach to Character Education." *Educational Leadership* (May 1996): 56–59.

Engel, Susan, & Marlene Sandstron. "There's Only One Way to Stop a Bully." *New York Times* (July 22, 2010). English, Fenwick. "Dumbing Schools Down with Data Driven Decision Making: A Deconstructive Reading of a Popular Educational Leitmotif." *National Forum of Educational Administration and Supervision Journal* (2001): 3–11.

Fagan, Amy. "Are Education Schools Amenable to Reform." *Fordham's Flypaper* (December 6, 2011). Available at: www.educationgadfly.net/flypaper/2010/12/event-highlights

Feistritzer, Emily. *The Condition of Teaching: A State by State Analysis*. Princeton, NJ: The Carnegie Foundation for the Advancement of Teaching, 1985.

"First National Bullying Summit." Washington, DC (2010). www1.whdh.com/news/articles/national/12002146408666/

Florida Education Coalition Crime and Violence Survey 1991–1992. *School Year, Juvenile Crime Surveys, Violence Florida Surveys*. Washington, DC: U.S. Department of Education, 1993. Forsyth, Patrick B., & Marilyn Tallerico. *City Schools Leading the Way*. Newbury Park, CA: Corwin Press, 1993.

Frazier, Calvin. *A Shared Vision: Policy Recommendations for Linking Teacher Education to School Reform*. Denver, CO: Education Commission of the States, 1993.

Friedman, Milton, & Rose Friedman. *Free to Choose a Personal Statement*. New York: Harcourt, Brace and Jovanovich, 1980.

Gabriel, John G. *How to Thrive as a Teacher Leader*. Alexandria, VA: Association of Supervision and Curriculum Development, 2005.

Gardner, Howard. *Frames of Mind: The Theory of Multiple Intelligence*. New York: Basic Books, 1983.

General Education in a Free Society, A Report of the Harvard Committee. Cambridge, MA: Harvard University Press, 1945.

Gehring, John. "Washington State Districts Issue Grades for Employability." *Education Week* (January 17, 2001): 12.

Gehring, John. "U.S. Seen Losing Edge on Education Measures." *Education Week* (April 4, 2001): 3.

Giroux, Henry A. *Corporate Culture and the Attack on Higher Education and Public School*. Bloomington, IN: Phi Delta Kappa Educational Foundation Fastback Series, 1999.

Goodlad, John I. *A Place Called School: Prospects for the Future*. New York: McGraw-Hill, 1984.

Goodlad, John I. *Teachers for Our Nation's Schools*. San Francisco: Jossey-Bass, 1990.

Goodlad, John I., & Timothy J. McMannon, Eds. The *Public Purpose of Education and Schooling*. San Francisco: Jossey-Bass, 1997.

Grissmer, David W., Ann Flanagan, Jennifer Kawata, & Stephanie Williamson. *Improving Student Achievement: What State NAEP Test Scores Tell Us*. MR-924-EDU. Santa Monica, CA: Rand Institute, 2000.

"Groundbreaking Teacher Preparation Standards to Be Used Beginning Next Year." *NCATE Accreditation* (May 15, 2000). Available at: www.ncate.org/2000/pressrelease.htm.

Hanushek, Eric A. "Assessing the Effects of School Resources on Student Performance: An Update." *Educational Evaluation and Policy Analysis* (Summer 1997): 141–164.

Hanushek, Eric A. "Have We Learned Anything New? The Rand Study of NAEP Performance." *Education Matters More* (2001). www.edmatters.orgHaughney, Kathleen. "Proposal Would Expand Florida Voucher Program" (February 12, 2010). www.newsserviceflorida.com/

Hirsch, E. D., Jr. *Cultural Literacy*. Boston: Houghton-Mifflin, 1987.

Hirsch, E. D., Jr. *The Schools We Need and Why We Don't Have Them*. New York: Doubleday, 1996.

Hoffman, Jan. "Online Bullies Pull Schools into the Fray." *New York Times* (June 27, 2010). www.nytimes.com/2010/06/28/style/28bully.htm

Holmes Group Consortium. *New Standards for Quality Teacher Education*. Washington, DC: U.S. Department of Education, 1984.

Holt, John. *Teach Your Own: A Hopeful Path for Education*. New York: Delacorte Press/Seymour Lawrence, 1981.

House, Ernest R. "A Framework for Appraising Educational Reforms." *Educational Researcher* (October 1996): 13.Hoxby, Caroline M. "*Would School Choice Change the Teaching Profession?*" *Journal of Human Resources* 37, no. 4 (Fall 2002): 846–891. www.nber.org/papers.

Hunt, James B., Jr. *What Matters Most: Teaching for America's Future*. New York: Teachers College, Columbia University, 1996.

Hunt, James B., & Thomas G. Carroll. "No Dream Denied: A Pledge to America's Children." National Commission on Teaching and America's Future (January 2003): 1–36.

"IDEA Funding: Time for a New Approach." Council for Exceptional Children (March 2003). www.Michigan.gov/documents/IDEAfunding

"If I Can't Learn from You—Ensuring a Highly Qualified Teacher for Every Classroom: Quality Counts." *Education Week* (2003): 76.

Johnston, Robert C. "Troubled Pennsylvania Districts Eye Dramatic Changes." *Education Week* (November 22, 2000): 18, 20.

Katz, Bruce, & Alan Berube. *Racial Change in the Nation's Largest Cities: Evidence from the 2000 Census*. The Brookings Center on Urban and Metropolitan Policy Survey. Washington, DC: Brookings Institute 2001.

Kaufman, P., et al. *Indicators of School Crime and Safety*." Washington, DC: U.S. Departments of Education and Justice, 2000.

Kleiman, Carol. "Diversity Heads for the Next Level." *Sun-Sentinel South Florida: Your Business* (2001): 13.

Kopp, Wendy. "Teach for America Brings Most Diverse Teacher Corps in History." *Cleveland.Com* (June 3, 2010). Available at: www.cleveland.com

Kozol, Jonathan. *Savage Inequalities: Children in America's Schools.* New York: Crown Publishing Company, 1991.

Lanier, J. *Tomorrow's Schools of Education.* A Report of the Holmes Group. East Lansing, MI: Michigan State University, 1995.

Lawton, Millicent. "Verbal, Math Scores on S.A.T. Up for Second Straight Year." *Education Week* (September 8, 1993): 10.

"Learn About Bullying: Deerfield Beach Middle School Students Are Beaten and Burned, It Needs to Stop." (March 19, 2010). Available at: www.msnbc.msn .com/ Leary, James. *Educators on Trial.* Farmington, MI: Action Inservice, 1981.

Leibbrand, Jane. "Accrediting Body Changing the Status Quo in Teacher Preparation." *National Council for Accreditation of Teacher Education Newsbriefs* (February 21, 2001) at: www.ncate.org/newsbrfs/dec_rept_release.htm.Levine, Arthur. *Educating School Leaders.* Washington, DC: The Education Schools Project, March 2005. Available at: www.wallacefoundation.org and www.edschools.org

Lewis, Anne C. "Washington Commentary." *Phi Delta Kappan* (April 2001): 567.

Lortie, Dan. *Schoolteacher.* Chicago, IL: University of Chicago Press, 2002.

Lyons, Kathleen, & Melinda Anderson. "U.S. Teacher Pay Rises Slightly: NEA Study Shows Salaries Declined in Some States." NEA News Release (February 20, 1997). Accessed at: www.nea.org/nr/nr.html.Mayer, Matthew J., & Michael J. Furlong. "How Safe Are Our Schools? *Educational Researcher* (January–February 2010): 16–26.

McCord, Nikki Rashada. "Safety of LGBT Students: Recommendations and Model Legislation." *NEPC* (September 30, 2010). Available at: www.nepc. colorado.edu

McKersie, William S. "Philanthropy's Paradox: Chicago School Reform." *Educational Evaluation and Policy Analysis,* no. 2 (Summer 1993): 109–128.

Miller, Amanda K. "Violence in U.S. Public Schools: 2000 School Survey on Crime and Safety." *Education Statistics Quarterly* 5, no. 4 (2004).

Nagourney, Adam. "LA School Set to Open at RFK Site." *The Arkansas Democrat Gazette*(September 5, 2010): 13 A.

Naisbitt, John. *Re-inventing the Corporation.* London: Guild Publishing, 1985.

"National Alliance for Public Charter Schools" (2010). www.publiccharters.org/

"National Campaign to Prevent Teen and Unplanned Pregnancy" (2008). www.thenationalcampaign.org

National Commission on Excellence in Education. *A Nation at Risk: The Imperative for Educational Reform.* Washington, DC: U.S. Government Printing Office, 1983.

National Council for Accreditation of Teacher Education. "New Teachers Say They Are Well Prepared." *Quality Teaching* (Spring 1997): 1–2.

National Council of State Legislatures. "NCSL Lack Force on No Child Left Behind Report." (Feb. 23, 2005). Available at: www.NCSL.org/programs/press/2005/NCLB_epec_summary.htm.

National Education Association. "Education Vital Signs." Southwest and U.S. Totals. Reprinted from National School Boards Association, *American School Board Journal.* (2006). www.asbj.com/evo/o6/EVSO6southwest.pdf.

National Education Association. "Rankings and Estimates a Report of School Statistics Update" (Fall 2009–2010). Available at: www.nea.org

National Governors' Association. *Time for Results in Education:* 1991. Washington, DC: 1991 Available at: www.jstor.org/

National Governors' Association, 1991. Report on Education. *Time for Results.* Washington, DC: Author, 1990.

National Research Council. *Knowing What Students Know: The Science and Design of Educational Assessment.* Washington: DC: The National Academics Press, Center for Education, 2010. Available at: www.books.nap.edu/books/0309072727/html/12.html.

"No Small Change: Targeting Money Toward Student Performance, Quality Counts." *Education Week* (2005): 7.

Nordlinger v. Hahn. 505 U.S. 1 (1992).

"Number of Public Charter Schools & Students, 2009–2010." National Alliance for Public Charter Schools" (September, 2009). www.publiccharters.org

Obama, Barack. "Commencement Address at Kalamazoo Central High School." (June 7, 2010). www.whitehouse .gov/issues/education/

"Oklahoma Alternative Certification." Oklahoma Department of Education Professional Standards (April 27, 2010). www.sde.state.ok.us/teacher/profstand/AltPlacement.html _oklahoma-alternative-certification.html

Olson, Lynn. "Education Schools Use Performance Standards to Improve Graduates." *Education Week* (May 11 2005): 1, 18.

Paulson, Amanda, & Stacy Teicher Khadaroo. "Education's Mr. Accountability." *The Christian Science Monitor* (August 30, 2010): 26–31.

Perrone, Vito. "The Life and Career of Ernest Boyer (1928–1995)." *Educational Leadership* 53, no. 6 (March 1996): 80–82.

Peters, Thomas J., & Robert H. Waterman. *In Search of Excellence: Lessons from America's Best Run Companies*. New York: Harper & Row, 1982.

Ponessa, Jeanne. "Despite Rocky Road, Ed. School Accreditation Effort on a Roll." *Education Week* (June 18, 1997): 8.

"Quality Counts." *Education Week: Editorial Projects in Education Research Center* 29, no.17 (January 14, 2010: 29 (17): 39.

Rand Corporation's of school effectivenessCharter Schools in Eight States; Effects on Achievement. San Monica, CA: Rand Corporation Rand (2009). 1987 www.rand.org

"Rankings and Estimates: Rankings of the States 2004 and Estimates of School Statistics 2005." Washington, DC: National Education Association Research, 2005. Available at: www.nea.org/edstats/images/05rankings.pdf

Paton, Dean. "States Prod Schools to Teach Relationships." *The Christian Science Monitor* (June 13, 2005): 2, 3.

"In Ranking, U.S. Students Trail Global Leaders." *USA Today* (December 7, 2010).

"Rankings and Estimates 2010." National Education Association (2010): 76.

Ravitch, Diane. *The Death and Life of the Great American School System*. New York: Basic Books, 2010.

Raywid, Mary Anne, & Libby Oshiyama. "Musings in the Wake of Columbine." *Phi Delta Kappan* (February 2000): 449.

Renee v. Duncan. 623 F.3d787 (2010).

Reports of the Course of Instruction in Yale College by a Committee of the Corporation and the Academical Faculty. New Haven, CT: Hezekiah Howe, 1828. Richardson, Joan. "A Carrot of a Different Color." *Phi Delta Kappa* (May 2010): 4.

Rose v. Council for Better Education. 770S.W2d. 186 (Kentucky, 1989).

Rosenthal, Neal H., & Ronald E. Kirtscher. *The Occupational Outlook Handbook 1992–1993*. Washington, DC: Bureau of Labor Statistics, 1992–1993.

Sarason, Seymour B. *The Predictable Failure of Educational Reform*. San Francisco: Jossey-Bass, 1990.

Sawchuk, Stephen, & Erik Robelen. "Stimulus Guidance Spotlights Teacher Evaluations." *Education Week* no. 28 (April 1, 2009).

Schmitt, Eric. "Whites in Minority in Largest Cities, the Census Shows." *New York Times* (April 30, (2001). Available at: www.puertoriopuirHerald.org

"School Modernization." Condition of America's Public School Facilities. National Center for Educational Statistics (2000) in National PTA." Washington DC: U.S. Department of Education, 2000.

Sergiovanni, Thomas J. *The Principalship: A Reflective Practice Perspective*. Boston: Allyn & Bacon, 1991.

Shane, Harold Gray, & M. Bernadine Tabler. *Educating for a New Millennium: Views of 132 International Scholars*. Bloomington, IN: Phi Beta Kappa, 1981.

Sizer, Nancy Faust, & Theodore Sizer. "A School Built for Horace." *Education Matters* (Spring 2001). Available: www.educationnext.org/2001/sp/26.html

Sizer, Theodore R. "Don't Tie Us Down." *Education Next* 5. Hoover Institution (Summer 2005.). Available: www.educationnext.org/20053/59.html

Sizer, Theodore R. *Horace's Compromise: The Dilemma of the American High School*. Boston: Houghton Mifflin, 1984.

Sizer, Theodore R. *Horace's School: Redesigning the American High School*. Boston: Houghton Mifflin, 1992.

Sizer, Theodore R. *Horace's Hope: The Future of the American High School*. Boston: Houghton Mifflin, 1996.

Smith, B. Othanel. *A Design for a School of Pedagogy*. Washington, DC: U.S. Department of Education, 1980.

Snyder, Thomas. *Digest of Educational Statistics*. Washington, DC: U.S. Department of Education, National Center for Educational Statistics, 2000.

Snyder, Thomas. *Teacher Quality Report*. Washington, DC: National Center for Educational Statistics, 1999.

Snyder, Thomas. *Condition of Education Survey*. Washington, DC: National Center for Educational Statistics, 1997.

Snyder, Thomas. *Digest of Educational Statistics*. Washington, DC: U.S. Department of Education, 1996.

"Special Education Inclusion." *Teaching and Learning* (November 5, 2001): 1–10. Available at: www.weac .org/resource/june96/speced.htm

"Special Needs, Common Goals, Special Education in an Era of Standards: Count Me In." *Education Week* and Pew Charitable Trusts (January, 2004): 7.

"State List of Accredited Institutions." *NCATE* (2011). Available at: www.ncate.org/of

Stricherz, Mark. "Top Oakland Administrators to Receive Bonuses Tied to Test Scores." *Education Week* (January 24, 2001): 5.

Stroud, Marcello. "Teach For America Fields Largest Teacher Corps in its 20-Year History." (May 24, 2010). Available at: www.teachforamerica.org/

Swearer, Susan M., Dorothy L. Espelage, Tracy Vaillancourt, & Shelley Hymel. "What Can Be Done About School Bullying? Linking Research to Educational Practice." *Educational Researcher* (January/ February 2010): 38–44.

Tallerico, Marilyn. "Governing Urban Schools." In *City Schools Leading the Way*. Edited by Marilyn Tallerico & Patrick B. Forsyth 239–240. Newbury Park, CA: Corwin Press, 1993, pp. 239–240.

Tanner, Daniel. *Progressive Education at the Crossroads: Crusade for Democracy*. Albany: State University of New York Press, 1991.

Marcello Stroud"Teach for America Brings Most Diverse Teacher Corps in History." *Com ://*"Teacher Salaries Stagnant as Health Insurance Costs Soar." *American Federation of Teachers News.* (December 31, 2004). Available from: jbass@aft.org Available: www.aft.org/ news/2004/salary_survey.htm Tewel, Kenneth J. *New Schools for a New Century*. Delray Beach, FL: St. Lucie Press, 1995.

"The National Campaign to Prevent Teen and Unplanned Pregnancy." (2008). www.thenationalcampaign.org/

"Today's NCLB Stories from AASA." American Association of School Administrators On Line(February 24, 2005). Available from: Npenning@AASA.org

Troyer, M. E., & C. R. Pace. *Evaluation in Teacher Education*. Washington, DC: American Council on Education, 1984.

U.S.CensusBureau.www.2010census.gov/2010censusdata

Viadero, Debra. "AFT Charter School Study Sparks Heated National Debate." *Education Week* (September 1, 2004): 9.

Waddell, Lynn. "Flap Erupts over Ads on School Websites." *Christian Science Monitor* (May 2, 2001): 2.

Walsh, Mark. "Appeals Court Curbs U.S. Rule on Alternative Certification." *Education Week* (October 6, 2010): 6.

Weber, James R. *Instructional Leadership: A Corporate Working Model*. Eugene, OR: ERIC Clearinghouse on Educational Management, June 1987.

Weber, R. M. "The Study of Oral Reading Errors: A Review of the Literature." *Reading Research Quarterly* 4 (1970): 96–119.

William T. Grant Foundation. *The Forgotten Half: Non-College Youth in America: An Interim Report on the School-to-Work Transition*. New York: William T. Grant Foundation Commission on Work, Family and Citizenship, 1988.

Wirt, John. *The Condition of Education Center for Educational Statistics*. Washington, DC: U.S. Department of Education, 2004.

Wirth, Arthur. *Education and Work for the Year 2000: Choices We Make*. San Francisco: Jossey-Bass, 1992.

Wolf, Shelby, Hilda Borko, Rebekah L. Elliott, & Monette C. McIver. "That Dog Won't Hunt! Exemplary School Change Efforts Within the Kentucky Reform." *American Educational Research Journal* (Summer 2000): 349–393.

Zerchykov, Ross. *School Boards and the Communities They Represent*. Boston, MA: Institute for Responsive Education, 1981.

Zirkel, Perry A. "Sorting Out Which Students Have Learning Disabilities." *Phi Delta Kappan* (April 2001): 639–641.

Zollers, Nancy J., R. Lille Albert, & Marilyn Cochran-Smith. "In Pursuit of Social Justice: Collaborative Research and Practice in Teacher Education." *Action in Teacher Education* (Summer 2000): 1–11.

CHAPTER 10

ISSUES IN MODERN AMERICAN EDUCATION

Even if only one child in ten could gain in intellectual effectiveness through a more favorable environment, we would still be bound to make the effort. . . . Individuals do differ greatly in their capacities, and each must be enabled to develop the talent that is in him [her]. We believe that every person should be enabled to achieve the best that is in him [her], and we are the declared enemies of all conditions, such as disease, ignorance or poverty, which stunt the individual and prevent such fulfillment.

John W. Gardner

School Desegregation	Civil Rights Movement	Campus Rebellion
1954 *Brown* case	1960s Martin Luther King, Jr.	1961–1968 Kennedy-Johnson legislation
1957 *Sputnik* issue	1961 John Gardner's *Can We Be Equal and* *Excellent Too?*	1966 Coleman Report
Criticisms of Arthur Bestor, James Conant, and Hyman Rickover	1963 Michael Harrington's *The Other America*	1978–2000s Affirmative Action Institutional Racism School as an Agency of Social Change Revisited

Figure 10.1   Time Line of Issues in Modern American Education

Anything that has already happened is history even if it happened only a moment ago. Making a good historical analysis of events just past is often more difficult than making one for those that occurred in an earlier period. Recent occurrences in social foundations and educational history are often surrounded by controversy. Very few modern events are free from criticism, and even the educational community often finds itself taking sides. Political groups get involved quite often in current educational concerns, and public opinion plays a vital role in numerous decisions. Although it was once rare for problems over the schools to result in litigation, it is now very common. Books that are critical of many aspects of education now become best-sellers while past critics wrote for much smaller audiences. Because education touches all of the American people and because the means of communication are expanding so rapidly, the current history of education is very much the history of controversial issues.

Chapter 2 included various positions in the philosophy of education. Philosophy is seldom universally accepted, so conflicting ideas and contradictory views are common. Pragmatists and idealists did not agree in the early twentieth century, and they do not agree today. The same can be said for schools of psychology like Gestalt and behaviorism. The fight over the legal status of private schools that led to the Oregon case of 1925 provides background for the issue of tax support to parochial schools and the legality of tuition tax credits for nonpublic education. The Oregon case occurred when there was bitter public reaction against parochial schools, which had existed in the United States for many years. Discrimination has been expressed in many ways, and direct efforts have been made to outlaw paro-

Equal Opportunity	Accountability	Return to Basics
1968 Issues over bilingual and multicultural education; accountability tests; compensatory education for the disadvantaged	1970 Charles Reich's *The Greening of America* Ivan Illich's *Deschooling Society*	1980s National critical reports, *A Nation at Risk, Action for Excellence, Making the Grade* 2000s Search for Civility, Comity, Consensus
1969 Arthur Jensen studied IQ and race	1973 Only 2,500 black doctorates in all fields	2001 No Child Left Behind Closing the educational achievement gap
1969 Theodore Roszak's *The Making of a Counterculture*	1979 John Goodlad's *What Are Schools For?*	2004 *Elkgrove v. Newdow*

chial schools. In 1925, the Oregon legislature passed a law that required all children to attend public schools through the eighth grade. The Society of Sisters of the Holy Names of Jesus and Mary and the Hill Academy brought suit against Governor Pierce in an effort to keep their schools. Although the state supreme court upheld the state law, the Supreme Court of the United States declared the action unconstitutional. It held that the state has a right to inspect and regulate private and parochial schools, but that the state does not have a monopoly on education. The Oregon case ruling has been unchallenged.

Issues involving the purposes or goals of education concern both the layperson and the professional educator in a democratic society. This kind of problem is the subject of philosophy of education, but it also involves values, norms, and attitudes that can be understood through sociology, economics, history, social psychology, and political science. Although various groups such as realists and pragmatists have clear-cut educational goals, the educational philosophy of the whole American people is not fixed and certain. In a fluid culture, the aims of education in one period of time are often altered considerably by the next generation.

The role of the teacher and that of the profession in addressing a problem or an issue concerning schools often consists of communication and clarification. The public may be unaware of the existence of problems, or there may be a misunderstanding of the exact nature of those problems. Difficulties concerning poverty, crime, taxation, employment, equal rights, academic freedom, racial integration, discipline, and so forth often have educational significance that is not clear to the casual observer. Arkansas became the first state in the nation to require yearly body mass index or BMI screening for all 450,000 public school students in an effort to deal with child obesity. Parents and students are encouraged to engage in healthy eating and exercise programs. School programs for healthy lifestyles are expanding. Explaining what the issues really mean and outlining possible consequences of various plans of action must often fall to educators. Analysis and clarification of hidden issues or underlying problems must often be undertaken before a solution can be reached. Obviously, past experience including knowledge of history can provide clues to the probable success or failure of alternatives.

A number of approaches can be taken to the history and understanding of current issues and challenges in American education. This chapter focuses on a number of well-known educational conflicts that have reached the courts. Litigation has always been important for educational policy, as in the Dartmouth College case of 1819 and the Kalamazoo high school decision of 1874. In contemporary society, many cases handled by the state and federal courts are vital to understanding recent educational history. Although each case is decided on its own merits, recent state and federal court education cases appear to reflect a trend toward conservatism, although President Obama's appointees may move the court to judicial activism. Current rulings give educators more support in creating and maintaining a safe school environment, controlling disruptive or threatening student behavior, and maintaining a proper learning environment. Many school districts have a zero tolerance policy for student misbehavior, especially for drug abuse. Earlier chapters examined the ideas of well-known philosophers, psychologists, and public officials who influenced education. This chapter deals with important modern educational critics and spokespersons for major organizations. Critics often serve as guides to significant educational problems. This chapter also focuses on a number of current educational issues for which educational institutions and teachers are accountable.

LITIGATION: THE COURTS AND PROBLEMS OF EDUCATION

Religion and Public Schools. Religion was the major subject in colonial schools, but with the separation of church and state, public schools could teach only interdenominational or nonsectarian religious principles. Still, the curriculum remained heavily influenced by religious writings, prayer, and Christian morality. Bible reading was considered nonsectarian in most communities. That a Protestant Bible was not acceptable to Catholics carried little weight, and Jews were also discriminated against in school programs. Before the twentieth century, minority groups often chose not to make an issue of religion in the public schools. If Catholic, Jewish, or other minority religious groups were unable to support their own schools, they normally accepted the rules of the public schools even when the requirements went counter to their own beliefs.

In the past few years, however, there have been a great number of court cases over the religious requirements or practices in public schools. Although the majority of the cases have decided against the inclusion of religious practices, a large number of Americans have felt that the schools are responsible for moral training that could hardly be given without reference to religion. Religious liberals and nonbelievers have attacked the practice of beginning the school day with prayer, and Jehovah's Witnesses have claimed that saluting the flag constitutes worship of a "graven image." There is no clear-cut division between patriotic and religious exercises; even the Pledge of Allegiance has contained the words "under God" since 1954.

FOCUS ON THE ISSUES

Church and State

The population of what is now the Republic of Ireland is overwhelmingly Roman Catholic. Because Catholic Ireland sided with Catholic English kings and lost wars first with Oliver Cromwell and later with William of Orange, it became subject to British rule. For more than a century, British overlords imposed unpopular restrictions upon the Irish people. Among the most odious was the requirement to support the Anglican Church. If an Irish farmer failed to pay the tithe to the local Church of England curate, the fee would be added to his land rent and he could be evicted if in arrears. Further laws prevented Catholics from attending colleges, entering the professions, owning land, voting, holding public office, or possessing a horse worth more than five pounds. The animosity so created was bitter and it is understandable that an independent Ireland refused to aid the British in World War II. Irish history furnishes an example of the kind of church–state relationship against which many of the American founding fathers rebelled. Jefferson and Madison were especially outspoken in their opposition to tax support for organized religion and demanded the adoption of the Bill of Rights before they would support ratification of the Constitution. The First Amendment requirement that no law shall be made for the establishment of religion or prohibiting its free exercise is one of the foundation stones of our nation.

Although no serious effort has ever been made to repeal the separation of church and state, many current educational issues involve religion. Prayer in public schools, keeping "under God" in the Pledge of Allegiance, censorship of curriculum materials, and the teaching of creationism are examples. Even more important is the question of using tax money for the support of church-related schools. The courts have long held that parochial schools could receive tax support only under the child benefit theory for services such as busing. Today, however, with strong support for parental control, tax money may be channeled to charter schools that have church connections. This process will continue to be subject to litigation. Further arguments related to religion and the schools can surely be expected.

What Do You Think?

1. How many religions are represented in our schools?
2. Might you have Catholics, Protestants, Jews, Buddhists, Islamics, nonbelievers, and others in the same classroom? How can a teacher avoid a conflict of interests, especially at the Christmas season?
3. Give examples of religious objections to the school curriculum from parents or students.
4. Many universities including the University of Arkansas have spirituality in the workplace programs. Identify how this may apply to issues like institutional racism, affirmative action, equality of opportunity, and school as an agency of social action. Use Internet searches for your responses.

On June 14, 2004, the U.S. Supreme Court overturned a 9th U.S. Circuit Court of Appeals ruling that found "under God" in the Pledge of Allegiance, when recited by public school students, violated the constitutional separation of church and state. The Supreme Court in *Elk Grove Unified School District v. Newdow* declined to decide the constitutional issue because the noncustodial father, Newdow, did not have legal standing to bring the suit on behalf of his daughter. The "under God" issue may be revisited in the future. Chaplains have been assigned to military units and "In God We Trust" has been stamped on coins. The major educational problem, however, concerns Christian Christmas programs, religious exercises, and the reading of Scripture as part of the public school program.

"For Goodness' Sake: Why So Many Want Religion to Play a Greater Role in American Life" (2001), a report of the Public Agenda Research Studies, found a majority of Americans believe religion has a place in the public schools, but tend to support a moment of silent prayer over nondenominational or overtly Christian prayers. The report finds most Americans are reluctant to isolate students whose faiths are different.

Attendance and Religion.   The issue of religion's role in education is centered on two quite controversial issues: the promotion of religious instruction in public schools and the use of public tax money to aid nonpublic schools. In 1919, Nebraska passed a law prohibiting private or parochial schools from teaching any subject in any language other than English. However, four years later, in *Meyer v. Nebraska*, the Supreme Court ruled that law unconstitutional. Although holding that the state can require attendance at some school, the Supreme Court stated that parents could send their children to private schools at which some subjects need not be taught in English. This was a landmark case concerning both religion and the language of instruction.

Two years later, the Supreme Court reinforced in *Pierce v. Society of Sisters* the right of parents to choose nonpublic schools. This case made unconstitutional a 1922 Oregon law that required all children between the ages of 8 and 16 to attend public schools. There has been no effort to outlaw private or parochial schools since 1925, and the *Pierce* doctrine remains in force.

The right of a student to be protected from rules that violate his or her religious freedom was at issue in the *Gobitis* case of 1938. The family objected to the school requirement of the Pledge of Allegiance as Jehovah's Witnesses. The court upheld the school board at first, but in 1943 reversed its position in *West Virginia State Board of Education v. Barnett*. Religious freedom thereafter became a valid reason for children to be excused from school activities that violate their religious freedom.

In 1947, approximately two million public school students were released to attend religious classes during some part of the school week. In *McCollum v. Board of Education of Champaign, Illinois*, in 1948, the Supreme Court held that releasing students to attend religious classes held in public school buildings was illegal. A later case in New York ended with a ruling that released time does not violate separation of church and state if religious classes are held outside the schools. Lawsuits have sometimes resulted in changing educational practices, as in the New York Regents' prayer case of 1962. Using the coercive power of the school to make children participate in religious activities has been held to violate the First Amendment. In the 1972 case of *Wisconsin v. Yoder*, the compulsory attendance law of the state was set aside to protect the free exercise of parents' religious views. The 2000 and 2004 36th Phi Delta Kappa/Gallup Poll found 52 to 54 percent of respondents oppose allowing parents to choose a private school for their child to attend at public expense. The 2010 Phi Delta Kappa/Gallup Poll found 68 percent of respondents support charters schools across several demographics including age, political affiliation, level of education, and even among public school parents (Bushaw & Lopez, 2010).

Uddin (2010) reports on a New York City controversy over Moslem request to close schools for holy days, Eid Ul-Adha and Eid Ul-Fitr, occurring at the end to the pilgrimage to Mecca and the end to Ramadan. The Moslem school population is over 100,000 or 12 percent of the New York City school population. Jewish holidays were allowed in the 1960s because 33 percent of the school population was Jewish. Mayor Blumberg fears that if too many groups claim religious holidays, student achievement levels would suffer.

Religion and Public Funding.   In the 1950s, the NEA and the American Association of School Administrators adopted resolutions opposing all efforts to use public funds for nonpublic education. NEA 2000–2001 resolutions reaffirmed the belief that voucher plans, tuition tax credits, or other funding arrangements to subsidize pre-K through 12 private school education can undermine public education. The NEA finds that federally or state-mandated parental option or choice plans compromise a commitment to free, equitable, universal, and quality education for every student. These positions were reaffirmed in 2010. Federal legislation provided school lunches for parochial schools in 1948, and the government allowed GI Bill and NDEA funds to be used for scholarships to nonpublic schools. The National Science Foundation made grants to private universities, and the Higher Education Act of 1965 gave money to church-related colleges for nonreligious purposes. Private schools also got libraries and instructional materials under the Elementary and Secondary Education Act of 1965.

In the *Cochran* case of 1930, the Supreme Court held that although direct aid to private and parochial schools was illegal, the state could use public funds to pay for transportation, lunches, textbooks, and health services that were of benefit to all children. This "child benefit" theory was also the basis in the *Everson* case for the use of taxes to pay for the transportation of students to Catholic schools. Recently, computer and technical equipment have been provided under the child benefit theory. *Everson* upheld *Cochran*; however, the Supreme Court was split, and the issue has not cooled.

Many advocates of the public schools fear that any aid to private and parochial schools will weaken public education. They illustrate the difficulty Americans had in obtaining tax support for public schools in the era of Horace Mann, and quote Thomas Jefferson on the necessity of keeping religion segregated from government. Several states now prohibit the use of tax money for any kind of aid to parochial schools, whether for child benefit or not. This issue is also tied to the question of tuition tax credits for parents who choose to send their children to private schools and for federal aid to nonpublic education.

Although Bible reading, nonsectarian prayers, and released time for religious instruction are illegal in public schools, the issue is not resolved. There is considerable pressure to "restore religion" to the public classroom. The conservative and liberal themes of religion and secularism will continue to be part of our nation's democratic dialogue in the future. The two appointments to the Supreme Court by Obama may result in more liberal future decisions on religious issues.

Some conservatives favor banning books that they feel do not support their definition of good child behavior. Because members of this group often send their children to private schools, they support vouchers or the deduction of tuition from income tax returns, as provided by law in Minnesota. Other states including Florida are currently proposing expanding the use of vouchers, although California and Michigan have defeated voucher proposals. Lower courts in Florida have ruled vouchers unconstitutional, and the state Supreme Court the reinforced lower courts by ruling vouchers unconstitutional in 2005. However, some 30,000 special needs and low-income poverty students continue to use vouchers in Florida. Governor Rick Scott has proposed expanding school voucher programs. Religious and other conservatives often oppose what they call "secular humanism"; they believe secular humanism has corrupted educational practices and the whole culture, and have formed parents' groups to rid the schools of "humanist" books. Well organized and well funded, the religious conservatives have taken their efforts into the courts and put great pressure on Congress to "restore prayer" to the public schools, with limited success.

It is important to note that the "moral majority" and the Christian Coalition are not monolithic organizations. Conservative Christians hold a variety of views. In "Christian Right Falls out of Unison on School Prayer," Felsenthal (1997) finds a diversity of opinions on the subject, with some believing religion is best left to the home and church. As the population grows more diverse, many other religions, such as the Moslem and Hindu faiths, are expanding their membership.

Evolution.   In *Epperson v. Arkansas* (1968), the court ruled that an antievolution statute is unconstitutional because evolution is a science rather than a secular religion, and students cannot be restricted from such information. Thirteen years later, on March 19, 1981, Governor Frank White signed the Arkansas Legislative Act 590, or The Balanced Treatment for Creation Science and Evolution Science Act, into law. In *McLean v. Arkansas Board of Education* (1982), a federal court ruled the act unconstitutional on the grounds that it had been passed to advance religion, that it had as a major effect the advancement of particular religious beliefs, and that it created for the state of Arkansas excessive and prohibited entanglement with religion. In *Edwards v. Aguillard* (1987), a Louisiana statute was rejected on similar grounds. The court ruled that giving equal time to creation science (intelligent design) and evolution was designed to discredit scientific knowledge and to prevent educators from disseminating such information, in violation of the First Amendment establishment clause. Several school districts, including Georgia, Kansas, and Pennsylvania, have recently moved to give equal time to "intelligent design" and evolution. The debate continues unabated and pro and con forces engage in political activism.

Control of the school curriculum through the selection or rejection of materials is an activity in which many groups are now engaged. Conservative groups putting pressure on school systems to reject certain textbooks include the Liberty Foundation, the Stop Textbook Censorship Committee, and the Educational Research Analysis. The last organization, headed by Mel and Norma Gabler, has had much visibility and influence.

On the liberal side are the American Civil Liberties Union, the Council for Democratic and Secular Humanism, People for the American Way, and the National Association for the Advancement of Colored People; in general, these groups support academic freedom and reject censorship. In addition, the National Organization for Women has recently become active in gender issues in textbooks.

Conservative and liberal groups have influenced textbook and curriculum content throughout our educational history. In the 1960s, the Supreme Court barred state-sanctioned prayer and Bible reading in public schools, in support of Jefferson's separation of church and state. The Supreme Court was silent on such issues for nearly two decades but indicated a new willingness to address First Amendment issues in the 1980s.

Lemon v. Kurtzman (1971) found that governmental enactments must have a secular purpose, the effects of which neither advance nor prohibit religion and do not involve excessive entanglement with religion. The *Lemon* test may be challenged in the future. In *Bown v. Gwinnett* (1995), federal courts upheld a Georgia legislative act allowing for a moment of quiet reflection in schools, as long as it is not over 60 seconds and is not intended as a religious exercise.

In 1984, President Reagan signed into law the Equal Access Act, which made it illegal to deny access to students who wish to conduct a meeting on the basis of religious, political, philosophical, or other contents of speech at such meetings. The Supreme Court in *Lamb's Chapel v. Center Moriches Union Free School District* (1993) ruled that if schools provide school facilities for some uses permitted by state law, religious groups must have the same access to these facilities.

On February 28, 2001, the U.S. Supreme Court heard a case, *Good News Club v. Milford Central School*, that denied use of school facilities to a religious youth group. The high court ruled on June 11, 2001, that school districts may not discriminate against religious groups who wish to use school facilities while secular groups can use such facilities. The court ruled that the **O** Milford School District violated the free-speech rights of the Good News Club. In *Christian Legal Society v. Martinez* (June 28, 2010), the Supreme Court in a 5-4 decision ruled that a public college does not violate the First Amendment by refusing to officially recognize a student organization unless it allows all students to join the group, even if that "all comers" policy requires a religious organization to admit gay students who do not adhere to the group's core beliefs.

Vouchers.   The voucher system is a plan for financing schools with tax money but with parents in control of that money. A voucher is a certificate issued to parents. The parents give the voucher to a school of their choice, and the school exchanges the voucher for payment by the government. The system was studied at Harvard University in the 1960s. Voucher plans were tried in the South after 1954 as a means of supporting segregated schools but were found unconstitutional. Some states have attempted to use a voucher system for supporting parochial schools, and cases are still pending on their legal status. Modern proposals for voucher plans guard against racial discrimination and the use of taxes to supplement tuition at expensive private schools.

Proponents argue that parents should have a choice as to which schools their children attend. They say the schools would become more competitive and establish many alternatives in curriculum and methods. They point out that without the voucher system only those wealthy enough to pay tuition can select schools for their children; the poor must accept whatever the local public schools offer. Properly regulated, a voucher system could bring innovation and reform to schools and give parents much more control over the education of their children. These arguments are especially strong in California, where a large segment of the population is supporting a law requiring that the state adopt the voucher system. Although the California and Michigan voters defeated voucher proposals in 2000, efforts to expand school choice continue. The Florida voucher system was recently ruled unconstitutional by the state supreme court, although special needs and low-income students continue to use vouchers.

Although research reports differ on the effectiveness of voucher programs, Jay P. Greene, senior fellow at the Manhattan Institute for Policy Research, in a 2001 report entitled "An Evaluation of the Florida A-Plus Accountability and School Choice Program," noted that the performance of students on academic tests improves when public schools are faced with the prospect that their students will receive vouchers. The Florida plan provides for students to choose a different public or private school if their school receives two failing grades on state standards during a 4-year period.

Bowman (2001) notes that national teachers' unions and a number of congressional Democrats helped defeat citizen initiative voucher plans in California and Michigan. Supreme Court cases *Simmons-Harris v. Zelman* (2000) and *Hibbs v. Winn* (2004) both addressed voucher issues. Vouchers will continue to be subject to litigation in the future.

Involuntary Segregation.   Involuntary segregation refers to excluding certain children from schools, usually on the basis of race. The problem of segregation is clearly linked to the period following the American Civil War and to the freeing of the slaves. Public schools for blacks and whites established during the period of Reconstruction in the South were quickly eliminated in the 1880s. Thereafter, southern states required that schools could not admit children from both races to the same classes, and segregation began.

Northern states did not usually have laws prohibiting racially integrated schools, but many northern schools were segregated because of population patterns. White students did not attend schools with a majority of black pupils until after the *Brown* case. Many schools in northern cities were all black or all white according to their location and the demography of the area. As Jonathan Kozol (2005, 2010) points out, Bronx, New York, and other communities continue to have segregated pockets of racial poverty and crime.

The prospect for social equality in the South at the time was so dubious that Booker T. Washington (1858–1915) thought blacks should accept segregation in return for some access to education. The *Plessy v. Ferguson* case of 1896 affirmed the principle that separate but equal facilities were legal. In 1906, W. E. B. Du Bois started the Niagara movement, which led to the 1909 organization of the National Association for the Advancement of Colored People (NAACP). In the 1930s, the NAACP began to challenge segregation laws on the grounds that facilities provided to black students were not even remotely equal to those of whites.

While not attacking the segregation laws on principle, the Supreme Court began to require admission of black students to southern professional schools, unless the states could prove that they had equal facilities for blacks within their borders. Finally in 1950, a direct challenge to segregated education was presented to the Court in *Sweatt v. Painter*. In this case, an applicant who had been denied admission to the University of Texas Law School solely on the basis of color claimed that the instruction available in the newly established state law school for blacks was markedly inferior to the instruction at the university; thus, equal protection of the law was denied. In a unanimous decision, the Supreme Court ordered the student's admission to the white school, indicating that it was virtually impossible in practice, at least in professional education, for a state to comply with the separate-but-equal formula.

The Brown *Decision on Segregation.* Following the decision in the *Sweatt* case, the NAACP and other organizations advanced the fight against segregation in public schools. This pressure resulted in several public school segregation cases. The Court proceeded with a great deal of circumspection and required an unusual amount of investigation by the counsels. Their deliberation was understandable; if segregation in public schools was determined to be a denial of equal protection of laws, it would in all likelihood be impossible to defend segregation in other sectors of public life. The legal foundation of the social structure of a great part of the nation was under attack. By 1954, it had become obvious to the public that black children in segregated states received a much poorer schooling than white students. In 1952, for example, Arkansas spent $102 for the education of each white child compared with $67 for each black child. Black colleges were often substandard, and few jobs were open to black students who had graduated from northern universities. Integration in the armed forces after World War II and the success of blacks who sued for entry into southern universities led to the Supreme Court decision of 1954, *Brown v. Board of Education.*

In this famous case, NAACP lawyer Thurgood Marshall argued that equality of educational facilities was not the question. Marshall claimed that prestige, teaching standards, the academic surroundings, and the inference of inferiority were important in educational equality. The Court agreed, saying that segregation was construed to deprive minority group children of equal educational opportunity. By its decision, the Supreme Court held that all laws concerning or permitting school seg-regation were in conflict with the Fourteenth Amendment and ordered involuntary segregation to cease within a "reasonable time." Several major cities like Baltimore, Washington, DC, and St. Louis made a complete transition to integrated schools on the basis of the 1954 decision.

This decision met with much opposition, especially in the South, as did most decisions involving integration. One of the frequent arguments against forced inte-gration is illustrated by an *American Bar Association Journal* article. Eugene Cook, attorney general of Georgia, and William J. Potter (1956) severely criticized the *Brown* decision. The opinion of the Court, said these critics, "did not hold that the old 'separate but equal' doctrine, laid down in *Plessy v. Ferguson*, was a bad law. It held that it was bad sociology."

Considerable progress toward desegregation was made in border states, but in the Deep South various measures designed to frustrate desegregation were tried. Boycotting or nonsupport of integrated schools, student assignment plans to mini-mize integration, and the temporary abolition of public schools, as in Prince Edward County, Virginia, took place. Integration of the teaching staff and token integration through bringing in a few minority-group students to all-white schools were com-mon attempts to meet legal requirements without basic change. Private academies were established in parts of the South in an effort to escape court-ordered integra-tion, especially in areas where black people were in the majority. The Supreme Court in *Brown v. Board of Education* (1955) ordered school integration with all deliberate speed.

De Facto *Segregation*.   A serious problem in many areas has been *de facto* segregation, or segregation based upon school district boundaries that encompass children from only one race. The problem of *de facto* segregation is by no means confined to the South; blacks, Mexican Americans, and other minority groups have been forced to live (often for economic reasons) in a single part or section of most cities. Racial boundaries tend to move rapidly so that schools that are planned to serve students from different races or ethnic backgrounds often end up being built in areas where only one race is present. Often some sort of educational park, cluster of school buildings, or central administration assignment of students has been used as an instrument for integration.

Heavy opposition to such efforts is often encountered. Many parents object to having their elementary school children attend schools other than those in their own neighborhoods or within walking distance of their homes. Some fear that inte-gration will have a negative effect on children, such as introducing them to foul language, crime, and drugs. Many school districts have experienced a loss of enroll-ment as a result of court-ordered desegregation plans. Parents move their families into suburban areas in order to avoid what they believe to be unfortunate aspects of school integration. Perhaps the greatest opposition has occurred when cities have attempted to solve the integration problem by busing students from one school to another in order to achieve some degree of racial balance. Los Angeles and Orlando, among other cities, now have a majority–minority population. Latinos and blacks are in the majority of formerly minority populations. However, these populations are not monolithic and have notable differences within them. A major problem for education has been the mandate given to schools to foster integration while the general public in many communities was unwilling to cooperate. Nevertheless, research indicates that whenever black, Hispanic, and white students can be placed together in positive and meaningful educational experiences at an early age, racial tension is reduced and human relations are improved.

Delays and circumventions in desegregation have not been confined to public schools. The attempt of Authurine Lucy to enter the University of Alabama in 1956 and the violence created by James Meredith's admission to the University of Mississippi in 1962 are illustrative of the problems of integration in higher education. Nevertheless, colleges and universities have been racially integrated with much less conflict than in public schools.

As the black movement for freedom and integration reached revolutionary levels, plans for school integration were set into motion throughout the United States. Some plans found general acceptance, but most efforts to move large numbers of children from one area of a city to another for integration of schools were bitterly opposed. With the passage of the Civil Rights Act in 1964 and the assassination of Martin Luther King, Jr., in 1968, desegregation entered a new phase. The Civil Rights Act specified that no person could be discriminated against on the basis of race, color, sex, or national origin in any program that received federal assistance. This meant that federal funding could be withheld from school districts or states that failed to adopt reasonable and acceptable plans for integration.

Some of the southern school districts with the greatest need for financial help have been the least willing to integrate. Plans involving the mass busing of children have drawn fire from parents, politicians, and the public. Federal courts and the Department of Health, Education, and Welfare have insisted upon prompt compliance with the law, but the struggle goes on in many communities. School buses were attacked and burned in Michigan. Riots over busing black students to South Boston High School in 1974 caused the closing of the school. Many state legislatures have issued laws against busing for racial balance, and Congress has come close to considering such a law. Meanwhile, schools attempt to follow legal guidelines and carry on the task of public education as best they can.

Although the Supreme Court has continued to uphold the *Brown* decision, militant resistance to busing has not died out, and many school districts still reflect segregation. Sometimes this situation occurs when the population of a city changes dramatically, as in the case of Newark, New Jersey, or Bronx, New York. The Court has held that school boards may not intentionally gerrymander a school district to encourage segregation (*Keyes v. Denver,* 1973), but some American cities are entirely white or black. In *Milliken v. Bradley* (1974), the Supreme Court reversed the lower federal court ruling, which said Detroit should adopt a metropolitan desegregation plan to include its suburbs. However, the Court in 1977 refused to review the decision of Judge Garrity in *Morgan v. Hennigan.* The Court let stand the placing of the school system in federal receivership because the Boston school board had intentionally increased segregation. Numerous other cases are still pending, and the

mood of the nation seems to be swinging away from support for court-ordered busing plans. Los Angeles was allowed to discontinue busing for racial integration in
1981. Nevertheless, desegregation reflects the multiracial society, and America will
not return to conditions that existed before 1954.

Affirmative Action.   Following close upon the efforts to end involuntary segregation came attempts to make college education and jobs accessible to a larger
number of disadvantaged minorities and to women. Affirmative action plans were established to recruit minority faculty and students in institutions of higher education.
Federal guidelines intended to increase minority enrollment led some institutions to
establish 10 percent minority quotas, allowing lower aptitude scores from minorities
to offset culturally biased tests.

Opposition to affirmative action appeared in 1972 from the Committee on Academic Nondiscrimination and Integrity, charging that policies favoring minority and
female candidates over others who were better qualified hurt professional performance. Although recognizing the evils of past discrimination, it objected to prefer-
ential minority admission standards.

In 1978, the Supreme Court agreed to hear *Regents of the University of California v. Bakke.* Bakke contended that the minority quota at Davis medical campus
had caused him to be rejected, although his scores were higher than those of the
admitted minority candidates. The Court ordered that Bakke be admitted on the
basis that his Fourteenth Amendment rights had been violated. However, it also
stated that race and background factors may be considered by institutions making
admissions decisions.

On June 24, 2003, the Supreme Court ruled on two University of Michigan
reverse discrimination cases. The Court upheld affirmative action and found race
could be a factor in admissions, if narrowly tailored to achieve diversity, and a com-
pelling state interest existed in the law school (*Grutter v. Bolinger*, 2003). The Court
found in *Gratz v. Bolinger* (2003) that the undergraduate admissions policy was too
mechanical and ordered a more individualized admissions policy. Justice O'Connor,
writing for the majority, noted that the Court was influenced by a massive outpour-
ing of support for affirmative action and opined that with an increasingly diverse
society, affirmative action might not be required in another 25 years.

Alexander and Alexander (2001) note the courts continue to use narrow focus
and strict scrutiny with diversity and race-based policies The Supreme Court in *Parents Involved in Community Schools v. Seattle School District No 1* (2000) in a 5-4
decision ruled that public schools may not use racial balance as a sole factor in
assigning students to schools. Race-conscious objectives to achieve diversity in
schools may be acceptable.

Litigation and Equality of Opportunity.   Although a growing part of the
educational budget for most school districts is federally funded, American school
support is largely state and local. Traditionally, the federal government has had no
role in school finance except where federal funds were involved. This changed
dramatically when using the Fourteenth Amendment equal protection guarantee.

The California Supreme Court ruled, in *Serrano v. Priest* (1971), that the state's system of financing public schools was discriminatory. The argument was that the quality of education provided was a function of school district wealth and therefore discriminated against poor children. Following *Serrano*, more than 50 suits in 30 states were filed, and many states had their local property tax systems struck down. Disparities among school districts' tax bases within states will continue to be litigated in the future.

Serrano v. Priest might have had more impact if the Supreme Court had taken a different stand in *San Antonio Independent School District v. Rodriguez* (1973). A Texas federal district court had ruled the Texas system of local property taxation illegal, as in the *Serrano* case. In 1973, the Supreme Court in a 5-4 decision reversed the district court decision and held that the system in Texas did not absolutely deprive poor people of education, nor did it discriminate against any definable category of the "poor." In spite of this support for the property tax, attention was brought to the inequality of educational opportunity within the states. Recent state and federal court rulings require equity provisions for financially burdened school districts. A Texas Supreme Court decision (*Edgewood v. Kirby*, 1989) required the state legislature to correct inequities in funding between financially burdened and affluent school districts. A Kentucky Supreme Court decision upheld a lower court (*Rose v. Council for Better Education*, 1988) that the state had failed to provide an efficient system of common schools, leading to the Kentucky Educational Reform Act of 1990, which provided for equity in taxation to ensure a guaranteed minimum level of financial support per pupil for all school districts. In a democratic society, it is hard to justify unequal financial support for education; thus, new laws have been proposed and others probably will be.

Changing educational practices and student characteristics have influenced modern litigation—for example, drug searches of students' persons or property by school officials. The Supreme Court held (*New Jersey v. T.L.O.*, 1985) that the Fourth Amendment applies to searches conducted by public school officials. However, school officials need not obtain warrants nor show probable cause before searching a student. The validity of a school search depends on its reasonableness under the circumstances. The Fourteenth Amendment clause pertaining to equal protection under the law also applies to the rights of students. Older practices of expelling students from school because they marry, are pregnant, or commit a crime are no longer legal, except recent federal court decisions are giving school authorities more power over student behavior. Zero tolerance policies, although being modified in many school districts, continue to be implemented to eliminate or reduce school violence. Federal courts support educators in maintaining an environment conducive to learning and rediscovering *in loco parentis* (the teacher and administrator stand in parental relationship to the student), although provision is made for students' civil rights.

Following the demand for accountability, schools were tested on the legality of new requirements for students. Some cases had to do with whether a diploma could be withheld from a student who had passed required courses but who was below par in performance. In *Debra v. Turlington* (1983), the Court ruled that functional

FOCUS ON THE ISSUES

Language

A little mouse was told that a great enemy of all mice exists in the world and that it may be identified by the sound it makes, which is "meyow." Listening, the mouse heard "meyow, meyow" and stayed safely inside. Later the mouse heard a sound that was "bow wow, bow wow." It said to itself, "Nothing was said about 'bow wow,' so that must be all right." The mouse went out and at once was pounced upon by a cat. The cat said, "There really is an advantage to being bilingual."

A silly story perhaps, but there is a lesson in it for all who plan to teach. English is the dominant language in the United States, and immigrants are expected to learn it if they are to succeed. Successive waves of foreigners from many non-English-speaking regions settled in America and mastered the native language. Only recently has the influx of Hispanics been so great that large areas of the nation, especially in California, Florida, and Texas, have become bilingual. Today, new citizens from Asian countries bring foreign languages to even geographically isolated American cities.

We are all familiar with problems children from non-English-speaking families have with school if instruction is provided only in English, which is the reason for bilingual programs throughout the nation. A greater issue is the lack of foreign language study in the American school curriculum. A great many Americans speak only English. Most secondary schools do not produce graduates fluent in any foreign language, although they may have classes in other languages for a year or two. Few other nations have a population limited to a single tongue. Certainly this needs to change as the global economy continues to require interaction with non-English speakers. The Chinese economy is rapidly growing and one-fifth of the world's population is Chinese. Few American students speak or study Chinese, but most students in China study English. Obviously, this puts us at a disadvantage in the global marketplace.

What Do You Think?
1. If all American schools require foreign language instruction, what in the curriculum might be reduced in order to provide the time for such study?
2. What proportion of American students come from families where a language other than English is spoken? Can we teach them English and also preserve their native tongue?
3. If you do not speak Spanish, how might you prepare to teach in a Latino school?
4. Identify ways in which we can address discrimination and prejudice against those with different language and culture.

literacy tests may be required as a prerequisite for a high school diploma, but the tests must be a valid measure of instruction. The Court also prevented statewide use of tests in Florida, until the state showed that discrepancies in passing rates of white and black students were not because of educational deprivations suffered by blacks before integration. In *Debra v. Turlington* (1984), Florida's high school exit exams were upheld, and by 1996 at least 16 states required students to pass competency tests in order to receive diplomas. Exit tests for graduation are becoming more common throughout the country as increased attention is paid to standards.

Other Significant Court Cases.   Although the most important influence of the courts has been directed toward desegregation, religion, and equality, there have

FOCUS ON THE ISSUES

Free Speech

A very small church based in Kansas has taken the position that all homosexual activity is the work of the devil and that all gays will go to hell. This is not unusual for conservative Christian congregations but this particular church has organized protests that seem to target individuals and groups that have nothing to do with the issue. In 2009, they staged a protest against gays and lesbians at the public high school in Moore, Oklahoma. Moore is a conservative city in a conservative region and certainly not a place where gay rights are advocated. The church in question then began to attack the military forces of the United States because of the policy that allows homosexuals to serve. The attacks did not focus on the "don't ask, don't tell" position of military or political leaders, but targeted funerals for soldiers killed in Afghanistan or Iraq. Church members carrying huge offensive signs appeared on the sidewalks across from religious institutions where the funeral for fallen heroes were taking place. These protests were disruptive to the services and those attending were upset. The general public was shocked and appalled. One father brought suit against the protesters and was successful in the lower courts, but an appeal was made to the Supreme Court on the basis of freedom of speech.

This illustrates a major problem with the structure of democratic institutions in modern society. The vast majority of Americans believe that the consternation caused by the funeral protests is not right and they should be stopped. The Constitution, however, is very strict about any limitation of freedom of expression. To falsely shout "Fire" in a crowded theater may not be protected but few other restrictions apply. The Supreme Court has the very difficult job of interpreting the law of the land when public opinion is opposed or divided. Certainly the people are not in agreement of issues like the death penalty or abortion. Educational history is full of examples such as litigation over racial integration of schools or Bible reading in the classroom. We must anticipate future court cases applying to education that will be greeted by some with joy and others with dismay.

What Do You Think?
1. Can the Supreme Court make decisions that are popular and also true to the law of the land?
2. Is there a way for public opinion to change the behavior of a radical minority outside of governmental or court action?
3. How can educators work to create an environment conducive to civility, compassion, and justice in communities with closed belief systems?

been several other areas of educational importance. A common practice in many American cities was testing children and then placing them in a fixed curriculum according to the ability group into which they fell. This practice, called "tracking," was found unconstitutional in *Hobson v. Hansen* (1967). The tracking system tended to promote segregation within schools, making it impossible for students to leave the assigned track.

Free speech, privacy, and due process under the law have been extended to children. In 1971, students in Columbus, Ohio, who were suspended for 10 days from school without a hearing, brought suit. In *Goss v. Lopez*, the Court held that high school students must be granted due process, including notice of the charges against them, and an opportunity must be provided for them to present their side of the story. Similar cases have protected children suspended for wearing long hair or violating school dress codes. The Family Educational Rights and Privacy Act of 1974 (also called the Buckley Amendment) requires schools to provide students over the age of 18 and parents of minors access to records. Quaker students in the Des Moines public schools were suspended for wearing black armbands to protest the Vietnam War (*Tinker v. Des Moines*, 1969). Modern courts have been active in matters concerning loyalty oaths, violations of civil liberties, and academic freedom. As a general rule, schools are prohibited from making any rule or regulation that impinges upon rights that students would enjoy if they were adults.

With large numbers of alien children entering the schools, especially along the Mexican border, litigation has emerged. In *Doe v. Plyler* (1978), a school district's policy excluding alien children was struck down. The Fifth Circuit Court of Appeals upheld the decision in 1980. In 1982, the Supreme Court permanently enjoined Texas from excluding undocumented alien children from tuition-free public schools, ruling all children must be served, whether or not they hold citizenship. Arizona, California, and other states are seeking to exclude illegal aliens from schools and medical care. Congressional legislation to limit public services for legal and illegal aliens is being discussed, but one would suspect continued support for the child benefit theory of assisting youngsters in need. However, it is becoming a national controversy.

Just as previously compulsory attendance was tested in the courts, so recently home schooling has become an issue. The Court found in *Stephens v. Bongart* (1937) that home instruction was not equivalent to public school instruction partly because of a lack of socialization opportunities. However, in *Massa* (1967), the Court ruled that socialization and social development had no place in determining home schooling and public education equivalence. In *Mazanec v. North Judson-San Pierre School Corporation* (1985), parents were found entitled to educate their children at home if they made a good-faith effort to meet certain minimum requirements. However, in *West Virginia v. Riddle* (1981), the court held that the state's interest in protecting children extends to home schools. With growing numbers of home and small religious schools, educators are concerned about the public school role in carrying the culture to all, a major theme in John Goodlad's "What Are Schools For?" Jackson, a high school girls' basketball coach, complained about school policies that he felt discriminated against his team in violation of Title IX, designed to ensure sexual equality in school programs. Fired, Jackson successfully sued, arguing that Congress intended Title IX to provide a protection for those who seek to protect the rights of women and minorities (*Jackson v. Birmingham Board of Education*, 2005). The Court's decision will protect those who expose violations of Title IX from retaliation.

Our society increases its sensitivity to concerns of those with varying lifestyles and belief systems. In a 5-4 decision, the Supreme Court in *Christian Legal Society v. Martinez* (2010) found that denying recognition of a religious student organization does not violate the first amendment. The Christian Legal Society required members to adhere to a faith statement that marriage should be between a man and a woman and to exclude homosexuals from membership. The court held that the Hastings Law School had a policy of nondiscrimination and organizational membership should be open to all comers. The Christian Legal Society was free to operate without access to school funds and facilities. Judge Alito dissenting sees further litigation in this area. In *Horne v. Flores* (2009), the Supreme Court in a 5-4 decision ruled that Arizona took appropriate steps to improve methods and instruction for English language learning. The Supreme Court reversed the court of appeals, which sought statewide increase in ELL funding. The issue will continue to be litigated.

In Loco Parentis. In the seventeenth, eighteenth, and nineteenth centuries, educators held parental power to discipline and regulate students. Although state and federal court decisions are case specific, *in loco parentis* may be revisited by the courts. The Supreme Court, in *Vernonia School District v. Acton* (1995), upheld school drug testing, noting that policy subjects are children committed to the temporary custody of the state as schoolmaster. The Court found that, in that capacity, the state could exercise a greater degree of supervision and control than over adults to maintain a safe and proper environment for learning.

Single-Sex Schools. In *United States v. Virginia Military Institute* (1996), the Supreme Court found that an exclusively male admission policy violated the Fourteenth Amendment equal protection clause, and that women have a right to full citizenship stature—equal opportunity to aspire, achieve, and participate in and contribute to society based on their individual talents and capacities. The 1996 Court's decision reviewed the nineteenth-century history of sexual discrimination in citing *Bradwell v. Illinois* (1873). In that case, the Court denied a woman the right to practice law: "In view of the peculiar characteristics, destiny and mission of woman, it is within the province of the legislature to ordain what offices, positions and callings shall be filled and discharged by men, and shall receive the benefit of those energies and responsibilities, and that decision and firmness which are presumed to predominate in the sterner sex." In the *Virginia Military* case, the Court found that women seeking a Virginia Military Institute quality education cannot be offered anything less than equal opportunity to afford them genuinely equal protection.

HISTORICAL OVERVIEW OF U.S. EDUCATIONAL CRITICS

Clashing views on controversial issues have characterized writing in the educational field for many years. Historically, the characteristic rigidity of institutionalized education has been criticized by progressives. However, business leaders and political conservatives have often attacked the schools for promoting socialistic ideas or for teaching about social issues. Liberal versus conservative arguments over curriculum, moral training, and rights of children have been in the educational literature for generations.

Curriculum matters interweave with methods and psychology. When Charles Eliot chaired the Committee of Ten in 1892, specific subjects prescribed for the high schools were Latin, Greek, English, German, French, Spanish, algebra, geometry, trigonometry, astronomy, meteorology, botany, zoology, physiology, geology, physics, chemistry, history, and physical geography. Critics pointed out the high school curriculum lacked vocational subjects, sociology, psychology, and the humanities. The committee was also highly influenced by the then-popular educational psychology stressing mental discipline. Later psychologists took issue with subjects chosen because of the alleged ability to train the mind. Others argued that a college preparatory curriculum did not serve a majority of high school students who were not college bound.

Critics of education in modern America highlight issues in contemporary schooling. Some find philosophical fault with the aims and purposes of education. Others attack teacher education, the curriculum, or the methods used. Many are concerned about the quality of programs and the products produced by schools. Critics are numerous, verbal, and well established in staunch positions with considerable public support. Some people think that modern critics perform a service by isolating problems and illuminating inadequate aspects of the educational system. Others say that responsible criticism requires offering attainable solutions and working within the system to achieve them. Clearly there are many more critics focusing on shortcomings rather than offering reasonable alternatives. Several critics provide poignant insight into the teaching–learning process and the total school environment, reaching education professionals who take them seriously and attempt change. Colleges of education have been especially sensitive to critics. Of course, critics also create anger, frustration, disgust, and other negative reactions both inside and outside the system.

Critics, 1950–1960s.   During the 1950s, the nation enjoyed a period of relative prosperity and tranquility. The reaction to the successful *Sputnik* launch ended the tranquil period. In the wake of fear and criticism, European schools were compared favorably with American ones. James B. Conant, former president of Harvard, called for high school reorganization with more emphasis on excellence. Admiral Hyman Rickover insisted that the major purpose of education is to produce the experts who create the technology and science upon which a modern nation depends for winning wars, hot or cold. Through such programs as the National Defense Education Act (NDEA), emphasis was placed upon science, technology, mathematics, foreign languages, and high standards.

Critics, 1970–1990s.   In the 1970s, dissatisfaction permeated the social order, and the grim realities facing the nation created a diversity of new educational criticisms. Fear of continuing war, loss of faith in government, Watergate, and the prospects of unemployment in a recessionary economy created uncertainty about the future. People began asking how to educate children to cope with the energy crisis, ecology problems, the depletion of natural resources, urban congestion, rising crime, a world population explosion, and a changing job market. Others focused on the developmental, creative, and human needs of individual students, especially children who to varying degrees are "victims" of society and therefore of the school system.

By 1980, distrust of "big government" caused dissatisfaction with social engineering and antipoverty programs. Inflation fueled demands for more job-related training, more efficient use of school time, and less busing for desegregation. The "moral majority" produced a new wave of attacks on teaching the theory of evolution, sex education, and values clarification. Multicultural studies and bilingual education became less popular. There were new demands for accountability. The reputation of education declined with ACT scores and many high school graduates proved unable to read beyond an elementary level. "Excellence" and a "return to basics" were the most popular slogans.

During the 1990s, SAT and ACT scores stabilized, educational reform and restructuring continued unabated, and cultural diversity was stressed. "Political correctness" was widely used to refer to the influence of various liberal groups. There was great national concern over the AIDS virus and the cancer-causing effects of cigarettes.

Modern Critics.   During the 2000s, as in the past, public schools and universities will be engaged in a wide variety of initiatives to provide an environment of educational excellence where all belong, learn, and succeed (Rogers, Arkansas, Public Schools, Mission Statement). For every initiative there will be counteracting forces. High-stakes testing is being rethought, with some states curbing the movement; the American Bar Association (ABA) has recommended ending one-size-fits-all solutions to complex problems confronting public schools, such as zero tolerance school policies. The ABA finds that zero tolerance policies may redefine students as criminals with unfortunate consequences. There will be continued efforts to deal with a multitude of issues confronting public school populations into the foreseeable future.

Seekers of Reform.   Advocates of change, including Samuel Bowles, Herbert Gintis, George Dennison, John Holt, Ivan Illich, Herbert Kohl, Jonathan Kozol, Theodore Roszak, and Charles Silberman, sought school reform from radical change to alternative education for at-risk students. Several of the critics wrote about the lives of minorities and students at risk. Their popular books gave visions and directions for needed school reform.

The Critics of Research.   Those with a critical eye, including Gerald W. Bracey, Huelskamp (the Sandia Report), and David Berliner, all provided analysis of the shortcomings, flaws, and manipulation of research results. Each researcher criticized the research behind educational reform reports including NCLB. Bracey had a yearly *Phi Delta Kappan* report on the need to improve research studies that drive educational policy. In one of his last interviews, Bracey noted that there is only one misconception really, which is that standardized tests are scientific and objective and are adequate instruments to evaluate children, teachers, schools, districts, states, and nations. Berliner referred to "manufactured crisis" and "myths" in reform reports.

No Child Left Behind Act (NCLB).   The Obama administration is proposing a new blueprint for Congress designed to soften the language of the original act. For example, the term *schools in need of improvement*, will be renamed challenged schools. The act may be renamed but testing for assessment will be maintained. In June 2010, the Supreme Court rejected a challenge to NCLB by school districts and teacher unions over funding (*School District of Pontiac, Michigan v. Duncan*, 2010).

The bill was cosponsored in 2001 by Representatives John A. Boehner (R-Ohio) and George Miller (D-California), and Senators Edward Kennedy (D-Massachusetts) and Judd Gregg (R-New Hampshire). Bush signed it the following year. NCLB includes annual testing for proficiency in reading and math from Grades 3 to 8 and one high school grade other than ninth. It has been extended to three tests in high school. It addresses Title I funding for schools based on poverty, teacher training and development with class size limits, educator legal protections from liability for "reasonable actions" to maintain order and discipline, reading programs in kindergarten through third grade, technology grants for computer training for poor and rural students, bilingual education funding to test students in reading and language arts in English after 3 years in school, and development of twenty-first-century community learning centers. The Elementary and Secondary Education Act was modified to require "highly qualified" teachers for school districts receiving Title I funding. By 2000–2008, states were required to give science tests to one grade within each of three levels of a K–12 education. NCLB includes a "safe harbor" provision for schools in which particular subgroups of students do not meet the annual measurable objective. As long as they can show significant progress toward proficiency, schools will not be identified as failing (needing improvement). Schools needing improvement are to be given technical assistance. Parents were given options including private tutoring and transferring to successful schools if there is no improvement after 3 years.

NCLB and NDRA also require school districts to release high school student information to recruiters. Russo (2004) finds parents are not familiar with act provisions; for example, many parents do not realize that they can "opt-out" of providing information to military recruiters. Members of the 111th Congress heard growing complaints from state education officials about provisions of the NCLB Act. The 112th Congress—faced with overhauling the financial regulatory system, the health care system, attempted assassination of an Arizona congresswoman, collective bargaining challenges, aftermath of the BP Gulf oil, spill as well as the usual educational social and political issues such as home schooling, charter schools, school prayer, teacher quality standards, and state accountability systems—will be challenged to reauthorize the Elementary and Secondary School Act. Arne Duncan, the Obama administration's education secretary, is seeking to expand charter schools and raise educational standards while emphasizing teacher quality and excellent in preparation programs with a divided 112th Congress.

Lindseth (2004) noted that school finance litigation is emerging to prove that funding for education is inadequate. Over 30 states are being sued for not providing adequate education in their schools. The Obama administration focused on low-income, at-risk, and special needs students in plans for reauthorization The Elementary and Secondary Education Act. The administration's blueprint for reauthorization includes more flexibility and less punitive policies ("Reading the Blueprint," 2010). Teacher union leaders have been critics of testing for assessment of achievement and Education Secretary Arne Duncan is meeting with them to work toward collaboration. There is speculation that union leaders want to change their image from being resistant to change and unwilling to cooperate. Popular films such as *Waiting for Superman*, and NBC's *Education Nation Summit*, have negative portrayal of unions and teachers (Murray, 2010). With a divided Congress and major budget deficits, there still will be an effort to compromise in reauthorization efforts (Parsons & Mascaro, 2011).

Race to the Top. The Obama administration's $4.35 billion federal grant program was designed to encourage states to improve education in the lowest performing schools in several areas: Adopting common academic standards and assessments that prepare students to succeed in the economy, workplace, and global marketplace; building data systems to measure student growth and success, and inform teachers and principals as to how they can improve instruction; recruiting; developing, rewarding, and retaining effective teachers and principals, especially where they are most needed; turning around our lowest achieving schools, which were targeted areas for school reform; supporting charter schools and focusing on math and science studies, which were main areas for judging states' applications for race to the top funding (Cavanagh, 2010). States were encouraged to submit proposals for innovative experimental programs to close the educational achievement gap. The Obama administration's 2011 budget includes an additional $1 billion for education to encourage prompt congressional action on the education act (Klein, 2010). Some state officials and advocacy groups criticized judges' methodology as inconsistent and arbitrary (Cavanagh, 2010). According to Secretary of Education Arne Duncan, districts with the lowest performing schools have four options:

- Replace the principal but keep the teachers and improve through professional development
- Close a school and hire a new principal who can hire back up to half of those teachers
- Close a school and open up under new governance
- Close a school and send children to a better school elsewhere

The next lowest 5 percent of the schools would be subject to targeted intervention. The rest of the schools would have state and local improvement programs (Garrett, 2010).

Critics with Other Viewpoints. Although no complete enumeration of modern educational critics is possible here, some of those with special points of view should be mentioned. Sylvia Ashton-Warner, author of *Teacher* (1963) and *Spearpoint: Teacher in America* (1972), is concerned with the meaning of equality and authority in education. Joseph Featherstone's *Schools Where Children Learn* (1968) warns about "faddishness" and questions whether schools can build a more equal society. The problem of relevance concerns George Leonard in *Education and Ecstasy* (1968). *Teaching as a Subversive Activity* (1969) by Neil Postman and Charles Weingartner deals with relevance and communication. William Glasser's *Schools Without Failure* (1968) and Sunny Decker's *An Empty Spoon* (1969) sound the same theme. Glasser's *The Quality School: Managing Students Without Coercion* (1998) stresses a humane, people-centered approach to all aspects of education in an age of conflict. Alfie Kohn in *The Schools Our Children Deserve: Moving Beyond Traditional Classrooms and Tougher Standards* (2000) and in *What Does It Mean to Be Well Educated?* (2004) discusses the excesses of a competitive high-stakes testing school environment and its effect on the quality of the learning environment. He finds schools are doing much better than they are given credit for and negative reporting tends to feed on itself. Linda Darling-Hammond's *Preparing Teachers for a Changing World* (2005) calls for balancing subject matter with assessments to meet the needs of diverse students. Marilyn Cochran-Smith's *Walking the Road: Race, Diversity, and Social Justice in Education* (2004) addresses conflicting philosophies of education and detailed roadmaps for democratic education.

Those who claim the schools have not been interested in humanistic psychology include Abraham Maslow and Carl Rogers. Another psychologist, Jerome S. Bruner, believes that too much emphasis has been placed on the structure of knowledge within the disciplines and not enough on structure in the context of learning and problem solving. Jean Piaget holds that learning takes place at various levels or stages of development depending upon both maturation and experience, and that too little attention has been given to the process of learning and too much to the content.

The wide range of criticisms of American education is not surprising in a rapidly changing, pluralistic, dynamic, and democratic culture. Some critics operate from a scholarly base within the profession, some represent philosophical causes, some are concerned about the role of the school in social change, and others attack education for its support of social values. Education is not an exact science and American society is dynamic and open; thus, criticism may be expected to continue. The problem for the professional educator is understanding exactly what the critics are saying and selecting the best ideas from a host of suggested alternatives.

The School as Agency for Social Action.
The school's role in social change is a philosophical issue, as Theodore Brameld and his critics are quick to point out. So many recent programs have seemingly developed to use education as a social institution for cultural change that the problem of purpose and function of schools has received new attention.

As James S. Coleman and Edgar Z. Friedenberg have insisted, demands and challenges for modern adolescents are very great. The impact of social change on the adolescent, pressures on middle-class teenagers, and the problem of youth values in an open society are major concerns for schools. Superimposed on these concerns are the special problems of low-income students, the children of the urban poor, and the youth from African American, Native American, or Latino families, who have more than their share of educational difficulties and are more apt to drop out of school. Various compensations have been tried for the culturally disadvantaged and to meet the needs of all children.

Ever since the Wechsler Scales for measuring adult intelligence were invented and the Army Alpha and Beta tests were given in World War I, mass testing has been used to establish norms. Many educators fear that both individual and group intelligence tests are misused in schools, but the first great objection to categorizing students by test scores came from those who charged cultural bias. It was argued that merely being from a middle-class white environment gave students an unfair advantage on these instruments. Efforts to construct culturally fair tests were followed by attempts to remove racism and sexism from textbooks. Most American public school textbooks before 1960 made minority people "invisible" and portrayed definite sex roles for youngsters.

Project Head Start, Vista, Job Corps, Talent Search, Teacher Corps, and Upward Bound are federally funded projects to help disadvantaged students. Job Corps centers were established to teach vocational skills to high school dropouts, while Upward Bound attempted to prepare disadvantaged youth for success in college. Other programs used federal funds for more teachers, buildings, and equipment in areas with concentrations of low-income or minority children.

The Coleman Report (Coleman 1966), Illich's *Deschooling Society,* (1971) and the work of Christopher Jenks indicate that these programs made very little lasting difference, with Illich suggesting that it is not possible for government-sponsored school programs to compensate for cultural differences. The Obama administration is focusing on raising standards, recruiting and retaining highly effective qualified teachers, and closing the achievement gap for low-income at-risk students and minority students.

Superimposed upon issues of government's role in aiding the culturally different were more emotional ones concerning race, heredity, and intelligence. Psychologist Arthur Jensen's 1969 article in the *Harvard Educational Review* suggested that black students average about 15 points below whites on IQ tests. Jensen tried to point out that his data were not a basis for judging the intellectual capacity of any individual, but the use of Jensen's studies to prove that integration must fail produced strong criticisms. Authors on both sides of the issue allowed emotions to overrule logic, and controversial articles continued to appear in the early 2000s.

Both the number of critics and the depth of their concern increased dramatically in the 1980s. The political and religious "new right" expressed an increasingly popular position, eschewing development of children's moral autonomy and supporting the teaching of what its supporters deemed to be "right." They had no problem with the idea that schools should indoctrinate "truth" and ethical behavior patterns in children. In practice, these conservative moralists defend educational programs that they believe will create moral character, patriotism, strict discipline, deference to authority, and opposition to secular humanism. They see the current schools corrupted with humanistic values and liberalism and often support home schooling, vouchers, and charter schools (93,500 in 40 states and the District of Columbia; Hendrie, 2005). In mid-2010 there were 4,600 charter schools in 39 states and the District of Columbia educating 1.5 million students (Toch, 2010).

While criticism of public schools continues, Linda Jacobson in *Education Week* (2001) noted areas of progress. Clinton's "early learning fund" was put into effect, quietly, as part of the 2001 federal budget. Local governments and community leaders can apply for funding of parenting programs, literacy promotion, and improved access to early childhood programs for children with special needs. The 2001 and 2005 budgets also provided for financial aid loan forgiveness for child-care providers, early childhood programs for high-poverty areas, as well as child-care assistance for low-income families.

ASSESSMENT AND ACCOUNTABILITY

The idea that schools and educators should be responsible for their actions is not new in American education. Annual reports of Horace Mann and the journal articles of Henry Barnard carried criticisms of inadequate or mistaken pedagogical efforts. Teacher training has been under fire since the development of normal schools and university departments of education. As early as 1898, the American Association of Manufacturers charged schools with "repressive brain stuffing," "dulling the intellect," and failing to provide youth with marketable skills. The business community has repeated the charge ever since. Educators have attacked each other, as in the progressive education rejection of the Herbartian lock-step methods and William Bagley's subsequent essentialist rejection of the progressives. Perhaps the main difference between the past and present is that today attacks are more widespread and rapid, which can be attributed to modern communication.

American public schools experience periods of ebb and flow both in public interest and public pressure. Following 1970, criticism of schools and teaching was linked to demands for accountability. It is a management concept, and is intended to hold someone responsible for performing according to terms previously agreed upon. Secretary of Defense Robert McNamara brought the unrelenting evaluative practices of business to government through his planning and budgeting system. In education, the founding of the accountability movement is usually credited to the works of Leon Lessinger (*Every Kid a Winner: Accountability in Education,* 1970).

The sudden popularity of accountability can be traced to growing dissatisfaction with school quality, a feeling that educators were closing ranks against public criticism, and the ever-increasing pressure for more tax dollars to finance education. Many educators have been quite negative about accountability, and the issues surrounding it continue to be argued in the twenty-first century. Total quality management and effective schools were popular themes in the mid-1990s, as the influence of business and industry efforts toward continuous product improvement and customer satisfaction were emphasized in education. William Byham's *Zapp in Education* (1992) was typical of the popular books on effective schools through empowerment.

As a theoretical concept, few would quarrel with accountability. Teachers obviously need to be responsible for what they do, and the educational profession does not object to evaluation. However, teachers do object to the idea that they are guilty of something punishable and the negative presumption that legislation is needed to make them do their jobs. More significantly, many unanswerable questions arise. Who is accountable? If the student fails to learn, is that always the teacher's fault and not the student's or the parents'? There is massive evidence that schools are responsible for only a part of the child's learning, and teachers are responsible for an even smaller part. For what are teachers accountable? Testable knowledge surely does not represent total learning. Incidental, collateral, and attitudinal learnings are not capable of being organized into objective sequences; thus, most accountability tests measure only a very limited part of what the student actually learns. John Goodlad pointed out that timeworn instruments of assessment and archaic criteria for evaluation are poor means for measuring pupil achievement. To whom are educators accountable? The answer to this would seem to be the clients (students, parents, and employers), but if teachers have no role in determining policy, accountability is unfair. Often government officials determine the criteria for accountability with no local input. If teachers are employees not consulted about school issues or practices, they can hardly be held professionally accountable.

The complexity of teaching is seldom fully understood by those seeking performance accountability. Student language deficiencies, violence, variable motivation, discipline, dysfunctional behavior, harassment, and discrimination are part of the culture of schools. Although these challenges have always been in our schools, severity of such issues is much greater now.

Laws and Lawsuits Focused on Accountability. Previously, teacher reputation was built on some estimate of "good" teacher behavior. Keeping order in the classroom and grading students fairly were examples of such behavior. Recently, the measure of "good" teaching has shifted to the ability of the teacher to produce specific behavioral changes in learners. California's Stull Act requires that the competence of teachers be partially measured by the performance of students. The implication is that when students do not learn, for whatever reason, the fault is the teacher's. Some critics see this idea as analogous to the ancient practice of paying physicians only if the patient recovers. Accountability has also been tested in the courts. In 1976, a student, allowed to graduate from high school, although unable to read at sixth-grade level, sued the San Francisco Unified School District, arguing that school personnel were negligent in failing to detect and correct his learning problem. In *Donohue v. Copiague* (1979), a student charged a New York school with failure to cope with his learning disabilities. The plaintiffs were unsuccessful in both cases, but clearly established the idea of holding teachers accountable to society for the quality and quantity of educational results. Courts in New York and Iowa have reaffirmed that teachers cannot be held liable for poor student performance, but demand for accountability has not diminished. McCarthy and Cambron-McCabe (1992) found that although none have yet been successful, some courts have found instances in which plaintiffs might recover damages in an instructional tort action. In general, courts have been loath to interfere with the administration of public schools.

In the 1970s, many states passed accountability laws. Some require student assessment via specific tests; others are broad and vague. Seven states involved in the Cooperative Accountability Project require evaluation, but specific measures are determined locally. Some educators fear that business-industrial models of accountability threaten teachers with punitive and often inoperable directives. Others see schools becoming more rigid and authoritarian, emphasizing test performance and nothing else. Sociologist Robert Havinghurst cautions against a simplistic accountability, making teachers totally responsible without considering other forces in the learning environment. Both the NEA and the National Commission on Teacher Education and Professional Standards have called accountability unprofessional, inhumane, and arbitrary unless the profession itself develops the standards and methods of measurement. The American Federation of Teachers (AFT) supports high standards and highly qualified teachers, but finds flaws in NCLB. Nevertheless, today most states require some form of assessment and accountability for public schools; most commonly, a standardized achievement test with failure resulting in loss of funding. This trend toward measuring and publishing public school achievement results may motivate teachers to "teach to the test."

The Learning First Alliance—comprised of a number of organizations including the National PTA, American Association of School Administrators, AFT, and American Association of Colleges of Teacher Education—issued a 2001 report raising questions about implementation of standards and accountability, concluding that in any large-scale effort to improve a complex system, there must be continuous reviews, or mid-course corrections, of progress and unintended consequences. There are dangers of excessive reliance on standardized test scores, especially for at-risk students. Student appraisal should use a variety of relevant information about student achievement.

Competency Tests for Teachers.   Along with accountability, the public has become concerned with eliminating incompetent teachers. Education colleges often require standardized assessments for certification to provide external evidence of skills and subject knowledge and for use with other performance data for teacher certification. Prior to 1978, when Florida passed a bill requiring a precertification comprehensive written examination, only a few states required beginning teachers to pass the National Teacher Examination (NTE) (currently the Educational Testing Services Praxis Series). Georgia, New York, Oklahoma, and Wisconsin had plans for some form of competency testing by 1981, and several other states were considering such requirements. After 1978, when the Supreme Court ruled that the NTE was not discriminatory (although more black teachers than white failed it), several states began to use it. NCLB seeks highly qualified teachers (college degree, full accreditation, specialization, and content knowledge) for all students by 2005–2006. This requirement will be adjusted to meet current state needs.

Some school districts administer their own prehiring tests to new teachers. The Dallas Independent School District had 50 percent failure rates on a 10th grade verbal and quantitative ability prerequisite. This alarming rate did little to enhance the public view of institutions that train teachers. However, these tests measure subject knowledge and not teaching skills. If universities are to be held accountable, the mathematics and geography departments are more vulnerable than departments of education. Although superior subject knowledge does not necessarily make a superior teacher, the public is right to demand that teachers be minimally competent in basic subjects. President Sandra Feldman of AFT favors entry-level testing of teacher candidates to improve the profession. She also calls for national standards for teacher tests. Both the AFT and the NEA oppose tests for teachers who are already in service. Ohio has a licensing plan requiring all new teachers to be evaluated on their performance, as well as on coursework and paper-and-pencil test scores. Their on-the-job performance will be based on interviews and observations of their instruction (Archer & Blair, 2001). Test pressures have led to instances of teacher dismissal for cheating on tests.

It has not been determined if tests should be criterion referenced, norm referenced, or both. Teacher candidates are now required to pass minimum competency tests in many states before certification. There are questions about the effectiveness of such tests in predicting classroom success and some concerns regarding the projected future teacher shortage. With a record national public school enrollment of more than 55 million during a major recession in 2010, Florida like other states have on the election ballot a proposal to increase class sizes and take other measures to operate with major funding cuts. A Florida legislative proposal to have teacher grade parents in terms of their parental involvement was controversial (CNN, 2011). It remained a proposal without implementation.

Started in 1987 by the Carnegie Foundation, the National Board for Professional Teacher Standards, chaired by Governor James B. Hunt of North Carolina, provides national teacher certification through teacher-developed portfolios and attendance at one of 200 nationwide assessment centers. The program, designed to improve teacher effectiveness, gave out its first certificates of advanced competency in 1995. Assessment includes commitment to students and student learning, knowledge of subject matter, managing and monitoring student learning, thinking systematically about their practice, and learning from experience and service as members of a learning community. Teachers provide classroom videos and participate in two days of performance-based assessment.

Curriculum Concerns.
The entire body of courses offered in the school program is the curriculum. Historically, studying curriculum is one of the best ways to understand what a school system tried to accomplish. Colonial New England schools taught religion, reading, and writing; Latin grammar schools concentrated on Latin, Greek, and theology. Core curriculum and student involvement in selection from a wide spectrum of courses was characteristic of progressive schools. In the 1950s, *Sputnik* and the NDEA produced a discipline-centered curriculum stressing science, mathematics, and foreign languages. With demands for civil rights and equal educational opportunities came a child-centered program with emphasis placed on ethical, social, and multicultural subjects. This program was followed by a "back to basics" movement with more formalized instruction and strict accountability. Within only 30 years, popularity shifted from Deweyan progressives to strict academicians to social reconstructionists to conservative essentialists. The future promises to be equally filled with conflicting demands for different curricular choices.

Since the mid-1960s, two schools of thought have dominated the curriculum controversy. One is the free, open, child-centered, humanistic, and socially oriented movement, theoretically grounded in the works of John Dewey, A. S. Neill, the social reconstructionists, and humanistic-existential authors. The other calls for standardized subject matter, no-nonsense basic education, high academic standards, and discipline-oriented schools. The philosophical foundation for this position reaches back to Plato and has been supported by twentieth-century perennialists and essentialists.

Modern speakers for the first movement include Edgar Friedenberg, Paul Goodman, John Holt, Herbert Kohl, and Charles Silberman. They oppose the conformity and docility characteristic of the subject-centered school. Accusing traditional schools of a meaningless curriculum and indifference to social issues, these authors demand relevant programs geared to the actual needs and desires of students. For them, curriculum content is less important than the process and the learner's ability to relate to the school activities. They wish to foster positive learning attitudes and practical people skills.

Authors like Jacques Barzun, Arthur Bestor, Mortimer Adler, Robert Hutchins, and James Koerner opposed this view, believing with James Conant and Admiral Rickover after *Sputnik* that the schools must concentrate on producing subject-matter experts and superior scholars to lead the technological society. Koerner, speaking for the Council for Basic Education, opposes progressive education's "soft" pedagogy and demands a return to "solid" academic subjects. The council argues against student-influenced curriculum, saying that adults know best what children should study. By 1980, the Council for Basic Education and the back to basics movement had gained vast public support, partly from parents disappointed with the information and skill levels of their public-schooled children and partly from the "moral majority," and questioned assumptions of an open, humanistic, child-centered, life-adjustment program. The Council for Basic Education and Education Planet websites provide information on national standards guidelines for curriculum. In calling for a return to "basics," Barzun (1945) has said, "Nonsense is at the heart of those proposals that would replace definable subject matter with vague activities copied from life or with courses organized around problems or attitudes." In our twenty-first century, some advocate the normal curve of probability based on standardized test scores (and support school districts in requiring students with low scores to repeat grade levels). Others support authentic assessment or a variety of achievement measures including portfolios and student-chosen projects. The former see high test scores as success indicators in a competitive environment; the latter see them as culturally biased instruments that lower self-esteem of poor test takers.

Curriculum Innovations and Methods.

Several emergent trends have provided persuasive arguments to broaden the public school curriculum. Not all schools have adopted new subjects, but sufficient demand is making new subjects important in curriculum development. New curriculum trends reflect interests in interdisciplinary approaches to schooling and a thrust toward individualization and relevance including career, consumer, environmental, multicultural, and substance abuse education. In addition, sex, character, and service learning education are in the emerging curriculum. Teachers are encouraged to use authentic assessment, conflict resolution, and observational training for dysfunctional behavior patterns (bullying, obesity) to meet the needs of a diverse student population. Many emerging curriculum trends have roots in the 1918 *Cardinal Principles of Secondary Education*.

The curriculum cannot be divorced from methods. The same subject matter used for a lecture and in discovery learning will produce very different results in students. Conservatives are generally more comfortable with traditional methods like lecture, textbook assignments, homework, standardized tests, and library reports. Liberals prefer laboratory methods like discovery learning, problem solving, and inquiry learning. The activity curriculum and child-centered curriculum are not popular with the back to basics movement, although both liberals and conservatives use individualized instruction. Computer-assisted instruction is acceptable to the subject-matter curriculum advocates so long as it stays on the subject. Team teaching, block scheduling, and flexible scheduling are most often found in progressively oriented schools. Businesses and communities often "adopt a school" by providing funds and volunteers for enrichment programs. The curriculum is interwoven with educational technology in which data gathering, storage, and dissemination improve educational delivery systems and assessment. Gewertz (2010) notes the three-quarters of the states have adopted a new set of common academic standards following the lead of the Council of Chief State School Officers and the National Governors' Association. This is a major stimulus for National Curriculum Standards.

Competency-Based Training and Performance Contracting.   Competency-based teacher education demands that public school students show mastery of fundamental subjects. Placing greater emphasis on reading, writing, and mathematics in elementary school and on English, science, history, and mathematics in secondary schools, supports minimum competency testing. Some schools have contracted with private teaching firms to improve educational performance. Such performance contracting (Texarkana in 1972) has produced disappointing results, but highlighted the public demand for improvement in student knowledge and skills. Project 81 in Pennsylvania is an example of a statewide attempt to ensure that all students meet graduation requirements as measured by competency tests.

Some schools and teachers use contracting with individual students as an instructional method. Giving grades for specific performances is most often used in progressive schools, but it is the same concept as specific competency graduation requirements. Minimum competency testing, which won public support in the early 1980s, is currently a widespread trend. Pay for performance gained popularity in 2011.

ISSUES OF INCLUSION

Educating the Exceptional Child.   In the eighteenth and nineteenth centuries, and even in the early twentieth century, special education children were often excluded from schools. Alexander and Alexander in *American Public School Law* (2001) cited cases in which imbecilic student behavior was grounds for expulsion, and academically disabled students were excluded from regular classes because of the depressing effect on teachers and schoolchildren. Thurlow and Johnson in the *Journal of Teacher Education* (2000) noted that the Individuals with Disabilities Education Act amendments of 1997 (NDEA, or Public Law 105-17) require states and districts to have students with disabilities participate in state and district assessments, and to report on their performance. As noted earlier, the 2004 Individuals with Disabilities Education Improvement Act (IDEA) requires greater consultation between private schools and district administrators, including recording and reporting the number of private schools with students with special needs. The number of children attending private schools determines a school district's IDEA funds that are allocated to private schools (McTighe, 2005).

In the twentieth century, vast gains were made in the diagnosis and treatment of students with special problems. Starting with programs for deaf or blind children, educational institutions developed a variety of effective methods for educating the exceptional child. The Rehabilitation Act of 1973 prohibits discrimination by failure to provide access and reasonable facilities for people with disabilities. The Americans with Disabilities Act of 1990 (ADA) mandated full availability to special telecommunications systems by July 1993 for over 26 million citizens with hearing and speech requirements. New facilities for children with disabilities were built, including ramps and restrooms to accommodate students in wheelchairs. Specialists trained to work with various learning disabilities have been in the schools for a little over a decade. Programs for students with mental retardation and students with trainable mental disabilities were developed to identify and help students with less pronounced difficulties, but the gifted and talented were ignored by many who assumed that they would learn in spite of the system.

In the early 2000s, litigation in the area of special education proliferated. In some cases, students and parents were suing school systems for providing special learning education services to disabled students and excluding regular students from the learning assistance. Lynn Olson (2005) notes that there are nearly 6 million students ages 6–21 receiving special education under Part B of IDEA. Of these, 67 percent have a specific learning disability (mainly dyslexia) or speech or language impairment.

Public Law 94-142.

In hearings for Public Law 94-142 (1975), it was noted that 1.75 million children with disabilities were excluded from school and another 4 million were not receiving full educational services. The law required exceptional learners to be placed in the least restrictive environment in which their educational needs could be satisfactorily served. Thus, children who previously spent their entire in-school time in special classes would be "mainstreamed" (spend at least part of the day in classes with nondisabled students). This strategy was intended to remove the stigma attached to students with disabilities, improve social relationships, provide nondisabled learning models, allow for a richer and more competitive environment, and learn to live in the "real" world. It also allowed more students to be served, provided more cost-effective education, and decentralized services to reduce transportation costs. Miller (2004) notes schools are struggling with the degree of responsibility for social as well as academic skills under the special education rubric. PL 94-142 requires all teachers to have a comprehensive system of professional development that includes special education courses and/or experiences that provide understanding of handicapped children with skills in assessment, curriculum design, teaching strategies, and instructional media (Patton & Braithwaite, 2010).

Funding Special Education.

Bruce Hunter of the American Association of School Administrators noted that when special education laws were created in the 1970s, no one considered "mission creep." As a result, the communally increasing

	Percentage of Students with Disabilities, Ages 6 to 21						
	1992–93	1993–94	1994–95	1995–96	2000–01	2005–06	2007–08
Regular class	39.8	43.4	44.5	45.4	46.5	53.7	58
Resource room	31.7	29.5	28.8	28.7	29.8	23.7	21.7
Separate class	23.4	22.7	22.4	21.7	19.5	16.7	15.0
Separate facilities	5.1	4.4	4.3	4.3	4.2	2.9	3.0

Figure 10.2 Classroom Placement of Students with Disabilities

Source: Cited in Marjorie Coeyman. *The Christian Science Monitor* (March 13, 2001): 20; National Center for Education Statistics. *The Condition of Education*. Washington, DC: Author, 1999; Thomas Snyder. *Digest of Educational Statistics*. Washington, DC U.S. Department of Education, 2004.

lists of impairments makes special education funding the fastest growing school expenditure (Miller, 2004). (For an idea of how fast regular classrooms have begun teaching students with disabilities, see Figure 10.2.)

IDEA bases the formula for state allotments through 2006 on demographics: How many children live in a state, and what percentage of them are living in poverty? The amendments seek to ensure that a portion of the IDEA funds are used to provide outreach and technical assistance to historically black colleges and institutions with a minimum 25 percent minority enrollment.

The 1997 amendments also address the challenge of dealing with children whose disability includes violence-prone behavior. Educational administrators continue to have difficulty interpreting IDEAs in terms of what special services are to be provided and how to fund them. The IDEA Reauthorization (July 2005) provides for comprehensive, coordinated early intervention programs for children in minority groups deemed to be subjected to overidentification and misidentification (Samuels, 2004).

From the early days of the republic, philanthropy has served the nation well. John Harvard gave a library and 300 pounds for Harvard; Horace Mann wrote of the stewardship theory of wealth, whereby those who attained wealth had an obligation to provide for others in need. The Bill and Melinda Gates Foundation has provided funds for worthy causes throughout the nation. The Kennedy Foundation provided funds for special education; Peabody College of Vanderbilt was a major recipient of the funding. In 2001, William T. Coleman and his wife Claudia gave $250 million for a cognitive-disabilities center at the University of Colorado. Coleman, founder of BEA Systems, a builder of Internet platforms, saw how a six-year-old niece with physical and mental disabilities responded by using a computer, and he wanted to make a difference in the lives of others in the field of assistive technology. Federal funding in 2008 covered 17.1 percent of estimated excess cost of education for children with disabilities. Shortfalls in funding has been assumed by states and local school districts (Individuals with Disabilities, 2010).

Benefits of PL 94-142: Is It Working?   There is no question about the benefit of mainstreaming's the exceptional child. If all classes were small and the learning specialist and the regular teacher always cooperated, there might not be controversy; unfortunately, this is not the case. Regular classroom teachers often feel that they are not prepared and do not have the time to work well with children with disabilities. An Individualized Education Program (IEP) is required for all mainstreamed exceptional children. This plan for education is cooperatively prepared by parents, teachers, and school officials, and covers the content, objectives, means of implementation, and evaluation of each student's program. The IEP cannot be altered without the consent of the child's review committee. Keep in mind that making and reviewing an IEP for each child requires much time and energy that might be devoted to other tasks. Teachers often feel that they must give most of their time to the special learners while they are present in the classroom. Parents of nondisabled children often complain that their children are getting less attention as a result of mainstreaming and that the presence of students with disabilities for large portions of the day reduces levels of expectation and diminishes excellence. Sometimes classroom teachers feel that they must work harder than the learning specialist, resulting in negative feelings. Although education colleges usually require a special education course, many classroom teachers feel unable to meet the needs of children with disabilities. It is not always clear just what responsibilities belong to whom, especially when the learning specialist is functioning as an observer to review the program's effectiveness. Mainstreaming seems to be working well in a number of school systems, although it also faces a good deal of criticism. Public acceptance is mixed.

Accessible Education.   The Council for Exceptional Children (CEC) noted in 1993 that full inclusion is a step on a continuum of services for all students with disabilities. Inclusion of students with mental or physical disabilities in regular classrooms throughout the school day is a meaningful goal to be pursued by schools and communities.

By 1993, universities and businesses had worked to remove barriers to facilities, providing elevators, sidewalk modification, easy access, and door-to-door transportation for people with disabilities. All institutions will be required to provide equal access in the future, although old buildings do not have to be upgraded for disability access until a renovation or remodeling project starts.

Increased Funding and Earlier Identification.   In 2004, the CEC worked to increase federal special education funds to 40 percent by 2000. Efforts are underway to help children succeed by fully funding the Individuals with Disabilities Act. The 2005 education budget proposed additional funds for Title I for disadvantaged students, specifically a 52 percent increase and an additional $1 billion for special education programs, a 75 percent increase since 2001. The $12.2 billion request for special education included support to improve educational and early intervention outcomes for children with disabilities (President Bush's FY 2005 Budget).

Mendez (2004) noted that the special education 2005 funding bill includes changes in discipline, identification, and teacher qualification. The update to IDEA will provide for disciplining special education students like other students, giving educators more freedom to exercise reasonable restraint as long as punishment is not for disability-related misbehavior.

In special education programs, earlier identification is being implemented to avoid misplacement. The number of students diagnosed with specific learning disabilities rose some 45 percent from 1987–1988 to over 2.8 million in 1998–1999. Coeyman (2001) reported that racial minorities make up a disproportionate number of special education placements, which may be from intentional or unintentional racial bias, noting that many special education classes involve lower expectations and less demanding curricula. A high-stakes testing environment is especially destructive for special education students, according to a report by the Civil Rights Project at Harvard University.

The percentage of mainstreamed disabled students in the United States has risen significantly since 1985; however, students with the most severe disabilities are placed more often in resource rooms, which are still favored over separate facilities.

Along with increased attention to inclusion, several current studies, including Mary Wagner and her colleagues', *What Happens Next? Trends in Postschool Outcomes of Youths with Disabilities* (1992), are designed to survey postschool outcomes. These studies indicate significant social independence and economic opportunity within five years of completing high school, even though most jobs held are low-skill, low-wage positions.

Fostering Giftedness.

Fostering Giftedness.   Demands for academic rigor, excellence, and intellectual development were loud in the era of the Cold War and *Sputnik*. James Conant argued in *The American High School Today* (1959) that the academically talented student was not being sufficiently challenged. In *Excellence: Can We Be Equal and Excellent Too?* (1961), John Gardner pointed out that excellence is needed not only in scientists and engineers but also in teachers, scholars, professional people, and social leaders. The White House Conference of 1955 stressed development of especially bright children. Science, mathematics, and foreign languages were considered the major areas of needed excellence. In *The Shopping Mall High School* (1985), Arthur Powell and colleagues covered most of the seemingly antithetical goals of making serious educational demands on students and graduating almost all of them.

Following the NDEA, interest in the gifted brought about a better understanding of the exceptionally bright student who largely found school boring and a waste of time. Intelligence tests failed to reveal special qualities such as creative ability. It was found that gifted and talented students often felt socially isolated and sometimes had difficulty in adjusting to group norms. Interest in the academically talented has continually increased since former U.S. Commissioner Sidney Marland submitted to Congress a 1972 report that recommended better education for the capable student. However, low funding slowed program development, until legislation was passed requiring special offerings to be made available for the gifted. Gifted and talented students must also be mainstreamed, but there is less controversy over this. By the turn of the twenty-first century, all schools provided some type of gifted and talented programming. Gootman (2010) notes that New York City is encouraging diversity in students taking gifted and talented tests. In 2009, children qualifying for gifted kindergarten programs rose by 45 percent. Nevertheless, low funding and a lack of trained teachers for the gifted have caused programs to lag far behind the level provided for students with disabilities.

Multicultural and Bilingual Education.
Issues developed in the 1970s regarding including multicultural studies in the curriculum and providing primary instruction in a language other than English, which continue today. The United States is a mosaic of cultures. Census Bureau statistics show Hispanics, 13.5 percent of the U.S. population (40 million), are projected to reach 24 percent (over 100 million) by 2050. A diverse African American population is the second-largest minority at 38.7 million. Native Americans, certain European minorities, Arabians, and Asian Americans are a growing part of the American population, with Asian Americans among the fastest growing. Some members of these groups have been assimilated into American mainstream culture, but others maintain their ethnic identity subculture. In many large cities there is a majority–minority population. "Minorities" are the majority in Los Angeles, Orlando, and other urban centers.

Multiculturalism and diversity are major areas of concern throughout the educational system from the National Council for the Accreditation of Teacher Education (NCATE) to public school and university administrations. Colleges of education, following NCATE standards, include multiculturalism within their education courses and also have courses and degree programs specifically targeting the topic. In the future, as the nation becomes more multiracial and multiethnic, it will be essential for its citizens to be accepting, appreciating, and understanding of the benefits provided by the rich human resources of diversity.

Historically, education has been used to bring foreigners into the national culture. Early arguments for public schools stressed the need to Americanize immigrants and ensure that all children speak English. Although this "melting pot ideal" did not result in uniform cultural patterns, the dominant Anglo-Protestant group did require conformity to its language, cultural preferences, and value orientation. Schools not only reflected middle-class interests but stressed white, Anglo-Saxon establishment norms. African Americans, Native Americans, and Hispanics, who were segregated rather than assimilated, did not fully participate in the majority society. In the early 2000s, movements toward total English immersion began, with California and Arizona implementing such programs while New York provided English immersion with optional bilingual education. Although total English immersion is controversial among bilingual specialists and English as a second language advocates, preliminary results with such programs are positive.

Cultural Awareness Education.
The civil rights movement called attention to discrimination, with African Americans first to demand equality of opportunity, soon followed by Hispanics and Native Americans. As part of the minority revolution, ethnic pride increased. Unique minority contributions were emphasized, together with ethnic histories and distinctive cultural patterns, leading to the cultural pluralism concept. Schools began offering cultural awareness programs, like black history and Hispanic studies.

Most American schools have incorporated multiculturalism into existing programs. Units dealing with Native Americans and Eskimos have been in the curriculum for years. Textbooks have been rewritten to include black and Hispanic role models, cultures, and special-attention events like Black History Month or Native American or Hispanic Heritage Week. International, social, and economic issues have fostered interest in global education. Minority–majority schools offer courses in ethnic studies or cultural pluralism. Education colleges encourage teaching values that support cultural diversity, ethnic awareness, alternative lifestyles, gender preference, and understanding of cultural pluralism with social action programs. Courses in diversity include efforts to encourage students to view the world through minority perceptions and to become engaged in efforts for social justice.

Bilingual and bicultural education grew out of problems non- and limited-English-speaking children were having in English-only schools, which most states required before the civil rights movement. In the 1960s, it was noted that large numbers of students failed or dropped out because the instruction was in a language foreign to them, especially in Texas, where Spanish-speaking students entered schools in which teachers spoke no Spanish. In 1968, the Bilingual Education Act was passed (with nearly $160 million appropriations by 1979), calling for instruction in two languages for non-native children. Bilingual education was supported in a 1974 Supreme Court case, *Lau v. Nichols*. Some Native American and Asian language projects were created, but most bilingual instruction is English-Spanish.

Minority and culturally diverse students often suffer from cultural clash in educational situations; for example, some Indian youngsters are taught silence in the presence of elders. In addition, Native American primary learning patterns are very different from those expected in most classrooms. Although Black English is not a bilingual program, students speaking a black dialect often have trouble acquiring standard English language. Educators need diverse instructional approaches with different ethnic groups; social justice issues are a concern for all.

Opposition to bilingual and multicultural education is widespread. Obviously the "back to basics" people are against spending time in pluralistic or multicultural studies instead of fundamental courses. Conservatives regard such studies as "frills" that should be eliminated from the basic curriculum. Others argue that the multiculturalism tends to promote cultural, social, and economic separation, and want the schools to emphasize the dominant core values and assimilate other cultures into mainstream America. Some feel that bilingual programs discourage the use of English by allowing children to function in school with another language.

Teaching Transcultural Values.   Despite these concerns, educators realize that equality is the basis of American society and that recognizing and appreciating the unique contributions of others, including African Americans, Native Americans, women, Hispanics, and Asian Americans, enhances communication and mutual appreciation.

As Dewey noted, schools are miniature societies. Forms of discrimination (sexism, racism, and classism) and cultural and linguistic conflicts are reflected in our schools. America's historical treatment of Hispanics, Asian Americans, and Native Americans has left wounds that still bleed. In *The Ethical, Legal, and Multicultural Foundations of Teaching* (1993), Fred Kierstead and Paul Wagner call for "transcultural" education, designed to provide for an interchange of cultural ideas in which multicultural education's divisive components would be replaced by the study of a culture's diverse contribution to humanity as a whole. Rather than stressing cultural differences within an American macroculture, transcultural education would study cultures' unifying themes and commonalities.

The Changing Role of Women in Education.   The equal rights for women cause has a history as long as that for minorities. Since Emma Hart Willard began a girls' boarding school in her home in 1814 and Mary Lyon opened Mount Holyoke Seminary in 1837, women have sought social justice. The following are a few leaders in women's search for equality.

Elizabeth Blackwell became the first American woman to earn the doctor of medicine degree, and astronomer Maria Mitchell was appointed the first female science professor at Vassar in 1862. Florence Bascom became a geologist with the U.S. Geological Survey in 1896 and a fellow of the Geological Society of America in 1894. In 1920, Florence Sabin, who took one of the first medical degrees from Johns Hopkins University, was the first woman to be elected to the National Academy of Sciences. Alice Evans was elected the first female president of the Society of American Bacteriologists in 1928, and Maria Mayer won the Nobel Prize in 1963 for physics research. Other prizes went to Rosalyn Yalow for medicine in 1977 and to Barbara McClintock in physiology and medicine in 1983.

Historian Darlene Clark Hine, editor of *Black Women in America: An Historical Encyclopedia* (2005), provides a reference book that describes the role of black women in American history from the seventeenth century to the present. From Africans put ashore from a Dutch ship at Jamestown in 1619 to Senator Moseley Braun's 1992 Illinois election, Hine provides detailed accounts of the struggles for progress and survival.

Edward Stevens and George Wood, in *Justice, Ideology, and Education* (1992), note that the civil rights movement, antiwar protests, and counterculture groups created a climate of liberation. Sexual discrimination has been addressed in Title IX of the Educational Amendments of 1972. Currently the *Educational Law Reporter* shows an increase in cases dealing with sex discrimination and harassment. Sexual harassment programs are held for employees in most of society's institutions.

The Civil Rights Act of 1991 includes a section dealing with civil rights and women's equity in employment, and the Glass Ceiling Act or Women's Equal Opportunity Act rewards firms demonstrating extensive efforts to create opportunities for women and minorities and assist them in reaching upper management positions. Major corporations, leading universities, and other institutions provide valuing-diversity workshops, seminars, and training sessions that deal with retaining and promoting culturally diverse employees. Sensitivity sessions are used to deal with issues of sexual harassment, as well as subtle forms of discrimination against women and minorities. The Supreme Court ruled in *Jackson v. Birmingham Board of Education* (2005) that individuals are protected from retaliation when they report unfair treatment of women.

Traditionally, the work of women has been viewed as less valuable than that of men. This view has helped keep teacher status and salaries low in a female-dominated profession. The selection of social studies teacher Christa McAuliffe for the ill-fated 1986 *Challenger* flight enhanced female educator prestige, but men still hold the majority of high-paying school administrative positions. In spite of decades of work to eradicate sexual stereotypes from textbooks and the National Organization for Women's (NOW) call for gender equity, discrimination still exists. Harvard President Lawrence Summers's remark about underrepresentation of women in science and math because of inherent gender differences led to virulent protests and profuse apologies (Fogg, 2005), but research shows girls are still discouraged from seeking careers in science and mathematics. In "Glass Ceiling Restricts Women" (1996), Lynne O'Shea notes the public education "glass ceiling"; women make up 75 percent of classroom teachers, but only 10 percent of superintendents nationwide. This situation will change in the future because of the increased number of women in educational administration graduate and doctoral programs. Successful women provide role models for girls and mentoring to help improve female status within society and the workforce. Jane Fonda donated $12.5 million for the establishment of an interdisciplinary research center at Harvard University's Graduate School of Education, which will specialize in exploring the effect of gender on learning and development in children.

Rimm and Kaufman in *How Jane Won: 55 Successful Women Share How They Grew* (2001) provide narrative accounts of how women overcome challenges to move from ordinary girls to extraordinary women. Goldberg, in a 2000 *Phi Delta Kappan* interview, "Restoring Lost Voices," notes Carol Gilligan's research with adolescent girls calling for amplifying children's voices by creating curriculum to engage in understanding of what they are saying and seeing. The National Women's Studies Association works to change women's lives through feminist education, with research at prekindergarten through postsecondary levels.

A large number of American women, especially single mothers, live in poverty. In *Women and Children Last* (1986), Hunter College Professor Ruth Sidel calls for a more humane set of social policies to deal with poverty, work and welfare, and the rights of women and children. Although much progress has been made, female equality in education and economics will continue to be an issue in the twenty-first century. Brimmer (2010) notes that the Obama administration's Secretary of State Hillary Clinton finds the global status of women a political, economic, and social imperative. Secretary Clinton has created a position of Ambassador at Large for Global Women's Issues. Women in China have benefited from economic growth and the communist view that females can hold important jobs, but they still suffer from the zero population growth policy.

Because families preferred boys, many females were aborted and today there is a shortage of women in many parts of the nation. Likewise in India, the old culture was male dominated. Hindu tradition required that girls obey their fathers and husbands and even supported suttee (burning of the wife when the husband died). These practices are no longer in vogue and Indian women have gained in status, but equity with males has not yet been achieved. This is even more true for the Arabic nations where Islam has not supported freedom or equality for women. American has made great strides toward gender equality but globally the gap between the sexes remains great.

TAKING SIDES TODAY AND TOMORROW

In this chapter, we have discussed issues, litigation, and contemporary critics. In every controversy, there is a connection to earlier issues, critics, or litigation. Nothing at issue in modern American education is without historical foundation. The current question of the federal government's proper role in educational matters relates to the Northwest Ordinance land grants and the Morrill acts. The caustic criticism of schools in Illich's *Deschooling Society* (1971) mirrors the centuries earlier attack on society and education in Rousseau's *Emile*.

The relationship between schools and the wider society is still debated. The 1870s appeal of Kalamazoo citizens to the courts used litigation to resolve educational conflict, as did the 1950s desegregation cases, the 1970s equal opportunity cases, and the twenty-first century lawsuits over financial support. Some aspects of the social and educational milieu stir up extreme public emotion and debate. An example is the *Roe v. Wade* case legalizing abortion, and the strongly held opinions about whether it should be upheld or reversed. Another is the question of whether small school districts with scarce resources must bear the whole cost of educating students with severe disabilities. Few object in principle to Public Law 94-142 and its mandates of a "least restrictive environment" education for children with disabilities. However, McCay Vernon cites a New Jersey situation in which educating one child with extreme hyperactivity places an added $1,500 per year tax burden on each citizen of the county. This problem has not been solved for the future, and is sure to be an issue for years to come.

Sometimes, a local reaction to a wider controversy can so divide a community that education is affected for a long time. In Kanawha County, West Virginia, textbook selection by two committees (from state-approved textbook lists) was forwarded to the board, which unanimously voted to accept it, and made the collection available for public review. By the winter of 1975, many of the books were labeled as "dirty, anti-Christian, or anti-American" by some parents and local groups, with local ministers divided on the issue. The flames were fanned by diverse opposing organizations: the NEA, the Council of Parents and Teachers, the NAACP, the National Library Association, the Ku Klux Klan, and the John Birch Society. The board finally banned books that depicted racial strife, demeaned patriotism, supported alien forms of government, debased religious or ethnic groups, encouraged sedition, or used offensive language. The judgment was so very broad that a great many books were removed from the schools.

Underlying this turbulent issue over textbooks were basic social conflicts. Kanawha County was made up of about 200,000 people; two-thirds were relatively affluent and one-third were rural, poor, Appalachian coal miners. This second group was denied an adequate standard of living and felt exploited. The schools, including the textbook committees, allowed them little or no involvement decisions. In the aftermath of the Kanawha County controversy, it is clear that a much deeper community conflict trigged textbook selection issues.

We can anticipate future educational arguments whenever there are serious values conflicts within the culture. In communities containing both fundamentalists and religious liberals, it is to be expected that creationists will pose arguments against evolution as the only credible theory of the origin of life. The conflict illustrates dominant group values resulting in variation in the quality of education different groups of children receive.

Many of the results of controversy on issues such as involuntary segregation are now history. However, heated debate continues on unfavorable comparisons of American and foreign students on standardized achievement tests. Decades of federal support for equalization programs like Head Start and Upward Bound did not support high levels of achievement. *A Nation at Risk* triggered an emphasis on competition, excellence, and high academic standards. Reagan administration Education Secretary William Bennett supported programs like the Great Books of the Western World and Mortimer Adler's Paideia proposal. The classical-perennialist curriculum of James Madison High School and the highly general liberal arts program became the 1980s model of quality secondary education. Regardless of its merits, critics like Floretta McKenzie, school superintendent in Washington, DC, argue the perennial approach fails to provide vocational training, job skills, and comprehensive instructional strategies to accommodate different learning styles of poorly motivated students. Dr. McKenzie is a prominent practicing educator and a leading advocate of minority education and equality who feels that the Great Books type of program leads to a dual system of education and increases the dropout rate, especially in states like Texas, where half of the 3.5 million school-age children are black or Hispanic.

John Gardner (1961) may have put it best when he asked, "Can we be equal and excellent too?" Access, achievement, and equity is the challenge of the future in a multiracial society with persistent pockets of poverty, crime, and violence.

With the 50 separate state educational systems, a continuing issue is providing equality of opportunity by eliminating differences in per capita dollars supporting each child within states. Courts have recently ruled that Arkansas, Texas, and Montana are in violation of required equalization rules. The fundamental problem is securing adequate taxation to support schools in areas where the economy is weak or other budget items, such as roads, get priority. Finding creative, innovative ways to finance schools, plus coping with increasingly expensive litigation in a litigious society, will continue to be a challenge.

George Sanchez found that Texas students with Spanish family names received on average one-fourth the years of formal education of those with Anglo family names. Well over five million children now come from homes in which English is not the primary language.

The composition of the Supreme Court affects affirmative action, diversity issues, and conservative versus liberal agendas. The Court's makeup will cause bitter debate when new nominees come up for Senate confirmation. School boards and school districts face divisive issues such as Christmas caroling, reciting the Pledge of Allegiance, prayers in schools, teaching religious history in schools, and a variety of parental concerns. These issues reflect an increasingly diverse society with multiple cultures and subcultures challenging traditional mores of society. The rapid increase in immigration is controversial in many states, but businesses want low-skilled, entry-level workers to fill jobs.

GAINING PERSPECTIVE THROUGH CRITICAL ANALYSIS

1. Name at least two ways educational controversies arise. How have past controversies been dealt with, and what strategies do past actions suggest for the present?

2. Identify at least three events that demonstrate the continuing problems of separation of church and state as it relates to religion in the public schools at home and abroad.

3. It has now been over 50 years since *Brown v. Board of Education*. Give your opinion regarding the effects of the 1954 decision on education today. Do you think we have unity within diversity or a more fragmented society? Give reasons for your answers. Discuss and answer the questions at the end of the Focus on the Issues features "Church and State" and "Language." These features are found within the chapter.

4. Choose two court cases that you think have made the greatest contribution toward improving the quality of opportunity in educational programs. Give two reasons why you selected the court cases.

5. Give the pros and cons of affirmative action. Identify recent Supreme Court cases on affirmative action.

6. Name three critics of education in America, and identify their major criticisms. (You could focus on high-stakes testing, obesity programs, English as a second language, immigration, English immersion vs. bilingual education, school financing, poverty, crime, gender issues, service learning, No Child Left Behind.)

7. Throughout our educational and social history there has been a trend to expanding rights, access, and opportunities to ever more of the population. Ethnic minorities, the disabled, the aged, those of alternative gender, and a multitude of other groups have seen increased affirmative action programs. Recently some school districts have been exploring inclusion of LGBT topics in civil rights programs and courses. Discuss our history and social foundations of expanded civil rights in school courses, programs, and educational aims.

HISTORY IN ACTION IN TODAY'S CLASSROOMS

1. Arrange a telephone interview (or an email correspondence) with a schoolteacher or administrator to determine his or her perceptions of future trends in education. Add these findings to your journal, and compare your findings with those of your classmates.

2. In your opinion, is the primary purpose of school to be an agency for social action or to impart basic knowledge through a planned curriculum, or both? Support your opinion with examples from the current literature in your field. Add the information to your journal.

BIBLIOGRAPHY

Most of the controversial issues in education are well covered in electronic databases such as ERIC and through search engines of the Internet.

Alexander, Kern, & M. David Alexander. *American Public School Law.* Belmont, CA: Wadsworth, 2001, 440, 539. Cases cited: *Watson v. City of Cambridge,* 157 Mass. 561, 32 N.E. 864 (1893) and State ex. rel. *Beattie v. Board of Education,* 169 Wis. 231, 172 N.S. 153 (1919).

Americans with Disabilities Act of 1990. Washington, DC: U.S. Department of Labor (1990). www.dol.gov

Archer, Jeff, & Julie Blair. "Performance Testing Being Readied for Ohio Teachers." *Education Week Quality Counts* (January 17, 2001): 14.

Archer, Jeff, & Julie Blair. "If I Can't Learn from You: Ensuring a Highly Qualified Teacher in Every Classroom." *Education Week Quality Counts* (2003).

Ashton-Warner, Sylvia. *Teacher.* New York: Simon & Schuster, 1963.

Ashton-Warner, Sylvia. *Spearpoint: Teacher in America.* New York: Knopf, 1972.

Barzun, Jacques. *Teacher in America.* Boston: Little, Brown, 1945.

Bender v. Williamsport, 475 U.S. 534, 106 S.Ct. 1326 (1986).

Berliner, David C. "Educational Psychology Meets the Christian Right: Differing Views of Children, Schooling, Teaching and Learning." *Teachers College Record* (Spring 1997): 381–416.

Berliner, David C., & Bruce J. Biddle. *The Manufactured Crisis: Myths, Fraud and the Attack on America's Public Schools.* New York: Addison Wesley, 1995.

"The Bible & Public Schools: A First Amendment Guide." Freedom Forum, The National Bible Association and First Amendment Center (November 11, 1999). Available at: www.firstamendmentcenter.org/about. aspx?id56261

Bloom, Benjamin. *All Our Children Learning.* New York: McGraw-Hill, 1980.

Bok, Sissela. *Lying: Moral Choice in Public and Private Life.* New York: Alfred A. Knopf, 1999.

Bowles, Samuel, & Herbert Gintis. *Schooling in Capitalist America.* New York: Basic Books, 1976.

Bown v. Gwinnett County School District, 112 F3d 1464 (11th Cir. 1997).

Bowman, Darcia Harris. "Republicans Prefer to Back Vouchers by Any Other Name." *Education Week* (January 31, 2001): 22.

Bracey, Gerald W. "Why Can't They Be Like We Were?" *Phi Delta Kappan* (October 1991): 104–117.

Bracey, Gerald W. "Our Eternal (and Futile?) Quest for High Standards. *Phi Delta Kappan* (December 2009–January 2010): 75–76.

Bracey, Gerald W. "The Third Bracey Report on the Condition of Public Education." *Phi Delta Kappan* (October 1993): 105–117.

Bracey, Gerald W. "The Tenth Bracey Report on the Condition of Education." *Phi Delta Kappan* (October 2000): 133–144.

Bracey, Gerald W. "The Thirteenth Bracey Report on the Condition of Education." *Phi Delta Kappan* (October 2003): 148–164.

Bracey, Gerald W. "The Fourteenth Bracey Report on the Condition of Education." *Phi Delta Kappan* (October 2004): 149–167.

Bradwell v. Illinois, 16 Wall 130: 142 (1873).

Brameld, Theodore. *Philosophies of Education in Cultural Perspective.* New York: The Dryden Press, 1955.

Brimmer, Ester. "Women as Agents of Change: Advancing the Role of Women in Politics and Society." U.S. Department of State (June 9, 2010). Available at: www.state.gov/p/io/rm/2010/142900.htm

Brown v. Board of Education, 347 U.S. 480 (1954).

Brown v. Board of Education, 349 U.S. 294 (1955).

Bruner, Jerome S. *The Culture of Education.* Cambridge, MA: Harvard University Press, 1996.

Bushaw, William, & Shane Lopez. *A Time for Change: The 42nd Annual Phi Delta Kappa/Gallup Poll* (September, 2010): 8. Available at: www.kappanmagazine.org

Byham, William C. *Zapp in Education.* New York: Fawcett Columbine, 1992.

"Cardinal Principles of Secondary Education." *National Education Association Report* (1918). www.archive .org

Cavanagh, Sean. "Race to the Top Now Faces Acid Test, Winners Brace for Challenge of Putting $4 Billion to Work." *Education Week* (September 1, 2010): 1, 16, 17.

Census Bureau (2011). www.census.gov

"Charter Connection." Center for Educational Reform (January 2005). Available at: www.edreform.com/home

Christian Legal Society v. Martinez, 561 U.S. _130. S.Ct. 2971 (2010).

"Civil Rights Act of 1991." Glass Ceiling and Women's Equal Opportunity (1991). www.Teaching AmericanHistory.org

Cochran Smith, Marilyn. *Walking the Road: Race, Diversity, and Social Justice in Education.* New York: Columbia University Teachers College Press, 2004.

Cochran v. Louisiana State Broad of Education, 281 U.S. 370 (1930).

Coeyman, Marjorie. "When Special Education?" *The Christian Science Monitor* (March 13, 2001): 15, 18.

Coleman, James. *Equality of Educational Opportunity.* Washington, DC: Government Printing Office, 1996. Referred to as the "Coleman Report."

Conant, James. *The American High School Today.* New York: McGraw-Hill, 1959.

Cook, Eugene, & William I. Potter. "The School Segregation Cases: Opposing the Opinion of the Supreme Court." *American Bar Association Journal* 42 (April 1956): 313.

Cordasco, Francesco. Council of Basic Education (now disbanded). *Bilingual Schooling in the United States: A Sourcebook for Educational Personnel.* New York: McGraw-Hill, 1976.

D'Amico, R., C. Marder, L. Newman, & Mary Wagner. *What Happens Next? Trends in Post School Outcomes of Youth with Disabilities.* Menlo Park, CA: SRI International, 1992.

Darden, Edwin C. "Prayer Falls on Hard Times." In *Legal Issues in Education Practice: Challenges and Opportunities in the 21st Century.* Education Law Association 2000 Conference Papers (2000): 6–10.

Darling-Hammond, Linda. *Preparing Teachers for a Changing World.* New York: John Wiley & Sons, 2005.

Davis v. Monroe County Board of Education, 526 U.S. 629, 119 S.Ct. 1662 (1999).

Debra v. Turlington, 564 F. Supplement 177 (1983).

Debra v. Turlington, 730 F.2d. 1405 (11th Cir. 1984).

Decker, Sunny. *An Empty Spoon.* New York: Harper & Row, 1969.

Dennison, George. *The Lives of Children: The Story of First Street School.* New York: Random House, 1969.

Doe v. Plyler, 458 F. Supp. 569 (E.D. Tex. 1978).

Donohue v. Copiague, 64 A.D.2d.29; 47 NYS 2d.440 (1979).

Edgewood v. Kirby, 777. S.W. 2d 391 (Tex, 1989).

Education Planet. Available at: www.educationplanet .com/

Edwards v. Aguillard, 482, U.S. 578 (1987).

Elk Grove Unified School District v. Newdow, 542 U.S. 1 (2004).

Engel v. Vitale, 370 U.S. 421 (1962).

Epperson v. Arkansas, 393 U.S. 97 (1968).

Everson v. Board of Education, 330 U.S. 1 (1947).

Featherstone, Joseph. *Schools Where Children Learn.* New York: Liveright Press, 1968.

Federal Glass Ceiling Commission. *Fact Finding Report.* Washington, DC: U.S. Government Printing Office (March 1995). Felsenthal, Edward. "Christian Right Falls Out of Unison on School Prayer." *Wall Street Journal* (February 24, 1997): A 24.

Finn, Chester, Jr., & Diane Ravitch. "Basic Instincts." *Wall Street Journal* (2006, February 27): A 14.

"Florida Legislator Wants Teachers to Grade Parents." CNN (January 26, 2011). Available at: www.CNN.com

Floretta McKenzie v. Christopher Smith, 771.F2d.1527 (1985).

Fogg, Piper. "Women and Science: The Debate Goes On." *The Chronicle of Higher Education* (March 4, 2005): A1, A8.

"For Goodness Sake: Why So Many Want Religion to Play a Greater Role in American Life." Public Agenda Research Studies (2001). Available at: www.publicagenda.org/specials/religion/religion.htm

Frahm, Robert A. "NAACP Opposes State Law." *Hartford Courant* (January 31, 2006).

Friedenberg, Edgar Z. *Sentimental Education.* New York. Review of Books, 1969.

Gardner, John W. *Excellence: Can We Be Equal and Excellent Too?* New York: Harper & Row, 1961.

Garrett, Rose. "NCLB Reauthorization: The New Blueprint" (March 16, 2010). www.edreform.com-educationissuestoday/

Gatti, Richard, & Daniel Gatti. *New Encyclopedia Dictionary of School Law.* West Nyack, NY: Parker Publishing Company, 1983.

Gewertz, Catherine. "Internet Tycoon Gives $250 Million for Cognitive-Disabilities Project." *Education Week* (January 24, 2001): 7.

Gewertz, Catherine. "Curriculum Producers Work to Reflect Common Standards." *Education Week* (August 25, 2010): 1, 20.

Glasser, William. *Schools Without Failure.* New York: Harper & Row, 1968.

Glasser, William. *The Quality School: Managing Students Without Coercion.* New York: Harper, 1998.

Goldberg, Mark E. "Restoring Lost Voices." *Phi Delta Kappan* (May 2000): 701–704.

Good News Club v. Milford Central School, 533 U.S. 98 (2001).

Goodlad, John. "What Are Schools For?" Bloomington, IN: Phi Delta Kappa Foundation, 1979.

Gootman, Elissa. "More Children Take the Tests for Gifted Programs, and More Qualify." *The New York Times* (May 4, 2009). Available at: www.nytimes.com/2009/05/05/education/05gifted.html

Goss v. Lopez, 419, U.S. 565 (1975).

Greene, Jay P. "An Evaluation of the Florida A-Plus Accountability and School Choice Program." New York: The Manhattan Institute for Policy Research. (February 2001). Available at: www.manhattan-institute.org/html/cr_aplus.htm

Gratz v. Bollinger, 539 U.S. 244 (2003).

Grutter v. Bollinger, 539 U.S. 306 (2003).

"Guidance on Religion in Schools Is Available." *Your School and the Law* 26, no. 7 (July 1996): 4.

Hendrie, Caroline. "Charter Authorizers Eye Rules on Closings." *Education Week* (February 2005): 1, 20.

Hibbs v. Winn, 542 U.S. 124 S.Ct. 2276 (2002).

Hine, Darlene Clark. *Black Women in America: An Historical Encyclopedia*. 2nd ed. Brooklyn, NY: Carlson Publishing (2005).

Hobson v. Hansen, 269 F. Supp (1967).

Holt, John. *How Children Fail*. New York: Pitman, 1964.

Holt, John. *What Do I Do Monday?* New York: Dutton, 1970.

Holt, John. *Freedom and Beyond*. New York: Dutton, 1972.

Horne v. Flores,129 S. Ct 2579, 557_____U.S. (2009).

Huelskamp, Robert M. "Perspectives on Education in America." *Phi Delta Kappan* (May 1993): 718–721.

Hurst, Marianne. "Fonda Gives Harvard Education School $12 Million." *Education Week* (March 7, 2001): 10.

"Individuals with Disabilities." *Federal Education Budget Project* (2010). Available at: www.febp.newamerica.net/background-analysis/individuals-disabilities-education

"Individuals with Disability Education Act." IDEA (2004). www.idea.ed.gov

"Guarantees All Children Age 3-21 Free Appropriate Public Education." Individuals with Disability Act Amendments 1997. www.insource.org

"Improving Student Learning in America's Public Schools." The Learning First Alliance (2011). www.learningfirst.org

Illich, Ivan. *Deschooling Society*. New York: Harper, 1971.

Jackson v. Birmingham Board of Education, 544 U.S. 167 (2005).

Jacobson, Linda. "Clinton's Early-Learning Fund Quietly Becomes Reality." *Education Week* (January 24, 2001): 22.

Jenks, Christopher. *Inequality. A Reassessment of the Effects of Family and Schooling in America*. New York: Harper Colophon Books, 1981.

Jensen, Arthur R. "How Much Can We Boost I.Q. and Scholastic Achievement?" *Harvard Educational Review* 39, no. 1 (Winter 1969): 1–123.

Jensen, Arthur R. "Reducing the Heredity-Environment Uncertainty." *Harvard Educational Review* 39, no. 3 (Summer 1969): 449–483.

Jones, R. L., Ed. *Mainstreaming and the Minority Child*. Reston, VA: Council for Exceptional Children, 1976.

Keys v. Denver, 413 U.S. 189 (1973).

Kierstead, Fred, & Paul Wagner. *The Ethical, Legal and Multicultural Foundations of Teaching*. New York: McGraw Hill, 2002.

Klein, Alyson. "Political Complexity, Political Calculus, Cloud ESEA Reauthorization Outlook" *Education Week* (May 19, 2010): 28–29.

Klein, Alyson. "Focus Turns to Congress After High Court's Denial of Challenge to NCLB Law." *Education Week* (June 16, 2010): 24.

Kohl, Herbert. *36 Children*. New York: New American Library, 1967.

Kohl, Herbert. *The Open Classroom*. New York: Vintage Books, 1970.

Kohn, Alfie. *The Schools Our Children Deserve: Moving Beyond Traditional Classrooms and Tougher Standards*. New York: Houghton Mifflin, 2000.

Kohn, Alfie. *What Does It Mean to Be Well Educated? And More Essays on Standards, Grading, and Other Follies*. Boston: Beacon Press, 2004.

Kozol, Jonathan. *Death at an Early Age: The Destruction of the Hearts and Minds of Negro Children in the Boston Public Schools*. Boston: Houghton Mifflin, 1967.

Kozol, Jonathan. *Free Schools*. Boston: Houghton Mifflin, 1972.

Kozol, Jonathan. *Illiterate America*. Garden City, NY: Anchor Press/Doubleday, 1985.

Kozol, Jonathan. *Savage Inequalities*. New York: Harper, 1992.

Kozol, Jonathan. *Amazing Grace: The Lives of Children and the Conscience of Nation*. New York: Harper, 1996.

Kozol, Jonathan. *Ordinary Resurrections Children in the Years of Hope*. New York: Crown Publishing Group, 2000.

Kozol, Jonathan. *Shame of the Nation*. New York: Crown Publishing, 2005.

Kozol, Jonathan. "State of Education." Lecture at University of Arkansas, Fayetteville (Summer 2010).

La Follette, Marcel Chotkowski. *Creationism, Science, and the Law: The Arkansas Case.* Cambridge, MA: MIT Press, 1993.

Lamb's Chapel v. Center Moriches Union Free School District, 508 U.S. 384 (1993).

Lau v. Nichols, 414 U.S. 563 (1974).

"Education for All Handicapped Children." Public Law 94-142 (1975). www2.ed.gov/policy

Leonard, George Burr. *Education and Ecstasy*. New York: Delacorte Press, 1968.

Lemon v Kurtzman, 403 U.S. 602 (1971).

Lessinger, Leon. *Every Kid a Winner: Accountability in Education*. New York: Simon & Schuster, 1970.

Lindseth, Alfred A. "Adequacy Lawsuits: The Wrong Answer for Our Kids," *Education Week* (June 9, 2004): 52.

Locke v. Davey, 540 U.S. 124 S.Ct. 1300 (2004).

Manno, Bruno V., Chester Finn, Jr., & Gregg Vanourek. "Beyond the Schoolhouse Door: How Charter Schools Are Transforming U.S. Public Education." *Phi Delta Kappan* (June 2000): 737.

Marland, S. P., Jr. (1972). *Education of the Gifted and Talented: Report to the Congress of the United States by the U.S. Commissioner of Education and Background Papers Submitted to the U.S. Office of Education*, 2 vols. Government Documents Y4.L 11/2: G36. Washington, DC: U.S. Government Printing Office.

Massa, 95 N.J. Super 382, 231 A.2d. 252 (Morris County Ct, 1967).

Mazanee v. North Judson-San Pierre School Corp, 614 F. Supp. 1152 (Nd Ind. 1985).

McCarthy, Martha M., & Nelda H. Cambron-McCabe. *Public School Law: Teachers' and Students' Rights*. Boston: Allyn & Bacon, 1992.

McCollum v. Board of Education of Champaign, Illinois, 333 U.S. 203 (1948).

McLean v. Arkansas Board of Education, 529 F.Supp. 1255 (1982).

McTighe, Joe. "New Idea Demands You Talk Shop with Private Schools." *Your School and the Law* (January 12, 2005): 5.

"Mission Statement." Rogers Arkansas School District (2011). www.rogersschool.net

Murray, Dave. "Teacher Unions, Duncan Announce Conference on Collaboration, but Are School Boards Left Out?" *The Grand Rapids Press* (October 16, 2010).

Mendez, Teresa. "A Special Compromise on Education." *The Christian Science Monitor* (November 22, 2004): 11, 12.

Meyer v. Nebraska, 262 U.S. 390 (1923).

Miller, Sara B. "Demand on Special Education Is Growing." *The Christian Science Monitor* (August 24, 2004): 1, 3.

Milliken v. Bradley, 418 U.S. 717 (1974).

Minersville School District v. Gobitis, 310 U.S. 586, 60 S.Ct. 1010 (1940).

Missouri v. Jenkins, 216 F.3d 720 (2000).

Mitchell v. Helms, (98–1648) 151 F 3d 347 reversed (2000).

Morgan v. Hennigan, 379 F. Supp. 410 (DC.Mass. June 21, 1974). "NEA 2000–2001 Resolutions." National Education Association (2000). Available at: www.nea.org/

New Jersey v T.L.O., 469 US. 325 (1985).

Nieto, Sonia. *Affirming Diversity*. New York: Longman, 1992.

"No Child Left Behind Act/ESEA." National Education Association (February 6, 2005). Available at: www .nea.org/esea/index.html

Noll, James. *Taking Sides: Clashing Views on Controversial Educational Issues*. Guilford, CT: Duskin, 1980.

Olson, Lynn. "States Revive Efforts to Coax NCLB Changes." *Education Week* (February 2, 2005).

Ormstein, Allan, & Daniel Levine. *An Introduction to the Foundations of Education*. 2nd ed. Boston: Houghton Mifflin, 1981.

O'Shea, Lynne. "Glass Ceiling Restricts Women." *Collegiate Times* (1996). Available at: www.dol.gov/oasam/programs/history

Parents Involved in Community Schools v. Seattle School District No.1, 551 U.S. 701 (2007).

Parsons, Chdristi, & Lisa Mascaro. "Obama's Education Plan An Early Test of Civility." *South Florida Sun Sentinel* (February 6, 2011): 5A.

Patton, James, & Ronald L. Braithwaite. "P.L.94-142 and the Changing Status of Teacher Certification/Recertification" *The Journal of Teacher Division of the Council of Exceptional Children* (April 1980): 43–47. Available at: www.deepdyve.com/lp/sage/p-l-94-142-and-the-changing-status-of-teacher-certification-Blu1TufOoN

Phi Delta Kappa/Gallup 2000–2004, 2010. Available at: www.pdkinti.org.

Piaget, Jean. *Play, Dreams and Imitation in Childhood*. New York: Norton, 1962.

Pierce v. Society of Sisters, 268 U.S. 510 (1925).

Plessy v. Ferguson, 163 U.S. 537 (1896).

Plyler v. Doe, 457, U.S. 202 (1982).

Postman, Neil, & Charles Weingartner. *Teaching as a Subversive Activity*. New York: Delacorte Press, 1969.

Powell, Arthur, Eleanor Farrar, & David Cohen. *The Shopping Mall High School*. Boston: Houghton Mifflin, 1985.

Pratte, Richard. *Pluralism in Education*. Springfield, IL: Charles C. Thomas, 1979.

"President Bush's FY 2005 Budget." The White House. www.georgewbush-whitehouse.archives.gov/infocus/budget/2005"Privatization of Public Education—From Vouchers to Outsourcing." National Education Association. www.nea.org/privatization/

Proctor, Samuel B., Ed. *A Man for Tomorrow's World: Addresses by Theodore Roszak and Alexander Frazier*. Washington, DC: Association for Supervision and Curriculum Development, 1970.

"Basic Rights Protection for Children with Disabilities." Public Law 105-17 (1999). www2.ed.gov

Race to the Top. Washington, DC: U.S. Department of Education, Spring 2011. Available at: www2.ed.gov/programs/racetothetop/index.html

Ravitch, Diane. *The Revisionists Revised: A Critique of the Radical Attack on the Schools*. New York: Basic Books, 1995.

Regents of the University of California v. Bakke, 438, U.S. 265 (1978).

"Religious Liberty, Public Education, and the Future of American Democracy." *Educational Leadership* (May 1995): 92–93.

Richey, Warren. "Can Religious Groups Hold Meetings in Public Schools?" *The Christian Science Monitor* (February 28, 2001): 1, 4.

"Rights Under 504 of Rehabilitation Act." The Rehabilitation Act of 1973. www.hhs.gov/ocr/504.html

Rimm, Sylvia B., & Sara Rimm Kaufman. *How Jane Won: 55 Successful Women Share How They Grew*. New York: Crown Publishing, 2001.

Rose, Lowell, & Alec M. Gallup. "The 32nd Annual Phi Delta Kappa/Gallup Poll of the Public's Attitudes Toward the Public Schools." *Phi Delta Kappan* (September, 2000): 42.

Rose v. Council for Better Schools, 790 S.W.2d, 186 60 EdLaw 1289 Rep (1989).

Rossow, Lawrence F., & Jerry Parkinson. "U.S. Department of Education, Office of Civil Rights, Sexual Harassment Guidance: Harassment of Students by School Employees, Other Students, or Third Parties." *School Law Reporter* 39, no. 5 (May 1997): 49–50.

Roszak, Theodore. *Where the Wasteland Ends: Politics and Transcendence in Postindustrial Society*. Garden City, NJ: Doubleday, 1972.

Roszak, Theodore. *The Making of a Counter Culture*. Berkeley, CA: University of California Press, 1995.

Roe v. Wade, 410 U.S. 113 (1973).

Russo, Charles J. "To Opt Out or Not to Opt Out? That Is the Military Recruiting Question." *Your School and The Law* (November 3, 2004): 1, 8.

Russo, Charles J., & Ralph Mawdsley. "U.S. Supreme Court Reviews Issue on School Access by Religious Groups." *Your School and the Law* (March 14, 2001): 1, 6.

Sack, Joetta L. "Special Education Costs Can Be Taxing for Districts." *Education Week* (March 14, 2001): 1, 32, 33.

San Antonio Independent School District v. Rodriguez, 411 U.S. 1 (1973).

Serrano v. Priest, 5 Cal.3d.584 P.2d 1241 (Cal. 1971).

Samuels, Christina A. "Renewed IDEA Targets Minority Overrepresentation." *Education Week* (December 8, 2004): 24, 28.

Sanchez, George. *Forgotten People: A Study of New Mexicans*. Albuquerque, NM: University of New Mexico Press, 1940.

School District of Pontiac Michigan v. Duncan, 584 F. 3d. 253 (6th Cir. 2010).

Sidel, Ruth. *Women and Children Last: The Plight of Poor Women in Affluent America*. New York: Viking, 1986.

Simmons-Harris v. Zelman, 234 F. 3d 945 (6th Cir. 2000).

Smuck v. Hansen, 132 U.S. App.D.C. 408 F.2d (1969).

"Special Education and Rehabilitative Services." FY 2005 Budget Summary. Available at: www.ed.gov/about/overview/budget/budget05/summary/edlite-section2b.html

"Standards and Accountability." Learning First Alliance (2003). Available at: www.learningfirst.org/news/standards/

Stephens v. Bongart, 189A 131 (N.J. Sup.Court 1937).

Stevens, Edward, & George H. Wood. *Justice, Ideology, and Education*. New York: McGraw-Hill, 1992.

Sundt, Melora. "Effective Sexual Harassment Policies: Focus on the Harasser and the Campus Culture." *Synthesis: Law and Policy* 4, no. 4 (1993): 333.

Sweatt v. Painter, 339, U.S. 629 (1950).

Swift, Matthew. "Reading the Blueprint: Mining the Research." *ASCD Education Update* (August 2010).

Taylor, Bonnie B. *Contemporary Legal Issues*. Denver, CO: ABC-CLIO, 1996.

Thurlow, Martha L., & David R. Johnson. "High-Stakes Testing of Students with Disabilities." *Journal of Teacher Education* 51, no. 4 (September/October 2000): 305–314.

Tinker v. Des Moines Community School District, 393 U.S. 503 (1969).

Toch, Thomas. "Reflections on the Charter School Movement." *Kappan* (May 2010): 70–71.

"Tracking Desegregation Issues, Charter Schools, Integration." Civil Rights Project UCLA (formerly Harvard). Westwood, CA: UCLA, 2011.

Travis, Scott. "Crowding to Ease, School District Says." *Sun-Sentinel South Florida* (March 24, 2001): 1 A, 12 A.

Tuttle v. Arlington Country School Board, 195 F3d.698 (4th Circuit 1999).

Tyack, David. *The One Best System*. Cambridge, MA: Harvard University Press, 1974.

Uddin, Asma. "The Other Muslim Controversy in New York City." (August 20, 2010). Available at: www.altmuslim.com/a/a/b/3913

United States v. Virginia Military Institute, 518,U.S.515 (1996).

"U.S. Circuit Court of Appeals Strikes Down Cleveland's Voucher Program." *Your School and the Law* (2001, January 3): 1, 5.

Vernon, McCay. "Improving the Lives of Both Deaf and Deaf Blind Individuals." *American Psychologist* (November 2006): 815–824. *Vernonia School District 47J v. Acton*, 515 U.S. 646 (1995).

Wagner, Mary, Ronald D'Amico, Camille Marder, Lynn Newman, & Jose Blackorby. *What Happens Next? Trends in Postschool Outcomes of Youth with Disabilities*. Washington, DC: Office of Special Education Program, U.S. Office of Education, 1992.

Walsh, Mark. "Public Sees Role for Religion in Schools." *Education Week* (January 17, 2001): 13.

Webb, Rodman, & Robert Sherman. *Schooling and Society*. 2nd ed. New York: Macmillan, 1989.

West Virginia State Board of Education v. Barnette, 319 U.S. 624 (1943).

West Virginia v. Riddle, 85 S.E. 2d 359, 361 (W. Va 1981).

Wisconsin v. Yoder, 406 U.S. 205, 92 (1972).

Wise, Arthur. *The Bureaucratization of the American Classroom*. Berkeley, CA: University of California Press, 1979.

"Working Through the Decade 1950-59." White House Conference (1955). www.timeline.com

Zelman v. Simmons-Harris, 536 U.S. 639 (2002).

Zirkel, Perry A. "Sorting Out Which Students Have Learning Disabilities." *Phi Delta Kappan* (April 2001): 639–641.

CHAPTER 11

GLOBALIZATION, TRENDS, AND GAINING PERSPECTIVE

Societies . . . are not machines and they are not computers. They cannot be reduced so simply into hardware and software, base and superstructure. A more apt model would picture them as consisting of many more elements, all connected in immensely complex and continually changing feedback loops. As their complexity rises, knowledge becomes more central to their economic and ecological survival.

Alvin Toffler

Industrial Era	Computer Age	Information Age		Post-Industrial Age
1969 *Apollo* moon landing	1970 Toffler's *Future Shock*	1980 Worldwide telecommunications networks		Socialization and basic learning through home computers and TV
	Transistor computer	1982	1990	
First-generation vacuum tube computer	*Explorer* launched	Naisbitt's *Megatrends*	Naisbitt's *Megatrends II 2000*	Social Justice Contingency Workforce Sexism
	Toffler's *Powershift*	Microcomputer in homes		

Figure 11.1   Time Line of Contemporary and Future Education

American teachers have always attempted to prepare their students for the future, even when they expected that future to mirror the present. What distinguishes the current teachings from those in the past is the accelerating rate of change and uncertainty about what the future world will be like. With the nation's schools connected to the Internet, what will be the most effective way of helping students monitor the quality of information accessed? In an interdependent connected world, how can educators address an increased backlash against globalization and its effect on poorer countries? We know that we must deal with lifelong learning, an information explosion, and a global economy, but knowledge of the future remains obscure while change occurs at an ever-more rapid rate. Even Einstein's theory of relativity is being challenged.

When this book's authors were boys growing up in different parts of America, there was no television and only limited radio. Warm summer nights were often spent gazing in wonder at the stars and planets. The Big Dipper was easily recognized, we knew the red planet was Mars, and we had a vague notion that the Milky Way was a galaxy. But we did not know—and could not have known—what every child with instant Internet access, courtesy of smaller, portable, wireless information, can know today. *Voyager* produced close-ups of distant planets. Deep-space probes by the Hubble telescope have revealed some 50 billion galaxies. Astronomers debate the meaning of black holes. More has been learned about our universe since the first moon landing than had been discovered in all prior human history. Back on earth, China has developed into the second largest economy with potential for world domination.

Perhaps nothing better illustrates the explosion of information than the July 4, 1997, *Pathfinder* landing on the surface of Mars. Within hours, pictures were being returned to Earth, placed on the Internet, and viewed by tens of thousands of people

2000				Communications Era
2000 Genetic engineering common	2001 International terrorism strikes U.S.	2005 Automated highways	2015 Human travel by light beam	2030 Mind-to-mind communication
				Nanotechnology
	Cultural wars	2012 Drugs for raising intelligence	Computers with human thought ability	
Microengineering				
2000 All students skilled in computer languages		Eight billion humans on Earth	2020 Worldwide guaranteed minimum income and world peace	Globalization Cheap energy from fusion

at hundreds of websites. Gone were the speculations of Martian canals on Mars and life forms such as those described in Wells's *War of the Worlds* (1898). Theoretical descriptions of Mars in reference books and texts were instantly obsolete as fact replaced conjecture.

The top three languages in the Internet usage in 2010 were English, Chinese, and Spanish. Chinese usage increased 1,277.4 percent while Spanish used increased 743 percent and English by 281 percent ("Internet World Stats," 2010). Modern teachers must develop problem-solving skills, teach how to evaluate information, and make a foundation for lifelong learning. Future survival depends on it. We face a global virtual reality technological age where a machine-generated reality offers new interactive learning. Computer games, holographs, and simulation serve as creative learning experiences as opposed to actual experiences.

History has its own intrinsic value, but most of us are interested in the past because of its practical value in understanding the present and its ability to suggest the probable course of future events. Children now entering kindergarten can reasonably expect to be alive and active well toward the end of the twenty-first century. Colleges that train teachers are currently working with teacher candidates who will directly influence the citizens of the twenty-second century. In periods of very slow cultural change such as the Middle Ages, significant spans of time were not critical. Today, with accelerating invention in many fields, the explosion of research and knowledge, careening technology, electronic communications networks, and computers, the rate of change does indeed approach Toffler's *Future Shock* (1970). The twenty-first century probably will be more different from the twentieth than twentieth was from the nineteenth. Children entrusted to the care of educators may expect changes that stagger the imagination. All indications point to an even faster rate of change that not even an economic depression could reverse. Because we cannot know the future in advance, it is necessary that we must prepare future citizens for as many alternatives as possible. It is extremely difficult to give future generations the skills and information (to say nothing of the attitudes and values) for future survival, but anticipation of future events seems fundamental to the attempt. Understanding different attitudes and values from a myriad of world cultures is absolutely essential.

The television series *Connections* shows how one scientific discovery led to another until the whole shape of technology, and even of human society, was drastically and unexpectedly altered. An illustration is the twelfth-century invention of the chimney, which made it possible to heat numerous rooms on more than one floor. One result was a dramatic change in architecture, because buildings no longer had to be built around one fireplace with a hole in the roof for smoke ventilation.

An educational example is the social revolution that took place in Athens during the fifth century B.C. A new class of rich people emerged, who made their money from banking, shipping, and the manufacture of goods for export. These men wanted to obtain an education for their sons similar to that provided for the young men from the old aristocratic families. For this purpose, they hired migrant teachers called *sophists,* such as Protagoras, Gorgias, and Antiphon. The sophists were skilled at teaching oratory and grammar, but they also criticized conventional morality, religion, and law. They taught practical ways of getting ahead in the world and clever means for evading rules. The sophists drastically changed the values and norms of Athenian society and eventually altered the entire social order. One might easily see a parallel between this social change and current events in oriental nations like China, Japan, and India. The revolt of the people of Egypt and other Middle East peoples is a modern example in the Arab world.

History can also be used as an instrument for analyzing and evaluating major forces or cultural trends in order to anticipate the future. Robert Heilbroner did exactly that in his books *The Future as History* (1959), *An Inquiry into the Human Prospect* (1975), *21st Century Capitalism* (1993), and *Visions of the Future* (1995). Heilbroner looked at long-standing trends in American culture as a means of defining the crucial problems that must be resolved to achieve a viable future. He gave detailed accounts of twentieth-century revolutions to show what must occur if liberal society is to survive. His second book looks at world economic trends, the challenges to political democracy, exploding population, environmental destruction, and obliterative weaponry. His third book suggests that capitalism relies on a mechanism for its economic coordination that is inadequate to meet the needs of our emerging world—namely, of globalization of production and an ecological encounter that will result in major institutional changes. Heilbroner's fourth book searches for unity within diversity to build a civilization more humane and decent than our own. He concludes that neither industrial capitalism nor Marxist socialism in their present forms has the necessary strength to avoid global catastrophe.

Jeremy Rifkin in *The Empathic Civilization: The Race to Global Consciousness in a World in Crisis* (2009) calls for a fundamental rethinking of economic and social

FOCUS ON THE ISSUES

Globalization

The vast majority of Civil War soldiers had not traveled outside the country of their birth before joining the army. Only a handful of World War I troops serving in France had visited Europe before the war. Such limited experiences, especially before the World Wide Web and television news coverage, fostered sectional interests, isolationism, and focus on the familiar local culture. Even today with daily reports from Afghanistan, Iraq, and Palestine; consumer goods of foreign manufacturers; easy global travel; and Internet access to the whole world, people may be thinking locally or nationally. If we are not of a global mind-set, many of our plans will fail. The impact of the automobile on American culture, for example, can scarcely be overemphasized. Not only do we love cars, but we are dependent upon them, especially in our sprawling western towns and cities where public transit is not available or feasible. Most of us understand how great the economic impact of the automobile production has been, but we are no longer dominant in that industry. Our roads are filled with machines made in Japan or South Korea, while those with American trademarks have parts made in Mexico to Taiwan. After the taxpayer bailout of General Motors, a large part of the successful recovery came from the sale of its product in China. Meanwhile, the rising demand for gasoline and declining crude oil reserves causes concern about the future of the combustion engine. As we seek new fields in places like Siberia and worry about disruption of supplies from the Middle East, other problems emerge, such as the huge BP oil spill in the Gulf of Mexico. Development of alternative fuels is progressing slowly, but only Brazil produces enough fuel from alcohol to power most of its vehicles. During the twentieth century, the lion's share of oil was consumed in the United States, with Europe a distant second. Now the demand for trucks and cars in the Orient has altered the equation. China's demand for oil products is second in the world and growing exponentially. Add to this the vast population centers of India and Indonesia, where cars will increase in number as soon as their growing economies will support ownership. Now, the production of cars and trucks for use in India and China has altered the equation. Add to this the vast population centers in India and Indonesia, where cars will increase in numbers as soon as their growing economies will support ownership. The window of time we have for solving the world's oil crisis is dramatically shrinking.

Equally significant is the impact of globalization on education. Call an American company about a problem with a product or bill and you will likely reach a representative in New Delhi, Sao Paulo, or Hong Kong. The person answering will often be fluent in English, well trained in a foreign university, and knowledgeable about your concern. The person contacted works for a fraction of American wages for the same job. The implications for career preparation in American schools are obvious. Our global culture and economy offers both opportunities and risks. To compete, our education must be excellent and must prepare us for lifelong learning.

What Do You Think?

1. If you were to buy an article of clothing such as a shirt at your local Wal-Mart, it will have been made by cheap labor in an Asian country. What is good and what is bad about this?
2. What are the implications of dependence among countries for the curriculum? For social skills? For knowledge of the world? For economic and social justice? For a contingency workforce? For sexism and discrimination?
3. It is anticipated that the Moslem population of the United States will reach 2.5 million in 2030. How might this influence teaching?

models moving from conflicts to compassionate cooperative human relations to protect and preserve our planet's precious resources. Richard Watson in *Future Minds:
How the Digital Age is Changing Our Minds, Why this Matters and What We Can Do
About it* (2010) analyzes the roll of technology in our society and calls for time out to
reflect and contemplate future trends and directions in our society. Both authors
envision more humanism, compassion, caring, and social justice in our society.

The record of predicting events is not a good one. Changes in human behavior
and value patterns are not as easy to predict as weather patterns or oil production.
As Harry Broudy (1961) puts it, "Human behavior cannot be extrapolated in any
simple linear fashion."

WORLD INTERDEPENDENCE

Wreaths stacked in rows along with toys, stuffed animals, tiny backpacks, and
other offerings lie in memoriam outside the remains of Beslan, Russia's School
Number 1, where 331 or more children, parents, and teachers were victims of terrorists (Weir, 2004). Terrorists' attacks on Madrid's commuter trains left 191 dead
and affected Spain's parliamentary elections. Recently the Islamic Commission of
Spain issued a *fatwa* (religious edict) finding that Osama Bin Laden's Al-Qaeda terrorist actions are totally prohibited and are the object of strong condemnation
within Islam ("Muslims," 2005). No nation is immune from terrorist attacks, as
proved in the 2005 subway bombings in London. Europeans also face a new threat
from homegrown alienated Islamic youth, who are threatening to wage a jihad
(Crawford & Johnson, 2004). In November 2009, a U.S. Army Major Nidal Malik
Hasan and psychiatrist, killed 13 people and wounded 30 others on a military base,
Fort Hood, Texas. Witnesses heard him shout "Allahu Akbar, God is Great" before
the killing (Wikipedia, 2011). On January 8, 2011, shot Congresswoman Gabrielle
Gifford in Arizona, killing several others including a federal judge (*Wall Street Journal*, 2011). Both instances reflect violence stemming from easy access to guns and
mental instability.

Periodically some Moslem scholars, clergy, and others issue fatwas declaring
that killing non-Islamic believers is the duty of all Moslems. Other Moslem scholars
deplore the use of violence as a political weapon. Children worldwide confront
scenes of horror daily, and some are targeted for death by terrorists. In time, current
cultural conflicts will be another footnote in history and hopefully some form of
democratic governance will emerge in the Middle East. However, whatever unfolds
will most likely differ from Western expectations.

Increasing legal and illegal immigration into the United States and Western
Europe is challenging educators. English as a second language (ESL), diversity, mul-
ticulturalism, and multiracialism will be essential issues for educators at all levels.
Some estimates of the illegal alien population range upward from 8–12 million
(Camartotas, 2004). Some states are seeking to limit immigration, some in Congress
are calling for increased border patrols, and former Senator and current Secretary of

State Hillary Clinton views immigration as the top future issue, calling for enhanced border security and better entry and exit systems (Limbacher, 2004).

The nation's educators are facing ESL challenges. In many school districts a multitude of languages are spoken. With an increasingly diverse society, the *National Collaborative on Diversity in the Teaching Force: A Call to Action* (2004) stressed the importance of eliminating institutional and individual racism in schools and colleges. The organization finds one of the resources necessary for improving the performance of students of color is a teacher workforce that is culturally competent and diverse. The 2004 report notes that the No Child Left Behind Act's requirement for "highly qualified" teachers needs to include minority faculty.

Marvin J. Cetron and Owen Davies in "Trends Now Shaping the Future" (2005) forecast some transforming issues:

1. The developed world economy will continue to grow for at least the next five years. (This appears overly optimistic in 2011 and 2012.)
2. The world population will reach 9.2 billion by 2050.
3. The developed world population, particularly the elderly, is growing dramatically.
4. Mass migration is redistributing the world's population.
5. Despite some xenophobic reactions to immigrants, there is growing acceptance of diversity. This is because of the unifying effect of mass media, which is promoting the growth of an integrated global society.
6. Militant Islam is spreading and gaining power.
7. Societal values are changing rapidly with more diverse family structures. Continuing urbanization will aggravate most environmental and social problems. Tourism and consumerism will grow rapidly in the future, while environmental sensitivity will expand as consequences of neglect become more apparent.

We must conclude from an historical perspective that science and the most sober human reasoning are conditioned to look only at the immediate past for causes of human problems.

Intellectual activity does not always merely follow change in the materialistic and technological spheres. Ideas, like those of the world's great religious leaders, have the power to change not only values but also priorities and views of the good life. Those who have really changed the world are the thinkers who have challenged basic theories, beliefs, values, and myths.

Scholars in many fields are speculating about the future and examining trends in the current world. Although much of the futuristic writing sounds warnings about what could happen, some works are optimistic. The ancient Chinese wrote symbols for the word *crisis* as a combination of *danger* and *opportunity*.

Faculty, administration, and student handbooks will grow in complexity as efforts are made to prevent, for example, excessive litigation regarding hate crimes, hate language, and racial and sexual harassment. Zero tolerance for deviant behavior, no matter how minor, will be designed to prevent crime and violence in schools, although there will be a growing backlash against excesses in the program. Educational

FOCUS ON THE ISSUES

Rapid Change

Google
Yahoo!
Cloud Computing
iPods iPads
YouTube/Facebook/blogs
Twitter
Legality of same-sex marriage
Cloned sheep
Sexting
e-readers

How many of the items in the list above are familiar? Probably all unless you do not view films, have Internet access, read widely, or watch television. The list is not very old. Students who have read the first seven editions of this textbook would have done so before any of the things on the list were known. A decade from now, your students will be able to make a list similar to this one but consisting of items unknown to us today. Those who teach must continue their education as a lifelong activity in order to keep up with their fields and understand the world of their students.

Things that shape our world and our perception of reality are both historical and current. We must blend important past events with current ones and incorporate future changes as they occur. Accelerating change makes information obsolete very quickly.

What Do You Think?

1. How does preparation for lifelong learning differ from becoming an expert in a field of knowledge?
2. Of those things listed, which (if any) will have a lasting impact and which will soon pass into obscurity?
3. This is the information age. What process do we use to transform information into knowledge and knowledge into wisdom?
4. How much confidence do we have in the truth and usefulness of our sources of information? How can we verify facts upon which we base decisions?

administration preparation will be oriented toward visions of organizations designed to facilitate change, empower people, and structure reform. Principals will be instructional leaders, developing networks and partnerships with universities, community groups, businesses, and civic organizations. Alternative teacher certification will become more popular as witness the growth of Teacher for America.

FUTURE TRENDS

Although we cannot be certain about the immediate future, much less long-range forecasts, certain trends in American education seem likely to continue. In addition, some worldwide forecasts have a high degree of probability that they will occur. If some degree of stability continues in the next decades, the following events seem likely to occur:

1. Education will continue throughout life. The 9-month school year will be replaced by ever-present learning opportunities. Mass media, electronic textbooks, the Internet, wireless cell phones, online degrees and courses, and information access systems will be used as educational aids at all educational levels. America's cyclical economic system will require continual job recycling. Former Governors Jeb Bush of Florida and Bob Wise of West Virginia are part of a 50-member *Digital Learning Council* working to develop a list of best practices for digital learning and to get states now to adopt them (McNeal & Samuels, 2010).

2. As alternative educational delivery systems expand, the old system of semester terms and units of credit will be altered. Means will be found to certify that the learner has the necessary level of skill and information to enter a new learning environment without showing academic credentials. Community colleges, vocational schools, and adult education will expand in the future to provide job skills for an ever-changing service and industrial economy.

   Colleges and universities will use adjuncts, contingency faculty now making up 50 percent of the nation's higher education faculty. Texas A & M University had a spreadsheet released in September 2010 weighing faculty annual salaries against students taught, tuition generated, and research grants obtained. With declining budgets, legislators and governors are demanding data to prove money given to colleges is well spent (Simon & Banchero, 2010).

3. Forty states now and more every year are adopting Common Core State Standards for English/language arts and mathematics (Griffith, 2011). The idea of a curriculum as broad as life itself, as Comenius suggested, in adult education and community colleges will provide students broad curriculum options. The seamless curriculum of the future will continue to be influenced by an increasingly diverse, multiracial, multicultural population with English-deficient and ESL students requiring a teaching force and a curriculum based on understanding their unique needs in cultural transformation, acceptance, and understanding. The Obama administration's Race to the Top is an effort to assure "highly qualified teachers" for all schools and tap into best practices for teaching learning excellence. A major effort is underway to improve instruction for at-risk, disadvantaged, diverse population students.

4. Learning facilitators will perform a variety of functions, and educational centers will have differentiated staffing for complete service schools offering learning and child care. Distance learning courses and degree programs will require more student collaboration, teamwork, and group work. An average of one in ten pupils in Grades K–12 is considered chronically absent from school. Most of those students

are from low-income at-risk disadvantaged families. Absenteeism and school dropouts are being addressed through school–family interventions in early grades (Sparks, 2010).

5. Accountability, assessment, and standardized high-stakes testing have been criticized as a prevalent factory model of education in the past, but will be used for the foreseeable future to measure achievement.

6. Age-specific compulsory learning institutions (schools) will be replaced by a variety of diversified learning environments. Children will be able to take responsibility for their own learning at a much earlier age. It will be common to find children and senior citizens in the same learning situations. Learning communities will emerge. Vouchers, charters, magnet schools, home schooling, and a variety of alternative educational systems will expand future school choice.

7. A contingent workforce with an ever-increasing number of part-time workers with little job security and few health benefits will require flexibility in educational aims, educational content, and length of schooling. Reddy (2010) notes that the number of people working part-time for economic reasons—workers who saw their hours cut back and those who were unable to find a full-time position—surged to 9.5 million, the highest on record in 2010. The reliance on temps may reflect a longer-run trend toward companies leaning on temps or contingent labor to fill most of their needs. A higher education contingent workforce has increased exponentially in recent years.

8. Technology will generate many new educational possibilities and challenges. Teenagers will be cautioned about the dangers of sexting. Chemical and electronic learning aids including brain stimulation will be used to help concentration and eliminate learning blocks. Skills required to quickly find and evaluate any information on any subject will become as common as reading is today. New companies will produce and market educational materials as well as entertainment computers and a myriad of new communication networks. An example is Achieve Communications, a company committed to bringing families and schools together online (www.webAdemic.com).

9. Education will stress understanding environmental forces that must be controlled in order to ensure the maximum realization of human potential and the good life. Students will become skilled at finding alternative solutions to major difficulties in problem-solving centers. Greater attention will be given to world understanding and to issues that involve all of the people on earth, although protests against globalization will continue. Roots of Empathy programs will provide new models of collaborative education such as mothers bringing babies to classes to encourage the development of empathic skills (Rifkin, 2010). At the same time, much educational activity will occur with small interest groups, or it will be directed toward the resolution of community problems. Ability to analyze data, think systematically, and realistically view future

possibilities will be universally needed skills. Respecting the rights of others—age, gender, culture, ethnicity—is a responsibility due from past to future generations.

10. Florida has provided online learning, virtual education, for all public K–12 students. Efforts are being made to provide guidelines, training, assessment, and evaluation of virtual school teachers ("Evaluating E-Educators," 2010). The National Education Technology Plan has a "Connected Online Communities of Practice" to improve teacher and leadership effectiveness, enhance student learning and increase productivity (Office of Educational Technology, 2011).

11. Globalization of trade will require educators to stress retraining, restructuring, and flexible responses to ever-changing international demands and challenges. Francis (2004) noted that for the first time on record, the United States has a deficit in high-tech trade. There are growing concerns about U.S. leadership in biotechnology, aerospace, scientific instruments, specialized industrial machinery, life sciences, optoelectronics, information and communication, electronics, flexible manufacturing, advanced materials, weapons, and nuclear technology. Technology follows Moore's law of doubling chip density and functionality every 18 months. Circuitry can be etched on a chip that is 28 nanometers wide; 5000 of these could fit into a single strand of human hair. The physical limits of current silicon-based technology will soon be reached and the true era of nano single atoms will appear (Stier, 2010).

12. Because of crime, violence, identity theft, and a variety of other challenges, most school districts require all future teachers to be fingerprinted. In addition, all populations of schools are provided policy handbooks depicting acceptable behavior with procedures for confidential reporting of violence and sexual harassment. The future trend is to add layers of protection for students, teachers, staff, and administration.

13. Alternative teacher certification preparation program will be assessed to determine the effectiveness of such programs (Cochran-Smith, 2005). High school seniors are training to work in Childhood Education Programs in Palm Beach, Florida, and being encouraged to consider teaching careers (Solomon, 2005). This model was used in the Lancaster or monitorial schools that originated in England and was popularized in the United States in the 1800s.

14. Phi Delta Kappa/Gallup Poll (2010) respondents wanted to recruit and retain highly qualified teachers and dismiss ineffective ones. There was a call for increased college attendance, finding ways to fix underperforming schools; encourage, expand, and develop top-quality charter schools throughout the country; and change the salary schedule to pay more to the best, more effective teachers. Future trends indicate more demand for accountability, merit pay, and improved academic achievement levels for all children, with pay for performance being considered.

In *Powershift* (1990), Toffler noted that for over 300 years the world was perceived as a great clock or machine, in which knowable causes led to predictable results. He believes we are witnessing one of the most important changes in the history of power, noting that it is clear that knowledge, a source of the highest quality of power, is gaining importance in our society and world. He projects that the most important power shift will occur in the hidden relationship between violence, wealth, and knowledge. In *War and Anti-War* (1993), Toffler calls for an understanding of the linkage between knowledge, wealth, and war.

Johnson and Kardos (2005) point to the need for flexible and collaborative workplaces to address the impending retirement of veteran teachers, rapid turnover rates among new teachers, and bridging the generation gap in the profession. Senior teachers can help retention rates by mentoring new teachers.

A growing number of states are placing responsibility on schools to help young people with tools they need to establish lasting healthy relationships. The Workable Peace Curriculum project in Partnership with the Program on Negotiations with Harvard Law School is developing a curriculum dealing with intergroup conflict and problem solving for the future ("Curriculum Materials," 2011).

The authors opine that students should view technology as a tool to enhance learning, not as an end in itself. Further, the move from data, to information, to knowledge, to wisdom requires persistent critical thinking and monitoring (filtering skills) to refine and evaluate information. Selecting data from the growing supply of information will be increasingly important in the future. The challenge for educators and society will be to resist the temptation to view technology as a cheap, quick fix to complex problems. A background of historical understanding and the appreciation of issues and conflicts of the past provide the best foundation we can have for predicting trends and preparing for a viable future. Rifkin (2009) in *The Empathic Civilization* finds human nature is more empathic oriented than conflict focused and sees education as the best route to a more humane society, taking care of our limited natural resources and sharing in an era of distributed capitalism. Perhaps the most important use of history and social foundations is showing us how far short of our own traditions and aspirations we have fallen and stimulating us to strive for a higher realization of our individual and collective potential in the world of the future.

GAINING PERSPECTIVE THROUGH CRITICAL ANALYSIS

1. What impact is the Internet having on educational instruction today? Give examples from your school experiences or current literature.
2. Analyze the increasingly global economy and identify pros and cons of internationalism. Address cultural conflicts at home and abroad.
3. Compare and contrast various methods of educational research. Give two examples of research projects that would be appropriate for each method.
4. Imagine you are 100 years in the future. In your vision, how do you think the current war on terrorism and the Iraqi conflict will have ended? How will education be impacted?
5. Identify gender, racial, demographic, language, and special needs in educating students in the

technological and communication skills needed in the future.

6. Describe the global culture of schools, including the trend toward having all teachers fingerprinted and surveillance systems installed to prevent student violence. In your school experience, have you found school districts distributing guidelines for expected student behavior together with provisions for confidentiality in reporting sexual harassment and violence?

7. Describe and analyze challenges and opportunities of the growing illegal immigrant population in the United States.

HISTORY IN ACTION IN TODAY'S CLASSROOMS

1. Visit a computer lab in your school. Discuss with those in charge of the lab how they are planning to keep up with the fast-changing field. Identify the problems they relate to you about adequate financing and quickly outdated hardware and software. Trace the history of educational technology.

2. In your journal, describe the classroom of the future. Use current literature in your field to support your ideas. Analyze global/international influences in our culture and our educational system.

3. Review copies of the *Educational Leadership* journal to find at least two alternative scenarios for the future of American education. Cover the multicultural, multidimensional, and multiracial components of our emerging demographics.

4. Identify the role of business/industry in building a compassionate, interdependent, global network for educators.

5. Analyze strengths and weaknesses of a technologically global-based educational system. Include inequities in classrooms and school districts in access and distribution of computers and software. Discuss and answer the questions at the end of the features "Globalization" and "Rapid Change." These features are found within the chapter.

6. Compare present and past conditions in schools for student safety and security. Interview a retired educator for your response.

BIBLIOGRAPHY

Academic Preparation for College: With Academic Preparation in English, the Arts, Mathematics, Science, Social Studies, and Foreign Languages. New York: The College Board, 1986.

Assessment of Diversity in America's Teaching Force: A Call to Action. Washington, DC: National Collaborative on Diversity in the Teaching Force, 2004.

Belsie, Laurent. "The Short, Simple Human Gene Map." *The Christian Science Monitor* (February 13, 2001): 1, 10.

Botkin, James, Mahdi Elmandjra, & Mircea Malitza. *No Limits to Learning: Bridging the Human Gap.* New York: Pergamon Press, 1979.

Boulding, Kenneth. *Equity and Efficiency in Economic Development.* Montreal: McGill-Queen's University Press, 1992.

Boulding, Kenneth. *Evolution, Order and Complexity.* London: Routledge, 1996.

Bowman, Jim, Fred Kierstead, Chris Dede, & John Pulliam. *The Far Side of the Future: Social Problems and Educational Reconstruction.* Washington, DC: World Future Society, 1978.

Boyer, William. *America's Future: Transition to the 21st Century.* New York: Praeger, 1984.

Boyett, Joseph, & Henry Conn. *Workplace 2000.* New York: Plume-Penguin, 1992.

Bright, James. *Practical Technology Forecasting.* New York: Industrial Management Center, 1978.

Broudy, Harry. *Paradox or Promise: Essays on American Life.* Upper Saddle River, NJ: Prentice Hall, 1961.

Broudy, Harry. *The Real World of the Public Schools.* New York: Harcourt Brace Jovanovich, 1972.

Bushwellere, Kevin, & Erik Faterni. "Technology Counts 2001: The New Divides." *Education Week* (May 10, 2001): 10–12, 62.

Camarotas, Steven A. "Economy Slowed But Immigration Didn't." *Center for Immigration Studies Backgrounder* (November 2004).

Cetron, Marvin. *Schools of the Future: How American Business and Education Can Cooperate to Save Our Schools.* New York: McGraw-Hill, 1985.

Cetron, Marvin J., & Owen Davies. "Trends Now Shaping the Future." *The Futurist* (March–April 2005): 27–42.

Cochran-Smith, Marilyn. "Taking Stock in 2005: Getting Beyond the Horse Race." *Journal of Teacher Education* (January–February 2005): 3–7.

Cole, Stephen. "Bill Coates Plots a Windows Future." *BBC News UK Edition* (January 21, 2005). Available at: news.bbc.co.uk/1/hi/programmes/click_online/4195177.stm

Commoner, Barry. *The Closing Circle: Nature, Man and Technology.* New York: Bantam Books, 1974.

"Congresswoman Gabrielle Giffords Shot." *Wall Street Journal* (January 8, 2011).

Cornish, Edward. *The Study of the Future: An Introduction to the Art and Science of Understanding and Shaping Tomorrow's World.* Washington, DC: World Future Society, 1978.

Crawford, David, & Keith Johnson. "Home Grown, New Terror Threat in EU: Extremists with Passports." *The Wall Street Journal* (December 27, 2004): A 1, A 5.

"Curriculum Materials." Workable Peace Curriculum (February 28, 2011). Available at: www.workable-peace.org/main-curriculum.html

Dillin, John. "As 'Good' Jobs Become 'Bad' Jobs, Congress Takes a Closer Look." *Christian Science Monitor* (June 18, 1993): 1, 4.

Dunn, Joe, & Howard Preston. *Future South—A Historical Perspective for the Twenty-First Century.* Urbana: University of Illinois Press, 1991.

Esfandiary, F. M. *Optimism One.* New York: Norton, 1970.

Esfandiary, F. M. *Up-Wingers.* New York: Popular Library, 1977.

"Evaluating E-Educators Evolving Skills." *Education Week Digital Directions* (Fall, 2010): 8.

Feinberg, Gerald. *The Prometheus Project: Mankind's Search for Long-Range Goals.* Garden City, NY: Doubleday, 1969.

"Foot Hood Shooting," *Wikipedia* (2011). Available at: www.en.wikipedia.org/wiki/Fort-Hood-shooting

Francis, David R. "U.S. Runs a Hi-Tech Trade Gap." *The Christian Science Monitor* (June 2, 2004): 1, 4.

Fuller, R. Buckminster. *Utopia or Oblivion: The Prospects for Humanity.* New York: Overlook Press, 1969.

Gates, Bill, & Collins Hemingway. *Business @ The Speed of Thought: Succeeding in the Digital Economy.* New York: Warner Books, 1999/2000.

Glines, Don. "Can Schools of Today Survive Very Far into the 21st Century?" *NASSP Bulletin* 73, no. 514 (February 1989).

Goodman, Paul. *Change in Organizations: New Perspectives on Theory, Research and Practice.* San Francisco: Jossey-Bass, 1982.

Griffith, David. "Catching Up With the Common Core." *Educational Leadership* (March 2011): 95.

Harman, Willis W. *An Incomplete Guide to the Future.* New York: Norton, 1979.

Heilbroner, Robert. *The Future as History.* New York: Harper & Row, 1959.

Heilbroner, Robert. *An Inquiry into the Human Prospect.* New York: W. W. Norton, 1975.

Heilbroner, Robert. *21st Century Capitalism.* New York: W. W. Norton, 1993.

Heilbroner, Robert. *Visions of the Future: The Distant Past, Yesterday, Today, Tomorrow.* New York: Oxford University Press, 1995.

Heilbroner, Robert. *The Age of Access.* New York: Tarcher/Putnam, 2000.

Heilbroner, Robert. *The Hydrogen Economy.* New York. Tarcher/Putnam, 2003.

Heilbroner, Robert. *The European Dream* New York: Tarcher/Putnam, 2005.

Helmer-Hirschberg, Olaf. *Social Technology.* New York: Basic Books, 1966.

Henderson, Hazel. *Creating Alternative Futures: The End of Economics.* New York: Berkeley, 1978.

Henderson, Hazel. *Building a Win-Win World: Life Beyond Global Economic Warfare.* San Francisco, CA: Berrett-Koehler, 1996.

Hendricks, Gay, & James Fadiman, Eds. *Transpersonal Education: A Curriculum for Feeling and Being.* Upper Saddle River, NJ: Prentice Hall, 1976.

Hipple, Theodore, Ed. *The Futures of Education 1975–2000.* Santa Monica, CA: Goodyear, 1974.

Illich, Ivan. *Deschooling Society.* New York: Harper & Row, 1971.

"Internet World Stats: Usage and Population Statistics" (2010). Available at: www.internetworldstats.com/stats7.htm

Johnson, Susan Moore, & Susan M. Kardos. "Bridging the Generation Gap." *Educational Leadership* (May 2005): 8–14.

Judy, Richard W., & Carol D'Amico. *Workforce 2020.* Indianapolis, IN: Hudson Institute, 1997.

Jungk, Robert. *The Everyman Project: Resources for a Humane Future.* London: Thames and Hudson, 1976.

Kadaba, Lini S. "Futurist (Joseph Coates) Identified Issues That Will Transform Corporations." *Tulsa World* (June 13, 1993): 4G.

Kerrey, Bob. *The Power of the Internet for Learning: Moving from Promise to Practice.* Washington DC: Report of the Web-Based Education Commission to the President and the Congress of the United States, December 2000.

Kierstead, Fred, Jim Bowman, and Christopher Dede, Eds. *Educational Futures: Sourcebook.* Washington, DC: World Future Society, 1979.

King, John, Ted Barrett, & Steve Turnham. "Inside Politics: Bush Calls for Changes on Illegal Workers" (January 8, 2004). Available at: www.cnn.com/2004/ALLPOLITICS/01/00/bush.immigration/

Kurian, George Thomas, & Graham T. T. Molitor, Eds. *Encyclopedia of the Future.* Old Tappan, NJ: Simon & Schuster, 1995.

Laszlo, Ervin. *The Systems View of the World: The Natural Philosophy of the New Developments in the Sciences.* New York: G. Braziller, 1972.

Leonard, George Burr. *Education and Ecstasy.* New York: Delacorte Press, 1968.

Limbacher, Carl. "Hillary Eyes Immigration as Top 2008 Issue." Newsmax.com (December 29, 2004). Available at: www.newsmax.com/archives/ic/2004/11/21/233417.shtml

McNeal, Michele, & Christiana A. Samuels. "Former Govs. Prod States on Digital Education." *Education Week* (October 18, 2010).

Meadows, Donella H. *Beyond the Limits: Confronting Global Collapse, Envisioning a Sustainable Future.* Post Mills, VT: Chelseas Green, 1991.

Meckler, Laura. "Giffords' Condition Still Improving." *Wall Street Journal* (January 14, 2011): A5.

Michael, Donald N. *Cybernation: The Silent Conquest.* Santa Barbara, CA: Center for the Study of Democratic Institutions, 1962.

Michael, Donald N. *The Unprepared Society: Planning for a Precarious Future.* New York: Harper & Row, 1970.

Montessori, Maria. *The Absorbent Mind.* Madras, India: Kalakshetra Publications, 1987.

Murphy, Dan. "In Iraq, 'Lawrence' Is a Must Read." *The Christian Science Monitor* (December 8, 2004): 1, 4.

"Muslims Who Condemn Al Qaeda." *The Christian Science Monitor* (March 15, 2005): 8.

Naisbitt, John. *Megatrends.* New York: Warner Books, 1982.

Naisbitt, John. *Re-inventing the Corporation: Transforming Your Job and Your Company for the New Information Society.* London: Guild Publishing, 1985.

Naisbitt, John. *Megatrends 2000: Ten New Directions for the 1990s.* New York: Morrow, 1990.

Naisbitt, John. *Global Paradox.* New York: Avon Books, 1994.

"National Education Technology Plan." Office of Educational Technology (March 2011). Available at: www2.ed.gov/about/offices/list/os/technology/index.html

"National Collaborative Diversity in the Teaching Force: A Call to Action" (October 2004). Available at: www.nea.org/assets/docs/HE/mf_diversityreport.pdf

Paton, Dean. "States Prod Schools to Teach Relationships." *The Christian Science Monitor* (June 13, 2005): 2, 3.

Peters, Thomas J. *In Search of Excellence: Lessons from America's Best-Run Companies.* Sydney, Australia: Harper & Row, 1984.

Peters, Thomas, and Robert Waterman. *In Search of Excellence: Lessons from America's Best Run Companies.* New York: Warren Books, 1982.

Phi Delta Kappa/Gallup Poll 2010, 2011. www.gallup.com/poll/142661/phi-delta-kappa-gallup-poll-2010.aspx and www.gallup.com/poll/149222/Platt, John R. *The Step to Man.* New York: John Wiley & Sons, 1966.

Platt, John R. "What We Must Do." *Science* (November 1969): 1115–1122.

Platt, John R. *Perception and Change: Projections for Survival.* Ann Arbor: University of Michigan Press, 1970.

Platt, John R. *The Next Twenty Years of Change.* Washington, DC: American Educational Research Association, 1979.

Polak, Fred. *Image of the Future.* San Francisco: Jossey-Bass, 1973.

Postman, Neil. *Teaching as a Subversive Activity.* New York: Dell, 1987.

Pulliam, John, & Jim Bowman. *Educational Futurism: In Pursuance of Survival.* Norman: University of Oklahoma Press, 1974.

Reddy, Sudeep. "Employers Increasingly Rely on Temps, Part-Timers." *The Wall Street Journal* (October 11, 2010).

Reimer, Everett W. *School Is Dead: Alternatives in Education.* Garden City, NJ: Doubleday, 1971.

Rifkin, Jeremy. *The End of Work: The Decline of the Global Labor Force and the Dawn of the Post-Master Era.* New York: G. P. Putnam & Sons, 1996.

Rifkin, Jeremy. *The Empathic Civilization.* New York: Jeremy F. Tarcher/Penguin, 2009.

Rubin, Louis, Ed. *The Future of Education: Perspectives on Tomorrow's Schooling*. Boston: Allyn & Bacon, 1975.

Samples, Bob. *The Metaphoric Mind: A Celebration of Creative Consciousness*. Reading, MA: Addison-Wesley, 1976.

Schumacher, E. F. *A Guide for the Perplexed*. New York: Harper & Row, 1977.

Schwartz, Eugene S. *Overskill: The Decline of Technology in Modern Civilization*. New York: Ballantine Books, 1972.

Scileppi, John. *A Systems View of Education: A Model for Change*. Lanham, MD: University Press of America, 1984.

Simon, Stephanie, & Stephanie Banchero. "Putting a Price on Professors." *The Wall Street Journal* (October 22, 2010).

Skinner, B. F. *Walden Two*. Englewood Cliffs, NJ: Prentice-Hall, 1976.

Solomon, Lois K. "Today's Students Future's Teachers." *South Florida Sun Sentinel* (February 15, 2005): 1B, 2B.

Sparks, Sarah D. "Early-Years Absenteeism Seen As Critical." *Education Week* (October 20, 2010): 1, 13.

Stier, Ken. "Save Our Semiconductors." *Time* (November 8, 2010): Global 6, 8.

Technology Standards for School Administrators Collaborative. "Technology Standards for School Administrators" (2001). www.aasa.org "Temps Getting More Work." *Tulsa World* (June 27, 1993): 2G.

Theobald, Robert. *An Alternative Future for America 2000*. Chicago: Swallow Press, 1970.

Theobald, Robert. *Futures Conditional*. Indianapolis: BobbsMerrill, 1972.

Theobald, Robert. *Turning the Century*. New York: Knowledge Systems, 1992.

Toffler, Alvin. *Future Shock*. New York: Random House, 1970.

Toffler, Alvin. *Learning for Tomorrow*. New York: Random House, 1974.

Toffler, Alvin. *The Third Wave*. New York: Morrow, 1980.

Toffler, Alvin. *The Adaptive Corporation*. New York: McGraw-Hill, 1985.

Toffler, Alvin. *Powershift: Wealth and Violence at the Edge of the 21st Century*. New York: Bantam, 1990.

Toffler, Alvin. *War and Anti-War*. New York: Little Brown, 1993.

Toffler, Alvin. *Creating a New Civilization: The Politics of the Third Wave*. Kansas City, MO: Turner Publishing, 1995.

Toffler, Alvin, & Heidi Toffler. *Creating a New Civilization: Politics of the Third Wave*. New York: Turner Publishers, 1995.

Toffler, Alvin, & Heidi Toffler. Interview. *StarTribune*, 1996. Available at: www.startribune.com/stonline/html/digage/toffler4.htm

Toffler, Alvin, & Heidi Toffler. "New Economy? You Ain't Seen Nothing Yet." *Wall Street Journal* (March 28, 2001): A 14.

Uchida, Donna, Marvin Cetron, & Floretta McKenzie. *Preparing Students for the 21st Century*. Bethesda, MD: World Future Society, 1996.

Uldrich, Jack. "Why Nanotechnology Will Arrive Sooner Than Expected." *The Futurist* (March–April 2002): 16–22.

Waskow, Arthur I. *Running Riot: A Journey Through the Official Disasters and Creative Disorder in American Society*. New York: Herder and Herder, 1970.

Watson, Richard. "Future Minds: How the Digital Age is Changing Our Minds." Boston: Nicholas Brealey Publishing, 2010.

Weir, Fred. "In Beslan, a Tense Bid for Calm." *The Christian Science Monitor* (October 14, 2004): 6.

Wells, H. G. *War of the Worlds*. New York: William Heinemann, 1898.

Wirth, Arthur. *Education and Work for the Year 2000: Choices We Face*. San Francisco: Jossey-Bass, 1992.

World Future Society, Ed. *The Future, Guide to Information Sources*. Washington, DC: World Future Society, 1979.

Zerchykov, Ross. *School Boards and the Communities They Represent*. Boston, MA: Institute for Responsive Education, 1981.

Zerchykov, Ross. *School-Community Relations*. Tempe: Arizona State University, 1994.

GENERAL ANNOTATED BIBLIOGRAPHY

Bailyn, Bernard. *Education in Forming of American Society*. Chapel Hill: University of North Carolina Press, 1960.

This critical essay on American history of education (from the cultural standpoint) surveys the main themes of educational history yet to be written. It contains a useful evaluation of earlier movements in American cultural history, such as Puritanism, philanthropy, race relations, and the growth of sectarianism.

Bowen, William G., & Derek Bok. *The Shape of the River*. Princeton: Princeton University Press, 2000.

This intensive research study and report on minority students at the nation's elite collegiate institutions includes recommendations for a consistent program of mentoring and support services to assist students at risk in study habits and skills needed for degree completion.

Boyles, Deron. *American Education & Corporations*. New York: Falmer/Taylor and Francis Group, 2000.

This book provides a critical analysis of the role of corporate America in education, with a focus on the power of advertising in a competitive economy.

Butts, Freeman. *The Education of the West: A Formative Chapter in the History of Civilization*. New York: McGraw-Hill, 1933.

This work is a very sound general history by one of the best-known American educational historians.

Butts, Freeman. *Public Education in the United States: From Revolution to Reform*. New York: Holt, Rinehart and Winston, 1978.

This work is outstanding for its detail and depth of study.

Caine, Renate Nummeal, & Geoffrey Caine. *Education on the Edge of Possibilities*. Alexandria, VA: Association of Supervision and Curriculum Development, 1997.

This overview of brain-based learning is designed to encourage teachers to move toward an information-delivery approach that is flexible, creative, and open to students' search for meaning (such as John Dewey introduced in the 1930s and 1940s).

Changeux, Jean-Pierre. *The Physiology of Truth: Neuroscience and Human Knowledge*. Cambridge, MA: Harvard University Press, 2004.

Collaborative skills and democratic values should be taught to maintain and retain a free pluralistic society. The book analyzes brain functions through interconnected processing systems that determine the quality of decision-making processes.

Coates, Joseph, & Jennifer Jarratt. *What Futurists Believe*. Mt. Airy, MD: Lomond, 1989.

This work profiles "futures" writings of leading authors in the field.

Cobb, Nina, Ed. *The Future of Education: Perspectives on National Standards in America*. New York: College Entrance Board, 1994.

This series of articles on national standards includes the effect of standards on teachers, educational policy, and subject matter associations.

Commager, Henry Steele, Ed. *Documents of American History*. New York: Appleton-Century-Crofts, 1963.

This work contains 665 noteworthy documents that were significant in the shaping of American history, including those pertinent to education.

Cremin, Lawrence. *The Wonderful World of Ellwood Patterson Cubberly: An Essay on the Historiography of American Education.* New York: Columbia University Teachers College, Bureau of Publications, 1965.

An interesting and delightful treatment of the first great American educational historian by a leading modern scholar in the same field.

Cremin, Lawrence. *American Education: The Colonial Experience 1607–1783.* New York: Harper & Row, 1970.

This work offers an analysis and description of the formative period of American education during the drive for independence.

Cremin, Lawrence. *Public Education.* New York: Basic Books, 1976.

This treatment of the history of American education gives attention to public policy, the emerging role of government, and the issues over control of schools.

Cremin, Lawrence. *American Education: The National Experience 1783–1876.* New York: Harper & Row, 1980.

This work offers an analysis and description of American education during the period of building and unifying the nation.

Cremin, Lawrence. *American Education: The Metropolitan Experience 1876–1980.* New York: Harper & Row, 1988.

This portrayal of American education as the nation achieved world-power status identifies three persistent elements of American education: popularization, multitudinousness, and politicization.

Cremin, Lawrence. *Popular Education and Its Discontents.* New York: Harper & Row, 1990.

This compilation of three essays explores increasing dissatisfaction with education, radical changes in society and education, and a continuing effort to solve social problems indirectly through education rather than through politics.

Curti, Merle. *The Social Ideas of American Educators.* Patterson, NJ: Pageant Books, 1959.

Part I's contents include Colonial Survivals and Revolutionary Promises, 1620–1820; New Conflicts and a New Solution, 1800–1860; Education and Social Reform: Horace Mann; Henry Barnard; The Education of Women; The School and the Triumph of Business Enterprise, 1860–1914; Education in the South; The Black Man's Place: Booker T. Washington, 1856–1916; William T. Harris, The Conservator, 1835–1908; Bishop Spalding, Catholic Educator, 1840–1916; Francis Wayland Parker, Democrat, 1837–1902; G. Stanley Hall, Evolutionist, 1846–1924; William James, Individualist, 1842–1910; Edward Lee Thorndike, Scientist, 1874–1949; John Dewey, 1859–1952; and Post-War Patterns. It includes a treatment of recent educational history, and provides an excellent social understanding of American educational development. Also useful is Merle Curti's The Growth of American Thought. New York: Harper & Row, 1951.

Curtis, Stanley J., & M. E. A. Boultwood. *A Short History of Educational Ideas.* 3rd ed. London: University Tutorial Press Ltd., 1964.

This standard text in Western educational history pays considerable attention to American education and American educational leaders. Helpful bibliographical information is given at the end of each chapter.

Diamond, Jared. *How to Succeed in History: Societies Don't Die by Accident—They Commit Ecological Suicide.* New York: Viking, 2004.

The UCLA Pulitzer Prize winner analyzes four ancient societies, finding ecological cannibalism led to their demise. Surviving societies, Diamond says, manage ecology effectively and anticipate problem areas.

Diaz, Carlos, Carol Marra Pelletier, & Eugene F. Provenzo, Jr. *Touch the Future . . . Teach!* New York: Pearson Education, 2006.

A culturally sensitive focus for the development of a community of learners in an expanding multicultural, multiethnic society. Viewing possibilities for educators to be agents of change in a global world community.

Didsbury, Howard F., Jr., Ed. *Future Vision: Ideas, Insights and Strategies.* Bethesda, MD: World Future Society, 1996.

These articles from the World Future Society 8th General Assembly explore a world of have and

have-not nations and possibilities for a more equitable and humane future.

Dworkin, Martin. *Dewey on Education*. New York: Columbia University Teachers College Press, 1959.

This best quick reference to the work of Dewey is for those who do not wish to use Dewey's own books. Also suggested is John Dewey's own Democracy and Education. *New York: Macmillan, 1916.*

Emery, Kathy, & Susan Ohanian. *Why Is Corporate America Bashing Our Schools?* Portsmouth, NH: Heinemann, 2004.

The authors examine corporate influence in education and the educational reform movement.

Epstein, Terrie. "Adolescents' Perspectives on Racial Diversity in U.S. History: Case Studies from an Urban Classroom." *American Educational Research Journal* (Spring 2000): 185–214.

This analysis of the challenge and opportunity of incorporating the historical experience of racial diversity into traditional narratives of U.S. history explores Eurocentrism and Afrocentrism in depth.

Evans, Harold Sir, Gail Buckland, & David Lefer. *They Made America: From the Steam Engine to the Search Engine, Two Centuries of Innovators*. New York: Little Brown, 2004.

This examination of the environment conducive to innovations in America identified aristocracy of strategic missionaries who were creative risk-takers and entrepreneurial adventurers.

Fantini, Mario. *Regaining Excellence in Education*. New York: Merrill/Macmillan, 1986.

This very good analysis of the reform movement in education results from A Nation at Risk *and other reports of the 1980s. It deals with future trends, as well as the responses of state and local groups to the demand for educational reform. Reports and sources are well documented and succinctly presented.*

Friedman, Thomas L. *The World is Flat: A Brief History of the Twenty-First Century*. New York: Farrar, Straus and Giroux, 2005.

An analysis of a world facing technological advances difficult to keep up with for governments and industry. Globalization is leading to an expanding democratic theory and practice, although international terrorism and networking is hampering that trend. A major contribution to interpretating and understanding the increasing collaboration across cultures and national boundaries.

Gaither, Milton. *American Educational History Revisited*. New York: Teachers College Press, 2003.

An overview of issues facing schools and society with an analysis of ideology, influence and contextualization, and diversity and controversy in the twentieth century.

Gatti, Richard, & Daniel Gatti. *New Encyclopedic Dictionary of School Law*. West Nyack, NY: Parker Publishing, 1983.

This complete analysis of laws and court cases that altered the shape of American education concentrates on the recent trends in the courts and the philosophical shifts that have created new trends in the relationship between schools and governing agencies.

Good, Harry, & James Teller. *A History of American Education*. 3rd ed. New York: Macmillan, 1973.

This detailed history of American education is especially useful for the period prior to the twentieth century.

Good, Thomas L., & Jere E. Brophy. *Contemporary Educational Psychology*. New York: Longman, 1995.

This excellent overview of the field focuses on the integration of theory and practice.

Goodlad, John I., & Timothy J. McMannon, Eds. *The Public Purpose of Education and Schooling*. San Francisco: Jossey-Bass, 1997.

This work offers an overview of major themes of educational reform movement in theory and practice.

Gutek, Gerald L. *Historical and Philosophical Foundations of Education*. Upper Saddle River, NJ: Merrill/Pearson Education, 2000.

This work covers three broad themes: major movements in world history, the biographies of leading educators, and philosophies and ideas that emerge

from their ideas. Each chapter identifies and analyzes major contributions to educational theory
and practice.

Hirsch, E. D., Jr. *The Schools We Need, Why We Don't
Have Them.* New York: Doubleday, 1996.

*This work is a call for rediscovery of William
Bagley's essentialism, which stresses the importance of common values and meanings crucial
to a democratic culture. Hirsch stresses bringing
our children closer to universal competence in
cultural literacy.*

Jacobs, Heidi Hayes. *Getting Results with Curriculum
Mapping.* Alexandria, VA: Association for Supervision and Curriculum Development, 2004.

*This book of readings in curriculum mapping is
designed to encourage dialogue among teachers
and to deal with measureable improvement in
student performance on a continuing basis.*

Johanningmeier, Erwin. *Americans and Their Schools.*
Chicago: Rand McNally, 1980.

*This superior text is both very detailed and inter-
esting. It would be an excellent choice for a text to
use in a graduate-level course about the history of
American education. Johanningmeier is an interesting author to read, and he puts to rest a number
of common myths about education in this nation.*

Judy, Richard W., & Carol D'Amico. *Workforce 2020.*
Indianapolis, IN: Hudson Institute, 1997.

*This work is an analysis of changing demographics
in the composition of the future workforce.*

Karier, Clarence J. *Shaping the American Educational State,
1900 to the Present.* New York: Free Press, 1975.

*This collection of essays and documents on the
most important forces at work in developing
the modern American educational system deals
with issues and problems as well as ideas and
movements.*

Knight, Edgar W. *Fifty Years of American Education.*
New York: Ronald Press, 1952.

*Other standard works on the subject by the same
author include* A Documentary History of Education in the South Before 1860. *Chapel Hill: University of North Carolina Press, 1949; and* Education
in the United States. *Boston: Ginn, 1951.*

Kohn, Alfie. *No Contest: The Case Against Competition.*
New York: Houghton-Mifflin, 1992.

*This work stresses the importance of cooperation
to improve student motivation in education and
enrich society.*

Kurian, George Thomas, & Graham T. T. Molitor, Eds.
Encyclopedia of the Future. Old Tappan, NJ: Simon
& Schuster, 1995.

*These 42 articles explore the future from a variety
of perspectives with forecasts and projections about
possible, probable, and preferable futures, from
H. G. Wells to Alvin Toffler.*

Levine, Daniel, & Robert Havinghurst. *Society and Education.* 6th ed. Boston: Allyn & Bacon, 1984.

*This very complete sociology of education calls
attention to the social forces in American education that have shaped modern conditions. It
provides the student of history with an in-depth
understanding of modern social attitudes and
trends.*

Lozer, Steven E., Paul C. Violas, & Guy Senese. *School
and Society.* New York: McGraw-Hill, 2002.

*This book contains historical and contempo-
rary perspectives on the evolution of American
education.*

Lucas, Christopher J. *Teacher Education in America: Reform Agendas for the Twenty-First Century.* New
York: St. Martin's Press, 1997.

*This work offers an analysis of trends in education
through historical background, teacher surveys,
and proposals for the teaching profession.*

Mayer, Frederic. *American Ideas and Education.* New
York: Merrill/Macmillan, 1964.

*This intellectual and social history of American
education is especially useful for the student of
ideas, attitudes, movements, and people. Mayer
includes a large number of quotations from educational leaders.*

McCown, Rick, Marcy Driscoll, & Peter Geiger Roop.
*Educational Psychology: A Learning-Centered
Approach to Classroom Practice.* New York: Allyn
& Bacon, 1996.

*This detailed analysis and record of the field
focuses on cultural diversity and gender issues.*

McGarrh, Kellie. *Hangin' in Tough: Mildred E. Doyle, School Superintendent.* Edited by Clinton B. Alison. New York: Peter Lang Publishing, 2000.

In Doyle's biography, McGarrh analyzes issues that interest educational historians and feminist scholars, such as women's struggles to acquire and keep administrative positions. Also analyzed are the differences in the way men and women operate in leadership positions and the impact of homophobia on those who are not stereotypically "masculine" or "feminine."

Meyer, Adolphe E. *The Educational History of the American People.* 2nd ed. New York: McGraw-Hill, 1967.

This very readable text presents the material in a refreshing way. It does assume some basic knowledge of American history on the part of the student.

Monroe, Paul, Ed. *A Cyclopedia of Education.* New York: Macmillan, 1911–1913.

This monumental five-volume work includes illustrations, charts, diagrams, and references. The work is dated but still the only one of its kind and a valuable source of information. It was reprinted in 1968 by Detroit's Gale Research, and a revised edition that will include modern material is in progress.

Morgan, Gordon D. *Toward an American Sociology.* Westport, CT: Praeger, 1997.

This work offers an interesting and informative analysis of sociology in light of its evolution throughout history.

Mulhern, James. *A History of Education.* 2nd ed. New York: Ronald Press, 1959.

Parts W and V of this work contain a wealth of material pertaining to the growth of (and the changes in) the American educational system.

Naisbitt, John. *Megatrends.* New York: Warner Books, 1982.

The student of history interested in the future will find in this book a very interesting presentation of the major forces operating to shape our world. Naisbitt describes the most important trends and suggests alternative courses of action to cope with them.

Noddings, Nel. *Philosophy of Education.* Boulder, CO: Westview Press, 1996.

This survey of contemporary trends and problems in philosophy of education includes a final chapter, "Feminism, Philosophy and Education," that summarizes the text from a feminist perspective, and in which Nel Noddings gives her personal convictions on the subject.

Perkinson, Henry. *Two Hundred Years of American Educational Thought.* New York: McKay, 1976.

This book contains one of the best accounts of the critics of education to be found.

Perkinson, Henry. *Since Socrates: Studies in the History of Western Educational Thought.* New York: Longman, 1980.

Perkinson gives a fresh account of the development of educational thought in the Western world, with stress placed on intellectual and cultural history.

Potter, Robert E. *The Stream of American Education.* New York: American Book, 1967.

Potter's book is one of the most complete single-volume treatments of American education available. It is especially useful for the study of current educational issues and problems.

Power, Edward J. *Main Currents in the History of Education.* 2nd ed. New York: McGraw-Hill, 1969.

This work offers a useful general treatment of major American educational ideas.

Power, Edward J. *The Transit of Learning: A Social and Cultural Interpretation of American Educational History.* Sherman Oaks, CA: Alfred Publishing Co., 1979.

This work offers a contextual treatment of curriculum development in the United States.

Power, Edward J. *Legacy of Learning: A History of Western Education.* Albany: State University of New York Press, 1991.

This work contributes to understanding the evolution of curriculum development in American education.

Pratte, Richard. *Ideology and Education.* New York: Wiley, 1977.

This useful account of the theories and philosophies of education treats individual thinkers and the social conditions that contributed to their ideas.

Ravitch, Diane. *Left Back: A Century of Failed School Reforms*. New York: Simon & Schuster, 2000.

From an historical, traditional, academic, and intellectual perspective, Diane Ravitch examines the progress movement, and finds the movement became a source of anti-intellectualism. Her models of educational excellence were William Torrey Harris, William C. Bagley, and Charles H. Judd, among others.

Ravitch, Diane. *The Language Police: How Pressure Groups Restrict What Students Learn*. New York: Alfred A. Knopf, 2003.

Professor Ravitch examines pressure group influence on curriculum and teaching methodology. She identifies pressure groups of the right and left, and their influence on the educational process.

Rippa, S. Alexander. *Education in a Free Society*. New York: Longman, 1997.

This well-developed, comprehensive approach to American educational history focuses on education in a free society.

Rusk, Robert, & James Scotland. *Doctrines of the Great Educators*. New York: St. Martin's Press, 1979.

This work offers a new account of the contributions to education made by those who really changed the basic conceptions about education.

Schmoker, Mike. *Focus: Elevating the Essentials*. Alexandria, VA: Association and Curriculum Development 2010.

A call for a consistent, coherent curriculum focused on learning essentials.

Shea, Mary, Rosemary Murray, & Rebecca Harlin. *Drowning in Data*. Westport, CT: Heinemann, 2005.

An examination of routes to improve assessment measures of student performance (including portfolios, benchmarking, and norm-referenced testing).

Shirky, Clay. *Cognitive Surplus: Creativity and Generosity in a Connected Age*. New York: Penguin Press, 2011.

Individual can use free time to gain information as well as to share and create it.

Sizer, Theodore R. *The Red Pencil: Convictions from Experience in Education*. New Haven, CT: Yale University Press, 2004.

Sizer has a commitment to educational reform, including performance-based assessments. He encourages educators to implement educational programs to improve student achievement. The Red Pencil includes Sizer's views about the value of family school choice, with financial support following the child.

Smith, L. Glenn, & Joan K. Smith, Eds. *Lives in a Narrative of People and Ideas*. New York: St. Martin's Press, 1994.

This work offers an overview of Western education through biographies of individuals who influenced educational theory and practice.

Spring, Joel. *American Education*. New York: McGraw-Hill, 2000.

This postmodern textbook has a context for knowledge through discussing the history of ideas and the impact of social and political forces.

Talbott, Stephen L. *The Future Does Not Compute: Transcending the Machines in Our Midst*. Sebastopol, CA: O'Reilly and Associates, 1995.

This book offers an analysis of the potential adverse effects of a computer-driven society on human values.

Thayer, V. T. *Formative Ideas in American Education*. New York: Dodd, Mead, 1965.

Professor Thayer presents the philosophic views and changing theories held by leading educators in the United States. The detail in which significant ideas are presented makes Thayer very good reading for serious educators.

Thernstrom, Abigail. *No Excuses: Closing the Racial Gap in Learning*. New York: Simon & Schuster, 2003.

Overview of challenges and opportunities facing policy makers to extend educational opportunity to all on equal terms.

Toffler, Alvin. *War and Anti-War*. New York: Little Brown, 1993.

This work offers a futurist's viewpoints on the impact of technology on the individual, society, and the world community.

Travers, Paul, & Ronald Rebore. *Foundations of Education: Becoming a Teacher.* 4th ed. New York: Allyn & Bacon, 2000.

This textbook is for prospective teachers and concerns historical, philosophical, and social perspectives on education. Dialogues between the two authors, a university professor, and a public school superintendent precede each chapter.

Tyack, David B., Ed. *Turning Points in American Educational History.* Waltham, MA: Blaisdell, 1967.

Some of the most significant writings and documents in the history of American education are presented in this book, with introductions by the author. This work is a well-selected collection of the most significant material about schooling in America.

Tyack, David B. *Seeking Common Ground: Public Schools in a Diverse Society.* Cambridge, MA: Harvard University, 2003.

An historical analysis of educational issues in a continuing search to find common unity within a diverse, pluralistic society.

Tyack, David B., & Larry Cuban. *Tinkering Toward Utopia: A Century of School Reform.* Cambridge, MA: Harvard University Press, 1995.

This critical analysis of educational reform movements is unlike the historical nature of most current reform arguments. (Most arguments on the topic result in both a magnification of present defects in relation to the past and an understatement of the difficulty of changing the system.)

Urban, Wayne, & Jennings Wagoner. *American Education: A History.* New York: McGraw-Hill, 1999.

Analysis and integration of historical events, including coverage of Native American traditions and southern education.

Wardle, Francis, & Marta I. Cruz-Janzen. *Meeting the Needs of Multiethnic and Multiracial Children in Schools.* New York: Pearson, 2004.

This book includes an analysis of the developmental needs of multiethnic, multicultural, and multiracial children in schools and society.

Warren, Donald, Ed. *History, Education, and Public Policy.* Berkeley, CA: McCutchan, 1978.

This collection of essays and documents gives a clear account of the way education and public policy in the United States are related.

Watson, Richard. *Future Minds: How the Digital Age is Changing Our Minds, Why This Matters and What We Can Do About It.* Boston: Nichols Bresley Publishing, 2010.

Explores need to place the digital age in proper perspective and use it as a tool to improve society rather than as an end in itself. To avoid being consumed by the connected age.

Webb, Rodman, & Robert Sherman. *Schooling and Society.* 2nd ed. New York: Macmillan, 1989.

This work offers an overview of education and its relation to society.

Weiner, Edie, & Brown, Arnold. *FutureThink: How to Think Clearly in a Time of Change.* New York: Pearson Education/Prentice Hall, 2005.

Analysis of future trends including middle-class global population growth, necessity of older people to become productive citizens in later years, expanding numbers of U.S. citizens opting to emigrate because of overseas opportunities, and growth of a latinized population. Prediction that by 2025 some 75 percent of Americans will live on the country's coasts and be subject to tropical storms.

Wirth, Arthur. *Education and Work for the Year 2000: Choices We Make.* San Francisco: Jossey-Bass, 1992.

This work offers an analysis of choices facing American society. Choices are offered between the status quo and the need for changing priorities to provide for increasing numbers of individuals at risk.

Zimmerman, Jonathan. *Whose America? Cultural Wars in the Public Schools.* Cambridge, MA: Harvard University Press, 2002.

This historical portrayal of various ethnic groups' contribution to America's educational history contains examples of how textbooks and curricula have been modified for a more inclusive narration of American progress in social and economic justice. Zimmerman finds American pluralism lessens overzealous religious and moral absolutism in culture and society.

Zmuda, Allison, Robert Kuklis, & Everett Kline. *Transforming Schools: Creating a Culture of Continuous Improvement*. Alexandria, VA: Association for Supervision and Curriculum Improvement, 2004.

The authors call for a competent system to highlight how systems thinking, collegiality, continuous improvement, and accountability are inextricably linked. Flexibility and a support system are essential for an organizational commitment to unqualified implementation of best practices in education.

GLOSSARY

Academic Freedom. The liberty of teachers and scholars to pursue scholarly questions without fear of control or chastisement by administrative personnel of educational or governmental institutions.

Academy. An American secondary school of the colonial and early national era that stressed practical subjects such as bookkeeping rather than the classics.

Accountability. The requirement that schools be responsible to the public for how well students do. This requirement is met through student testing.

Acculturation. Integrating into the dominant society through acclimating to its culture, mores, and folkways.

Activity Curriculum. A school program or curriculum chosen by the students themselves with the guidance from the teacher. The activity curriculum was used in some schools associated with progressive education.

Apperceptive Mass. The term used by the philosopher-psychologist Herbart to describe interlocking related or associated ideas in the subconscious part of the mind.

Assessment. Efforts to measure, through quantitative and qualitative devices, the effectiveness and achievement levels of teachers, students, and administrators.

Associationism. The school of psychology holding that learning should emphasize the relationships of concepts or ideas. Herbart was an associationist in this sense.

Authentic Assessment. Student assessment balanced among a variety of evaluation measures designed to relate educational theory to real-life issues.

Axiology. The study of moral ethical standards and judgments.

Behaviorism. A school of psychology started by John B. Watson in 1912 that assumes nothing about people or animals and bases its conclusions entirely upon the observed reactions or "behavior" of subjects when they are exposed to a given stimulus.

Blended Learning. A student learns in part at a school away from home and in part through online delivery systems.

Block Scheduling. Flexible scheduling designed to improve educational outcomes. It is designed to expand time allocated for specific subjects.

Chaos Theory. Belief that human history, once viewed as having some rational base of predictability, is rather continuing epochs of change, disturbance, flux, and flow. As a result, unpredictability of complex phenomena as paradigm shifts occur creates less stability and more intellectual upheavals.

Charter Schools. Public schools formed by parents, teachers, administrators, or other interested parties to provide innovative learning environments with reduced bureaucratic regulations. There are over 700 charter schools operating in 25 states with charter school laws, and the numbers continue to rise.

Child-Centered School. A school in which the primary concern is with developing the whole child rather than with subject matter. John Dewey and the progressive educators developed child-centered schools in which they tried to follow the natural needs, interests, and abilities of children.

Child Study Movement. The scientific study of the nature of children and learning, which G. Stanley Hall began around 1900.

Coeducational Colleges. Coeducation was given an impetus by Oberlin College in 1833. By the 1860s, women gained more support for college entrance by Cornell University's Andrew D. White. Prior to 1833, there were female academies and colleges.

Collective Bargaining. A provision for negotiating with a school board by which teachers are represented not as individuals but as a group. A union or a professional organization may be the bargaining agency.

Common School.   A school for all of the people. In the United States, free, public, elementary schools were the first "common" schools, but the term is now also applied to public high schools.

Common State Standards.   Consistent nationwide expectations of students in math and science. Other subjects will follow.

Compensatory Education.   Systematic efforts to overcome problems of the culturally different student, as with Head Start or bilingual teaching.

Competency-Based Teacher Education.   A requirement that teachers demonstrate, before they are certified, minimum competency in the subjects they will teach. Competency testing of students to see how well they can perform is now often required before graduation.

Comprehensive High School.   A secondary school that attempts to cater to the needs of all students by offering more than one course of specialization in its program. Comprehensive high schools usually have a college preparatory course and one or more scientific or vocational courses that are terminal.

Compulsory Education.   School attendance that is required by law on the theory that it is for the benefit of the commonwealth to educate all the people. Today, the practice is under attack by critics.

Constructivism.   Similar to Jerome Bruner's discovery learning, this theory stresses encouragement of multidimensional learning environments to assist students in developing critical thinking skills that can be transferred from theory into practice.

Core Curriculum.   A program in which the different subjects of the curriculum are related to a central group of studies. History and geography are combined into the social studies core. Model core curricula often relate foreign languages with other subjects.

Cultural Assimilation.   Integration through language or culture of the dominant society.

Curriculum Mapping.   A technique for examining what is taught, how instruction occurs, and when instruction is delivered. It serves as a framework for examining decision making and the purposes of schooling.

Cyber Bullying.   Online, texting, or cell phoning hurtful, hateful messages.

Dame School.   A low-level primary school in the colonial and early national periods usually conducted by an untrained woman in her own home. Dame school teachers taught only the bare fundamentals, for which they received small fees or presents.

***De Facto* Segregation.**   A condition of segregation or separation of races into different schools caused by district boundaries that include children from only one race in a given school. This differs from segregation *de jure*, which is a legal requirement for segregated schools (illegal since 1954).

Deism.   The belief, held by many liberal colonial leaders, that God created the world and then withdrew to let it operate according to natural law. This means that man is on his own because God does not interfere with the affairs of men.

Developmental Stage.   The theory that learning depends upon the maturity of the learner and that it is necessary to reach a certain level of development (physical or mental or both) before certain kinds of learning can take place.

District System.   A scheme of school organization, originating in Massachusetts, in which the local geographical unit or district is the legal authority for a school or schools. Modern districts, within state systems, are the legal areas covered by the services of a given school or schools.

Diversity.   Cultural, ethnic, physical, and mentally challenged uniqueness in student learning styles, coping strategies, and multiple intelligences.

Dropouts.   Students leaving school at all levels before grade and college completion.

Early Childhood Education.   Any systematic effort to teach a child before the normal period of schooling begins. Froebel and Montessori were pioneers in the field. Project Head Start is a modern example of early childhood education.

Education.   As used by futurists, it refers to that for which there are no known answers, as opposed to training.

Empirical Principle.   The belief, as expressed by John Locke, that the measure of the truth of an idea is its comparison with commonsense reality. Many nonempirical theories hold that logic, revelation, or innate feelings test truth.

The Enlightenment.   A pattern of thought that protested against authority in religious and secular life. The Enlightenment stressed science, reason, and the dignity of all men, and it helped to create the shift of thought that made the American Revolution possible.

Epistemology.   The study or theory of the nature and limits of knowledge.

Essentialism. An educational theory that is a protest against progressive education and consists of an effort to identify the most important practical skills that are then taught to children as the basic or essential subjects.

Experimental Schools. Schools in which new methods or materials are tried in an effort to select the best. Universities, school systems, or private groups can conduct experimental schools. Normally, careful records are kept in order to measure the progress of pupils using a new curriculum or technique against those using more established ones.

Faculty Psychology. The belief, which was the basic psychology of educators in the nineteenth century, that the mind is divided into separate faculties or powers such as willing, memory, and reasoning. Exercise of the faculties was supposed to strengthen the mind; thus, the study of Latin grammar would transfer to or improve the ability to use logic.

Formative Evaluation. Using evaluation methods, including student feedback, to improve instruction. It provides information to assist students throughout their learning process.

Futurism. A philosophical position and a movement in education designed to shift emphasis from the current era to the needs that will emerge in a period of rapid change.

General Education. Education that is not specialized and that is designed for general living or good citizenship rather than preparation for a vocation. There is an issue over just what should be included in general education as well as how many years should be devoted to it.

Goals 2000. Efforts to encourage more effective schools by stressing broad-based learning outcomes for all students in public schools.

Governmental Gridlock. Political infighting that blocks legislation or governmental action.

Graded School System. A division of schools into groups of students according to the curriculum or the ages of pupils, as in the six elementary grades. Early schools were not graded, and a substantial number of modern elementary schools are experimenting with nongraded systems, although grading is still the common practice.

Great Awakening. A religious revival in colonial America that was responsible for the creation of many schools and church-related colleges. Jonathan Edwards is credited with starting the Great Awakening among Puritans in about 1733.

Herbartian Method. The formal system of presenting subject matter to students by the American followers of Herbart, using the five formal steps of preparation, presentation, association, generalization, and application.

High School. High school emerged from the Latin grammar school and originally provided for college preparatory studies. They were given popular impetus by the 1874 Michigan supreme court *Kalamazoo* case, which found that city high schools were part of the state public school system.

High-Stakes Testing. Reliance on standardized test results to measure student achievement and grade schools.

Hornbook. A single printed page—containing the alphabet, syllables, a prayer, and other simple words—that was used in colonial times as the beginner's first book or preprimer. Hornbooks were attached to a wooden paddle for ease in carrying and covered with a thin sheet of transparent horn for protection.

Humanism. A movement to attain knowledge of life and institutions through the study of the Latin and Greek classical authors. Humanism influenced the American colonies and had a profound effect on the development of American schools. Modern humanism is concerned with the needs and values of people.

IDEA. The Individuals with Disabilities Education Act stipulated that public schools provide a free and appropriate education for students with disabilities.

Idealism. A major school of philosophy that holds that only ideas are real and that objects cannot exist outside the mind. Idealism was used by Berkeley to signify the opposite of realism. Jonathan Edwards and W. T. Harris were American idealists who influenced education.

Inclusion. Full inclusion of disabled students in regular classrooms.

Industrial Revolution. The transition from an agrarian to an industrial society and the machine age.

In-Service Training. Continuing education for teachers who are actually teaching or in service. Such training can be conducted in a school as a workshop or extension course, or teachers can attend classes in a university at night or during vacation periods.

Intelligence Quotient (IQ). A number that is obtained by dividing mental age (found by a standard or normal test) by chronological age. Intelligence quotients are widely used for placing children in school programs, although they are by no means perfect measurements.

Internet.   Worldwide computer network, formerly used by military and academic researchers on a limited basis.

Involuntary Segregation.   Forced separation of students on the basis of race, color, or creed. Racial segregation cannot be required by law in the United States since the Supreme Court decision in the 1954 *Brown* case.

Kindergarten.   A "garden of children" or an institution where small children can grow and develop. The term was coined by Froebel, who began the first schools for children ages four, five, and six years. Kindergartens appeared in America about the time of the Civil War and are now schools for five-year-olds.

Knowledge Revolution.   The tremendous explosion of information in almost every field, which is so great that it is difficult for scholars to be aware of the new knowledge discovered in their own and related fields. The knowledge revolution is accompanied by a vast increase in sources of information, especially computers.

Laissez-Faire.   The idea, based on Adam Smith's *Wealth of Nations*, that the government should not interfere in any way with the laws of supply and demand. *Laissez-faire* theory holds that the best government is one that governs least.

Land Grant College.   Colleges or universities founded or supported by a gift of public land. The Morrill Land Grant Act of 1862 established many American agricultural and mechanical colleges.

Latin Grammar School.   A classical secondary school with a curriculum consisting largely of Latin and Greek, the purpose of which was preparation for college.

Lock-Step.   A rigid or uniform organization and curriculum in which each grade or course is the foundation for each higher grade or course and in which there is no flexibility. The influence of the American Herbartianists led to the lock-step in our public schools after 1890.

Logic.   A science that deals with rules of valid critical thinking. Also, the analysis of common fallacies in language usage.

Looping.   Teachers staying with students from first to second or higher grade levels and then repeating the cycle with other students; similar to the one-room school concept of our educational history.

Lyceum.   Associations for the dissemination of knowledge (arts, literature) and cultural advancement. First organized by Josiah Holbrook in 1862.

Mainstreaming.   The process, required by Public Law 94-142, of placing exceptional learners in the least restrictive learning environment. This means that students with disabilities spend at least part of each day in a "regular" classroom.

Melting Pot.   The assimilation of immigrants into mainstream culture and total immersion into the dominant language.

Mental Discipline.   A theory, associated with faculty psychology and transfer of training, that holds that the mind must be disciplined or exercised through drill, memorization, and the study of difficult subjects.

Metaphysics.   The search for reality, truth, and meaning of existence.

Middle School.   A modern school organizational plan. Middle schools can be imposed between elementary and junior high schools, or they can replace junior high schools. A 4-4-4 plan uses the term *middle school* for the middle 4 years.

Modular System.   Flexible schedule in a school, organized around modules of time (usually 15 minutes each), to allow for different time periods for various subjects and individual needs.

Monitorial Schools.   Schools developed by Joseph Lancaster and Andrew Bell in which one teacher taught a number of bright students or monitors who, in turn, taught other groups of children. Monitorial schools were brought to America in the early national period in an attempt to provide cheap charity education for poor students.

Multiculturalism.   Appreciation and understanding of diverse populations—culture, race, ethnicity, gender, age, social class—and providing a climate for academic and social success.

Multitrack System.   The educational program, found in Europe and in the American colonies, that provided one kind of education for the wealthy elite and another kind for the ordinary people.

A Nation at Risk.   One of a series of national reports in the early 1980s that were critical of American schooling. These reports created a demand for excellence and a movement for school reform.

Naturalism.   In philosophy, the belief that the world contains only forces that require no supernatural explanation. In education, the belief that children should be free to follow their own interests, desires, and needs. Rousseau was a naturalist in education.

No Child Left Behind Act.   Accountability for student achievement through monitoring progress through assessment measures. This led to efforts to improve achievement levels for at-risk, minority, and English-as-a-second-language students through federal funds and guidelines. Modification is expected on reauthorization because of criticism from school district administrators about penalties for not meeting NCLB guidelines.

Nongraded School. A school that is not divided into specific grades for each age group. Nongraded schools can have children grouped according to social needs, ability, or progress, or not grouped at all.

Normal School. An American teacher-training school or college. Nineteenth-century normal schools were often 2-year institutions on about the same level as high schools. Modern teacher-training colleges are 4-year institutions, and many offer graduate training.

Object Lessons. Teaching by means of objects and activities rather than through abstract symbols and words. Edward Sheldon first introduced the object lesson of the Swiss educator Pestalozzi in America at the Oswego Normal School in 1850.

Old Field School. A colonial educational institution developed in Virginia by families who would cooperate to build an elementary school on one of the fallow "old fields." These schools were the counterparts of district schools in New England.

Open Classroom. A modern educational innovation in which self-contained classrooms are replaced with an open plan with individualized instruction and freedom for the child to move about the school.

Outsourcing. Using specialized expertise for school management needs—for example, using Marriott Food Services to provide school lunches. Sanitation, bookstores, school management, and the like have been turned over to private organizations.

Parochialism. Limited, restricted view of individuals and society; an isolationistic tendency.

Parochial Schools. Denominational schools. An early founder of parochial schools was Elizabeth Seton.

Pay for Performance. Salary based in part on student achievement levels.

Pedagogy. The scientific study of education, or the curriculum of teacher-training institutions with regard to how to teach.

Perennialism. A term used by Theodore Brameld to describe a position that opposes pragmatism and progressivism and that looks toward a restoration of the absolute or ultimate value system of ages past. Robert Hutchins and many Catholic educators can be described as perennialists.

Political Correctness. Sensitivity to needs, interests, and diversity of at-risk students and specific populations, sometimes used to infer excessive single-interest political groups and educational power blocks.

Pragmatism. The school of philosophy that holds that only the practical results of a belief give it meaning and that arguments that have no practical consequence are meaningless. Charles Peirce coined the term, and John Dewey is a good example of a pragmatist in education.

Programmed Learning. Any learning device that can be used by a student in such a way that a reaction to his or her activities is immediately supplied. These devices range from simple, printed notebooks to computer-assisted instruction, and the learner is not dependent upon a teacher in order to progress.

Progressive Educators. A term applied to a group of educators who objected to subject-centered schools, followed the philosophy of John Dewey, and applied the doctrines of Rousseau, Pestalozzi, and Froebel to education. Francis W. Parker was an early progressive, but the term is usually associated with members of the Progressive Education Association, which was founded in 1918.

Project Method. The method of William H. Kilpatrick and his followers. Any learning activities in which pupils have an opportunity to choose, direct, or plan their own work under conditions similar to those of real life.

Rate Bill. A scheme for supporting schools that provided a transition from fees to tax support. Each child was charged a rate or graduated amount for schooling, according to what the parents were able to afford.

Sapiential Authority. A term used by futurists like Theobald to mean authority based in truth, or the value of information in itself rather than upon status or position.

Scientific or Sense Realism. An effort to relate education to the "real" or commonsense world, started by scientific thinkers like Copernicus, Galileo, and Bacon. John Locke and Benjamin Franklin were scientific realists who influenced American schools.

Sectarianism. A term that refers to religious denominations. Early schools in America were under the control of particular church groups or sects until the Bill of Rights required that public schools be secular because of separation of church and state.

Secularism. The principle of religious freedom applied in such a way that the sphere of influence of religious groups or religious leaders does not extend to public institutions like the schools.

Single-Track System. An educational program in which all the students have the same kind of educational opportunity rather than one school system for the elite and another for the masses.

Skype. Global communication networking through advanced computer technology.

Social and Future Philosophy. The exploration of the accelerating world of change, which is especially concerned with the study of the school as a social institution and concepts including freedom, human rights, leadership, ideology, power, equity, and justice. The exploration of possible, probable, and preferable futures and analysis of alternative scenarios for the future.

Social Darwinism. The theory of evolution applied to society rather than to biology. Sumner and Spencer used social evolution to justify the existing social conditions and the concentration of wealth in the hands of the few.

Social Fragmentation. Excessive focus on differences to the detriment of tolerance, comity, civility, and unity essential for democratic theory and practice.

Social Reconstruction. The belief that society can be made over or changed. Some social reconstructionists in education have held that the schools can reconstruct society. Theodore Brameld believes that schools should have some role in social change.

Special Education. A school program designed for the child who is exceptional, that is, either gifted or below normal in ability. The study of exceptional children is now well established, and most American school systems have special-education classes.

Subject-Centered School or Curriculum. The traditional educational program that is organized around subject matter or around major concepts in the organized fields of knowledge or disciplines. It is in opposition to the child-centered curriculum, which emphasizes children's individual differences, needs, and interests.

Summative Evaluation. Judging student learning through examinations at the end of a program or course. As a result, there is less room for student learning throughout the course or program of study.

Sunday School. A movement started by Robert Raikes in England and transferred to the United States in the early 1800s that attempted to teach the fundamentals to children who worked in factories during the week.

Synergy. The impact of change in one aspect of the culture on other seemingly unrelated aspects.

Tabula Rasa. As used by John Locke, the theory that children have no innate ideas at birth and that the mind comes to be furnished with ideas through the sense organs or sensation. All learning comes through experience, and the mind is blank at birth.

Team Teaching. A plan by which several teachers, organized into a team with a leader, provide the instruction for a larger group of children than would usually be found in a self-contained classroom. Team members can handle classes together, or one member can teach a large number of children while the others work with individuals.

Terminal Education. Education or schooling that is not designed to lead to further or higher schooling. High school vocational programs that lead directly to jobs rather than to college are examples of terminal education.

Theocracy. Civil and political power vested in the same person or group. Separation of church and state in America is guaranteed by the Bill of Rights, but the early New England governments were theocracies.

Time-on-Task. An effort to improve schools by paying close attention to the time students actually spent paying attention to their subjects as opposed to time devoted to activities such as passing in halls or listening to announcements.

Transfer of Training. The theory, associated with faculty psychology and mental discipline, that learning one subject will aid or transfer to the study of another subject.

Utilitarianism. In education, the doctrine that the school curriculum should be governed by its usefulness for vocational success or public utility.

Vocational Education. Training that is intended to prepare the student for a particular job or to give a basic skill needed in several vocations.

Voluntary Segregation. The practice of establishing a school or other institution that is not for the use of the general public but that is under the control of a specific group. Parochial and private schools are examples of voluntary segregation.

Vouchers. Providing families with a voucher that can be used in public or private schools of their choice.

World Wide Web. Linkage of information channels worldwide that assists in disseminating and organizing information.

Zero Tolerance. Infractions of school rules and regulations that result in immediate disciplinary action regardless of whether the student act is a major or minor infringement of school policy.

INDEX